POLITICAL PARTIES
IN AMERICAN HISTORY
1789–1828

Political Parties in American History

Volume 1

1789–1828

Edited by

WINFRED E. A. BERNHARD

General Editor: MORTON BORDEN

G. P. PUTNAM'S SONS, New York

CAPRICORN BOOKS, New York

For
· SENTA H. BERNHARD
and
ELIZABETH A. BERNHARD

CONTENTS

GENERAL EDITOR'S PREFACE

"On the preservation of parties," wrote an anonymous Antifederalist to the *Maryland Gazette*, "public liberty depends." The warning is as appropriate today as it was in 1788. Deep in the American mind is an unusual dichotomy concerning party politics. On one hand, it is regarded at best as an entertainment, a subject of humor, and at worst as a dirty business, corrupting and compromising, the endeavor of self-seeking, power-hungry individuals. On the other, it is recognized as essential both to the operation of government and as an institutional cement joining Americans of every persuasion. The same citizens who take a passionate interest in elections exhibit a pronounced distrust of their representatives.

Thus, political parties have developed and matured, frequently been challenged, transformed or replaced by others, and have been denounced and denigrated by critics throughout our history. To understand the origins, natural history, and current state of parties is the purpose of these volumes. Particularly in the twentieth century minority groups who were never granted equality or permitted to participate in the American success story have come to demand their place at the political table. How well parties respond to these demands and how effectively they function as an agency of social change have become the crucial issues of the 1970's.

MORTON BORDEN

PREFACE

The initial volume in the series *Political Parties in American History* relates to the emergence and ultimate dissolution of the first American party system in the nearly forty years between the establishment of the federal government and the election of Andrew Jackson to the Presidency. In its entirety this is a period in which a new experiment in nationhood was constantly being tested. An untried, uncertain country, weak in the eyes of Europe, with a precarious future, had changed into an assured nation, its government under the Constitution established, its economy expanding, and its independence of Europe proved. National unity, despite various challenges, had not yet succumbed to sectional hostility. A society oriented to the patrician outlook and structure of the eighteenth century in a generation had become ebulliently democratic, shifting many of its values in the process. The evolution of political parties had virtually coincided with the evolution of the federal government.

The selections in this anthology are indicative of the renewed attention historians and political scientists are giving to parties, recognizing their essential role in a democratic society. The history of parties, once narrowly construed as the history of elections, has, in recent years, been reconsidered and altered. Political scientists, borrowing approaches from the behavioral sciences, have based their analyses of parties on "empirical propositions and theories of a systematic sort, tested by closer, more direct, and more rigorously controlled observations of political events."[1] Out of this new methodology have grown numerous behavioral and sociological investigations of individuals and groups engaged in the quest for political power through the party. While political scientists have been largely oriented to the present, they have raised provocative questions about sociopolitical developments which are affecting current conceptions of the political process in early American history. The influence of the new approach is evident in this volume of readings, though the traditional has not been slighted.

What justification can there be for analyzing long-past political developments when the American party has changed significantly from its beginnings? Should party history be a required "tonic" for students of history to take like the proverbial springtime dose of sulfur and molasses?

A valid rationale for the study of party history is that it sweeps the reader toward a larger understanding of the behavioral patterns of the human being involved in this case in political activity. Too often political parties are relegated to a subsidiary position in political analysis because they have been considered "the fever curve in the pathology of politics."[2] The profound concern in contemporary society about the functioning of democracy, especially the participation of the mass of citizens in voting and in decision-making, has given a fresh emphasis to the connection between parties and democracy. So closely intertwined are representative government, democracy, and political parties that a leading political scientist, Avery Leiserson, emphatically asserts, "the study of political parties is virtually a prerequisite to a realistic understanding of the problems of democracy, both in theory and in action."[3]

The chief objective in bringing this collection together is to stimulate the reader to investigate further the fascinating history of the Federalist and Democratic-Republican parties, so vital in evaluating the complex developments of the Early National Period. From the extensive literature on parties, I chose the writings of historians and political scientists who lucidly present significant ideas and interpretations. The decision was made to reprint as many of the articles and chapters as possible in their entirety rather than to include fragments from a multiplicity of sources. With the interests of the general student of history in mind instead of the specialist, I tried to achieve a balance from the point of view of topics and of periods. Both the influence of individuals and that of the electorate at large are discussed; the impact of foreign and domestic issues is presented; and the party at the state and at the national level is critically examined.

The arrangement of the selections, beyond the initial introductory section, is designed to emphasize the beginnings of the two parties in the early 1790's, the growth to maturity, and the changing nature of the first party system in the 1820's. Suggestions for additional readings, dealing with political as well as party developments, are in the bibliographies appended to each section of the book. It is hoped that the reader will find the interpretations in this anthology challenging and useful in formulating his own opinions regarding early political parties.

At this point I wish to express my thanks, very briefly, to those who have helped bring this project into being. Morton Borden, as general editor of the series, has been resourceful in ideas and has revealed qualities of patience unusual among editors. In completing this volume, I am greatly indebted to my wife, Betty Kromer Bernhard, for her imaginativeness, her critical acumen, and her constant interest.

Amherst, Massachusetts

WINFRED E. A. BERNHARD

NOTES

[1] Robert A. Dahl, "The Behavioral Approach in Political Science: Epitaph for a Monument to a Successful Protest," *American Political Science Review*, Vol. LV (December, 1961), p. 766.

[2] Sigmund Neumann, "Why Study Political Parties?" in *Modern Political Parties: Approaches to Comparative Politics*, Sigmund Neumann, ed. (Chicago and London, University of Chicago Press, 1956), p. 1.

[3] Avery Leiserson, "The Place of Parties in the Study of Politics," *American Political Science Review*, Vol. LI (December, 1957), p. 949.

Part I

APPROACHES TO A CONCEPT
OF PARTY

This introductory section analyzes the salient elements of the embryonic American two-party system. Of the essays reprinted here, the first relates to the process of party formation while the second concerns the intellectual climate in which parties struggled to grow. The selections not only explore the background of party history but also offer an overview toward an explicit concept of party.

In his essay "Parties and Nation-Building in America," William N. Chambers presents an interpretation of the preconditions and the generative forces leading to the unexpected emergence of the Federalist and the Democratic-Republican parties. Examining these political groups in action, he relates the party experience of the 1790's to the general question of party influence on the pattern of growth of any new nation. Richard Hofstadter in "A Constitution Against Parties," considers political preconceptions of the eighteenth century in arriving at a synthesis of attitudes toward parties. Prevalent antiparty ideas, he observes, created a negative medium which strongly affected the growth and acceptance of an opposition party.

For the political observer, too often a rigid and, therefore, distorting definition of party has substituted for an authentic concept of party. Because it has remained perpetually fluid, reflecting the diversities and complexities of its human components, party can be seen clearly only through a close examination of it as an institution, as an influential organism, and as a product of historic forces. To scrutinize past attitudes toward party, within the political and social framework of the time, is also enlightening. Historians as much as social scientists have had difficulty reaching agreement on what constitutes a political party. Henry Steele Commager has wisely observed, "it is perhaps easier to say what a party is not than to say what it is."[1]

The undercurrent of distrust toward parties, so evident in the eighteenth century, may be observed in a contemporary twentieth-century form. In the popular convictions of today parties are often considered per se corruptive, essentially undemocratic, and irresponsible. Why has there been antipathy; how is past and present mistrust alike or different? In the long range what effect has public criticism had on the function of party?

Dissatisfaction with party, at present, is shaped by the belief that neither of the major parties has been sufficiently sensitive to the transcendent social problems which engulf the individual. Feeling that parties are ineffective and are controlled by powerful political cliques, some might agree with David Hume, the Scottish philosopher of the mid-eighteenth century, who expressed concern regarding "the difficulty of extirpating these weeds, when once they have taken root in any state."[2]

In reacting negatively to political parties, the generation of the Founding Fathers was responding to an image of parties based as much on theories of politics as on reality. Their political experiences, in an era when politics often rotated around the fortunes and interests of ruling Colonial families, ephemeral, coalescing "factions," and town "juntos," accentuated a deep-seated distrust of men banded together for political purposes. The infusion of English ideas about parties and the American interpretation of English politics under the Stuart and Hanoverian rulers helped convince the eighteenth-century American that parties indeed were morally unsound. Later events in the American political scene of the 1790's merely corroborated feelings born much earlier.

The picture of party became static and categorical. Every society, so the argument ran, tended to break into self-centered groups rivaling each other for control of the state. These inherently undesirable factions developed into parties which had a corrupting influence and threatened the stability of the Republic. Parties gave vent to man's worst nature, his passions; parties also promoted conflict and inevitably led to chaos if they were given freedom and were not curbed. There was a widespread conviction "that the common good was somehow defined by the state and that political parties or factions—organized opposition to established government—were seditious."[3]

Adverse attitudes had been sustained by a prevailing belief that the ideal public figure was not the party man but the man who dedicated himself to public service without any attachment to party. At the same time, with the rise of "parties" in Congress and in the states, there was a growing consciousness of the inevitability of party, a gradually increasing recognition of political opposition as an acceptable part of the political process. Not until the two-party system evolved into democratically oriented, highly organized, and professionally directed groups in the

1820's and later did old animosities toward the idea of party substantially subside.

The panorama of early party development is seen in sharpest perspective in relation to modern party. What long-range changes have occurred in party? What vestiges remain? In short, what has the first party system contributed to its political descendants? A cursory glance at modern party may generate comparisons as the reader plunges into the selections in this volume.

The major parties, constituting the principal elements of the contemporary party system, reflect the value judgments of modern America in relation to technology and society. Ostensibly the system includes two equal, competitive parties; actually, one or the other party may dominate, or the two parties may be in equilibrium. Both parties are coalitions of separate and diverse political interests—a congeries of voluntary political organizations, of varying composition and strength, brought together under the umbrella of a national party name.

A distinguishing feature of parties is decentralization in organizational structure and in locus of power. This lack of centralization has proved advantageous to the local party units as power is concentrated at the base of the organization rather than in a national leadership which exercises strict control over state, county, and local committees. Only during a national nominating convention or a Presidential election does either of the parties have cohesiveness and unity of purpose. Since authority is diffused and party discipline difficult to maintain, ambitious or dissident party members can often assert their independence of the upper echelon of leaders with impunity.

With the growing political sophistication of the electorate, concepts of party leadership and the image of leaders are changing from past norms. Yet the underlying function of party leaders remains the same: maintaining an effective political organization, mobilizing both party and voter, and winning elections. Many local leaders feel, however, that their activity in promoting community welfare or interpreting party position is more important than their traditional task of vote getting.

In its relationship to the voter, the party must take into account the needs and interests of large blocs of people, trying to balance conflicting goals, yet win over the individual voter. Parties are thus broadly based, recruiting their party workers and voting affiliates from all socioeconomic levels. Although parties are not considered democratic in their internal structure or operation, they strive to appeal to a wide segment of the electorate, reflecting the democratizing effect of mass participation in politics. As the Federalists belatedly discovered, a party must avoid elitism if it is to survive.

Within limits the modern party can rely on a strongly entrenched voter loyalty which often persists from one generation to the next. While each party remains distinctive, the effort to win over the uncommitted voters has led to muting of ideology and the adoption of similar political positions and tactics. In contrast with the Federalists and Democratic-Republicans, the major parties have avoided taking emphatic ideological stands or being innovative, preferring to win elections by getting the greatest amount of public support.

The party exists to win control of the government at any level through peaceful election contests. The ultimate object of both parties is to determine governmental policies and to gain patronage rather than to acquire power for its own sake. Considered from another position, the primary function of parties is to control the inevitable struggle for power in politics and to moderate the clashes. As an integral part of its activities the party keeps the electoral process workable, making political democracy viable.

The effect of party on many voters is negligible except where patronage or appointment to office is involved. In state and national governments parties do exert influence on legislative and executive policies as well as on legislative procedures. Their role as causative agents in the legislative process should not be exaggerated. Contemporary parties seem to be better able to muster their forces to win elections (and the accompanying power) than to carry out their policies, coherently and effectively, once they have a majority. Lack of unified party organization limits their ability to determine national policy in domestic and foreign affairs. Yet party influences, however indirect and subtle they are, do lead to political cooperation and compromise. Where they have maintained their competitive aspects, the two major parties have not been irresponsible wielders of power but have supported national interests and political democracy. In the opinion of Sigmund Neumann, an eminent political scientist, the modern party "is *the great intermediary which links social forces and ideologies to official governmental institutions and relates them to political action within the larger political community.*"[4]

NOTES

[1] Henry Steele Commager, "The American Political Party," *American Scholar*, Vol. XIX (Summer, 1950), p. 309.

[2] David Hume, "Of Parties in General," in *The Philosophical Works*, Thomas H. Green and Thomas H. Grose, III, eds. (1882; reprint ed., Aalen, Germany, Scientia Verlag, 1964), p. 127.

[3] Bernard Bailyn, "Political Experience and Enlightenment Ideas in Eighteenth-Century America," *American Historical Review*, Vol. LXVII (January, 1962), p. 350.

[4] Sigmund Neumann, "Toward a Comparative Study of Political Parties," in *Modern Political Parties: Approaches to Comparative Politics*, Sigmund Neumann, ed. (Chicago and London, University of Chicago Press, 1956), p. 396.

PARTIES AND NATION-BUILDING

IN AMERICA*

William N. Chambers

Early American party history frequently has been treated as narrative. In this selection, William N. Chambers, an outstanding political scientist, has provided a new dimension of inquiry into the evolution of the first party system by developing a hypothesis of party origins and by analyzing the effectiveness of parties as functioning organisms. He presents evidence to show that a sense of national identity, the presence of liberal values, and citizen participation in politics were essential to the appearance of permanent parties. Considering the Federalist and Republican parties the first truly modern parties, he tests their accomplishments against general norms of party performance, concluding that on balance they had a positive influence which intensified the nationalizing forces in American life. William Chambers is Edward Mallinckrodt Distinguished University Professor at Washington University, St. Louis. His scholarly works include Old Bullion Benton, Senator from the New West *(1956) and* Political Parties in a New Nation *(1963). He is also co-author of* The American Party Systems—Stages of Political Development *(1967).*

Political parties emerge out of certain sets of conditions, confront certain problems or loads in the political system, and perform interrelated functions which may include functions contributing to political integration. What the conditions are determines in part the shapes party structures will take, the functions they will perform, and how they will perform them. Yet the way in which political elites and party leaders handle

* Reprinted by permission of Princeton University Press. From William N. Chambers, "Parties and Nation-Building in America," in *Political Parties and Political Development*, Joseph La Palombara and Myron Weiner, Social Science Research Council, eds. (copyright © 1966 by Princeton University Press; Princeton Paperback, 1968), pp. 79-106.

6

political loads also determines the result in part and the impact parties may have on political development in general. In short there is a reciprocal relationship between political development and loads on the one hand and the effects of party action on the other. This relationship carries profound consequences for the political system, particularly in the era of national formation or nation-building.[1]

Once political parties emerge, they may take on stable structures and establish stable patterns of interaction which constitute party systems. It is probably more useful for analysis to think in terms of developing party systems rather than simply of parties. For the United States it is certainly true that the relationship between parties and national integration can be understood only in terms of the party system and the net balance of integrative and malintegrative consequences of that system as a whole. Approached in this way, early American experience provides a useful laboratory. The United States constituted the first modern "new nation" in the sense that the American people were the first to throw off colonial rule, establish an independent polity, and achieve a fresh national identity. It was also the United States that brought into being the first modern political parties and party system with the emergence of the Federalist and Republican formations within two decades of the assertion of independence.[2] In short, American development presents a case study of nation-building and party-building of great potential use in general and comparative political analysis.[3] The address to these phenomena here will be to discuss the context and conditions out of which early American parties arose, the shape parties took and the functions they performed, the character of the party system, and the net impact that system had on national integration. The effect of parties on integration was a kind of end-product of the totality of functions the parties performed and of their relationships with one another.

The discussion will focus on the Federalists and Republicans in the 1790's, the crucial party-building decade. Neither of these formations survived beyond the period around 1820, and the first American party system was followed by a second system in the Jacksonian era in the 1830's. Yet the parties of the 1790's marked the way for later Democrats, Whigs, and second Republicans and for the party systems they evolved. These parties and systems showed important similarities to their predecessors as well as some differences.

1. Basic Conditions in Party Development

Political parties in America did not spring from growing resistance to colonial rule from 1763 to 1776 in a manner that is familiar in many new nations in Asia and Africa today. In the revolutionary struggle sharp divisions did develop between Patriots and Loyalists. The Patriots established committees of correspondence in the thirteen colonies or states, formed the Continental Congress as a coordinating agency for the revolutionary effort and as a quasi-government thereafter, and undertook other means of agitation, cooperation, and action. Yet the Patriots did not become a party in the full sense and did not persist as a distinct political formation past the period of the struggle for independence. Cleavage between so-called Federalists and anti-Federalists appeared in the controversy over the ratification of the new Constitution in 1788-1789. Yet once again these alignments did not take on party form, and the actual contest over ratification was waged among a pluralistic congeries of leaders and groups that varied significantly from place to place in the thirteen state arenas involved. In the internal politics of the several states, moreover, the contest for power was waged by a variety of factional formations rather than by parties. Only relatively advanced Pennsylvania developed something like a party system.[4]

Thus the first American parties, or national parties, emerged out of new conflicts only in the 1790's. In terms of economic groups, what distinguished Federalists from Republicans were cleavages between mercantile, investing, and manufacturing interests and certain segments of agriculture on the one side and most planting and agrarian interests on the other. Differences also arose out of disagreements over the degree to which power should be consolidated in the new national government; over proposed policies to promote economic growth and capitalist development through government action; and over the extent to which foreign policy should be oriented toward traditionalist-monarchist England or revolutionary-republican France. Lastly, conflict grew out of contentions between leading personalities such as the Federalists Alexander Hamilton and John Adams on the one hand and the Republicans James Madison and Thomas Jefferson on the other, contentions that were sometimes as petty as they were colorful; and out of cleavages among a variety of other group, sectional, religious, local, and personal interests and persuasions. The whole story does not require retelling in its historical detail.[5] The Federalists and Republicans also developed out of a set of basic conditions, which are more to the point here.

As a general theory or hypothesis, the most basic conditions associated with the development of political parties in the modern sense may be summarized under four major headings:

1) The emergence or prospect of a significant national or common political arena, within which influence or power may be sought with reference to the decision-making centers and the offices of a common political system.

2) The development of differentiation or complexity within the political system in terms of divergences in group structures and conflicts of interest and opinion and in terms of governmental structures and functions.

3) The emergence of social structures and of ideologies or utopias which permit or encourage some form of popular or mass politics and a substantial electorate.

4) A sense of felt need to develop political structures to establish relationships between leaders and popular followings if leaders are to win and hold power and governmental functions are to be performed.

This statement of conditions can readily be related to the American instance by mediating the general theory through statements of particular sets of conditions which, taken together, constitute an immediate-conditional or relative-historical explanation for the emergence of the first American parties. The recital of American conditions will be summarized[6] as a set of middle-range generalizations about American political development.

1) A national political arena was opened with the ratification of the new Constitution and the establishment of the national government in 1789.

Even in the colonial years a considerable degree of intercolonial communication and what might be called continental consciousness, or proto-national identity, had begun to emerge on the American scene.[7] This development at once helped to sustain and received new impetus from the Revolutionary War effort and the Continental Congress of 1775-1789. The limited powers of this Congress, however, together with the fact that it could not exercise direct power over citizens but was only a quasi-government which depended on the states, and the fact that the Congress consisted of delegates appointed by state legislatures rather than of representatives chosen by the voters, kept it from providing a truly national political arena. The new general government with its single indirectly elected executive and its representative two-house Congress did become the center of a rapidly developing national arena. It was in and around this government that groups, leaders, and parties struggled and the great issues of the day were fought out.

2) The indigenous pluralism within the American nation produced a high degree of differentiation among groups, social strata, and states or sections and a complex interplay of interests, loyalties, sentiments, and opinions; and most of these forces quickly found expression in politics and turned increasingly to the national scene.

The cross-currents which the pluralism of early American life threw up were complex indeed. There were small-freehold farmers and great planters owning thousands of slaves; merchants, shippers and shipbuilders, importers and exporters, investors, and struggling manufacturers; artisans or "mechanics"; varied ethnic stocks and different religious faiths; would-be "aristocrats" and nascent "democrats," and sanguine "Gallomen" and sober "Anglomen"; states competing with one another; and a host of subgroupings, such as near-subsistence farmers or farmers who looked to the market. There extended across the new nation a congeries of interests that had to be given expression and accommodated if the system was to sustain itself and perform its functions; and parties developed in considerable part as a response to such felt needs. Certain interstate comparisons are also revealing in connection with this condition for party formation. Indices are difficult to assign, but Pennsylvania exhibited a particularly high degree of differentiation in the interplay of interests, which helps to explain the fact that Pennsylvania alone developed a state party system in the 1780's and also moved rapidly toward shaping local units of the national parties in the 1790's. A significant degree of complexity might also be attributed to New York, for example, where the pace of national party development was second only to that of Pennsylvania; but in New York old patterns of domination by great families and clique politics, characteristics which were much less in evidence in Pennsylvania, impeded party development.[8] It may be suggested as a hypothesis that the higher the degree of differentiation of group and other relationships is in a political system, the greater is the probability for the development of political parties, though this probability may be reduced by the presence of other impeding conditions. Such differentiation certainly existed in American national politics by the 1790's, as various group interests took on nation-wide form and sought national expression.

Substantial differentiation also characterized the national government. It was not only formally separated into executive, legislative, and judicial branches with distinct prescribed powers but the two houses of Congress had different electoral foundations and constituencies and somewhat different functions. The Constitution also provided among the various organs of government an intricate set of checks or reciprocal relationships that in effect constituted a further differentiation of functions. Again, parties arose in part in response to the problems leaders faced in trying to operate this complex governmental machinery effectively.

3) Social structures and basic perspectives in the American experience provided a strong impetus for popular involvement in politics, demands for representation and mechanisms of consent, and the emergence of a substantial electorate.

In comparison with contemporary European societies American society was remarkably open, atomistic, affluent, and fluid. It was not bound to feudal traditions, graded structures of estates or classes, or old corporate configurations. Most men owned a piece of farm land or other property as a foundation for individual independence; a vast continent and its wealth of resources offered unprecedented opportunities; distances between rich and poor were not so great as they were in Old World societies; social distinctions and deference patterns were not so sharp or rigid, and there was no genuine aristocracy or fixed hierarchy; and social mobility was a frequent fact as well as a hope. Distinctions there were, particularly between great planters and lesser farmers and Negro slaves in the South; and where social gradations were particularly sharp and persistent, patterns of deference held on longer than they did elsewhere. Yet distinctions were generally on the wane, partly as a result of economic opportunity and partly because of the democratization that had accompanied the Revolution and swept many states in the 1780's. This development was furthered by the impact of the social outlook, *ethos*, or mood that Hartz has aptly called the American "liberal tradition." This fundamental perspective, with John Locke as its ideologue, was to develop steadily in American conditions from a utopia to an increasingly common general ideology and foundation for emerging consensus; and in drafting the Declaration of Independence, which became the basic statement of the American creed, Jefferson drew on Lockian ideas as "the common sense of the subject." The liberal tradition placed heavy stress on such important if sometimes conflicting values as free individualism, opportunity, individual achievement, equalitarianism, and liberal democracy.[9] It is not surprising that movement toward democratic participation, representation, and consent was rapid, and it is also not surprising that these forces brought the emergence of an extensive electorate in state after state. In terms of interstate comparisons all of these forces and particularly the stress on equalitarianism and a mass base for politics were especially pronounced in Pennsylvania, where party action developed most rapidly. On the other hand equalitarianism and the extension of suffrage took hold more slowly in the Southern states, where full-scale party structures and action came comparatively late, although even there the impact of remaining tax or property qualifications on suffrage has been exaggerated by older historians.

It may be suggested as a further general hypothesis that the greater the degree to which equalitarian political ideologies and extended suffrage obtain, the greater is the probability that political parties will develop in the absence of other, impeding factors. Recent research findings for the American case indicate that after the Revolution the great majority of white adult males in an era of widely held agricultural property could vote. Not all of them did, but the democratic impulse and keen party competition brought voting participation in the period 1799-1802 and after to the substantial proportion of 39 per cent or more of white adult males in important elections, a level that was not to be exceeded until new party rivalry appeared in the Jacksonian era.[10] Moreover access to other avenues to the political arena was comparatively open. Freedom of political belief, expression, and action was also generally accepted, despite important uncertainties and exceptions in the early years.

4) Within the context of these conditions, a sense of felt need gradually arose for efficient means to represent and combine interests, amass power, conduct elections, and manage government.

Innumerable obstacles stood in the way of party development, and no one set out to construct parties with a blueprint in mind. Men thought in terms of devices to meet immediate needs, or bickered about immediate interests; many important political figures including George Washington spoke out against the idea of parties. The process of party-building was one of groping expediencies as well as brilliant innovations, and it was some time before leaders came to think consciously in party-building terms. Yet in the space of a few years after the ratification of the Constitution in 1789 stable structures were evolved, and the Federalist and Republican formations emerged as parties.

This analysis is hardly unique in its basic terms. It is consistent with suggestions contained in the classical work of Ostrogorski, with the emphasis Weber puts on the relationship between popular or mass politics and "parties of politicians," and with many of the ideas offered by Duverger.[11] Yet the summary here is based primarily on investigation of the American instance. Circumstances will certainly reveal variations from context to context in the significance of any one condition in the development of political parties even though the general pattern of relevant conditions may remain constant. Indeed it may be argued that generic conditions as they affect the development of parties can be firmly established only in terms of comparative historical processes carefully analyzed through a theoretically oriented historiography or time-oriented science of political development. As V. O. Key puts it: ". . . a conception of the party system must take into account its dimension of time. It may be useful to think of the party system as an historical process rather than as patterned and static institutional behavior. . . . if the party process is viewed through time, additional aspects of the working of party [systems] may be identified."[12] This, presumably, is the task of developmental political science or analytical history.

A possible factor in party development as it has operated in many new nations today should be noted. This is the effect of external influences on the peoples of developing areas who are seeking to achieve the modernization that most Western societies have already accomplished. The adaptation of foreign ideas or models as part of the European legacy, including general models for political parties, has played a significant part in political development in Asia and Africa today, although of course local conditions continue to have profound effects.[13] Such mimetic elements were virtually absent in the early American experience. The terms "Whig" and "Tory" had been in use in England for a century or more, but they denoted broad persuasions and shifting alliances of factions or personal clique-"connexions," in the old spelling and the old style, rather than parties as such; suffrage remained extremely narrow; and these early English political formations did not develop continuing and pervasive structures to provide stable links between leaders at the parliamentary center and substantial popular followings in the nation as a whole. It was not until the rise of the Liberal and Conservative formations after the limited first Reform Act of 1832 that England may be said to have arrived at genuine political parties. Nor were modern party models available in the 1790's in other European countries. In short the Federalist and Republican formations in the United States had to find their own way toward party structure and party action.

II. Political Development, Party Structures, and Party Functions

The argument that American parties in the 1790's were the first modern parties is more than a mere historiographical contention. It involves conceptions of what a political party is and does and of how American parties were related to the whole question of political development, and a conceptual distinction between party politics and faction politics. Political development may be understood as a movement toward a political system which is capable of handling the loads it confronts, characterized by significant differentiation of structures and specificity of functions, increasingly centralized and able to maintain itself. It may not be as easy to measure political development as it would be to measure economic development, for example, yet one might argue that a highly developed political system is characterized by some measure of rationalized political efficiency, defined as a substantial degree of coherence in policy output and a capacity for innovation in the face of new problems.[14] Parties and party systems may have an important impact on the course of such development.

In the American case the emergence of parties marked a significant elaboration of structures and a movement toward relative political efficiency. Before the advent of parties politics was a pluralistic, kaleidoscopic flux of personal cliques like those that gathered around the great magnate families in New York, caucuses of the sort that came and went in many New England towns, select and often half-invisible juntas in the capitals or courthouse villages in the Southern states, or other more or less popular but usually evanescent factions. All of these political formations in their pluralistic variety may be brought under the general heading of faction politics. With few exceptions such old-style "connexions" or multiple factions were characterized by lack of continuity from election to election, by tenuous or shifting relationships between leaders in government on the one hand and the electorate on the other, by comparatively narrow ranges of support from interest groupings, and thus by a confusing degree of raw, unaggregated pluralism in politics. One result was that it was difficult for the voters to hold any one group of men responsible for the direction of public policy. Another was that policy-making was generally erratic or incoherent except where it was under the control of a dominant "connexion," clique, or junta.

The advent of the Federalists and Republicans as comprehensive parties, on the other hand, brought a new dualistic order into politics. The parties emerged as durable, differentiated, visible, rationalized formations which developed stable operating structures. Continuing relationships were evolved between leaders and cadre at the center of government and between lesser leaders and cadre in the states, counties, and towns; and in turn between this structure and broad popular followings in the electorate. It is appropriate in the American instance to consider the structure of leaders and cadre as "the party," or party proper, and its supporters or adherents in the public as its following. At the beginning American parties accomplished little toward organization strictly construed as a regularized differentiation of internal functions and corresponding division of labor. Indeed the Federalists never achieved significant organization, although the Republicans by the late 1790's and early 1800's devised party caucuses, conventions, and committees in several states which foreshadowed the full development of organization proper in the Jacksonian era. Yet both party structures in the 1790's did reach out to amass stable popular followings of considerable range and density that carried them well beyond the fluid and limited support pre-party factions had enjoyed. Lastly, both parties developed distinctive sets of in-group perspectives with emotional overtones, or ideologies, that helped to bind party structures together and popular followings to the parties. In short the first American parties can be described as developing historical patterns of stable structures linked to broad popular followings, with distinguishing ideologies, and as structures that were able and ready to perform crucial political functions. It is in terms of this general idea of what a party is that the Federalists and Republicans may be thought of as the first modern parties.[15]

In the functions they came to perform the first American parties exerted an important influence on the course of political development in general. In the process of nation-building any people is likely to face a number of interrelated problems which impose significant loads on the political system. Among the most salient of these we may list the following:

1) Establishing and maintaining a national authority, or the operating political system itself.

2) Expressing and aggregating interests as essential functions and, if possible, containing conflict within a spectrum which will prevent immobilism or disruption.

3) Meeting the "crisis of participation" and meeting related problems of coordinating political action in a politics of popular participation.

4) Recruiting and training at all levels new leaders who are capable of managing the problems or loads at hand.

5) Effecting a "pay-off," in Lipset's terms, or meeting the "crisis of distribution" in order to maintain the political system by convincing at least substantial segments of the population that it is an instrument through which they may accomplish their objectives.

6) Arriving at a position with reference to possible opposition to governing elites within the polity.

Each problem noted here certainly does not carry the same weight in every emerging nation, but the loads are sufficiently universal in political development to give an analysis of their impact a general relevance. How political parties affected the way each was met in the American instance can be recounted briefly.

First, although parties did not establish the national constitutional authority in the United States, they did much to assure its effective operation. Despite controversy over the balance of federal and state powers in the new political system, both Federalists and Republicans worked within it. Both parties also discountenanced periodic eruptions of violence for political purposes; thus, for example, party spokesmen did not take up the violence of the Whisky Insurrection of 1794 or the Fries Rebellion of 1799 as a weapon of opposition but condemned it instead. As time passed, parties and party leaders also came to manage the structures of the central government, establish informal connections between its separated agencies, and staff its offices. In short, the parties filled gaps in the constitutional structure of national authority in a constitutional manner and thus performed a crucial constitutional function.

Second, parties dealt effectively with one of the major problems of the new American polity in expressing and aggregating conflicting interests. Given the manifold pluralism and sectional divisions on the American scene, and given a continuation of the politics of raw group pressures and of factions, conflicts of interest might have brought immobilism in the political system along with severe strains or social disruption. Both the Federalists and the Republicans amassed followings which included national coalitions or combinations of interests and opinions, however, held together by working formulas of agreement or compromises, and the Federalists enjoyed at the outset a far wider range of group support than early historians were willing to attribute to them.[16] Conflict continued in party channels, but within viable limits.

Third, early American parties helped to meet the load of popular participation and related problems. Many Federalists were far from happy at the prospect of having to curry votes in order to hold power, but they adjusted at least in part to the imperatives an increasingly open, liberal society imposed. Their Republican opponents meanwhile actively encouraged popular involvement in politics and made the emerging general ideology of liberal democracy a particular ideology for their party, thereby winning an increasingly large following that helped to make them a dominant party after 1800. Indeed the Federalists tended to remain a "party of notables," in Weber's phrase, maintained a condescending tone, and were inclined to view elections as referenda on the policies they had already forged in government. On the other hand the Republicans, partly a "party of notables" but also and increasingly a "party of politicians," revealed a responsiveness to sentiments and opinions among their followers and in the electorate which made them what may be called a "popular party," a party highly sensitive to such currents. Yet both parties turned to general propaganda to inform voters and influence public opinion, most significantly through partisan media at the capital like the *Gazette of the United States* (Federalist) and the *National Gazette* (Republican) and satellite newspapers in the states, although the Republican *Gazette* was soon replaced by the Philadelphia *Aurora* as a national party organ. Moreover both parties gradually evolved procedures to coordinate action in the nomination of candidates and the conduct of election campaigns, and to appeal to and bring out the vote.

Fourth, the parties brought up leaders or enlisted new cadres who helped to manage political business throughout the political system. The roster of major leaders includes such brilliant figures as Hamilton, Adams, Jefferson, and Madison at the party "point," in the capital; editor-politicians like John Fenno, Philip Freneau, Benjamin Franklin Bache, or Noah Webster; such Congressional leaders as Fisher Ames, Theodore Sedgwick, James Monroe, or Albert Gallatin; and scores of prominent local leaders like John Jay in New York or Alexander Dallas in Pennsylvania. Yet the parties, particularly the Republicans, also developed national behind-the-scenes cadre figures like John Beckley, who served the Republicans as a kind of informal national chairman, and untold legions of lesser cadre in the supportive echelons of the party phalanx, in the states, counties, and towns. Most early American party managers were young, and many were intellectuals to a greater or lesser degree. The average age of nine representative Federalist leaders in 1792, when incipient parties were beginning to take recognizable form, was

44, and the average age of thirteen representative Republican leaders was 36. Nearly all had attended college at a time when higher education was not common, and most had significant intellectual talents as writers or in other areas. One of the most remarkable devices for bringing forward political leadership came with the growth of indigenous Democratic or Republican societies as formal political associations in several states and cities. These societies had a short life and never became mass-membership units in the Republican party as such;[17] but they provided a useful training ground for new political elites.

Fifth, parties also provided mechanisms to assure that the new political system produced a pay-off. They not only quickly developed to the point where they could provide representation for important interests, but as each party partly emerged out of controversy over important national issues each maintained different positions on these issues. On economic policy, for example, Hamilton and the Federalists advocated government measures to encourage hothouse capitalist development even at the expense of economic inequality within the society, while Jefferson and most Republicans were content to speak for a predominantly agricultural economy as the foundation of an equalitarian simple-republican order even at the cost of a slow pace of national economic growth. In the positions they took on these and other issues the two parties in effect provided the electorate with a choice. In the coherence and innovation they brought into government they also helped to shape reasonably consistent courses for public policy. A comparison of Congressional behavior before and after the development of national parties makes clear the transition from confusion to some measure of order and coherence in policy decisions.[18] No group perhaps got all it wanted, but all important groups had some means to express their demands; and serious dysfunction was avoided.

Sixth, American parties arrived at the acceptance of opposition. To be sure, not only Hamilton but also many other Federalist leaders were suspicious or impatient of opposition, and the Alien and Sedition Acts of 1798, which Adams as well as extreme Federalists supported, were aimed at Republican critics. Yet no general program of repression was undertaken, and when the Republicans won the presidency and both houses of Congress in 1800 the Federalists yielded power in 1801 without recourse to force. Despite overheated rhetoric in the campaign and later Congressional maneuvers to make Aaron Burr president instead of Jefferson, it was the first instance of such a peaceful transition in modern politics.[19] Meanwhile the Republicans in opposition had followed a wholly peaceful course, had carefully avoided overtones of disruptive separatism in the Kentucky and Virginia Resolutions of Jefferson and Madison that censured the Alien and Sedition Acts, and had come rather more readily than the Federalists to the acceptance of opposition after they won power. American parties achieved a *modus vivendi* of adjustment to opposition and peaceful rivalry instead of repression or violence.

In short, parties helped to meet many of the loads the new nation faced and did so in an ideological spirit of open, innovative, and pragmatic accommodation.[20] Parties moreover contributed to political development as a whole by providing mechanisms for the rationalization of politics through the party structures and by helping to introduce a measure of political efficiency which faction politics could scarcely have achieved. Within the general scheme advanced by Almond and Coleman for the analysis of non-Western or underdeveloped as well as Western or developed societies,[21] the first American parties may be said to have undertaken important aspects of the crucial functions of socialization, recruitment, interest articulation, interest aggregation, communication, and rule-making. The intricate machinery of the Constitution could scarcely have functioned as it did without the role parties and the party system played.

It is possible to offer a conceptual generalization based on the American experience. The American parties of the 1790's took the form of cadre structures rather than mass-membership parties, in Duverger's terms; and they did not perform as comprehensive a range of internal functions as many parties in new nations in Asia and Africa have undertaken today, or at least not so intensively point by point.[22] Other differences in specific structure and function could be pointed out from party system to party system. Yet it may also be argued that the American experience lays bare useful generic aspects of the process of party development. If this is the case, all modern parties may be thought of, in a conceptual hypothesis, as historical instances of social formations directed toward the acquisition of governmental power whose definitive characteristics are stable structures, stable relationships linking leaders and popular followings, performance or an offer to perform a wide range of crucial functions in the political system, and the generation of in-group perspectives or ideologies. The specific shape of parties will vary with conditions, loads, and responses, but all modern parties seem likely to exhibit at an irreducible minimum the four general characteristics suggested by the American case.

III. Party Systems and Party Roles

The ultimate impact parties have depends on the party system. Whether there is one party or more than one makes a difference; the kinds of relationships that exist between parties where more than one appears also count; and so does the kind of leadership that develops within the parties. Thus one-party systems will have their own consequences; the impact of plural party systems may differ in societies characterized by widely-shared agreement as compared with societies riven by the centrifugal forces of bipolarized pluralism,[23] and a party system marked by intransigence is likely to produce quite different results from one in which pragmatic adaptation is the mode. Few if any of these matters can be taken as wholly foreordained, at least in the early stages of political development.

Continuing competition between the Federalists and Republicans in the 1790's produced the first modern two-party system. The American experience suggests that the defining characteristic of stable competitive two-party systems is continuing interaction between the parties in which each must take the other into account in its conduct, particularly as it touches on their relations with the electorate in their bids for power and their relations to the centers of government authority. The character of this interaction may be put in terms of four interrelated criteria:

1) The existence of continuing conflict between parties, at once based on and implying the development of policy positions and ideologies which appear as "we-they" perspectives. Differences between parties in policy and ideology may be relatively broad or relatively narrow.

2) The provision of stable links or connections between elements in the public or electorate on the one hand and government on the other as the parties contend with one another.

3) The conduct of party conflict short of social disruption, with at least some degree of acceptance of the idea of a loyal opposition. If party conflict passes beyond the bounds of the spectrum suggested here, it is difficult to conceive of the parties as operating within a stable system, because the seeds of the breakdown of the system or its transition to a different kind of system would always be present. In a stable competitive party system there must at a minimum be some kind of agreement to disagree without recourse to repression or disruption.

4) The existence of a reasonable chance for "out" parties to win governmental power and become "in" parties, and therefore the possibility of the alternation of parties in power. Where one party holds an unassailable dominant position even though opposition exists, we can scarcely speak of a genuinely competitive system.

In the United States the first parties established a pattern of dual party competition. This pattern gave way in the 1800's to a period of Republican ascendency in which the Federalists grew less and less able to provide a significant national challenge to the governing party of Jefferson, Madison, and Monroe; and this pattern of one-party dominance in turn gave way to a new period of faction politics as the Republicans themselves suffered disintegration. In the Jacksonian era, however, new parties revived the pattern of dual party competition, and it has persisted in America despite periodic third-party challenges in the national arena and variations in state arenas. In its broad form the model of a stable competitive party system derived from the early-American experience and suggested here may serve as a basic model of such systems in general,[24] within which variations in particular characteristics may be taken into account.

Political parties may also be thought of as tending toward democratic or plebiscitarian poles in their behavior and roles in the party system. The issue hinges on the different ways parties respond to the load of participation in the course of political development. On the one hand the attitude of political elites may be that mass involvement in politics is something to be contended with through manipulation or control. This may be accomplished through parties as directing and mobilizing but not responsive structures; by molding interests and opinions rather than by giving them open expression; and by elections as formal referenda rather than effective choices. On the other hand elites may adjust to or stimulate patterns of effective participation in the power structure, assume attitudes or responsiveness to a variety of freely expressed interests and opinions in the party system, and view elections as open choices on broad policy options, which in turn should have an effect on public policy. Given their inclination to look upon elections as referenda on policies they had already forged, the Federalists tended toward a plebiscitarian outlook—or a restricted plebiscitarian outlook if one includes their additional inclination to view with misgivings the emergence of a sizable electorate—while the Republicans moved toward an increasingly democratic response. Yet the bent of social structure, Lockian ideology, and the polity tended to push the party system as a whole along a democratic course. The fact that parties developed in a competitive system in which each party had to appeal to a substantial electorate if it was to gain power also provided an internal dynamic in the party system itself which moved it still further in a democratic direction. The existence of open and continuing Federalist and Republican rivalry at virtually all levels of government meant that the party system provided a choice for the public or electorate. This opportunity for choice became the fulcrum of democratic consent and control in the American experience.

Variations in structure between the Federalists and Republicans are also relevant to the question of democratic and plebiscitarian patterns. The Federalists persisted in their notabilistic structure; they were internally created, in Duverger's phrase, originating as they did in and building out from a powerful nucleus at the center of government; and they never developed great sensitivity to popular demands. Because the Republicans were relatively free from such notabilistic characteristics, they developed more and more as a "popular party." Although they too built out from the center of government, they were also in an important part externally created, out of indigenous elements in the states and localities, in a manner Duverger finds unusual for cadre parties; and they were inclined to see elections as expressions of the popular will even to the point of investing them with a Lockian mystique. In the relationships the Republican party evolved with its popular following important patterns of two-way communication emerged, and what was said at either end of lines of communication was likely to be heard and considered at the other, at the top as well as at the bottom. In part such relationships emerged out of the fact that the Republicans grew up in opposition and were faced with the necessity of mobilizing support to counter the advantages in power the Federalists enjoyed as a government party. The result, however, was a further impetus toward democratization of the American party system.

Lastly, the democratic bent in the development of American parties found expression in the manner in which the parties performed political functions. Their style was more specific than diffuse, more instrumental than affective, and their appeal more general than particular, although personal ties continued as an important undercurrent in party life; and American parties developed in a direction that stressed mass appeals and popular mobilization in elections. Moreover the fact that the parties had a comprehensive governmental structure to work through meant that they enjoyed significant opportunities to carry popular choices in policy into effect once they had won office. Indeed the Federalists and Republicans probably achieved a higher degree of efficiency on this count than later American parties have done when internal factionalism has worked against coherent translation of national electoral choices into governmental decisions.[25]

For the democratic and plebiscitarian alternatives the crucial point is the role party systems as a whole play. They may provide channels for open recruitment, effective participation, and effective representation, or they may not; if they do, they may exhibit a substantial measure of intraparty democracy. They may provide meaningful, relatively orderly, continuing options on policy as well as leaders among which the public or electorate can choose, or they may not; if they do, they offer choices as the operative meaning of interparty democracy. It may be argued as a general hypothesis that competitive dual-party systems carry a stronger probability not only of democratic consent but of democratic control than do pluralistic multiparty systems, in the sense of the translation of broad popular choices into public policy; whereas multiparty systems or dual systems with a high incidence of intraparty factionalism are less efficient in promoting democratic control because the clarity of either-or alternatives is lacking and parties or factions must enter into *ad hoc* coalitions to govern. Yet these features and problems of consent and control are not involved at all in any effective sense in plebiscitarian systems, where domination replaces meaningful consent and manipulation replaces free choice.

IV. Parties and National Integration

In an important sense nearly every aspect of the discussion of American nation-building and party-building here is related to the question of integration. It remains, however, to isolate and analyze the elements involved from the point of view of this particular aspect of political development.

Most broadly, national integration may be taken as a process of incorporating various parts of a society into a functioning whole. Where a relatively high degree of integration obtains, a political system can perform essential functions with a substantial measure of acceptance, order, and efficiency. Integration also tends to proceed by phases, meeting various problems, so to speak, as it moves from lower to higher stages.

Among these we may note the growth of obedience and loyalties to the nation which transcend loyalties to its parts; the reduction of barriers between various parts of the whole, the opening of communication, and ultimately the toleration of differences within unity; the emergence of faith in the political system; and the emergence of shared values and perspectives, or consensus. Where norms or promises of democracy exist, integration appears to require general access to effective participation in the processes of the political system. Successful integration in a society of any complexity also appears to require some rationalization of political processes so that the variety of elements in the nation may be related effectively to a single government. These aspects of political development will be taken here not as integration itself, or as "participation integration" and "process integration"; but as requisites for national integration, construed as the process of incorporation of parts into a whole. This notion of integration in general has been put suggestively by Deutsch in a summary of possible stages: "Open or latent resistance to political amalgamation into a common national state; minimal integration to the point of passive compliance with the orders of such an amalgamated government; deeper political integration to the point of active support for such a common state but with continuing ethnic or cultural group cohesion and diversity; and, finally, the coincidence of political amalgamation and integration with the assimilation of all groups to a common language and culture. . . ." [26]

National integration may be found in different dimensions at different junctures in time. Much also depends on the sequence and clustering of issues. If a developing polity faces all at once the loads of establishing legitimacy and achieving some measure of integration and also the problems of participation and distribution and of rationalizing political processes, serious strains are likely to occur.[27] In the American case the timing of issues was fortunate. It was no easy task to amalgamate thirteen previously separate, often squabbling states into a single nation. Yet the emergence of communication among the colonies and various sections even before the Revolution, the development of a continental consciousness, the Revolutionary experience and American tribulations after 1783 as a lonely republic in a generally hostile world, the existence of a substantial measure of cultural as well as linguistic identity, the rise of economic interdependence, and the increasing sway of the liberal tradition all helped toward the development of national identity in a way that few new nations in Asia or Africa today have enjoyed.[28] The federal character of the new national political system under the Constitution, with

its explicit recognition of diversity within unity, marked another important step. Finally the charismatic legitimacy George Washington brought
to the new government, and his refusal to allow his personal appeal to
be converted into a foundation for perennial power, also did much to
smooth a transition from personal foundations for legitimacy to rational
foundations in a legal-constitutional order. It was only after most of these
phases in the process of integration had been passed through or were
underway that other loads came to the fore in the nation as a whole.
There was already a significant development toward integration before
national political parties appeared.

Many aspects of party action did more to hinder this development than
to advance it. The Federalists and Republicans not only expressed but
even exacerbated cleavage in their representation of conflicts of interest
in the society and in their maneuvering for office and power; in the way
in which they helped to pit men against one another "like two cocks,"
as Jefferson put it in describing his relations with Hamilton in the cabinet;
and by contributing to a general heating-up of the political atmosphere.
Indeed conflict is inherent in competitive party systems as they have been
described here because such systems provide open channels for the clash
of interests, sentiments, and opinions which already exist in the population and introduce new elements of antagonism on their own in their
continuing rivalry for power. The we-they perspectives of parties, the
stress on the virtues of "our" leaders and policies and symbols and the
evil of "theirs," are all likely to stir strident outcries among rival partisans. Moreover early American party cadres were not always above sharp
dealing and even occasional fraud in elections in the scramble for power;
there was at least one occasion in the 1790's when invective between
partisans in the American Congress came to blows; the suspicion and
partisan motives which spawned the Alien and Sedition Acts carried over
into the partisan strains of the election of 1800; and party conflict exacerbated personal dislikes, leading Burr and Hamilton to a duel in which
the latter was killed. It was such aspects of political rivalry that Washington condemned when he spoke out against "the spirit of party" as a
spirit sure to "distract the public councils." There is no discounting the
malintegrative impact of such aspects of party rivalry in the American
case.

Yet it is important to note two additional elements in this connection,
which may be expressed as general hypotheses. First, it may be that
parties of the general American type, by channeling the conflicts which
already exist within the society and subjecting them to mediating struc-

tures, reduce on the whole the amount of conflict that would otherwise occur even though they generate distinctively partisan cleavages on their own. Second, it may be that such parties by expressing conflict openly in a patterned manner within the rules of the political system promote integration by facilitating rhetorical modes of expression as channels of social and psychological catharsis, thereby drawing off potential strains in the political system as a whole. In any case the American polity weathered the storms of its formative period and has weathered all such storms but one that blew up over the most continually divisive issue in American life, the place of the Negro in the national community—and in that one the loosing of the national and integrative ties of the party system in 1860 was the prelude to civil war in 1861.[29] Although parties in the 1790's scarcely ushered in a millennium of harmony, conflict was kept within peaceful bounds.

In this connection the place of ideology requires some specification. Federalists and Republicans were divided ideologically on many questions of domestic policy. Issues of world politics such as the Jay Treaty with England in 1795 touched off frenzies of logomachy in which each party hinted that the other verged on treason, and Washington thought that the Jay Treaty controversy agitated the public to a point that equaled the excitements of the revolutionary era itself. Extreme or "High" Federalists in the late 1790's could scarcely stomach the thought of the Republicans gaining power, and a few of them in the early 1800's even toyed with abortive schemes for the secession of New England from the union as an answer to Republican ascendency. Yet by and large ideology among party leaders took the form of giving vent to emotional release in rhetoric; and as a controlling element in behavior it did not reach the point of ultimate intransigence. Extremist Federalists remained a minority in the party as a whole, and John Adams as a party leader as well as President insisted on following a moderate course in foreign policy; Jefferson's conduct in office has been described as a triumph of practical adaptation over ideological inflexibility—"what is practicable," he himself commented, "must often controul what is pure theory." On the whole ideological divisions between Federalists and Republicans were sharper than they have usually been between major American parties, but not sharp enough to produce disruptive consequences in the polity.

In their competition, meanwhile, early American parties made significant contributions to some of the crucial requisites for national integration. They helped to fulfill the democratic promises of the American liberal tradition by providing effective channels for popular participation.

They assisted in meeting the problem of distribution by their transmission to government of the demands of important groups across the nation and in the states and localities. They contributed to solving the problem of orderly management in a complex polity by their conduct of nominations and elections and by helping to manage the agencies of the national government. In short, parties helped to realize a measure of political efficiency which could never have been achieved through faction politics.

As integration was involved in the problem of establishing constitutional legitimacy and the evolution of a viable national consensus, parties also performed directly integrative tasks in their relation with the public in several ways:

1) By supporting the new constitutional order in its hour of uncertainty and testing, even in the face of disagreements over specific interpretation of the Constitution itself.

2) By strengthening and maintaining communication and a sense of shared stakes among different groups in the several states. Thus, for example, both Massachusetts men and Virginians could join across state lines in being either Federalists or Republicans, though there were more of the former in Massachusetts and more of the latter in Virginia. Without national parties malintegration among the several states might have persisted far longer than it did.

3) By undertaking recruitment and socialization, or bringing up and training new elites to man posts in the political system and providing popular education in politics on an informal basis.

In these ways parties helped to promote a sense of political community and efficacy and thereby further strengthened the new government. If they did not perform a range of directly integrative functions comparable to those that parties have undertaken in many new nations today, this was in part because the American problem of integration was less demanding by the time parties appeared.

In the final analysis, however, the effect of parties on national integration depends on the role of the party system as a whole. The fruitful issue for analysis appears to be not a general either-or question of whether parties integrate or don't integrate. The question is: Under what conditions do party systems of what kinds promote a net balance of integration or of nonintegration, and in what ways? It is the contention here that the first American party system, despite the malintegrative results of certain aspects of party action, produced a net balance of integrative results. This was the case in large part because of certain salient features of the system itself and their consequences.

First, there is the fact that the Federalists and the Republicans took on the form of stable, broad-gauge parties as contrasted with shifting, narrow factions. Thus the parties and their followings operated as broadly inclusive combinations of interest groups. In the long-term interaction of the parties in competition for support these combinations could be held together only by political brokerage and compromise in the party structures and in their relations with their followings. The net result was that the party system turned group conflict from unlimited pluralistic into manageable dualistic channels before it reached the decision-making centers of government. As compared with the tensions of deadlock that might have ensued if indigenous pluralism had continued unchecked, party dualism reduced malintegrative strains.

Second, because the parties developed as formations given more to the practical pursuit of power and office than to ideological intransigence, they tended to conduct conflict within a moderate range. They did so in part as a result of the moderate bent of American politics generally and in part out of the exigencies of their interaction in the party system itself. Yielding too much to the views of extremist groups or leaders threatened the loss of important blocs of votes that were essential to political success. The result was a tendency to push the party system toward moderation or centralism and to limit the ambit of extremist elements. All of these forces combined to produce a net balance of integrative results, particularly as compared with the degree of malintegration that would have followed from constant extremes in party policy or action. In this context the party system also arrived at the acceptance and legitimization of a coordinated political opposition.

Third, by providing instruments for electoral consent and democratic choice the party system helped to drain off dissatisfaction before it reached the point of serious disaffection. It opened avenues of expression for those who were at the moment out of power as well as in, gave hope to the "outs" that they might become "ins" as a result of electoral choices, provided concrete mechanisms through which the far-flung national electorate could hold someone responsible for the conduct of government, and offered working tools for a peaceful change of elites if the electorate wished it. It is hard to imagine how major national elections could have been managed in a satisfactory manner without the machinery of operating democratic choice the party system made available. By 1800, for example, widespread dissatisfaction with Federalist leaders and policies had built up within many important groups in the population, however much parties intensified it. If the party system had not existed to help effect a transfer of power to the Republicans in a way the dispersed mechanisms of faction politics could scarcely have done, dissatisfaction might have grown to seriously disruptive proportions or turned to violence, as earlier antagonisms toward ruling elites and their policies had done in the Regulator movement in North Carolina, in Shays' Rebellion in Massachusetts, or in the Whisky Insurrection and the Fries Uprising. On balance again, the party system may be said to have reduced potential disaffection and disruption, with a net gain for integrative over malintegrative consequences.

Lastly, parties in the party system operated within the rules of the developing polity as a whole, with the obvious integrative results which this fact entailed.

This analysis of the American experience suggests as a general hypothesis that a democratic two-party system can produce a net balance of integrative impacts on political development if the parties embrace a wide range of interests and opinions in their followings held together by pragmatic adjustment, if they keep conflict within moderate bounds, and if they are ready to operate within a larger basic agreement or an accepted set of fundamental rules. The hypothesis contains a substantial set of "ifs," however; and they raise a final important question.

V. Leadership, Purposes, and Political Styles

The net impact of early American parties on national integration was what it was to an important degree because of key features which the party system came to exhibit as a whole—notably the features just outlined here, and its pragmatic development in general. It remains to explore why, or how, the American party system took on these particular characteristics; why, or how, it came to operate within the rules.

A large part of the explanation lies in the comparatively narrow range of conflict American conditions produced and in the rise of the American liberal tradition toward national consensus. The distribution of interests and opinions tended to fall into a curve of dualistic centrality, with most interests and opinions encompassed in two central peaks of concentration which tapered off into much lower measures of extremes, as it were, rather than into a bimodal curve of disruptive extremes or a centrifugal scattering of disruptive drives.[30] Such matters of social fact, prevailing ideology, a relatively limited spectrum of social conflict, and the distribution of interests may be taken as a necessary condition in any explanation of how the American party system came to perform as it did. Yet the explanation as a whole goes beyond such matters and brings us again to the responses of American party leaders to the conditions and loads they faced.

Particularly in a period of national formation, what leaders do and how they do it may have a crucial impact. In the American case the bulk of party leaders were guided by purposes and convictions which included a deep concern for the future of the new nation or the success of its "republican experiment," as well as by concerns for more immediate or particular political goals. Moreover they had before them the example and counsel of Washington, who served far more as a moderator than he did as a mobilizer or dramatizer, as many later prophet-leaders of nationalism have. In the long run American party leaders avoided pushing issues and ideologies to the breaking-point of violence or disruption, as they might have done, and upheld the Constitution and the rules of the polity; and when the test of 1800 came the Federalists as a whole accepted the result rather than resort to force to prevent it. In short, no major party leader was ready to chance the destruction of the new nation in order to gain partisan or factional advantage. The role of leadership in this connection is underscored by the fact that the story might have been quite different if men like the intransigent ultra-High Federalists of Connecticut, for example, had dominated in national party leadership.

Lastly, American party leaders developed unusual skills in intergroup adjustment and combination, in compromise, in aggregating as well as mobilizing interests, and in the practical rationalization of political methods and processes; and through such skills they helped to establish patterns of adjustment as well as of conflict in the party system. These crucial matters of purpose, commitment, and skill became the foundations of the basically pragmatic style the preponderance of American party leaders achieved. It is in important part the lack of such commitments, skills, and styles that has prevented many new nations in Asia or Africa today from establishing a viable measure of national integration and efficiency, and many nations in Latin America from managing peaceful transfers of power by democratic procedures. If there are lessons for developing nations today that may be learned from the early American experience in political development, they lie in large part here—in the area of leadership and in the manner in which leaders conduct politics in general and party politics in particular.

Considered as a whole, the response of American party leaders to the problems of nation-building and party-building was more than a reflex action to social conditions and emerging ideology. It was also a creative element operating in reciprocal interaction with these elements, an active and positive factor itself. It was forwarded by human purposes, modes of behavior, and shared hopes, notably the hope of building a strong nation and making the republican innovation work in a hostile world. Rivals though they were and spokesmen of strongly different points of view, Hamilton the Federalist and Jefferson the Republican were outstanding examples of this creative personal element, one by virtually inventing a program to point the nation toward economic growth, the other by embodying the spirit of American nationhood and liberal democracy. If the total historical process in its groping, its occasional pettiness, and its conflict as well as its creative aspects was by no means all smooth and orderly, it did bring the United States from uncertainty to stable nationhood, from faction politics to working party politics, and to a political system that was cohesive, internally legitimate, and autonomous, in Deutsch's terms.[31] The measure of integration early America achieved was in part a byproduct of underlying forces. It was also in part the result of active responses to conditions and loads by political leaders.

NOTES

[1] See the introductory chapter to this volume by Joseph LaPalombara and Myron Weiner, *passim*.

[2] Cf. Seymour Martin Lipset, *The First New Nation: The United States in Historical and Comparative Perspective*, New York, 1963, pp. 16-98; and William N. Chambers, *Political Parties in a New Nation: The American Experience, 1776-1809*, New York, 1963, pp. 1-169. Substantially all of the data concerning American party development on which this paper rests is presented in the latter work, particularly in instances when other citations do not appear here.

[3] See Karl W. Deutsch and William J. Foltz, eds., *Nation-Building*, New York, 1963, p. 3, for concepts of "national growth," "national development," and "national-building."

[4] Among other sources, see Elisha P. Douglas, *Rebels and Democrats*, Chapel Hill, 1955; Allan Nevins, *The American States During and After the Revolution*, New York, 1924; Frederick W. Dallinger, *Nominations for Elective Office in the United States*, New York, 1903; Ralph Volney Harlow, *The History of Legislative Methods in the Period Before 1825*, New Haven, 1917; Forrest McDonald, *We the People: The Economic Origins of the Constitution*, Chicago, 1958. In particular, McDonald gives a careful, long-term account of politics in each state as it led up to the politics of ratification. See also George D. Luetscher, *Early Political Machinery in the United States*, Philadelphia, 1903; other monographs and studies cited in Chambers, *op. cit.*, pp. 211-212, 214-215.

[5] Valuable monographs on early American party development and related phenomena include Joseph Charles, *The Origins of the American Party System*, Williamsburg, 1956; Noble E. Cunningham, Jr., *The Jeffersonian Republicans: The Formation of Party Organization, 1789-1801*, Chapel Hill, 1957, and *The Jeffersonian Republicans in Power: Party*

Operations, 1801-1809, Chapel Hill, 1963; and Manning J. Dauer, *The Adams Federalists*, Baltimore, 1953, which covers far more than its title suggests. See also the early classic by M. Ostrogorski, *Democracy and the Organization of Political Parties*, New York, 1902, and the histories by Edgar E. Robinson, *The Evolution of American Political Parties*, New York, 1924; Wilfred E. Binkley, *American Political Parties: Their Natural History*, 4th ed., New York, 1962; and Herbert Agar, *The Price of Union*, Boston, 1950.

⁶ For another statement of these conditions and some of the methodology involved in the analysis, cf. William N. Chambers, "Party Development and Party Action: the American Origins," *History and Theory*, Vol. 3, No. 1 (1963), pp. 111-117.

⁷ Richard L. Merritt, "Nation-Building in America: the Colonial Years," in Deutsch and Folz, eds., *op. cit.*, pp. 66-72.

⁸ For aspects of political development in Pennsylvania in the early years and into the nineteenth century, see Harry Marlin Tinkcom, *The Republicans and Federalists in Pennsylvania, 1790-1801*, Harrisburg, 1950; Russell J. Ferguson, *Early Western Pennsylvania Politics*, Pittsburgh, 1938; Sanford W. Higginbotham, *The Keystone in the Democratic Arch: Pennsylvania Politics 1800-1816*, Harrisburg, 1952, and other sources cited in Chambers, *op. cit.*, pp. 214-216, 218.

⁹ Louis Hartz, *The Liberal Tradition in America*, New York, 1955, pp. 17-22, 35-96, *passim*; see also Lipset, *op. cit.*, *passim*.

¹⁰ Cf. Edmund S. Morgan, *The Birth of the Republic, 1763-1789*, Chicago, 1956, pp. 93-94; Chilton Williamson, *American Suffrage from Property to Democracy 1760-1860*, Princeton, 1960; Richard P. McCormick, "New Perspectives on Jacksonian Politics," *American Historical Review*, Vol. 65 (1960), pp. 288-301.

¹¹ Max Weber, "Politics as a Vocation," in H. H. Gerth and C. Wright Mills, eds., *From Max Weber: Essays in Sociology*, New York, 1946, pp. 99-104; Maurice Duverger, *Political Parties: Their Organization and Activity in the Modern State*, New York, 1955, *passim*; Ostrogorski, *op. cit.*, *passim*.

¹² V. O. Key, Jr., *Politics, Parties, and Pressure Groups*, 5th ed., New York, 1958, p. 222.

¹³ See, e.g., John H. Kautsky, *Political Change in Underdeveloped Countries: Nationalism and Communism*, New York, 1962; Gabriel A. Almond and James S. Coleman, eds., *The Politics of Developing Areas*, Princeton, 1960; Immanuel Wallerstein, *Africa: the Politics of Independence*, New York, 1961, pp. 63-79; Thomas Hodgkin, *African Political Parties*, London, 1961, pp. 38-48.

¹⁴ See Samuel H. Beer, "New Structures of Democracy: Britain and America," in William N. Chambers and Robert H. Salisbury, eds., *Democracy in the Mid-Twentieth Century: Problems and Prospects*, St. Louis, 1960, pp. 30-59.

¹⁵ For a fuller elaboration of the distinction between faction politics and party politics, and of the concept of party as durable structure and rationalized performance of key functions, see Chambers, *Political Parties in a New Nation*, pp. 17-33, 39-51, and pp. 97-98, 106-110.

¹⁶ Dauer, *op. cit.*, *passim*; for the decline of Federalist support, Shaw Livermore Jr., *The Twilight of Federalism: the Disintegration of the Federalist Party, 1815-1830*, Princeton, 1962; also Binkley, *op. cit.*, pp. 29-51.

¹⁷ See Eugene Perry Link, *Democratic-Republican Societies, 1790-1800*, New York, 1942; and Cunningham, *The Jeffersonian Republicans*, pp. 49-55.

¹⁸ [William Maclay], *The Journal of William Maclay*, New York, 1927, contains interesting material from the pen of an inside observer; also, Dauer, *op. cit.*, where useful tables of voting behavior are set forth, Appendix III; and Charles, *op. cit.*, p. 94.

¹⁹ Lipset, *op. cit.*, pp. 36-45.

²⁰ Cf. Chambers, *Political Parties in a New Nation*, pp. 117-119, for a more detailed exposition of the role of ideology in general and party ideology in particular.

²¹ Almond and Coleman, *op. cit.*, pp. 16-17, 26-58, *passim*.

²² See, e.g., Hodgkin, *op. cit.*, pp. 125-148, 155-165.

[23] See Giovanni Sartori, "European Political Parties: the Case of Polarized Pluralism," LaPalombara and Weiner, Ch. 5.

[24] For a more detailed elaboration of this schema and some of its implications, and also for the decline of the Federalists and the disintegration of the Republicans, cf. Chambers, *op. cit.*, pp. 143-147 ff., 191-208.

[25] For a particularly vigorous critique of this aspect of American party and governmental action, see James MacGregor Burns, *The Deadlock of Democracy: Four Party-Politics in America*, Englewood Cliffs, N.J., 1963, *passim*; for other views see William N. Chambers, *The Democrats, 1789-1964: A Short History of a Popular Party*, Princeton, 1964, for a brief case study of America's oldest party, and George Mayer, *The Republican Party, 1854-1964*, New York, 1964, for the Democrats' durable rival; also, the general histories by Agar and Binkley, already noted.

[26] Deutsch, "Nation-Building and National Development: Some Issues for Political Research," in Deutsch and Foltz, eds., *op. cit.*, pp. 7-8.

[27] LaPalombara and Weiner, *op. cit.*, Ch. 1.

[28] Merritt, *op. cit.*, pp. 6-72; Lipset, *op. cit.*, pp. 23-35, 61-66; Almond and Coleman, *op. cit.*, pp. 149-152, 239-246, 366-368, *passim*; Wallerstein, *op. cit.*, pp. 85-101.

[29] See Roy Franklin Nichols, *The Disruption of American Democracy* (New York, 1948), *passim*, for a valuable analysis of the breakdown of parties as the precursor of the Civil War; also, Arthur Schlesinger Jr., *The Politics of Upheaval*, Boston, 1960, for the political strains which followed the Great Depression of 1929 and the role of party politics.

[30] Cf. Sartori, *op. cit.*, pp. 9-14.

[31] Deutsch, *op. cit.*, pp. 11-12.

A CONSTITUTION

AGAINST PARTIES*

Richard Hofstadter

Richard Hofstadter is recognized as a perceptive analyst of American intellectual developments. In The Idea of a Party System, *he presents an array of original interpretations regarding the effect of ideas on the evolution of party. Hofstadter suggests, in the chapter included here, that a deep concern about preserving "liberty" from the encroachments of "power" led to structuring of the Constitution as an antiparty instrument of government with the expectation that the dangers of parties would be checked. Although their positive value was not readily acknowledged, parties became essential to the proper operation of the constitutional system. Richard Hofstadter, author of such provocative books as* Social Darwinism in American Thought *(1944) and* The American Political Tradition *(1948), received a Pulitzer Prize for his* Anti-Intellectualism in American Life *(1963). At the time of his death in 1970, he was De Witt Clinton Professor of American History at Columbia University.*

I

That political parties did not hold a respectable place in eighteenth-century American political theory was a reflection of the low estimate put upon their operation in practice. Wherever the Americans looked, whether to the politics of Georgian England, their own provincial capitals, or the republics of the historical past, they thought they saw in parties only a distracting and divisive force representing the claims of

* Originally published by the University of California Press; reprinted by permission of the Regents of the University of California. From *The Idea of a Party System: The Rise of Legitimate Opposition in the United States, 1780-1840*, by Richard Hofstadter (copyright © 1969 by the Regents of the University of California): Chapter 2, "A Constitution Against Parties," pp. 40-73.

unbridled, selfish, special interests. I do not intend here to try to penetrate the thickets of eighteenth-century politics either in England or in the American provinces. We long ago learned not to identify the Whigs and Tories of the eighteenth century with the highly developed British political parties of modern times, and not to imagine that England had a well-developed two-party system at the close of the eighteenth century or even during the early decades of the nineteenth. Modern parties have grown up in response to (and in turn have helped to stimulate) the development of large electorates, and their institutional structures are in good measure an outgrowth of the efforts necessary to connect the parliamentary party and the mass party. The modern party is, in this respect, the disciplined product of regular party competition in the forum of public opinion. It also deals with legislative issues, over which the established parties differ. But this concern with issues and legislation—and hence with competing programs—which we now take for granted as a focus of party politics did not have at all the same degree of development in the politics of late eighteenth-century England or of the American colonies.[1] It is the need to legislate frequently that imposes a constant discipline within a parliamentary body, as it is the need to carry issues to an electorate of considerable size that requires permanent organizations within the constituencies.

Although a suddenly enlarged electorate, active political contests, and the presence before Parliament of important issues coincided with a strong tendency toward a two-party system in the early eighteenth century, this state of affairs, which began to wane after the death of Queen Anne, was a matter of the rather distant past by the time of George III's accession. British politics in the era of George III, with the cabinet system not yet developed, with its relatively small electorate, its pocket boroughs, its connections of leading families, its management by purchase and arrangement, its lack of highly focused issues, its multiple, shifting factions, its high proportion of unaligned members of Parliament, bore only a vague germinal relation to the highly developed modern British party system. Historians may argue about details, but even as late as the 1820's, Richard Pares once suggested, one should perhaps speak only of a tendency toward a two-party system. The modern procedure for a change of ministry was first foreshadowed, though in a rudimentary way, only in 1830, when Wellington's cabinet was forced to resign and give way to the Whig ministry headed by Earl Grey.[2] An adverse vote in the House of Commons now became established as the occasion for the end of a ministry, but it was not until 1868 that a prime minister (in this case Disraeli) first took the popular verdict in an election as a clear mandate and resigned without testing his position in Parliament. It was only after the Reform Acts of 1832 and 1867 that Britain moved toward the extended electorate of the sort that had been established in the United States. Efforts to organize machinery to mobilize a large electorate, which had reached a high state of development in the United States by the 1820's were being made in England during the 1860's. In party development, therefore, the United States proved to be the avant-garde nation.

Though today we think of the party system, party organization, and party identifications among the electorate as being much more fully developed in Britain than in the United States, it is easy to see why eighteenth-century Americans found in the state of English politics little that was edifying and less to imitate. However we may now assess the English political system in the last half of the eighteenth century, it seems safe to say that most Americans saw in it even less merit than it had, that they regarded it with a certain self-righteous puritanism, emphasizing its evil and corrupt character, which they contrasted with the robust and virtuous character of their own politics. Although there were still Anglophiles of a sort, one finds few Americans near the close of the century who could, with Hamilton, look upon English political culture, with all its faults, as the most advanced in the West, or who could understand why he thought it was the only government in the world that united "public strength with individual security."[3] One can find perhaps none at all who could see in the historic division between Whigs and Tories any precursor of the highly functional party system of the future.

On the eve of the Revolution, most colonials thought of recent English history simply as a story of moral degeneracy, political corruption, and increasing despotism, marking a sharp and perhaps irreversible decline from the glories of that earlier England whose principles had been the inspiration of American liberties. Indeed one reason for the Revolution was the felt necessity of severing connections with a state that was losing the pristine purity of its constitution and was cutting itself adrift upon the seas of corrupt and tyrannical government. Americans saw this corruption when they visited the mother country; they read about it in the English political pamphleteers; they saw it at work on their own premises in the behavior of the Customs Commissioners during the 1760's. Benjamin Franklin had commented on the increasing "corruption and degeneracy of the people" in England during the 1750's, and shortly before Lexington and Concord was still complaining about "an extream corruption prevalent among all orders of men in this rotten state.'' All he could see was ''Numberless and needless places, enormous salaries, pensions, perquisites, groundless quarrels, foolish expeditions, false accounts or no accounts, contracts and jobbs'' which ''devour all revenue and produce continual necessity in the midst of natural plenty.'' James Otis thought that the House of Lords was filled with peers who had not risen above what they learned at Oxford and Cambridge—''nothing at all but whoring, smoking, and drinking''—and that the Commons were ''a parcel of button-makers, pinmakers, horse jockeys, gamesters, pensioners, pimps, and whore masters.'' John Adams believed that the virtue of England was done for: ''Corruption, like a cancer . . . eats faster and faster every hour. The revenue creates pensioners, and the pensioners urge for more revenue. The people grow less steady, spirited, and virtuous, the seekers more numerous and corrupt, and every day increases the circles of their dependents and expectants, until virtue, integrity, public spirit, simplicity, and frugality, become the objects of ridicule and scorn, and vanity, foppery, selfishness, meanness, and downright venality swallowing up the whole society.'' Jefferson, writing under the stress of wartime animosity in his *Notes on Virginia*, concluded that Great Britain was nearly finished: ''The sun of her glory is fast descending on the horizon. Her philosophy has crossed the channel, her freedom the Atlantic, and herself seems passing to that awful dissolution whose issue is not given human foresight to scan.''[4]

II

Although the Americans thought of their own political condition as being much healthier than England's—it was in the New World that they expected old English liberties to be preserved—they thought they had no reason to attribute the comparative soundness of their own politics, as they saw it, to any evidences of party government. Though many historians would probably want to make an exception for Pennsylvania, and some perhaps for New York, most would agree with the general judgment that ''no colony had what could be appropriately designated as a party structure.''[5] Certainly if a rigorous definition of party structure is laid down, demanding not merely parliamentary factions in the assemblies but clearly developed and permanent mass parties, this judgment would hold.

A great deal of political energy went into the repeated battles with the royal governors, and this put a premium on methods of organization that united rather than divided the assemblies. In the conduct of their struggles, and in securing legislation, the colonists had recourse to more or less disciplined caucusing groups, sometimes called "Juntos" which made life difficult for the governors but greatly increased the effectiveness of those who wanted to assert colonial prerogatives. After 1776, with royal governors out of the way, the state legislatures, released from the unifying discipline imposed by the struggle for their prerogatives, were more free to break up into factional groupings. Political contests could now take on more clearly the form of struggles between rival groups of citizens within the state. But of course many respectable men saw this period as one of alarming disorder, and they could see little promise of good in the local factionalism that developed. "To many, the very word 'party' carried anti-republican connotations."[6]

Pennsylvania, which had the closest thing to a two-party system, was sometimes pointed to as an example of the evil effects of party strife under constitutional government. Madison, for example, in the Fiftieth *Federalist*, cited the "two fixed and violent parties" of Pennsylvania as a primary reason for the failure of that state's Council of Revision. The state had been "for a long time before, violently heated and distracted by the rage of party," Madison pointed out, and this was a difficulty that the other states must also expect to experience.[7] Yet one may wonder about the justice of this judgment on Pennsylvania. The factions in Pennsylvania may have been as bad as they were thought to be—the politics of that province had always been contentious—but the existence of parties did not prevent the Pennsylvanians from going through the fires of the Revolution, the British ensconced on their very doorstep, without slipping into tyranny or giving way to indiscriminate reprisals, or from emerging with a free and quite democratic constitution.

No doubt the factors that combined to produce free government were numerous, and party conflict was only one of them. Provincial factionalism had its seamy side and its social costs; and the pre-party factions may be criticized by contrast with the highly developed parties of a later day. But factional differences taught the Americans to argue, polemicize, legislate, and on occasion to make compromises; the modern political party is an evolutionary product resting on a large fund of political experience, of which this early factional politics was a part.

The truth seems to be, however, that free government could struggle along with or without these rudimentary forms of party. Virginia must here concern us especially; and Virginia—which, along with Connecticut, was the least faction-ridden of the colonies—represents the strongest challenge to the notion that the political party had to be a decisive force in the development of a free state. If we compare the political culture of the Old Dominion, which was, after all, the political culture that the Virginia dynasts knew best, with most other colonies, we are impressed by its partyless condition and the relative uneventfulness of its domestic politics in the eighteenth century up to about 1763. One may argue whether the government of colonial Virginia was brilliant, but it was certainly competent as governments went then and as most of them go now; and Virginia bequeathed to the new nation an impressive, if preponderantly parochial, gallery of talents, unmatched by any of the other states.

It is Virginia that may serve to remind us that, for all the claims that have been made for the "democratic" character of colonial politics, colonial society was a deferential society and its politics were ordered accordingly. In his elegant little study of the methods of political control in Washington's Virginia, there was one conception for which Charles S. Sydnor had no use, beyond a need to explain its absence, and that is the conception of party. In eighteenth-century Virginia men were elected not because of the group they were associated with or what they proposed to do about this or that issue but because of what they were. An election promise might be made here or there—though political promises were rather frowned on and might even be made the object of investigation or cause an elected candidate to be refused his seat—but in the main men put themselves forward on their social position and character and manners, and on their willingness to treat their constituencies in the right and liberal fashion, not least on their willingness to ply them with rum punch. It was rare for a man to run on issues or policies; and no one could run on factional identifications, since these were thin, ephemeral, and spare of meaning.[8]

"Perhaps the most striking characteristic of Virginia politics between 1689 and 1763," writes Jack P. Greene in his study of the Southern colonial assemblies, "was its tranquillity." Even the governors, he concludes, were in the main able, prudent, and moderate. The aristocracy was tightly knit and mutually accommodating. There was no serious rivalry between the Council and the Burgesses. Sectional divisions there were, but before the Revolution they were not of grave consequence. Class differences there were also, and occasional personal rivalries, but they produced no parties, not even permanent factions, and St. George

Tucker was able to recall with satisfaction long after the Revolution that he had never seen anything in the Burgesses "that bore the appearance of *party spirit.*"[9]

A generation nurtured in this environment had no successful example of party government anywhere in its experience, but it had an example of a partyless government of a free and relatively benign character, and the statements of the Virginia dynasts about party, though conventional among their entire generation in America as well as in their own particular cherished locale, have a uniquely firm root in Virginia soil.

III

Let us turn from the state of practice to the state of theory. The Founding Fathers, thinking along lines drawn by the old struggle against British authority, by the works of dissenters, radical Whigs, and libertarian publicists, and by the violent pre-Revolutionary controversy itself, were concerned with one central issue: liberty versus power. Because men are fallible, wicked, and self-aggrandizing, they thought, power tends always to extend itself and to encroach upon liberty. "From the nature of man," said George Mason at the Federal Convention, "we can be sure that those who have power in their hands . . . will always, when they can, . . . increase it." "Power," said Madison, "is of an encroaching nature."[10] The basic problem of republicanism, as most of them saw it, was to protect liberty by devising foolproof checks upon power. The basic problem of good American republicans like Madison, who nevertheless wanted a stronger Union, was to protect liberty by checking power, without at the same time weakening government to a point at which its stability would be in danger.

Liberty, then, was the basic value. As to what it consisted of, Americans sometimes assumed so much that their passionate claims for liberty seemed to mask a demand for license or anarchy. But they would have answered that liberty prevailed when men were free to exercise their natural rights. As an answer to the abstract question, What is liberty? this was enough for them, and they had no difficulty at all in spelling out what natural rights were or what institutions threatened liberty or sustained it. It was endangered by many things they saw in contemporary England: monarchy and aristocracy, a standing army, corruption, bribery, and patronage, a decadent state of morals. It could best be protected under a government which had within it a strong popular house in the legislature, a broad freehold suffrage, a system of mutual checks and balances among the arms of government, an independent judiciary, explicit guarantees of rights (among these, civil and religious liberties and trial by jury), and frequent (some said annual) elections.

The necessity of checks on power is a theme struck over and over. But it is important that for the Fathers these checks had to be built *into the constitutional structure itself*. They were not content—and still less were the people they had to persuade—to rest their hopes on those checks that might arise in the political process alone, and this is one reason why they put no faith in party competition. Their hopes were pinned on a formal, written system of internal checks and balances, the precise enumeration of limited powers, and the explicit statement of constitutional guarantees, such as the opponents of the Constitution insisted on adding to it. Such informal forces in politics as the temper of the public, the process of opposition, the institutionalization of party structures, which to us seem so vital in democracy, seemed to them too slender a reliance, too inadequate a substitute for explicit constitutional specifications.

Here, it is important to realize, the ideas about constitutional structure that prevailed in America were derived both from Anglo-American experience and from the traditions of classical political thought. What had come down as the authoritative prescription of just and stable government from the times of Polybius and Aristotle was the idea of mixed government—that is, a government that would incorporate representation of the three basic orders in society. The three indispensable arms of government would act for the sovereign, the nobility, and the people. The prevalent eighteenth-century passion for balanced government, which was founded on the conviction that liberty and justice would be most secure if the elements of the state and of society were counterposed in such a way as to check and control each other, was sought for in constitutional systems that separated the powers of government and put the several arms of government in a state of watchful mutual tension. The necessary mutual checks would thus be provided by the elements of the constitution, and not by parties, which were indeed usually thought of, when they were thought of at all, as forces likely to upset the desired constitutional balance by mobilizing too much force and passion in behalf of one limited interest.

When they were thought of at all: in classical political theory, in the great books from Aristotle and Machiavelli to Locke and Montesquieu, which were read by the Founding Fathers when they consulted literature for political wisdom, parties played only an incidental, illustrative historical role, usually as examples of some difficult problem or some historical mischief. Most of the classical political writers had mentioned party here and there, but none of them discussed parties at substantial length or offered a theory of the role of the party in the state. Even such empirically minded thinkers as Aristotle and Machiavelli had little to say on the subject;[11] and so strong was this tradition that even as late as 1861, long after his own country was well launched upon the development of its two-party system, John Stuart Mill could write an entire treatise, *Considerations on Representative Government*, in which he never elaborated upon the role of party. Indeed, it was the great cumulative and collective merit of writers like Bolingbroke, Hume, Burke, and Madison that they showed a new understanding of the importance of party and a strong disposition to move it somewhat closer to the center of concern in political thought.

However, the point remains that in the thinking of the Founding Fathers, the truly useful and reliable antitheses of politics, the counterpoises upon which they were disposed to rely for liberty and stability, were still embodied not in the mutual checks of political parties but in the classic doctrine of the separation of powers, in the mutual checks of the houses of legislature, or in the checks exerted upon each other by the executive and the legislature, and in that exerted by the judiciary over the other two. Checks were to be built into planned constitutional forms instead of being left to the hurly-burly of politics. James Madison, for example, assuring the Federal Convention that the new constitution would have safeguards against the betrayal of trust by officials, explained: "An obvious precaution against this danger would be to divide the trust between different bodies of men, who might watch and check each other." John Jay, speaking for the Constitution in the New York ratifying convention, said: "The two houses will naturally be in a state of rivalship. This will make them always vigilant, quick to discern a bad measure, and ready to oppose it."[12] It was two *houses*, not two parties.

While most of the Fathers did assume that partisan oppositions would form from time to time, they did not expect that valuable permanent structures would arise from them which would have a part to play in the protection and exercise of liberties or in reconciling the stability and effectiveness of government with the exercise of popular freedoms. The solution, then, lay in a nicely balanced constitutional system, a well-designed state which would hold in check a variety of evils, among which the divisive effects of parties ranked high. The Fathers hoped to create not a system of party government under a constitution but rather a constitutional government that would check and control parties.

This conviction, as Cecelia Kenyon has pointed out, was shared by both sides in the debate over the adoption of the Constitution. Although Federalists and Anti-Federalists differed over many things, they do not seem to have differed over the proposition that an effective constitution is one that successfully counteracts the work of parties. The Anti-Federalists often expressed a sweeping opposition to the idea of political organization as such, and, as Miss Kenyon has observed, "the contemporary opponents of the Constitution feared parties or factions in the Madisonian sense just as much as did Madison, and . . . they feared parties in the modern sense even more than Madison did. They feared and distrusted concerted group action for the purpose of 'centering votes' in order to obtain a plurality, because they believe this would distort the automatic or natural expression of the people's will."[13]

IV

We have come now to the point at which we can examine the problem of party as it was expressed in the minds of the Virginia dynasts. It seems fitting to begin with Madison: he was a more systematic, and I believe a more deliberate and profound thinker than Thomas Jefferson; as the philosopher of the Constitution, he gives the clearest and most authoritative statement of the conflict between the rationale of the Constitution and the spirit of party; and, as the man who began, before Jefferson, to play the central role in organizing what came to be considered Jefferson's party, he illustrates even more sharply than Jefferson our central paradox of party government instituted by anti-party thinkers.

The great achievement of Madison was to provide for his contemporaries a statement of the checks-and-balances view of government in which a pluralistic view of society itself was linked to the plural constitutional structure. Like John Adams, he saw with great clarity the importance of supplementing the internal balance of the Constitution with the external balance of the various interests and forces that made up society.

Here Madisonian pluralism owes a great deal to the example of religious toleration and religious liberty that had already been established in eighteenth-century America. The traditions of dissenting Protestantism had made an essential contribution to political pluralism. That fear of arbitrary power which is so marked in American political expression had been shaped to a large degree by the experience men of dissenting sects had had with persecution. Freedom of religion became for them a central example of freedoms in general, and it was hardly accidental that the libertarian writers who meant so much to the colonials so often stemmed from the tradition of religious dissent. In the colonies, Americans fought unrelentingly against the proposal to introduce an Anglican episcopate among them, an idea that excited in their minds a remarkable terror that religious liberty, and then all liberty, would be invaded. In their campaign against an American episcopate, the colonials cooperated with dissenters in the mother country with such admirable system and regularity that they established a veritable trans-Atlantic Protestant anti-episcopal union, whose members gave a great deal of thought to the problems of liberty, toleration, and pluralism.[14]

In 1768 an Anglican chaplain was quoted by one of his anti-establishment opponents in New York as having said that American experience showed that "republican principles in religion naturally engender the same in civil government." It was an appropriate remark. The whole Protestant enterprise had made for the decentralization of structure within the churches themselves, and at the same time within the structure of society. There were no longer a State and a Church standing together as unified, firm ordered hierarchies, but two spheres of values that could sometimes compete. The presence of dissenters, and the necessity of appeasing them in the interests of secular stability, meant that the imperatives of the state and those of the church might not coincide, and that the latter might in some respects be sacrificed for the former. The presence of a variety of theologies, a plurality of views within Protestantism itself, also made toleration a necessary precondition for the secular values of peace and social stability. The coexistence of the sects and the growth of toleration led to a premium on argument and persuasion, as against main force. The dissenters, with the law against them and no other instrument of suasion available to them, had had to defend their interests in this way. It became clear in England that there could no longer be such a thing as a single enforceable orthodoxy. Even error had to be tolerated, and if error could be endured where profound matters of faith were concerned, a model had been created for the political game, in which also one might learn to endure error in the interests of social peace.[15]

Of course the advancing secularism of educated men brought strong reinforcement to this tendency. One notices the common sense of relief shared by such different theorists of party as Bolingbroke, Hume, and Burke at the passing of the old religiously inspired, bigotry-animated political divisions of the seventeenth century, and Hume indeed had made a central principle of it in his political writings. The advanced, enlightened, more or less secular man could take a genial view of the competitions of sects, so long as they were all free and not at each others' throats. So Franklin, a Deist, patronized the churches, and Jefferson in time forged a curious political alliance between Enlightenment liberalism and the passion of the minority sects for religious freedom.[16]

The intellectual transition from the pluralism engendered by religious denominations to that of parties was clearly illustrated by William Livingston in New York during the 1750's. A young man still in his late twenties when he started writing in 1752, Livingston was soon to cut quite a figure in the politics of the province as a partisan in the De Lancey-Livingston party battle. The De Lanceys were Anglicans, the Livingstons and their allies Presbyterians and keen enemies of episcopacy. In 1752 Livingston launched his *Independent Reflector*, a journal which aped the style of the *Tatler* and the *Spectator* but which took much of its argument from *Cato's Letters*. Though a strong partisan, Livingston had been put off by dogmatic doctrinal religion at Yale. His Presbyterianism was qualified by a certain broad tolerance of other dissenting groups and yet fortified by an intense, almost anti-clerical animus against the Anglican Church. His own doctrines on faction were hewn out of the current orthodoxy. ("Unspeakably calamitous have been the consequences of party-division. It has occasioned deluges of blood, and subverted kingdoms.") But still, as an ardent partisan, Livingston, like Bolingbroke with his country party to end all parties, had to have an exception: "To infer . . . that the liberties of the people are safe and unendanger'd, because there are no political contests, is illogical and fallacious." We all have a right to look into the conduct of our superiors, and if we find in them "a combination of roguery" it is our common right to "form a party against their united strength: and such a party, I hope we may never want the spirit to form."[17]

Livingston, who never lacked such spirit, was roused to one of his keenest efforts in 1753 during the controversy over the founding of King's College (later Columbia). He was afraid that the college, should it receive a charter from the Crown, would become an exclusively Anglican institution, "an academy founded in bigotry and reared by partyspirit." He proposed instead that the college should be created by the legislature, and established on such a non-sectarian basis that all the groups in the province could use it together, and that all the youths sent there could be educated free of indoctrination in any particular set of religious or partisan tenets. *"For as we are split into so great a variety of opinions and professions; had each individual his share in the government of the academy, the jealousy of all parties combating each other, would inevitably produce a perfect freedom for each particular party."* Next to a patriot king and wise laws, Livingston argued, "an equal toleration of conscience is justly deem'd the basis of the public liberty of this country. And will not this foundation be undermined? Will it not be threatened with a total subversion, should one party obtain the sole management of the education of our youth?"[18]

Note that the term "party" is applied by Livingston more or less indifferently to a religious or a political group, a circumstance that arises not only out of their interconnection in the provincial politics of New York but also, and more importantly, out of his understanding of the principles of mutuality involved both in religious liberty and civic peace. For him libertarian principles in religion did indeed have a bearing on the problems of civil government.

A similar awareness of the relation between multiple sects and liberty is evident in a remarkable address before a convention of the Congregational clergy of Rhode Island delivered by the Reverend Ezra Stiles in 1760 and published the following year. Stiles was really addressing the Congregational world of New England, which, though badly divided for twenty years by the effects of the Great Awakening, was still united in its anxiety about episcopal incursions. In *A Discourse on the Christian Union* Stiles pleaded for an ecumenical tolerance. "Every sect," he said, "have a right to vindicate their particular forms." Theological differences, which he hoped to minimize among good Christians, might survive, but: "Their conviction . . . is not to be laboured by the coercion of civil or ecclesiastical punishment, but by the gentle force of persuasion and truth—not by appeals to the tenets of parties and great men; not by an appeal to the position of Arminius or Calvin; but by an appeal to the inspired writings." In arguing that even church councils or consociations had no authority over individual churches, Stiles added strikingly: "Coercive uniformity is neither necessary in politics nor religion." This conclusion was premised upon a remarkable statement of harmony in plurality: "Providence has planted the British America with a variety of sects, which will unavoidably become a mutual balance upon one another. Their temporary collisions, like the action of acids and alcalies, after a short ebullition will subside in harmony and union, not by the destruction of either, but in the friendly cohabitation of all. . . . Resplendent and all-pervading TRUTH will terminate the whole in universal harmony. All surreptitious efforts and attempts on public liberty will unavoidably excite the public vigilance of the sects, till the terms of general union be defined and honorably adjusted. The notion of erecting the polity of either sect into universal dominion to the destruction of the rest, is but an airy vision . . . all the present sects will subsist and increase into distinct respectable bodies, continuing their distinctions for a long time yet to come in full life and vigor. Indeed mutual oppression will more and more subside from their mutual balance of one another. Union may subsist on these distinctions, coalescence only on the sameness of public sentiment, which can again be effected in the Christian world only by the gentle but almighty power of truth. . . . The sects cannot destroy one another: all attempts this way will be fruitless—they may effect a temporary disturbance, but cannot produce a dissolution—each one subserves the mutual security of all. . . . Nothing however will content us but actual experiment—this experiment will be made in one century, and then perhaps we shall be satisfied.''[19]

It remained for James Madison to make still more explicit than Livingston or Stiles the analogy between the religious and the civic spheres. From his earliest days Madison had had a deep and passionate commitment to religious liberty. The Madison family was never warmly disposed toward the Anglican establishment in Virginia, and Madison's father appears to have been unsympathetic to the persecution of Baptists that raged during James's youth in neighboring Culpeper County. Madison himself, who was tutored by a Princeton-educated Presbyterian, made the significant choice to go to Princeton rather than to Anglican William and Mary. His undergraduate years at Princeton coincided with the regime of President John Witherspoon, who was later to be a signer of the Declaration of Independence. Although his religion was more severe than Madison's, Witherspoon may have heightened his antipathy to establishments. At Princeton Madison also appears to have read Voltaire surreptitiously, and of all the Voltairean aphorisms that he might have chosen to fasten upon, he became particularly fond of Voltaire's saying that in England one sect would have produced slavery and two a civil war, but that a multiplicity of sects caused the people to live at peace.[20] He was also apparently familiar with William Livingston's *Independent Reflector*, which was often read at Princeton. When he went back to Virginia, it was as a firm advocate of religious liberty and an alert foe of an Anglican episcopate. The editors of his papers have concluded that religious issues were more important than economic ones in stimulating his earliest interest in politics. When he began to correspond with a college friend from Pennsylvania, William Bradford, it was religious issues that chiefly aroused him, and he began to make unfavorable comparisons between Virginia's persecutions and the broad tolerance displayed in Pennsylvania.

At twenty-three, he denounced "that diabolical Hell conceived principle of persecution" and the Anglican clergy for abetting it, and professed that this troubled him more than any other public issue. Concerning a new outbreak of persecution in Culpeper County he wrote to Bradford in January 1774: "There are at this [time] in the adjacent county not less than five or six well-meaning men in close [jail] for publishing their religious sentiments which in the main are very orthodox. I have neither patience to hear, talk, or think of anything relative to this matter, for I have squabbled and scolded, abused and ridiculed about it to so little purpose, that I am without common patience." By contrast he admired "that liberal catholic and equitable way of thinking as to the rights of Conscience, which is one of the characteristics of a free people" that he believed to be prevalent in Pennsylvania. Later it was Madison who would take the leadership in the struggle to go beyond the limited principle of toleration to espouse complete religious liberty and achieve disestablishment in the first constitution of Virginia.[21]

As Madison was well aware in the less discouraged moments of his maturity, an answer to the "hell-conceived principle" was already apparent in America. The growth of a multiplicity of denominations and sects had made religious freedom a practical necessity, and had provided the political forces to make it possible. Madison's insight into the strength and viability of a pluralistic society seems at least to have been heightened by, if it did not derive from, the model already before him of various religious groups coexisting in comparative peace and harmony. He told the Virginia ratifying convention of 1788 that the remarkable freedom of religion now achieved "arises from that multiplicity of sects, which pervades America, and which is the best and only security for religious liberty in any society. . . . The United States abound in such a variety of sects, that it is a strong security against religious persecution, and it is sufficient to authorize a conclusion that no one sect will ever be able to outnumber or depress the rest."[22]

A monopolistic religious establishment, Madison saw, is in a position to persecute, just as a single interest in society or a single arm of government, when unchecked, is in a position to be tyrannical. A plurality of sects militates against religious oppression just as a plurality of varying social interests militates against political oppression. Madison put this

analogy very explicitly in Number 51 of *The Federalist*, where he spoke
of the desirability of guarding against the oppression of minorities by
a single consolidated majority. This, he thought, could be done in the
proposed federal republic of the United States "by comprehending in
the society so many separate descriptions of citizens as will render an
unjust combination of a majority of the whole very improbable, if not
impracticable." While all authority in the proposed republic, he went
on, "will be derived from and dependent on the society, the society itself
will be broken into so many parts, interests, and classes of citizens, that
the rights of individuals, or of the minority, will be in little danger from
interested combinations of the majority. *In a free government the security
for civil rights must be the same as that for religious rights. It consists
in the one case in the multiplicity of interests, and in the other in the
multiplicity of sects*. The degree of security in both cases will depend
on the number of interests and sects; and this may be presumed to depend
on the extent of country and number of people comprehended under the
same government."[23]

<h2 style="text-align:center">V</h2>

The best statement of Madison's pluralism, of course, is in the familiar
Number 10 of *The Federalist*, a work which shows a powerful obligation
to the theory of party laid down in David Hume's essays.[24] Madison's
basic concern in that essay was to show that a large federal union would
be better than a small republic at sustaining free representative government; but his point of departure was the problem of controlling parties
and the "violence" and threat to liberty that are connected with them.
Always, in *The Federalist* the fundamental thing government has to control is the "assertive selfishness of human nature." But the basic manifestation of this selfishness in political life is the party, or faction. Possibly the greatest of the many advantages that would come with a well-
constructed Union, Madison argued, was "its tendency to break and control the violence of faction." (Madison, it should be noted, used the
terms party and faction as synonyms.)[25] The classical problem of the
republics known to previous history, their instability, injustice, and confusion, had already been much remedied by the constitutions of the
American states, he admitted. But now complaints were being heard
everywhere by public-spirited men that "the public good is disregarded
in the conflicts of rival parties"—and particularly that measures were
being decided "by the superior force of an increased and overbearing

majority." Such injustices were largely if not wholly the consequence of "a factious spirit" in government. "By a faction," Madison goes on, "I understand a number of citizens, whether amounting to a majority or a minority of the whole, who are united and actuated by some common impulse of passion, or of interest, adverse to the rights of other citizens, or to the permanent and aggregate interests of the community."[26]

How best to remedy this state of affairs? You can destroy liberty, which makes faction possible, but that remedy is clearly far worse than the disease. You can try to give all citizens the same opinions, passions, and interests, but that is impracticable. Men have different faculties and different abilities in acquiring property; and protecting these faculties is the first object of government. But out of these differences arise different kinds and degrees of property, hence differing political interests and parties. "The latent causes of faction are thus sown in the nature of man." Passions will make men form factions and "vex and oppress each other." But different propertied interests—landed, moneyed, mercantile, manufacturing, debtors, and creditors—are the most common and durable sources of factions. "The regulation of these various and interfering interests forms the principal task of modern legislation, and involves the spirit of party and faction in the necessary and ordinary operations of government."

This last sentence, because of the ambiguity of the word "involves," has led some readers to think that Madison had found, after all, a strong positive function for parties. But it is one thing to say that legislation or government cannot be carried on without having parties make their appearance—i.e., that they are *involved*—and another that they are *valuable* in the process; and I think the whole context of Madison's work, with its pejorative definition of party and its many invidious references to party, make it clear that it was the former meaning he was trying to convey.

Since the causes of faction cannot be safely or wisely removed, Madison was saying, we have to look for relief in the means of controlling its effects. The most dangerous faction is the most powerful, the majority faction, and it is above all the tyranny of the majority that we must be concerned with. A minority faction, he admitted, could be temporarily obstructive, and could even convulse society. But in the normal course of events in a republic, it will be outvoted, and it will be "unable to execute and mask its violence under the forms of the Constitution." However, a majority faction can sacrifice the public good and the rights of other citizens to its ruling passion, and it is this above all that must be prevented. "To secure the public good and private rights against the danger of such [majority] faction, and at the same time to preserve the spirit and form of popular government, is then the great object to which our inquiries are directed."

How can this be done? It is useless to rely on enlightened statesmen: they may not always be there; and it is the very essence of good constitution-making to provide safeguards against ordinary human frailties.[27] The answer lies in a representative republic, which will avoid the turbulence of direct democracy, and in an extensive republic rather than a small one.

In making this last point, Madison was trying to establish a view which thus far had had the status of a heresy. It was standard eighteenth-century doctrine—made canonical by Montesquieu though questioned by Hume—that republican governments, whatever their merits, are not strong enough for the government of an extended territory. Madison was concerned to assert the opposite: that an extended territory such as that of the United States bodes well for the survival and stability of representative republican government precisely because, being large, it embraces a healthy and mutually balancing variety of economic and social interests. It is just this plurality and variety that he believes will prevent the emergence of a cohesive and oppressive majority. "Extend the sphere, and you take in a greater variety of parties and interests; you will make it less probable that a majority of the whole will have a common motive to invade the rights of other citizens; or if such a common motive exists, it will be more difficult for all who feel it to discover their own strength, and to act in unison with each other."[28]

In a large federal republic, Madison argued, a majority faction was less likely to be achieved than in a small one. The greater variety of parties is the greatest security "against the event of any one party being able to outnumber and oppress the rest." Thus the parties themselves are mobilized against the great danger of party. A multilateral equipoise, a suspended harmony of conflicting elements, very Newtonian in conception, is established. In Pope's words:

> Not chaos-like, together crushed and bruised
> But, as the world harmoniously confused
> Where order in variety we see,
> And where, though all things differ, all agree.

With the Madisonian formulation, thinking on the role of party had thus reached a stage of profound but fertile ambiguity. To unravel the ambiguity would require an entire additional generation of political experience.

VI

Certain aspects of the Madisonian model require comment here, since they point to difficulties unresolved either in the theory or the construction of the Constitution. Madison is not, for example, wholly clear by just what mechanism the formation of an oppressive majority is to be prevented. It is not certain whether he is saying that in a properly balanced society under a properly balanced constitution it will be impossible for a majority to form at all, or whether he simply believes that the majority, if formed, will be too weak or too impermanent, or both, to execute its "schemes of oppression." But more important than this is the question whether Madison has left room enough in his ingenious model for the formation of a majority sufficiently effective to govern at all. If the "energetic" government he and Hamilton sought was to become a reality, it would surely carry out a number of policies of sweeping consequence for the people, policies which in most cases would be the object of doubt and dispute. How could any such policies be formed and executed, if not through the periodic formation of majority coalitions? Again, how could they be better legitimated under a republican system than by reference to the majority will? Madison himself would soon enough begin to see the cogency of these questions.

Another problem that has stimulated much comment is that Madison seems to show so little fear of minority tyranny or even of minority obstruction, both of which he dismisses in a phrase. He does not address himself to the possibility that, since majorities are to be weak and precarious, a large, aggressive minority, though incapable of taking the reins of government, might veto whatever policy it likes, and thus in effect tyrannize over the majority.[29] There is, in short, no protection of the majority against grave deprivations imposed by the minority. (And as we shall see in due course, Madison was forced to confront this possibility near the end of his life, when he was compelled by his opposition to nullification to rephrase his view of the majority.) Neither, it must be added, does Madison address himself to the possibility that a minority interest in the population, by virtue of superior wealth, organization, and influence, can actually come into the firm possession of power against a pluralistic and divided majority. Yet within a few years after the Constitution was in operation this was precisely what the leaders of the emergent Republican party were saying about the Federalists.

Then, again, Madison's argument hardly anticipates the next step in the political game. What was he to say about the dangers of a majority coalition when his own party, the Republicans, had finally organized one? Were the Republicans a faction or party in the sense in which Madison had used that word? Were they too, then, a danger to liberty? Were they a danger to liberty when, having two of the arms of government and finding the opposition entrenched in the third, the judiciary, they tried to subordinate the third arm also? Was this a fatal invasion of the sacred principle of the separation of powers?

There is another set of problems arising from the tension between Madison's two great objectives, to create a more "energetic" national government and to protect liberty. Professor Alpheus T. Mason has remarked that *The Federalist* was a "split personality." Certainly there was a breach between Hamilton's clear and uncluttered concern for greater governmental energy and his tendency to consider that in a country like America liberty would be sure to take care of itself, and Madison's passionate desire, without sacrificing energy, to check the majority, to be sure that liberty was secured in a more certain way than had ever been done in the history of republics.[30]

The balance of social interests, the separation and balance of powers, were meant to secure liberty, but it was still uncertain, after the instrument had been framed and ratified, whether the balance would not be too precarious to come to rest anywhere; and whether the arms of government, separated in the parchment, could come together in reality to cooperate in the formation and execution of policy. As we shall see, a mechanism had to be found, for example, by which men could put together what God, in the shape of the Constitution, had sundered—to make it possible for the President and Congress to work in harness. Both the Federalists and the Republicans had to find a solution to this—the Federalists by making Hamilton a kind of prime minister to bridge the gap, and the Republicans by having President Jefferson exert through his agents and his direct influence a great power in Congress. The framers, discussing the method of election of the President, had expressed a good deal of concern that this should not happen—that the Executive should not be in league with, or the leader of, a party. But both sides, in order to make policy, found the agency of party a practical necessity. And in the end it seems doubtful whether this Constitution, devised against party, could have been made to work if such a functional agency as the party had not sprung into the gap to remedy its chief remaining deficiencies.

At an early point, then, parties were to become a part of the machinery of government in a manner that went well beyond Madison's resigned acceptance of them as evils that would always be there. In a country which was always to be in need of the cohesive force of institutions, the national parties, for all their faults, were to become at an early hour primary and necessary parts of the machinery of government, essential vehicles to convey men's loyalties to the State under a central government that often seemed rather distant and abstract. So much so that we may say that it was the parties that rescued this Constitution-against-parties and made of it a working instrument of government. When Lord Bryce came to evaluate American government in *The American Commonwealth*, he noted: "The whole machinery, both of national and State governments, is worked by the political parties. . . . The spirit and force of party has in America been as essential to the action of the machinery of government as steam is to a locomotive engine; or, to vary the simile, party association and organization are to the organs of government almost what the motor nerves are to the muscles, sinews, and bones of the human body. They transmit the motive power, they determine the direction by which the organs act. . . . The actual working of party government is not only full of interest and instruction, but is so unlike what a student of the Federal Constitution could have expected or foreseen, that it is the thing of all others which anyone writing about America ought to try to portray."[31]

A final word must be said about the character of Madison's pluralism. His was a pluralism *among* the parties, whereas the course of our national history has produced a pluralism *within* the parties. It was natural for Madison in 1787-88 to think of the country as having not merely a wide variety of interests but also a rather wide variety of party groupings and subgroupings within the states. Historians will almost certainly disagree about the details, but Forrest McDonald's delineation of the various political factions existing during the Confederation may be suggestive. He found, leaving out a miscellany of very small factions, one state (Pennsylvania) with two parties, five states with two major factions, five with three or four major factions, and one (Delaware) with multiple cliques.[32] We need not be surprised that Madison's thought had to be adapted to this existing political disorganization—thirteen states, each in its way a kind of separate political interest, and all together containing within them something like thirty discernible political groupings. What Madison did not see in advance was that the Constitution, by focusing more attention on nationwide issues, and indeed by itself first becoming a nationwide issue, would become a major force, perhaps *the* major force, in creating two great parties, and thus ironically making more probable the very majority coalition he so much feared; and, still more ironically, putting first Jefferson and then himself at the head of such a majority. What happened in due course, as it is so easy for us to see, was that our social pluralism made itself effective within each of the two major parties, a process that was strikingly evident in the Jeffersonian ranks by 1804, if not earlier. In our politics each major party has become a compound, a hodgepodge, of various and conflicting interests; and the imperatives of party struggle, the quest for victory and for offices, have forced the parties themselves to undertake the business of conciliation and compromise among such interests. This business goes on not merely in the legislative process, where Madison expected it would, but also in the internal processes of the great political parties themselves.

Madison's pluralism, then, had substantial merits as a generalized model, but as to the parties it was mislocated. Envisaging political parties as limited, homogeneous, fiercely aggressive, special interests, he failed to see that the parties themselves might become great, bland, enveloping coalitions, eschewing the assertion of firm principles and ideologies, embracing and muffling the struggles of special interests; or that they might forge the coalitions of majorities that are in fact necessary to effective government into forces sufficiently benign to avoid tyranny and sufficiently vulnerable to be displaced in time by the opposing coalition. Liberty, he had always understood, would sustain a political atmosphere in which a conflict of parties would take place. The reverse of that proposition, the insight that underlies our acceptance of the two-party system, that the conflict of parties can be made to reinforce rather than undermine liberty, was to be well understood only in the future.

NOTES

[1] Cf. Richard Pares: ". . . In the eighteenth century Cabinets existed to govern rather than to legislate, and parties to sustain government rather than legislation; . . . when a minister legislated, even on important matters, he often did so as an individual, not only technically but politically. It did not often happen that a party's programme consisted of legislation, or that the merits of a legislative proposal were, in any sense, put before the electorate." *King George III and the Politicians* (1953), 195. Cf. J. H. Plumb, *Sir Robert Walpole: The Making of a Statesman* (1956), 250-251.

[2] Pares, *King George III*, 191; cf. 182-207. The fluctuations and gradual growth of opposition and party politics are traced in Archibald S. Foord, *His Majesty's Opposition,*

1714-1830 (1964). On tendencies toward party in early nineteenth-century England, see Austin Mitchell, *The Whigs in Opposition, 1815-1830* (1967), especially chapters 1-3, and Norman Gash, *Reaction and Reconstruction in English Politics, 1832-1852* (1965), chapters 5-6.

³ Hamilton citing Necker to the Federal Convention, Max Farrand, ed., *Records of the Federal Convention of 1787* (1911), I, 288. On the elements of English freedom as of 1815, see Elie Halévy, *England in 1815* (ed. 1946), 588-591, and 108-200, passim.

⁴ For Franklin, Otis, and Adams, see H. Trevor Colbourn, *The Lamp of Experience* (1965), 72, 97, 130-131; for Jefferson, his *Notes on Virginia* (1785), ed. by T. P. Abernethy (1964), 66. Colbourn is especially illuminating on American versions of English and European history. See also Cushing Strout, *The American Image of the Old World* (1963), 12-17, 25-29, 33-38; William L. Sachse, *The Colonial American in Britain* (1956), 204-207; Edmund S. Morgan, "The Puritan Ethic and the American Revolution," *William and Mary Quarterly*, 24 (1967), 14-19.

⁵ Clarence Ver Steeg, *The Formative Years, 1607-1763* (1964), 273.

⁶ Richard P. McCormick, *Experiment in Independence*, 79; see chapter IV of his work for an excellent account of political machinery in the 1780's. Carl L. Becker, in his *History of Political Parties in the Province of New York, 1760-1776* (1909), considered that parties, not very clearly defined, came into being in the 1760's, but concedes that before that date New York was still in the thrall of "aristocratic methods of political management." See 11-18.

⁷ *The Federalist*, ed. by B. F. Wright (1961), 353-354. On the party struggle before 1766, see Theodore Thayer, *Pennsylvania Politics and the Growth of Democracy, 1740-1776* (1953).

⁸ See C. S. Sydnor, *Gentlemen Freeholders* (1952), especially 106-108, 115, 120-121. On the nature and significance of deferential society, see the brilliant essay by J. R. Pole, "Historians and the Problem of Early American Democracy," *American Historical Review*, 67 (1962), 626-646. On the transition from the politics of deference to those of public opinion and party debate in England and America, see Lloyd Irving Rudolph, "The Meaning of Party," doctoral dissertation, Harvard University, 1956.

⁹ Jack P. Greene, *The Quest for Power* (1963), 29-30; see also David Alan Williams, "Political Alignments in Colonial Virginia, 1698-1750," doctoral dissertation, Northwestern University, 1959, and Thad W. Tate, "The Coming of the Revolution in Virginia: Britain's Challenge to Virginia's Ruling Class," *William and Mary Quarterly*, 19 (1962), 339-340, 343.

¹⁰ Farrand, *Records*, I, 578; *The Federalist*, Number 48, 343. On the theme of power and liberty, see Bernard Bailyn, *The Ideological Origins of the American Revolution* (1967), and on the late acceptance of parties in formal political theory, Austin Ranney, "The Reception of Political Parties into American Political Science," *South-Western Social Science Quarterly*, 32 (1951), 183-191.

¹¹ It is a point that deserves further exploration, but what seems to dominate in the classical tradition is the sense that parties will normally be more or less identical with one of the orders in the state. Machiavelli generally speaks of a party as being identical with an order. Cf. *The Prince* in *The Prince and the Discourses* (Mod. Lib. ed., 1940), 35, 119; he refers to two hostile groups within the nobles as "factions." *Ibid.*, 42. In *The Discourses* he writes: "In every republic there are two parties, that of the nobles and that of the people; and all the laws that are favorable to liberty result from the opposition of these parties to each other, as may easily be seen from the events that occurred in Rome." *Ibid.*, 119. "Democracies," Aristotle had written, "are only exposed to sedition between the democratic party and the oligarchical, and there are no internal dissentions—at any rate none worth mentioning—which divide democratic parties against themselves." *Politics*, V, chap. 2, 16.

¹² Farrand, *Records*, I, 421, 260; Jonathan Elliott, *Debates in the Several State Conven-*

tions (1888), II, 285. Cf Madison in Number 51, where he argues that one should so contrive "the interior structure of the government as that its several constituent parts may, by their mutual relations, be the means of keeping each other in their proper places." Again, the way to avoid excessive legislative predominance is "to divide the legislature into different branches; and to render them, by different modes of election and different principles of action, as little connected with each other as the nature of their common functions and their common dependence on the society will admit." *The Federalist*, 355, 357.

[13] See her "Introduction" to her documentary anthology, *The Antifederalists* (1966), cx; cf. lv, lxxxv, xciii-xciv; see also her essay, "Men of Little Faith: the Antifederalists on the Nature of Representative Government," *William and Mary Quarterly*, 12 (1955), 40; cf. 13, 36.

During the debates over the ratification of the Constitution, factions and parties were occasionally mentioned, and almost always invidiously, by spokesmen on both sides, though more often by Federalists than by Anti-Federalists. Elliot, *Debates*, II, 14, 71-72, 168, 248, 253-254, 266, 292, 310, 317, 320, 322, 532; III, 37, 46, 87, 90, 107-108, 125, 233, 282, 290, 310, 316, 492, 583; IV, 38, 40, 59, 60, 66, 74-75, 127, 329.

[14] For a full account of this movement, see Carl Bridenbaugh, *Mitre and Sceptre* (1962).
[15] *Ibid.*, 306 n, 52.
[16] For this alliance see Sidney E. Mead, "American Protestantism during the Revolutionary Epoch," *Church History*, 12 (1953), 279-297.
[17] *The Independent Reflector*, ed. by Milton Klein (1963), 146, 148. On the significance of this controversy, see Klein's Introduction and Richard Hofstadter and Walter P. Metzger, *The Development of Academic Freedom in the United States* (1955), 187-191.
[18] *Independent Reflector*, 184, 195, 213: italics added. An Anglican spokesman, William Smith, saw the issue as follows: "As to the political uses of national establishments, he must indeed be a very shallow politician who does not see them. The statesman has always found it necessary for the purposes of government, to raise some one denomination of religion above the rest to a certain degree. This favor'd denomination, by these means, becomes as it were the creature of the government, which is thus enabled to turn the balance and keep all in subjection." Bridenbaugh, *Mitre and Sceptre*, 152. And this is precisely what the dissenting factions intended to prevent.
[19] *A Discourse on the Christian Union* (1761), 53, 95, 96-97; cf. Bridenbaugh, *Mitre and Sceptre*, chap. 1. "Our grand security," Stiles wrote to a Saybrook minister in 1767, "is in the multitude of sects and the public Liberty necessary for them to cohabit together. In consequence of which the aggrieved of any communion will either pass over to another, or rise into new sects and spontaneous societies. This and this only will learn us wisdom not to persecute one another." Edmund S. Morgan, *The Gentle Puritan: A Life of Ezra Stiles, 1727-1795* (1962), 252.
[20] In the *Lettres Philosophiques* Voltaire had written: "If there were only one religion in England, one would have to fear despotism; if there were two, they would cut each other's throats; but they have thirty, and they live happy and in peace."
[21] *Papers*, ed. by W. T. Hutchinson and W. M. E. Rachal I (1962), 101-106, 107, 111-113, 159, 170 ff.; Irving Brant, *James Madison: The Virginia Revolutionist* (1941), 65-77, 85, 128-130, 243 ff. On religious persecution in Virginia, see William Taylor Thom, *The Struggle for Religious Freedom in Virginia: the Baptists* (1900) and Garnett Ryland, *The Baptists of Virginia, 1699-1926* (1955), chap. III.
[22] Elliot, *Debates*, III, 330: see also *Writings*, Hunt, ed., II, 185; V, 176. For a much later statement on pluralism and tolerance in connection with the founding of the University of Virginia, see *Writings*, IX, 125-127.
[23] *The Federalist*, 358; italics added; cf. Farrand, *Records*, I, 134-136 for his speech in the Convention of 1787; and *Writings*, V, 123-129 for his speech in the Virginia Convention.

²⁴ For the text, see *The Federalist*, 129-136. The composition of this remarkable essay had gone on for some period of time. The basic analysis had been stated and restated in letters and in his "Observations" of April 1787. See *Writings*, II, 273, 346-347, 366-369; V, 28-32. It is important also, on this theme, to read *The Federalist*, Numbers 14, 37, 47, 48, 50, and 51.

²⁵ For example: ". . . and the most numerous party, or, in other words, the most powerful faction must be expected to prevail." *The Federalist*, Number 10, 132. See, on this, the useful textual comparisons made by Gottfried Dietze in *The Federalist: A Classic on Federalism and Free Government* (1960), 119 n; Dietze also points out (106) that Hamilton and Jay used the terms in the same way, cf. B. F. Wright in his edition of *The Federalist*, 33.

²⁶ Note that where Burke had defined party as based on principles aiming to advance the common interest, Madison defines it as based on passions or interests that threaten the general welfare.

²⁷ Cf. Hume, *Essays*, I, 99: "But a republican and free government would be an obvious absurdity, if the particular checks and controls, provided by the constitution, had really no influence, and made it not the interest, even of bad men, to act for the public good."

²⁸ In *The Federalist*, Number 9, Hamilton had tackled the same problem by trying to show that even Montesquieu had seen the confederation of republics as an answer to the problem of size.

²⁹ See Robert A. Dahl, *A Preface to Democratic Theory* (1956), 27-29, and more generally, chap. I, "Madisonian Democracy."

³⁰ Alpheus T. Mason, "The Federalist—A Split Personality," *American Historical Review*, 57 (1952), 625-643, especially 636 ff.

³¹ *The American Commonwealth*, 3d ed. (1897), I, 6; II, 3, 4.

³² Forrest McDonald, *We the People* (1958), chap. II. On Delaware, however, see John A. Munroe, *Federalist Delaware* (1954), 97-109, who finds two basic factions here also.

Part II

NASCENT PARTIES, 1789-1796

The brief span of years between the first federal elections and the end of Washington's Presidency was highly significant in the growth of a party system. In this period, the first symptoms of an emergent opposition party became evident. With surprising rapidity within a few years the party struggle between Federalists and Democratic-Republicans in Congress and in several states was normative. Stark differences over Hamilton's financial system, the French Revolution, and relations with Great Britain belied expectations of a general consensus and continuing harmony within the nation, producing, instead, increasing political cleavage. A pluralistic society with varied interests and outlook generated white-hot political emotions, yet the nation did not break up into fragments. The sense of nationhood, engendered by the revolutionary experience, the commitment to republicanism, and the veneration of the Constitution were among the cohesive forces having a strong centripetal effect. Nevertheless, political contentiousness and divisiveness over issues helped produce parties. By 1796, even though antagonism to the idea of party remained lively, strides had been made, often unconsciously, toward a two-party system.

The selections constituting this section focus on various aspects of party development. In "New Jersey's First Congressional Election," Richard P. McCormick analyzes the methods of conducting an election in the preparty period, as well as the efficacy of election machinery in protecting the public will. An excerpt from the late Joseph Charles' classic study *The Origins of the American Party System* critically assesses Alexander Hamilton's objectives and the virulent Congressional opposition to his financial system. Norman K. Risjord's study "The Virginia Federalists" investigates social, economic, and geographic differences in Virginia to explain the existence of a nationally oriented, anti-Jeffersonian political party in the state. In "John Beckley: An Early American Party Manager," Noble E. Cunningham, Jr., vividly portrays

Beckley in his role as professional politician and organizer of the Republican Party. The final selection, "Washington's Farewell, the French Alliance, and the Election of 1796," by Alexander DeConde deals with the effect of French influence on American party politics during a crucial election period.

A fundamental and simple question—when did American parties begin?—has raised a recurring debate among historians. No consensus has resulted largely because of historians' individual views of causation in political history and the difficulty of precise definition of parties. The question can be effectively rephrased and extended. What social forces lay beneath, what specific issues evoked parties in the postrevolutionary period?

Although contending groups formed in Colonial assemblies over local problems, in the strictest sense it would be a misconception to designate them as organized, ongoing parties. The politics of the Revolution and the Confederation years were divisive enough to result in the coalescence of political groups within the prefederal Congresses, but there was insufficient stability or continuity to distinguish these interest groups as parties. Jackson T. Main, however, in his latest book, *Political Parties Before the Constitution*, has examined political alignments at the state level during the 1780's and suggests that, in many states, divisions over basic political and economic issues were creating local legislative parties.

A traditional explanation attributes parties to differences over the Constitution in the politically effervescent period 1787-1789. According to this interpretation, federalist and antifederalist parties, struggling over ratification, were the progenitors of the later Federalists and Democratic-Republicans. Charles Beard in his noted work *Economic Origins of Jeffersonian Democracy* argued that economic class differences between capitalist and agrarian groups gave impetus to the rise of parties. In his view the same underlying economic cleavages made the parties of the 1790's the "lineal descendants" of the constitutional divisions.[1] Once almost universally accepted, this interpretation has lost much of its former popularity in light of more sophisticated political research. Historians reject the "notion of continuous flow," to use William N. Chambers' phrase, seeing instead that different issues of a later period produced new and more permanent political groups.

As early as 1825, John Quincy Adams, in his "Parties in the United States," explained American party division on the basis of "principles of social repulsion." In addition to the natural human tendency to divide politically, he found ethnic diversity, historical traditions, religious distinctions, and the existence of free and slaveholding areas as causes of party divisions. Federalists, in his view, were men of wealth and aristocratic outlook whose *raison d'être* was the protection of property, while Republicans were the majority who advocated democratic principles and championed the French "cause of human rights."[2]

Adams' multicausal explanation of party origins is not out of step with modern historical scholarship, which emphasizes sociological as well as political factors in the development of political parties. Contemporary investigation underscores the fact that no single issue can account for party divisions. The origins must be sought in the gradual formation of party nuclei in Congress, in the impact of major issues, and in the complexities of state and local politics.

Symptoms of party growth were abundant between 1792 and 1796. Under Madison's leadership in Congress opponents of Federalist policies began to cooperate, and a "Republican interest" evolved to counter the Federalist "friends of order." Crises over foreign affairs, notably the Genêt mission, the war crisis of 1794, and Jay's Treaty, led to a sharper definition of parties. As Harry Ammon has brought out, the Genêt affair first forced the nascent parties to move out of their Congressional orbit to appeal for public support. Federalist leaders were especially active in using the furor to undermine the Republicans.[3]

Party activity increased as the tempo of political life accelerated. Electioneering intensified in the contests of 1794 and 1796; the Democratic-Republican societies, as pressure groups, stimulated the spread of the Republican Party; Republican organizations developed noticeably in New York and New Jersey. Both parties, anxious to win over voters, utilized an intensely partisan press to sway the public. Multidimensional social, political, and economic differences were being expressed more and more through parties and in the struggle for political power. While the structure of parties remained skeletal in comparison with the post-1800 period, foundations were being laid, stone by stone, for the future.

Who then were Federalists and who were Republicans in the period under consideration? Generalization, in the absence of extensive politicosociological data, is at best tenuous, but it is important to summarize the similarities, as well as the differences, between the two party groups. To conceive of Federalists as an elite of conservative-minded businessmen or of Republicans as the democratically inspired supporters of the "common man" would be highly distorting. Nor is it correct to view them as ins versus outs—in other words, parties of no positive differences in principle or objectives.

Both political parties were strongly committed to the success of the experiment in republican government no matter how vehemently they accused each other of disloyalty to American principles. Epithets such as "Tory" or "Jacobin," so frequently in use, concealed an underlying loyalty on the part of most Federalists and Republicans to the continued independence of the nation. Among other characteristics of the parties were similarities in structure and approach. Both developing parties had elite leadership groups, yet drew on a heterogeneous following from various levels in society, widely scattered geographically. Federalists, as well as Republicans, formulated a rationale of government which served as an ideological bond for diverse elements within the parties. Their ideas were derived logically from axioms about the nature of man in society and the kind of ideal government best suited to man's needs. To ardent participants the parties and their principles were diametric opposites, whatever basic similarities in organizational techniques and electioneering methods these two components of the party system had.

As the Federalist Party developed, it attracted men of commerce, shipowner as well as merchant, to it. New business types such as bankers and speculators gave it strong support; professional men, especially lawyers, and often Congregational ministers in New England were firm in their Federalist beliefs. Skilled laborers in urban communities such as New York and Western settlers in the trans-Appalachian areas of the Southern states were prone to Federalism. The agrarian element too was highly important to Federalist success. Small New England farmers, Pennsylvania Germans, South Carolina merchant planters, and commercial farmers in the west of Virginia remained a source of strength into President Adams' administration.

These disparate social and economic elements were not tightly woven together, as has already been suggested, in a highly organized party. At best there seemed to be a congeries of local or state groups united with Federalists in Congress by a commonly held political position and an ideology: a staunch support of the Constitution, a demand for an energetic government deriving its powers from a broad interpretation of the Constitution, advocacy of Hamilton's financial program, unyielding opposition to French Revolutionary influences, and veneration of Washington.

Federalist ideology posited the concept that most men were fundamentally incapable of governing themselves wisely and were likely to follow will-o'-the-wisps, leading to the downfall of the Republic. Since man was inherently fallible and given to evil, authority had to prevail; otherwise freedom would succumb to despotism. Champions of a well-ordered social structure in which deference to the natural leadership of men of education, property, and family position was to be expected, Federalists were certain that they alone were a bulwark against the excesses and inherent tyranny of popular rule. Government in Hamilton's view should be not by a broadly based party, but by the talented few who would act for the common good. Consequently, the Republican opposition was not legitimate; it was instead visible evidence of insidious attempts to subvert government and infuse abhorrent French ideas into society.

To whom, in turn, did the Republicans appeal? Former antifederalists found Republican opposition to Hamiltonian centralization very congenial. Opponents of high finance, with its dangers of taxation and corruption, turned to Madison as their spokesman. Hostility to Britain and adulation for France helped crystallize the Republican Party in the battles over foreign policy after 1793. But it was the emotion-laden Jay's Treaty which could provoke an ardent Jeffersonian Republican, Dr. Nathaniel Ames of Dedham, Massachusetts, to state pungently in his diary in 1795. "The President Washington ratified the Treaty with Britain. . . . Better his hand had been cut off when his Glory was at its heighth—before he blasted all his Laurels!"[4]

Small farmers in the Southern and Mid-Atlantic states and slaveholding planters formed the backbone of the early Republican Party. From 1794 on, Federalist leaders were uneasy about the "Jacobin" spirit in urban seaport communities and the gains Republicans were making in some of them. Philadelphia, influenced by the Democratic-Republican societies, was largely Republican, while New York City added the support of mechanics, tradesmen, and some professional people to the upstate Republican yeomanry. In Massachusetts and Connecticut communities, however, Republicans, at this time, were few and far between.

With the same intellectual heritage as the Federalists, the Republicans developed more positive views of humanity than their opponents. Man, in optimistic Republican eyes, was capable of perfection and could be trusted with liberty and self-government. Education was the touchstone, according to Republicans, which enabled man to rise above ignorance and to govern wisely. Fearing the growth of an aristocracy of wealth, the Republicans were convinced that the Federalists in power would trample down liberty in their quest for monetary gain. Unless the Federalist tendency to resort to financial and military power to carry on government were curbed, there was grave danger that the states would be dominated by an omnipotent central government. An effective counterweight to this threat, Republicans believed, was to oppose everything which undermined the preservation of the rights of man and republican government. In a practical way, simplicity in operating the government and limiting national power would further these ideals.

By the election of 1796 both parties had emerged out of the chrysalis stage. Washington's retirement from the Presidency spurred "the party racers to start," as one observer commented. With a national forum to debate major issues and with an increasingly politically conscious electorate participating in political activity, political parties were certain to expand in influence. Slowly, almost haltingly, the nation had come to a reluctant acceptance of parties. The next years after 1796 would see only an intensification of party, not its extirpation.

NOTES

[1] Charles A. Beard, *Economic Origins of Jeffersonian Democracy* (New York, Macmillan, 1915), p. 32.

[2] John Quincy Adams, *Parties in the United States* (New York, Greenberg: Publisher, 1941), pp. 1-2, 11-12, 15. The manuscript was not published until this edition appeared.

[3] Harry Ammon, "The Genêt Mission and the Development of American Political Parties," *Journal of American History*, Vol. LII (March, 1966), pp. 725-726, 731.

[4] Diary of Nathaniel Ames, August 14, 1795, Dedham Historical Society, Dedham, Massachusetts.

NEW JERSEY'S FIRST

CONGRESSIONAL ELECTION, 1789:

A Case Study In Political Skullduggery*

Richard P. McCormick

Elections are a key to the democratic process, revealing many facets of political parties in action and giving a unique insight into the behavior of the electorate. Ideally, elections are a means of expressing the popular will with respect to leaders and, to a degree, governmental policies. In this article Richard McCormick, professor of history at Rutgers University, cogently discusses the first federal election in New Jersey in the context of the functioning of the political system. Missing none of the drama of this hot election contest, he concentrates on its overall significance, concluding that the lack of adequate safeguards in the election machinery vitiated the wishes of a majority of the voters. An effective mode of conducting elections, he suggests, is essential if democracy is not to be thwarted. Richard McCormick, widely known for his studies in political history, is the author of Experiment in Independence: The History of Voting in New Jersey *(1953) and* The Second American Party System *(1966).*

The functioning of the electoral machinery available to the American people at various periods in their history for the expression of their will is a field of study that has received less attention than it merits. Even those who style themselves "political historians" have been prone to make much of issues, alignments, and personalities and to neglect the intricate processes that form the working core of democracy. Republican government is distinguished by its reliance on techniques for permitting eligible voters to choose those who will be the authentic representatives

* Reprinted by permission from Richard P. McCormick, "New Jersey's First Congressional Election, 1789: A Case Study in Political Skulduggery," *William and Mary Quarterly*, 3d Ser., Vol. VI (April, 1949), pp. 237-250.

of the majority in the public councils. Upon the adequacy of those techniques, therefore, rests the efficiency of this form of government. When the existing electoral machinery is immaturely developed or readily corrupted by fraudulent manipulation, the popular will is frustrated, negatived, or, at best, inaccurately recorded. Moreover, the machinery itself is a factor in determining what issues will be emphasized, what kinds of alignments will develop, and what types of personalities will dominate.

An illuminating case history of electoral practices in the earliest days of the Federal Republic is found in the first congressional election in New Jersey. Although devoid of broad significance in the usual sense, this contest abundantly illustrates not only the elementary character of election machinery at the time but also the readiness with which such machinery could be "used" by scheming men. Adding to the interest in the New Jersey case is the fact that it presented the First Congress with a complicated election dispute, the solution of which was to occasion the new House of Representatives no little difficulty.

The background of the election can be sketched briefly. The basic political cleavage in the state was along sectional lines, with East Jersey opposed to West Jersey. The result of historical, geographic, social, cultural, and economic differences between the two regions, the division had long been fairly clear-cut on questions of internal policy. During the mid-eighties East Jersey was in control of the government and enacted a series of financial measures, among them a loan-office law, over the protests of the West Jersey minority in the legislature. On the matter of ratifying the Constitution, however, the state had exhibited rare unanimity, chiefly because all classes and sections expected to benefit from a tariff that would enable the Federal government to pay its debts and release the states from burdensome requisitions. In 1789 the balance between the contending forces was delicate, and the political chieftains of West Jersey, especially, looked to the election which would choose the representatives to the First Congress with great interest.[1]

The machinery for selecting New Jersey's first congressmen was set in motion by the legislature that met in October, 1788. A bill to provide for the choosing of presidential electors, senators, and representatives, introduced early in the session, was the subject of behind-the-scenes controversy for three weeks. The question at issue was whether representatives should be voted for in a general or in district elections. The members from the western counties, taking a confident all-or-nothing attitude, favored the general method, which was eventually adopted on November 21.[2]

The law provided that any qualified voter might nominate four candidates by delivering a list of names to the clerk of the court of common pleas in each county who would in turn transmit them to the governor for publication. The election was to be conducted by ballot under the same regulations that applied to state elections. In charge of the election in each county was the sheriff, who was assisted by a group of inspectors —one from each town—elected by the assembled voters when they came to the polling place on the first day of the canvass. The other election officials were three clerks chosen by the inspectors. In most counties the poll would be opened at the county seat and would be adjourned from there to other specified locations. The number of polling places varied from two to eight in a county, with a total of fifty-three in the state as a whole. As to franchise requirements, any voter who was challenged by the inspectors had to swear or affirm that he was of full age, worth £50 clear estate, and one year resident in the county. The election was to begin February 11, 1789; of great importance in view of later developments was the fact that no date was set for closing the polls. Responsibility for counting the ballots and determining who were the successful candidates was assigned to the governor and his privy council.[3]

The character of the campaign that was to be waged over the four congressional seats began to take form even before the legislature adjourned. Early in the session an agreement had been effected among the political chieftains of West Jersey and a few powerful men in East Jersey. This combination had been responsible for the adoption of the general election scheme and had been active also in the senatorial contest.[4] Its crowning achievement, however, was the placing in nomination, with the sanction of a large group in the assembly, of a four-man slate which became generally known as the "Junto ticket" or the "West Jersey ticket."[5] The quartet was made up of two men from East Jersey—Elias Boudinot of Elizabethtown and James Schureman of New Brunswick —and two from West Jersey—Thomas Sinnickson of Salem and Lambert Cadwallader of Trenton. All except Sinnickson, who was a prosperous merchant, had served in the Continental Congress; all had been outspoken critics of paper money; all were destined to become firm Federalists. The ticket was to receive almost universal support in the western counties; Schureman alone was popular in East Jersey.[6]

The popular leaders in East Jersey were unable to come to any agreement on a slate that they could back in opposition to the Junto.[7] Instead, many tickets were nominated in the northern counties. Most of them included the names of Abraham Clark, signer of the Declaration of

Independence, state legislator, member of the Continental Congress, and champion of paper money, and Jonathan Dayton, Revolutionary officer, member of the Constitutional Convention, and speculator extraordinary in public lands and securities.[8] In some counties strong combinations were formed in behalf of a particular group of candidates, but there was nothing comparable to the near-unanimity that prevailed in West Jersey. Dayton alone of the East Jersey non-Junto candidates had a small number of loyal campaigners in the southern part of the state.[9] In all, some fifty-four men were placed in nomination, although many subsequently announced their withdrawal from the race.[10]

The campaign was not characterized by debate over pertinent issues but rather by attacks on personalities and appeals to sectional jealousy. The Junto ticket was presented to the people as being staunchly Federalist, and the foes of the Junto, particularly Clark and Dayton, were depicted as being unfriendly to the new Constitution. There is little evidence that such a distinction in fact existed.[11] Rumors and accusations of all kinds were actively propagated in the press, through handbills, and by word of mouth. The Junto was condemned as a "secret cabal" of "great men" who should be taught not to meddle in politics.[12] Elias Boudinot was denounced for having drawn "many thousands of dollars out of the public treasury to decorate his palace, profusely furnish his table, and clatter through the streets in a chariot" while he was President of the Continental Congress.[13] The serious charge was made against Jonathan Dayton that he had been heavily involved in illegal trade during the war.[14]

No one came in for more abuse than did Abraham Clark, the foremost political figure in East Jersey. Wide circulation was given to handbills containing sworn statements that Clark had openly declared his hostility to the Constitution and to General Washington and that he had tendered depreciated certificates in payment of a debt to a Quaker merchant.[15] In answer to these attacks, Clark readily admitted that he had had some early doubts about the Constitution, but he insisted that he had in no way opposed ratification and that he was willing to leave to Congress the matter of recommending amendments. He dismissed the insinuation that he was inimical to Washington and flatly denied the tender story. In his own behalf, he asserted that his letters had been "taken up and secreted" by his malicious opponents. Too, he scorned the erroneous report, printed in a Trenton paper, that he had withdrawn from the campaign.[16]

The campaign was obviously a heated one, with no holds barred. So general was the indulgence in vituperation that the editor of the *Bruns-wick Gazette* was moved to remark that scarcely a single candidate "escaped the lash of some slanderous tongue."[17] The principal active supporters of individual candidates were motivated by considerations of personal loyalty and friendship and by a desire to win power in the competition for office. Family alliances and close social relationships among groups of leading men were at the base of political factions. The electorate was influenced largely by sectional considerations. In essence, the contest was between the Junto slate of West Jersey and Clark and Dayton of East Jersey. It was the familiar contest that had long dominated Jersey politics.[18]

It was in the manipulation of the actual election that political skulduggery reached its peak—or its depth. The Junto had the superior organization, and it spared no efforts, legal and otherwise, to garner votes. The key figure in the group was Joseph Ellis, a member of the council from Gloucester, who was credited with having originated the whole plan.[19] Others who figured prominently in the inner workings of the machine were Elias Boudinot and his brother, Elisha; Richard Stockton, son of the "Signer" and Boudinot's nephew; John Chetwood, close friend of Boudinot's and Council member from Essex; Joshua Maddox Wallace, John Lawrence, James Kinsey, Caleb and William Newbold, and Richard S. Smith of Burlington; and Franklin Davenport of Gloucester. Not a few of these men were tainted with toryism; all subsequently became Federalists.[20]

The strategy of the Junto was simple. Realizing that they would secure relatively few votes in East Jersey, they schemed to get every possible vote in the five lower counties. In order that the managers in Burlington and Gloucester might be apprized of what was necessary to be done, a daily communication was maintained with Boudinot and Chetwood, who reported on the state of the polls in the northern counties. A printed ballot, probably an innovation, was prepared to be given to the voters. Election inspectors and clerks in West Jersey were Junto men, and they were not above refusing tickets that did not contain the prescribed four names. To insure a maximum vote, the polls were moved around the circuits not once but twice. Ballots were collected also at places not authorized by law.[21] "Everybody," wrote William Bradford from Burlington, "seemed to be *positively* charged with the Electioneering Spirit, & ready to communicate it at the slightest approach."[22]

The greatest difficulty confronting the Junto was to persuade the "rigid" Quakers to turn out and vote.[23] The argument used to overcome this obstacle was that Clark, Dayton, and their cohorts were bellicose Presbyterians who would visit all sorts of oppression on the peaceable Quakers once they gained control of the government. Such propaganda was effective. "The Poor Friend being alarmed at the situation of his Society," reported Joseph Bloomfield, "finds 'Freedom' takes the Printed junto-Ticket, & away He goes, with such of his Neighbors as He can influence by telling them the same melancholy tale—to keep out the bloodthirsty Presbyterians and to prevent War, Blood & Slaughter."[24]

The supporters of Dayton were not idle in West Jersey, but their efforts were in vain. Joseph Bloomfield, Dr. John Ross, and some others from Burlington; the Reverend Andrew Hunter of Woodbury; the Ogdens and the Daytons of Elizabethtown; Robert Lettis Hooper of Trenton; John N. Cummings of Newark; and Jonathan Rhea of Monmouth all visited the polls in the western counties and sought to bring in voters for their candidate.[25] These men were, with Dayton, members of the Society of Cincinnati; most were former army comrades. Some of them later became Federalists—like Dayton—while others joined the Democratic-Republicans.[26]

The climax of the election came late in February. The voting had begun throughout the state on the eleventh, and by the twenty-third seven counties, all those to the northward of Trenton with the important exception of Essex, had closed their polls and reported their returns. The totals showed over 5,000 for Schureman, 4,000 each for Clark and Dayton, and less than 1,000 each for Boudinot, Cadwallader, and Sinnickson. The Junto ticket was clearly not popular in East Jersey.[27] The West Jersey politicos proved themselves more than equal to the occasion. They had originally assumed that the maximum vote in the five lower counties would be about 5,000 with Burlington providing 1,500 of that total.[28] When a courier from Boudinot in Elizabethtown arrived in Burlington with the final figures from East Jersey, the Junto managers went into action.

It had been planned to close the Burlington poll on the twenty-first of February and that in Gloucester on the twenty-third. Instead, the ballot boxes, in the custody of zealous inspectors, were sent once more around the circuit in each county in order to round up sufficient votes to overbalance the 4,000 that Clark and Dayton had already obtained plus the 2,500 they were expected to get when Essex made its return. "The Bell-Wethers of Cadwallader & Boudinot are riding night and day for this purpose," Bloomfield informed Dayton from Burlington. "If your Essex-

Election is not closed," he advised, "you must turn out 3,000 votes, or I fear we shall not succeed in our wishes. Had the Polls in this County & Gloucester closed as first intended, there would have been not more than 3,000 votes taken in this & Gloucester County."[29] His analysis was correct. Not until March 4 did the Burlington election end, by which date 2,826 votes had been cast. "The fear of injuring a Cause which they were anxiously engaged to support," Joshua Maddox Wallace ingenuously explained to Boudinot, "induced our Inspectors to close the Poll. Unless more Votes than you expect are taken in Essex, the Western Ticket is safe."[30]

The supporters of Clark and Dayton in Essex County, which was the center of opposition to the Junto, were fully aware of the devices that were being employed in West Jersey, and they were determined not to be outdone. On March 12, they petitioned the officials in charge of the election in the county to keep the poll open "so long as it is probable that the keeping it open will serve to counteract and frustrate the combinations against us; as we wish to remain unrepresented, until we can have a Fair Election, rather than submit to a representation, in which we have no confidence."[31] This request was granted, and not until April 27—more than ten weeks after the voting had begun—did the balloting end.[32] The election had turned into a farce; James Madison was restrained when he commented on the "very singular manner" in which it had been conducted. Walter Rutherfurd was more exact. "Poor Jersey," he lamented, "is made a laughing stock of."[33]

The complicated problem of determining the results of the election lay with the governor and his privy council.[34] Evidently assuming that all the returns would be in by that date, Governor Livingston called four of his councilors to Elizabethtown on March 3. At this time he laid before them the results of the voting in the seven counties that had reported. Immediately a dispute developed within the group, with two councilors friendly to Clark and Dayton arguing that the election should be decided on the basis of these scanty returns and two others insisting that the votes from the whole state were needed. Unable to come to any agreement, the meeting adjourned, and the governor announced another privy council session for March 18.[35]

When the privy council met again on March 18, the election scene, of course, had changed. The uninhibited endeavors of the Junto had given the Schureman-Cadwallader-Boudinot-Sinnickson ticket a majority of some seven thousand votes in the five lower counties. Sensing defeat for Clark and Dayton, Essex had refused to close the polls. The privy council had before it, then, the returns from twelve counties only. According to law, it was supposed to determine the four persons having "the greatest Number of Votes from the whole State, to be the Persons duly chosen" to represent New Jersey in Congress.[36] Obviously it could not comply with the letter of the statute as long as Essex withheld its votes. With twelve members in attendance, the privy council wrestled with the knotty tangle and finally decided "to cast up the whole number of votes from the twelve Counties . . . leaving the decision of the legality of the election of the four Persons who have the Majority of Voices from the twelve Counties . . . to those to whom it appurtains . . ." Thereupon Schureman, Cadwallader, Boudinot, and Sinnickson were named as the four highest, and Governor Livingston was advised to issue a proclamation embodying this equivocal verdict. Vigorously dissenting from this decision were three pro-Clark councilors who took the not illogical position that if March 3 had not been the proper time to decide the election, then the privy council should wait until all of the counties had been heard from.[37] On the day following the meeting, Governor Livingston issued his proclamation announcing the verdict of the privy council and leaving the "decision of the legality of the election . . . to whom it appertains."[38] Thus the final disposition of the matter was by implication left up to Congress.

The disgruntled followers of Clark and Dayton in East Jersey were disposed to contest the verdict of the privy council. Protests against the outcome of the election were aired in the press, and soon petitions were circulating throughout the northern counties calling upon the House of Representatives to investigate the canvass.[39] On April 28 these petitions were presented to the House. The next day they were referred to the committee of elections with instructions to "report a proper mode of investigating and deciding thereupon."[40] Subsequently, the adherents of the Junto introduced counterpetitions, which were handled in the same manner.[41]

A month went by before the House, occupied with the more important task of creating the structure of the new government, took further notice of the New Jersey election. Finally, on May 25, approval was given to a report from the committee of elections empowering that group to receive proofs and allegations respecting the charges made in the petitions and to report the facts to the House.[42] Not until almost two months later did the committee make any further report.[43] Then it notified the House of its findings and stated that certain allegations in the petitions required the testimony of witnesses. The question was, how should it go about procuring such testimony? Fisher Ames, a member of the committee, proposed that the judges of the Supreme Court of New Jersey be commissioned to take depositions. This precipitated an interesting debate, in the course of which suggestions were made that a special commission should be sent to New Jersey, that both parties to the dispute should be heard by counsel before the whole House, and that the committee of elections should be authorized to send for evidence, papers, and records. There was even some discussion of whether or not the House possessed the power to take cognizance of proceedings in New Jersey under an election law of that state. At the end of the debate, Ames' proposal was negatived, but the House adjourned without providing the committee with any positive answer to the question raised.[44]

Despite the fact that it lacked clearly defined powers, the committee evidently decided on its own initiative to grant a hearing on August 13 to the petitioners against the election and to their counsel. Present at the hearing to testify were Abraham Kitchell, member of the council from Morris, Jacob Arnold, assemblyman from the same county, and Peter Haring, councelor from Bergen. Their testimony, as it was given in response to questions by their counsel, centered mainly around the privy council meeting of March 3.[45] Elias Boudinot was present, and at the end of the hearing he "moved for a further day merely to shew that the Essex Election had been carried on with violent designs to prevent a Representation." The committee refused this request, because, according to Boudinot, they did not think it "worth while."[46]

Five days after the hearing, the committee of elections made known its findings to the House. Embodying six points, the brief report merely listed chronologically the main events of the election and its aftermath; it contained no recommendations. The only action taken at the time was to lay the report on the table.[47]

After more than four months of delay, the House finally made its decision on the New Jersey case early in September. The committee report was taken up for consideration on the first. Several motions were made and withdrawn as various members expressed their views on the subject.[48] In the words of the *Gazette of the United States*, "no determinate principle of discussing the subject" was agreed upon. The debate was continued on the second, and it ended with the adoption by a large majority of a resolution declaring the sitting members to have been "duly elected and returned to serve" in the House.[49] "The principle which lead the House was," according to Elias Boudinot, "that the Governor and Council would have been inexcusable if they had not delayed the

Matter, when they found but 7 Counties had returned their Lists."[50] The decision had not been easily made. "I have seldom kept my mind in suspense till the vote was called," wrote Fisher Ames. "In this case I remain still in suspense, inclining sometimes *pro*, sometimes *con*."[51] After months of uncertain floundering when confronted with an unprecedented problem, Congress had settled an election contest in which it had little interest and announced a verdict that represented a weak avoidance of real issues.

The whole episode demonstrated the extent to which democratic expression could be influenced by the character of the available electoral machinery. Loose franchise requirements, inadequate and poorly distributed polling facilities, partial election officials, lax balloting regulations, and ambiguous provisions for closing the election and counting the votes were but some of the major flaws in the mechanism. There existed every opportunity for determined political managers to pile up votes in a brazenly calculated manner. Because the machinery was faulty, it cannot be said that the election represented the popular will of the people of New Jersey. Indeed, there is the strongest presumption that the *vox populi* was frustrated. Although the New Jersey situation may not have been typical, it was doubtless not unusual. The solution to the problem of assuring the people's will honest expression through efficient electoral machinery lay in the future. The solving of that problem was to be essential to the functioning of truly republican government.

NOTES

[1] For an elaboration of the political situation in New Jersey at this time, see my unpublished doctoral thesis, "Experiment in Independence: New Jersey in the Critical Period, 1781-1790," University of Pennsylvania, 1948.

[2] *Votes and Proceedings of the General Assembly of the State of New-Jersey, Thirteenth Session, First Sitting* (Trenton, 1788), 62; *Journal of the Proceedings of the Legislative-Council of the State of New-Jersey, Thirteenth Session, First Sitting* (Trenton, 1788), 7-18; Robert Lettis Hooper to Jonathan Dayton, Nov. 11, 1788, Miscellaneous Papers, New York Public Library (NYPL); Elias Boudinot to James Kinsey, Nov. 20, 1788, New Jersey Manuscripts, III, New Jersey Historical Society (NJHS).

[3] *Acts of the . . . General Assembly of the State of New Jersey, Thirteenth Session, First Sitting* (Trenton, 1788), Acts of Nov. 21, 29, 1788; *Acts . . . , Eighth Session, First Sitting*, Act of Dec. 16, 1783. The procedure in this congressional election differed in three important respects from the machinery that had been maintained in the past. Formerly, *viva voce* voting had been employed in eight of the thirteen counties. Too, the number of polling places in the state was increased from twenty-nine to fifty-three. This change was especially important in the western counties, where the polling facilities were

actually trebled. Finally, this election marked the first time the people of the state had voted as a whole for any officials.

⁴ Elias Boudinot to James Kinsey, Nov. 20, 1788, New Jersey Manuscripts, III; William Bradford to Mrs. [Elias] Boudinot, Dec. 5, 1788, Wallace Papers, I, Historical Society of Pennsylvania (HSP).

⁵ "A Freeholder" in (Elizabethtown) *New Jersey Journal*, Dec. 10, 1788; Samuel Dick to Gov. William Livingston, Jan. 7, 1789, Livingston Papers, Massachusetts Historical Society (MHS); John Stevens, Jr., to John Stevens, Sr., Dec. 23, 1788, Stevens Papers, Stevens Institute of Technology (SIT).

⁶ The original nomination lists for the counties of Middlesex, Somerset, Sussex, Burlington, Gloucester, and Cumberland, preserved among the papers of William Livingston in the Massachusetts Historical Society, detail the candidates nominated in each of those counties and who nominated them. Consequently they indicate the stand taken by important persons in the election and the relative strength of the different candidates in various counties.

⁷ John Mehelm to William Livingston, Feb. 20, 1789, Livingston Papers.

⁸ "A Freeholder," *New Jersey Journal*, Dec. 10, 1788; "A Free Elector," *ibid.*, Jan. 7, 1789; "A Correspondent," *ibid.*, Jan. 21, 1789; *Brunswick Gazette*, Jan. 6, 27, 1789; Nomination lists, Livingston Papers. It is significant that many of the tickets proposed in East Jersey coupled the names of Clark and Dayton, who are generally called "radicals," with those of Schureman and Sinnickson, who were strongly conservative. Too, some of the most "respectable characters" placed Clark's name on their lists.

⁹ "Letters of Martin B. Bunn to Abraham Clark," *Brunswick Gazette*, Feb. 23 to Sept. 15, 1789. These letters, seven in number, were written by an opponent of Clark. They contain a wealth of information on the campaign in general and on the contest in Somerset in particular. The pseudonym, "Martin B. Bunn," was probably derived from the names of Ephraim Martin, Robert Blair, and Edward Bunn, three legislators from Somerset who were friendly to Clark.

¹⁰ *New Jersey Journal*, Jan. 21, 28, 1789; *Brunswick Gazette*, Jan 27, 1789.

¹¹ Samuel Dick to William Livingston, Jan. 7, 1789, Livingston Papers. None of the surviving personal correspondence relating to the campaign would indicate that fidelity to the Constitution was a serious issue.

¹² "A Freeholder," *New Jersey Journal*, Dec. 10, 1788; "A Free Elector," *ibid.*, Jan. 7, 1789.

¹³ "A Candid Enquirer," *New Jersey Journal*, Feb. 11, 1789.

¹⁴ Joseph Bloomfield to Jonathan Dayton, Feb. 23, 1789, Gratz Collection, HSP.

¹⁵ *New Jersey Journal*, Feb. 4, 1789; *Brunswick Gazette*, Feb. 10, 1789.

¹⁶ *New Jersey Journal*, Feb. 4, 1789; *Brunswick Gazette*, Feb. 7, 1789.

¹⁷ *Brunswick Gazette*, Mar. 24, 1789.

¹⁸ John Rutherfurd to Robert Morris, Jan. 13, [1789], Robert Morris Papers, Rutgers University Library (RUL).

¹⁹ Joseph Bloomfield to Jonathan Dayton, Feb. 28, 1789, Miscellaneous Manuscripts, RUL; "Triumph," *New Jersey Journal*, Mar. 18, 1789.

²⁰ Joshua M. Wallace to Elias Boudinot, Mar. 6, 1789, Wallace Papers, VI.

²¹ Joseph Bloomfield to Jonathan Dayton, Feb. 23, 1789, Gratz Collection; John Lawrence to Elias Boudinot, Feb. 16, 1789, Emmet Collection, NYPL; J. M. Wallace to Elias Boudinot, Mar. 6, 1789, Wallace Papers, VI.

²² Bradford to Elias Boudinot, Feb. 17, 1789, Wallace Papers, I.

²³ The Burlington Quarterly Meeting early in 1789 called the attention of Friends to the minute that had been adopted by the Philadelphia Yearly Meeting in 1758 advising Friends against holding public office. Many with "tender consciences" believed they could not participate in elections. Minutes of the Burlington Quarterly Meeting, Feb. 23, 1789, Friends Book Store, Phila.; Ezra Michenor, *A Retrospect of Early Quakerism, being*

extracts from the records of Philadelphia Yearly Meeting and the meetings composing it (Philadelphia, 1860), 274; "John Hunt's Diary," *Proceedings of the New Jersey Historical Society*, LIII (1935), 111.

[24] Joseph Bloomfield to Jonathan Dayton, Feb. 28, 1789, Miscellaneous Manuscripts, RUL. This letter is printed in full in *The Journal of the Rutgers University Library*, IV (1941), 48-50.

[25] Joseph Bloomfield to Jonathan Dayton, Feb. 23, 1789, Gratz Collection; Bloomfield to Dayton, Feb. 28, 1789, Miscellaneous Manuscripts, RUL.

[26] List of members of the Society of Cincinnati in the State of New Jersey, July, 1788, File D:227, NJHS; Walter R. Fee, *The Transition from Aristocracy to Democracy in New Jersey, 1789-1829* (Somerville, N.J., 1933), *passim*.

[27] *New Jersey Journal*, Feb. 25, 1789; *Brunswick Gazette*, Mar. 3, 1789.

[28] James Kinsey to Elias Boudinot, Feb. 16, 1789, Miscellaneous Manuscripts, RUL.

[29] Joseph Bloomfield to Jonathan Dayton, Feb. 23, 1789, Gratz Collection.

[30] J. M. Wallace to Elias Boudinot, Mar. 5, 1789, Wallace Papers, VI. The polls were still open in Gloucester and, perhaps, in Salem and Cape May, but they had all closed before March 12. According to Bloomfield, there had been 1,802 ballots cast in Burlington and about the same number in Gloucester up to February 23. When the election finally ended the two counties had polled over 5,300 votes. This approximated the total from Bergen, Middlesex, Somerset, Monmouth, Morris, Hunterdon, and Sussex, whose combined population was more than twice that of the two southern counties. It is significant that in the state election held in October, 1787, the total vote in Burlington was only 258. See Henry C. Shinn, "An Early New Jersey Poll List," *Pennsylvania Magazine of History and Biography*, XLIV (1920), 77-81. Actually, the Burlington vote of 2,826 was equivalent to about 80 per cent of the adult white male population.

[31] *Brunswick Gazette*, Mar. 24, 1789.

[32] *New Jersey Journal*, Mar. 11, 1789; Essex election return, Apr. 30, 1789, Livingston Papers.

[33] *The Writings of James Madison . . .* , Gaillard Hunt, ed. (New York, 1902), V, 330; Rutherfurd to John Stevens, Sr., Mar. 13, 1789, Stevens Papers.

[34] The privy council, composed of members of the council, met irregularly at the summons of the governor to advise him on such matters as granting pardons, signing pay warrants, and issuing proclamations. It had never before had any part in determining elections.

[35] The manuscript minutes of the privy council in the State Library at Trenton make no mention of this meeting on March 3. The full story of the session, however, is related in "Evidence given before the Committee [of Congress] on [the] New Jersey Election, Aug. 13, 1789" (in the handwriting of Elias Boudinot) in the Livingston Papers. It seems that the supporters of Clark and Dayton, sensing a tie in the privy council, had roused Peter Haring—member of the council from Bergen—before daybreak on March 3 and had persuaded him to ride to Elizabethtown to attend the meeting in the hope that he would break the tie by voting for the determination of the election. Haring appeared, but the governor refused to put the question to a vote.

[36] *Acts of the General Assembly . . .* , *Thirteenth Session, First Sitting*, Act of Nov. 21, 1788.

[37] Minutes of the Governor's Privy Council, Mar. 18, 1789, State Library, Trenton. The vote totals from the twelve counties were: Schureman, 12,537; Cadwallader, 8,685; Boudinot, 8,603; and Sinnickson, 8,240. See *Pennsylvania Packet*, Mar. 24, 1789. In the eight counties to the northward of Trenton the totals for the Junto candidates were: Schureman, 6,751; Cadwallader, 985; Boudinot, 1,462; and Sinnickson, 479. In the same eight counties (which had seventy per cent of the state's white population) the votes for Clark and Dayton were respectively 7,242 and 6,708. The belated returns from Essex, where some 3,000 ballots had been cast, were: Clark, 2,762; Dayton, 2,984; Schureman, 1,274;

Boudinot, 448; Sinnickson, 124; and Cadwallader, 17. These figures clearly indicate the sectional character of the election contest. Moreover the percentage of those voting would seem to be surprisingly high in view of the property qualification. For the state as a whole, nearly one-half of the adult white males voted. In Burlington and Essex, where the election fever was highest, the percentages of adult white males voting were seventy-eight per cent and ninety per cent respectively. These fantastically large figures indicate that when votes were needed and the election officials were amenable, the property qualification was an unimportant barrier.

[38] *Brunswick Gazette*, Mar. 19, 1789. An interesting problem arose in connection with the commissions of the four congressmen. Boudinot took his seat in the House on March 23, but three days later he had not yet received a commission. James Schureman wrote to Livingston on March 28 expressing his embarrassment about the lack of a commission, and indicated that he was hesitant about going to Congress without one. Evidently commissions were subsequently granted, but the phrase "duly chosen," contained in the election statute, was omitted from them. There is a draft of a commission in the Livingston Papers, dated March 21, 1789, from which the significant phrase is also lacking. Journal of Elias Boudinot in Congress, March-August, 1789, Boudinot Papers, HSP; John Chetwood to William Livingston, Mar. 26, 1789; James Shureman to Livingston, Mar. 28, 1789, Livingston Papers; "One of Seven Thousand" in (New York) *Daily Advertiser*, July 31, 1789.

[39] "Essex," *New Jersey Journal*, Mar. 18, Apr. 1, 1789; "Triumph," *ibid.*, Mar. 18, 1789; "A Lover of Order," *ibid.*, Mar. 25, 1789; *Brunswick Gazette*, Mar. 24, 1789.

[40] *Journal of the House of Representatives of the United States*, [1st Cong., 1st Ses.] (New York, 1789), 27-28. Brief treatments of the New Jersey election case by Congress may be found in M. St. Claire Clarke and David A. Hall, *Cases of Disputed Elections in Congress, 1789-1834* (Washington, 1834), 38-44; Chester H. Rowell, *A Historical and Legal Digest of all the Contested Election Cases in the House of Representatives from the First to the Fifty-Sixth Congress, 1789-1901* [56th Cong., 2nd Ses., House Doc. 510] (Washington, 1901), 38, 772; Asher C. Hinds, *Precedents of the House of Representatives of the United States . . .* (Washington, 1907), I, 978-981. The committee of elections—the first standing committee created by the House—was selected April 13. *House Journal*, 16.

[41] *House Journal*, 40, 43. Elias Boudinot believed the protests against the election were "only designed to keep the People's Passions up for another Election," but he initiated the counterpetitions and sought to have them signed "by the best People of known good character." Boudinot to Elisha Boudinot, Apr. 14, 1789, Gratz Collection.

[42] *House Journal*, 48-50. Earlier, on April 29, the House had prescribed a mode of procedure for handling the South Carolina election contest (Ramsay *vs*. Smith) which differed in many respects from that prescribed for the New Jersey case. Lacking firm precedent, Congress was obviously uncertain about how it should proceed. *House Journal*, 17, 21, 28, 40-41, 48-49.

[43] *House Journal*, 75-76.

[44] The fullest report of the debate of July 15 is in the *Daily Advertiser*, July 16, 1789. A slightly different version is given in the *Gazette of the United States*, July 18, 1789.

[45] "Evidence given before the Committee [of Congress] on [the] New Jersey Election, Aug. 13, 1789," Livingston Papers. This document contains Elias Boudinot's detailed notes on the hearing. The hearing is referred to in no other sources.

[46] Elias Boudinot to Elisha Boudinot, Aug. 15, 1789, Boudinot Papers, III. The witnesses were represented by "Messrs Winser [?], ı Aaron Ogden with Coll [Colonel Matthias] Ogden." The Ogdens were brothers; Aaron had married Jonathan Dayton's sister. "Winser" cannot be identified. There is evidence that the petitioners at one time had sought to obtain Alexander Hamilton as their counsel. Elias Boudinot to Elisha Boudinot, Apr. 14, 1789, Gratz Collection.

[47] *House Journal*, 104-105. The report was accompanied by certain supporting docu-

ments, including the election lists for each county. A diligent search of the governmen
archives failed to reveal these documents, which may have been destroyed in the fire o
1814.

    [48] *House Journal*, 120; *Pennsylvania Packet*, Sept. 4, 1789; *Gazette of the United States*
Sept. 2, 1789.
    [49] *House Journal*, 120; *Gazette of the United States*, Sept. 5, 9, 1789; *Daily Advertiser*
Sept. 2, 3, 1789.
    [50] Boudinot to William Livingston, Sept. 2, 1789, Livingston Papers.
    [51] Ames to George R. Minot, Sept. 3, 1789, *Works of Fisher Ames*, Seth Ames, ed
(Boston, 1854), I, 70.

ALEXANDER HAMILTON*

Joseph Charles

Alexander Hamilton remains a controversial personality in American party history. Was he a farseeing leader of the Federalist Party, or did he merely use the party to further his consuming ambitions? In a brilliant analysis, Joseph Charles insists that Hamilton's financial program is indefensible, economically and politically. Since his goal of effecting a bond between conservative moneyed groups and the national government was not identical with the interests of the Federalists at large, Hamilton failed to unite a large element of the populace behind the movement to establish a strong national government. Hamilton's activities thus implanted the seeds of party difference, helped consolidate the Republican opposition, and seriously undermined the Federalists. Joseph Charles, author of The Origins of the American Party System, *was at the time of his death in 1952 a dedicated student of early American history despite an active career in the Department of State.*

The characters of Burr and Jefferson are supposed to be the great puzzles of the early national period. Jefferson is held up in general textbooks on American history as the classic example of inconsistency, of departure in office from principles laid down while in opposition. Yet neither of these men is more puzzling, if we raise the question of ultimate purposes, than is Hamilton, and neither appears more inconsistent than Hamilton if we put some of his most important words and actions side by side.

* Reprinted by permission of the University of North Carolina Press. From *The Origins of the American Party System: Three Essays* by Joseph Charles (Williamsburg, Va., Institute of Early American History and Culture, 1956). Copyright © 1956 by the Institute of Early American History and Culture: Chapter I, Section 2, "Alexander Hamilton," pp. 7-36.

In Numbers 12 and 21 of *The Federalist* Hamilton all but promised his readers that no excise or land tax would be levied under the new Constitution.[6] Yet an excise was an early part of the economic program, and from 1795 on, he was advocating policies which could only be paid for by a land tax.[7]

Generally regarded as the high priest of sound and conservative financial policies, Hamilton was apparently untroubled by the condition of our paper money in 1795-96,[8] which, taken with our general financial condition at that time, seemed even to Federalists to constitute a dangerous problem.[9] A little later he appears to have been urging fiat money as a means of helping the government out of its financial difficulties; for in August, 1798, he wrote to Wolcott, the Secretary of the Treasury:

> For these and other reasons [scarcity of money for the interior needs of the government], which I have thought well of, I have come to the conclusion, that our Treasury ought to raise up a circulation of its own. I mean by the issuing of Treasury notes payable, some on demand, others at different periods, from very short to pretty considerable,—at first having but little time to run. . . .[10]

The only assiduous pamphleteer among the public figures of the first order at that time, and a man who had been more important in helping to finance and direct partisan newspapers than any other leader in either party, Hamilton wrote in 1802, ". . . they [the Federalists] erred in relying so much on the rectitude and utility of their measures as to have neglected the cultivation of popular favor, by fair and justifiable expedients."[11]

In *Federalist* 11 Hamilton had written, "Let Americans disdain to be the instruments of European greatness! Let the thirteen States, bound together in a strict indissoluble Union, concur in erecting one great American system, superior to the control of all transatlantic force or influence, and able to dictate the terms of the connection between the old and the new world!"[12] Yet during the negotiation and the struggle for the ratification of the Jay Treaty, as during the years 1798-99, Hamilton must at least have thought our interests inseparable from Great Britain's and our support to be had on her own terms, if he did not, as his opponents charged, put her interest above that of this country.[13]

On the question of the ability of the American people to govern themselves and of the part that they were to have in the new government, many of Hamilton's utterances from 1787 to 1789 were in sharp conflict with his later words and policies. In a speech at the New York Constitutional Convention he said:

> . . . We have been told that the old Confederation has proved inefficacious, only because intriguing and powerful men, aiming at revolution, have been for ever instigating the people and rendering them disaffected to it. This, sir, is a false insinuation.
>
> I will venture to assert that no combination of designing men under heaven will be capable of making a government unpopular which is in its principles a wise and good one, and vigorous in its application.[14]

Earlier in the same speech he had stated:

> After all, we must submit to this idea, that the true principle of a republic is that the people should choose whom they please to govern them. Representation is imperfect in proportion as the current of popular favor is checked. This great source of free government, popular election, should be perfectly pure, and the most unbounded liberty allowed.[15]

Yet as soon as there was popular opposition to any of his measures, Hamilton claimed that it was stirred up by men who wanted to destroy the government. A combination of designing men was his favorite explanation for the opposition to government policies which began to appear by 1793.[16] In practice he believed in free elections no longer than they supported his policies, for in 1800 he tried to nullify the popular vote. At that time the practical issue was not only that which Mr. Allen Johnson stated, the question whether or not a political opposition was to be allowed to exist.[17] The more important point was whether or not, when a political opposition had been successful at the polls, the choice of the voters was to be followed. Hamilton appeared willing to go to any lengths to circumvent the popular vote in 1800 when he saw that the Federalists would be defeated by following it.[18]

Such contradictions and inconsistencies as these are not of great importance except as they reflect the fundamental problem which is raised by contrasting Hamilton's general views on government with the policies which he followed. While the Constitution was being adopted, no one spoke of the interest of the whole country or of the necessity for concessions by every group, interest, and section more persuasively than did Hamilton. It was his pride that he was able to "think continentally." Yet the High-Federalist measures from 1796 to 1800, which were only the last of a series of steps that had narrowed the base of Federalist support and had made the party hated over large sections of the country, were those of a body of men who looked to him for leadership. It seems likely that a study of Hamilton which was based directly upon what he did or tried to do would be very different from one based upon his writings or the customary accounts of him.

Among the fundamental problems raised by a study of Hamilton's political behavior is the question whether his contributions to *The Federalist* represent his ideas of the way in which the new government would operate, or whether these essays were merely clever propaganda for the adoption of the Constitution. Did Hamilton in the years from 1787 to 1789 envisage a nation unified in sentiment by mutual concessions, by a genuine concern for the interests of the whole, as some passages of *The Federalist* might lead one to believe? Did he really believe in the representative government and free popular elections of which he spoke so favorably in the New York Constitutional Convention?[19] Further, did Hamilton's fundamental views and purposes change between 1787 and 1800, or did they remain the same, concealed part of the time behind a calculated misrepresentation, a clever soothing of "the great beast"? These questions are important, for Jefferson is supposed to have been the hypocrite, the wily politician of the time, and Hamilton, whatever his faults, always to have been frank, open, honest, and manly.

We cannot give a definite answer to these questions, but it is worthwhile recording that Hamilton did not render his lip service, if such it was, to representative government until after he had tried in the Constitutional Convention to win support for a plan of government which was only a thinly veiled elective monarchy.[20] When Hamilton found that he could not win a following for this scheme, he gave the Constitution which was drafted his heartiest support. His enemies later claimed that he did so only because he hoped that in the right hands the new government might be made into something which, in operation, would closely resemble the government he had championed. In 1802 he wrote a letter to Gouverneur Morris which would imply that he had never had any faith in the Constitution. He described it as "a frail and worthless fabric which I have been endeavoring to prop up."[21] Such facts as these do not necessarily furnish the explanation of Hamilton's policies. They do not prove the contention of his enemies that he was trying while in office to bring about a monarchy or a dictatorship. But Hamilton's known views on government, his open statements to intimates, do raise the question of his fundamental purposes and entitle us to ask whether, for example, the measures of his economic program, so important to the new nation, were intended to further or subvert the type of government which most well-informed men thought they were supporting when they voted to accept the Constitution.

Such fundamental problems as these have not been clarified; they have not even been set forth by Hamilton's biographers.[22] Thus the standard works on Hamilton evade the main issues which his career raises; and his rightful place in our history, once these issues are raised, becomes a subject for controversy.

Hamilton's whole career invites further study because of his transcendent importance in the forming of our government, but no part of it is of so great importance as that between 1789 and 1800. For those who are interested in the question of party development, his policies and views from 1789 on are probably the most important single problem. If we look at the issues with which public opinion during those years was most concerned and which were the immediate causes of party division, we shall see that there was not one of them in which Hamilton did not play a leading part. The questions were:

1. Should we pass the various measures which made up Hamilton's economic program, 1790-93?[23]
2. Should we declare our neutrality in the war between France and England in 1793, or should we act in accordance with our treaty with France?
3. Should we ratify and put into effect the Jay Treaty?
4. Should we give the Administration crisis powers, 1798-99?

We are for the moment particularly concerned with the first of these crucial questions with which Hamilton was intimately connected. Before going into the details of the various parts of his economic program, however, it is necessary to take a general view of the measures it included and to point out some of their more obvious consequences. When the new government was established, it inherited large debts dating back to the Revolution: debts which were owed to our own citizens, to the French government, and to banking houses in Holland. Under the Articles of Confederation we had for some years failed to pay even the interest on some of these debts. In addition to this burden, the states had separate debts which also went back to the Revolution. Some of the states had been as delinquent as Congress in meeting their obligations, while others had made considerable progress in repaying theirs. Hamilton's first step was to fund the national debt, that is, to determine the interest and principal due to each creditor and, since the creditors could not be paid immediately, to issue to them new bonds which were now the basis of the national credit. Although his second step, called Assumption, was included in the Funding Bill as actually passed, it provided for the assuming of the debts of each of the states by the national government, thus, of course, adding to the total of the national debt. His next step was to establish a national bank in which the government owned stock, though it had to go further into debt to acquire this stock.

The main sources of revenue which Hamilton provided for the new government came from indirect taxes on imported goods and from an excise tax laid on liquor made in this country. The choice of these sources of income entailed far-reaching consequences. Since most of our trade was with England and a high volume of imports was necessary for revenues, friendly relations with England became essential to the national credit of the new government. It could not seek a high degree of economic self-sufficiency, nor could it take any diplomatic step which might offend England without grave risks. On the other hand, the Excise Act, as it was passed and administered under Hamilton's influence, brought about the Whiskey Rebellion. As will appear later, there was no point in Hamilton's economic program which is not important for the political as well as for the economic historian. Nowhere do we draw nearer the central issue of the 1790's, the question of what kind of government and society we were to have in this country, than in the study of Hamilton's economic policy.

As we have seen, Hamilton's whole program rested on the funding of the debt, and the manner in which this was done is highly important. The basis of his plan was to issue negotiable bonds to the full amount of the various evidences of indebtedness which would be presented to the national government, without regard to the question of original ownership, the degree of previous depreciation of the security, or the relation between real and nominal value of money at the time that the loan had been made or the service rendered to the government. It may seem wise to us that Hamilton did not attempt to solve the difficult questions which would have been involved in such readjustments of the debt, but according to Channing, probably nine-tenths of the congressmen expected, when they went to the first meeting of Congress, that there would be

some sort of revision or scaling down of the debt.[24] The degree of infla-
tion which had existed during most of the Revolutionary period, the fan-
tastic prices which the government had frequently been forced to pay
for goods and services, had caused many to suppose that the government
would adopt some arbitrary ratio of old debts to new securities, rather
than promise to pay in good money a debt that had been accumulated
largely in terms of depreciated Continentals. There appears, however,
to have been little question among members of the House as to the desirability of paying the face value of each security presented. The only
important question raised was who should be paid.

The only modification of Hamilton's plan of funding which was seriously debated was that some attempt be made to discriminate between
the original holders and the speculators who had purchased securities
from these holders, usually at a fraction of their value and frequently
with information from members of the government that the debt was to
be paid in full.[25] Madison, who had until this point been very close to
Hamilton, took the position that there must be a discrimination between
speculators and original holders, who were usually soldiers and their
families or creditors who had furnished supplies and money at the time
when the cause looked darkest. In a speech made on the public credit
in February, 1790, he said:

> A composition, then, is the only expedient that remains; let it
> be a liberal one in favor of the present holders, let them have
> the highest price which has prevailed in the market; and let the
> residue belong to the original sufferers. This will not do perfect
> justice; but it will do more real justice, and perform more of the
> public faith, than any other expedient proposed.[26]

Hamilton had declared that the national credit was of one piece, that
if the smallest part of it suffered injury or could be called into question,
the whole was damaged;[27] and Madison's scheme of discrimination was
treated in the House as though it were an effort to prevent the government
from meeting its just obligations, even though the government would not
have owed any less had discrimination been adopted. It was the representatives closest to Hamilton—Sedgwick and Ames of Massachusetts, Laur-
ance of New York, Boudinot of New Jersey, and William L. Smith of
South Carolina—who pushed the Funding Bill through in the form in
which Hamilton wished it enacted. Their speeches, which were largely
monotonous declamations on the nation's honor and which thus had little

bearing upon the only important point raised, that of discrimination, probably did not affect the outcome; the twenty-nine members out of sixty-
four who owned securities needed only four votes from the unorganized
remainder of the House to pass the bill.[28]

In view of the charges made later against the Republicans, it is important that we should note that their opposition was not to the funding
of the debt. They objected to the failure to discriminate between the original holders and the speculators. Likewise, the most serious objection of
Madison and Jefferson to Assumption was to the details of the scheme,
the manner in which the debt of the states was to be assumed, rather
than to Assumption itself. The plan to establish the Bank was the first
of Hamilton's measures which they met with unequivocal opposition.
"Discrimination" justly describes the attitude they showed toward these
earlier measures of his financial program.

The greatest opposition to the manner in which the debts were funded
came from the Southern states[29] and from Pennsylvania. In those states
many who had been strongest in their support of the Constitution
denounced the funding scheme in the strongest terms when it had become
apparent that there was to be no attempt to discriminate between
speculators and original holders. Benjamin Rush, who had been one of
the strongest and most influential supporters of the national Constitution
in Pennsylvania, believed shortly after the Funding Bill was passed that
his state was very much opposed to it. "The Quakers & Germans who
now govern directly or indirectly both our city and state, possess very
few certificates; and we have more widows, orphans, and soldiers among
us who have parted with their certificates than any city in the union."
He felt, moreover, that Pennsylvania had been betrayed by those among
her representatives who had supported Funding. He stated that both
Clymer and Fitzsimmons, the most influential of the representatives from
Pennsylvania in the first Congress, "left the city last fall determined on
discrimination," but that the latter had now become "the midwife of
a system every principle of which will be reprobated when established
in our state."[30] Sedgwick's account of the struggles he had with the
Pennsylvania delegation, before he could bring them around to support
these measures, bears out Rush's remark.[31]

In addition to the causes which Rush gave for Pennsylvania's opposition to Funding, there was the fact that Madison's suggestion for discrimination at no time received a fair hearing. The Pennsylvanians knew
that it was not impossible to work out an equitable plan of discrimination

between original and present holders, because they had done so with their own state debt. This plan of discrimination was at that time in operation. When Madison's similar proposal was denounced as impracticable, John Nicholson, who had worked out the details of the system of discrimination which was accepted by the Pennsylvania legislature, sent Madison a copy of this plan and said that it had been printed and was being distributed to the public.[32] The *Pennsylvania Gazette* ran a widely quoted series of articles upon the effects that might be expected to follow Hamilton's method of funding:

> Such injustice and oppression [as the funding scheme occasioned] may be colored over with fine words, but there is a time coming when the pen of history will detect and expose the folly of the arguments in favor of the proposed funding system as well as its iniquity. . . . If the balance still due the army is paid them, it would spread money through every county and township of the United States, if paid to the speculator, all the cash of the United States would soon center in our cities and later in England and Holland.

A few weeks later the same writer, *A Farmer*, stated that it would "be impossible for farmers to borrow money to improve their lands, for who will lend money to an individual for 6 per cent when government securities will yield from 8 to 12 per cent."

" 'The farmers,' he continues, 'never were in half the danger of being ruined by the British government than they now are by their own.' "[33]

The evidences of opposition to the funding system throughout the South, where the speculators had made their richest haul, are so numerous that there is no need to labor the point. Similar feeling, so general in Pennsylvania, was probably one of the strongest bonds in the future political unity between that state and the South. The opinion of the measure held by those opposed to Funding, that it was rooted in calculated injustice, was strengthened by later developments. In 1795, when $1,181,000 was disbursed by the government on interest and capital payment on the public debt, the four original New England states received $440,800 of this amount. Massachusetts alone received much more than all the states south of the Potomac; Connecticut, more than Virginia, North Carolina, and Georgia combined.[34] The distribution of securities stirred up sectional feeling, and the way in which money was raised to pay the debt caused additional bitterness. Even in the late 1790's, Republican writers still found Funding a useful subject, and Joel Barlow, one of the most effective of them, wrote:

> Besides the magnitude of our debt, the manner of funding it has had a pernicious influence on the policy of our government with foreign powers. The payment of the interest was made to depend in a great measure on the duties to be levied on imported merchandise, which were by law appropriated for fifteen years to this object. This made every stock-holder a partizan of our commercial connections with that country whose commerce with us was supposed principally to secure this revenue; however injurious those connections might become to the general interest of the United States. It is greatly owing to this unfortunate measure that our commerce has suffered so much during the present war from English and French depredations. For no one will deny that the latter were occasioned by our tame submission to the former.[35]

Popular feeling against Funding apparently died out quickly in the prosperity of the early 1790's, but later, when grievances against the Administration and the Federalist party became frequent, complaints of the evil effects of Funding were usually to be heard among them.

The funding system, which was the basis of Hamilton's whole financial program, did not arouse so much controversy as did the next step in the fulfillment of his plans, that by which the debts of all the states were to be assumed by the Federal government. A good deal of the opposition which Funding itself raised, as it was some time in coming to a head, vented itself on this second measure. Assumption was designed ostensibly to regulate the accounts between the debtor and the creditor states, but its other effects were so far-reaching that this must have seemed insignificant among them. It was like using a cannon to kill a mouse. If the national government was to pay the debts of the states,[36] it was obvious that the former would effectually dominate the revenue sources of the country, which under the Constitution were to be jointly tapped by state and Federal governments. With this step taken, the individual states lost a large degree of their autonomy. Regarded from any point of view, Assumption meant a degree of consolidation and subordination of state to national authority which few had hitherto contemplated.

The general and uncritical shouldering by the new government of all claims against the Confederacy, which had been the distinguishing feature of the Funding Bill, had brought to the public view a debt of about 50 millions, and Assumption had added 22-1/2 millions. Nearly 11 millions of this turned out to have been added unnecessarily, as Henry Adams shows.[37] The total debt of the government would have been around 60 millions, instead of over 70, if the precise nature of the account of each state with the old Confederacy had been ascertained before the debts were assumed. It was not generally known at the time how much the failure to investigate these circumstances was costing the government, but even without this knowledge the new total of the funded debt was sufficient to cause much anxiety. Apprehensive questions were asked by many who, on the whole, favored the measure: What interest would this debt bear? What proportion of the national revenue would be necessary to meet it? Could it ever be discharged? Questions such as these were asked. Other objections arose because of the way in which speculators had profited by buying up state securities; for their operations in the state funds, if not larger, were at least bolder than their operations in acquiring government securities. Many of these speculators were believed to live in New York and Massachusetts, states which would have profited greatly by having their debts assumed by the government even without this additional gain to their individual citizens. Virginia and Pennsylvania were discharging their debts satisfactorily, and their opposition to the measure formed a bond which later events were to strengthen. South Carolina alone of the Southern states was a large gainer by Assumption, and had it not been for the support of her members, Assumption would have had no chance from the beginning.[38] The immediate advantages or disadvantages for their individual states appear to have been uppermost in men's minds in their calculations upon this subject. Its larger implications and more important consequences were to be revealed little by little over a period of some years.

The striking fact which has been generally ignored in the contest over Assumption is that the strongest opposition both inside the House and out came from men who had been most active in their support of the Constitution. Indeed, there were probably not more than half a dozen men in the first House of Representatives who had opposed the Constitution, Burke of South Carolina, Bloodworth of North Carolina, Bland and Griffin of Virginia, Heister of Pennsylvania, and Gerry of Massachusetts being the only members who had played prominent parts in the struggle against it. Of these six men three, Burke, Bland,[39] and Gerry, supported Assumption. On the other hand, Gilman and Livermore of New Hampshire; Hartley, Muhlenberg, and Scott of Pennsylvania; Madison and most of the rest of the Virginia delegation; all of the North Carolina delegation except Bloodworth; and Abraham Baldwin, Matthews, and Jackson of Georgia were active supporters of the Constitution, yet they opposed Assumption to the finish. We cannot discover whether the three New York members who voted against Assumption supported the Constitution or not. From what we do know about them it would seem probable that all three, Floyd, Hathorn, and Van Rensselaer, supported the Constitution. Perhaps the most striking fact in the whole effort to get Assumption accepted is that the four members of the House from Maryland and Virginia who changed their votes on Assumption after the famous dinner at which Jefferson and Hamilton discussed the subject with them had all been supporters of the Constitution.[40]

The line which is asserted by some to run from the supporters of the Constitution to the Federalist party and from its opponents to the Republican was broken on this occasion, and with these basic measures of Hamilton's financial program a new principle of division appeared in national politics. At the Constitutional Convention the basic division which appeared had not been sectional, but between the large and the small states. Once the great compromise of the Constitution was made, by which each state was represented in the Senate by two men and in the House according to population, there was no longer any ground for a conflict of interest between the large and small states. The former basis of division, which it had been feared would make any union impossible, did not appear in Congress; and until the first measures of Hamilton's financial program were proposed, there did not seem to be any recurring basis of division among the members of the House of Representatives. Of the first session of Congress, before the proposal of any of the measures of Hamilton's program, Madison wrote:

> In general, the interests and ideas of the Northern and Southern States have been less adverse than was predicted by the opponents or hoped by the friends of the new Government. Members from the same State, or the same part of the Union, are as often separated on questions from each other as they are united in opposition to other States or other quarters of the Continent.[41]

The atmosphere of harmony was not restricted to the House of Representatives but was apparent everywhere, even among those who had opposed the adoption of the Constitution. Madison wrote to Washington in November, 1789:

As far as I can gather, the great bulk of the late opponents are entirely at rest, and more likely to censure a further opposition to the Government, as now administered, than the Government itself. One of the principal leaders of the Baptists lately sent me word that the amendments had entirely satisfied the disaffected of his sect, and that it would appear in their subsequent conduct.[42]

And William Bingham wrote to Hamilton only a few days later, "The present Period is very favorable for carrying into Effect a System of Taxation, as the Affection of the People are so rivetted to the New Government, that their minds will be easily conciliated to all its operations."[43]
All the evidence would indicate that the second session of the first Congress, to which the Funding and Assumption Bills were presented, found the people of the whole country extraordinarily united in support of the new government.[44] They realized that this was perhaps their last chance to obliterate the pettiness and selfishness of the past few years, the full dangers of which seem to have become apparent only as the people rose above themselves and experienced a new union and harmony.
This spirit of union and harmony was shattered, both inside the House of Representatives and among the public at large, by the measures of Hamilton's financial program. A sharp sectional division appeared in the voting upon the measures of that program, a division which foreshadowed the first phase in the growth of national parties. There were two votes against Assumption from New Hampshire but none from the other New England states. There were three votes against it from New York, none against it from New Jersey, and four against it from Pennsylvania. Thus from the Northern states there were nine votes against the measure, while there were twenty-four in favor of it. In the South there were for Assumption one vote from Delaware, two from Maryland, two from Virginia, and five from South Carolina.[45] These make a total of ten for the bill, while eighteen were against it, but we should remember that the four votes from Maryland and Virginia had to be arranged, and that South Carolina was by no means so Federalist upon other measures as upon this. On the Excise Bill there were but two votes in opposition in New York and the states to the north. There were four votes against it from Pennsylvania, making a total from the Northern states of six against the bill, while twenty-eight were for it. In the South there were one vote for the bill from Delaware, one from Maryland, four from Virginia, and one from South Carolina, which made a total of seven for the measure, and there were fifteen against it from the representatives of that section.[46]

On the bill to establish the Bank there was but one vote in opposition from the Northern states, that of Grout of Massachusetts, making the total of those states thirty-three to one. The vote of the Southern states on this measure was six for it, nineteen against it.[47] Nothing like this sectional division had been seen in the voting before these measures were introduced.

It cannot be assumed, however, that the strong support which New England representatives gave Hamilton's measures in the House reflected the sentiment of their section accurately. There is ample evidence from the best Federalist sources[48] that even in the most conservative circles of New England there was much doubt as to the wisdom of Assumption and a good deal of opposition to it. Nothing could show the scope and audacity of Hamilton's economic program as it appeared to his contemporaries so well as the fact that many members of the groups who were supposed to benefit most from Assumption feared that here Hamilton was going much too fast. According to Samuel Henshaw, Stephen Higginson "liked the plan generally, but was fearful that it was too rigid, prompt and energetic for this early period of our national existence."[49] Gouverneur Morris thought that Hamilton was not only going too fast, but in the wrong direction as well. He wrote from London when he heard that Assumption had been suggested, "To assume the payment of what the States owe, merely because they owe it, seems to my capacity not more rational, than to assume the debts of corporations, or of individuals." Later in this letter he said, "If the individual or community be in debt, or not in debt, to others, is a circumstance which the public, the Union, America, in short, has nothing to do with."[50]

Gouverneur Morris's letter shows that other Federalists than those from New England were opposed to Assumption when it was proposed, but the strongest protests against it from those who were to remain loyal Federalists appear to have come from Massachusetts. The prevalence of opposition in conservative circles there raises the question of how the measure got the unanimous vote of the Massachusetts members. At least a part of the answer lies in the exertions of Theodore Sedgwick, the most strenuous of Hamilton's supporters in the first Congress. One of his own letters gives the following account of the methods by which Assumption was put through: "During the passage of the assumption bill we had several hairbreadth escapes from ruin. My colleague Gerry, who is the veriest quiddle in nature, would be frequently seduced by the enemy." A motion had been offered excluding all notes not presented by the original holders unless the owner would swear that he had not purchased between certain dates. "This was a kind of self-denying purgation ordinance designed to declare the purity of the members, and was therefore precisely of a nature to operate on his mind." Gerry was in favor of this bill, and Sedgwick labored with him privately to give it up, "telling him it was supported by insidious men," but Gerry was not convinced. "I was finally obliged to get up in the House and tell him what I had so often before said to him, and concluded by declaring that if he persisted he should stand responsible to Massachusetts for the failure of this measure so beneficial to our constituents. This had its effect and to his utter disgrace he was obliged to abandon his object."[51] This letter from Sedgwick shows the part that Hamilton's intimate associates in Congress played in getting his favorite measures adopted, a part which was frequently quite as important as that ascribed to them by their opponents.

We have been concerned with the immediate repercussions of Hamilton's program, both in the House and among the more well-informed of the general public, rather than with its long-run effects upon the growth of parties. But it should be apparent that a measure which so seriously alarmed many of those from the section which it benefited most, a measure which was later found to have increased the debt unnecessarily and to have led to a more scandalous use of official influence and information for the benefit of speculators than even the Funding Bill, contained ample ammunition for the party battle which was soon to break out. The threats of disunion if the bill were not passed and such coercion as Sedgwick applied to Gerry on the floor of the House showed an eagerness for the passing of this measure which was to cause more bitterness later than at the time.

If we view Hamilton's program for a moment in its relation to the later growth of political parties, we are struck by a curious circumstance. The basic measures of his plan, Funding and Assumption, have been treated by historians and economists in almost every respect except that of their effect on public opinion. On the other hand, the effects on public opinion of two less important measures, the establishment of the Bank and of the excise system, are frequently remarked upon. The former had immediate effects in dividing opinion by producing the first complete expositions of the opposing views of the Constitution which were to become the official creeds of the two parties; the latter had its effect by bringing about the Whiskey Rebellion. These later measures came at a time when party division was already well on its way, and they have tended to obscure the effects of Funding and Assumption. The

greater importance of the earlier measures is due to the fact that so much
of later Federalist policy grows out of them. It is in studying these
policies, which so frequently went directly in the face of the main currents of opinion, that we shall find the first milestones in the growth
of parties.

Perhaps the most important single effect, as far as the growth of parties
is concerned, of the establishment of the Bank and the setting up of the
Excise was that these measures, instead of redressing the balance between
sections and interests which many thought had been so disturbed by
Hamilton's first measures, gave additional advantages to New England
and the moneyed group. They brought no solace to the sections and
groups most outraged by Funding and Assumption. In New England only
the large distillers of West Indian molasses were affected by the Excise,
and they had already been placated by favorable concessions in the duty
paid on both foreign liquors and those made in this country from foreign
materials. Large areas of the South and of western Pennsylvania, however, found little comfort in any of the provisions of the Excise on whiskey, particularly after the provision exempting stills of less than fifty-
gallon capacity was removed in 1792. The smallest details of the excise
system seemed designed to work hardship, since almost all those accused
under it had to make long journeys for trial; and as soon as it became
apparent that no attention was to be paid to the numerous petitions to
have the Excise Bill changed or withdrawn, it was evaded and defied.
Thus in the last parts of Hamilton's program, where he could have
afforded concessions which might have alleviated some of the bitterness
caused by his fundamental measures, he passed by the opportunity and
extended the privileges of the few and the burdens of the many which
were implied in its framework.

Having examined Hamilton's program in its relation to public opinion
and the later growth of parties, we turn to the economic reasoning by
which Hamilton supported the various parts of his program. "In the 'Vindication of Funding' . . . he . . . adds that if a government borrows
a hundred dollars, it spends it, and that is capital; while the bond may
be sold, and is another. Thus the credit of government produces a new
capital of a hundred dollars."[52] Sumner says of this reasoning, "These
notions show a remarkable amount of confusion in regard to money, capital, and debt, in the mind of a man who has a great reputation as a
financier."[53] And of the reasoning by which Hamilton defended Assumption, Sumner says, ". . . although it was creditable to his sense of justice,

[it] is not strong when regarded from the political point of view. It remained true that he was reaching out for a duty which did not necessarily devolve upon him, and was exposing the Federal Government to a new trial, when he thought he was winning strength for it."[54]

Concerning Hamilton's arguments for a close connection between the Bank and the government, Sumner writes:

> There was no need, in the case of the Bank of the United States, of allowing subscriptions in the public debt. The public debt was all provided for independently of the bank. . . . The government of the United States never realized any gain whatever from this device. The expectation was unfounded and illusory, and the opposition were justified in saying that if it had been real, it would have been derogatory to the government.
>
> Another very great vice in Hamilton's bank was the arrangement by which the United States government, being itself at the time impecunious, subscribed stock in the bank and gave its notes for the subscription.[55]

Sumner sees in this precedent the rise of the most vicious practices of government finance, which did not come to an end until the establishment of the independent sub-treasury system. Elsewhere he states, "In these passages [from the letters, newspaper articles, and the Federalist reports on public credit and on the national bank] we see that he was under the dominion of the most vicious fallacies with regard to money and banking, and that his idea of a bank did not go beyond some of the vulgar misconceptions about it."[56]

In his famous letter to John Sullivan in 1780, urging the establishment of a national bank, Hamilton stated that this country was then in the same condition as France before Law's Mississippi scheme: "The foundation [of that scheme] was good, but the superstructure too vast"; and that we should select the good in this and other plans, "avoiding the defects and excesses. Something on a similar principle in America will alone accomplish the restoration of paper credit. . . ."[57] He seems even in later years to have maintained the attitude toward government finance which is revealed in this statement.

Oliver Wolcott, one of Hamilton's closest disciples, was appalled at the financial condition of the national government when he succeeded

Hamilton as Secretary of the Treasury. In September, 1795, he wrote to Hamilton saying that public affairs were in a critical state and that he did not see how the affairs of the Treasury were to be managed:

> Our foreign resources are dried up; our domestic are deeply antici-
> pated, at least as respects the bank. Banks are multiplying like
> mushrooms. The prices of all our exports are impaired by paper
> negotiations and unfounded projects, so that no foreign market
> will indemnify the shippers. Our commerce is harrassed by the
> war, and our internal revenue unproductive of the expected sums,
> owing to prejudice, combination, and the want of competent
> officers. Usury absorbs much of that capital which might be calcu-
> lated upon as a resource, if visionary speculations could be
> destroyed.[58]

Hamilton seemed unconcerned by this grave financial situation and answered Wolcott, "The worst evil we can struggle with, is inefficiency in the measures of government."[59] At the time of Fries' Rebellion he put what seems to have been his idea at this time even more clearly: "The consideration of expense is of no moment compared with the advantages of energy."[60]

Hamilton's financial program and his later policies are usually defended as having been indispensable, not because they contributed energy to the government, but because they were the embodiment of sound finance. Hamilton is pictured ordinarily as a man of profound insight into the principles of economics and finance, who was content to let the chips fall where they might. If his policies cannot be defended by this reasoning, if his economic tenets and reasoning were defective, or if he was inclined to subordinate financial policy to other purposes, we should see what the objects were that he sought to gain. If the energy which they imparted to the government is to be the criterion for judging his financial measures, we should inquire into what he meant by energy.

Oliver Wolcott, as Hamilton's assistant in the Treasury Department, wrote a letter to his father about the time that Assumption was first presented to the House of Representatives, which is frequently considered as expressing Hamilton's purposes at this time:

> I can consider a funding system as important, in no other way
> than as an engine of government. The only question is what the

engine shall be. The influence of a clergy, nobility and armies, are and ought to be out of the question in this country; but unless some active principle of the human mind can be interested in support of the government, no civil establishments can be formed, which will not appear like useless and expensive pageants, and by their unpopularity weaken the government which they are intended to support. . . .

For these reasons I think the State debts ought to be assumed, as without the assumption the political purposes which I have enumerated, cannot be attained. This will indeed increase the debt in the United States, to a degree which will be very inconvenient. The taxes necessary to pay the interest will be burdensome, and they will appear to be just, only to those who believe that the good attained is more important than the evil which is suffered.[61]

The reasoning sounds like that of Hamilton; his other statements that it was necessary to have propertied men financially interested in the new government[62] would seem ample warrant for the assumption that Wolcott has given here a faithful paraphrase of Hamilton's purposes as expressed in his economic program. When we look at Hamilton's first measures in this light, instead of thinking of them as having been the sole means of saving national credit, their fitness for their real purpose is evident, and it is only then that the artistic economy with which they were fashioned can be justly appreciated. If Hamilton's method of applying Funding and Assumption raised the debt to a higher total than the establishing of national credit would have required, it may also have given an opportunity to interest that many more moneyed men in the new government. By refusing to discriminate between original holders and speculators, he secured for the latter their great profits. From any point of view, a more perfect device for the concentration of wealth at that time could hardly have been conceived. As Rexford Tugwell and Joseph Dorfman put it:

The reports of Hamilton in 1790 and 1791, taken together, constitute a theoretical plan which is just beginning to be appreciated. The economic organization logically involved was grand and imperial in scope. A fully negotiable funded debt, drained originally from the small-property classes and met by taxes paid by the masses, was to be used by an emerging moneyed class to create profitable speculative enterprises in lands, industry, and finance.[63]

From the point of view of the interest of the country as a whole, the axioms upon which Hamilton's program rested may be false, the reasoning by which it was supported, defective or strained; but from the point of view of the creation and strengthening of a moneyed interest, his whole plan was flawless both in conception and execution.

The working out of Hamilton's economic program in the realm of practical politics, the specific relations between it and his later policies, and the effects of both on the development of parties, will be treated in the course of this study; but the question of his larger ends, his ultimate purposes as revealed in this system, may be profitably considered here. If this system was primarily "an engine of government," what sort of engine was it?

If we look at the career of Hamilton as a whole, a few dominant ideas, each of which would support the others in the circumstances of that time, are evident. Hamilton put his trust in the privileged classes and considered their interests as inseparable from those of society as a whole. He wanted a close collaboration between this country and England. He aimed at the closest possible union, even a high degree of consolidation, between the different parts of this country, and he wanted a powerful central government. These aims were so closely related in the conditions of the time that they are perhaps aspects of the same plan, and he probably thought of them as different means toward a single goal. The economic program which he advanced furthered these aims in every respect. It made for the supremacy of the propertied classes; it involved as much consolidation and as great a centralization of power as would have been accepted at that time; and it brought in its train intimate commercial and diplomatic relations with Great Britain. All Hamilton's fundamental views are implied in this program, and it is here that we see them most closely integrated.

Sumner states that those parts of Hamilton's system which were not necessary for the financial integrity of the new government were incorporated because of "political expediency,"[64] but this pale term is inadequate to explain the passionate conviction with which Hamilton defended his whole scheme, his fear that if a single part of it were not adopted or were abandoned, the whole would be weakened.[65] This devotion to his system sprang from his conception of what society should be, and his knowledge that the whole of the system was necessary before the special interests of the moneyed group could be so enmeshed in those of the general public that it would be impossible for anyone to attack the former without laying himself open to the charge that it was in reality the latter against which he was laying stealthy designs. Hamilton was incidentally strengthening and consolidating interests friendly to his policies which would be powerful in Congress, but he was primarily concerned with putting the nation on the path he thought it should follow.

The questions of who supported Hamilton's financial program and why they did so are perhaps as important in a study of the formation of parties as is any analysis of Hamilton's purposes in urging this program. The passing of his basic measures has sometimes been attributed to the greed of speculating congressmen and the influence of other speculators. Yet the fact that many congressmen did hold government and state securities, the values of which were greatly increased by Funding and Assumption, is no proof that they were speculators, or that they had made use of official information to acquire securities which they knew would be affected by measures pending. Within little more than a year after the passing of Funding and Assumption, the Republicans began to charge that Federalist congressmen had made precisely this use of their official positions, but in the absence of better evidence than the Republicans were able to present in support of these charges, they were labeled as those of men so hostile to the new government that they would go to any length in an attempt to discredit it.

The question whether or not congressmen were speculators and not merely security holders was not cleared up at the time, but a letter of Andrew Craigie offers conclusive evidence that a number of congressmen did make use of their official positions to aid their speculations in government securities in 1789 and 1790. Craigie states in this letter that the consideration of the government debt was delayed until these men could get their affairs in shape to reap the greatest possible benefit from the new measures. Craigie was a Boston speculator who, during much of the time that the first Congress was in session, stayed in New York in a boarding house with six New England congressmen, numbering among them Hamilton's strongest supporters. In January, 1790, while Congress was beginning its considerations of Hamilton's first report, Christopher Gore, also deep in speculation, said of Craigie, "Should a bill of sale be given of Congress, Andrew surely would pass as appurtenant,"[66] and perhaps no better authority than Craigie's could be found for the statement which he made on the speculations of congressmen to one of his associates in September, 1789. He wrote that Congress would not deal with the debt until after the recess for several reasons, among which he included the following: "Besides there are many who are interested in delaying the Business either because they have borrowed large sums of the debt which they have to purchase or because their private arrangements are not in readiness for speculation."[67]

The fact that congressmen were speculating in the government funds and that such large speculators as Craigie and William Duer were in a position to know the inmost secrets of Congress and the Treasury is important as showing that there was a basis of fact for later Republican charges, but it does not serve to explain clearly the basis of party division; for neither of the first national political parties deserves to be judged by or identified with its camp followers. The Federalist party, particularly in these years, rested upon a much broader base than that offered by speculators. The passing of Hamilton's program can be attributed to interested speculators and their associates in Congress in only a superficial sense. According to later Republican charges, the honest, disinterested congressmen were divided fairly evenly on many of Hamilton's measures, the balance being turned by those who were in a position to profit directly, as was the case with the members who had bought state securities in the expectation that Assumption would be adopted. Thus even by the later admission of Hamilton's opponents, who were only too prone to identify Federalism and speculation, there were many in Congress who supported his measures without any prospect of profiting from them except as they promised to benefit the country as a whole. It is by directing our attention to supporters of this sort that we shall get the greatest light on the relation of Hamilton's measures to the process of party formation.

The men who supported Hamilton's program from a motive other than direct personal gain may be roughly divided into those who remained Federalists and those who finally went over to the opposition though they had supported Hamilton's early measures. The first group was made up of men who, though they might think specific measures unwise, welcomed the larger implications of Hamilton's financial program as well as those of his later policy, as they became increasingly clear to them. As these men saw them, Hamilton's measures were designed to restore control to the conservatives without openly challenging the current popular dogmas of government. Hamilton would have yielded the battle as far as declamation and political theory were concerned, lest his commanding position on a more decisive field be endangered. With the

promulgation of his program, the more astute conservatives realized that
they had found a daring and resourceful leader. There were groups in
every state who had opposed any change in the relation of classes during
and since the Revolution, to whom that movement meant primarily the
preservation of the social structure of colonial times with themselves
occupying the first, rather than the second or third, places; and the
leaders of such groups were not slow to grasp the implications of Hamilton's program. Gouverneur Morris once remarked to John Jay, "Finance,
my friend, all that is left of the American Revolution grounds there,"[68]
and if he was thinking of the American Revolution as a social movement,
this remark might well serve as the motto of Hamilton's economic program. Those who wanted the preservation of an old-world society with
the additional advantage of exploiting a new continent could not have
done better than to give Hamilton their undivided allegiance. He merited
Talleyrand's tribute: "Il avait deviné l'Europe."[69]

It should be noted, however, that all conservatives in the United States
are not to be identified too closely, nor for too long a period, with Hamilton's supporters. Some men of very conservative views who had upheld
his early measures later joined his opponents when they became convinced that they had been deceived in his purposes. Such men as John
Dickinson, John Langdon, George Wythe, and Charles Pinckney, conservative leaders in their respective states in 1789, had gone over to the
opposition by 1796. Others, like Rush and Madison, equally strong supporters of the Constitution, were alienated by Hamilton's earlier
measures. A consideration of the political affiliations of the most prominent men in the country from 1789 to the end of the decade shows that
from the time of Hamilton's first measures there was much shifting from
one party to the other.

The effect of Hamilton's measures upon those who, though hostile to
Hamilton, remained in the Federalist party should also be considered.
John Adams, who hated banks,[70] the moneyed interest, and in fact
Hamilton's whole conception of the basis of government, supported his
early measures although he distrusted them. In supporting measures
which he did not like but which seemed to him necessary for the success
of the new government, Adams probably represented more accurately
than Hamilton ever did the views of the rank and file of those who
remained Federalist, but a crusty personality and a mass of abstruse political theory such as his were not designed to bring public sentiment to
a focus, no matter how strong it was potentially. Since he could not
make an articulate political force of those whose views he represented,

the solid, homely, and indigenous aspects of Federalism were largely obscured, and Hamilton's party leadership was not challenged until the party split in 1799. Hamilton's policy divided his erstwhile supporters while it united his opponents, and the true measure of his importance in the formation of political parties can be judged only by following both the growth of the Republicans and the disintegration of the Federalists. It may be noted in passing that since Hamilton's measures did not preserve the degree of unity which the conservatives had attained in 1789, efforts to treat the political division of the 1790's in strictly economic terms are likely to be highly misleading.

It is customary to contrast Hamilton's views of society with his own humble and uncertain origins on a small West Indian island, but any reflection upon the highly centralized economic control, the hierarchies of the caste system, and the dependent position of these sugar islands in the mercantile scheme should serve to explain Hamilton's vision of the perfect state. We can see in the purposes of his mature years the perfect, if inverted, reflection of the circumstances and vicissitudes of his youth. More than most men, Hamilton deserves to be discussed in terms of his purpose as a whole. Instead of following this procedure, however, both those who attack and those who defend him are likely to concentrate on the personal aspects of his policies, upon his motives, instead of judging the whole as a policy of creative statesmanship.

The great reliance of Hamilton's defenders has been upon his personal honesty and unselfish devotion to the United States, the assumption being that as long as we grant him these qualities, his policies were not open to attack. Both defense and criticism of him have echoed the partisan language of the 1790's, and both have been equally beside the point which is of primary significance for us. He himself construed attacks upon his system as efforts to convict him of personal dishonesty, and he defended all his measures, particularly to Washington, from the impregnable fortress of his personal honor; but if we wish to see how his program divided public opinion at the time, we merely cloud the issue by entering into the question of his own integrity and disinterestedness. His political enemies would have had a powerful weapon if they could have shown that he profited personally from policies that they wished to have overthrown, but that is the only importance, as far as the history of the country is concerned, of the question of Hamilton's personal character. Hamilton honest was a much more powerful adversary than Hamilton as an interested speculator, and a conspicuous integrity was indispensable for the part that he wished to play in the new government. This fact does not mean that he had to restrain a desire for personal enrichment lest it conflict with his other aims. He cared little for money either as a citizen or a statesman;[71] he saw it only as a means. A man can have only one dominating urge, and Hamilton's was for power and influence. He did not need money for his own purposes as long as he had the support of those who had money. Again we go wandering off into the labyrinth of the merely personal if we are too concerned as to whether Hamilton's desire for power was selfish, or whether he only wanted a government which was the embodiment of power and thought his measures the best way of attaining it. We may grant every contention of his admirers in support of the latter thesis and still see that such a single-minded pursuit of power terminates either in revolt and disunion or in the Leviathan state. Though primarily concerned with the creation of a powerful state, Hamilton seems never to have asked himself how powerful a state could be if it were not based on the loyalty, affections, and best interests of all of its citizens.

NOTES

[6] Vols. XI, XII of Henry Cabot Lodge, ed., *The Works of Alexander Hamilton*, 12 vols. (New York, 1904), hereafter cited as Lodge, *Hamilton's Works*, contain *The Federalist*. For Hamilton's promise on the excises, see *Federalist* 12, *ibid.*, XI, 92; on land taxes, see *Federalist* 12, 21, *ibid.*, 92, 166.

[7] Though Hamilton in *Federalist* 12 explained that no excise would be levied because the "genius of the people" hated excises, he seems to have welcomed the rebellion against his excise as an occasion for displaying the military power of the state. Leland DeWitt Baldwin, in his book *Whiskey Rebels* (Pittsburgh, 1939), does not say what he believes to have been Hamilton's motives in forcing the issue on the matter of the Excise in 1794, but he gives evidence which would support the conclusion that for political reasons Hamilton was glad of the opportunity to crush resistance to central government by force at that particular time. See especially pp. 110-12, 184, 220-21, 234-35. On p. 269 he states, "If Hamilton was actually trying to pacify the West the circumstances surrounding the issuance of the processes served in July, 1794, certainly showed political ineptitude; an accusation not lightly to be made against him."

[8] See correspondence for those years between Hamilton and Oliver Wolcott, Secretary of the Treasury, in George Gibbs, ed., *Memoirs of the Administrations of Washington and John Adams* (New York, 1846), hereafter cited as Gibbs, *Memoirs*; John Church Hamilton, ed., *The Works of Alexander Hamilton*, 7 vols. (New York, 1850-51), hereafter cited as Hamilton, *Hamilton's Works*; Hamilton Papers, Library of Congress, hereafter cited as Hamilton Papers, LC. Wolcott was greatly disturbed by our financial condition at this time. See Wolcott to Hamilton, Dec. 8, 1796, Hamilton, *Hamilton's Works*, VI, 175-76.

[9] John Adams to his wife, Philadelphia, Feb. 15, 1796. "The money of the country, the paper money, is the most unpleasant object I see. This must have a remedy, and I fear it will be western rebellion, or the opposition to the treaty." Charles Francis Adams, *Letters of John Adams. Addressed to His Wife*, 2 vols. (Boston, 1841), II, 202. See below for Wolcott's letter showing the way in which he viewed our situation.

[10] Hamilton to Wolcott, New York, Aug. 22, 1798, Hamilton, *Hamilton's Works*, VI, 349.

[11] *Ibid.*, 541.

[12] Lodge, *Hamilton's Works*, XI, 88.

[13] See Joseph Charles, *The Origins of the American Party System; Three Essays* (Williamsburg, Va., 1956) The Jay Treaty, part 2.

[14] Lodge, *Hamilton's Works*, II, 29.

[15] *Ibid.*, II, 27-8; XI, 308-09; XII, 91-2.

[16] *Ibid.*, V, 190-91.

[17] "For a season it seemed as though the Republican party was to be denied the right to exist as a legal opposition, entitled to obtain power by persuasion. . . . They [the Republicans] won, therefore, for all time that recognition of the right of legal opposition which is the primary condition of successful popular government." Allen Johnson, *Union and Democracy* (Boston and New York, 1915), 119.

[18] Stephen Van Rensselaer to Hamilton, Albany, Mar. 15, 1799. "The Assembly have a bill for electing Electors of the President & Vice-President—it will pass—are you of the opinion that it would be proper for the Senate to concur? Unless New York gives us a different representation the federalists are lost—Whether we have any object now since the late conduct of the President—you are a better judge than we. If it is however necessary that we should still persevere pray let me hear from you. Our friends are extremely pressing that I should write to you on the subject." Hamilton Papers, LC.

It is generally known that Hamilton wrote to Jay, May 7, 1800, after the Republicans had won the election for the New York State Assembly, urging that Jay call together the old assembly, which was Federalist, and have them choose the electors, even though this procedure would have been contrary to law. In the same letter Hamilton shows that he was depending on the Federalists in the Pennsylvania State Senate to prevent the taking of an electoral vote, which would have been Republican. Lodge, *Hamilton's Works*, X, 371-74.

Federalist efforts to prevent the passage of the law necessary for a choice of electors in New York were known to the Republicans at the time. See John Dawson to Madison, Philadelphia, Dec. 12, 1799, Madison Papers, Library of Congress. Hereafter cited as Madison Papers, LC.

[19] See second quotation from Hamilton's speech at the New York Constitutional Convention, above.

[20] Lodge, *Hamilton's Works*, I, 347-69.

[21] Hamilton to G. Morris, Feb. 27, 1802, *ibid.*, X, 425.

[22] William Graham Sumner, *Alexander Hamilton* (New York, 1890); John Church Hamilton, *The Life of Alexander Hamilton* (Boston, 1879); Henry Cabot Lodge, *Alexander Hamilton*, in John T. Morse, Jr., ed., *American Statesmen*, VII (Boston, 1882); Frederick Scott Oliver, *Alexander Hamilton: An Essay on American Union*, new ed. (New York, 1916).

[23] By Hamilton's economic program I mean Funding, Assumption, the Excise Bill, and the bill establishing the Bank. Hamilton's plans for encouraging manufacturing in this country are not treated here. They were not carried out, perhaps because of the mishaps which befell the Society for Establishing Useful Manufactures (see Joseph Stancliffe Davis, *Essays in the Earlier History of American Corporations* [vol. XVI in *Harvard Economic Studies*, Cambridge, 1917], I, 349-504 *passim*; hereafter cited as Davis, *American Corporations*), but it seems more probable that his plans for establishing manufacturing, at least in the near future, were abandoned for other reasons. The change might have come about because a large volume of imports was necessary to maintain government revenue, because Hamilton found himself more dependent for political support on merchants than he had expected to be, or because during the European wars of the early 1790's American capital tended to be engrossed in European trade instead of being invested in the United States.

²⁴ Edward Channing, *A History of the United States*, 6 vols. (New York, 1905-32), IV, 69. This is a point of great interest and importance, and it is to be regretted that Channing did not indicate the evidence upon which he based his conclusion. The letters of William Bingham and Stephen Higginson ("Letters from Two Business Men to Alexander Hamilton on Federal Fiscal Policy, November, 1789," James Wettereau, ed., *Journal of Economic and Business History*, III [1930-31], 667-86, hereafter cited as "Letters from Two Business Men"), in which both men urge substantially the method of funding which Hamilton followed, would suggest that it was not generally taken for granted among moneyed men that such a plan would be adopted. There seems, however, to be very little definite evidence as to the sort of arrangement which had been generally expected before Hamilton's plan was announced.

²⁵ See quotations from Andrew Craigie, in Davis, *American Corporations*, I, 188-89.

²⁶ Gaillard Hunt, ed., *The Writings of James Madison*, 9 vols. (New York, 1900-10), V, 444. Hereafter, Hunt, *Madison's Writings*.

²⁷ See "First Report on Public Credit," Lodge, *Hamilton's Works*, II, 227 ff.

²⁸ The yeas and nays were apparently not called on the Funding Bill, so it is impossible to know how the individual members voted.

²⁹ As strong a supporter of the Constitution as Henry Lee, then governor of Virginia, wrote to Madison from Berry Hill, Apr. 3, 1790, while the measures were before Congress, saying that he would rather "see the Union dissolve than submit to the rule of a fixed insolent northern majority." Gaillard Hunt, ed., *Disunion Sentiment in Congress in 1794* (Washington, 1905), Introduction, 10. See also letter of Dr. Stuart to Washington concerning opposition in Virginia, Abingdon, Jun. 2, 1790, Worthington Chauncey Ford, ed., *The Writings of George Washington*, 14 vols. (New York and London, 1889-93), XI, 482-84 *n*; Edmund Randolph to Madison, Mar. 6, 1790, Madison Papers, LC; Madison to Monroe, Apr. 17, 1790, *ibid.*; Edmund Randolph to Madison, May 20, 1791, *ibid.*; Beverly Randolph to Madison, Jul. 12, 1791, *ibid.*

³⁰ Rush to Madison, Philadelphia, Apr. 10, 1790, Madison Papers, LC. The comments of Rush raise the question of how much of the debt remained in the hands of the original holders at the time it was funded, a point of the greatest significance if we are interested in the later political effects of Funding. Those who had had to part with their securities, particularly those whose securities had been bought by speculators who had been informed of the steps that were to be taken in regard to the debt, were probably among the most decided enemies of Hamilton and his later measures. Hamilton, in his "Vindication of the Funding System" (Lodge, *Hamilton's Works*, III, 20-21), states that in 1786-87, when New York State holders of Continental securities had an opportunity to trade them in for state securities on advantageous terms, "it appeared that about two-thirds of the debt remained in the hands of the original proprietors." He thought that alienation had been less in New England and Maryland than in New York, no greater in Pennsylvania and New Jersey, but that a more considerable alienation had taken place south of Maryland. Hamilton's estimate of the amount of alienation seems to be far smaller than that of anyone else who commented upon it at the time. R. J. Meigs wrote to Madison, Marietta, Feb. 1, 1792, that he thought that the old army had disposed of seven-eighths of its securities before announcement of redemption. Madison Papers, LC. Pelatiah Webster, who later favored discrimination between original holders and speculators, wrote in Jan., 1785, "It is a matter of public notoriety and general belief, that almost the *whole* of the *widows, orphans, soldiers*, and other *distressed public creditors*, have sold their securities, which are now in the hands of speculators, who are known to be very numerous, and many of whom have a vast amount of them." Quoted in Davis, *American Corporations*, I, 180-81. Noah Webster expressed similar sentiments in a letter of Mar. 5, 1787, to Governor James Bowdoin of Massachusetts, *ibid.*, 180 *n*. And in Jul., 1788, Andrew Craigie wrote, "The greater part of the public debt is held by rich people who can afford to keep their Interest." *Ibid.*, 181.

[31] Sedgwick to his wife, New York, Mar. 22, 1790. "The truth is we have not only to support our measures but we have also our party to keep in order. Without the delegation of Pennsylvania it is impossible to succeed. Mr. Fitzsimmons and Mr. Clymer the only men in it are but unexpectedly called home and how soon they will return is uncertain. Wadsworth, too, has thought it more to his interest to speculate than to attend to his duty in Congress and is gone home." Sedgwick Papers, Massachusetts Historical Society. Hereafter cited as Sedgwick Papers, MHS. Writing to his wife again on the state of the Assumption Bill, Apr. 13, 1790, Sedgwick said, "The event of assumption during the present session grows every day more and more uncertain. . . . Our great difficulty is with the delegation of Pennsylvania. They have no hesitation in declaring that they believe the assumption to be indispensable to the welfare of the country, but they seem to consider the measure as unpopular in that state and have not the firmness of spirit to give a decided preference to the welfare of the people over their own popularity." *Ibid.* Other evidence of sentiment in Pennsylvania against the funding scheme among those whom we should expect to be in favor of it is to be seen in the fact that a number of public creditors living in Pennsylvania who had petitioned Congress to take steps "for the revival of public credit and the advancement of the national honor" (see *Annals of Congress*, [Washington, 1834-56], Aug. 28, 1769) joined next year in a remonstrance against the Funding Act (see *Finance in American State Papers* [Washington, 1832-61], I, 76). The general opposition to Funding and Assumption throughout the South is well known, but little attention has been called to the similar feeling in Pennsylvania, though the opposition of the Pennsylvania public creditors is pointed out by Charles Franklin Dunbar in "Some Precedents Followed by Alexander Hamilton," *Quarterly Journal of Economics*, III (1888), 32-59.

[32] Nicholson to Madison, Feb. 17, 1790. "The practicability of effecting a separate provision for original holders, I am well convinced of. I have carried into effect a similar plan in Penna. adopted by the legislature with respect to their *depreciation debt* and with a few alterations it might be done with great exactness and very little difficulty." Madison Papers, LC.

[33] Articles signed *A Farmer* in *Pennsylvania Gazette* (Philadelphia), Jan. 27, Feb. 3, 1790. Quoted by Margaret Woodbury, *Public Opinion in Philadelphia, 1789-1801*, in *Smith College Studies in History*, V (Oct., 1919-Jan., 1920), 45-46. Second quotation in Miss Woodbury's words.

[34] See Charles Austin Beard, *An Economic Interpretation of the Constitution of the United States* (New York, 1913), 36.

[35] Joel Barlow, Paris, Dec. 20, 1799, *Two Letters to the Citizens of the United States* (New Haven, 1806), 76-77.

[36] It is interesting to note that this measure was not undertaken as a result of petitions to Congress from state creditors that the national government assume the debts of the states. While the measure was under consideration some of the men who were most in favor of Assumption were terrified lest some of the state governments most in debt should undertake to provide completely for their creditors and thereby defeat Assumption.

[37] Henry Adams, *The Life of Albert Gallatin* (Philadelphia and London, 1880), 168.

[38] See Madison to Edmund Pendleton, New York, Mar. 4, 1790, *Letters and Other Writings of James Madison*, 4 vols. (Congress Edition, Philadelphia, 1865), I, 508-9 (hereafter cited as Madison, *Letters*), for an account of the way in which particularly Massachusetts and South Carolina would profit from Assumption.

[39] See *Annals of Congress*, Jul. 24, 1790. Bland was not present at the final vote on Assumption, but he was in favor of the measure. He wrote to Patrick Henry, Mar. 9, 1790, "that having sworn to support the constitution he was voting for every measure of energy and consolidation; that government once assumed over so extensive a dominion must fall into anarchy or be supported with vigor." Hunt, *Madison's Writings*, VI, 8 *n*. (Hunt's wording.)

[40] For evidence that Richard Bland Lee and Alexander White of Virginia, Daniel Carroll and George Gale of Maryland, were the four men whose votes were changed, see Richard

Henry Lee to William Lee, New York, Jul. 27, 1790, James Curtis Ballagh, ed., *The Letters of Richard Henry Lee*, 2 vols. (New York, 1911-14), II, 535.

[41] Madison to Jefferson, New York, May 9, 1789, Madison, *Letters*, I, 466.

[42] Madison to Washington, Orange, Nov. 20, 1789, *ibid.*, 496.

[43] "Letters of Two Business Men," 679.

[44] For evidence of widespread approval of the Constitution at the time of its adoption in Portsmouth, New Hampshire, and Boston, places where there had been much opposition and where the Republicans were to be strong, see Lawrence Shaw Mayo, *John Langdon of New Hampshire* (Concord, New Hampshire, 1937), 216-21, and John C. Miller, *Sam Adams, Pioneer in Propaganda* (Boston, 1936), 384.

[45] *Annals of Congress*, Jul. 26, 1790.

[46] *Ibid.*, Jan. 27, 1791.

[47] *Ibid.*, Feb. 8, 1791.

[48] John Quincy Adams to John Adams, Newburyport, Mar. 19, 1790, Worthington Chauncey Ford, ed., *The Writings of John Quincy Adams*, 7 vols. (New York, 1913-17), I, 48; same to same, Newburyport, April 5, 1790, *ibid.*, 50; Christopher Gore to Rufus King, Boston, Jan. 24, 1790, Charles R. King, ed., *The Life and Correspondence of Rufus King*, 6 vols. (New York, 1894-1900), I, 385 (hereafter cited as King, *Correspondence*); same to same, Boston, May 30, 1790, *ibid.*, 388; Nathaniel Gorham to Sedgwick, Jan. 12, 1790, Sedgwick Papers, MHS; same to same, Jan. 23, 1790, *ibid.*; Henshaw to Sedgwick, Boston, Jan. 27, 1790, *ibid.*; same to same, Boston, Jan. 30, 1790, *ibid.* Two letters from Henry Van Schaack to Sedgwick, Pittsfield, May 3, 1794, and Feb. 13, 1797, indicate that Assumption continued to be used by the opposition in their attacks on the Administration and that the Federalists were not able to meet all their arguments. In the first of these letters Van Schaack urges Sedgwick to get an abstract from the Treasury books to give him additional information to refute skeptics. The second letter suggests that he had been reading Gallatin's "A Sketch of the Finances of the United States" (Henry Adams, ed., *The Writings of Albert Gallatin*, 3 vols. [Philadelphia, 1879], III, 69-207; hereafter cited as Gallatin, *Writings*) and that he had been partially convinced, for the time, by it. *Ibid.*

[49] Henshaw to Sedgwick, Boston, Feb. 14, 1790, *ibid.*

[50] Gouverneur Morris to Robert Morris, London, Jul. 31, 1790, Jared Sparks, ed., *Life of Gouverneur Morris with Selections from His Correspondence and Miscellaneous Papers*, 3 vols. (Boston, 1832), III, 11-13. Hereafter, Sparks, *Life of G. Morris*.

[51] Sedgwick to Ephraim Williams, Philadelphia, Jan. 31, 1793, Sedgwick Papers, MHS.

[52] Sumner, *Alexander Hamilton*, 150.

[53] *Ibid.*

[54] *Ibid.*, 157.

[55] *Ibid.*, 164.

[56] *Ibid.*, 167.

[57] Lodge, *Hamilton's Works*, III, 332-33. (On p. 319 Lodge mistakenly describes this letter as written to Robert Morris.)

[58] Wolcott to Hamilton, Philadelphia, Sept. 26, 1795, Hamilton, *Hamilton's Works*, VI, 39-40.

[59] Hamilton to Wolcott, New York, Oct. 3, 1795, *ibid.*, 40.

[60] Hamilton to McHenry, New York, Mar. 18, 1799, Lodge, *Hamilton's Works*, VII, 69.

[61] Oliver Wolcott to Oliver Wolcott, Sr., New York, Mar. 27, 1790, Gibbs, *Memoirs*, I, 43.

[62] Hamilton to Sullivan, 1780 (only date given): "The only plan that can preserve the currency is one that will make it the *immediate* interest of the moneyed men to co-operate with government in its support." Lodge, *Hamilton's Works*, III, 332.

[63] Rexford Guy Tugwell and Joseph Dorfman, "Alexander Hamilton: Nationmaker," *Columbia University Quarterly* (XXIX and XXX, 1937 and 1938), XXX, 63-4.

[64] ". . . assumption stood upon a very different footing [from funding]. It was a matter

of political expediency, not of simple financial rectitude; and its expediency remains in doubt to this day." Sumner, *Alexander Hamilton*, 154.

⁶⁵ In the spring of 1796 a bill was moved in Congress which would have authorized the sale of bank stock owned by the government, the proceeds to be used to pay off a sum due from the government to the bank. Hamilton wrote to Wolcott, May 30, 1796, "I perceive Congress are invading the Sinking Fund System. If this goes through, and is sanctioned by the President, the fabric of public credit is prostrate, and the country and the President are disgraced. Treasury bills and every expedient, however costly, to meet exigencies, must be preferable in the event to such an overthrow of system." Hamilton Papers, LC.

⁶⁶ Remark quoted from Christopher Gore by Bassinger Foster, Jr., in letter to Craigie, Boston, Jan. 15, 1790, Craigie Papers, Vol. I, American Antiquarian Society, Worcester.

⁶⁷ Craigie to Daniel Parker, *ibid.*, Box III, Miscellaneous.

⁶⁸ Lodge, *Hamilton's Works*, II, 289 is one of several places where this remark is quoted without any reference to the date or the circumstances in which it was made. There is, therefore, no evidence that Morris had Hamilton's program in mind when he made this statement.

⁶⁹ Gertrude Franklin Atherton, *The Conqueror: Being the True and Romantic Story of Alexander Hamilton* (New York, 1916), quoted on title page.

⁷⁰ Adams to Benjamin Rush, Quincy, Aug. 28, 1811. "Funds and banks I never approved, or was satisfied with our funding system; it was founded on no consistent principle; it was contrived to enrich particular individuals at the public expense. Our whole banking system I ever abhorred, I continue to abhor, and shall die abhorring."

He continues later in the same letter, "A national bank of deposit I believe to be wise, just, prudent, economical, and necessary. But every bank of discount, every bank by which interest is to be paid or profit of any kind made by the deponent, is downright corruption. It is taxing the public for the benefit and profit of the individuals; it is worse than old tenor, continental currency, or any other paper money." Charles Francis Adams, ed., *The Life and Works of John Adams*, 10 vols. (Boston, 1850-56), IX, 638. Hereafter cited as Adams, *Works*. And in a letter to John Taylor of Caroline, Quincy, Mar. 12, 1819, Adams wrote, "I have never had but one opinion concerning banking, from the institution of the first, in Philadelphia, by Mr. Robert Morris and Mr. Gouverneur Morris, and that opinion has uniformly been that the banks have done more injury to the religion, morality, tranquillity, prosperity, and even wealth of the nation, than they can have done or ever will do good. They are like party spirit, the delusion of the many for the interest of a few." *Ibid.*, X, 375.

⁷¹ Of the personal affairs of Hamilton at the time of his death Gouverneur Morris wrote to Robert Morris, Morrisania, Jul. 20, 1804, "His affairs are sadly deranged. He has made a considerable purchase of land in no very eligible situation and of a quality inferior to some which is now on the market. After paying and binding himself to pay he found a heavy mortgage which he was obliged to take up and of course to encumber himself still more. His country house has according to custom cost him much more than he thought it would." Morris concluded that under the best of circumstances Hamilton would have been several years clearing off these encumbrances. (Letterbooks of Gouverneur Morris, Library of Congress.) Thus there were other reasons in addition to Hamilton's personal honesty which caused him to die poor.

THE VIRGINIA FEDERALISTS*

Norman K. Risjord

The underlying basis of bipartisanism and the political behavior of the electorate are continually intriguing topics. In an incisive analysis of the Virginia Federalist Party, Norman K. Risjord tests Charles Beard's famous thesis that economic interests are the basic determinants of political differences. He concludes that this interpretation offers only a partial and oversimplified explanation when applied to Virginia, where political divisions were based on long-standing social and geographic patterns in addition to the economic. By a roll-call technique he establishes that the Virginia Federalist Party maintained its greatest strength in areas where needs were best met by the national rather than the state government. At present a professor of history at the University of Wisconsin, Norman Risjord is the author of a study of Southern conservative Democratic-Republicans, The Old Republicans *(1965).*

Partially obscured by the furor over Charles A. Beard's interpretation of the Constitution has been a subtle, but widespread, assault upon Beard's other important piece of research, *The Economic Origins of Jeffersonian Democracy.* Contemporary scholars, searching for the roots of American political parties, have generally rejected Beard's argument that there was a continuity of issues and attitudes from the 1780's to the 1790's.[1] But, oddly enough, they have generally ignored Beard's secondary assumption—implicit in his work on the Constitution—that the Antifederalists and their Republican descendants were the party of the people, while the Federalists represented special class and financial interests. To be sure, Beard himself obscured this implication by his open admiration for Hamilton's "realism" in appealing to economic interests.

* From Norman K. Risjord, "The Virginia Federalists," *Journal of Southern History*, Vol. XXXIII (November, 1967), pp. 486-517. Copyright 1967 by the Southern Historical Association. Reprinted by permission of the Managing Editor.

But the implied evaluation of parties, vastly extended by later historians writing in the Progressive tradition, remained indelibly impressed upon the popular mind.[2]

It must be admitted that Beard's appraisal of the party struggle as basically a contest of "fluid capital versus agrarianism" was grossly oversimplified. He ignored the rural support given to Federalists and the strong entrepreneurial element among Republicans.[3] Yet students of early political parties have been so preoccupied with the mechanics of leadership, organization, machinery, and propaganda that they have generally ignored the underlying social and economic interests that determined political attitudes, and they usually accept without question the Jeffersonian bias engraved upon the popular mind by Beard, Claude G. Bowers, and Vernon Louis Parrington. The purpose of this essay, then, is to test these various themes of current scholarship by a close examination of the Federalist party in Virginia.

In arguing for continuity Beard's difficulty was that he relied primarily upon Federalist sources and Federalist-minded historians like John Marshall and Albert J. Beveridge, all of whom had a vested interest in demonstrating that the critics of the Washington administration were really opponents of the Constitution itself. Yet those historians who argue that there was no connection between the factional divisions of the 1780's and the parties of the 1790's rely for support largely on the shifting positions of the leadership, with Jefferson and Madison providing the best examples. To sort out the political attitudes of the party rank and file is extremely difficult, but an approximation can be achieved by examining the subsequent careers of the delegates who composed the ratifying conventions.

In Virginia, eighty-six delegates (plus three Kentuckians) voted in favor of the Constitution in 1788; of these thirty-eight remained Federalists and twenty-three became Republicans.[4] The remainder either dropped out of sight or, as in the case of Edmund Randolph, shifted sides so often as to defy categorization. Of the seventy-three (plus six Kentuckians) who voted against the Constitution in Virginia, forty can be subsequently identified and every one became a Republican except William Cabell, a minor figure who never held political office, and Patrick Henry.[5] Even Henry remained bitterly opposed to most of the measures of the Washington administration until he lost his followers to Jefferson and Madison. Then, in a bitter old age, he yielded to an ardent Federalist courtship and agreed to run for the Assembly, only to die before he could take his seat.[6] Approximately the same percentage of each group (fifty-one Federalists and forty Antifederalists) had subsequent careers in the executive, legislative, or judicial branches at either the state or federal levels.[7]

It is thus apparent that the party which supported the Constitution did indeed ultimately subdivide into Federalists and Republicans as asserted by most recent historians. But these figures also suggest that only a minority of Constitutionalists went over to the Republican side, and the rank and file of that party came mostly from the ranks of Antifederalism. Several of the delegates did not represent the prevailing sentiment in their constituencies, of course, and others were elected without a prior commitment on the Constitution. A conservative estimate, nevertheless, is that at least half, and possibly as many as two-thirds, of the Republican voters in the mid-1790's had been opponents of the Constitution. To some extent this was even true of the party leadership. Of the nine supporters of the Constitution who later served in Congress, five became Republicans and four remained Federalists; of seven Antifederalists who served in Congress, five became Republicans and two died before party organizations were formed. It is also significant that the first five United States senators elected by the Virginia Assembly were former Antifederalists, and not until 1799 did the Assembly choose as senator a Republican who had been a supporter of the Constitution. Federal and Antifederal organizations—if, indeed, there ever were any—did not evolve into permanent parties, but the division of popular sentiment in Virginia did persist with fair continuity.

One explanation for this is that the political and economic issues which divided Virginians in the 1780's did not suddenly disappear upon the ratification of the Constitution. Such perennial problems as the debts owed to British merchants, Indian depredations on the frontier, and the opening of the Mississippi divided Virginians into warring factions in the 1780's and continued to agitate the politics of the state for nearly a decade after the Constitution was ratified. Most of these issues ultimately involved the question of nationalism—the relative advantages to be secured by centralized government—and that was also the essence of the debate over the Constitution. Those who had witnessed the humiliations of governmental incompetence during the Revolution demanded a stronger government that could win a respected position among the nations of the world. This group included such ranking military officers as Horatio Gates, Daniel Morgan, James Wood, and Ebenezer Zane, who provided much of the political leadership for the Shenandoah Valley and the northwestern section of the state through the

1790's. Others, more closely associated with the state regime, felt little need for additional federal authority. And many, including some like George Mason and James Monroe who had favored strengthening the central government, pointed to the lack of a Bill of Rights as evidence that the Constitution had gone too far in the direction of centralization.

The Federalists pushed the Constitution through a hostile ratifying convention partly through the impressive credentials of their leadership (Washington, Madison, Edmund Randolph, and John Marshall) and partly through the persuasive argument that the Constitution would go into effect regardless of what Virginia did. But Patrick Henry was not so easily suppressed. In the months after the Constitution was approved he united the various antinationalist elements behind a call for a second federal convention. The purpose would be to amend the Constitution, adding a Bill of Rights and removing the power of direct taxation. In the next session of the General Assembly during the fall of 1788 Henry threatened to boycott the division of the state into congressional districts until the House of Delegates adopted resolutions favoring a second convention. A Federalist substitute motion referring the problem of amendments to Congress was defeated, 50 to 72, and the House proceeded to adopt Henry's resolutions by voice vote.[8]

Even the adoption of a Bill of Rights by Congress in the following year failed to impress Henry and his following. Virginia's Antifederalist senators, Richard Henry Lee and William Grayson, promptly issued a broadside denouncing the proposed amendments as inadequate and predicting that the state governments would soon be annihilated by overriding central authority.[9] When the Assembly again took up its duties in Richmond in the fall of 1789, Patrick Henry moved to postpone consideration of the amendments until the following session. His motion was rejected "by a great majority," and the House proceeded to approve without a roll call the twelve amendments submitted. Undaunted, Henry then introduced a resolution requesting Congress to add to the Bill of Rights all the other amendments suggested by the Virginia ratifying convention. The effect would have been further restrictions on the power of the federal government, especially in the field of taxation. This effort failed on a tie vote, 62 to 62, which was broken when the speaker, Thomas Matthews of Norfolk, voted nay. Reporting on Virginia politics to the President on December 6, Attorney General Edmund Randolph believed that this vote showed "the strength of the parties, and that in the house of delegates the antifederal force has diminished much since the last year."[10] Senate rejection of four of the amendments, however, postponed Virginia's approval of the Bill of Rights until 1791. The final addition to the Constitution of nine amendments guaranteeing the rights of citizens and a tenth which seemingly guaranteed the rights of states did not entirely satisfy the antinationalists, however. As late as 1793 a resolution requesting Congress to consider the rest of the amendments suggested by the Virginia ratifying convention was postponed in the House of Delegates by a narrow margin of 63 to 54.[11]

The contest concerning alteration of the Constitution was soon overshadowed by the adverse reaction among Virginians to various measures of the Federalist administration. Rumors of the pomp and ceremony that attended the President's weekly levees aroused criticism among those who feared for the security of republican principles.[12] Alexander Hamilton's fiscal policies provoked a violent reaction in Virginia. Even staunch Federalists such as Henry Lee (a speculator himself) abhorred the mounting national debt, felt cheated by the assumption program, and mistrusted the Bank. In the House of Delegates a resolution condemning assumption of state debts as "repugnant to the Constitution" passed on November 3, 1790, by 75 to 52.[13]

The root of this division was still the fundamental issue of domestic centralization, though in a new form. But in the following years the problems provoked by the French Revolution and the outbreak of war in Europe provided an entirely new set of divisive issues. A polarization of feeling between pro-British and pro-French elements enhanced the factional division among Virginians and contributed to the organization of political parties.[14] The appearance of French emissary Edmond Charles Genêt in the spring of 1793 occasioned an explosion of pro-French feeling among Virginians that benefited greatly the Jeffersonian Republicans. President Washington's proclamation of neutrality, which was designed to put a damper on the Genêt mission, was widely criticized for its timing. More extreme Republicans even doubted the constitutional power of the President to declare a state of no-war. The furor died quickly in the course of the summer when Genêt discredited himself by disobeying the orders of the President in regard to fitting out French privateers in American ports. When the Assembly met in the fall of 1793, Governor Henry Lee recommended that it adopt a resolution supporting the President's policies. Embarrassed Republicans submitted a resolution in the House of Delegates that foreign policy was not a fit subject for commentary by a state legislature, but the House rejected this and adopted by 77 to 48 a Federalist resolution praising the neutrality proclamation as "a politic and constitutional measure, wisely adopted at a criti-

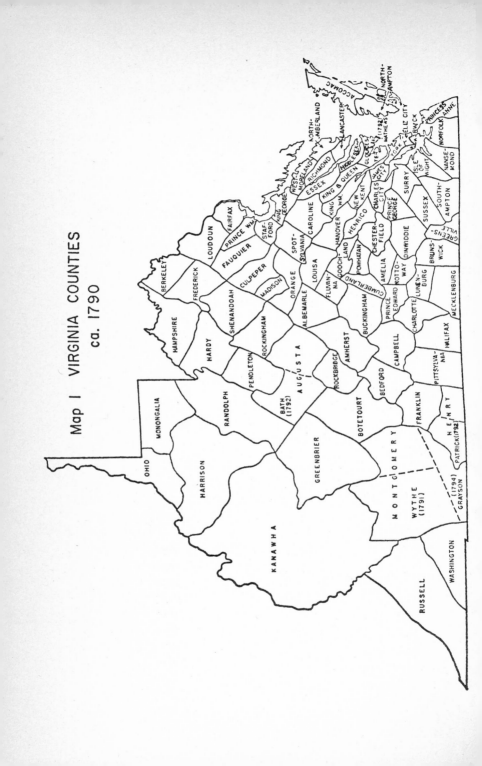

Map I VIRGINIA COUNTIES
ca. 1790

cal juncture. . . ." No doubt a number of Republicans supported the resolution in order to avoid the taint of being excessively pro-French, but Governor Lee nevertheless considered the division a vote of confidence in the President.[15]

Taken together, the various roll calls of the House of Delegates between 1788 and 1793 reveal a factional division in Virginia politics. Several of the votes (those involving the summoning of a second federal convention) reveal attitudes toward the Constitution itself, while others involve issues (assumption of state debts, foreign affairs) that provoked the birth of formal political parties. By combining them it is possible to determine the extent of continuity in Virginia politics in the years after the Constitution was ratified but before party organizations were fully formed. A simple index has been devised to determine the degree of nationalist/Federalist or antinationalist/Republican sentiment among Virginia counties represented in the House of Delegates.[16] If there were no connection between the factions of 1788 and the parties of the 1790's, then the random voting of delegates would place nearly all the counties at the center of the index and the resulting map would contain a meaningless assortment of "divided" counties. The index, however, actually reveals a clear pattern of voting, and the resulting map bears a remarkable similarity to the vote on the Constitution (see Maps 2 and 3).[17] It is thus evident that the division of popular sentiment in Virginia between nationalists and antinationalists preserved a significant amount of continuity from the 1780's into the 1790's.[18] Fundamental political issues, based on social and economic differences, tended to divide Virginians into fairly well-defined geographical sections.

In their economic basis, and to a lesser extent in their social structure, the Federalist counties differed substantially from the rest of Virginia. The Eastern Shore and the region between the Potomac and the Rappahannock extending west to the Blue Ridge were areas undergoing an agricultural revolution. Among the first to experience the frustrations of exhausted soils and declining yields due to overconcentration on tobacco, these counties began shifting from tobacco to wheat, corn, and other cereal grains well before the Revolution. Accompanying this diversification was the adoption of progressive agricultural techniques—the use of gypsum, deep plowing, and crop rotations—stemming from the experiments of the Maryland planter John Beale Bordley in the 1770's and propagated after the Revolution by the Loudoun County planter John A. Binns. Such was the extent of this agricultural revolution that by 1795 the merchants of Alexandria were exporting ten times as much flour as

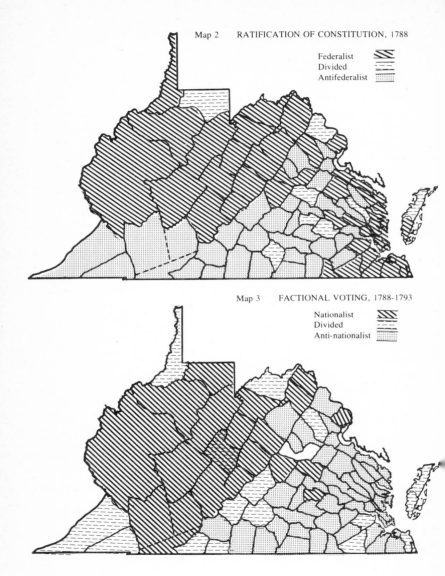

Map 2 RATIFICATION OF CONSTITUTION, 1788

Federalist
Divided
Antifederalist

Map 3 FACTIONAL VOTING, 1788-1793

Nationalist
Divided
Anti-nationalist

tobacco.[19] Since the primary markets for such exports were the West Indies and southern Europe, the merchants and planters of the region looked to the federal government for aid in expanding their commercial outlets. In contrast, the tobacco planters in the Piedmont and Southside, their markets in Britain and France relatively secure, saw little advantage in a strong central government over which they had little control.[20]

Agricultural reform in the nationalist counties was accompanied by a constant search for improved methods of transportation and marketing. In 1785 various planters and merchants of the Northern Neck united with leaders of the Shenandoah Valley to form the Potomac Company. George Washington was installed as first president of the company, but the initial meeting of stockholders was presided over by Alexander White, later a prominent Valley Federalist. Over the next decade the company constructed roads through Loudoun and Fairfax counties, cleared obstructions from the Potomac, and built canals around the falls. By 1795 flatboats could navigate the Potomac thirty miles above Cumberland, Maryland, and as far as sixty miles up the Shenandoah River. The soils of these counties were generally considered to be the richest in the state, and with the opening of the Potomac land prices rose dramatically in the 1790's. The result was an economic unity based on internal improvements, as Alexandria became the commercial hub of northern Virginia. The numerous and energetic merchant class of the region was also politically active—Leven Powell, wealthiest merchant in Loudoun County, is generally credited with organizing the Federalist party in the Northern Neck during the 1790's.[21]

Tied commercially to the Northern Neck, another center of Virginia Federalism included the counties of the Shenandoah Valley, those in the Alleghenies just west of the Valley (hereafter referred to as the Allegheny slope counties), and those along the valley of the Kanawha River. Populated largely by Scotch-Irish Presbyterians and Germans, both Lutheran and sectarian, this region possessed substantial ethnic and religious differences from the rest of Virginia. Unlike the Piedmont, which was settled by Tidewater planters moving inland, the counties west of the mountains were populated by emigrants moving southward along the Great Valley from Maryland and Pennsylvania. Lacking the pride of locality characteristic of eastern Virginia, they tended to be more nationalist in outlook. The economic structure of this region also differed substantially from that of eastern Virginia. In the Shenandoah Valley the size of the average farm was 229 acres, as against an average of 284 for the Piedmont; slaves made up about 15 per cent of the population in the Valley and about 5 per cent in the mountain counties, compared with about 50 per cent east of the Blue Ridge.[22] As in the Northern Neck the merchants and farmers of the western counties united in their affection for the federal government, which alone could provide the protection and aid necessary in marketing their crops of grain, whiskey, and hemp.[23]

In contrast to the Northern Neck, where the Federalist merchants and planters gradually lost control of their counties in the course of the 1790's, western Federalism was more solidly grounded on a foundation of popular support. The rank and file of the party consisted of middle-class, commercial farmers (the subsistence farmers of the southwest usually voted Republican), whose economic and political interests were seldom served by the eastern planter gentry who controlled the state. Though western Federalism was primarily an agrarian movement, its leadership, interestingly enough, was almost invariably mercantile. In a region of small farmers the village merchant, lawyer, or physician alone possessed the local stature to qualify him for election to the General Assembly or Congress. Social, economic, and political interests thus united to make the counties in the Potomac, Shenandoah, and Kanawha watersheds the bulwark of Virginia Federalism until after the War of 1812.

The explosive political issues of the 1790's gradually weakened the Federalist party east of the Blue Ridge, but had little effect on Federalist strongholds in the West. The excises of 1791, which created widespread disaffection throughout the Allegheny Plateau, had relatively slight impact on the mountain counties of Virginia—perhaps because Virginia Federalists in Congress took pains to explain to their constituents that the added duties were needed to finance expeditions against the Indians.[24] The Whiskey Rebellion itself found little support in (West) Virginia. Though the excise was generally unpopular, most western farmers preferred peaceful political action to active resistance.[25] During the height of the insurrection at Pittsburgh a Federalist member of the House of Delegates reported from Clarksburg to Governor Henry Lee that ''a very great majority [in Harrison County] are averse to proceedings so destructive to good order, and subversive of the rights of a free, independent people.'' The citizens of Morgantown organized a defense of the city against the depredations of rebels from Pennsylvania seeking to force Virginians into the insurrection.[26] In the end, the counties composing present-day West Virginia contributed about a thousand men to the army that suppressed the rebellion, while Federalist leaders, such as Daniel Morgan, were prominent members of Governor Lee's army staff.[27]

Western Virginians remained loyal to the Federalist party because it served their interests. Scattered discontent with the fiscal system and the excises was soon dissipated amidst the general satisfaction in the West with Washington's Indian policies. The Southern Indians were pacified by generous treaty settlements, and the ravages of the Ohio tribes, which created widespread alarm in northwest Virginia,[28] were ended by the successful campaign of Anthony Wayne at Fallen Timbers in 1794. On Washington's retirement from office, aged Arthur Campbell, who had led an army of debt-ridden frontiersmen into open rebellion a decade before, seized the occasion to express his appreciation to the President, "especially for the share of attention you have paid to the safety and prosperity of the Western Country. . . ." Revealing some of the old rhetorical fire that had charmed the West for a generation, he concluded: "Our Wives our Children, and vast property now pass and repass in safety, as it were in full view of our late enemies. The hand that was used to raise the bloody Hatchet, now meets the wearied Traveller with greetings and a supply of provisions."[29] The signing of Pinckney's Treaty with Spain in 1795 pushed back Spanish territorial claims and promised an end to Spanish intrigues among the Southern Indians. Even more important to Virginians, it opened the Mississippi River and granted the right to deposit goods at New Orleans. This satisfied the demands of Virginia frontiersmen and brought to an end an issue that had convulsed Virginia politics for a decade.

Closely related to the Indian problem was the treaty with Great Britain signed by John Jay in November 1794. The treaty is often, and no doubt correctly, regarded as the key to the formation of party organizations, but in Virginia its only effect was to alter the pre-existing factional alignment by shrinking the extent of Federalist support. Only two features of the treaty directly affected Virginians—the establishment of a commission for the settlement of prewar debts and British agreement to evacuate the northwest posts. Both issues had troubled Virginia politics since the end of the war. Moreover, the two were related, for the British justified their retention of forts in violation of the peace treaty on the ground that Americans violated the treaty first by refusing to pay their debts. Through the 1780's a creditor faction led by Madison and George Mason demanded debt payment on the grounds that repudiation would have a disastrous effect on trade and frighten potential investors.[30] But efforts to provide for debt collection in annual installments and open the state's courts to British lawsuits were killed by the opposition of Patrick Henry and Richard Henry Lee. The alignment in the Assembly on this issue

followed generally the division between nationalists and antinationalists.[31]

By 1786, after "repeated disappointments," Madison was ready to
give up, but his cause obtained new life the following year when the
delegates from western Virginia deserted the debtor faction and voted
in favor of repealing all laws in conflict with the peace treaty. Alarmed
by sporadic warfare along the Ohio frontier, the Westerners suspected
that the British posts along the Great Lakes were giving moral and logisti-
cal support to the Indians. A repeal of the statutes which conflicted with
the peace treaty by denying British suitors access to Virginia courts, they
hoped, would induce the British to evacuate their forces from American
soil. The maneuver failed, but the (West) Virginians supported the Constitution in 1788 largely on the promise that a strong national government
would have power to vanquish the Indians and remove the British.[32] During the early 1790's the position of each side, frontiersmen and indebted
planters, hardened. Shocked by the defeats of Josiah Harmar and Arthur
St. Clair, Westerners grew frantic at the prospect of war with England
in early 1794.[33] At the same time the old debtor faction led by Patrick
Henry was reinforced by anti-British Republicans. "The late debates concerning British debts," Attorney General Randolph reported in 1793,
"have served to kindle a wide-spreading flame. The debtors are
associated with the antifederalists, and the discontented federalists; and
they range themselves under the standard of Mr. Henry, whose ascendancy has risen to an immeasurable height."[34] It was clear that eastern
Virginia planters were prepared to react violently to any effort to compromise the debt problem.

Publication of the Jay Treaty in the spring of 1795 dealt a heavy blow
to Federalism in Virginia. Establishment of a commission to settle debts
seemed to be a surrender of the interests of Virginia planters, and the
treaty's failure to mention neutral rights was a tacit acceptance of British
interpretations of international law. The Republicans organized mass
meetings which drew up petitions and passed resolutions of protest. Party
organizations appeared at the local level, and party lines hardened. In
November 1795 the House of Delegates adopted by a vote of 100 to
50 a resolution approving the conduct of Virginia's senators in voting
against the treaty. A map of the vote (Map 4) reveals the same basic
sectional pattern that had characterized Virginia politics for a decade.
But it also reveals a considerable shrinkage in Federalist support. The
Federalists were virtually wiped out in the Piedmont and in the region
south of the James, indicating the unanimity of sentiment among tobacco

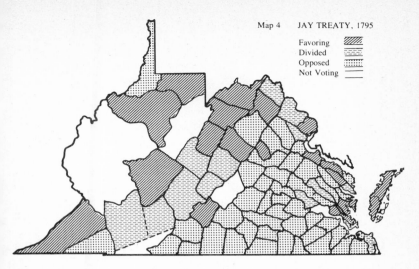

Map 4   JAY TREATY, 1795

Favoring
Divided
Opposed
Not Voting

planters on the debt provisions. The western vote, though distorted some-what by absenteeism, appears to reflect a general satisfaction with the removal of the British from the northwest posts. The only Federalist gains were in the Northern Neck (Loudoun, Prince William, and King George). This area, along with the Williamsburg peninsula and the Eastern Shore, had been part of Madison's creditor faction in the 1780's, and no doubt it was pleased with the limited access to the West Indies market granted by the treaty (although that provision was deleted by the Senate). The increase in Federalist strength there was also due in part to the develop-ment of a party organization centered in Alexandria.

The imbroglio with France resulting from the Jay Treaty provoked a wave of nationalism which temporarily strengthened the Virginia Federal-ists. Since France, unlike England, posed no immediate threat to the sea-board or the frontier, Virginia nationalists could permit themselves the luxury of outrage at the humiliating treatment administered to the Ameri-can commissioners in Paris. Few Virginia Federalists articulated this feeling better than young Charles Fenton Mercer, a future leader of the party who was then completing his education at Princeton. Like most Virginians, he had long possessed a basic sympathy for France, but he was dismayed by the "corruption of those principles which created the revolution." France was no longer the model republic, Mercer told his brother-in-law, for its initial idealism had been perverted by the corrupt usurpations of the Directory, the creation of a vast army, and the tendency toward military despotism. A nation bent on conquest understood nothing but force, he concluded, and the humiliating treatment of the American commissioners demonstrated the futility of negotiating from weakness: ". . . if the President wished for peace he did well in recommending to Congress a preparation for defense[,] did well to express his sense of the injustice of the French government. A government not to be won by submission must be made to respect the rights of others through fear. We have seen the effect of a submissive policy in the present contest of Europe and it was time that we should open. our eyes."[35]

In Congress the four Virginia Federalists uniformly supported the administration's defense program—creation of a naval department, suspension of commerce with France, tax increases, and enlargement of the army and navy. But only one, Thomas Evans of the Eastern Shore, voted for the Alien and Sedition Laws.[36] In Richmond, John Marshall denounced the measures of domestic repression as " 'useless . . . [and] calculated to create unnecessary discontents and jealousies.' "[37] But these acts seemed to have little immediate effect on Virginia public opinion. In the congressional elections of 1799 Virginia returned eight Federalists (out of a total of nineteen representatives), the largest number ever obtained by the party in that state.[38] In the House of Delegates the Federalist minority rose from the fifty who had defended the Jay Treaty to over sixty. These modest gains suggest that nationalism provoked by the undeclared war with France was a more important factor in shaping public opinion in Virginia than were the errors committed by the Federalist administration in Philadelphia. They suggest also that the famous resolutions of 1798 had little immediate propaganda value, even in Virginia.

Drawn up by James Madison and introduced into the House of Delegates by John Taylor, the Virginia Resolutions of 1798 provided the first opportunity in a decade for a full-dress debate on the fundamental issue of nationalism versus states' rights. The Federalists, representing the merchants and small farmers of the Potomac and Shenandoah valleys, struck hard at the philosophical and legal flaws at the root of Madison's generalizations. To them the compact theory of government outlined in the resolutions was nothing more than an attempt to perpetuate the rule of the planter gentry. "[I]n the name of Heaven!" exclaimed General Daniel Morgan, "are their [the Republicans'] Views honest? I think not. . . . does it not appear that those people—disappointment [sic] at not being elevated in the Genl. Government, wish to cut it to pieces, in order that they may rule & tyranize over a part."[39]

This notion was advanced with telling effect on the floor of the House of Delegates by Edmund Brooke of Prince William. Though he disapproved of the Alien and Sedition Acts and agreed with the Republicans' defense of individual liberty, Brooke taunted the majority on their refusal to protect the rights of the citizen at the state level. In a conflict between the national and state governments he would unhesitatingly give his allegiance to "The government of the United States . . . because, in the government of the United States, the representation of the people of this state is more pure and more equal than it is, or could possibly be in the state government under the existing state constitution."[40] This line of argument had been developed earlier by a Valley Federalist, Archibald Magill, who launched an attack on the compact theory itself. If the states alone are parties to the constitutional compact, he pointed out, the people are excluded from the formation of government, a situation, he noted, which had a parallel in the General Assembly where representation was determined by counties rather than population.[41]

Former Governor Henry Lee singled out another flaw in the compact theory. He begged the Assembly to confine itself to a petition for repeal of the Alien and Sedition Laws, or at most to refer the issue to the federal judiciary. To declare the laws null and void was to invite civil disobedience and chaos. He predicted that "if the principle of obeying the will of the majority was once destroyed, it would prostrate all free government." The threat of a minority veto implicit in the resolutions deeply concerned most Virginia Federalists. General Daniel Morgan predicted that "Instead of an extensive, united nation, respectable among all the powers on the Globe, we shall dwindle into a number of petty divisions, an easy prey for domestic Demagogues and foreign Enemies. . . ."[42]

The resolutions were adopted by the House of Delegates by a vote of 100 to 63.[43] The vote reveals the fundamental sectional pattern that had persisted throughout the decade. Though Federalist strength increased somewhat over the vote on the Jay Treaty, it had evaporated in two key areas—the Tidewater part of the Northern Neck (except for Henry Lee's Westmoreland County) and the Williamsburg peninsula. Federalist gains among counties south of the James, which had occasionally appeared in the nationalist column before 1793, were only temporary. The Federalists also lost support among the farmers along the Ohio River (Harrison and Ohio counties) and in the southwest. No longer menaced by Indians, the subsistence farmers of this region (or, more accurately, "semisubsistence," since they often had one small cash crop) adopted a more provincial, antinationalist outlook and remained predominantly Republican thereafter.

The ingenious combination of nationalism and democracy erected by the Federalists in the debate on the Virginia Resolutions reflected the sectional interests they represented. Merchants and farmers in the Potomac, Shenandoah, and Kanawha watersheds looked to the national government because their demands seldom received sympathetic treatment in Richmond; they were ignored in Richmond because they lacked (or at least the western counties lacked) proper representation. Because they reflected these interests better than the Republicans, the Federalists remained a power in the west in Virginia throughout the Presidencies of Jefferson and Madison, but as they became increasingly tied to regional interests they doomed themselves to a permanent minority status. Their devotion to nationalism and democracy was thus a product of their regional distribution, rather than a profound ideology. The two principles might have served as the philosophical foundations for a strong and prosperous party, but the Federalists lacked the perception and the organizational capacity to capitalize on the idea. Instead their numbers declined rapidly in the next few years.

The superiority of Republican party organization, the success of Republican propaganda, and the obvious achievements of the Jefferson administration were primarily responsible, but the Federalists contributed to their own decline by irresponsible actions. In Congress the Virginia Federalists generally approved of Adams' peace overtures toward France in the spring of 1800, but they also voted to retain the provisional army, favored continuing commercial retaliation against France, and divided four to two in favor of extending the Sedition Law.[44] In the election contest between Jefferson and Burr they voted five to one in favor of Burr on all the early ballots. Even on the final ballot, when moderates to the northward and in South Carolina withheld their votes, three Virginians continued to support Burr.[45] This departure from moderation became utter irresponsibility two years later when four Virginia Federalists (including two from the west) voted against a resolution carrying into effect the Louisiana Purchase. The appropriation for the purchase passed the House of Representatives by 85 to 7, but in the minority were three Virginia Federalists holding out even after New England gave in.[46] These actions on the national level tarnished the party image and decimated Federalist sentiment in Virginia. In the election of 1805 only one Federalist was returned to Congress, and the party's strength in the Assembly declined to twenty-five by the end of Jefferson's first term in office.

The pattern of county voting during Jefferson's Presidency was the culmination of the tendencies noted in the vote on the Virginia Resolutions of 1798. Federalist sentiment was reduced to the Eastern Shore, the upper Potomac, and the Allegheny slope, areas that remained Federalist through interest, voting habit, and the institutionalization of parties until after the War of 1812. In the case of the Eastern Shore, a feeling of separateness from Virginia and association with predominant Federalism in Delaware and the Eastern Shore of Maryland were additional factors. In the Tidewater there were only isolated pockets of Federalism after 1800, due largely to the continuing influence of prestigious families (Henry Lee in Westmoreland and the Christians in New Kent). The Richmond Federalists, though highly vocal, remained a minority that seldom won a local election after 1800.

Federalism might have withered and died out in Virginia if the Jeffersonians had pursued an active policy of political and social reform to meet the demands of the small farmers of the northwest. Shortly after Jefferson was elected the Assembly was presented with numerous petitions from the west demanding reapportionment of the legislature. In January 1803 a bill to establish twenty-four senate districts with an equal number of free, white inhabitants in each was rejected by the Jeffersonian majority, 52 to 72.[47] The following year a resolution recommending a constitutional convention was rejected, 72 to 87.[48] Western Federalists were quick to blame these defeats on eastern Republicans. They particularly objected to the demand that three-fifths of the Negro slaves be counted in ascertaining population. This was enough to make one Valley Federalist advocate a division of the state because he was being forced to pay extra taxes for the maintenance of slavery and a slave patrol in Richmond, and then "when a proposition was made to obtain an equal representation in the senate (which would increase the western members from four to nine) these low-land republicans (or more properly speaking high-flying aristocrats) opposed it, and insisted that if any alteration was made, their negroes should be represented also."[49]

Western Republicans who dared to side with the eastern gentry were reminded of their apostasy at election time. One unfortunate Hampshire Republican went down to defeat after suffering a series of accusations that he was too "anxious to gain the favour of those conspicuous characters residing in the lower counties; *they* pretend to be violent republicans, but are in fact the greatest aristocrats in the United States."[50] The Jeffersonian failure to respond to this deep-rooted feeling left the Federalists with a solid foundation of support in the Potomac, Shenandoah, and Kanawha valleys, ready to take advantage of further errors by the ruling Republicans.

British depredations on the high seas, climaxing with the *Chesapeake* incident, provided new grounds for criticism of Jeffersonian doctrine. "All history agrees in the fact," observed a Valley Federalist, "that under weak and relaxed administrations, insults are not only offered from abroad, but rebellious spirits at home [Aaron Burr] are encouraged to project schemes of usurpation, and aggrandizement." Another suggested that if the President had invested his surplus funds in the navy instead of an unholy effort to acquire West Florida the nation would receive more respect abroad.[51] Virginia Federalists vigorously defended the nation's neutral rights, but they had little to suggest in the way of policy, except a mutual forbearance on the lines of the Monroe-Pinkney Treaty. The experiment in commercial retaliation, on the other hand, surrendered the nation to "a tribe of political economists" and imposed serious hardship on Virginia farmers.[52] In the spring elections of 1808 counties on the Northern Neck and Eastern Shore, only recently converted to the Republican interest, returned to the ranks of Federalism. In the presidential contest of that year many opponents of the embargo threw their support to James Monroe. In October Dr. James McClurg, former delegate to the Federal Convention, presided over a meeting of Richmond Federalists which endorsed Monroe on the grounds that he offered the prospect of better relations with Great Britain.[53] This suggestion was generally followed by Federalists in the Northern Neck and Eastern Shore, but counties in the Valley and northwest favored instead the Federalist candidate Charles C. Pinckney. In Congress the number of Virginia Federalists elected in 1809 jumped to five,[54] and in the House of Delegates Federalist strength arose to thirty members, a figure that remained remarkably stable throughout Madison's eight years in office.

These gains of 1809 were preserved because the Federalist regions had little interest in a quarrel with England. The Eastern Shore was badly exposed and traditionally hostile to Jeffersonian policy. The counties along the Allegheny slope were remote from the maritime conflict and too distant from Indiana to feel much concern over British intrigues among the Indians of the Northwest. Both regions, moreover, prospered from the war in Europe; prices for their major products—flour, beef, pork, and hemp—held up better than other American exports throughout the prewar period.[55] Yet a fundamental nationalism prevented Virginia Federalists from engaging in the sort of obstructionist tactics that typified New England opposition. In Congress the Virginians uniformly opposed all measures of commercial retaliation, but they generally supported such defensive measures as fortification of harbors and maintenance of the navy.[56]

Since the votes of Virginia Federalists were normally cast in silence —James Breckinridge and Daniel Sheffey alone achieved any sort of stature in Congress—it is difficult to determine their attitude toward the war with England. The best indication is a speech by Daniel Sheffey in the House of Representatives on January 11, 1813, on a bill to raise an additional military force of 20,000 men. Sheffey made a clear distinction between a war for national rights and a war for empire. He offered to support any army intended for defense against foreign invasion or to suppress the Indians, and he considered the existing military establishment sufficient for both. But the conquest of Canada, he felt, was not worth the expense, even if it could be accomplished. The nation did not need more land and would have difficulty governing a foreign territory. Sheffey concluded by outlining his own terms for a settlement with Britain. He would remove the impressment issue by prohibiting the employment of British seamen on American vessels but insist on British abandonment of the principle. A settlement could then be reached if the United States would abandon its insistence on the absolute immunity of its flag, thereby permitting the British to enforce their blockade and carry on their war with Napoleon.[57]

Such proposals, perhaps unacceptable to a majority of Americans at the time, were nevertheless a reasonable alternative and evidenced a responsibility in opposition that characterized the actions of Virginia Federalists throughout the war. In the Twelfth Congress they voted invariably against a large army that might be used for offensive purposes, but generally supported the navy and the militia.[58] In 1812, when talk of Canada filled the air, they unanimously opposed any increase in taxes or authorization for loans. But two years later when British assaults on Washington and the New York frontier changed the character of the war they supported a bill imposing additional taxes.[59] The same pattern emerged in the General Assembly. Uniformly opposed to the war at its inception, the Federalists in the House of Delegates cast thirty votes against a resolution approving the belligerent stance of the House Foreign Relations Committee in December 1811, and they voted against all efforts to increase the military forces of the state.[60] But in December 1814 a bill levying additional excises to finance Virginia's share of the war effort passed the House, 127 to 25. Only four Virginia Federalists opposed it; the rest were Republicans from the traditionally antinationalist regions of the Southside and southwest. A month earlier, when the Republicans introduced a resolution denouncing British peace terms and pledging support for the war, the Federalists sought unsuccessfully to soften the tone of the resolution lest it embarrass the peace commissioners, while still pledging support for the war.[61]

Moderate, responsible opposition such as this enabled the Federalists in Virginia to maintain their party strength through the war. Five Federalists were returned to Congress in 1813 and four in 1815.[62] In the House of Delegates the number of Federalists dropped to less than twenty during the war but climbed back up to thirty in 1815. At a time when the Hartford Convention and the "Blue Lights" symbolized the intransigent sterility of the declining Federalist party in New England, the party in Virginia remained a viable political force. In 1817 three Federalists (all new men) were elected to Congress,[63] and in the House of Delegates nineteen Federalists could be found voting against a congratulatory address to President Madison on his retirement. Indeed, as late as 1821 there were eighteen Federalists voting against a resolution denying the jurisdiction of the Supreme Court in the case of *Cohens* v. *Virginia*.[64] Such organization as the party possessed evidently disappeared after the war,[65] and in the 1820's they became indistinguishable from Republican nationalists (see Map 5).[66]

The various legislative elements of the postwar nationalism—the Second Bank of the United States, the protective tariff, and internal

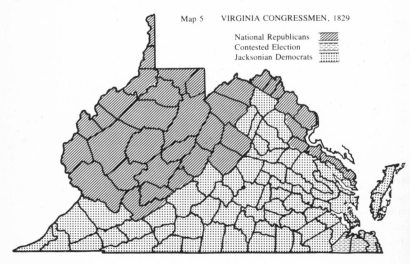

Map 5   VIRGINIA CONGRESSMEN, 1829

National Republicans
Contested Election
Jacksonian Democrats

improvements—divided Virginia political sentiment along regional lines that closely paralleled the sectional division of the 1790's. Districts that deserted the Federalists after 1800 often elected Republican nationalists, such as John P. Hungerford, a former Federalist who represented the Northern Neck in the postwar period, and Thomas Newton, the perennial congressman from Norfolk. The most articulate and consistent Republican exponent of the postwar nationalism was Henry St. George Tucker, who was elected to Congress in 1815 from the northern Shenandoah Valley (Frederick and Shenandoah counties).

The support given to any particular federal program, of course, varied with regional interests. The Northern Neck, Eastern Shore, and middle Tidewater had scant use for internal improvements, but in 1816 these districts gave solid support to the tariff and, to a lesser extent, the Bank. Similarly, the Federalists who represented the small farmers and village merchants of the west ignored the Bank and the tariff, but they were vitally interested in a comprehensive program of road construction and river improvement.[67] Since the 1790's the types of aid which Virginia nationalists sought from the federal government had changed with the times—they were less preoccupied with trade treaties and Indians and more concerned with transportation facilities and federal protection of household manufactures. Nevertheless, if the congressional votes on the tariff and internal improvements are combined, the sectional division of Virginia in 1816-18 was almost identical to the vote on the Jay Treaty twenty years before.[68]

Within the ranks of Virginia nationalists party differences remained important. Many Republican nationalists, though generally in favor of a bank and a tariff, were hostile to the construction of roads and canals that would enhance the migration to the West and further diminish the marginal utility of eastern lands. The Federalists, on the other hand, consistently championed the western demand for transportation facilities. As early as 1800 Congressman Henry Lee introduced a resolution to inquire into the expediency of constructing post roads throughout the United States, but nothing came of the idea.[69] On the state level before 1812 internal improvements did not become a political issue because both parties and all regions supported the chartering of turnpike and canal companies. But in 1812 Charles Fenton Mercer proposed to set aside a general fund for internal improvements financed by dividends from the shares of stock owned by the state in various canal companies and the Bank of Virginia.[70] The proposal was lost amidst the general preoccupation with the war, but in 1815 Mercer headed a committee which recommended a comprehensive program of internal improvements to stimulate the expansion and growth of the state.[71] An act creating a fund for internal improvements was passed without difficulty. Although the only roll call appeared on a motion to postpone, the vote is instructive. Both parties voted for internal improvements, the Federalists by 32 to 1, the Republicans by 77 to 51. More significant is the fact that six eastern Federalists favored internal improvements and only one opposed, while Republicans from west of the Blue Ridge divided 17 to 16 against internal improvements.[72] This abdication of responsibility to western constituents left the field to the Federalists.

When the issue appeared on the national level in 1817, the Federalists were quick to respond. Daniel Sheffey, betraying none of the doubts of its constitutionality that plagued Virginia Republicans, found authority in the power of Congress to regulate commerce and provide for the national defense. He believed that under a national program "Local ambition, jealousy, and animosity will be lessened; the Union will be strengthened, because national benefit will be added to national security, as an additional motive for us to remain one people." Revealing a far-sighted understanding of the potential of economic growth, he suggested the government might even finance the program by borrowing money at interest because "The capacity of the people to pay taxes would be increased in proportion as the price of transportation of their products to market would be diminished—a result which must follow a well-organized and liberal system of internal improvement."[73] President Madison's veto of the Bonus Bill prompted an extended debate in Congress, in which the Virginia Federalists Edward Colston, James Pindall, and Charles F. Mercer assumed primary responsibility for answering the constitutional misgivings of the Virginia Old Republicans.[74]

The Federalist support for internal improvements was paralleled by a demand for political and social reform on the state level, again in response to the interests of their small-farmer constituents. A revision of the state constitution of 1776 had long been regarded as a necessity, for the large and populous western counties were grossly under-represented. Even prominent Republican leaders such as Jefferson and Thomas Ritchie approved the idea, but during Jefferson's administration, when the Republicans were in solid control of the state, nothing was done. In 1804 a resolution to summon a constitutional convention was rejected by the Republican majority in the House of Delegates. The proposal reappeared in January 1812 but was rejected by an even larger majority, both parties evidently considering it inopportune in view of the impending war.[75]

The war delayed only temporarily the rising demand for constitutional reform. In 1815 the city of Winchester revived the issue by sending to the Assembly a strong petition demanding representation by population, a reduction in the size of the House of Delegates to one hundred members, and extension of the suffrage to all free, white, adult males. When the House rejected a convention bill in the spring of 1816, Valley newspapers carried an address suggesting that popular meetings assemble on the Fourth of July in each county to select two delegates for a convention in Staunton on August 19. The address claimed bipartisan support, but the most prominent authors were Valley Federalists.[76] The Staunton convention was attended by sixty-nine delegates from thirty-six counties (including twelve east of the mountains) representing a substantial majority of the population of the state. The meeting adopted a memorial, with only one dissenting vote, asking the Assembly to summon a constitutional convention. Although many of the delegates were Republicans, western Federalists controlled the machinery of the convention. The presiding officer was James Breckinridge, and Daniel Sheffey dominated the debates.[77] It was clear that the Federalists had moved into the policy vacuum left by the Republicans and made electoral reform their own.

Impressed by the rising chorus of protest, the House of Delegates in January 1817 at last adopted a bill authorizing a popular referendum on the advisability of a convention. Both parties favored the measure, the Federalists by 21 to 4, the Republicans, 82 to 56. The bill was moderate enough, providing only for a referendum on the possibility, but in a gesture toward democracy, the House adopted an amendment authorizing the convention to extend the suffrage as well as redistrict the state. The amendment squeaked through, 79 to 76, the Republicans favoring it by 68 to 65, the Federalists dividing evenly, 11 to 11. Neither side covered itself with glory on the issue of democracy, but it is noteworthy that two eastern Federalists favored suffrage extension, while eight western Republicans opposed it.[78]

When the Senate rejected the bill, the reform movement collapsed for a decade. Continued Federalist interest in the program is nonetheless evident from the debates in the constitutional convention of 1829-1830. Though only a handful of old Federalists attended the convention, they were prominent advocates of the western position in demanding manhood suffrage and representation based exclusively on white population. The most articulate spokesman for western interests was Philip Doddridge, prominent Federalist from Wheeling since 1800 and member of the House of Delegates since 1815.[79] Nor were such democratic inclinations confined to Federalists from west of the Blue Ridge. William H. Fitzhugh and Charles F. Mercer of Loudoun County defended the western position, and Robert B. Taylor, Federalist lawyer from Norfolk, advocated manhood suffrage with such vigor that his constituents protested and forced him to resign his seat.[80] In fact, John Marshall was the only Federalist to defend the eastern position in the debate. On the final vote he was joined only by Thomas Marshall and John Scott of Fauquier, while eleven former Federalists voted against the constitution.[81]

Education was another reform on the Federalist agenda after 1815. Publicly-financed common school education in Virginia dates from 1811 when the Assembly established a "Literary Fund" for the education of the poor. The fund remained small and ineffective until after the war when Charles F. Mercer took up the cause; in the 1820's his work was continued by his Federalist associate from Loudoun County, William H. Fitzhugh. In 1816 he wrote a report for a special committee of the House of Delegates which suggested that the Literary Fund be greatly expanded. Mercer recommended that refunds from the federal government due the state for its participation in the war be invested and the interest used to maintain a free grammar school in every county.[82] A year later the Assembly authorized a comprehensive state-wide system of grammar schools and academies, including the establishment of a state university. The bill passed the House of Delegates, 66 to 49. Federalists supported it by 14 to 2; Republicans were almost evenly divided, favoring it by 52 to 47. It is a delightful irony—and one which Mr. Jefferson may not have appreciated—that the initial authorization for the University of Virginia was passed only with Federalist help.[83]

This thesis can, of course, be carried too far, for there are many examples of reform thought in the Republican party, perhaps most obviously, the political, educational, and antislavery views of Jefferson himself. It is nevertheless clear that neither party in Virginia had a monopoly on progressive reform, democracy, or virtue. To that extent the Jeffersonian bias characteristic of much recent scholarship would seem to be unjustified. It is quite possible—indeed, probable—that the Virginia Federalists were not typical of Federalists everywhere, but an examination of them raises enough questions to suggest the need for further study of political issues and ideologies at the state level.[84]

On the other hand, Beard and the Progressive historians, though clearly oversimplistic in identifying the party conflict as a contest of "fluid capital versus agrarianism," were generally correct in discerning fundamental economic, social, and geographical cleavages in American politics—cleavages that were responsible for a considerable degree of continuity in voting behavior. Virginia throughout the period from 1788 to 1829 (and perhaps beyond) was divided essentially into national and antinational regions, and party allegiance was determined by local conditions and local needs. The party battles may have been conducted within a general framework of common assumptions, but the strife was nonetheless there. To the participants it was a clash of very real interests that involved their lives, their livelihoods, and their destinies.

NOTES

[1] Joseph Charles in a doctoral dissertation that was posthumously published as *The Origins of the American Party System: Three Essays* (Williamsburg, 1956) was among the first to question the continuity theme, and his views are supported with only minor variations by Noble E. Cunningham, Jr., *The Jeffersonian Republicans: The Formation of Party Organization, 1789-1801* (Chapel Hill, 1957) and by various studies on the state level: Harry Ammon, "The Republican Party in Virginia, 1789 to 1824" (unpublished Ph.D. dissertation, University of Virginia, 1948); Harry M. Tinkcom, *The Republicans and Federalists in Pennsylvania, 1790-1801: A Study in National Stimulus and Local Response* (Harrisburg, 1950); and Paul Goodman, *The Democratic-Republicans of Massachusetts: Politics in a Young Republic* (Cambridge, 1964).

[2] Merrill D. Peterson, *The Jefferson Image in the American Mind* (New York, 1960), 320-29, 347-50; Robert E. Thomas, "A Reappraisal of Charles A. Beard's *An Economic Interpretation of the Constitution of the United States*," *American Historical Review*, LVII (January 1952), 370-75.

[3] Manning J. Dauer, *The Adams Federalists* (Baltimore, 1953), 18-25; Bray Hammond, *Banks and Politics in America from the Revolution to the Civil War* (Princeton, 1957), 144-226, *passim*.

[4] Here and elsewhere I am excluding from consideration the delegates from counties in Kentucky, even though they participated in Virginia politics until Kentucky became a state in 1792.

[5] Appendices showing the methods used to determine the political affiliation of members of the ratifying convention and of the Assembly were too long to be included in this article, but copies may be obtained from the author upon request. In general, they include lists of key roll-call votes on party-determining issues, lists of presidential electors and county corresponding committees in the *Calendar of Virginia State Papers*, and various newspaper and manuscript sources.

[6] Washington at one point offered him the State Department and the attorney generalship and ended up by pleading with Henry to enter Congress or the Assembly. Washington to Edward Carrington, October 9, 1795; Washington to Henry, October 9, 1795; Henry Lee to Washington, July 17, 1795; Washington to Henry, January 15, 1799, in Washington Papers (Manuscript Division, Library of Congress). Cabell was an Antifederalist opponent of Madison in Albemarle County in 1788-1789 and may have followed Henry into the Federalist camp.

[7] The collective-biography technique has several shortcomings, most important of which

is that it disregards the question of whether delegates actually represented their constituencies. Both Beard and Forrest McDonald have been criticized for neglecting this by Lee Benson, *Turner and Beard: American Historical Writing Reconsidered* (Glencoe, Ill., 1960), 163-74, 200-202. To mitigate this difficulty I have combined the collective-biography technique with an index of average county voting over a period of years in order to obtain a reasonable approximation of popular sentiment (see footnote 16).

⁸ Virginia, House of Delegates, *Journal, 1788*, pp. 42-44 (November 14) [hereinafter cited as *JHD*]; Charles Lee to Washington, October 29, 1788, in Washington Papers.

⁹ Madison to Washington, December 5, 1789 (Lee-Grayson broadside, September 28, 1789, enclosed), in Washington Papers.

¹⁰ Madison to Washington, December 5, 1789; Randolph to Washington, November 22, 26, December 6, 11, 15, 1789, *ibid.*; *JHD, 1789*, pp. 90-91, 101-102 (November 30, December 5).

¹¹ *JHD, 1793*, pp. 117-18 (December 6).

¹² David Stuart to Washington, June 2, 1790, in Washington Papers.

¹³ Lee to Hamilton, August 12, 1791; September 10, 1792, in Alexander Hamilton Papers (Manuscript Division, Library of Congress); *JHD, 1790*, pp. 35-36 (November 3).

¹⁴ Harry Ammon, "The Formation of the Republican Party in Virginia, 1789-1796," *Journal of Southern History*, XIX (August 1953), 283-310.

¹⁵ *JHD, 1793*, pp. 30, 31, 69 (November 1, 15); the quote is from page 31.

¹⁶ A note on methodology: There are several difficulties involved in roll-call analysis of early state legislatures. Prime among these is the paucity of significant roll calls (seldom more than one or two per session), which precludes the use of sophisticated analytical techniques involving matrix clusters or Guttman scaling. For this reason a period of years has been used (1788-1793), even at the risk of producing a static picture, in order to obtain enough roll calls to provide a statistical basis. The year 1793 was selected as a terminal date in order to keep the time span as short as possible since the statistical approach inevitably hides temporal change (to include roll calls after 1793, for instance, would obscure the undeniable decline of Federalist strength). Terminating in 1793, moreover, avoids the polarizing impact of party organizations. Since it is generally conceded that formal party machinery was not developed until after 1793, each delegate before that time was presumably voting according to the dictates of his conscience or the conceived interests of his constituents.

An additional difficulty peculiar to Virginia politics is that the annual elections for the Assembly produced a high rate of turnover in the House of Delegates. It is not possible, therefore, to determine a voting pattern for a significant number of individuals, and the investigator must seek instead a pattern among counties. Since each county was represented by two delegates (the three boroughs of Richmond, Williamsburg, and Norfolk each had one), a meaningful index must take into account problems of absenteeism, as well as delegates from the same county voting on opposite sides of an issue. The following scale was devised to determine the degree of nationalism (or antinationalism) in the votes of each Virginia county between 1788 and 1793:

4—both delegates voting nationalist

3—one delegate voting nationalist and one not voting

2—delegates divided or both absent

1—one delegate voting antinationalist and one not voting

0—both delegates voting antinationalist

The total score for each county can then be divided by the number of roll-call votes in order to determine the average degree of nationalism, and the politics of the county can then be characterized with the following index:

2.8-4.0—Nationalist/Federalist

1.7-2.7—Divided

0.0-1.6—Antinationalist/Republican

[17] The vote on the Constitution, June 25, 1788, is taken from Hugh Blair Grigsby, *The History of the Virginia Federal Convention of 1788* . . . (2 vols., Richmond, 1890-1891: Virginia Historical Society, *Collections*, IX-X), I, 345-46. Only ten counties (out of eighty-four counties and three boroughs) reversed themselves in their votes on the Constitution and their subsequent political behavior. A deviation of 11 per cent is statistically tolerable, but the shift itself reveals a pattern. Nine of the counties changed from being pro-Constitution in 1788 to being antinationalist thereafter. Four of these are in the southeast corner of the state (Norfolk, Nansemond, Isle of Wight, and Greensville); despite the presence of the commercial center of Norfolk, the vast majority of the people in each of these counties were tobacco farmers whose interests were similar to those of the neighboring counties of the Southside, a predominantly antinationalist region. Two others (Caroline and New Kent) were in the middle Tidewater, another predominantly antinationalist region. The remainder (King George and Northumberland in the Northern Neck and Shenandoah in the Valley) produced voting patterns that were exactly on the borderline between "antinationalist" and "divided," and all three periodically sent Federalists to the Assembly until 1800. The one county (Montgomery) which shifted from Antifederalist in 1788 to "nationalist" thereafter was in the southwest. This reversal may have been due in part to the movement of population southwest along the Valley from heavily Federalist Botetourt and Bedford after 1788, and in part it may have reflected satisfaction with the policies of the Washington administration which kept the Southern Indians pacified.

[18] The division on the Constitution itself reflected a sectional division of the state that had lasted through the 1780's: Jackson T. Main, "Sections and Politics in Virginia, 1781-1787," *William and Mary Quarterly*, 3d. Ser., XII (January 1955), 96-112.

[19] Harrison Williams, *Legends of Loudoun: An Account of the History and Homes of a Border County of Virginia's Northern Neck* (Richmond, 1938), 159-60; Fairfax Harrison, *Landmarks of Old Prince William: A Study of Origins in Northern Virginia* (Berryville, Va., 1964), 408-10. Bordley's works were read and his suggestions often adopted in Virginia: Horatio Gates to General [Adam] Stephen, July 25, 1784, in Horatio Gates Papers (New-York Historical Society).

[20] Agricultural reform, of course, was not a Federalist monopoly (witness the writings of John Taylor and the activities of James M. Garnett in founding county agricultural societies), and it did spread gradually into the Antinationalist counties. It is therefore only a partial explanation for the sectional division, and it did not prevent the defection of Northern Neck counties to the Republicans after 1795.

[21] Freeman H. Hart, *The Valley of Virginia in the American Revolution, 1763-1789* (Chapel Hill, 1942), 156; Harrison, *Landmarks*, 408-10, 547; Williams, *Legends*, 179. For contemporary comment on soil fertility, agricultural innovations, and the importance of opening the Potomac, see Edward Carrington to Hamilton, October 4, 1791, in Harold C. Syrett and Jacob E. Cooke (eds.), *The Papers of Alexander Hamilton* (11 vols. to date, New York and London, 1961-), IX, 275-78; David Stuart to Washington, November 18, 1791; Burgess Ball to Washington, February 9, 1795, in Washington Papers.

[22] *First Census, 1790* (Philadelphia, 1791), 48-49; Hart, *Valley of Virginia*, 15, 163. The Piedmont average, moreover, disguises the prevalence of large plantations amidst the small holdings of "poor whites"; the average in the Valley, on the other hand, was closer to the mean.

[23] Alexander White, a Valley Federalist, sought to include a protective duty on hemp in the tariff of 1789. *Annals of Congress*, 1 Cong., 1 Sess., 158 (April 16, 1789).

[24] Alexander White to David Shepherd, April 26, 1791, in David Shepherd Papers, Draper Collection (State Historical Society of Wisconsin, Madison).

[25] Burgess Ball to Washington, August 19, 1794, in Washington Papers.

[26] John Haymond to Lee, September 4, 1794, in *Calendar of Virginia State Papers* (11 vols., Richmond, 1875-1893), VII, 294; Samuel T. Wiley, *History of Monongalia County, West Virginia* . . . (Kingwood, W. Va., 1883), 96.

[27] Thomas C. Miller and Hu Maxwell, *West Virginia and Its People* (3 vols., New York, 1913), I, 206; Charles H. Ambler, *A History of West Virginia* (New York, 1933), 185.

[28] Henry Lee to Washington, April 29, 1793, in Washington Papers.

[29] Arthur Campbell to Washington, November 15, 1796, *ibid.*

[30] Madison to Jefferson, August 20, 1784; Madison to Monroe, May 29, 1785, in Gaillard Hunt (ed.), *The Writings of James Madison* (9 vols., New York, 1900-1910), II, 64-65, 143-44; George Mason to Arthur Lee, March 25, 1783, in Kate Mason Rowland, *The Life of George Mason, 1725-1792* (2 vols., New York, 1892), II, 40.

[31] *JHD, 1783*, p. 129 (June 20); *JHD, 1784*, p. 41 (June 7); Madison to Monroe, December 24, 30, 1785, in Hunt (ed.), *Writings of James Madison*, II, 205-207, 210-12; Main, "Sections and Politics in Virginia," 103-104.

[32] Madison to Jefferson, December 4, 1786, in Hunt (ed.), *Writings of James Madison*, II, 293-94; Jackson T. Main, *The Antifederalists: Critics of the Constitution, 1781-1788* (Chapel Hill, 1961), 229.

[33] Joseph Neville to Col. Benjamin Biggs, April 3, 1794, in Benjamin Biggs Papers, Draper Collection.

[34] Randolph to Washington, June 24, 1793, in Washington Papers.

[35] Mercer to James M. Garnett, June 18, 1798, in Charles Fenton Mercer Papers (New-York Historical Society).

[36] *Annals of Cong.*, 5 Cong., 2 Sess., 1553-54, 1772, 1925, 2028-29, 2171 (April 25, May 18, June 13, 21, July 10, 1798). Daniel Morgan, James Machir, and Josiah Parker did not record a vote on the Alien and Sedition Laws; and Machir did not vote on the direct tax.

[37] Albert J. Beveridge, *Life of John Marshall* (4 vols., Boston and New York, 1916-1919), II, 389.

[38] Thomas Evans (Eastern Shore), Samuel Goode (central Southside), Henry Lee (Northern Neck), John Marshall (Richmond and Peninsula), Robert Page (northern Valley), Josiah Parker (Norfolk), Leven Powell (Loudoun-Fairfax), and Edwin Gray (lower James). Gray's politics was a matter of uncertainty even to contemporaries. He soon became a Republican, but at least he was "elected as the federal candidate": Edward Carrington to Washington, May 10, 1799, in Washington Papers. Though several of these districts contained a large proportion of Republican counties, the presence of sizable Federalist minorities (suggested by the county votes before 1795) and the personal stature of Marshall and Lee helped these districts to swing temporarily into the Federalist column.

[39] Daniel Morgan to Benjamin Biggs, Philadelphia, February 12, 1799, in Biggs Papers, Draper Collection.

[40] *Debates in the House of Delegates, upon . . . the Alien and Sedition Laws* (Richmond, 1818 [1798], 79. Brooke's assertion was correct, for the congressional districts drawn up in 1793 were fairly proportional, approximately 30,000 to 35,000 whites in each.

[41] *Ibid.*, 67-74.

[42] *Ibid.*, 110-17, 177; Morgan to Biggs, February 12, 1799, in Biggs Papers, Draper Collection.

[43] *Debates in the House of Delegates*, 183-84.

[44] Beveridge, *Marshall*, II, 428; Leven Powell to Major Burr Powell, December 11, 1799, in "The Leven Powell Correspondence," *John P. Branch Historical Papers of Randolph-Macon College*, I (June 1903), 231-33; *Annals of Cong.*, 6 Cong., 1 Sess., 369, 419-20, 531-32 (January 10, 23, February 20, 1800); 2 Sess., 975-76, 1049-50 (January 3, February 21, 1801).

[45] Washington *National Intelligencer*, February 18, 1801.

[46] *Annals of Cong.*, 8 Cong., 1 Sess., 488-89, 548-49 (October 25, 29, 1803). The

four Virginia Federalists in the Eighth Congress were Thomas Griffin (Yorktown and Eastern Shore), Joseph Lewis, Jr. (Loudoun-Fairfax), James Stephenson (northern Valley), and Thomas Lewis (Kanawha). Lewis' election was contested by Republican Andrew Moore, who was seated by the House on March 5, 1804. *Ibid.*, 1092.

[47] *JHD, 1802-1803*, pp. 59-60 (January 19, 1803). Voting for the bill were twenty-seven Federalists and twenty-five Republicans; voting against it were six Federalists and sixty-six Republicans.

[48] *JHD, 1803-1804*, pp. 71-72 (January 9, 1804). Voting for the convention were twenty-two Federalists and fifty Republicans; voting against it were thirteen Federalists and seventy-four Republicans. J. R. Pole, "Representation and Authority in Virginia from the Revolution to Reform," *Journal of Southern History*, XXIV (February 1958), 16-50, especially page 25, agrees that apportionment, rather than suffrage, was the pre-eminent issue until 1829.

[49] Martinsburg *Berkeley and Jefferson Intelligencer*, March 18, 1803.

[50] "A [Federal] Republican," *ibid.*, April 1, 1803; see also "Cato" and "A Voter," *ibid.*, April 15, 22, 1803.

[51] *Ibid.*, March 20, August 14, 1807.

[52] *Ibid.*, August 7, October 9, 1807; September 9, 1808.

[53] Richmond *Enquirer*, October 18, 1808.

[54] James Breckinridge (Botetourt-Kanawha), Joseph Lewis, Jr. (Loudoun-Fairfax), Daniel Sheffey (southwest), James Stephenson (northern Valley), and Jacob Swoope (central Valley).

[55] The price of flour, the primary staple export of the Shenandoah-Potomac region, is a good index. After dropping to a low of $4.25 a barrel at Alexandria during the embargo, the price rose to $6.75 in the spring of 1809 and then settled at $6.00 for the rest of the year. After Macon's Bill Number Two repealed all restrictions on trade, the price rose to $9.50 in the summer of 1810 and then hovered around $8.50 through the year 1811. These figures were taken from a monthly sampling of prices listed in the Martinsburg *Berkeley and · Jefferson Intelligencer*, the Charlestown *Farmer's Repository*, and the Richmond *Enquirer*.

[56] See votes on Macon's bills, *Annals of Cong.*, 11 Cong., 2 Sess., 1354-55, 1484-85, 1931 (January 29, March 5, April 19, 1810); on bill to complete harbor fortifications, *ibid.*, 1 Sess., 256-57 (June 9, 1809); and on an amendment to preserve the navy's frigates, *ibid.*, 2 Sess., 1977 (April 25, 1810).

[57] *Ibid.*, 12 Cong., 2 Sess., 680-702.

[58] *Ibid.*, 1 Sess., 691, 800-801, 999, 1003-1005, 1084-85 (January 6, 17, 27, 28, 29, February 21, 1812); 2 Sess., 440-41, 449-50, 843-44, 946 (December 22, 23, 1812; January 14, 30, 1813).

[59] *Ibid.*, 1 Sess., 1092, 1108-12, 1114-15, 1145-46, 1147-55 (February 25, 27, 28, March 3, 4, 1812); 2 Sess., 907-908, 919-20 (January 26, 27, 1813); 13 Cong., 3 Sess., 704 (December 1, 1814).

[60] *JHD, 1811-1812*, pp. 69-71 (January 8-9, 1812); *JHD, 1812-1813*, pp. 162-63, 166 (December 17, 1812; February 13, 1813).

[61] *JHD, 1814-1815*, pp. 59-61, 124 (November 9, December 20, 1814). Colonel William Bentley of Richmond, who had served in the Revolution, expressed the fundamental nationalism of Virginia Federalists in a letter to Thomas Ritchie. Though he had opposed the declaration, he felt that since the war was "*constitutionally* declared" it was the "duty of every *real federalist* to exert all the means in his power to prosecute [it] with vigor and effect." Richmond *Enquirer*, February 12, 1814.

[62] Federalists in the Thirteenth Congress were James Breckinridge (Botetourt-Kanawha), Hugh Caperton (southern West Virginia), Joseph Lewis, Jr. (Loudoun-Fairfax), Daniel Shef-

fey (southwest), and Francis White (northern Valley). Federalists in the Fourteenth Congress were James Breckinridge, Joseph Lewis, Jr., and Daniel Sheffey (re-elected), and Magnus Tate (northern Valley).

[63] Federalists in the Fifteenth Congress were Edward Colston (Berkeley-Jefferson), Charles F. Mercer (Loudoun-Fairfax), and James Pindall (northwest).

[64] *JHD, 1816-1817*, pp. 224-25 (February 22, 1817); *JHD, 1820-1821*, p. 181 (February 9, 1821).

[65] This is evidenced by the extent to which an able, articulate Federalist like Charles F. Mercer was permitted to assume a position of leadership in the House of Delegates.

[66] The House of Delegates in the years 1821-1830 unfortunately conducted no roll-call votes on party-determining issues, such as a congratulatory address to Monroe on his retirement or to Jackson on his accession. Newspapers generally omitted party labels when carrying election data after 1820, possibly in an effort to promote harmony. Most Federalists co-operated. As early as 1818 a Valley Federalist supported the Republican candidates for the House of Delegates with a plea for an end to party strife, and a year later Congressman Edward Colston promised to support the Monroe administration when it was in the right and oppose it only when he considered it to be in the wrong: Charlestown *Farmer's Repository*, April 29, 1818; March 24, 1819. As a result, the only identifiable party division seems to be at the national level. Map 5 is a portrayal of the districts of congressmen elected in 1829, divided by parties into National Republicans and Jacksonian Democrats. The "contested election" was a case where the National Republican took the seat and in 1830 the House of Representatives voted to seat the Jacksonian Democrat. The primary change from earlier maps is in the Eastern Shore—lower Peninsula district, but this seems to be a temporary aberration of this election. Within a few years thereafter Henry A. Wise became the perennial Whig congressman from this district.

[67] Daniel Sheffey admitted the Bank was constitutional, but he believed it would not solve the problem of a national currency. Three Virginia Federalists voted against the Bank; one did not vote: *Annals of Cong.*, 14 Cong., 1 Sess., 1219, 1343-44 (March 14, April 6, 1816). Two years later Charles F. Mercer opposed a bill authorizing additional vice-presidents for the Bank on the grounds that its expanded activities would bring it into greater conflict with the state banks, though he owned no stock in state banks: *ibid.*, 15 Cong., 1 Sess., 1752-55 (April 16, 1818). All Virginia Federalists voted against the tariff in 1816 and again in 1818: *ibid.*, 14 Cong., 1 Sess., 1352 (April 8, 1816); 15 Cong., 1 Sess., 1743 (April 15, 1818).

[68] Thomas P. Abernethy, *The South in the New Nation, 1789-1819* ([Baton Rouge], 1961), 430, 432, maps the votes in Congress on the tariff and internal improvements. These maps are not entirely accurate, since the Eastern Shore was combined with the lower Peninsula (Williamsburg-Newport News) in one congressional district, represented by Burwell Bassett, a Republican who voted for the tariff.

[69] *Annals of Cong.*, 6 Cong., 1 Sess., 621 (March 10, 1800).

[70] *JHD, 1812-1813*, pp. 56-57 (December 15, 1812).

[71] On the committee of nineteen were only four Federalists, but a majority of the Republicans were easterners. Mercer, himself an easterner, evidently made the difference. *JHD, 1815-1816*, pp. 9, 64, 73-78 (December 5, 23, 28, 1815).

[72] *Ibid.*, 158 (February 15, 1816).

[73] *Annals of Cong.*, 14 Cong., 2 Sess., 886-91 (February 6, 1817); quotations are from pages 890 and 891.

[74] *Ibid.*, 15 Cong., 1 Sess., 1278-82, 1284-1318, 1340-50 (March 11, 12, 13, 1818).

[75] *JHD, 1811-1812*, pp. 94-95 (January 23, 1812).

[76] Oren Frederic Morton, *The Story of Winchester in Virginia* . . . (Strasburg, Va., 1925), 98-99; *JHD, 1815-1816*, pp. 167-68 (February 9, 1816); Alexandria *Herald*, July 21, 1816; Charlestown *Farmer's Repository*, June 5, 1816. The address "To the People of the Commonwealth of Virginia" was signed by twenty-two persons, all but four from

est of the Blue Ridge. There were eight Federalists, five Republicans, and the rest I
ave not been able to identify. The Federalists were all members of Congress or the Assem-
ly, whereas most of the Republicans were obscure individuals who were identified only
y their occasional attendance at county political meetings.

[77] *JHD, 1816-1817*, pp. 86-87 (December 13, 1816); Charles H. Ambler, *Sectionalism
 Virginia from 1776 to 1861* (Chicago, 1910), 96.

[78] *JHD, 1816-1817*, pp. 168-70 (January 24, 1817).

[79] Lyman Draper's sketch of Philip Doddridge, in Va. MSS, Vol I, Draper Collection;
 oddridge to Biggs, December 4, 1799, in Biggs Papers, *ibid.*

[80] Hugh Blair Grigsby, *The Virginia Convention of 1829-30* (Richmond, 1854), 71; W.
 . Elliott, "Robert Barraud Taylor," *John P. Branch Historical Papers*, III (June 1910),
 63-67.

[81] Grigsby, *Virginia Convention*, 96-97.

[82] *Ibid.*, 71; *JHD, 1815-1816*, pp. 113-15 (January 12, 1816).

[83] *JHD, 1816-1817*, pp. 214-15 (February 18, 1817). The final act chartering the univer-
 ity was passed on January 19, 1819, by a vote of 143 to 28: *JHD, 1818-1819*, p. 112.
 nly one Federalist was opposed; most of the Republicans came from the traditionally
 ntinationalist areas south and southwest of the James.

[84] David H. Fischer, *The Revolution of American Conservatism: The Federalist Party
 the Era of Jeffersonian Democracy* (New York, 1965), has made an important start
 this direction, but his preoccupation with congressional politics and tendency to identify
 ll Federalists as "conservatives" leave many questions unanswered.

JOHN BECKLEY: AN EARLY AMERICAN
PARTY MANAGER*

Noble E. Cunningham, Jr.

Thomas Jefferson has traditionally been regarded as the founder of the Democratic-Republican Party. As the result of comprehensive investigation into the early history of the Republican Party, Noble E. Cunningham, Jr., professor of history at the University of Missouri, contends that Madison, rather than Jefferson, was the leader who, with the aid of relatively little-known political figures, shaped the party during its earliest years. In the following essay, Cunningham directs attention to the place of the individual in the process of party formation. John Beckley, in the author's view, was a man of unusual political talents whose historical importance has been unnecessarily obscured. Few of Beckley's contemporaries had his singleness of purpose in politics, channeling Republican energies to win critical elections. Cunningham's two major studies on the Republican Party are The Jeffersonian Republicans: The Formation of Party Organization *(1957) and* The Jeffersonian Republicans in Power: Party Operations, 1801-1809 *(1963).*

For a number of years while serving the national government, Thomas Jefferson made hurried notes of official happenings, private conversations, and other information that came to his attention. These memoranda, often scribbled on loose scraps of paper taken from his pocket at the moment, were made most regularly during the period when he was Secretary of State. Years later Jefferson collected these notes into what he called the "Anas," and as such, posterity has often seen fit to publish them.[1] Historians have frequently found occasion to refer to

* Reprinted by permission from Noble E. Cunningham, Jr., "John Beckley: An Early American Party Manager," *William and Mary Quarterly*, 3d Ser., Vol. XIII (January, 1956), pp. 40-52.

these isolated scraps of notes, and not a few impressions conveyed by the "Anas" have found their way into the current of American history. One of these impressions, most unmistakably derived from the "Anas," concerns John Beckley, of whom Jefferson made mention on a number of occasions while Secretary of State.

While Jefferson served in Washington's first Cabinet, Beckley, who had been clerk of the Virginia House of Delegates when Jefferson was Governor of Virginia, held the first clerkship of the House of Representatives.[2] A young man of thirty-two in 1789, he already had had much experience as clerk of governmental assemblies, committees, and popular gatherings. When the freeholders of Henrico County, Virginia, assembled at the courthouse in Richmond, November 1774, to choose a committee of safety, John Beckley, then only seventeen, had been appointed clerk.[3] When the same freeholders gathered a year later to resolve that no provision, fuel, or naval stores be allowed to be water-borne from the county without the approval of the Committee of Safety, Beckley again had been the clerk;[4] and in February 1776, Beckley had been appointed assistant clerk of the Committee of Safety of Virginia.[5] As revolutionary Virginia advanced from colony to independent statehood, Beckley had served as assistant clerk to the Council of State of Virginia,[6] assistant clerk to the Privy Council,[7] and clerk of the Senate.[8] In October 1779, Beckley had been chosen clerk of the House of Delegates,[9] where he served until his election as clerk of the United States House of Representatives in 1789.[10] His experience in Virginia prepared him well for that position.

Beckley performed the duties of his new post with ability and industry. One member of Congress wrote of "the Facility with which he could turn to any Paper which had ever been committed to his care," and declared that "there never was a more correct & diligent clerk . . . who so happily united Accuracy with Dispatch."[11] Another contemporary reported that "His articulation was distinct, his elocution commanding, and his parliamentary knowledge accurate and extensive."[12]

It was not, however, Beckley's competence and efficiency in the House that Jefferson noted in the "Anas," but rather his activities as a political intelligence agent. Beckley had early become infected with the party spirit which the debates in Congress seemed to generate. When his Virginia friends began forming an opposition group, he resolutely lined up with them and soon became one of the most active partisans of what contemporaries were coming to call the "Republican interest."[13] He was a bitter foe of Alexander Hamilton, whom he regarded as an "*extraordinary* man . . . with a comprehensive eye, a subtle and contriving mind, and a soul devoted to his object";[14] and he was fond of using the adjectives "insidious" and "contemptible" in reference to Hamilton.[15]

As clerk of the House, Beckley was in a position to watch every move in Congress with much more facility than most of the members. His eyes fell on papers few others chanced to see; his ears picked up bits of conversation meant never to be heard outside a confidential circle. After watching the men who had been "a good deal closetted with the Secretary" of the Treasury and piecing together evidence "from hints drop't," Beckley could report that "Accident has led me to the knowledge of a circumstance which confirms the suspicion that Mr. H[amilton] is the author" of the "late insidious attack on Mr. Jefferson."[16] Likewise he could report that he "happened to see" a publication signed "Civis" brought to the office of the Secretary of the Treasury "by a servant of his" and that he was told it appeared to be in the handwriting of one of Hamilton's clerks.[17]

Everywhere he went, Beckley had the happy facility of obtaining all sorts of information "about men and things," as Benjamin Rush once said.[18] In Philadelphia he learned from printers the identity of certain writers in the press; he heard from merchants about transactions with the Treasury.[19] He made frequent trips to New York and seldom failed to return without some revealing piece of political intelligence.[20] Whether rumor or fact, all was recounted to Jefferson, who faithfully recorded his friend's reports and filed them among the "Anas" notes. Again and again, Jefferson would make the memorandum, "Beckley tells me. . . ."[21] The following entry recorded in 1793 is typical:

> Mar. 31. Mr. Beckley tells me that the merchants bonds for duties on 6. mo. credit became due the 1st. inst. to a very great amount. That Hamilton went to the bank on that day and directed the bank to discount for those merchts. all their bonds at 30. days, and that he would have the Collectors credited for the money at the Treasury. Hence the Treasury lumping it's receipts by the month in it's printed accts. these sums will be considered by the public as only recd. on the last day, conseqly. the bank makes the month's interest out of it. Beckley had this from a mercht. who hd a bond discounted & who supposes a million of dollars worth were at the bank here. . . .[22]

It was Beckley who supplied Jefferson with information about the financial interests of congressmen. In the spring of 1793, he communicated to Jefferson a "list of paper men" in Congress, carefully noting the Bank stockholders and directors and those who were "suspected only,"[23] and he kept Jefferson advised of all new discoveries which he made about the legislators.[24]

In consequence of the frequent memoranda that Jefferson, while Secretary of State, made of the confidential reports which Beckley carried to his office, Beckley has gone down in history as a mysterious person who carried tales and worked behind the scenes;[25] actually, he merits attention less as a political informant than as one of the leading party-organizers of the 1790's. At ease in the realm of practical politics and a skillful organizer, he could manage an election campaign with the same methodical competence with which he performed the duties of the clerkship of the House. John Beckley was a man who knew how to win elections and to advance a party cause.

No ordinary man, Beckley was an alumnus of the College of William and Mary,[26] one of the early members of Phi Beta Kappa,[27] and a close friend of Jefferson, Madison, and Monroe.[28] When in 1792, Benjamin Rush wrote a letter of introduction to Aaron Burr of New York, he pointed out specifically that Beckley "possesses the confidence of our two illustrious patriots Mr. Jefferson and Mr. Madison."[29] While Monroe was Minister to the French Republic, Beckley was one of a small group of friends to whom Monroe sent special reports about the course of events in France.[30]

Beckley was well versed in public affairs and political theory; shortly after the election of 1800 was decided, he sent to the President-elect a lengthy and detailed letter setting forth the principles which he believed should guide Jefferson's administration. To insure the republican character of the government, Beckley urged:

> 1st: That all political relations, by treaty, with foreign nations should be avoided.
>
> 2d: That simple commercial connections on a basis of perfect reciprocity and the most conducive to the principles of free commerce should be pursued.
>
> 3d: That the defensive system of protecting commerce by a limited navy, embargo, suspension of intercourse, and fortified

ports and harbors, is the most sure, safe, cheap, and effectual.
4th: That protecting duties for the encouragement of manufactures ought to be imposed as far as revenue considerations will
admit, and the Alien laws repealed.

5th: That the agricultural interest be promoted, by repeal of
Excises and Land tax, to effect which rigid economy should be
enforced in all the departments of Government, all unnecessary
establishments put down, sinecure offices abolished, and all
speculation on the public wants, by jobs and contracts done away.

6th: That a new organization of the Executive departments of
Government be made,

1st: by a revision and amendment of the Constitution of each.

2d: by new, simple, and effectual interior regulations.

3d: by changes of men in office and new appointments so
as *gradually*, but certainly & effectually, to place the Executive
administration in the hands of decided republicans, distinguished
for talents & integrity.[31]

These suggestions illustrate the thoughtful, even scholarly, side of the
character of Beckley, who, like so many of the Jeffersonian party leaders,
was strongly attached to specific principles of government. But Beckley
was ever the practical politician: his peculiar forte was the election campaign, the party battle.

Beckley spent much of his time and energy in partisan activities, working to win elections, doing everything he could to advance the Republican
faction as it grew from a weak coterie of political leaders to the well
organized party that elected Jefferson to the presidency in 1800. Thus,
in the election year 1792, Beckley journeyed to New York to confer
with Aaron Burr,[32] relayed information from New York and Pennsylvania to Madison and Monroe in Virginia, and actively promoted cooperation among Republicans in New York, Pennsylvania, and Virginia
in support of a common candidate for the vice-presidency.[33]

As party conflict quickened in the 1790's, Beckley spent many hours
circulating political pamphlets, some of which he wrote himself. In a
letter to Madison in May 1795, he explained: "I enclose eight copies
of the 'Political Observations.' I brought two dozen from New York and
have distributed them all. I expect 50 more in a day or two, and shall
scatter them also—they were bought and dispersed in great numbers
there, and are eagerly enquired after by numbers here—it will be repub-

lished in Boston, Portsmouth, Vermont, and at Richmond. Some careless delay has attended the little statement of fact by 'a calm observer,' but I have written to Col. Burr and expect to see it shortly. . . ."[34] If it may be concluded—from Beckley's intimations to Madison and the suspicions of contemporaries[35]—that Beckley was the "calm observer," it was under this guise that he wrote a series of articles suggesting that President Washington had received Treasury advances at times in excess of his lawful annual salary.[36]

During the contest over the Jay Treaty, Beckley was active in organizing the opposition. To Madison, he wrote at the height of the dispute:

> I have been and am still much occupied in a removal from my late residence to a new house in 8th Street South of Walnut, which I have purchased, besides I am at this moment confined to my room by a tumour on the leg. I do not however omit my endeavor to assist the common cause of republicanism & our country as endangered by the impending treaty. . . . we have already dispersed in Circular letters, all over the States, a petition to the H. of Represent[ative]s without, as yet, the smallest suspicion from our opponents. All our movements are kept secret until they have reached their ultimate destination, and we now meditate an address to the people in this same mode. . . .[37]

As the presidential election of 1796 approached, Beckley became extremely active. Assuming the management of the Republican campaign in Pennsylvania, he bent every effort to bring victory to Jefferson and his party. It is in this contest that Beckley appears at his best as a party worker, a practical politician, and a campaign manager.

In September 1796, as soon as he learned that Washington's retirement was to be officially announced, Beckley went into action. He was convinced that the short notice the President had given of his retirement was "designed to prevent a fair election, and the consequent choice of Mr. Jefferson." But it would not produce that effect, he believed, if Pennsylvania would "make but a reasonable exertion."[38] He wrote at once to a trusted and influential political friend in central Pennsylvania, General William Irvine of Carlisle. Having served as a brigadier general in the Revolutionary army, a delegate to the Continental Congress, and a member of the federal House of Representatives, he could be relied upon to carry much weight in his district. To Irvine, Beckley explained:

. . . the general sentiment is in favor of Jefferson, and I think a little exertion by a few good active republicans in each *County* would bring the people out, and defeat the influence of your little rotten towns such as Carlisle, Lancaster, York, &c. A silent, but certain cooperation among the country people may do much. In my next I will send you a list of the republican Electors, that have been agreed upon for this State, and hope you will be able to scatter a few copies thro' *some proper hands.* . . . From Georgia, No. Carolina, South Carolina, Virginia, Kentucky & Tennessee we expect a unanimous vote—half Maryland & Delaware, some in New Jersey, and several to the Eastward —so that if Pennsylvania do well the Election is safe. In the City & County [of Philadelphia] we expect to carry the republican ticket by a large Majority. Have you any western friends that you could drop a line to, to assist us? . . . Cannot an effectual exertion be made? It is now or never for the republican cause.[39]

The next week, as he had promised, Beckley sent the list of Republican electors which had been agreed upon in Philadelphia. "A few Copies of the lists of Electors, with the names plainly written, dispersed in a few judicious hands in the Country, and copies of them scattered about in different neighbourhoods, would do great good, if the people are warned of the day, and [if] a few popular men will endeavour to bring them out. By next post I will endeavour to send you some handbills, by way of address to the people of Pennsylvania, shewing the strong reasons there is for this States having a Southern, rather than an Eastern president."[40] Pennsylvania, he repeated, must decide the election; he hoped that "every exertion" would be made.

It is interesting to note the attention Beckley gave to winning the support of leading men who could be counted on to have influence with their neighbors. He placed much reliance on tickets being "dispersed in a few judicious hands" and on "a few popular men" bringing the people out on election day. It was important that campaign tickets be placed in *"proper hands."*

Beckley was not content, however, to place complete reliance on influential citizens to carry the election. His publicity campaign to familiarize the voters with the Republican ticket is probably not to be equalled in any election of the 1790's. Tickets were scattered across the state by the thousands, and political handbills were sent out from Philadelphia in bundles. On October 17, Beckley wrote Irvine again:

By old Doctor Nesbit, I have forwarded to you a packet with
handbills, which I must tax your goodness to put under way for
the Western Country, so as to reach it before the Election for
Electors. You best know what characters to address them to. In
a few days a select republican friend from the City will call upon
you with a parcel of tickets to be distributed in your County. Any
assistance and advice you can furnish him with, as to suitable
districts & characters, will I am sure be rendered. He is one of
two republican friends, who have undertaken to ride thro' all the
middle & lower counties on this business, and bring with them
6 or 8 thousand tickets. It is necessary at the same time to aid
the common object by getting all our friends to write as many
tickets as they can, in their respective families, before the Elections. . . . .

I enclose you a few copies of the ticket to disperse among such
good friends, as will exert themselves, to get as many copies
before the Election, as they can.[41]

Three weeks before the election, Beckley could boast that "our republican ticket is pushing with infinite zeal & earnestness,"[42] and he could
report to Madison that "30,000 tickets are gone thro' the State, by
Express, into every county."[43] The distribution of a total number of
tickets equal to about one-third of the voting population[44] reveals the
extensive circulation given to the Republican ticket. It appears even more
impressive when compared with the actual number of Pennsylvania voters
—slightly more than twelve thousand—who participated in the presidential election of 1796.[45] In addition to the party tickets, handbills were
printed and widely distributed. On one occasion, a thousand copies of
a single political address were printed and circulated throughout the
state.[46] The shrewdness of this early party manager appears in the careful
plans he made for the selective distribution of that address. To avoid
the possibility of effective Federalist rebuttal from Philadelphia, he urged
distribution in the other parts of the state first. To Irvine he wrote: "Enclosed are 6 copies of an address to the people of Pennsylvania—by next
mail on friday, or by first *certain* opportunity, will forward you 100
more. It will be most advisable however to push them on over the Mountain, before they are circulated below, which will prevent any counter
address. 1000 Copies are struck & will be dispersed in such manner that
they may appear first above, before they can come back to the
City."[47]

Beckley left little to chance in his preparations. The election law required that the names of the fifteen electors for whom a freeman voted be hand-written on his ballot; printed tickets were not acceptable at the polls. Beckley, therefore, not only covered the state with printed tickets from which the voters could conveniently and accurately copy the names, but he urged all Republican friends to write as many tickets as possible, and to employ members of their families in the task. These written tickets could be put into the hands of voters who appeared at the polls without prepared ballots.

In a period when "electioneering" was only beginning to be accepted as a proper part of the political life of the country, not a few men would have stood aghast had they been fully aware of the activities of Beckley. His well laid plans, his large-scale campaign, his whole system of political campaigning reveal a skillful party manager whose ability and industry few contemporaries could match.

When Jefferson won fourteen of Pennsylvania's fifteen electoral votes in 1796, Beckley could look back with satisfaction upon a successful campaign, but as unfavorable returns from other states reached Philadelphia, he could only lament that "After all our exertions I fear Jefferson will fail altogether. . . ."[48]

Soon Beckley himself was to feel the effect of the Federalist victory. When Congress met in May 1797, Federalists, aware of Beckley's activities in behalf of Jefferson, blocked his re-election and denied him, by one vote, the clerkship he had held since 1789.[49] Jefferson lamented this "loss of the ablest clerk in the U.S.,"[50] and John Page of Virginia delcared that "as much of a Democrat as I am I would not have voted against B[eckle]y if he had been the most insolent Aristocrat & desperate Tory that could be found in the United States."[51] But the Federalists were in control, and a Republican partisan was removed.

Beckley's services to the party, however, were not forgotten. After the Republican victory in the state elections in Pennsylvania in 1799, Jefferson wrote to Governor Thomas McKean recommending that his friend be given an office under the new administration, because of "the talents, diligence & integrity with which he has conducted himself in office, and . . . his zealous attachment to good principles in government."[52] McKean responded with appointments to the Mayor's Court of the City of Philadelphia and to the Orphans' Court of the County—two clerkships that would be equal in income, if not in importance, to the lost position.[53]

In the election of 1800, Beckley was active once again, this time as chairman of the Republican Committee of Correspondence for Philadelphia.[54] His anonymous pamphlet, *An Address to the People of the United States; with an Epitome and Vindication of the Public Life and Character of Thomas Jefferson*, written for that campaign, was widely circulated.[55] Extracts, especially the epitome of Jefferson's life, were among the most frequently reprinted pieces in the Republican press.[56] Beckley there described Jefferson as "a man of pure, ardent and unaffected piety; of sincere and genuine virtue; of an enlightened mind and superior wisdom; the adorer of our God; the patriot of his country; and the friend and benefactor of the whole human race."[57] In August 1800, Beckley sent a dozen copies of the pamphlet to Monroe in Virginia, explaining:

> To you, as a friend, I must apologize for the inaccuracies & inefficiencies of the "Epitome"—destitute of Materials, oppressed by sickness myself and the death of an only child, having only designed a brief newspaper essay, and being urged by friends to give it its present form, and believing that it is materially found in fact, I determined to send it forth. 1000 copies were struck for me, 1000 more by the printer. 1000 at New York, 1000 in Connecticut & 1000 in Maryland, have since been struck, and imperfect as it is, it will I trust do some good.[58]

The Republican victory of 1800 and the election of Jefferson regained for Beckley the clerkship of the House,[59] where he was to serve until his death at the age of fifty, on April 8, 1807.[60] In addition, President Jefferson gave his old friend and supporter the post of Librarian of Congress.[61] Here Beckley gave vent to his partisan spirit by making it difficult for Federalists in Congress to obtain documents from the library.[62]

In or out of office, Beckley never withdrew from the fascinating world of politics.[63] A partisan always, he worked ceaselessly for party ends in a time when that kind of allegiance was only beginning to be looked upon as a virtue. A skillful electioneer, both a product and a promoter of the newly developing party system in the United States, Beckley was an early prototype of a now familiar figure—the party manager.

NOTES

[1] Notes made during the years 1791-1806 are included in the "Anas," arranged and edited by Jefferson in 1818. The "Anas" are printed in *The Writings of Thomas Jefferson*, ed. Paul Leicester Ford (New York, 1892-99), I, 154-339.

[2] Beckley defeated S. Stockton, of New Jersey, who had the same number of votes on the first ballot. See Madison to Washington, Apr. 6, 1789, *The Writings of James Madison*, ed. Gaillard Hunt (New York, 1900-10), V, 339; *Annals of Congress*, 1 Cong., 1 Sess. (Apr. 1, 1789), 96.

[3] *Virginia Gazette* (Dixon and Hunter), Feb. 11, 1775, supplement, reporting meeting of Nov. 17, 1774. This is the earliest reference to John Beckley that this writer has uncovered. Whether or not Beckley was born in Virginia seems uncertain. Beckley's obituary appearing in the *National Intelligencer and Washington Advertiser*, Apr. 10, 1807, states that he was born in Great Britain and came to this country under the protection of an uncle at the age of eleven.

[4] *Virginia Gazette* (Purdie), Nov. 24, 1775, reporting meeting of Nov. 6, 1775.

[5] "Journal of Committee of Safety of Virginia," Feb. 7, 1776, in *Calendar of Virginia State Papers and Other Manuscripts* (Richmond, 1875-93), VIII, 76.

[6] Beckley took the oath of office Dec. 23, 1776. *Journals of the Council of State of Virginia*, ed. Henry R. McIlwaine (Richmond, 1931—), I, 298.

[7] Appointed July 2, 1777. *Ibid.*, I, 445.

[8] *Virginia Gazette* (Dixon and Hunter), Dec. 12, 1777; *Virginia Gazette* (Dixon and Nicholson), Feb. 26, 1779.

[9] *Journal of the House of Delegates of the Commonwealth of Virginia; Begun and Held at the Capitol . . . the Fourth of October in the year of our Lord one thousand seven hundred and seventy-nine* (Richmond, 1827), p. 5.

[10] *Calendar of Virginia State Papers*, IV, 540. Beckley also served as secretary of the Virginia Convention of 1788. Hugh Blair Grigsby, *The History of the Virginia Federal Convention of 1788 with Some Account of the Eminent Virginians of that Era who were Members of that Body*, ed. R. A. Brock (Richmond, 1890), I, 64.

[11] John Page to William Blackburn, May 29, 1797, John Page Papers, Duke University Library.

[12] *National Intelligencer and Washington Advertiser*, Apr. 10, 1807.

[13] Aaron Burr to James Monroe, Sept. 10, 1792, James Monroe Papers, II, 199, Library of Congress; Beckley to James Madison, Sept. 10, 1792, James Madison Papers, New York Public Library.

[14] Beckley to Madison, Oct. 17, 1792, Madison Papers, N. Y. Pub. Lib.

[15] Beckley to Madison, Sept. 2, 10, 1792, Madison Papers, N. Y. Pub. Lib. In 1797, it was Beckley who, according to Monroe, released the Hamilton-Reynolds notes to James Thomson Callender, the publication of which led to Hamilton's public confession of his affair with Mrs. Reynolds in order to disprove charges of speculation in government securities while Secretary of the Treasury. See James Monroe to Aaron Burr, Dec. 1, 1797, quoted in Philip Marsh, "Hamilton and Monroe," *Mississippi Valley Historical Review*, XXXIV (1947), 467.

[16] Beckley to Madison, Sept. 2, 1792, Madison Papers, N. Y. Pub. Lib.

[17] Beckley to Madison, Sept. 10, 1792, *ibid*.

[18] Rush to Aaron Burr, Sept. 24, 1792, *Letters of Benjamin Rush*, ed. Lyman Butterfield (Princeton, 1951), I, 623.

[19] Jefferson, "Anas," July 18, Mar. 23, 1793, *Writings of Jefferson*, ed. Ford, I, 245, 225.

[20] Jefferson, "Anas," June 7, 1793, *ibid.*, I, 231-232; Beckley to Madison, Sept. 10, Oct. 17, 1792, Madison Papers, N. Y. Pub. Lib.; see also Madison to Jefferson, July 13, 1791, on a trip Beckley made to the Eastern states in 1791, Madison Papers, XIV, 26, Lib. Cong.

[21] See Jefferson, "Anas," *Writings of Jefferson*, ed. Ford, I, 223, 225, 231-232, 233, 244-245, 272.

[22] *Ibid.*, I, 225.

[23] *Ibid.*, I, 223. Charles A. Beard in *Economic Origins of Jeffersonian Democracy* (New York, 1915), pp. 166-167, gave Jefferson the credit for compiling this list, indicating Jefferson's particular concern in the matter. "It is not apparent how Jefferson secured this information," wrote Beard, "but it would seem from the footnotes which he adds that he derived it from personal inquiry and through the inquiries of his friends. Whether he had access to the Treasury and Bank books through a clerk or a partisan is a matter for conjecture." There seems, however, to be no need for speculation; Jefferson clearly wrote at the head of this roster of stockholders: "The following list of papermen is communicated to me by Mr. Beckley." See Jefferson's notes, Mar. 23, 1793, Jefferson Papers, LXXXII, 14232, Lib. Cong., and "Anas," *Writings of Jefferson*, ed. Ford, I, 223.

[24] Jefferson, "Anas," Mar. 25, 1793, *Writings of Jefferson*, ed. Ford, I, 223n.

[25] Historians have taken little note of Beckley; some effort to rescue him from obscurity has been made by Philip Marsh, "John Beckley, Mystery Man of the Early Jeffersonians," *Pennsylvania Magazine of History and Biography*, LXXII (1948), 54-69.

[26] *A Provisional List of Alumni, Grammar School Students, Members of the Faculty, and Members of the Board of Visitors of the College of William and Mary in Virginia, from 1693 to 1888* (Richmond, 1941), p. 7. There seems to be no basis for assuming that Beckley attended Eton, as stated by Grigsby, *History of the Virginia Federal Convention of 1788*, I, 64, and accepted by others (e.g., Marsh, "John Beckley," p. 54). An examination of the Eton Register covering the years 1750-1790 by Harold A. Tarrant, clerk of the Old Etonian Association, failed to reveal the name of John Beckley. Harold A. Tarrant to the author, Apr. 24, 1953.

[27] Beckley was initiated into the Society as the thirty-second member, Apr. 12, 1779, and took a very active part in the early years of the Society. See "Original Records of the Phi Beta Kappa Society," *William and Mary Quarterly*, 1st Ser. (1896), 215, 226, and Oscar M. Voorhees, *The History of Phi Beta Kappa* (New York, 1945), pp. 15, 18, 19.

[28] See especially the letters of Beckley to Madison and Monroe in Madison Papers and Monroe Papers, N. Y. Pub. Lib.

[29] Rush to Burr, Sept. 24, 1792, *Letters of Benjamin Rush*, I, 622.

[30] See Monroe to Dr. George Logan, June 24, 1795, in *The Writings of George Washington*, ed. John C. Fitzpatrick (Washington, 1931-44), XXXV, 128n.

[31] Beckley to Jefferson, Feb. 27, 1801, Jefferson Papers, CIX, 18801-02.

[32] Beckley to Madison, Sept. 10, Oct. 17, 1792, Madison Papers, N. Y. Pub. Lib.

[33] Beckley to Madison, Oct. 17, 1792, *ibid.* It was Beckley who the year before secured a copy of Thomas Paine's *The Rights of Man* and arranged its reprinting in Philadelphia. Jefferson to Madison, May 9, 1791, *Writings of Jefferson*, ed. Ford, V, 331-332; Jefferson to Thomas Mann Randolph, July 3, 1791, *The Writings of Thomas Jefferson*, eds. Andrew Lipscomb and Albert E. Bergh (Washington, 1903), XIX, 77-78.

[34] Beckley to Madison, May 25, 1795, Madison Papers, N. Y. Pub. Lib. *Political Observations* was a pamphlet written by Madison, probably at the insistence of Beckley. See Madison to Monroe, Jan. 26, 1796, *Letters and Writings of James Madison* (Congressional edition, New York, 1884), II, 74.

[35] See Oliver Wolcott to Oliver Wolcott, Sr., Nov. 19, 1795, George Gibbs, *Memoirs of the Administrations of Washington and John Adams, edited from the Papers of Oliver Wolcott* (New York, 1846), I, 268. The question of Beckley's authorship is discussed in Marsh, "John Beckley," pp. 59-62.

[36] Donald H. Stewart, "Jeffersonian Journalism: Newspaper Propaganda and the Development of the Democratic-Republican Party, 1789-1801," unpubl. diss., Columbia Univ., 1950, p. 983.

[37] Beckley to Madison, Sept. 10, 1795, Madison Papers, N. Y. Pub. Lib.

[38] Beckley to William Irvine, Sept. 15, 1792, William Irvine Papers, XIII, Historical Society of Pennsylvania.

[39] Beckley to Irvine, Sept. 15, 1796, *ibid.*

[40] Beckley to Irvine, Sept. 22, 1796, *ibid.*

[41] Beckley to Irvine, Oct. 17, 1796, *ibid.*

[42] Beckley to Monroe, Oct. 17, 1796, Monroe Papers, N. Y. Pub. Lib.

[43] Beckley to Madison, Oct. 15, 1796, Madison Papers, N. Y. Pub. Lib.

[44] This estimate is based on statistics for the year 1793. The Constitution of Pennsylvania adopted in 1790 provided that every freeman of the age of twenty-one years who had resided in that state for two years and within that period had paid a state or county tax was eligible to vote. *Federal and State Constitutions*, comp. Francis N. Thorpe (Washington, 1909), V, 3096. Tax rolls, therefore, are a fairly accurate basis for estimating the number of qualified voters in the state. In 1793, according to an official enumeration of taxpayers required by the Constitution every seven years, there were 91,115 taxpayers. George D. Letuscher, *Early Political Machinery in the United States* (Philadelphia, 1903), p. 12. Making allowance for the names of women listed on the tax rolls, estimated at less than one per cent (*ibid.*, p. 13n.), the number of eligible voters was probably not far from 90,000 in 1793.

[45] Certified returns from the office of the state secretary of Pennsylvania, *Federal Gazette*, Baltimore, Nov. 30, 1796.

[46] Beckley to Irvine, Oct. 4, 1796, Irvine Papers, XIII.

[47] *Ibid.*

[48] Beckley to Irvine, Dec. 16, 1796, *ibid.*

[49] *Annals of Congress*, 5 Cong., 1 Sess. (May 15, 1797), pp. 51-52; *Virginia Argus*, May 23, 1797, supplement.

[50] Jefferson to Madison, May 18, 1797, *Writings of Jefferson*, ed. Ford, VII, 125.

[51] John Page to William Blackburn, May 29, 1797, Page Papers.

[52] Jefferson to McKean, Jan. 9, 1800, Jefferson Papers, CVI, 18163.

[53] McKean to Jefferson, Mar. 7, 1800, *ibid.*, CVI, 18210.

[54] Beckley to Alexander J. Dallas, Nov. 7, 1800, Dallas Papers, Hist. Soc. Pa.

[55] Beckley acknowledges authorship of this pamphlet in a letter to William Burwell, June 28, 1805, in Jefferson Papers, CL, 26289-90. The pamphlet was signed "Americanus."

[56] *American Mercury*, Hartford, Sept. 4, 1800; *Sun*, Pittsfield, Mass., Oct. 21, 1800; *Bee*, New London, Conn., Sept. 24, 1800; *Raleigh Register*, Sept. 23, 30, Oct. 7, 1800.

[57] [John Beckley], *An Address to the People of the United States; with an Epitome and Vindication of the Public Life and Character of Thomas Jefferson* (Philadelphia, 1800), p. 32.

[58] Beckley to Monroe, Aug. 26, 1800, Monroe Papers, N. Y. Pub. Lib.

[59] *Annals of Congress*, 7 Cong., 1 Sess. (Dec. 7, 1801), p. 310.

[60] *National Intelligencer and Washington Advertiser*, Apr. 10, 1807.

[61] Beckley was appointed on Jan. 26, 1802, three days after Congress authorized the appointment of a librarian. Lucy Salamanca, *Fortress of Freedom: The Story of the Library of Congress* (Philadelphia, 1942), p. 45.

[62] See *William Plumer's Memorandum of Proceedings in the United States Senate 1803-*

1807, ed. Everett S. Brown (New York, 1923), entry of Dec. 23, 1806, pp. 537-538.

[63] Two years before Jefferson's second term was to expire Beckley was promoting the interest of Monroe for the Presidency and sending him confidential reports. Beckley wrote to Monroe in 1806: "I trust the *confidential* letter I wrote you during the Session via New York per packet has come safe to hand. It was not signed and was written in the 3d person, so as to guard *vs* accidental miscarriage. I unfolded the intrigues which caused us so much agitation during the Session, and the initials used I was confident you could not mistake." Beckley to Monroe, July 13, 1806, Monroe Papers, N. Y. Pub. Lib.

WASHINGTON'S FAREWELL, THE FRENCH

ALLIANCE, AND THE ELECTION OF 1796*

Alexander DeConde

What effect does a nation's foreign affairs have on political parties? Alexander DeConde, a prominent specialist in American diplomatic history, explores the intricacies of the election of 1796 in light of emotion-laden Franco-American relations. He finds that French intervention in American politics, designed to affect the outcome of the election, was posited on the assumption that a triumphant Republican Party would reverse the pro-British trend of American foreign policy. In French eyes, this course alone would save the Franco-American Alliance of 1778. DeConde's astute dissection of the tangled foreign interrelationships shows that French activity was countered by the influence of Washington's Farewell Address. Two of DeConde's numerous studies on diplomatic topics relate to the Early National period. They are Entangling Alliance: Politics and Diplomacy Under George Washington *(1958) and* The Quasi-War: The Politics and Diplomacy of the Undeclared War with France, 1797-1801 *(1966). At the University of California, Santa Barbara, Alexander DeConde is professor of history.*

When in 1789 George Washington became the nation's first president the French alliance was the cornerstone of American foreign policy. It largely had made possible American independence and had established American foreign policy orientation. At the end of Washington's second term, in fact as he prepared his farewell to public life, the life-giving alliance was practically dead and the United States was virtually at war with France. Why, in eight formative years, did such a drastic reversal

* From Alexander DeConde, "Washington's Farewell, the French Alliance, and the Election of 1796," *Mississippi Valley Historical Review,* Vol. XLIII (March, 1957), pp. 641-658. Copyright 1957 by the Mississippi Valley Historical Association. Reprinted by permission of the Managing Editor, *Journal of American History.*

in foreign policy take place?[1] A full answer to this question would be long and complex; yet by looking closely at the election of 1796 and by reviewing the Farewell Address in its political context we may find a partial answer as to how the alliance received its mortal wound. We may also find additional reason for revising the traditional interpretation of the Farewell Address as a wise, timeless, and unbiased warning to the nation.

The blow from which the alliance never recoveredwas the Jay Treaty of 1794.[2] While this Federalist-negotiated treaty averted a war with England, a war which Federalists feared, the major objectives which John Jay had been expected to win were not realized. Because it failed to obtain specific concessions on impressments, ship seizures, and Indian raids on the frontier, the treaty infuriated Republicans and others who still nurtured a Revolution-bred hatred of England.[3] At the same time it blighted Franco-American relations. Successive French revolutionary governments were convinced that the Jay Treaty violated the Franco-American treaties of 1778 and that the American government had accepted it against the will of an overwhelming public sentiment. Believing that the bulk of the American people were pro-French even though Washington's Federalist government was pro-English, the French sought to arouse their allies, the American people, to their true interest. This true interest was alliance with France and disassociation with England, America's natural enemy and France's major antagonist in war since February, 1793.[4]

To arouse the American people in defense of the 1778 alliance the French Directory in June, 1795, sent to the United States a new minister, a young man in his early thirties, Pierre Auguste Adet. To the French the Jay Treaty created an intimate alliance between the United States and France's worst enemy. In Adet's instructions, therefore, the idea that the treaty violated the French alliance stood out as the foremost grievance against the Washington administration.[5]

Despite French anger, and despite Adet's attempts to prevent ratification, the Senate approved the Jay Treaty eleven days after Adet had landed in Philadelphia. Two months later, while Adet continued his efforts to kill it, Washington ratified the treaty.[6] England accepted the ratified treaty and in April, 1796, after a long, last-ditch battle in which Adet used all the influence he could muster against the treaty, the House of Representatives voted funds to implement it. To Adet as to other Frenchmen this meant the end of the 1778 alliance and another triumph for England and English gold.

Not knowing that Washington already had decided to retire from the presidency, Adet now saw the overthrow of Washington and his Federalist administration as the only salvation for the 1778 alliance. Adet and the French Directory viewed the Washington administration as the captive of English policy; to save the alliance it had to be replaced by a pro-French Republican administration.[7] Charles Delacroix, French foreign minister, advocated inciting an uprising against Washington to break the Jay Treaty and to invigorate the alliance. Thomas Jefferson, he believed, would replace Washington and thus France would command the influence in the United States which she deserved. Prospects for the defeat of Washington were good, he believed, since the President, once the idol of the American people, had become to some an object of scorn and even hatred as the result of the Jay Treaty; already the journals attacked him, his principles, and his conduct.[8]

Taking into account what it conceived to be the temper of American popular opinion, and with the objective of destroying English influence in the United States and salvaging the 1778 alliance, the French government intervened actively in the presidential election of 1796. Through Adet and other French officials in the United States the Directory openly supported the Republican party and wherever possible attacked the Federalist party.[9] French intervention in the election became, therefore, one of the main issues in the campaign of 1796. The fate of the alliance hung on the outcome of the election.

The decision of the Directory to intervene in the 1796 election, while a decisive factor, contributed but one element to the complex politics of the election. Domestic issues and the Jay Treaty itself contributed others. Final acceptance of the treaty plunged Franco-American relations to their lowest depths since independence and marked a great political triumph for Federalists. Yet to Republicans all hope of ultimately defeating the treaty did not appear lost. Seeing the extent of the Jay Treaty's unpopularity, Republican leaders believed that it would make an excellent campaign issue in the 1796 election as an unrivaled party rallying point for national sentiment. Thomas Jefferson, James Madison, and other party leaders believed that popular opinion remained still largely pro-French and anti-British. Being politicians they reacted logically. Their party had ready-made national issues; they had only to exploit them properly and victory would be theirs. Republicans, consequently, carried over into the election of 1796 their campaign against the Jay Treaty and the pro-British "system" of Alexander Hamilton.[10]

Granted the logic and appeal of the Republican campaign plan, a towering obstacle—the person and prestige of George Washington—stood in the way of success, as was clear to the French. So deep was the impression Washington had made on fellow Americans that to attack him would be to risk injuring the attacker. Twice he had been chosen president without a dissenting vote. Had he so desired he could undoubtedly have held office for a third term, for, as a foreign observer remarked, "there is a Magic in his name more powerful in this Country than the Abilities of any other man."[11] No man, moreover, was better aware of this than Jefferson. "Republicanism," he advised, "must lie on it's [sic] oars, resign the vessel to it's pilot [Washington], and themselves to the course he thinks best for them."[12]

Despite Washington's great political strength the situation in 1796 was far different from 1789 and 1792; Washington probably could have had a third term, but not by unanimous choice. In political battles over neutrality, the Jay Treaty, and other issues, he had divested himself of nonpartisanship. To Republicans and Francophiles the guise of being above party and of working for the welfare of the nation as a whole, in view of his intimate connections with his Federalist subordinates and his consistent practice of acting in accord with their principles, appeared the sheerest hypocrisy.[13] In town and country some men now spat at the mention of his name, denounced him as a monocrat and an Anglomaniac, and prayed for his removal from office. Washington in 1796 had become a central figure in emerging party politics; his was a principal target for the violent personal politics of the time; and to the French he was the main barrier to reactivation of the 1778 alliance.[14]

So bitter was feeling between English and French partisans that domestic issues drifted into relative insignificance. In their conviction that the Federalist administration did not truly represent the American people, the French were encouraged by pro-French partisans among Republicans who indicated that the Federalist government would topple if only France were to take a strong stand.[15] As the election year of 1796 opened, Republicans intensified their attacks against the Federalist administration. The Jay Treaty and the loud cry of aristocracy, monarchy, and plutocracy aroused deep popular emotions. Mutual hatred characterized the two large political segments of the American public.

With his government under fire on both domestic and foreign policy and with himself the target of unrestrained scurrility, Washington found the demands of his office increasingly difficult to endure. Publicly he maintained a dignified silence, but privately he revealed the strain.[16] Even he had come to see that the myth of nonpartisanship was shattered, and that his concept of an administration above party and the tumult of politics had been illusory. Foreign relations had exploded the myth while serving as a catalyst in the formation of national political parties. This was an issue capable of transforming the opposing local alliances of Federalist and anti-Federalist into integrated national parties—an emotional foreign policy issue capable of capturing public imagination in a way which abstruse problems of finance could not.[17]

Despite his increasing distaste for the office and the increasing speculation about his not wishing to be a candidate for a third term, the President remained silent as to future plans. Leaders of both political parties, however, had little doubt that he would not run. "He gave me intimations enough," asserted John Adams, "that his reign would be very short." Early in 1796, and even before, both parties had laid tentative plans which did not include Washington as a candidate.[18]

The attacks on Washington grew increasingly bitter during the year. Opponents charged that he had betrayed a solemn pledge to France by destroying the French alliance. Personal attacks accused him of taking more salary than was allotted him. His mail was tampered with for political advantage, and forged letters of 1777 were refurbished and printed as genuine. Particularly cutting was Tom Paine's bitter attack from Paris, which city was the source, Federalists were convinced, of the anti-Washington campaign.[19] Jefferson, too, had lost patience with the exalted role of Washington. The President, he wrote, like Samson had had his head "shorn by the harlot England."[20]

Despite pressures to stay and ride out the storm, Washington disclosed in May, 1796, that he intended definitely to retire.[21] If he had nurtured at all the desire to seek a third term it was killed by the acid criticism to which he had been subjected. The President decided not to seek a third term not only because he sought retirement in his old age but also because he was disgusted with the abuse from political opponents. "The true cause of the general's retiring," declared one of his staunchest supporters, "was . . . the *loss of popularity* which he had experienced, and the further loss which he apprehended from the rupture with France, which he looked upon as inevitable."[22]

Once the decision to retire was made, Washington turned to Hamilton, as usual, for advice. When, he asked, would be the best time for publication of his farewell to the nation? Hamilton, with his eye on the coming election, advised that the public announcement be held off as long as possible. "The proper period now for your declaration," wrote Hamilton, "seems to be *Two months* before the time for the Meeting of the

Electors. This will be sufficient. The parties will in the meantime electioneer conditionally, that is to say, *if you decline*; for a serious opposition to you will I think hardly be risked."[23]

Three months before the gathering of electors Washington announced to the nation his intention to retire. Although in 1792 he had planned a valedictory to the nation and James Madison had drafted one, the September, 1796, version, in which Hamilton's hand was prominent, became a piece of partisan politics directed specifically against Republicans and Francophiles who had made Washington's last years miserable. At the time, it was recognized for what it was: a political manifesto, a campaign document. The 1792 version, drawn up before popular passions had been stirred by war in Europe, did not, for example, stress politics nor did it touch on foreign affairs. In the 1796 version partisan politics and foreign affairs were central.[24]

Washington's specific target in foreign affairs, heartily seconded by Hamilton, was the alliance with France. He struck at Adet's partisan activities, at French meddling in American politics (while passing over British meddling), and at the allegedly dangerous implications of the French alliance. Washington told Hamilton that had it not been for the status of "party disputes" and of foreign affairs he would not have considered it necessary to revise his valedictory. He was convinced that a warning to the nation was necessary to combat foreign (French) intrigue "in the internal concerns of our country." It is indeed easy "to foresee," he warned, "that it may involve us in disputes and finally in War, to fulfill political alliances." This was the crux of the matter; Washington believed that the French alliance was no longer an asset to the country.[25]

Washington's valedictory trumpeted the Federalist answer to Republican accusations that the administration had sold the country to the British; it countered the anti-administration furor over the Jay Treaty; it was a justification and defense of his policies. As such it was designed and as such it became the opening blast in the presidential campaign, contrived to prevent the election of Thomas Jefferson. The Farewell laid the basis for Federalist strategy of using Washington's great prestige to appeal to patriotism, as against the evil of foreign machinations, to make "Federalist" and "patriot" synonyms in the minds of the electorate. Under the banner of patriotism the Farewell spearheaded the attack on the opposition party and on French diplomacy.[26]

In the address Washington opened with the announcement that he would not be a candidate for a third term and then stressed the advantages of union and the evils of political parties. Having in mind, undoubtedly, the French Republic, he advised against "a passionate attachment of one Nation for another." Such "sympathy for the favourite nation," he warned, leads to wars and quarrels "without adequate inducement or justification." Then followed the oft-quoted "Great rule of conduct" that with foreign nations we should have "as little *political* connection as possible." While stressing fidelity to "already formed engagements," he announced that "'tis our true policy to steer clear of permanent Alliances with any portion of the foreign world." Washington deplored the growth of political opposition, chastised the public for its attachment to France, and concluded with a defense of his foreign policy, particularly his much criticized policy of neutrality which was based on the Proclamation of April 22, 1793. He called this the "index" to his plan or policy.[27]

Although cloaked in phrases of universal or timeless application, the objectives of the address were practical, immediate, and partisan. Men often attempt to rationalize their partisan political views in pronouncements studded with timeless patriotic appeals; so it was with Washington and Hamilton. The valedictory bore directly on the coming election, on the French alliance, and on the status of Franco-American relations in general.

While expressed cogently and linked forever with Washington's name, the main ideas and foreign policy principles of the Farewell were not unique with either Hamilton or Washington. They were prevalent Federalist ideas on current foreign policy and politics, and can be found expressed in various ways in the polemical literature of the time. The concept of no entanglement with Europe, for instance, was a common one among Federalists and others. More often than not it was a universalized reaction against a specific annoyance—the French alliance. Stated as non-involvement with Europe an attack against the alliance had great psychological appeal. In time this specific meaning was lost and only the generalization remained.[28]

As partisans had expected, Washington's words stoked an already hot political situation. "It will serve as a signal," exclaimed New England Federalist Fisher Ames, "like dropping a hat, for the party racers to start."[29] The Farewell was indeed soon under partisan attack. Washington's advice for the future, taunted William Duane, "is but a defence for the past." Referring to the warning against "permanent alliances," he exclaimed, "this extraordinary advice is fully exemplified in your departure from the spirit and principle of the treaty with France, which was declared to be permanent, and exhibits this very infidelity you reprobate in a most striking and lamentable light." The President had not, Duane continued, "adhered to that rigid and neutral justice which you profess—every concession to Britain in prejudice of France was a deviation from neutrality." Much of the evil which Washington attributed to faction, he claimed, came from the Federalist party. "Your examples of party influence are uniformly drawn from occasions wherein your personal opinions, your pride and passions, have been involved."[30] As to Washington's advice to steer clear of permanent alliances, why, critics asked, was it unwise to extend the nation's political engagements? Was not the Jay Treaty a political connection, practically an alliance with England?[31]

To James Madison—who earlier had feared that under Hamilton's influence the address would become a campaign document—the valedictory confirmed his assumptions; it was all politics. Under the complete influence of the British faction, Madison wrote, Washington obviously sought to destroy the French alliance. "It has been known," he continued, "that every channel has been latterly opened that could convey to his mind a rancor against that country [France] and suspicion of all who are thought to sympathize with its revolution and who support the policy of extending our commerce and in general of standing well with it. But it was not easy to suppose his mind wrought up to the tone that could dictate or rather adopt some parts of the performance."[32]

Minister Adet believed wrongly that the address would arouse the indignation of pro-French "patriots" and would not have the effect on the people that the British faction hoped it would. He consequently plunged into the campaign to see to it that the address would not have its intended effect.[33] Looking upon John Adams as an enemy of France and a friend of England, he electioneered brazenly for Jefferson. The future conduct of France toward America, he made clear to Americans, would be governed by the election's outcome.[34]

Beginning at the end of October and timing himself carefully, Adet began publication of a series of public manifestoes designed to influence the electorate. He conjured up the prospect of war with France, stressing that Jefferson's election would eliminate such a possibility. With the Quakers of Pennsylvania, Federalists lamented, Adet's strategy of fear worked. Fearing a Federalist-sponsored war against France, Quakers cast their votes for Republicans.[35] "French influence never appeared so open and unmasked as at this city [Philadelphia] election," cried William Loughton Smith, Hamilton's congressional mouthpiece. "French flags, french cockades were displayed by the Jefferson party and there is no doubt that french money was not spared. . . . In short there never was so barefaced and disgraceful an interference of a foreign power in any free country."[36]

Adet's procedure was to write an official note to the Secretary of State and then to send a copy for publication to Benjamin Bache's Philadelphia *Aurora*. In his note of October 27, for example, he protested against American foreign policy and appealed to the people to renew their friendship with France by disavowing the Jay Treaty and honoring the French alliance.[37] A few days later (November 5) the pages of the *Aurora* carried Adet's second manifesto, dubbed by Federalists the "cockade proclamation." In the name of the Directory it called on all Frenchmen in the United States—in the land of an ally—to mount the tricolored cockade, symbol of liberty. Those who did not so give public evidence of their support of the French Republic were to be denied the services of French consuls and the protection of the French flag. Immediately the tricolored cockade blossomed in the streets. Americans as well as Frenchmen wore it as a badge of devotion to the French cause. It became, in short, a symbol of republicanism.[38]

Ten days later Adet followed the "cockade proclamation" with his last and most florid note, which he again sent simultaneously to the Secretary of State and to Bache's *Aurora*. In it he announced that as a result of the Jay Treaty his function as minister had been suspended and that he was returning to France.[39] Adet had timed his announcement so that it might have a maximum political influence, particularly on the electors who were soon to meet to choose Washington's successor.[40]

Adet's notes and Secretary of State Timothy Pickering's replies were used as campaign ammunition by both sides. Federalists, of course, were furious. They denounced Adet's pronouncements for what they were— brazen electioneering maneuvers by a foreign agent. John Adams, against whom the last note was directed, found "it an instrument well calculated to reconcile me to private life. It will purify me from all envy of Mr. Jefferson, or Mr. Pinckney, or Mr. Burr, or Mr. any body who may be chosen President or Vice President."[41] William Cobbett, violent Francophobe and anti-Jeffersonian, published Adet's note under the title of *The Gros Mosqueton Diplomatique; or Diplomatic Blunderbuss*. He ran with it, of course, an adverse commentary.[42]

Friends of France, according to Adet, were delighted. Republican leaders were willing and even eager to use the issue of the French alliance to gain votes. But, contrary to Adet's opinion, they were not happy with the French minister's personal interference. Madison, for instance, maintained that Adet's note announcing his return to France worked "all the evil with which it is pregnant." Its indiscretions, he added, gave comfort to Federalists who had the "impudence" to point out that it was "an electioneering maneuver," and that "the French government had been led into it by the opponents of the British treaty."[43]

Adet did not realize that his activities worked mainly to injure the cause he sought to aid. French popularity, according to competent observers, decreased as a result.[44] Disgusted by Adet's conduct, Washington drew even closer to the British. One piqued New England writer went so far as to declare that since Adet's electioneering on behalf of Jefferson "there is not an elector on this side of the Delaware that would not be sooner shot than vote for him." And Philip Key maintained that Adet's meddling "irretrievably diminished that good will felt for his Government & the people of France by most people here."[45]

Unaware of any adverse reaction, Adet and his intimates believed that his actions and the Directory's measures would influence the presidential electors decisively in favor of Jefferson.[46] What Adet and the Directory had not taken into account was that invariably when a foreign diplomat takes sides openly in the domestic politics of the nation to which he is accredited he makes the party leader he seeks to aid appear to be the pawn of a foreign government. Such a charge, whether or not true, gives the opposition the opportunity of patriotically denouncing foreign interference and of posing as the defender of national honor against foreign subversives. So it was with the Adet case. His activities seemed to confirm the very warnings of foreign interference that were stressed in Washington's Farewell Address.

Sensing the opportunity, Federalists attacked the French alliance, denounced French domestic interference, and pitted the patriotism of Washington and Adams against the Jacobin-tainted Republican campaign. Voters were importuned to beware of foreign influence; to "decide between the address of the President and the [French]"; to follow Washington's counsel. Adet and the Directory, they were told, wished to draw the nation into war and to sever the western from the Atlantic states. No doubt clouded the Federalist mind; the Union was in danger.[47]

Federalist warnings, persistent though they were, did not stop French interference in American politics; nor did the interference end with the choosing of electors in November. Few of the electors were pledged to a specific candidate, so the campaign continued with increasing tumult until December 7, when the electors cast their ballots. Adet, having suspended his diplomatic functions, remained in Philadelphia to continue his anti-administration campaign. He and the Republicans hammered at similar themes, stressing that if Adams were elected the errors of the Washington administration would be continued, since Adams was committed to Washington's tragic policies; and that such policies would lead to war with France.

Candidate Adams, on the other hand, believed that only time would tell whether "the French Directory have only been drawn in to favor the election of a favorite, or whether in their trances and delirium of victory they think to terrify America, or whether in their sallies they may not venture on hostilities." He advised that under the circumstances "Americans must be cool and steady if they can."[48]

But Americans were not cool and steady. In newspapers and elsewhere they debated the French alliance, the mounting crisis with France, and the possibility of war.[49] Hamilton, as was his practice in time of crisis, wrote articles for the press to reply to Adet's manifestoes, to defend administration foreign policy, and to attack the French alliance.[50] Another prominent Federalist, Noah Webster, editor of the *American Minerva,* wrote a series of articles in which he also attacked the alliance. His articles were reprinted and widely circulated. In the Federalist press, in fact, attacks on the alliance now became common. Webster in his articles stressed that France had equated the term ally with that of vassal; "an *open* enemy," he declared, "is less dangerous than an *insidious friend.*" Although the British, too, had injured the United States, Webster maintained that the American connection with Great Britain was stronger than the French alliance because "our connection with her is solely *an alliance of interest.* This is the true basis of all national connections. We are therefore in no danger from Great Britain."[51]

In the first week of February, 1797, the American people finally learned the results of the election. Although the Federalist victory was narrow, it was enough to sink French hopes for a revived alliance. By "three votes" John Adams, who wisely had perceived that he was "not enough of an Englishman, nor little enough of a Frenchman, for some people," was elected second president of the United States.[52]

Jefferson, however, captured the second highest electoral total and became vice-president.[53] America's first contested presidential election therefore, although a clear-cut Federalist victory, gave some comfort to Republicans and struck fear into Federalist ranks. But Republican strength had not been sufficient to overturn the government and hence to reverse the course of Franco-American relations. To staunch Hamiltonian Federalists this aspect of the election was indeed sweet. In various election post-mortems, in New England in particular, such Federalists rejoiced that the "French party is fallen," and that the French alliance was at last valueless. Even Adet, one of them pointed out, "avows, and it is rather a tough point to avow, that our treaty is disadvantageous." Now he might inform the Directory that it has "been deceived by the revolutionary Americans in Paris; that we (at least the Yankees) have not been traitors, and have ceased to be dupes."[54]

With the Federalist victory, narrow though it was, the Farewell Address had done its work. The French alliance which had been drawn to last "forever" and which had been the core of American foreign policy when Washington launched the federal government was practically dead as he prepared to leave office. Despite French and Republican efforts to the contrary, and in large part because of the impact of Washington's Farewell, the basic foreign policy orientation of the United States remained pro-British.[55] The Farewell Address now belonged to posterity and posterity has given it meanings to fit its own problems.

NOTES

[1] A few months after Washington had left office, the French, in taking stock of the defunct alliance of 1778 and the serious state of American relations, asked the same question. Louis-Guillaume Otto, "Considérations sur la Conduite du gouvernement des Etats-Unis envers la France, depuis 1789 jusqu'en 1797" [Paris, June 17, 1797], Archives des Affaires Etrangères, Correspondance Politique, Etas-Unis (Reproductions in the Library of Congress), XLVII, 401-18.

[2] For background on the Jay Treaty see Samuel F. Bemis, *Jay's Treaty: A Study in Commerce and Diplomacy* (New York, 1923); Frank Monaghan, *John Jay: Defender of Liberty* (New York, 1935), 361-404; Joseph Charles, "The Jay Treaty: The Origins of the American Party System," *William and Mary Quarterly* (Williamsburg), Ser. III, Vol. XII (October, 1955), 581-630; Bradford Perkins, *The First Rapprochement: England and the United States* (Philadelphia, 1955), 1-6.

[3] That the treaty violated the "rights of friendship, gratitude and alliance which the republic of France may justly claim from the United States" was a foremost criticism of Jay's work, a criticism which had great popular appeal. See the memorial emanating from a mass meeting of citizens in Philadelphia, July 25, 1795, cited in Margaret Woodbury, "Public Opinion in Philadelphia, 1789-1801," *Smith College Studies in History* (Northampton, Mass.), V, nos. 1-2 (1919-1920), 88. "Junius Americanus," in New York *Herald,* reprinted in *Virginia Herald and Fredericksburg Advertiser,* June 26, 1795, attacked the administration for neglecting France and surrendering to Great Britain's tyranny. For a French commentary on American public opinion in regard to the Jay Treaty see François de La Rochefoucauld-Liancourt, *Travels through the United States of North America in the Years 1795, 1796, and 1797* (2 vols., London, 1799), I, 381-82.

[4] See, for example, Joseph Fauchet to Committee of Public Safety, April 19, 25, 1795, Frederick J. Turner (ed.), *Correspondence of the French Ministers to the United States, 1791-1797* (American Historical Association, *Annual Report,* 1903, Vol. II, Washington, 1904), 649-50, 662-63. For an astute French analysis of the status of the alliance at the time of the Jay negotiations see Philippe A. J. Létombe to Commission of Foreign Rela-

tions, [1794], Archives des Affaires Etrangères, Correspondance Politique, Etats-Unis, XL, 241-47.

⁵ Adet's instructions, dated October 23, 1794, are in Turner (ed.), *Correspondence of French Ministers*, 721-30. For biographical details on Adet see *Nouvelle Biographie Générale* (Paris), I (1852), 278; Jean Kaulek (ed.), *Papiers de Barthelemy: Ambassadeur de France en Suisse, 1792-1797* (6 vols., Paris, 1886-1910), VI, 151 n. Adet was second choice for the American mission. Alphonse Bertrand, "Les Etats-Unis et la Révolution Française," *Revue des Deux Mondes* (Paris), XXXIII (May 15, 1906), 422 n.

⁶ Adet wrote that "the President has just countersigned the dishonor of his old age and the shame of the United States." Adet to Committee of Public Safey, September 2, 1795, Turner (ed.), *Correspondence of French Ministers*, 776-77. The despatch is printed in translation in Gilbert Chinard (ed.), *George Washington as the French Knew Him* (Princeton, 1940), 106-109. In France, of course, Washington's support of the Jay Treaty was considered a tragic mistake and inimical to the 1778 alliance. See George Duruy (ed.), *Memoirs of Barras: Member of the Directorate*, trans. by Charles E. Roche (4 vols., London, 1895-1896), II, 103 (entry of March 22, 1795); Michele de Mangourit to ———, December 23, 1795, Archives des Affaires Etrangères, Correspondance Politique, Etats-Unis, XLIV, 554. In the United States, Washington's signing of the treaty infuriated Republicans; Republican newspaper editors embarked on a concerted effort to make public life so unpalatable that Washington would virtually be driven from office. See the diary of Dr. Nathaniel Ames, August 14, 1795, in Charles Warren, *Jacobin and Junto* (Cambridge, 1931), 12, 63; Donald H. Stewart, "The Press and Political Corruption during the Federalist Administrations," *Political Science Quarterly* (New York), LXVII (September, 1952), 436. William Vans Murray, a moderate Federalist, believed that Washington ran the "risk of the most alarming discontent if he ratifies & war if he does not." William Vans Murray Papers, Commonplace Book, August 15, 1795 (Princeton University Library, microfilm copies).

⁷ Adet to Minister of Foreign Relations, May 3, 1796, Turner (ed.), *Correspondence of French Ministers*, 900-906.

⁸ "Rapport au Directoire Exécutif par le Ministre des Relations Extérieures," January 16, 1796, Archives des Affaires Etrangères, Correspondance Politique, Etats-Unis, XLV, 41-51. Part of the document is printed in Samuel F. Bemis, "Washington's Farewell Address: A Foreign Policy of Independence," *American Historical Review* (New York), XXXIX (January, 1934), 257-58.

⁹ "Mémoire sur les effets du dernier traité des Etats-Unis et de l'Angleterre, et les remèdes à employer," [May, 1796], Archives des Affaires Etrangères, Correspondance Politique, Etats-Unis, XLV, 323-51; Adet to Minister of Foreign Relations, May 3, 1796, Turner (ed.), *Correspondence of French Ministers*, 900-906.

¹⁰ Phineas Bond, British consul in Philadelphia, for example, maintained that it was pretty well understood that Republican opposition to the Jay Treaty was planned by Jefferson "for the double purpose of promoting the interests of France and of advancing" his candidacy for president. Bond to Lord Grenville, May 4, 1796, British Foreign Correspondence: America (Henry Adams Transcripts, Library of Congress). See also Harry Ammon, "The Formation of the Republican Party in Virginia, 1789-1796," *Journal of Southern History* (Lexington, Ky.), XIX (August, 1953), 309-10.

¹¹ Robert Liston, British minister in Philadelphia, to Grenville, October 13, 1796, Henry Adams Transcripts. The quotation is from Henrietta Liston to James Jackson, October 16, 1796, Bradford Perkins (ed.), "A Diplomat's Wife in Philadelphia: Letters of Henrietta Liston, 1796-1800," *William and Mary Quarterly*, Ser. III, Vol. XI (October, 1954), 604.

¹² Jefferson to James Monroe, June 12, 1796, Paul L. Ford (ed.), *The Writings of Thomas Jefferson* (10 vols., New York, 1892-1899), VII, 80; James Madison, too, complained of Washington's prestige. Madison to Jefferson, May 22, 1796, Madison Papers (Library of Congress), XIX, 68, cited in Nathan Schachner, *Thomas Jefferson: A Biography* (2 vols., New York, 1951), II, 581.

[13] John Quincy Adams believed that Republican efforts to associate Washington with "an English party" was "a party manoeuvre," a trick "to make their adversaries unpopular by fixing upon the odious imputations." Adams to Joseph Pitcairn, March 9, 1797, Worthington C. Ford (ed.), *Writings of John Quincy Adams* (7 vols., New York, 1913-1917), II, 140.

[14] See, for example, Lexington *Kentucky Gazette*, September 26, 1795; John B. McMaster, *A History of the People of the United States* (8 vols., New York, 1883-1913), II, 289. While opposing him, many of Washington's critics still recognized his virtues. One, for instance, remarked that "the best man that ever lived possessing the influence of the P[resident], is a dangerous man; the more so if guided in any of his measures by others who may not be so virtuous. God grant we may never have cause to say 'curse on his virtues; they have undone his country'." Joseph Jones to James Madison, February 17, 1796, Worthington C. Ford (ed.), "Letters from Joseph Jones to Madison, 1788-1802," Massachusetts Historical Society, *Proceedings* (Boston), Ser. II, Vol. XV (1902), 155.

[15] At this time La Rochefoucauld-Liancourt, for example, reported that the common people in the United States were overwhelmingly pro-French and anti-British. *Travels*, II, 64-65, 139.

[16] See, for example, Washington to Jefferson, July 6, 1796, and to Charles C. Pinckney, July 8, 1796, John C. Fitzpatrick (ed.), *The Writings of George Washington, 1745-1799* (39 vols., Washington, 1931-1944), XXXV, 120, 130.

[17] Ammon, "Formation of the Republican Party in Virginia," *Journal of Southern History*, XIX (August, 1953), 300.

[18] The quotation is from John Adams to Abigail Adams, March 25, 1796, Charles F. Adams (ed.), *Letters of John Adams Addressed to His Wife* (2 vols., Boston, 1841), II, 214. Republicans shared the same rumors. Madison to Monroe, February 26, 1796, *Letters and Other Writings of James Madison* (4 vols., Philadelphia, 1865), II, 83; Madison to Monroe, May 14, 1796, Gaillard Hunt (ed.), *The Writings of James Madison* (9 vols., New York, 1900-1910), VI, 301 n. For about a year George Hammond, the British minister, had heard rumors that Washington would retire in 1797. Hammond to Grenville, January 5, 1796, Henry Adams Transcripts.

[19] John Quincy Adams to John Adams, August 13, 1796, Ford (ed.), *Writings of John Quincy Adams*, II, 21; Paine to Washington, July 30, 1796, Philip S. Foner (ed.), *The Complete Writings of Thomas Paine* (2 vols., New York, 1945), II, 691-723. For other details see Nathaniel W. Stephenson and Waldo H. Dunn, *George Washington* (2 vols., New York, 1940), II, 409; McMaster, *History of the People of the United States*, II, 249-50.

[20] Jefferson to Philip Mazzei, April 24, 1796. See Howard R. Marraro, "The Four Versions of Jefferson's Letter to Mazzei," *William and Mary Quarterly*, Ser. II, Vol. XXII (January, 1942), 24-25; Schachner, *Jefferson*, II, 578-79.

[21] Washington to John Jay, May 8, 1796, Fitzpatrick (ed.), *Writings of Washington*, XXXV, 36-37.

[22] William Cobbett, *Porcupine's Works* (12 vols., London, 1801), IV, 444 n. The italics are in the original.

[23] Washington to Hamilton, June 26, 1796, Fitzpatrick (ed.), *Writings of Washington*, XXXV, 103-104. See also Washington's letter to Hamilton, May 15, 1796, *ibid.*, 50; Hamilton to Washington, July 5, 1796, *ibid.*, 104 n, and in Henry Cabot Lodge (ed.), *The Works of Alexander Hamilton* (9 vols., New York, 1885-1886), VIII, 408-409. Republicans recognized that Washington's delayed announcement of retirement was a political scheme emanating from Hamilton. Noble E. Cunningham, "The Jeffersonian Party to 1801: A Study of the Formation of a Party Organization" (Ph.D. dissertation, Duke University, 1952), 142.

[24] A copy of Madison's suggestions for the 1792 version of the Farewell Address is incorporated in Washington to Hamilton, May 15, 1796, Fitzpatrick (ed.), *Writings of Washington*, XXXV, 51-61; the September 19, 1796, version is on pp. 214-38. For a

detailed analysis of the address and its various contributors see Victor H. Paltsits (ed.), *Washington's Farewell Address* (New York, 1935). Usually Washington's advice on foreign policy is taken as the substance of the Farewell. See Albert K. Weinberg, "Washington's 'Great Rule' in Its Historical Evolution," in Eric F. Goldman (ed.), *Historiography and Urbanization* (Baltimore, 1941), 113. Marshall Smelser, in "George Washington and the Alien and Sedition Acts," *American Historical Review*, LIX (January, 1954), 326, and in "The Jacobin Phrenzy: Federalism and Liberty, Equality, and Fraternity," *Review of Politics* (Notre Dame), XIII (October, 1951), 476, and Joseph Charles, in "Hamilton and Washington: The Origins of the American Party System," *William and Mary Quarterly*, Ser. III, Vol. XII (April, 1955), 262, have placed the Farewell in its context as a political document.

[25] Bemis, "Washington's Farewell Address," *American Historical Review*, XXXIX (January, 1934), 262-63. Washington understood that basic in any nation's foreign policy was self-interest, and that at this stage of American development it was to the nation's advantage, particularly from his Federalist viewpoint, not to be bound by the French alliance. Sound though this view may be in the perspective of mid-twentieth century, in 1796 it appeared to political opponents to be a partisan political view. To Republicans, loyalty to the alliance and hostility to England appeared the best means of promoting national self-interest. Roland G. Usher, "Washington and Entangling Alliances," *North American Review* (New York), CCIV (July, 1916), 29-38; James G. Randall, "George Washington and 'Entangling Alliances'," *South Atlantic Quarterly* (Durham), XXX (July, 1931), 221-29.

[26] Wilfred E. Binkley, *American Political Parties: Their Natural Histories* (New York, 1943), 51. For a stimulating discussion of the Farewell Address which vigorously attacks the persistent myth that Washington's words constituted an inspired charter for a permanent foreign policy based on isolationism, see Louis B. Wright, "The Founding Fathers and 'Splendid Isolation'," *Huntington Library Quarterly* (San Marino), VI (February, 1943), 173-78.

[27] The quotations follow the text printed in Fitzpatrick (ed.), *Writings of Washington*, XXXV, 214-38.

[28] For a discussion of this point see Weinberg, "Washington's 'Great Rule' in Its Historical Evolution," in Goldman (ed.), *Historiography and Urbanization*, 109-38. The foreign policy ideas reflected in the Farewell were not even unique American principles; they can be found in the writings of certain eighteenth-century *philosophes*. See Felix Gilbert, "The 'New Diplomacy' of the Eighteenth Century," *World Politics* (Princeton), IV (October, 1951), 13-14, 28. For earlier expressions of the idea of non-entanglement with Europe, see the discussions relative to the congressional resolution of June 12, 1783, in Samuel F. Bemis, *The Diplomacy of the American Revolution* (New York, 1935), 166-67, and Alexander DeConde, "William Vans Murray's *Political Sketches:* A Defense of the American Experiment," *Mississippi Valley Historical Review* (Cedar Rapids), XLI (March, 1955), 637-38.

[29] Fisher Ames to Oliver Wolcott, September 26, 1796, George Gibbs (ed.), *Memoirs of the Administrations of Washington and John Adams, edited from the Papers of Oliver Wolcott, Secretary of the Treasury* (2 vols., New York, 1846), I, 384-85.

[30] [William Duane], *A Letter to George Washington, President of the United States: Containing Strictures on His Address of the Seventeenth of September, 1796, Notifying His Relinquishment of the Presidential Office*, by Jasper Dwight of Vermont [pseud.] (Philadelphia, 1796), 31, 40-45. In later years politicians and others referred to Washington's advice as an enduring guide to policy. See, for example, Henry Cabot Lodge's address of February 16, 1916, at Morristown, New Jersey, entitled, "Washington's Policies of Neutrality and National Defence," in his *War Addresses* (Boston, 1917), 117-36.

[31] John C. Hamilton, *History of the Republic of the United States of America, as Traced in the Writings of Alexander Hamilton and of His Contemporaries* (7 vols., New York,

1857-1864), VI, 536-37. Although Americans viewed the Farewell in many instances as purely a political document, this is not to deny that some men wanted a genuine neutrality which would save the United States "from the exactions and insolence of both" England and France. See, for example, James Kent to Moss Kent, September 19, 1796, William Kent (ed.), *Memoirs and Letters of James Kent* (Boston, 1898), 174.

[32] Madison to Monroe, September 29, 1796, quoted in Irving Brant, *James Madison: Father of the Constitution, 1787-1800* (Indianapolis, 1950), 442. As Washington had anticipated, opponents claimed that the motive behind the Farewell was his knowledge that if he ran he would not be re-elected. McMaster, *History of the People of the United States,* II, 290-91. Federalists were convinced that Republicans created French animosity against Washington for political reasons. See Timothy Pickering to John Quincy Adams, December 9, 1796, Pickering Papers (Massachusetts Historical Society, Boston); John Quincy Adams to John Adams, April 4, 1796, Ford (ed.), *Writings of John Quincy Adams,* I, 484. Young Adams praised the address. He wrote Washington that he hoped "it may serve as the foundation" for future American policy. Letter of February 11, 1797, *ibid.,* II, 119-20. Samuel F. Bemis, "John Quincy Adams and George Washington," Massachusetts Historical Society, *Proceedings,* LXVII (1945), 365-84, maintains that young Adams' ideas influenced Washington and the Farewell.

[33] Adet to Minister of Foreign Relations, October 12, 1796, Turner (ed.), *Correspondence of French Ministers,* 954; Bemis, "Washington's Farewell Address," *American Historical Review,* XXXIX (January, 1934), 263.

[34] Adet to Minister of Foreign Relations, September 24, 1796, Turner (ed.), *Correspondence of French Ministers,* 947-49. The Directory, of course, approved of Adet's meddling and counted on Jefferson's election. Delacroix wrote to Adet on November 2, 1796, that his despatches confirmed what the Directory had expected would result from its measures directed against Washington's government. Archives des Affaires Etrangères, Correspondance Politique, Etats-Unis, XLVI, 355-57. The British, too, had a vital stake in the election. Bond to Grenville, May 4, 1796, Henry Adams Transcripts. For a discussion of the 1796 election with emphasis on John Adams and domestic politics see Manning J. Dauer, *The Adams Federalists* (Baltimore, 1953), 92-111.

[35] Fisher Ames to Christopher Gore, December 3, 1796, Seth Ames (ed.), *Works of Fisher Ames* (2 vols., Boston, 1854), II, 206; John Adams to Abigail Adams, December 4, 1796, Adams (ed.), *Letters of John Adams to Wife,* II, 231; Oliver Wolcott to Oliver Wolcott, Sr., November 27, 1796, Gibbs (ed.), *Wolcott Papers,* I, 400-401.

[36] William Loughton Smith to Ralph Izard, November 8, 1796, in Ulrich B. Phillips (ed.), "South Carolina Federalist Correspondence, 1789-1797," *American Historical Review,* XIV (July, 1909), 785.

[37] Adet to Pickering, October 27, 1796, *American State Papers, Foreign Relations* (6 vols., Washington, 1832-1859), I, 576-77. For Pickering's response of November 1, 1796, see *ibid.,* 578; see also Pickering to Rufus King, November 14, 1796, Charles R. King (ed.), *The Life and Correspondence of Rufus King* (6 vols., New York, 1894-1900), II, 108-109.

[38] The proclamation is in Archives des Affaires Etrangères, Correspondance Politique, Etats-Unis, XLVI, 352, and is reprinted in Cobbett, *Porcupine's Works,* IV, 154-55. Adet's promulgation of the "cockade proclamation" was under orders from his home government. Adet to Minister of Foreign Relations, November 12, 1796, Turner (ed.), *Correspondence of French Ministers,* 967.

[39] Adet to Pickering, November 15, 1796, *American State Papers, Foreign Relations,* I, 579-83.

[40] Adet to Minister of Foreign Relations, [November, 1796], Turner (ed.), *Correspondence of French Ministers,* 969-70.

[41] Adams to Abigail Adams, November 27, 1796, Adams (ed.), *Letters of John Adams to Wife,* II, 229.

[42] Reprinted in Cobbett, *Porcupine's Works,* IV, 137-206.

[43] Madison to Jefferson, December 5, 1796, Madison Papers, quoted in Brant, *Madison: Father of the Constitution,* 445. See also Fisher Ames to Christopher Gore, December 13, 1796, cited in Harry M. Tinkcom, *The Republicans and Federalists in Pennsylvania, 1790-1801: A Study of National Stimulus and Local Response* (Harrisburg, 1950), 173.

[44] Liston to Grenville, November 15 and December 9, 1796, Henry Adams Transcripts. Liston complained that Republicans charged that British gold was being used in the election and confessed "that a persevering repetition of such accusations has at last the effect of procuring them a degree of credit." A prominent Republican Unitarian clergyman was surprised at how people cursed the French at this time. *The Diary of William Bentley* (4 vols., Salem, Mass., 1905-1914), II, 207 (entry of November 8, 1796).

[45] For the observation on Washington, Henrietta Liston to James Jackson, 1796, Perkins (ed.), "Diplomat's Wife in Philadelphia," *William and Mary Quarterly,* Ser. III, Vol. XI (October, 1954), 605. The quotations are from "The People," Hartford *Connecticut Courant,* reprinted in *New Hampshire and Vermont Journal: or, The Farmer's Weekly Museum* (Walpole, N. H.), November 22, 1796, and Philip Key to James McHenry, November 28, 1796, in Bernard C. Steiner, *The Life and Correspondence of James McHenry* (Cleveland, 1907), 202. Congressman Robert Goodloe Harper wrote to his constituents that if there had been no other objection to Jefferson than French exertions on his behalf it would have been sufficient to oppose him. Letter of January 5, 1797, Elizabeth Donnan (ed.), *Papers of James A. Bayard, 1796-1815* (American Historical Association, *Annual Report,* 1913, Vol. II, Washington, 1915), 25. Later, certain French officials came to believe that the activity of Adet coupled with that of his predecessors plus the seeming duplicity of the French government brought victory to the Federalists in 1796. Even Jefferson, it was pointed out, came to believe that the French sought to destroy the American Constitution. See James A. James, "French Opinion as a Factor in Preventing War between France and the United States, 1795-1800," *American Historical Review,* XXX (October, 1924), 46.

[46] Adet to Minister of Foreign Relations, [November 22, 1792], Turner (ed.), *Correspondence of French Ministers,* 972.

[47] "Americanus," in *Gazette of the United States* (Philadelphia), reprinted in New York *Herald,* December 3, 1796. William Vans Murray, commenting on a letter from James McHenry, November 19, 1796, Murray Papers, Library of Congress.

[48] John Adams to Abigail Adams, December 4, 1796, Adams (ed.), *Letters of John Adams to Wife,* II, 231. A basic charge directed against Adams was that he was too closely connected to the British party. "Cassius," in Philadelphia *New World,* October 28, 1796, cited in Woodbury, "Public Opinion in Philadelphia," *Smith College Studies in History,* V, 126.

[49] William Willcocks, "To the People of the United States," *The Minerva,* reprinted in New York *Herald,* December 28, 1796, January 18, 1797, maintained that France from the beginning had sought to involve the United States in war. Some Federalists saw in the difficulties with France the virtue that the nation might be cured "of extraneous attachments," that the embarrassing French alliance would be destroyed. Chauncey Goodrich to Oliver Wolcott, Gibbs (ed.), *Wolcott Papers,* I, 417. Republican congressman from Virginia, John Clopton, warned his constituents against Federalist "efforts to foment a prejudice in the public mind against the French nation." Clopton to Isaac Youngblood, January 24, 1797, John Clopton Papers (Duke University Library).

[50] Under the signature "Americanus," Hamilton on December 6, 1796, published "The Answer," his reply to Adet. Lodge (ed.), *Works of Hamilton,* V, 348-62. Under the signature "Americus," he published a series of articles, beginning January 27, 1797, entitled "The Warning," in which he warned against French influence and the alliance. *Ibid.,* 363-92.

[51] Webster's articles were entitled: "To the People of the United States," and ran from

December, 1796, through February, 1797. Harry R. Warfel, *Noah Webster: Schoolmaster to America* (New York, 1936), 229. The quotations are from *The Minerva*, reprinted in New York *Herald*, December 17 and 28, 1796.

[52] John Adams to Abigail Adams, December 12, 1796, in Charles F. Adams, *The Life of John Adams* (2 vols., rev. ed., Philadelphia, 1891), II, 208. The electors' ballots had been announced on the first Wednesday in January but were not counted formally until the first Wednesday in February.

[53] Adet realized before the meeting of electors that Jefferson, "in spite of the intrigues against him," would become vice-president. Although he rejoiced in Jefferson's election he understood that the Virginian was drawn to France primarily because he feared England. Even Jefferson, declared the French minister, "is an American, and as such, he cannot sincerely be our friend. An American is the born enemy of all the peoples of Europe." Adet to Minister of Foreign Relations, December 31, 1796, Turner (ed.), *Correspondence of French Ministers*, 982-83.

[54] *New Hampshire and Vermont Journal*, March 7, 1797.

[55] The son of the new president caught a glimpse of the Farewell in the future of American foreign policy. The failure of the French in their attacks against Washington in the election of 1796, he believed, should reveal to them the "temper" of the American people. "Can France possibly believe," he asked rhetorically, "that Mr. Jefferson, or any other man, would dare to start away from that system of administration which Washington has thus sanctioned, not only by his example, but by his retirement?" John Quincy Adams to Joseph Pitcairn, January 31, 1797, Ford (ed.), *Writings of John Quincy Adams*, II, 95-96.

Part III

CONTENDING FOR POWER,
1796-1801

From the retirement of Washington as President to the climactic election of Jefferson to office in 1801, party activity accelerated. Major political issues, the product of complex relations with France, captured public attention and evoked a heightened level of political participation. With the formation of party organizations in various states, party influence in both state and national elections became more apparent. Amid the extreme competition for power between Federalists and Republicans, the hope, once widespread, that the nation could exist without parties all but vanished. Instead, differences over domestic and foreign policies flared, political positions hardened, and sectional animosities in party politics multiplied.

The selections in this part center on an increased political tempo, the interweaving of foreign policy with party politics, and the culmination of party rivalry in the election of 1800. As the readings make evident, the Republican challenge reached a peak of intensity by 1800, resulting finally in the first transfer of national political power under the new government. Historian Paul Goodman in the initial article investigates the influence of the existent social structure on party participation by comparing the social background of Federalist and Republican Congressmen. Alfred Young's essay "The Mechanics and the Jeffersonians: New York, 1789-1801" stresses the political significance of the skilled workingman as a determining force in the development of the New York Republican party. The chief concern of Jacob E. Cooke in his article "Country Above Party: John Adams and the 1799 Mission to France" is the impact on the Federalist Party of Adams' resumption of diplomatic negotiations with France. Dumas Malone's "Politics and Libel, 1800" presents Jefferson's activities during the election campaign, contrasted with Federalist tactics in state politics, in the courts, and in the press. In the last selection, "Charge and Countercharge: The Election of 1800," Morton Borden dissects the involved political maneuvering which followed the election deadlock between Jefferson and Aaron Burr.

In the evolution of political attitudes, party growth gained momentum. Man—so the eighteenth century fervently believed—could and must use reason to effect good government. In actuality, however, man's passions, not a well-tempered reason, governed the political process. A reflection of the strong influence of emotions was the stark, if not diabolical view Federalist and Republican partisans held of each other. Each might base political responses or actions on the fictitious image of the opposing party conjured up in the mind. Venting their antipathies and anxieties in newspapers, pamphlets, and speeches, they created a hostile political atmosphere, deeply tinging party politics at the same time that they were providing the historian of the future with colorful examples of the overheated political mind. Political issues, easily emotionalized, inevitably became divisive; political ideology which had helped define parties now strained national unity to the point that some disgruntled groups seriously considered secession from the Union.

Americans of the period, certain that they had a unique opportunity to determine the future of their experiment in republican government, could not lightly accept the outlook of their political opponents, nor could either party be confident that its rival would not subvert republican principles once it acquired power. The determination to make the republican form of government succeed resulted in "a peculiarly volatile and crisis ridden ideology, one with little resilience, little margin for error, little tradition of success behind it, and one that was vulnerable both psychologically and historically."[1]

The election of 1796 had revealed the gradual maturing of parties. Two parties, confronting each other in the campaign, had carried their competitiveness beyond the Congressional scene into the country at large. In both the Presidential and Congressional contests the candidates had clearly been identified with a party, and even electors no longer considered themselves apart from political affiliations. At this juncture, however, neither party was highly organized. Hamilton's efforts to bypass John Adams as the Federalist Presidential candidate in favor of Thomas Pinckney was an awkward scheme, yet it signified the beginning of a rift that the Federalists would not be able to overcome. In the aftermath of the election Jefferson regarded Adams's victory as a "barrier against Hamilton's getting in."[2] Republicans likewise were not entirely united in their political support. Pennsylvania and New York party members had maneuvered to support Aaron Burr instead of Jefferson. To one Federalist, at least, it was certain that in backing Burr, Republicans only wanted "to make a Cat's paw of him."[3]

The Presidency of Adams was not merely a prologue to the election of Jefferson in 1801; in the history of party development it is notable as a period in which the Federalist Party sacrificed its unified force to fragmentation. By a margin of three electoral votes Adams eked out a victory over Jefferson, but it was a victory overshadowed by lingering hostilities and by mounting intraparty strife. Symptomatic of the stresses within the Federalist Party was the divergence between the moderates, largely agrarian-oriented, who sided with Adams and an ultra wing, the High Federalists, who coalesced around Hamilton and were prone to advocate extreme policies. With serious implications for the future of the Federalists the intense feeling between Adams and Hamilton was not allayed after the election of 1796. Rather it became a major motif of early party history. Perhaps it was fortunate for the cause of the Republicans that Jefferson did not win the election as the next four years of political opposition served to strengthen both party methods and organization. For the moment, however, the Federalists were in the saddle, booted and spurred, and were capable of riding hard against their opponents.

Although Adams was sensitive to the manifestations of these personal rivalries, he was also cognizant of the continuing import of foreign interference in American affairs. Party politics swung in a balance, inevitably affected by foreign issues and entanglements. Near the beginning of his term in office John Adams noted: "At the next election, England will set up Jay or Hamilton, and France, Jefferson, and all the corruption of Poland will be introduced unless the American spirit should rise and say we will have neither John Bull nor Louis Baboon."[4]

Party antagonisms were still inflamed in 1797 as a result of the Jay Treaty controversy, and the sharpening of French hostility toward the United States made the situation even more bitter. Each party was driven to reaffirm its ideological response to the implications of the French Revolution. For the Republicans the Revolution still symbolized the furthering of democracy; for the Federalists it only evoked the specter of the Reign of Terror. Uncompromisable opinions such as these had an inordinate influence in polarizing parties.

In the wake of Federalist agitation for a strong anti-French policy in 1797 came the notorious XYZ Affair. The revelation of the high-handed treatment of an American diplomatic mission by the French generated a wave of public resentment and nationalistic fervor which momentarily raised the Federalist Party to a crest of popularity. With the intensification of hostility to France, the High Federalist wing of the party won strong support among the moderates, who then gravitated to the Hamiltonian position of advocating war with France. Even though the party had control of Congress in the spring of 1798, a Federalist Congressional caucus decided that it was inadvisable to risk pushing a declaration of war since the majority was not sufficiently secure.

In a feverish atmosphere Federalist war measures providing for a provisional army and enlarged navy, a land tax, and a suspension of commerce with France were pushed through Congress. Federalists, determined to stifle the sources of "Jacobinism"—pro-Republican aliens and a scurrilous Republican press—rapidly passed the four Alien and Sedition Acts. The leading historian of the acts suggests that the Federalists, "wishing to eliminate political heresy, . . . decided to stamp out any criticism which had even a remote tendency to undermine the authority of their administration and lead to an 'overthrow' of their party at the polls."[5]

The party gains of one moment were quickly washed away by repercussions of the Alien and Sedition laws. Amid contention for political power, prosecutions of Republican editors for violating the libel law heartened the Federalists but gave the Republican Party a political issue of major proportions which launched the campaign of 1800.

Often viewed as "the Revolution of 1800," the election was, in the eyes of contemporaries, a contest over fundamental principles of government which would determine the future of the nation. By 1800 party lines and structure had crystallized greatly in comparison with 1796. In the opinion of William N. Chambers, the national party system only reached its full development in 1800, when it "became at once a center and an active engine of political conflict."[6] Among the many aspects of the political contest, the accelerated activity of the Republicans, the split among the Federalists, and the postelection transition to Republican control of the national government command attention.

Actually the election of 1800 consisted of a congeries of state elections over a span of months in which "thousands upon thousands of votes . . . were dictated by neighborhood feuds, local hatreds, state politics, and ethnic heritage."[7] Republican advances in such states as New Jersey, New York, and Pennsylvania were vital to the Republican victory in 1800, yet the Republican tide did not run swiftly throughout the country. Federalists might shudder as New England Republicanism spread from port towns to countryside; at best, however, it was only beginning to have strength. Improvements in party organization, active state party leaders, and effective use of propaganda were keys to Republican strides in New Jersey. In New York Burr's adroit political moves, his talent in winning support of businessmen, and his constant electioneering forged a political organization which overcame defeat in 1799 and delivered New York's electoral votes to the Republicans. Gains in Pennsylvania were in large part a result of public antipathy to the land tax, the

Alien and Sedition laws, as well as Federalist handling of the local Fries' Rebellion in 1799. Federalism was being constantly eroded.

Republican momentum alone did not bring about the Federalist defeat at the national and state levels. Inner conflicts, lack of purposefulness, and a loose political organization were important factors. Many years after the event, John Quincy Adams asserted that the Federalist schism began over the question of increasing the size of the army; actually no single factor was responsible. Personality differences between high-ranking party leaders, a diffused concept of how a party should function, and differences over foreign policy created the rift. In light of the strong support many Federalist voters gave Adams in 1800, it is not entirely clear to what extent the party lost *because* of these internal difficulties. A crucial factor was that the Federalists, in general, had not mastered the technique of party building as well as their adversaries.

In the confusion of the election, one facet of politics was overlooked. Despite the intransigence and scheming of the Federalists, desperately seeking to avoid a total loss of power, it was possible to effect a peaceful transfer of political power from one party to another. This may have occurred as one political scientist, the late Morton Grodzins, suggests because "parties were vehicles through which other moderating factors made themselves felt,"[8] but the truly significant aspect of the contest was that the election did not result in an overturn of the party system.

NOTES

[1] John Howe, Jr., "Republican Thought and the Political Violence of the 1790's," *American Quarterly,* Vol. XIX (Summer, 1967), p. 165.

[2] Thomas Jefferson to James Madison, January 1, 1797, Madison Papers, Vol. XX, Library of Congress.

[3] Benjamin Goodhue to Caleb Strong, December 24, 1796, Caleb Strong Papers, Forbes Library, Northampton, Massachusetts.

[4] John Adams to Abigail Adams, March 17, 1797, Charles Francis Adams, ed., *Letters of John Adams Addressed to His Wife* (Boston, Little and Brown, 1841), Vol. II, pp. 251-52.

[5] James M. Smith, *Freedom's Fetters: The Alien and Sedition Laws and American Civil Liberties* (Ithaca, Cornell University Press, 1956), p. 147.

[6] William Nisbet Chambers, *Political Parties in a New Nation: The American Experience, 1776-1809* (New York, Oxford University Press, 1963), p. 149.

[7] Leonard L. Richards, "John Adams and the Moderate Federalists: The Cape Fear Valley as a Test Case," *North Carolina Historical Review,* Vol. XLIII (Winter, 1966), p. 30.

[8] Morton Grodzins, "Parties and the Crisis of Succession in the United States: The Case of 1800," in *Political Parties and Political Development,* Joseph L. Palombara and Myron Weiner, eds. (Princeton, Princeton University Press, 1966), p. 317.

SOCIAL STATUS OF PARTY LEADERSHIP:

THE HOUSE OF REPRESENTATIVES, 1797-1804*

Paul Goodman

To delineate parties more clearly than in the past, political analysts are developing new techniques, making quantitative comparisons on the basis of sociological data. By utilizing this approach, Paul Goodman presents a lucid cross-sectional view of party leadership in Congress. He examines family origins, education, occupations, and other sociological elements to determine the social status of members of the House of Representatives. The Federalist and Republican parties were dissimilar in social composition, he notes, with the Federalists often having the advantage of coming from more secure social strata than the Republicans, but regional variations were sufficiently evident to preclude wide-sweeping generalizations. Goodman's investigations raise important questions for further analyses of the bases of party allegiance and cohesiveness. In The Democratic-Republicans of Massachusetts *(1964), Goodman, who is professor of history at the University of California at Davis, shows in greater detail the correlation between social and political forces in the shaping of the Republican Party in a strongly Federalist state.*

An earlier investigation of the social sources of party development in Massachusetts suggested that Jeffersonian Republicans drew their leadership and support from ambitious, upwardly mobile elements excluded from positions of power and prestige by an entrenched and privileged Federalist elite.[1] A coalition of diverse groups, Bay State Republicans spoke for those anxious to gain access to power and to participate more fully in the governance of the Commonwealth. To test more precisely and systematically the hypothesis that the social status of Federalists was

---

* Reprinted by permission from Paul Goodman, "Social Status of Party Leadership: The House of Representatives, 1797-1804," *William and Mary Quarterly*, 3d Ser., Vol. XXV (July, 1968), pp. 465-474.

higher than that of Republicans, and to determine its usefulness outside
the Bay State, a quantitative analysis of the status of party leadership
was undertaken whose findings are reported below.[2]

Between 1797 and 1804 a little over two hundred and fifty men served
in the House of Representatives. They constitute an important sample
of political leadership during the emergence of the first American party
system. By the late 1790's Congress had become sharply polarized
between Federalists and Republicans, reflecting the growth of party
rivalry at the national capitol and in the constituencies. Because most
congressmen during these years affiliated with one of the two parties
and party preference was relatively stable, this group is particularly
appropriate for study.

Some historians have suggested that age may significantly influence
political behavior. Thus Stanley Elkins and Eric McKitrick argued that
age was one of the critical differences between the supporters and opponents of the federal constitution. They contended that the "young men
of the Revolution" were less influenced by provincial attachments and
perspectives and more impressed by the desirability of centralizing political power because of experiences in national affairs during and
immediately following the Revolution.[3] Whatever the validity of this
thesis for the ratification controversy, age differences were not significant
among partisan leaders in the following decade.[4] The average age of
Federalists in the Fourth, Fifth, and Sixth Congresses was 44, 43, and
44, and of Republicans, 43, 43, and 45. National averages, however,
may obscure differences within sub-divisions of the Union, but sectional
comparisons in this case do not greatly alter the general picture. The
eight-year differences between New England Federalists and Republicans
in the Sixth Congress was unusual, for generally the age differential
within sections was narrow and showed little consistency from one Congress to the next. (See Table 1)

Far more striking differences emerged by comparing the generational
level of Republicans and Federalists. Few party leaders were foreign born
or came from families which had recently migrated to America. Congressmen of both parties came from families that had been in America
an average of 123 years. Federalist families, however, had been in
America some thirty years longer than Republican families. The sharpest
difference was in the middle states where Federalist families had arrived
an average of twenty-nine years earlier than had Republican families.
In New England the Republican families had arrived ten years earlier
than Federalist families, but Southern Federalists could trace their ances-
try back fourteen years further than Republicans. The data themselves

Table 1

AVERAGE AGE OF CONGRESSMEN, 4th-6th CONGRESSES *a*

	Federalists			Republicans		
Congress	4th	5th	6th	4th	5th	6th
Number of Congressmen	(52)	(60)	(62)	(57)	(48)	(47)
New England	42.8	44.7	46.3	45.3	43.5	54.0
Middle States	47.9	43.3	43.4	44.3	44.6	46.9
South *b*	41.7	39.7	41.9	42.0	42.8	41.2
U.S.	44.1	43.3	44.3	42.96	43.3	44.5

a Ages were calculated at the beginning of each Congress.

b The South includes Maryland, Virginia, North and South Carolina, Tennessee, Kentucky, and Georgia.

do not tell us how large a generational difference is significant. One might hypothesize that among leadership elements, older families generally enjoyed higher social status than younger families, having had more time to accumulate wealth and influence. Hence generational level may be an index of social standing. If so, Republican leadership in the middle states, where the generational gap was greatest, was less well established than Federalist leadership. But generational level is at best a crude and perhaps not entirely reliable indicator of social status. It is likely that many older families for one reason or another were less successful in achieving and sustaining high social status than others of similar or lesser longevity. (See Table 2)

Other more reliable indices support the hypothesis that the social status of Federalist leadership was higher than that of Republican leadership, except in the South. About 71 per cent of the occupations engaged in by Federalist fathers were high-ranking compared to 69 per cent for Republican fathers, a similarity owing to the large number of Southerners in the Republican sample which obscures significant differences between the parties in other sections. In the South fathers of both Federalist and Republican congressmen engaged in high-ranking occupations with somewhat greater frequency than their colleagues in other regions, 76 per cent for Federalists, 77 per cent for Republicans. In New England and the middle states Federalist fathers engaged in high-ranking occupations with much greater frequency than did Republican fathers: 68 per cent of the Federalist fathers engaged in high-ranking occupations compared to 40

Table 2
GENERATIONAL LEVEL OF CONGRESSMEN IN 1797
(AVERAGE NUMBER OF YEARS FAMILY IN AMERICA) *a*

	Federalists 56 Congressmen	*Republicans* 59 Congressmen
New England	151 years	161 years
Middle	118	89
South	120	106
U.S.	138	107

a Generational level was calculated from the year of arrival of the first generation from which the congressmen descended, according to the sources. The accuracy of genealogical data is open to a good deal of skepticism because of the inclinations of both genealogists and their subjects to gild the family tree, and because of the possibility of errors arising from the complexity and difficulties in tracing accurately. But for purposes of this analysis, it is reasonable to assume that errors and bias infect equally Federalist and Republican data, and the important thing is not absolute generational levels but the comparative generational levels of the two groups of partisans.

per cent of the Republicans; 72 per cent of the middle states Federalist fathers held high-ranking occupations compared to 33 per cent of the Republican fathers. (See Table 3)

Turning from fathers to sons, we see that differences in occupational rank persisted into the next generation. Both Federalist and Republican congressmen advanced their occupational status, but Federalists widened the gap, moving up further than their opponents. Some 88 per cent of occupations engaged in by Federalist congressmen were high-ranking, a gain of 17 per cent over their father's occupations, compared to 80 per cent high-ranking occupations for the Republicans, a gain of 11 per cent. Again intrasectional comparison shows striking differences except in the South. Among New England congressmen, 89 per cent of the Federalist occupations were high-ranking compared to 67 per cent for Republicans; and in the middle states, 83 per cent of the Federalist occupations were high-ranking in contrast to 63 per cent of the Republican occupations. Outside the South Republican congressmen moved more rapidly in advancing from the middle-ranking occupations of their fathers to high-ranking ones than did Federalists, but they had much further to go to close the gap which still remained. Republicans outside the South thus generally engaged in occupations that enjoyed less prestige than those of their political rivals. (See Table 4)

These differences in occupational ranking reflect differences in the fre-

Table 3

OCCUPATIONS OF FATHERS OF CONGRESSMEN BY
RANKING OF OCCUPATION *a*

| Occupation | Federalists (69 Occupations) | | | | Republicans (59 Occupations) | | | |
	New Eng.	Middle	South	U.S.	New Eng.	Middle	South	U.S.
High-ranking *b*	68%	72%	76%	71%	40%	33%	77%	69%
Middle-ranking *c*	32	28	24	29	60	67	23	31

a Tables 3-6 are based on all occupations held by congressmen for whom data were available, including multiple occupations for some individuals. Because of the inadequacy of occupational data and problems in interpreting and handling them, these tables are at best crude approximations of occupational status. Greater precision would be possible if we knew more about the occupational histories of the congressmen and their fathers, including the father's occupation at the time of the son's birth and the father's highest occupational attainment, and the congressmen's occupation at time of election and the highest occupation attained and longest held. Since multiple occupations were common, and since occupational status was shaped in part by the totality and succession of occupations engaged in, it might have been useful to distinguish which commanded primary commitment. An equally vexing problem encountered in Tables 3 and 4 was determining whether an occupation was high- or middle-ranking. The sources often distinguish between planters and farmers, merchants and shopkeepers, but there is no way of knowing how comparable were the criteria used for choosing one occupational description rather than another. Additional details describing an individual's wealth, style of life, and position in his community helped form an impression of whether he was high- or middle-ranking.

b In distinguishing between high-ranking and middle-ranking occupations I have followed Aronson, *Status and Kinship in the Higher Civil Service,* chaps. 3, 4. High-ranking occupations included landed gentry, merchants, ship builders, professional men, mill owners, and bankers. Professional men included judges, lawyers, doctors, teachers, and ministers.

c Middle-ranking occupations included artisans, farmers, and shopkeepers.

quency with which the two groups and their fathers engaged in certain *types* of occupations. The fathers of Federalist congressmen were more likely to have been professionals than Republican fathers, even in the South. Some 16 per cent more of the Federalist occupations were professional. The most marked differences occurred in the middle states where only 17 per cent of Republican occupations were professional compared to 44 per cent of the Federalist occupations. Commercial occupations were a bit more important among Federalist fathers, but manufacturing and the mechanical arts were slightly more important among Republican

Table 4
OCCUPATIONS OF CONGRESSMEN BY RANKING
OF OCCUPATIONS

Occupation	Federalists (162 Occupations)				Republicans (150 Occupations)			
	New Eng.	Middle	South	U.S.	New Eng.	Middle	South	U.S.
High-ranking *a*	89%	83%	92%	88%	67%	63%	94%	80%
Middle-ranking *b*	11	17	8	12	33	37	6	20

a High-ranking occupations included landed gentry, merchants, ship builders, professional men, financiers, land speculators, and iron masters.

b Middle-ranking occupations included artisans, farmers, innkeepers, teamsters, clerks, and laborers.

Table 5
OCCUPATIONS OF FATHERS OF CONGRESSMEN

Occupation	Federalists (69 Occupations)				Republicans (59 Occupations)			
	New Eng.	Middle	South	U.S.	New Eng.	Middle	South	U.S.
Professional	35%	44%	41%	39%	50%	17%	23%	23%
Commercial	35	28	12	27	0	12	29	22
Manufacturing;Mechanical arts	9	0	6	6	0	12	6	8
Agricultural	21	28	41	28	50	59	42	47

fathers. Whereas the professions were the largest source of occupations among Federalist fathers, agriculture dominated the occupations of Republican fathers: 19 per cent more Republican fathers engaged in agricultural occupations than did Federalist fathers.

Just as there was a shift from lower to higher ranking occupations between the two generations, there were shifts in the *types* of occupations

Table 6
OCCUPATIONS OF CONGRESSMEN

| Occupation | Federalists (162 Occupations) | | | | Republicans (150 Occupations) | | | |
	New Eng.	Middle	South	U.S.	New Eng.	Middle	South	U.S.
Professional	69%	54%	50%	59%	46%	37%	44%	42%
Commercial	18	22	8	16	27	28	9	17
Manufacturing; Mechanical arts	4	7	2	4	7	11	1	5
Agricultural	9	17	40	20	20	24	46	35

engaged in by the fathers and sons. Both Republican and Federalist congressmen deserted other occupations for the professions, and at about the same rate. Consequently, the occupational differential between the generations persisted with remarkable stability: 17 per cent more of the occupations engaged in by Federalist congressmen were professional than those engaged in by Republicans while 15 per cent more of the Republican occupations were agricultural. Again both groups engaged in commerce, manufacturing, and the mechanical arts with similar frequency. Occupational differences were not great in the South, but considerable in New England and the middle states. Federalist membership in the professions accounts for a good deal of their higher occupational rank.

The occupational data, however, may understate the social distance between Federalists and Republicans, since we have more information about the former than the latter—162 Federalist occupations as against 150 Republican occupations—probably because those of lower status left fewer traces.

Educational achievement is another index of social status, and the data generally support the hypothesis that the Federalists' social status was higher than that of the Republicans, except in the South. Eighteen per cent more Federalists completed college than did Republicans. More than twice the percentage of Southern Republicans completed college (25 per cent) than did Southern Federalists, but in New England 20 per cent more Federalists completed college and in the middle states 7 per cent more Federalists received degrees. From another perspective, nearly half the Federalist congressmen completed college whereas a little over a fourth

Table 7

EDUCATIONAL ACHIEVEMENT OF CONGRESSMEN

| | Federalists (128 Congressmen) | | | | Republicans (125 Congressmen) | | | |
	New Eng.	Middle	South	U. S.	New Eng.	Middle	South	U. S.
Completed College	77%	31%	11%	46%	57%	24%	25%	28%
Attended College	0	6	22	8	0	5	14	10
Primary-secondary Schooling	21	43	36	31	29	53	34	39

of the Republicans did. Republicans were thus not as well educated as Federalists. (See Table 7)

Though the data available for comparing ethnic identity are less plentiful, they suggest important differences. Persons of English extraction were dominant among the Federalists. They were also the largest element among the Republicans, but not nearly as important because Jeffersonians included significant numbers of Irish or Scotch-Irish and Germans. Fourteen per cent of the Republicans were Irish or Scotch-Irish compared to 4 per cent of the Federalists. Ethnic differences appear more striking in intraregional comparisons. In the middle states and the South, where the population was ethnically more heterogeneous than in New England, there was greater ethnic diversity among congressmen of both parties. In the middle states, 26 per cent of the Federalist congressmen identified were English and 27 per cent were non-English, but among middle states Republicans only 8 per cent were English whereas 47 per cent were non-English: both the Germans and Irish or Scotch-Irish Republicans outnumbered those of English extraction. In the South, however, 7 per cent more Republicans were of English extraction than were Federalists, though Southern Republicans included a substantial percentage of Irish and Scotch-Irish. The greater degree of ethnic diversity among Republicans is consistent with the generational differences noted above, since the non-English elements began migrating to America later than did the English. (See Table 8)

Data on religious affiliation are meager, either because a large percentage of congressmen had no denominational attachment or because such

Table 8
ETHNIC IDENTITY OF CONGRESSMEN

| | Federalists (128 Congressmen) | | | | Republicans (125 Congressmen) | | | |
	New Eng.	Middle	South	U. S.	New Eng.	Middle	South	U. S.
English	49%	26%	25%	36%	29%	8%	32%	24%
Welsh	2	3	3	2	7	5	1	3
Scottish	0	6	8	4	0	5	4	4
Irish, Scotch-Irish	4	6	3	4	7	13	15	14
Dutch	0	9	0	2	0	5	0	2
German	0	3	0	1	0	16	1	6
French	0	0	0	0	0	0	3	1
Swiss	0	0	0	0	0	3	0	1

information rarely appears in the sources. The findings must therefore be considered tentative. The combining of data indicating definite and probable religious affiliation suggests that both groups possessed denominational ties with similar frequency: 33 per cent of the Federalists and 31 per cent of the Republicans. Among both groups Episcopalians and Presbyterians appeared most frequently: 10 per cent of the Federalists were Episcopalians and 9 per cent of the Republicans, and another 10 per cent of the Federalists were Presbyterians as were 7 per cent of the Republicans. The small percentage of Federalists who were Congregationalists (6 per cent) suggests that the paucity of data may distort the picture, since New Englanders, who accounted for 45 per cent of the Federalist group, were more likely to have been church members than were congressmen from other parts of the Union and presumably were generally Congregationalists. No Federalists were Baptists, Methodists, or Lutherans, and no Republicans were Unitarians, Catholics, or German Reformed; 4 per cent of the Federalists were Quakers compared to 1 per cent of the Republicans, but 4 per cent of the Republicans were Lutheran and Dutch Reformed respectively, whereas 1 per cent of the Federalists were.

Indices of social status, such as generational level, occupational rank of fathers and sons, the type of occupations engaged in, ethnic identity, and educational achievement suggest that Republican leaders in New England and the middle states came from social strata other than those from which Federalists were drawn. Republicans came from families more recently arrived in America, they were generally less well educated, engaged in occupations of lower rank, were less likely to be professionals, and were more often members of non-English ethnic groups. But in the South the indices of social status show considerably less difference between Federalists and Republicans in contrast to conditions in the other two regions. Southern congressmen of both parties engaged in high-ranking occupations with similar frequency, as was also true of their fathers. Southern Federalists were somewhat more likely to be professionals than Southern Republicans but the latter were better educated. Finally, Southern Republicans came from families which had migrated later than Federalist families and though a greater percentage of the Republicans were of English extraction, they included a sizeable group of Irish and Scotch-Irish. These data suggest that there was no clear-cut status differential between Federalists and Republicans in the South.

Family prominence, unlike the above measures of social status, is more subjective. A congressman's family was considered "prominent" if at least during the immediately preceding generation it had achieved distinction in terms of wealth, learning, professional accomplishments, or political importance. Sixty-seven congressmen, of whom 58 per cent were Federalists and 42 per cent were Republicans, came from families considered prominent by this test. But though prominent Federalist families appeared with similar frequency in the three regions, with New England accounting for 35 per cent of the Federalist total and the middle and southern states for 30 per cent and 33 per cent respectively, 68 per cent of the prominent Republicans came from the South and the rest from the middle states.

Quantitative analysis tends to support the hypothesis that Republican leadership except in the South came from elements less well established in their communities than were their rivals. They were often upwardly mobile, as indicated by rapid movement of Republican congressmen into occupations ranking higher than those engaged in by their fathers. Federalists were also moving up, so fast that Republicans did not catch up. From a national perspective, the Republicans were a heterogeneous coalition whose New England and middle state elements were socially inferior to their important Southern leadership. These data, however, do not, and perhaps cannot, explain *why* the parties attracted leaders from different social strata outside the South, nor do they reveal why New

England and middle state Republicans made common cause with their social superiors to the South. Quantification is useful, but it cannot answer many of the most important and interesting questions about political behavior in the early republic which are concurrently being investigated by more traditional historical methods.

NOTES

[1] Paul Goodman, *The Democratic-Republicans of Massachusetts, Politics in the Young Republic* (Cambridge, Mass., 1964).

[2] The pioneering quantitative study of the social status of political elements in the early Republic is Sidney Aronson's *Status and Kinship in the Higher Civil Service* (Cambridge, Mass., 1964). Because Aronson studied appointments to federal office, his group was probably not as representative of party leadership as were congressmen, since both Adams and Jefferson attempted to choose their appointees from among the upper strata. See also David Fischer, *The Revolution of American Conservatism* (New York, 1965), appendix I. Data for this study were drawn from the *Dictionary of American Biography* (New York, 1928-1944), *The Biographical Dictionary of the American Congress* (Washington, 1928), *The National Cyclopaedia of American Biography* (New York, 1893), state and local histories, the various state historical journals, and genealogies. Because of inadequacies in the data—greater for some analytical purposes than for others—and difficulties in interpreting them, the findings are at best approximations. Quantification in this study yields neither scientific precision nor dispenses with the necessity to make numerous judgments, many of which are impressionistic.

[3] Stanley Elkins and Eric McKitrick, "The Founding Fathers: Young Men of the Revolution," *Political Science Quarterly*, LXXVI (1961), 181-216.

[4] Party identification of congressmen is based on the compilation of legislative roll call votes in Manning J. Dauer, *The Adams Federalists* (Baltimore, 1953), appendix III. I have altered the party identification of five congressmen where the data cast doubt on Dauer's designation. Thompson Skinner, listed as a Federalist, *ibid.*, 290, was a Republican. Three others designated as Federalists more often than not voted Republican: Benjamin Taliaferro, Edward Grey, and Willis Alston. Thomas Tillinghast has been shifted from the Republican to the Federalist column.

THE MECHANICS AND THE JEFFERSONIANS:
NEW YORK, 1789-1801*

Alfred F. Young

In explaining early political development, historians have given relatively little attention to the voting behavior of particular social groups. Yet Alfred Young in the study presented here reveals how important the mechanics or skilled craftsmen of New York City were in determining Federalist and Republican Party fortunes. He argues convincingly that the political alignment of the early 1790's did not fit the stereotype of rich merchant versus poor workingman. Rather it was a complex grouping of mechanics allied with the upper classes in the Federalist Party. Disenchantment with Federalist national policies and successful Republican political tactics gradually won over the mechanics to Republican allegiance. Their shift to Republicanism, in Young's assessment, was not complete by 1800 but had an eroding effect on Federalism. Obviously the Federalist concept of party did not encompass a broadly based party in which the interests of the mechanics were strongly protected. Alfred Young, a professor of history at Northern Illinois University, is the author of The Democratic Republicans of New York *(1967), a work of major importance in the history of early American parties.*

In 1789, on the eve of George Washington's inaugural, New York was a solidly Federalist town. In the Congressional election of 1789, the city chose a Federalist by a vote of 2,342 to 373; in the gubernatorial poll it voted against George Clinton, anti-Federalist Governor, 833 to 385.[1] And the mechanics of all ranks were overwhelmingly Federalist. They poured forth to celebrate Washington's inauguration just as they had marched in 1788 to celebrate ratification of the Constitution. They were active in nominating Federalists and they voted Federalist.[2]

* From Alfred F. Young, "The Mechanics and the Jeffersonians: New York, 1789-801," *Labor History*, Vol. V (Fall, 1964), pp. 247-76. Reprinted by permission of Alfred . Young and the Managing Editor, *Labor History*.

"Almost all the gentlemen as well as all the merchants and mechanics," Virginia's Senator Grayson observed in 1789, "combined together to turn [George Clinton] out" while the "honest yeomanry" alone supported him.[3] In 1790 anti-Federalists did not even go through the motions of nominating Assembly or Congressional candidates.

From 1789 to 1801 the major thrust of New York City politics was the effort of the anti-Federalists, then the Republicans, to win back the following they enjoyed in the immediate post-war years and establish a new one among the rapidly expanding electorate.[4] Of necessity this was an effort to win support among the mechanics.

For the old anti-Federalist leaders this was a formidable task. George Clinton, the party chieftain and Governor since 1777, was an Ulster county lawyer and landholder whose reputation was built on his services in the Revolution as a staunch Whig, wartime Governor and foe of Tories.[5] Anti-Federalist political support came primarily from the independent small farmers of Long Island, the west bank of the Hudson and the upper Hudson valley.[6] In New York City the small circle of Clintonian leaders, while men of lowly origins, were all successful merchants, as their homes in the fashionable part of lower Manhattan attested.[7] John Lamb, for example, was Collector of the Port, a lucrative position;[8] Marinus Willett was the county sheriff,[9] Melancton Smith was busy with various speculations, some of them in William Duer's group.[10] Henry Rutgers was born to wealth which made him one of the city's largest landlords.[11] Only one officer of the General Society of Mechanics and Tradesmen, John Stagg, their old radical Whig compatriot, acted with the Clintonians; while the only artisan in their circle,[12] Ezekial Robbins, a wealthy hatter, was not even a member of the Mechanics Society.[13] They had, in fact, better connections among merchants than mechanics.

In 1791-92 when the Livingston family defected from the Federalists to form a coalition with the old anti-Federalists, they brought with them no special strength among the mechanics. They were city merchants and lawyers, and owners of tenanted estates in the upper Hudson valley. Indeed before the Revolution, in 1768-69, the Delancey faction had been able to win over mechanics against William Livingston of the famed "whig triumvirate,"[14] and in 1774-76 the radical mechanic factions usually were at loggerheads with conservatives led by Robert R. Livingston (senior and then junior), Philip Livingston and John Jay and William Duane, related to the Livingstons by marriage.[15] The memory of Chancellor Robert R. Livingston's veto of the charter for the General Society of Mechanics in 1785 was even fresher.[16] Moreover Aaron Burr, the young lawyer sent to the United States Senate in 1791 by the Livingstons and Clinton, in 1785 was the only city Assemblyman who had voted against the charter.[17] Thus the loose coalition that became the "republican interest" as far as New York City politics went—the Clintons, the Livingstons and Burr—were in reality three factions in search of a following.

They found this following in stages in a long uphill battle. Their first victory did not come until the end of 1794 when they won the Congressional seat by a vote of about 1,850 to 1,650.[18] They did not win an Assembly election until 1797, and in the closing years of the decade all the elections were nip and tuck. In the famous "battle of 1800"—the election that determined that the state's electoral votes would be cast for the Jefferson-Burr ticket—the Republicans took the assembly by 3,050 to 2,600 and squeaked through the Congressional race 2,180 to 2,090 votes. Not until 1801 did they win a majority of the £100 freeholder electorate privileged to vote for Governor. Thus even at the end of the Federalist era, New York was not quite a safe Republican town; Federalists in defeat retained a sizable following. Analysis of the election returns leads to the conclusion that the mechanics who in 1789 were overwhelmingly Federalist, by 1800-01 were divided: most were Republican; a good number stayed Federalist. The task, then, that confronts the historian is to explain how various segments of the mechanic population left the house of Federalism in response to the successive issues of the 1790s.

I

Through most of Washington's first administration, from 1789 through 1792, the honeymoon of mechanic Federalist and merchant Federalist continued. The sources of Federalist popularity among mechanics were several. Federalists were the party of the Constitution; they also appeared as the party of the Revolution. The Tories in their camp took a back seat; Colonel Alexander Hamilton ran the party and it was not missed that John Laurence, their first Congressman, had married the daughter of the famed "Liberty Boy," Alexander McDougall.[19] Federalists were also the party of George Washington, an object of universal veneration while the city was the nation's capital in 1789-90. "Poor men love him as their own," said a character in a play by the New York dramatist, William Dunlap.[20] The fact that the city was the capital also helped; anti-Federalists complained that the Federalist "electioneering corps" included "the masons, stone cutters, the carpenters and the mortar carriers" employed in refurbishing city hall as Federal Hall.[21]

In drawing up slates at election time Federalists accommodated mechanics. In the 1789 election when mechanics and merchants each nominated an Assembly ticket, Hamilton presided over a meeting of delegates from both groups which drew up a satisfactory coalition ticket.[22] Hamilton claimed, with apparent impunity, in *Federalist* Essay Number 35 that "Mechanics and manufacturers will always be inclined with few exceptions, to give their votes to merchants, in preference to persons of their own professions and trades. Those discerning citizens are well aware that the mechanic and manufacturing arts furnish the materials of mercantile enterprise and industry."[23] But just to make sure, for years Federalists ran one or more leading mechanics, including leaders of the General Society, on their annual Assembly ticket.[24]

In their policies in the first Congress, Federalists made good on some of their promises during the ratification controversy. The city's mechanics petitioned for tariff protection at once, pointing out to their brethren that "foreign importations were highly unfavorable to mechanic improvement, nourishing a spirit of dependence, defeating in a degree the purpose of our revolution and tarnishing the luster of our character."[25] Congressman Laurence neatly balanced the interests of his constituency, pleading for higher duties on beer, candles, hemp, and cordage (manufactured by the city's artisans), for lower duties on rum, madeira, and molasses (imported by the West Indies merchants), couching the latter plea on behalf of the poor—"that part of the community who are least able to bear it."[26] Early in 1792 Congress passed another mildly protective tariff bill while the anti-Federalist position was sufficiently blurred for Hamilton to be able to claim that "this faction has never ceased to resist every protection or encouragement to arts and manufactures."[27]

Hamiltonian finance was generally supported in the city as in the state as a whole. Funding drew only a few whimpers of protest in the city; in fact it was John Stagg, the Clintonian mechanic, who helped squelch a petition that appeared among veterans on behalf of Madison's proposals for discrimination.[28] Assumption struck sparks only among the old anti-Federalist foes of "consolidation." While Hamilton's "Report on Manufactures" does not seem to have drawn any special accolades from mechanics, his overall performance as Secretary of the Treasury gave him a prestige that outlasted his party's. On his retirement in 1795 a group of building craftsmen offered to build him a house at their own expense,[29] and after his death in 1804 the General Society went into mourning for six weeks.[30]

The first sign of a serious mechanic alienation from the merchants came in 1791, when the General Society's new petition for incorporation was "treated with contemptuous neglect" by the State Assembly which in the same session granted a charter to the Bank of New York, the merchants' favorite. Some of the old mechanic consciousness, last apparent in 1785-86 when the charter was first rejected, now revived. "Mechanics," said a writer in Greenleaf's anti-Federalist organ, "those who assume the airs of 'the well born' should be made to know that the mechanics of this city have equal rights with the merchants, and that they are as important a set of men as any in the community."[31] Another man pushed the issue further:

Who will deny that a republican government is founded on democratic principles? . . . That the manufacturing interest, from its nature is, and ever will remain of the democratic denomination, none can deny. Why then incorporate large monied interests, and no democratic ones? Should we not have a wholesome check to the baneful growth of aristocratic weeds among us?[32]

In the Spring elections of 1791 the mechanics refused to go along with the merchants ticket, nominating instead a slate that included one of their officers and two leaders of the burgeoning Tammany Society. Four of their candidates won—"our motley city representatives," Robert Troup called them in his alarmed report to Hamilton.[33] And the following year the mechanics charter sailed through the legislature.

Once chartered, the society grew from about 200 members in 1792 to about 600 in 1798, most of them master craftsmen. Chartered "only for charitable purposes" as the society regretfully explained, it occasionally made small loans to its members besides acting as a benefit society.[34] And while it eschewed partisan politics, it nonetheless had the effect it anticipated of "uniting us as brethren in common interests."[35]

Mechanics expressed some of this same spirit by flocking into the Tammany Society, described confidentially by its organizer as "a political institution founded on a strong republican basis whose democratic principles will serve in some measure to correct the aristocracy of the city."[36] Founded in 1789, it had 300 members by the Fall of '91; and perhaps 200 more by 1795, among whom mechanics were the most numerous. Its first chief Sachem was William Mooney, an upholsterer and paper hanger.[37] Its leaders stressed its democratic rather than its class character. Tammany "united in one patriotic band," William Pitt Smith of the Columbia faculty exclaimed, "the opulent and the industrious—the learned and the unlearned, the dignified servant of the people and the respectable plebeian, however distinguished by sentiment or by occupation."[38] The organization was not political, and its leadership at first was predominantly Federalist. But the fact that anti-Federalists were active in Tammany and the Assemblymen elected in 1791 were Tammany figures were both omens of its political potential.[39]

The little appreciated "bank war" and "panic" of 1792 brought to a boil such disillusionment with the Federalist honeymoon as then existed.[40] After the Bank of the United States was chartered and a threat of a coalition of its New York branch with the Bank of New York loomed in 1791, there was a movement to charter a third bank led by "the disappointed in the direction of the existing banks," foremost among whom were the Livingstons.[41] While the origins of the venture were speculative, "men of all classes flocked" to subscribe to its stock, as Edward Livingston claimed in extolling its advantages to "persons of small capital" and victims of the lending "favoritism" of the Bank of New York.[42] Hamilton fought the new venture desperately; by March he knew that the "bank mania" was "made an engine to help the governor's [Clinton's] re-election."[43] In April the "prince of speculators," William Duer, Hamilton's recently resigned Assistant Secretary, collapsed, and the bubble inflated by speculation in bank stock, securities, and land burst. Duer brought down with him not only leading merchants like the Livingstons but a host of common folk from whom he had borrowed to the hilt: "shopkeepers, widows, orphans, butchers, carmen, gardeners, market women," a businessman recorded, "even the noted bawd Mrs. McCarty." All business, including that of construction, halted; and "the mechanics began to feel the effect of the failures."[44] Small wonder, then, that a mob of about 400-500 threatened Duer's life at the debtor's jail,[45] or that Republicans "made bitter use" of Hamilton's "attachment to Colonel Duer" in the elections.[46] In the gubernatorial poll of 1792 Clinton ran better than he ever had in the city, receiving 603 votes, to 729 for John Jay, or 44 per cent of the total.[47]

In the Congressional election late in 1792 William Livingston—elected previously as a Federalist Assemblyman—offered the Federalists their first national challenge. "That whore in politics," as a Hamilton's informant called him,[48] Livingston made a special appeal to the Mechanics Society for support, claiming to be responsible for their charter. He was also identified with an unsuccessful appeal to make New York City's appointive mayor elective.[49] In a cloudy campaign in which party lines were not clearly drawn, Livingston received 700 votes to 1,900 for the successful Federalist, John Watts.[50]

Through these minor political crises, the leaders of the Mechanics Society did not break with the Federalists. They turned down Livingston's plea for support; it was not only "repugnant to their objects to participate in elections," but he was "an improper person."[51] Similarly they refused to endorse Governor Clinton in 1792[52] or Melancton Smith when he successfully sneaked into the Assembly in 1791. In the Spring of 1793 several officers of the Mechanics Society, including Robert Boyd, the radical Whig blacksmith, were still on the Federalist Assembly ticket giving the party an easy victory.[53] In short, at the end of the first Washington administration, despite a smouldering discontent with Federalism in the city, mechanics of the substantial sort and mechanics as a whole had not left the house of Federalism.

II

The parting of the ways came in Washington's second term, and the precipitant was Federalist foreign policy. The French Revolution was an initial stimulus in 1793. When the French frigate *L'Embuscade* did battle with the English man of war *Boston* off Sandy Hook some nine boatloads of New Yorkers went out to cheer the French victory while on the shore fistfights broke out between "Whig" and "Tory" cartmen.[54] The arrival of Citizen Edmund Genêt prompted the first open mass meeting of the decade and a welcoming committee was formed whose secretary was White Matlack, a well-to-do brewer and iron manufacturer.[55] As a young doctor walked through the poor east side section, he heard "a dram shop full of Frenchmen singing 'Carmagnole.' The next shop I came upon some person was singing 'God Bless Great George' and which immediately procured a parcel of hearty curses upon his majesty from the rest of the company."[56]

Actually it was Britain and not France that proved the real catalyst. By early 1794, because the thin wall of Federalist tariff protection was not holding the line against the competition of British manufactures, craft groups once again dispatched petitions to Congress.[57] Then news of massive British depredations against American ships and of a British threat to renew Indian war electrified all classes; it brought the possibility of war to the state's unprotected frontier and the city's unprotected harbor. Thus Republican proposals—in Congress, Madison's old bill for discrimination against British shipping; in New York, Governor Clinton's demand to fortify the harbor and the Livingstons' strident cry for war—caught full sail the most violent wave of Anglophobia since the Revolution.[58] At a meeting sponsored by Republicans, White Matlack was the principal speaker and mechanics were so prominent that a

Federalist satirist derided the "greasy caps" in a mock epic poem. At each good point made by a speaker, he jibed:[59]

> Hats, caps and leathern aprons flew
> And puffs of wondrous size and jerkins blue

In the same flurry of patriotism the city's Democratic Society came into being: its leaders were merchants and lawyers; its members, according to one of them, "are composed of and mingle with every class of citizens"; its meetings, according to a Federalist critic, were attended by "the lowest order of mechanics, laborers, and draymen."[60]

A dramatic change in city opinion was apparent in the Spring of 1794 when the Commissioners of Fortifications, headed by Governor Clinton, called for volunteer labor to erect a fort on Governor's Island.[61] For weeks, the Republican paper reported, "hardly a day has passed . . . without a volunteer party of fifty to one hundred" putting in a day's labor.[62] A British visitor described it vividly:

> Marching two and two towards the water side . . . a procession of young tradesmen going in boats to Governor's Island to give the state a day's work . . . drums beating and fifes playing . . . with flags flying. Today the whole trade of carpenters and joiners, yesterday the body of masons; before this the grocers, school masters, coopers and barbers; next Monday all the attorneys and men concerned in the law, handle the mattock and shovel the whole day, and carry their provisions with them.[63]

And of course he could have added more: The Democratic Society, Tammany, the General Society of Mechanics, "all the true Republican carpenters," "the patriotic Republican sawyers," "the patriotic sailmakers"—so they called themselves in the papers—the journeymen hatters, cordwainers, peruke makers, hairdressers, tallow chandlers, tanners and curriers; in short, it was the Constitutional parade of 1788 all over again but under different leadership. And there was also something new: the most recent immigrants to the city styling themselves "Irish laborers," "English Republicans," and the "patriotic natives of Great Britain and Ireland."[64]

The Republicans reaped a political harvest quickly. Early in April 1794, Chancellor Robert R. Livingston advised his younger brother, Edward, not to run again for the Assembly. "The mechanics and cartmen" were Federalist: "I find no class of people on which you can depend."[65] A few weeks later in elections held after the work on the fort had just begun, Federalists won but the Republican vote unexpectedly zoomed from a high of 500 in 1793 to a range of 1,200 to 1,400.[66] Then in the Congressional poll of December 1794-January 1795 Edward Livingston risked a race against John Watts, the Federalist incumbent. A lawyer and city resident, a member of the aristocratic Hudson Valley family known as "Beau Ned" (the young dandy),[67] he was presented to the voters as "the poor man's friend," a "good Whig," and "a good Republican and true friend of the French." Watts was described as a "Tory," "a paper man," "an opulent merchant" and "a friend to British measures."[68] The year before, when Livingston ran for the Assembly, he received 214 votes; he now won 1,843 to 1,638.[69]

In this changing climate the General Society of Mechanics and Tradesmen shifted perceptibly. John Stagg, the Clintonian and radical Whig, was returned as President; later he presided at the public meeting at which Livingston was nominated.[70] At its Fourth of July dinner in 1794, the society toasted "the republican societies of the City of New York"; the following year it accepted an invitation from the Democratic Society for a joint celebration of Independence Day with them, Tammany and the Coopers Society. A committee worked out the details of an observance that was repeated every year thereafter: a parade to a church (militia officers seated in front of the pulpit, the mechanics to the right of the center aisle, the Democrats to the left, Tammany and the Coopers off to either side aisle), a ceremony consisting of the reading of the Declaration of Independence followed by a patriotic oration by a Republican leader.[71] The typical mechanic could now be portrayed in Republican hues: he was, according to a writer in the Republican paper, a hard working man who eschewed high living, opposed the "haughty well born," saved to buy a lot in the suburbs for his old age, and enjoyed a family gathering at home where his children beat time to "Yankee Doodle" and "Carmagnole."[72]

Thus, the first Republican breakthrough came in a revival of "The Spirit of 76." Over the next few years Republicans had great difficulty transferring this new strength, which came on a national issue, to state elections.[73] They were also unable to sustain mechanic Republicanism on national questions, as the vicissitudes of the Jay Treaty fight of 1795-96 illustrated. A "town meeting" protesting the treaty was attended by from 5,000 to 7,000 people. It was held at the noon lunch hour when, according to an irate Federalist, "our demagogues always fix their meetings in order to take in all mechanics and laborers—over whom they alone have influence."[74] The poorer workers were especially noticeable:

cartmen with their horses, "the hodmen, and the ash men and the clam men," as were recent immigrants—Scotsmen, Irish, English and French.[75] When the vote was taken to damn the Treaty, according to one contemporary, "there was not a wholecoat" among them. The Livingstons were "supported by a few of the principal citizens, the rest being made up of men of the lower class." Others claimed, however, that the leaders did not have "a majority of the lower class," or that several hundred sided with Hamilton.[76] By the Spring of 1796, after Washington signed the Treaty and Republicans in the House threatened to hold up its enforcement, anti-Treaty sentiment faded. Playing on the fear of war and threatening economic coercion, Federalists were able to collect some 3,200 signatures on a pro-Treaty petition.[77] Republicans by contrast turned out less than half of the previous year's opponents at a public rally, one-third of whom, a Federalist charged, "as is usually the case were negroes, sweeps, boys, Frenchmen, and curious people." The "merchants and traders," he insisted, and "the substantial mechanics" backed the Treaty.[78]

The claim was probably justified. In the Congressional election at the end of 1796 James Watson, a wealthy merchant, received the Federalist nomination after four others had turned it down because, in Hamilton's words, "he had gotten a strong hold of most of the leading mechanics who act with us."[79] Edward Livingston recovered his lost ground to win a second term by a safe margin of 2,362 to 1,812 votes. But his vote, a contemporary accurately put it, came from wards "chiefly inhabited by the middling and poorer classes of the people."[80] Thus at the end of the second Washington administration the city's working population was split: the Federalists retained a good section of the "substantial mechanics" while the Republicans had the "middling and poorer classes" in an unstable constituency.

III

Republicans did not consolidate this foothold until they mastered the art of exploiting the class antagonisms of the poor, threats to the economic interests of particular crafts, and the aspirations of new immigrants.

Poverty in New York went hand in hand with population growth and economic progress.[81] The city, the worldly-wise LaRochefoucauld observed in 1796, "like all great towns contains at once more riches and more wretchedness than towns less populous and commercial."[82] A petition from one group of workers pointed out that "house rent, fuel, provisions and prices of everything necessary for the support of a family have been rising." In the winter of 1796-97 some 600 unemployed journeymen petitioned for public assistance because many "by reasons of large families" were "in want of sufficient fire and wood."[83] For newcomers housing was the worst problem. The upper-east side near the shore—the seventh ward—was the city's worst slum. As a doctor described it, it had "narrow, crooked, flat, unpaved, muddy alleys" filled with swamps, stagnant water, "little decayed wooden huts," some inhabited by several families; all was wafted by an intolerable stench from garbage piled in the streets, putrefying excrement at the docks and a tan yard in their midst.[84] Understandably, when a yellow-fever epidemic claimed 700 lives in the summer of 1795, it was here that the toll was heaviest.[85]

Discontent bred of such conditions was ready for political exploitation. By 1795 there were 900 more voters in the £100 electorate for a total of 2,100 but there were 2,300 more 40 shilling renters, or a total of 5,000. Moreover, the poorer voters were concentrated in the newly-built parts of town, the fifth and especially the seventh wards along the East River, and the fourth and especially the sixth to the west along the North (or Hudson) River. In the seventh, known as the "cartman's ward," there were 870 40-shilling voters to 311 £100 voters; in the sixth the proportion was 1,298 to 223. Here was the Republican potential.[86]

The pent-up class feeling erupted in the election of the Spring of '96 which, as Hamilton put it, "in view of the common people . . . was a question between the rich and the poor because of the 'vile affair of whipping Burke and McCredy'."[87] Thomas Burk and Timothy Crady—Federalists could not get their names straight—were ferrymen, recent Irish immigrants who got into an altercation with Gabriel Furman, an arrogant Federalist alderman of the wealthy first ward. Accused of the crime of "insulting an alderman" they were tried without due process before a court of three aldermen and a Federalist Mayor intent upon making an example of the "impudent rascals," and were sentenced to two months in jail (Burk got twenty lashes as well).

William Keteltas, a young Republican lawyer, took this case of the "oppression of the innocent poor" to the State Assembly, demanding impeachment of the city official.[88] After a Federalist committee exonerated them and Keteltas turned his guns on the Assembly, he was called before the Bar of the House and asked to apologize. He refused and was found guilty of contempt, whereupon the tumultuous crowd that had jammed the Assembly carried him off to jail in a handsome arm chair midst cries of "The Spirit of '76." An issue of class justice had been transformed into one of free speech. After a month of agitation from "the iron gate," Keteltas was released and escorted home by a cheering crowd. That was a Tuesday; on Friday Republicans nominated him as one of their twelve Assembly candidates. When Federalists mocked the "ragamuffins" who paraded for Keteltas, Republicans claimed them as "the men by whose mechanical labours the necessaries and conveniences of life are produced in abundance"; it was "such men as these [who] were the triumphant victors at Breed's Hill, at Saratoga, at Yorktown." The Federalists won, but the Republican slate hit its highest peak thus far.[89]

In the September 1796 municipal elections Republicans for the first time capitalized on local issues. The Common Council was in the hands of conservative Federalist merchants elected by a tiny handful of voters.[90] Republicans railed at the Mayor and Council for dispensing arbitrary justice, failing to curb forestalling in the markets, neglecting to keep the streets clean, and increasing expenditures and taxes. They elected two men, both of whom were disqualified on technicalities, then re-elected one of them, Jacob Delamontagnie, a secretary of the Democratic Society, by an even wider margin.[91]

Early in 1797 Republicans took up the cause of a single craft, the seventy-five members of the Association of Tallow Chandlers and Soap Makers, whose factories the state legislature ordered removed from the city proper to the outskirts of towns—on the grounds that their fumes were a cause of epidemic. The chandlers petitioned the Assembly. The Republican Brockholst Livingston became their counsel, and at their request Dr. Samuel Latham Mitchill, the Columbia scientist and Tammany orator, prepared a pamphlet-length treatise exonerating the chandlers' "pestilential vapors," blaming the fever on "septic acid vapors," his favorite theory.[92] The chandler issue boiled through March; in April the Republicans nominated Mitchill for the Assembly on a slate that included a tanner, a hatter, a sailmaker, and the two aldermen elected in the wake of the Keteltas affair. Federalists capitulated, endorsing half the Republican ticket, an unheard of event, and Republicans won their first Assembly election of the decade, their vote ranging between 1,600 and 2,100 to a scant 600 to 700 for the Federalists.[93] In 1800 Dr. Mitchill, the tallow chandlers' hero, was the successful Republican candidate to replace Edward Livingston in Congress.

Republicans also won over another group, the cartmen. Numbering more than 1,000 by 1800, they were known for their "quick tempers" and "mistreating their horses." Normally they chafed under the regulations of the city fathers.[94] In the ferryman affair a doggerel verse on

broadside reminded the cartmen of their own trouble with Major Richard
Varick:[95]

> He often sits upon a bench
> Much like unto a judge, sir.
> And makes the wretches bosom wrench
> To whom he owes a grudge, sir.
>
> But now he does a great offense
> It is no thing to mock at
> He takes away the cartmen's pence
> And puts them in his pocket.

By 1798 the cartmen were Republican enough for the Federalists to gerry-
mander the outlying seventh ward ("the cartmen's ward") out of the
city into the Westchester Congressional district. In the 1799 Assembly
elections Federalist merchants stood at the polls and "used all their influence with the cartmen" with some success.[96] The next year "Independent Cartman" appealed to his brethren not to submit again to such
merchant pressure: who will do the work if not us? "Will their puny
clerks carry the burdens which we do?"[97] The cartmen resisted and as
a result there were only eighteen cartmen in the crowd when Hamilton,
in 1801, appeared at a meeting of cartmen and appealed to "my dear
fellow citizens."[98]

From the mid-'90s on, Republicans also spoke in clear tones to the
city's new immigrants. Federalists were not without experience in dealing
with nationality groups politically.[99] But to the French, Scots, English,
and especially the Irish recent arrivals who ran up the cost of charity
at the alms house, hated England and allegedly brought in yellow fever,
Federalists were cool or hostile.[100] Republicans, by contrast, formed the
"Society for the Assistance of Persons Emigrating from Foreign
Countries." They turned out en masse to welcome Joseph Priestley and
in their press, Irish and Scots could read reports of struggles for liberty
in their native lands.[101] Congressman Livingston, during the xenophobia
of 1798 to 1800, eloquently opposed the Alien Law, even introducing
a petition from Irish aliens of New York, and in the Assembly Aaron
Burr fought the proposed constitutional amendment to bar Federal office
to naturalized citizens.[102] The political fruits fell accordingly. "The poor
Irish and French," one Federalist was convinced, were enough to carry
the sixth and seventh wards for Jefferson in 1800.[103]

IV

In the closing years of the decade Republicans also picked up some of the issues that from the 1780s on had been of concern to master mechanics. For one, they committed themselves to tariff protection. In the General Society a committee headed by the Republican sailmaker, George Warner, drafted a letter lamenting the growth of foreign importations; they were "an influence highly unfavorable to mechanical improvement, nourishing a spirit of dependence, defeating in a degree the purpose of our Revolution, and tarnishing the luster of our national character"—the very language was that used by Federalist mechanics in 1789.[104] In 1801 a mass meeting of "the mechanics and manufacturers of New York City" sent a memorial to Congress beseeching the "protecting hand of government."[105] As the reign of Jefferson approached, "A Song for Hatters" expressed the expectations of other artisans:[106]

Before the bad English Treaty,
Which Jay with that nation has made
For work we need make no entreaty
All Jours were employed at their trade.

Philadelphia she then had a hundred
New York she had fifty and more
In the first scarce the half can be numbered
In the last there is hardly a score. . . .

And what has occasion'd this failing,
And caus'd us to fall at this rate
'Tis the English, whose arts are prevailing
With our Great rulers of state. . . .

When shortly in our constitution
A Republican party will sway
Let us all then throw in a petition
Our grievance to do away. . . .

That our party in Congress may now rule
Let each voter for liberty stir
And not be to England a base tool
When Jefferson aids us and Burr.

Republicans again took up the cause of freer banking facilities. But where the Livingstons' frontal assault of 1792 failed, Aaron Burr in 1799 managed the camouflaged Bank of Manhattan through the legislature with finesse.[107] While the new bank was primarily of concern to aspiring merchants, it is symptomatic of the mechanic interest in credit that some two dozen members of the Mechanics Society were among the charter stock subscribers.[108] The new bank, Republicans boasted, broke the "banking monopoly" and struck a blow at usury, an object of special contempt to many working class patrons of the city's money lenders.[109]

From 1797 on, Republicans also committed themselves clearly to direct representation of master mechanics on their Assembly tickets. In 1798 they repeated their success of the previous year by running four artisans on their ticket; in 1799 they ran six new ones. Even the famous all-star slate Aaron Burr assembled for the battle of 1800 had a place on it for George Warner, sailmaker, Ezekial Robbins, hatter, and Phillip Arcularius, tanner.[110]

The inroads Republicans made among mechanics of all types was confirmed by Federalist tactics from 1798-1801. For a while during the "half war" with France and the "reign of terror," Federalists basked in a glow of X.Y.Z. patriotism as some mechanics turned against the Republicans—now the so-called "French party"—just as they had deserted the Federalists in 1794-95 as the British party. It was almost a second honeymoon of mechanic and merchant as the Mechanics Society toasted "Millions for defense, not one cent for tribute," Tammany substituted "Yankee Doodle" for "The Marseillaise," and mechanics paraded en masse in Washington's funeral cortege. But the Federalist attitude to Republican mechanics was by this time fatally ambivalent. Besides threatening mechanics with the loss of their jobs, they beat the nativist drums, challenging naturalized aliens at the polls and attempted to suppress the city's two Republican papers. At election time when they sought to woo mechanics, Republicans warned about "the avowed despisers of mechanics who may for a few days intermingle with honest men in order to deceive them."[111] Federalists also voted the poor from the alms house and courted free Negroes with promises of office holding and "enormous supplies of home crackers and cheese."[112] And in the election of 1800 when Hamilton was unable to induce men of "weight and influence" to run, he arranged an Assembly slate filled with unknown artisans: a ship chandler, a baker, a bookseller, a potter, a shoemaker, a leather inspector, and spoiled the image only by including Gabriel Furman "the man who whipped the ferrymen."[113] Federalist tactics thus can only be described as desperate and to no avail. Mechanic interest was unsurpassed

TABLE NO. 3

THE NEW YORK CITY ELECTIONS OF 1800 AND 1801

| | 1800 | | | | 1801 | | | |
| | Assembly | | Senate | | Assembly | | Governor | |
Ward	Rep.	Fed.	Rep.	Fed.	Rep.	Fed.	Rep.	Fed.
1	172	245	47	130	208	222	82	145
2	200	434	74	213	217	375	112	209
3	250	438	75	185	284	365	104	194
4	412	330	124	179	426	274	145	162
5	458	370	139	147	545	313	170	148
6	814	363	187	108	919	267	289	89
7	786	485	231	164	1052	353	364	145
Total Vote	3092	2665	877	1126	3651	2169	1266	1090

Sources: for 1800, *American Citizen*, May 5, 1800; for 1801, *Republican Watch-Tower*, May 6, 1801.

in the voting in the Spring of 1800: "All business was suspended, even the workmen deserted the houses they were building";[114] yet Federalists lost the city.

The election returns for 1800 and 1801 indicate that the mechanics were preponderantly Republican yet were divided in their allegiances. The fact that there were two categories of voters—the £100 freeholders alone qualified to vote for Senators and Governor, and the 40 shilling renters allowed to vote only for Assemblymen—enables us to differentiate roughly the voting patterns of the various strata of mechanics. (see Table 3) First, about two thirds of the Republican vote—in 1800, about 2,200 of 3,100 votes; in 1801, 2,400 of 3,600 votes—came from the Assembly voters, the 40 shillings renters who in effect were the poorer mechanics, the cartmen, petty tradesmen and journeymen. Secondly, about one half of the total Federalist vote came from this same group—in 1800, 1,300 of their 2,600 votes; in 1801, 1,100 of 2,150 votes. Thirdly, Republicans also had significant support among the £100 freeholders who included the master craftsmen—43 per cent or 876 voters in 1800, 54 per cent or 1,266 voters in 1801. As a Republican editor proudly pointed out, this refuted the Federalist contention that Jefferson and Burr were supported only by "persons of no property."[115]

Analysis of the returns by wards confirms this political division among both prosperous and poorer mechanics. In the sixth and seventh wards with the greatest proportion of poor voters and recent immigrants, where Republicans made their greatest effort to get out the vote,[116] they received more than half of their total city vote in 1800 and 1801. Yet Federalists also had a following here, 800 voters in 1800, reduced to 600 the following year. By contrast, the second and third wards at the bottom of Manhattan, the centers of the fashionable wealthy merchant residences,[117] through the entire decade gave the Federalists almost a two to one margin. The fourth and fifth wards, the midtown on both the west and east side, which were probably the most "middling" in the city, divided about evenly between the two parties. In 1802 Republicans confirmed the class basis of their support in the poorer wards when they divided the city into two Congressional districts. They created their own safe district by placing the sixth and seventh wards in together with the fourth, giving the first, second, third and fifth wards to the Federalists in a district which also included Brooklyn and Richmond. Federalists did not even run a candidate in the Republican district, while Republicans ran one in the Federalist area with "no hopes of success."[118]

By 1800-01 Republican support among mechanics, it is reasonable to hypothesize, came from: 1.) master craftsmen and journeymen in many trades, especially the less prosperous ones; 2.) craftsmen as a whole in trades whose interests Republicans espoused, such as tallow chandlers and shoemakers; 3.) craftsmen in those trades most in need of protection from British manufacturers such as hatters and tanners; 4.) cartmen as a whole; 5.) newer immigrants, especially the Irish,[119] French [120] and to a lesser extent the Scots,[121] and English, 6.) mechanics who had been patriots in the Revolution and responded to the revival of the "Spirit of '76."

The numerically smaller following of the Federalists may well have come from 1.) the more "substantial mechanics" in many trades to whom Hamilton's appeal for the Federalists—as the party that brought "unexampled prosperity"—was meaningful;[122] 2.) craftsmen least in need of protection, such as the building trades; 3.) poorer tradesmen most closely dependent on and most easily influenced by merchants, such as the service trades; 4.) American-born mechanics and New England migrants who felt their status threatened by the influx of "foreigners";[123] 5.) new immigrants, anxious to differentiate themselves from their radical countrymen, especially the English;[124] and 6.) mechanics of a loyalist or neutralist background who were made uneasy by the revival of anti-Toryism.

V

The New York Republicans, it should be clear, did not become a labor party. The Clintons, Livingstons and Burrites, and other merchants, land-holders, lawyers and office holders ruled the party. Moreover, they had the support of a substantial segment of the merchant community, although not the men at the apex of economic power in the city.[125] Nor did the mechanics become even an organized wing of the party, bargaining for nominations as they had with the Federalists early in the decade. Republi-cans always found a place for a few mechanics on their twelve-man Assembly slate and for many others on their electioneering committees. Mechanics were members, though not leaders, of the Democratic Society and leaders as well as members of the Tammany Society. George Warner, sailmaker, or Matthew Davis, printer,[126] were speakers at the annual Republican celebration of Independence Day; James Cheetham a former hatter,[127] was influential as an editor and pamphleteer; and early in the 1800s a number of tanners were active enough to win a reputation as the "tannery yard clique" and "the swamp clique." But there was no assertive workingmen's faction among the Republicans as there would be in the Jacksonian era.[128] And mechanic support was as much the prod-uct of the courting by Republican politicians as it was of the demands of the labor movement.

Nor were Republicans put to the severe test of choosing between wage workers and master craftsmen in labor disputes. Republicans, it is appar-ent, were sympathetic to the craft organizations. They celebrated the Fourth with the Mechanics and Coopers Societies, pleaded the cause of the Association of Tallow Chandlers, and opposed the use of prison labor to manufacture shoes, an issue close to the hearts of cordwainers.[129] While there were a few strikes late in the decade, there was no trial of "a combination of labor" as "a criminal conspiracy" until 1809-10.[130]

Nonetheless Republican thought was unmistakably shaped by the par-ty's mechanic constituency. There was, to be sure, a tinge of agrarianism to some Republicans: a glorification of the yeomanry among the upstate anti-Federalist leaders; an idealization of the rural virtues in the aristocrat-ic landholder Robert R. Livingston[131] (who signed his newspaper articles "Cato"); a contempt for the hateful city in the poet-editor, Philip Freneau.[132] But, understandably, Chancellor Livingston, who fearfully vetoed the Mechanics Society charter in 1785, praised the aggressive tal-low chandlers in 1797 as "those respectable and useful citizens."[133] By the late 1790s, when Republican writers analyzed the political alignment of social classes, they found a place for mechanics in the Republican coalition. The concept might be that "farmers and mechanics & co" were the "laborers, men who produce by their industry something to the common stock of commodity" opposed by the unproductive classes,[134] or it might be that "farmers, merchants, mechanics and common laboring men" have a "common interest" against "the great landholders and monied men."[135] The General Society of Mechanics and Tradesmen, for its part, found a place for a picture of a plowman on its membership certificate side by side with a house carpenter and a shipwright, all beneath a slogan "By Hammer and Hand All Arts Do Stand."[136]

Perhaps the New York Republican leaders, who were neither agrarian-minded nor commercial-minded in the strict sense, will be best understood as spokesmen for productive capital. Three of the four merchant presidents of the Democratic Society, for example, invested in such productive ventures as a linen factory, a thread factory, a mine and spermaceti candle works.[137] Chancellor Livingston, who is well known for promoting the steamboat, also experimented with manufacturing paper and reducing friction in millstones. "Mechanicks is my hobby horse," he told Joseph Priestley.[138] He was the President and Samuel L. Mitchill the Secretary of the Society for the Promotion of Argiculture Arts and Manufactures. Mitchill was also a pioneer in industrial chemistry, and sympathized with the goal of protection for American manufactures. He congratulated Hamilton on his "Report on Manufactures" in 1792; as Republican chairman of the House Committee on Commerce and Manufactures, in 1804 he sponsored a tariff program.[139]

New York Republicans also took up the social reforms favored by their mechanic constituents. Tammany, for example, at one dinner toasted in succession "The speedy abolition" of slavery, "a happy melioration of our penal laws" and "the establishment of public schools."[140] William Keteltas, the hero of the ferrymen's *cause célèbre*—when incarcerated in the debtor's prison—edited a paper, *Prisoner of Hope,* which pleaded the debtor's plight.[141] Edward Livingston, in his first term in Congress, began the reform of the criminal code, a subject that would become a life-long concern.[142] Contrary to the contention of some historians, Republicans also lent active support to abolition.[143] Reform was bipartisan and several measures came to fruition when John Hay was Governor, but the urban Republicans imparted a warm humanitarianism to a frosty anti-Federalism and a crusading egalitarian flavor to the genteel philanthropic humanitarianism of the city's merchants and ministers.

Equally important Republican orators instilled the environmentalist concepts of the enlightenment that justified a permanent program of reform.[144]

Neither mechanics nor Republicans made much of an issue of political reform, especially during George Clinton's long tenure as Governor from 1777-95. The restrictive suffrage provisions in the state constitution and its unique Council of Appointment and Council of Revision were occasionally discussed but not widely protested.[145] Typically, when Tunis Wortman examined the question of abolishing the property qualification to vote, in his political treatise of 1800, the city's leading democratic theorist contented himself with summarizing the pros and cons and ended by saying the question was "not decided."[146] In 1801, when Republicans sponsored the first constitutional revision convention, they permitted universal male suffrage in the election of delegates, but restricted the convention itself to reforming the Council of Appointment.[147]

After 1801, their mechanic constituency cautiously beckoned the Republicans towards reform on the municipal level where only freeholders of £20 or more were permitted to vote for aldermen and the Mayor was appointed. For a while Republicans were content to broaden suffrage in their own way. Wortman as county clerk was observed "running to the poll with the books of the Mayor's court under his arm, and with a troop of ragged aliens at his tail." He was also one of the organizers of "faggot voting," a process by which a group of propertyless Republicans were qualified to vote by the joint temporary purchase of a piece of real estate.[148] When the courts ruled out faggot voting, Republicans demanded that the voting qualifications be lowered at least to the 40 shilling leasehold requirement in Assembly elections; they also asked for the elimination of plural voting and voice voting and for the popular election of the Mayor.[149] By 1804 they won all but the last of these demands.[150]

It might be argued that Republicans did more within the framework of the existing political institutions to provide a greater place for mechanics. Like the old anti-Federalists, Republicans were generally distrustful of the wealthy. Unlike the anti-Federalists, who had confidence only in the yeomanry, Republicans included a role for mechanics among the *Means for the Preservation of Political Liberty*, as George Warner entitled his oration. The trouble, as this sailmaker put it, was that "tradesmen, mechanics, and the industrious classes of society consider themselves of too little consequence to the body politic."[151] Republicans defended the right of mechanics to scrutinize political affairs in "self-created" societies and to instruct their representatives at "town meetings." When Federalists mocked such pretensions, Republicans delighted in taunting them with their own epithets, signing their newspaper articles "one of the swinish multitude" or "only a mechanic and one of the rabble." Republicans also upheld the election of mechanics to public office against Federalist scoffers who "despise mechanics because they have not snored through four years at Princeton."[152]

The mechanic vote and viewpoint guaranteed that Republicans, in their political philosophy, would abandon the old anti-Federalist suspicion of the Constitution. For converts from Federalism like the Livingstons there was never any problem. Other Republicans straddled the constitutional question: Keteltas said he was "neither a Federal nor anti-Federal."[153] Wortman, however, was tempted to revert to the old anti-Federalist view, and to indict the Federalists of '98. He began to collect materials for a book that would expose "the secret convention of 1787 and its members . . . , [and the] intrigues and artifices made use of, for the purpose of compelling the adoption of the constitution." But the book that appeared in 1800—Wortman's *Treatise Concerning Political Inquiry and the Liberty of the Press*—was a libertarian disquisition devoted to the Constitution and Bill of Rights.[154] Republicans could hardly have done otherwise, for their mechanic supporters were men who had paraded for the Constitution in 1788 or had since migrated to the new democracy in order to seek its blessings. To George Warner, the sailmaker and soldier, "the same American spirit which animated to the contest the heroes of the Revolution" prevailed in directing the national convention of '87 to the constitutional establishment of the liberty we at this day enjoy."[155] Thus the city's Republicans, like the mechanics, were both nationalistic and democratic in their outlook.

And now to return to the question posed in the introduction as to the character and continuity of the political conflict between the years 1774 and 1801. Beyond any question, in the 1790s the mechanics were important in New York City politics. Charles Beard's observation that "neither the Republicans nor the Federalists seem to have paid much attention to capturing the vote of the mechanics" was based on inadequate evidence. In the effort to construct the party conflict as one of "agrarianism" vs. "capitalism," Beard did not allow a sufficient place for the mechanics to whom even Jefferson referrred sympathetically as "the yeomanry of the city."[156] Carl Becker's projection of the conflict of the 1760s into 1790s was misleading in another way. The implication of the continuity of mechanic allegiances—radical Whig to anti-Federalist to Jeffersonian—is insupportable. Mechanics who clearly were Federalist in

1788 remained safely Federalist until 1794 and the substantial mechanics a good deal longer, many of them through 1801 and beyond. Mechanics did not always behave as one unified class in politics. Nor can the Republicans be understood as a mechanic party if that was Becker's implication. And yet Becker's thesis remains attractive. There was an intense struggle in New York City in the 1790s for "who shall rule at home," and if not strictly a class conflict, within it were the elements of a clash between "the privileged and the unprivileged" involving the mechanics as Becker suggested. The plot, dialogue and even character types of the 1790s bear a striking resemblance to the drama of the pre-Revolutionary era. Once again the battle cry that stirred the mechanics was British policy, the cause was American Independence, and the ideology was patriotism or "the Spirit of '76." Other insistent mechanic demands thread through the last three decades of the century: for democratic participation, for social recognition, for protection for American manufactures. The new leaders of the 1790s, the Livingstons, resumed something of their pre-war position as aristocratic republicans at the head of the "popular party." The new mechanics' hero of the late 1790s, William Keteltas, was Alexander McDougall of 1769 all over again, a second "John Wilkes of America." The methods, too, were similar: the town meetings, the popular political societies, the churning printing presses. The symbolism of the July Fourth celebration perhaps completes the picture. Thus Jeffersonian Republicans of New York City, with due allowance for the rhetoric of politics, could claim that they were heirs to the "Spirit of '76" and that the "revolution of 1800" was indeed the consummation of the Revolution of 1776.

NOTES

[1] *Greenleaf's New York Journal and Patriotic Register,* Apr. 9, 1789 (hereafter cited as *New York Journal*); [New York] *Daily Advertiser,* Apr. 27, 1789.

[2] In 1788 Federalist legislative and convention candidates were endorsed at meetings of master carpenters, and at a meeting of "the respectable mechanics and tradesmen," *Daily Advertiser,* Apr. 24, 28, 29, 1788.

[3] William Grayson to Patrick Henry, June 12, 1789, W. W. Henry, ed., *Life, Correspondence and Speeches of Patrick Henry* (3 vols., New York, 1891), III, pp. 389-95.

[4] For a brief survey, Sidney Pomerantz, *New York, an American City, 1783-1803* (Columbia University Studies in History, Economics and Public Law, No. 442, New York, 1938), chs. 2, 3.

[5] E. Wilder Spaulding, *His Excellency George Clinton, Critic of the Constitution* (New York, 1938), chs. 7-12.

[6] E. Wilder Spaulding, *New York in the Critical Period, 1783-1789* (New York, 1932), chs. 5, 12. Forrest McDonald, *We The People. The Economic Origins of the Constitution* (Chicago, 1958), pp. 283-300.

[7] For the leaders see "Minutes of the Republican Society" (1788), John Lamb Papers, N. Y. Hist. Soc. and Box 5 of Lamb Papers, *passim*.

[8] Isaac Q. Leake, *Memoirs of the Life and Times of General John Lamb* (Albany, 1850), pp. 296-98, 351-55; *American State Papers, Miscellany*, I, pp. 57-58, 60-62, for Lamb's income as collector.

[9] Daniel E. Wager, *Col. Marinus Willet: The Hero of the Mohawk Valley* (Utica, 1891), pp. 45-47.

[10] Robin Brooks, "Melancton Smith, New York Anti-Federalist, 1744-1798" (unpub. doctoral diss., University of Rochester, 1964), ch. 2.

[11] L. Ethan Ellis, "Henry Rutgers," *Dictionary of American Biography*, VIII, pp. 255-56; "Tax Lists or Assessments on the Real and Personal Property" (New York City, June, 1796), Ms, N.Y. Hist. Soc., in particular for the seventh ward.

[12] See Roger Champagne, "The Sons of Liberty and the Aristocracy in New York Politics, 1765-1790" (unpub. doctoral diss., University of Wisconsin, 1960), p. 481. For Stagg on Clinton's election committee, *New York Journal*, Apr. 2, 1789.

[13] "Minutes of the General Society of Mechanics and Tradesmen," Dec. 1, 1794, Dec. 23, 1795 (typescript at the office of the Society, New York City); for his house see James Wilson, *Memorial History of the City of New York* (4 vols., New York, 1891-93), III, pp. 150-52.

[14] Roger Champagne, "Family Politics versus Constitutional Principles: The New York Assembly Elections of 1768 and 1769," *William and Mary Quart.*, 3rd ser., XX (1963), 57-79; Milton Klein, "William Livingston: American Whig" (unpub. doctoral diss., Columbia University, 1954), chs. 13, 15.

[15] Becker, *New York, 1763-1776, passim.;* Champagne, "Sons of Liberty," ch. 7 and pp. 439-40.

[16] George Dangerfield, *Robert R. Livingston of New York, 1746-1813* (New York, 1960), p. 197; for the veto, Charles Z. Lincoln, ed., *Messages From The Governors* (Albany, 1909), II, [1777-1822], pp. 228-233.

[17] Nathan Schachner, *Aaron Burr: A Biography* (New York, 1937), pp. 84-85.

[18] The returns for this and subsequent elections are given below.

[19] Charles W. Spencer, "John Laurence," *Dictionary of American Biography*, VI, pp. 31-32.

[20] Cited in Martha Lamb, *History of the City of New York* (2 vols., New York, 1880), II, p. 352.

[21] "Civis," *New York Journal*, Apr. 9, 1789.

[22] Miscellaneous Notes and Memoranda for April, 1789, Alexander Hamilton Papers, N.Y. Hist. Soc.; for the nominations, *Daily Advertiser*, Apr. 8 ff., 1789.

[23] Jacob Cooke, ed., *The Federalist*, Essay 35, (Middletown, Conn., 1961), p. 219.

[24] The mechanics elected as Federalist Assemblymen and the year of their election were: 1789: Anthony Post, carpenter and President of the General Society; Francis Childs, printer of the Federalist *Daily Advertiser* and Vice President of the Society, and Henry Will, pewterer, an incorporator of the Society; 1790: William W. Gilbert, silversmith, and Will; 1791: John Wylley, tailor, and Will; 1792: Gilbert and Wylley; 1793: Robert Boyd, blacksmith, Richard Furman, painter and glazier and Jotham Post, either a druggist or carpenter; 1794: Furman and Post; 1795: Furman, Post and Alexander Lamb, a cartman; 1797: (ticket defeated); 1798: Furman; 1799: John Bogert, iron monger, Jacob Sherred, painter, Anthony Steenback, mason and Anthony Post, carpenter; 1800 and 1801, defeated; see *New York Civil List* (Albany, 1869 edn.), 130-148 for assemblymen; for identifications, see *New York Directory* (New York, annually) and "Minutes of the General Society of Mechanics and Tradesmen, 1785-1832," *passim*. For a published list of the members of the Society, Thomas Earle and Charles C. Congden, eds., *Annals of the General Society of Mechanics and Tradesmen of the City of New York, 1785-1889* (New York, 1892, appendix.

[25] A letter to the Mechanics Society of Boston in "General Society of Mechanics Min-

utes," at November 18, 1788; the petition is in *American State Papers: Finance* (Washington, 1832), I, pp. 8-9.

26 Joseph Gales and W. C. Seaton, eds, *The Debates and Proceedings in the Congress of the United States, 1789-1824* (42 vols., Washington, 1834-56), 1st Cong., 1st sess., Apr. 14, 1789, 131, 133-34, 150, 153; Apr. 24, pp. 205-06. Hereafter cited as *Annals of Congress.*

27 An unpublished ms. fragment (1794) in Hamilton Papers, Lib. of Congress, Microfilm, also reprinted in Beard, *Economic Origins*, pp. 246-47.

28 *Daily Advertiser*, Feb. 3, 22, 1790. Stagg was active in putting down the movement in the Society of Cincinnati.

29 Griffith J. McRee, *Life and Correspondence of James Iredell* (2 vols. New York, 1857), II, p. 442.

30 Martha Lamb, "The Career of a Beneficent Enterprise," *Magazine of American History*, XX: 2 (Aug., 1889), 94. I have found no evidence of mechanic testimonials in a search through the Hamilton Transcripts, Col. Univ. Lib. I am indebted to Harold Syrett, Editor of The Hamilton Papers, for the opportunity to make use of the transcripts. Nor is there any such evidence in Broadus Mitchell, *Alexander Hamilton, The National Adventure, 1788-1804* (New York, 1962) or in John C. Miller, *Alexander Hamilton, Portrait in Paradox* (New York, 1949).

31 A Friend to Equal Rights, *New York Journal*, Mar. 30, 1791.

32 "Leonidas," *ibid.*, Feb. 22, 1792.

33 For nominations, *New York Journal*, Apr. 13, 16, 1791; *Daily Advertiser*, June 2, 1791; Robert Troup to Alexander Hamilton, June 15, 1791, Hamilton Transcripts, Col. Univ. Lib.

34 "Minutes of the General Society," *passim*. The usual loan was £100 or £150; on Mar. 2, 1796, the society had £500 on loan, on Mar. 7, 1798, £1250.

35 A letter to the Mechanics Society of Providence, *ibid.*, at Nov. 7, 1792. For the charter see *Laws of the State of New York*, 13th sess., ch. 26.

36 John Pintard to Jeremy Belknap, Oct. 11, 1790, cited in Edwin P. Kilroe, *Saint Tammany and the Origins of the Society of Tammany . . .* (New York, 1913), pp. 136-37.

37 Peter Paulson, "The Tammany Society and the Jeffersonian Movement in New York City, 1795-1800," *New York History*, XXXIV (1953), p. 50.

38 William Pitt Smith, "An Oration Before the Tammany Society, May 12, 1790," *New York Magazine or Literary Repository*, I (1790), pp. 290-95, at 294.

39 For the officers see *New York Directory* (1789-1792), Pintard was elected to the Assembly in 1790 and failed in 1791 when William Pitt Smith and Melancton Smith were elected. See *New York Journal*, Apr. 22, 1790, *Daily Advertiser*, June 2, 1791.

40 Alfred Young, "The Democratic Republican Movement in New York State, 1788-1797" (unpub. doctoral diss., Northwestern University, 1958), ch. vii and Joseph S. Davis, *Essays in the Earlier History of American Corporations* (2 vols., Harvard Economic Studies, XVI, Cambridge, Massachusetts, 1917) II, ch. 2.

41 Alexander Macomb to William Constable, Feb. 21, 1792, Constable Papers, N. Y. Pub. Lib.; see also Seth Johnson to Andrew Craigie, Jan 21, 1792, Craigie Papers, III, No. 70, Amer. Antiq. Soc.

42 Reported in Johnson to Craigie, Jan. 22, 1792, *ibid.*, No. 71; see also "Decius," *New York Journal*, Feb. 15, 1792 and a spate of articles, *Daily Advertiser*, Feb. 7-29, 1792, *passim*.

43 See Alexander Hamilton to William Seton, cashier of the Bank of New York, Jan.18, 24, Feb. 10, Mar. 19, 21, 1791; the quotation is from James Tillary to Hamilton, Mar. 1, 1792, all in Hamilton Transcripts, Col. Univ. Lib.

44 Johnson to Craigie, Mar. 25, Apr. 18, 1792, Craigie Papers, III, Nos. 73, 76, Amer. Antiq. Soc.; *New York Journal*, Mar. 28, 1792.

45 Benjamin Tallmadge to James Wadsworth, Apr. 19, 1792, Wadsworth Papers, Conn. Hist. Soc. and ms. fragment [Apr. 1792], N.Y.C. Misc. ms., Box 14, N.Y. Hist. Soc.

[46] James Watson to James Wadsworth, Apr. 3, 1792, Wadsworth Papers, Conn. Hist. Soc. and Johnson to Craigie, Apr. 15, 1792, Craigie Papers, III, No. 75, Amer. Antiq. Soc.

[47] *Daily Advertiser*, June 2, 1792.

[48] James Tillary to Hamilton, Jan. 14, 1793, Hamilton Transcripts, Col. Univ. Lib.; for Livingston, Wilson, *Memorial History of the City of New York*, III, pp. 79-80.

[49] *Journal of the Assembly of the State of New York*, 15th sess., 151; "Atticus," *New York Journal*, June 17, 1792.

[50] *New York Journal*, Feb. 20, 1793. Livingston was not endorsed by anti-Federalist or Republican leaders either for Congress or for the Assembly the following spring; see Philip Ten Eyck to John B. Schuyler, Apr. 3, 1793, Schuyler Papers, Misc., N. Y. Pub. Lib.

[51] "General Society Minutes," Jan. 9, 1793; *New York Journal*, Jan. 12, 1793.

[52] See the election committees in *New York Journal*, Feb. 25, Mar. 21, 1792.

[53] *Ibid.*, May 29, June 1, 1793.

[54] Alexander DeConde, *Entangling Alliance: Politics and Diplomacy Under George Washington* (Durham, N.C., 1958), pp. 269-70.

[55] *New York Journal*, Aug. 7, 10, 1793; Rufus King to Alexander Hamilton, Aug. 3, 1793, Charles King, ed., *The Life and Correspondence of Rufus King* (6 vols., New York, 1894-1900), I, p. 493.

[56] Alexander Anderson, "Diary," Jan. 9, 1794, Ms., Columbiana Col., Col. Univ. Lib.; see also entries for July 31, Aug. 8, 1793.

[57] *Annals of Congress*, 3rd Congress 1st sess. Petitions were received from the following New York City artisans: manufacturers of hand bellows (Feb. 3, 417), nail manufacturers (Feb. 21, 458), hatters (Mar. 5, 478). From other cities petitions came from manufacturers of metal buttons, tobacco, hemp, nails, paint, bar iron, glass, hats, and hosiery, 482, 1023, 1131, 432, 256, 475, 452, 453, 456, 523, 522. For support for protection from Tammany, see *New York Journal*, Nov. 27, 1795.

[58] DeConde, *op. cit.*, ch. 3. John C. Miller, *The Federalist Era, 1789-1801* (New York, 1960), ch. 9.

[59] *New York Daily Gazette*, Mar. 4, 1794; "Acquiline Nimblechops," [pseud.] *Democracy, An Epic Poem* . . . (New York, 1794), attributed, falsely, I believe, to Brockholst Livingston.

[60] William Woolsey to Oliver Wolcott, Jr., Mar. 6, 1794, cited in Eugene P. Link. *Democratic Republican Societies, 1790-1800* (Columbia Studies in American Culture, No. 9, New York, 1942), 94; "Address . . . by the Democratic Society of New York," May 28, 1794, Broadside, N.Y. Pub. Lib. Of 43 men known to be members of the Society, a very incomplete number, it has been possible to identify them as follows: merchants, 14; craftsmen, 12; public officials, 2; lawyers, 4; teachers, 2; unidentified, 13. For analysis of the comparable Philadelphia society in which 32.8% were craftsmen, see *ibid.*, pp. 71-73.

[61] "Proceedings of the Commissioners of Fortifications for the City of New York and its Vicinity," (1794-1795), Ms., N.Y. Hist. Soc.

[62] *New York Journal*, May 10, 1794.

[63] Henry Wansey, *The Journal of an Excursion to the United States of North America in the Summer of 1794* . . . (Salisbury, Eng., 1796), reprinted in Bayrd Still, ed., *Mirror for Gotham* (New York, 1956), pp. 65-66. I have changed the order of several sentences.

[64] See *New York Journal*, Apr. 26, 30, May 3, 7, 10, 24, 28, June 18, 21, 1794. See also I. N. P. Stokes, comp., *Iconography of Manhattan Isle* (6 vols., New York, 1915-1928), V, 1307.

[65] Robert R. to Edward Livingston, Apr. 10, 1794, R. R. Livingston Papers, N. Y. Hist. Soc.

[66] *New York Journal*, June 7, 1794.

⁶⁷ William Hatcher, *Edward Livingston: Jeffersonian Republican and Jacksonian Democrat* (Baton Rouge, 1940), ch. 1; Charles H. Hunt, *Life of Edward Livingston* (New York, 1964), chs. 1-3.

⁶⁸ William Miller, "First Fruits of Republican Organization: Political Aspects of the Congressional Elections of 1794," *Penn. Mag. Hist. and Biog.*, LXIII (1939), 118-43; Young, *op. cit.*, pp. 616-20.

⁶⁹ *New York Journal*, Feb. 7, 1795 cf. to returns, *ibid.*, May 29, June 1, 1793.

⁷⁰ *New York Journal*, Nov. 26, 29, Dec. 3, 1794.

⁷¹ *New York Journal*, July 5, 1794; "General Society of Mechanics Minutes," June 3, 24, July 1, 1795 and for the seating arrangements, June 7, 1798.

⁷² "See to That," *New York Journal*, Dec. 27, 1794.

⁷³ For returns in the 1795 gubernatorial elections, *New York Journal*, June 3, 1795.

⁷⁴ Benjamin Walker to Joseph Webb, July 24, 1795 in W. C. Ford, ed., *Correspondence and Journals of Samuel Bacheley Webb* (3 vols., New York, 1894), III.

⁷⁵ Grant Thorburn, *Forty Years Residence in America* . . . (Boston, 1834), 37-40.

⁷⁶ Seth Johnson to Andrew Craigie, July 23, 1795. Craigie Papers, III, No. 97, Amer. Antiq. Soc.; "Slash," *New York Journal*, July 25, 1795 for the remark about "not a wholecoat"; Benjamin Walker cited in footnote 74.

⁷⁷ Alexander Hamilton to Rufus King, Apr. 24, 1796, Hamilton Transcripts, Col. Univ. Lib. For pressure by insurance underwriters, "Circular letter by Nicholas Low, Archibald Gracie and Gulian Verplanck, New York, May 3, 1796," Broadside, N.Y. Pub. Lib.

⁷⁸ William Willcocks, a New York City Federalist Assemblyman, in *Albany Gazette*, May 2, 1796.

⁷⁹ Hamilton to Rufus King, Dec. 16, 1796, Hamilton Transcripts, Col. Univ. Lib.

⁸⁰ "Impartial History of the Late Election," *New York Journal*, Dec. 27, 1796; *Argus*, Jan. 20, 1797.

⁸¹ Pomerantz, *op. cit.*, 199-225; Morris, *Government and Labor in Early America*, 200 ff.

⁸² F. A. F. de La Rochefoucauld-Liancourt, *Travels Through the United States of America, in the Years 1795, 1796, 1797* (2 vols., London, 1799), II, p. 205.

⁸³ "Petition of the Repackers of Beef and Pork to the State Legislature, Jan. 24, 1795," Misc., Ms., N.Y.C. No. 86, N.Y. Hist. Soc.; "Jehosphapet," [New York] *Evening Post*, Jan. 14, 1795; "To the Inhabitants of the City of New York," *Argus*, Jan. 14, 1797.

⁸⁴ Dr. Elihu Hubbard Smith, "Letters to William Bull . . . on the Fever" in Noah Webster, Jr., comp., *A Collection of Papers on the Subject of Billious Fevers* (New York, 1796), pp. 66-74.

⁸⁵ Matthew Davis, *A Brief Account of the Epidemical Fevers* (New York, 1796), pp. 58-67 for a list of the dead, 6, 16-17 for housing. For verification, Dr. Richard Bayley, *An Account of the Epidemic Fever* (New York, 1796), 59-66, 122 and *Argus*, Oct. 17, 1795.

⁸⁶ For the electoral census of 1795 by wards, see Supplement to the *Daily Advertiser*, Jan. 27, 1796.

⁸⁷ Hamilton to Rufus King, May 4, 1796, Hamilton Transcripts, Col. Univ. Lib.

⁸⁸ For a full account, Young, *op. cit.*, ch. 20; for a brief account, Pomerantz, *op. cit.*, pp. 263-68.

⁸⁹ *New York Journal*, Apr. 15, 19, 22, especially "A Dialogue Between an Old Tory and a Young Republican," *ibid.*, Apr. 22.

⁹⁰ Pomerantz, *op. cit.*, pp. 64-76.

⁹¹ In the *New York Journal*, "An Elector," Sept. 20; "A Citizen," Sept. 22; "A Freeholder," Sept. 22; and an editorial paragraph, Sept. 29, 1796; for the contested election, Arthur Peterson, ed., *Minutes of the Common Council of the City of New York* (19 vols., New York, 1917), II, pp. 284-86; Pomerantz, *New York*, pp. 120-22.

⁹² For the petition, Assembly Papers, Box 5, No. 113, New York State Lib.; for news-

paper accounts, *New York Journal*, Feb. 18, 23, Mar. 8, 11, 1797; Samuel L. Mitchill, *The Case of the Manufacturers of Soap and Candles in the City of New York Stated and Examined* (New York, 1797); Mitchill to Robert R. Livingston, June 9, 1797, Misc., ms., N.Y. Hist. Soc.; Livingston to Mitchill, July 18, 1797, R. R. Livingston ms., N.Y. State Lib.

[93] *New York Journal*, June 4, 1797.

[94] Kenneth and Anna M. Roberts, trans. and ed., *Moreau de St. Mary's American Journey (1793-1798)* (New York, 1947), pp. 124-25, and 127, 158-59, 162 for other observations on labor in the city; "Regulations of the Cartmen . . . 1795," Broadside, Lib. of Congress.

[95] "The Strange and Wonderful Account of a Dutch Hog" (New York, 1796), Broadside No. 7765, N.Y. State Lib.; Varick was Dutch for hog.

[96] Peter Jay to John Jay, May 3, 1799, John Jay Papers, Col. Univ. Lib.

[97] "An Independent Cartman," *Republican Watch-Tower*, Apr. 30, 1880 and in the same issue "To the Cartmen of New York," "To the Cartmen," by "Eighteen Hundred," and report of a meeting; "Leonidas" *ibid.*, Mar. 14, 1801 claimed that only 1,150 of 1,500 votes were cast in the 1800 election as a result of threats.

[98] "A Cartman," *Republican Watch-Tower*, Apr. 25, 1801.

[99] To take the Germans as an example: In 1788 Federalists candidates were endorsed "at a very numerous meeting of Germans" (*Daily Advertiser*, Apr. 28, 1788); in 1790 the German Society, claiming to be rebuffed by the merchants, offered support to the mechanics' ticket if they nominated a German (*New York Gazette*, Apr. 20, 1790).

[100] See Alfred Young, "New York City in the Hysteria of 1798 to 1800" (unpub. master's thesis, Col. Univ., 1947), pp. 92-101.

[101] "Society for the Assistance of Persons Emigrating From Foreign Countries . . . June 30, 1794," Broadside, N.Y. Hist. Soc.; for their constitution, *New York Journal*, June 25, 1794 and philosophy, Thomas Dunn, A.M., *A Discourse . . . October 21, 1794 Before the New York Society* . . . (New York, 1794); for Priestley's welcome, Edgar Smith, *Priestley in America, 1794-1804* (Philadelphia, 1920), pp. 21-40.

[102] *The Speech of Edward Livingston on the Third Reading of the Alien Bill* (Philadelphia, 1798) also in *New York Journal*, July 14, 1798; *Annals of Congress*, 5th Congress, 1st Sess., Feb. 12, 1799, p. 2884; Schachner, *Aaron Burr*, 152.

[103] Phillip Livingston to Jacob Read, Feb. 23, 1801, reprinted in *Col. Univ. Quart.* XXIII (June, 1931), p. 200.

[104] "General Society of Mechanics Minutes," Jan. 16, Feb. 6, Feb. 20, Mar. 6, Apr. 3, 1799 reprinted in Earle and Congdon, eds., *Annals*, pp. 241-42. The letter was drafted, agreed to, and reconsidered at a special meeting, then rejected. Thus there was a division in the society on the question which may also account for the first recorded contest for officers, Jan. 4, 1800. The fact that George Warner, an active Republican, was chairman of the drafting committee leaves no doubt as to the Republican position.

[105] *American Citizen*, Mar. 19, Mar. 21, Apr. 10, 1801. George Warner was secretary to this committee; another petition was sent to the state legislature requesting bounties for the production of sheep to encourage the wool industries, signed by a number of Republicans, *American Citizen*, Feb. 14, 1801.

[106] "A New Song," by J. C. [James Cheetham, hatter and co-editor of the paper], *Republican Watch-Tower*, Feb. 21, 1801; for other evidence of Republican support for manufactures, Minutes of the Tammany Society, Dec. 1, 1800, ms., N.Y. Pub. Lib., for a debate; *Argus*, Nov. 27, 1795 for a Tammany toast; *New York Journal*, Apr. 15, 1797, June 8, 1799.

[107] Beatrice Rubens, "Burr, Hamilton and the Manhattan Company," *Polit. Sci. Quart.*, LXXII (1957), 578-607 and LXXIII (1958), pp. 100-125.

[108] Bank of Manhattan, *A Collection of 400 Autographs Reproduced in Facsimile from the Signatures of the Original Subscription Book of the Bank of Manhattan* (New York, 1919).

[109] *New York Journal*, Jan. 8, Feb. 12, 15, 1800; "Philander," *American Citizen*, Apr. 28, 29, 1800; for a debate, Minutes of the Tammany Society, Mar. 31, 1800, ms., N.Y. Pub. Lib.

[110] The mechanic candidates on the Republican ticket were: for 1797: Phillip Arcularius, tanner, Ezekial Robbins, hatter, and George Warner, sailmaker; for 1798: Arcularius, Robbins, Arthur Smith, mason, and John Wolfe, boot and shoemaker; for 1799: Joshua Barker, manager of an air furnace, Ephriam Brasher, goldsmith, John Brower, upholsterer, Matthew Davis, printer, Benjamin North, carpenter, and William Vredenbergh, grocer. For excellent details: Anne B. Seeley, "A Comparative Study of Federalist and Republican Candidates in New York City" (Unpublished master's thesis, Col. Univ. 1959). Of 16 Republican candidates of mechanic background nominated over the entire decade Mrs. Seeley found the tax evaluations of about half of them to be high, e.g., £1200 to 5850 and about half to be low, £100 to 400.

[111] *Argus*, Apr. 20, 1799; see James Smith, *Freedom's Fetters. The Alien and Sedition Acts* (Ithaca, N.Y., 1956), pp. 204-220, 385-417; Young, "New York City in the Hysteria of 1798-1800," *passim*.

[112] "To a Certain Man," *American Citizen*, Apr. 24, 1801.

[113] Matthew L. Davis to Albert Gallatin, Apr. 15, 1800, Gallatin Papers, N.Y. Hist. Soc.; see also Robert Troup to Rufus King, Mar. 9, 1800, in C. King, ed., *Correspondence of Rufus King*, III, pp. 207-08.

[114] Peter Jay to John Jay, May 3, 1800, Jay Papers, Col. Univ. Lib.

[115] *American Citizen*, May 4, 1801; see also Aaron Burr to William Eustis, Apr. 28, 1801, Eustis Ms., Mass. Hist. Soc.

[116] For 1800 Matthew L. Davis to Albert Gallatin, May 1, 1800, Gallatin Papers, N.Y. Hist. Soc. Notices of meetings: *American Citizen*, Apr. 22, 25, 1800; Peter Jay to John Jay, May 3, 1800, Jay Papers, Col. Univ. Lib.; John C. Miller, *Alexander Hamilton*, p. 512.

[117] Wilson, *Memorial History of New York*, III, 150-52, for a list of 250 homes assessed at over £2000 in 1798; Stokes, *Iconography of Manhattan Island*, V, p. 1374; Beard, *Economic Origins*, pp. 382-87, erred in lumping the first with the second and third; it was more mixed; see "Impartial History of the Late Election," *New York Journal*, Dec. 27, 1796, for comment that remains valid for 1800.

[118] Editorial, *American Citizen*, Apr. 30, 1802.

[119] For Republican organizations among the Irish: for the United Irishmen of New York, *Time Piece*, July 6, Aug. 30, 1798 and *Argus*, Mar. 18, 1799; for "Republican Irishmen," *American Citizen*, July, 1800 and July 9, 1801; for Hibernian Provident Society, *Republican Watch-Tower*, Mar. 18, 28, 1801; for Hibernian Militia Volunteers, Link, *op. cit.*, p. 184.

[120] For the variety of political opinions among the French see F. S. Childs, *French Refugee Life in the United States: An American Chapter of the French Revolution* (Baltimore, 1946), pp. 70-75; *Moreau de St. Mery's American Journey, passim;* for a French newspaper of a Republican cast see George P. Winship, "French Newpapers in the United States from 1790 to 1800," *Bibliographic Society of America Papers*, XIV (1920), pp. 134-47.

[121] For the Caledonian Society, decidedly Republican, see [New York] *Evening Post*, Dec. 22, 1794; *Argus*, Dec. 3, 1795; *New York Directory for 1796*, unpaged; for a conservative Scot's observations on the "hot characters" among his fellow migrants, Grant Thorburn, *Forty Years Residence*, pp. 23, 37-40, 92.

[122] New York *Commercial Advertiser*, Apr. 11, 1801 and *An Address to the Electors of the State of New York* (Albany, 1801).

[123] See the toasts of a "Yankee Fraternity," *Daily Advertiser*, July 10, 1798.

[124] For a short-lived Federalist paper founded by a recent English migrant, John Mason Williams, see [New York] *Columbian Gazette* (April 4-June 22, 1799), especially the prospectus April 6 and valedictory, June 22.

[125] Alfred Young, "The Merchant Jeffersonians: New York as a Case Study," (unpub. paper delivered before the Miss. Valley Hist. Ass'n., Apr., 1954).

[126] Matthew Davis, while best known as Burr's amanuensis for *Memoirs and Correspondence of Aaron Burr*, was a printer, publisher of the short-lived [New York] *Evening Post* (1795), then co-publisher of [New York] *Time Piece* (1797). He was active in Tammany and the Mechanics Society, was the Independence Day orator in 1800, and the organizer of the Society for Free Debate (1798).

[127] James Cheetham, a recent English immigrant and a hatter by trade, became co-editor of *American Citizen* and *Republican Watch-Tower* (1800-ff), a leading pamphleteer and the first biographer of Thomas Paine (1809).

[128] Frank Norcross, *History of the New York Swamp* (New York, 1901), 8-11; Lee Benson, *The Concept of Jacksonian Democracy: New York as a Test Case* (Princeton, 1961); Walter Hugins, *Jacksonian Democracy and the Working Class: A Study of the New York Workingman's Movement, 1829-1837* (Stanford, 1960).

[129] "A Shoemaker," *American Citizen*, Apr. 23, 1801; "To the Shoemakers," *Republican Watch-Tower*, Apr. 22, 1801; "A Shoemaker to the Journeymen Shoemakers," *ibid.*, Apr. 25; Report of the Comissioners of the Prison, *Albany Register*, Mar. 3, 1801.

[130] Richard Morris, "Criminal Conspiracy and Early Labor Combinations in New York," *Polit. Sci. Quart.*, LVII (1937), pp. 51-85.

[131] Robert R. Livingston, "Address to the Agricultural Society of the State of New York," *New York Magazine*, VI (Feb., 1795), pp. 95-102.

[132] Lewis Leary, *That Rascal Freneau. A Study in Literary Failure* (New Brunswick, N.J., 1941), pp. 260-65, 275.

[133] Robert R. Livingston to Samuel L. Mitchill, July 18, 1797, Livingston Ms., N.Y. State Lib.; for the veto see note 16 above.

[134] "To Farmers, Mechanics and other Industrious Citizens," *Time Piece*, May 14, 1798.

[135] "Scrutator," *New York Journal*, Apr. 19, 1797.

[136] Lamb, "The Career of a Beneficent Enterprise," *op. cit.*; a membership certificate is on exhibit at the General Society, New York City.

[137] Henry Rutgers established a "bleach-field and thread manufactory" (*Daily Advertiser*, May 12, 1791); James Nicholson was chairman of the New York Manufacturing Society (*New York Directory for 1790*, p. 135) and was interested in a textile venture (Joseph Garlick to Nicholson, Mar. 15, 1798, Misc. Ms., Nicholson, N.Y. Hist. Soc.); Solomon Simpson had an interest in the New York Iron Manufacturing Company, was part owner of a lead mine and a founder of the American Minerological Society and co-owner of a spermaceti candle factory (Morris Schappes, "Anti-Semitism and Reaction, 1795-1800," *Pubs. of the American Jewish Hist. Soc.*, XXVIII, Part 2 [Dec., 1948], 115-16).

[138] Dangerfield, *op. cit.*, pp. 284-289.

[139] Lyman C. Newall, "Samuel Latham Mitchill," *Dictionary of American Biography*, VII, pp. 69-70; Mitchill to Hamilton, Dec. 3, 1792, Hamilton Transcripts, Col. Univ. Lib.; Joseph Dorfman, *The Economic Mind in American Civilization, 1606-1865* (New York, 1946), I, pp. 324-25.

[140] *New York Journal*, "Extraordinary" page, Dec. 6, 1794; for the Mechanics Society reform sentiment see "Minutes of the General Society," July 1, 1795.

[141] *Forlorn Hope*, Mar. 24-Sept. 13, 1800; for a rival debtor's paper also edited by a Republican, see *Prisoner of Hope*, May 3-Aug. 23, 1800.

[142] *Annals of Congress*, 4th Cong., 1st Sess., pp. 254-55, 257, 304-07, 1394.

[143] See Young, "Democratic Republican Movement," pp. 768-69.

[144] Tunis Wortman, *An Oration on the Influence of Social Institutions Upon Morals and Human Happiness . . . before the Tammany Society May 12, 1795* (New York, 1796); and DeWitt Clinton, *An Oration on Benevolence Delivered before the Society of Black Friars . . . November 10, 1794* (New York, 1795).

[145] I saw no signs of interest in suffrage reform in the Minutes of the Mechanics or Tammany, the toasts offered at their celebrations or in the expressions of the Democratic Society; for pro universal suffrage articles in *Time Piece:* "On Some of the Principles of American Republicanism," May 5, 1797; "Political Creed," Aug. 21, 1797; "Communication," Oct. 6, 1797; and "Universal Justice," Nov. 10, 1797.

[146] Tunis Wortman, *Treatise Concerning Political Enquiry and the Liberty of the Press* (New York, 1800), pp. 195-97.

[147] Jabez Hammond, *History of Political Parties in the State of New York* (2 vols., Cooperstown, 1846), I, ch. 6.

[148] John Wood, *A Full Exposition of the Clintonian Faction* (Newark, 1802), 20-21; Pomerantz, *op. cit.*, pp. 208, 134.

[149] James Cheetham, *Dissertation Concerning Political Equality and the Corporation of New York* (New York, 1800).

[150] Pomerantz, *op. cit.*, 133-145; Chilton Williamson, *American Suffrage From Property to Democracy 1760-1860* (Princeton, 1960), pp. 161-64.

[151] George Warner, *Means for the Preservation of Public Liberty . . . delivered before the Mechanics, Tammany, Democratic and Coopers Societies, July 4, 1797* (New York, 1797), pp. 12-13.

[152] *Argus,* Apr. 8, 1799.

[153] "A Dialogue Between 1776 and 1796," *New York Journal,* Jan. 29, 1796.

[154] Tunis Wortman to Albert Gallatin, Feb. 12, 1798, Gallatin Papers, N.Y. Hist. Soc. For the book see Leonard Levy, *Legacy of Suppression, Freedom of Speech and Press in Early American History* (Cambridge, Mass., 1960), pp. 283-89.

[155] Warner, *Means for the Preservation,* pp. 9, 19; in the same pro-Constitution vein see Samuel L. Mitchill, *An Address . . . July 4, 1799* (New York, 1800), pp. 7, 20; Matthew L. Davis, *An Oration . . . July 4, 1800* (New York, 1800), 15; for a hint of the old anti-Federalist attitude, George Eacker, *An Oration . . . July 4, 1801* (New York, 1801), pp. 10-11, all delivered before the several societies.

[156] Beard, *op. cit.*, p. 466; Jefferson to Thomas Mann Randolph, May 6, 1793, Paul L. Ford, ed., *The Writings of Thomas Jefferson* (10 vols., New York, 1892-1899), VI, p. 241.

COUNTRY ABOVE PARTY:

JOHN ADAMS AND THE 1799 MISSION TO FRANCE*

Jacob E. Cooke

    President John Adams ex post facto considered his decision to send a second peace mission to France in 1799 the wisest and most objective act of his entire career. Professor Jacob E. Cooke, a noted Hamiltonian specialist, has vigorously challenged this widely accepted view. He contends that the "war party" contingent among the Federalists was not enough of a threat to warrant a precipitous diplomatic peace move on Adams' part, a move which only promoted the disruption of the Federalist Party. Adams' failure to see himself as leader of a unified Federalist Party is manifest in his unilateral decision-making and in his alienation of important party leaders. In light of the realities of French foreign policy, Cooke concludes that the Convention of 1800 between France and the United States was not the great diplomatic triumph Adams thought it was. Associate editor of The Papers of Alexander Hamilton, *Jacob Cooke is MacCracken Professor at Lafayette College. He has written extensively on early American politics and is currently engaged in a biographical study of Tench Coxe.*

    The story of the diplomatic history of the administration of John Adams, as often related, is a tale of high intrigue and sinister plots. It goes something like this:

    After the rejection of the envoys which Adams sent to France in 1797 in a last-ditch effort to resolve French American differences peaceably, the United States tottered on the brink of a formal war with France. The leaders of the Federalist party—Alexander

   * Reprinted by permission of Jacob E. Cooke and Moravian College. From *Fame and the Founding Fathers,* Edmund P. Willis, ed. (Bethlehem, Pa.; Moravian College, 1967). Copyright 1967 by Moravian College. Jacob E. Cooke, "Country Above Party: John Adams and the 1799 Mission to France," pp. 53-77.

> *Hamilton   chief   among   them—and   the   President's   own*
> *cabinet—warmongers all—embraced an opportunity to strike a*
> *blow at the perfidious French and their pernicious American*
> *allies, the Republicans. The dupe of no man, John Adams soon*
> *unravelled the sinister plot Hamilton and his cohorts in the*
> *President's Cabinet were concocting and determined to thwart it.*
> *In a bold bid for peace and presidential independence, he*
> *appointed a new mission to France which, despite the insidious*
> *efforts of the Hamiltonian cabal to prevent its departure, saved*
> *the country from militarism and preserved the peace.*

However unfair this parody may be, it does point up assumptions about Adams' administration which increasingly have become axioms to be demonstrated rather than hypotheses to be proved. I have found that the record yields evidence to support a different interpretation and if my account is also a distorted one it may still serve to question the continued acceptance of what I find to be largely partisan history.

Twentieth-century historians have been virtually unanimous in their praise of Adams' decision to reopen negotiations with France, a smaller number has been critical of the manner in which he announced his decision,[1] but virtually none of them[2] has followed the lead of nineteenth-century Federalist historians who attributed the break up of the Federalist party to it.[3] Biased as these filiopietistic historians undeniably were, there may be more substance in their assessment of the impact of Adams' decision than more recent historians have been prepared to admit.

On February 18, 1799, President Adams, without previously consulting his Cabinet, members of Congress, or other leading Federalists, cryptically announced to the Senate the nomination of "William Vans Murray, American Minister resident at The Hague, to be minister plenipotentiary of the United States to the French Republic."[4] If ever the hackneyed word "bombshell" has been applicable to a presidential message it surely describes this one. Leading senators were momentarily stunned—Theodore Sedgwick could only explain the nomination as "the wild and irregular start of a vain, jealous, and half frantic mind";[5] Timothy Pickering sorrowfully noted that "we have all been shocked and grieved";[6] and Harrison Gray Otis merely asked: ". . . is the man mad?"[7]

The shock and the sense of outrage expressed by such Federalist leaders cannot be explained as the bitter reaction of disappointed men suddenly deprived of a war for which they longed. The surprise was genuine and the criticism of the President, however intemperate, was understandable. In the summer of 1798 Adams, with the hearty approval and close cooperation of Federalist leaders, had taken a new departure in American foreign relations. Confronted with unmistakable proof of French contempt for the United States and her apparent willingness to provoke a war, Adams and the Federalists adopted a program designed to thwart the French menace by building up the country's defenses. Further negotiations were not ruled out, but in view of the treatment meted out to Charles C. Pinckney in 1797 and to the XYZ envoys in 1798 the Federalists agreed that they should be renewed only if it were unmistakably clear that the French wished a settlement. "I will never send another minister to France," Adams said on June 21, 1798, "without assurances that he will be received, respected, and honored as the representative of a great, free, powerful and independent nation."[8] Whatever Adams' inner thoughts about the wisdom of his party's program, Federalist leaders, in and out of Congress, were unaware during the next six months of any impending change in policy.

In his annual message of December 8, 1798, Adams informed Congress that "nothing is discoverable in the conduct of France which ought to change or relax our measures of defense," but he went on to announce a subtle change in foreign policy which few congressmen could have missed. Retreating from his inflexible position of the previous June, the President said that: "It must be left with France (if she is indeed desirous of accommodation) to take the requisite steps."[9] Federalist congressmen, however, keenly aware of the French duplicity and intransigence which had undermined negotiations in 1797 and 1798 refused to endorse Adams' open door policy. The House of Representatives politely reminded the President that "the wisdom and decision which have characterized your past administration, assure us, that no illusory professions will seduce you into any abandonment of the rights which belong to the United States, as a free and independent nation."[10] The Senate, even more emphatic, summarized the history of French hostility toward the United States and concluded that "these facts indicate no change of system or disposition; they speak a more intelligible language than professions of solicitude to avoid a rupture, however ardently made."[11] Adams was thus warned that the Congressional leaders of his party objected to a revival of the conciliatory policy of 1797 and 1798 and would approve another French mission only if they were unequivocally convinced that France was willing to negotiate in good faith. They were reassured, however, by the President's firm reply that "I have seen no real evidence of any change of system or disposition in the French Republic toward the United States."[12]

During the three succeeding months, Congress swiftly proceeded to carry out the President's recommendations for invigorated war preparations[13] and Adams' behavior, save in one instance,[14] did little to suggest that he was preparing to act on the hint thrown out in his message of December. To the contrary, on January 21, 1799, he submitted to Congress a report from his Secretary of State on U.S.-French relations (promised in his annual message) which was a bitter arraignment of French policy, a policy designed, in Pickering's words, "to fleece us" to gratify French "avarice and revenge" and to "satiate its ambition." "I hope we shall remember," Pickering remarked grandiloquently, that "the tiger crouches before he leaps upon his prey."[15] If Adams was contemplating the reopening of negotiations, approval of such a statement was, to say the least, injudicious for it could only serve to mislead Congress, the public, the Republican opposition, and his own advisers. Three weeks later, he suggested even more strongly that he had no intention of reopening negotiations with France. On February 15, in announcing to Congress that an objectionable French decree[16] (news of which had been submitted in a message of January 28, 1799), had been suspended, Adams said, that "it should be remembered that the *arrêt* . . . of the 2d of March, 1797,[17] remains in force . . : and that this *arrêt* accomplished the same purpose as that which the French ostensibly had disclaimed in the suspension."[18] Three days later he announced the nomination of William Vans Murray.

Just as the addresses from Congress should have suggested to Adams the necessity of strong and skillful presidential leadership in guiding his country toward the peace table, so too should the attitude of his Cabinet, which reflected the opinion of an influential wing of his own party, have suggested the political pitfalls of renewed negotiations. Although they were not opposed to negotiations, Adams' advisers, as we shall see, strongly opposed the appointment of another minister to France. Adams was undeniably correct in asserting that responsibility for the conduct of the country's foreign relations resided in the President and not in his Cabinet, but he was just as surely politically obtuse in disregarding the opinions of leaders of his own party, Cabinet members among them.

Some historians doubtless would object to this conclusion on the grounds that Murray's appointment was necessary to thwart the extremists of Adams' own party who were clamoring for a war with France.[19] But the disagreement between the President and other Federalist leaders was not a conflict between proponents of peace and warmongers. That a "war party" existed is undeniable, but that it was as large or influential as is often supposed is doubtful.[20] Take, for example, the members of Adams' Cabinet, who usually are described as "High Federalists," a group customarily regarded as the war party. Although James McHenry thought a declaration of war "indispensable" and Benjamin Stoddert considered it desirable,[21] no member of the Cabinet suggested that the President recommend it. Timothy Pickering argued that the state of U. S.-French relations and American public opinion were "incompatible with a recommendation to declare war against France." Such a recommendation, he said, would be "inexpedient because of France's disposition to retract many of its demands" and because Congress would be unwilling to accede to it. Although Pickering believed that "our country ought not to be exposed to a third ignominious repulse," he was convinced that the French were prepared to send a minister to the United States.[22] Oliver Wolcott, on whose recommendations Adams heavily leaned in his annual message, emphatically rejected the idea that war was necessary, recommending instead, "that it is the true policy of the government to retain its present position, to invigorate the system of defense, and to baffle skill by skill."[23] Adams rejected this argument, on the face of it moderate enough and doubtless expressing the opinion of a majority of Federalists, because, as he later recalled, he "thought the proposition intended to close the avenues to peace, and to ensure a war with France."[24] Nor did Hamilton advocate a declaration of war. Despite its persistence for a century and a half, the accusation, as Broadus Mitchell has remarked, is "baseless."[25] Hamilton's considered and consistent opinion on negotiations was given to Lafayette to whom he wrote that American overtures for peace were sincere and "that it is in the power of France, by reparation to our merchants for past injury, and the stipulation of justice in the future, to put an end to the controversy."[26] Evidence on this point could be multiplied but it would only point to the conclusion that one can make Hamilton a warmonger only by quoting him out of context, a task, I might add, at which many of our historians have been extraordinarily skilled.[27]

Why, then, did Adams decide to reopen negotiations?[28] He earlier had received news of the Directory's willingness to settle differences with the United States from a number of independent sources—from Elbridge Gerry and George Logan, Americans recently returned from France, and from Joel Barlow, Nathaniel Cutting, and Richard Codman, Americans resident in France.[29] But, as Adams later said, "The testimonies of Mr. Codman, Mr. Cutting, Mr. Barlow, and Mr. Logan, and all other private communications, though they might convince my own mind, would have had no influence to dispose me to nominate a minister, if I had not received authentic, regular, official, diplomatic assurances."[30] These assurances were contained in a three-way correspondence between William Vans Murray, U. S. minister to the puppet government at The Hague, Louis André Pichon, French secretary of legation there, and Talleyrand, French foreign minister. "Whatever Plenipotentiary the government of the United States might send to France," Talleyrand wrote to Pichon, "would be undoubtedly received with the respect due to the representative of a free, independent, and powerful nation."[31] Many Federalists—senators, congressmen, and Cabinet members among them—insisted that Talleyrand's assurances, far from satisfying the requirements of Adams' message of June 21, 1798, were unofficial. They were neither endorsed by the Directory, it was pointed out, nor communicated through regular diplomatic channels. Despite his later disclaimer, Adams must at the time have subscribed to this view. In his message of February 18, 1799, nominating Murray, he said: "If the Senate shall advise and consent to his appointment, effectual care shall be taken in his instructions that he shall not go to France without direct and unequivocal assurances from the French government, signified by their minister of foreign relations, that he shall be received in character."[32] When under pressure from Federalist congressmen Adams agreed only a few days later, to name a three-man commission instead of a single envoy he imposed similar conditions.[33] James McHenry, biased as he undoubtedly was, was surely correct in saying that Adams "considered the measure, at the moment of recommending it to the Senate, as resting on sand and of dubious issue."[34]

It may well be, as Adams said, that such an invitation to the peace table could not be ignored, but the manner in which he chose to accept it was politically inept. As Fisher Ames remarked, "The step . . . ought to have been known, if not approved, by the chief officers and supporters of government in Congress."[35] Adams was sincerely convinced, however, that he could alter the course of foreign policy only by keeping his intentions secret and presenting his advisers and Congress with a fait accompli. "I knew that if I called the heads of departments together, and asked their advice," Adams explained:

> three of them would very laconically protest against the measure. The other two would . . . modestly and mildly concur with them. The consequence would be, that the whole would be instantaneously communicated to . . . the Senate, and . . . the House of Representatives; the public and the presses would have it at once, and a clamor raised, and a prejudice propagated against the measure, that would probably excite the Senate to put their negative on the whole plan.[36]

Such an explanation reveals more about the President's own mental cast than about his Cabinet's loyalty. Why, one is entitled to ask, did he object to disagreement with his advisers? If he knew the press and public would be opposed to the measure should he not have explored more carefully the best manner of effecting it?

Had Adams been bent on dividing his party, he scarcely could have acted more effectively. As Page Smith has said, "A measure which he had hoped would isolate the extremists threatened seriously to demoralize the whole party."[37] To many Federalists, Adams was abandoning a policy to which he had committed himself only eight months earlier and in which his party fervently believed. Instead of leading his party by persuasion he appeared bent on destroying it by dictation; instead of educating Federalist leaders on the wisdom of his policies, he appeared eager to engage in a power struggle with them.[38] Had Adams cautiously prepared his party for a change in policy, had he been willing to exercise leadership unremittingly rather than fitfully, had he reached a decision after discussion with party leaders in and out of Congress, had he been willing to heed their recommendations for the preconditions that should precede negotiations, even had he been more prudent in selecting a time and a manner for announcing his decision, he might well have won the cooperation of all but a small minority of Federalists.[39]

Despite Adams' insistence on the necessity of shock tactics, there were alternatives open to him, alternatives which would have achieved the goal of negotiation without sacrificing party unity. Such alternatives were suggested by Washington and Hamilton and, unlikely political bedfellow though he may have been, John Quincy Adams. Writing to the Secretary of State on October 6, 1798, J. Q. Adams "urgently advised" that preliminary negotiations be carried on at The Hague by authorizing Murray to carry on discussions with an accredited representative of the Directory "to make certain that France was ready to offer terms which would ensure the success of a final negotiation. . . ."[40] Writing shortly after Adams' surprise announcement, Washington echoed this suggestion. "Had we approached the antechamber of this Gentleman [Talleyrand] when he opened the door to us, and there waited for a formal invitation into the Interior, the Governments would have met upon equal ground, and we might have advanced or receded according to circumstances without commitment. . . ."[41] Hamilton, regarded by Adams as implacably hostile to peace, was not so much opposed to negotiations as to Adams' method of instituting them. In view of the treatment accorded Charles C. Pinckney and the XYZ envoys, Hamilton believed that the French should have been required to send an envoy to the United States "with adequate powers and instructions,'' a step which he was convinced they were willing to take.[42] Since Adams objected to such a policy, however, Hamilton's alternative proposal was the same as Washington's: "He might secretly and confidentially have nominated one or more of our ministers actually abroad for the purpose of treating with France; with *eventual* instructions predicated upon appearances of an approached peace."[43]

The result of Adams' independent action was something of a political paradox: while alienating prominent Federalist leaders, he apparently enhanced his popularity among the party's rank and file.[44] But popularity of executive decisions counted for far less in the 1790's than later. The President then did not possess the influence nor command news media and other resources by which he subsequently could take advantage of favorable public opinion to consolidate his party behind him and bring dissident party leaders into line. However much Adams deplored the fact, the cohesion of the Federalist party depended on the support of party leaders, and most of the leaders of his party opposed him. They were, as Henry Cabot Lodge once remarked, "all men of ability and determination, and they possessed an amount of political weight and actual power that it is now difficult to conceive. In their hands rested the power to ruin the President and destroy the party. . . ."[45]

Since the best test of presidential success is a pragmatic one, Adams' decision to reopen negotiations may deserve the praise which historians have lavished on it. But if Adams was wise he also was very lucky. His decision was, as I have said, based on faith more than evidence, faith that Talleyrand, whose duplicity in the XYZ affair was patent, could be trusted to keep his word, faith that the foreign minister was indeed speaking for the Directory, and faith that France's disadvantages in Europe would work to the advantage of the United States. As things turned out, Adams did receive the definite assurances his critics demanded, and his mission negotiated a peace which temporarily ended the Franco-American dispute. That this was owing to fortuitous events over which the President had no control and of which he was ignorant measurably diminishes his accomplishment. His success was made possible by those Federalists he later disdained and by Napoleon Bonaparte, for just as the Federalists' preparedness program had paved the way for negotiations, so Napoleon's desire to acquire Louisiana assured their success.

The sequel to Adams' nomination of commissioners to negotiate with France frequently has been misunderstood. One familiar account has it that Adams immediately instructed his Secretary of State to draw up their instructions but that Pickering, stubbornly determined to prevent their departure, ignored the President's repeated requests and procrastinated for months on end.[46] The instructions finally were prepared and the commissioners sent on their way only after an irate President, realizing that his arrogant Secretary of State was seeking to subvert the Administration's policies, rushed to Trenton and took charge himself. This stereotyped account follows Adams' own interpretation[47] of the events of 1799, but it is at odds with the historical record.

However much they may have disliked Adams' decision to send envoys to France, his official family neither disputed his right to make it nor tried to undermine it. As Oliver Wolcott said: "After the President had decided that the assurances were sufficient, the officers were directed to prepare the instructions. The orders were executed with promptitude and sincerity; the expediency of the measure was, at least by me, dismissed. The only question was, respecting the terms of a treaty between the United States and a powerful European nation."[48] Nor did Hamilton, despite Adams' suspicions, connive with "all his confidential friends" to "prevail on the President to violate" his pledge to reopen negotiations should assurances be received.[49] When he first heard of Adams' appointment of a new mission, Hamilton had written that "as it has happened, my present impression is that the measure must go into effect . . ."[50] and although he would have preferred, as I have said, that negotiations be handled in another manner, he did not attempt to defeat the President's plan. With receipt of news that the Directory had been overturned, as we shall see, both Hamilton and the Cabinet did warmly urge Adams to suspend the mission, but these governmental changes had led the President himself to question its expediency.

The long delay in the departure of the commissioners was actually attributable to the President rather than to the "insidious and dark intrigues" of Hamilton[51] or the intransigence of Timothy Pickering. Pickering made no secret of his disagreement with Adams' decision to send the peace mission,[52] but he did not intentionally delay it. The delay was owing, as I have said, to Adams' insistence that the French give unequivocal and formal "assurances" that the American envoys would be received and treated with respect. No less than four months were required for William Vans Murray, to whom this task was assigned, to receive his instructions, secure the required assurances, and transmit them to the State Department.[53] If Pickering was slow in preparing instructions for the envoys it thus was because there was no need for speed; if Adams neither prodded Pickering nor stipulated a deadline for their preparation it was because he felt no sense of urgency. The assurances were received from Murray on July 30, 1799,[54] and Pickering immediately forwarded them to the President who replied on August 6 asking that the instructions be prepared "as promptly as possible" and submitted to the heads of departments for "their corrections, if they shall judge any to be necessary."[55] When Pickering reported on August 23 that the instructions would be ready in a few days, Adams neither complained nor commented on the delay.[56] At this point Pickering temporarily had to suspend the conduct of official business because of a yellow fever epidemic which forced government officials to flee Philadelphia. But on September 10, 1799, as soon as he was settled in his temporary office in nearby Trenton and had had time to confer with his colleagues, he sent the instructions.[57]

Some two weeks earlier however, news had reached the Secretary of State that "a very portentous scene . . . appeared to be opening" in France, possibly "another explosion," and after consulting the Cabinet he suggested to the President that the mission be temporarily suspended.[58] This recommendation could only have confirmed the President's independent decision to delay the departure of the envoys,[59] for on September 16, three days before he received Pickering's letter, Adams informed his Secretary of State that "The revolution in the Directory, and the revival of the clubs and private societies in France, and the strong appearances of another reign of Democratic fury and sanguinary anarchy approaching, seem to justify a relaxation of our zeal for the sudden and hasty departure of our envoys."[60] Doubtless prompted by a letter from Benjamin Stoddert of September 13 (a letter whose meaning persistently has been misunderstood),[61] Adams reluctantly decided that he should go to Trenton to discuss the problem with his advisers.[62] "I pray you to write to the Attorney General to meet us," he wrote to Pickering. "We must be all together, to determine all the principles of our negotiations with France and England."[63]

The President arrived in Trenton on October 10, having stopped over a few hours in Windsor, Conn., to talk to Chief Justice Oliver Ellsworth, one of the commissioners appointed in February, and having been delayed in Hartford where he contracted "a most violent cold, attended with constant fever."[64] On the evening of the 15th he met with his Cabinet in order to put the instructions which had been prepared for the envoys in final form, but, as Wolcott said, he was "silent on the question whether the mission ought to proceed."[65] The meeting adjourned shortly after 11 o'clock. Early the next morning Pickering, to his astonishment received a note ordering him to deliver "the instructions, as corrected last eve-

ning, . . ." to the envoys and to request them to leave for France by Nov. 1.[66]
What had happened in so brief a time to remove Adams' doubts about
the expediency of such an act? He later denied that his determination
ever had wavered, and pictured himself as resolutely resisting the stub-
born determination of his Cabinet to thwart his plans for peace. "I was
astonished, I was grieved, I was afflicted, to see such artificial schemes
employed, such delays studied, such embarrassments thrown in the way,
by men who were, or at least ought to have been my bosom friends
. . ."[67] he recalled. Yet the arguments of the Cabinet, open and plausible
as they were, cannot objectively be construed as "artificial schemes"
or contemplated "embarrassments." For more than a month Adams had
apparently believed, as did they, that the turmoil in France warranted
a suspension of the mission. No foreign news which might have led him
to change his mind had been received; no ostensible change in the domestic situation could have influenced him. Priding himself on his independence, suspicious of cabals, the virtually unanimous opinion of his
advisers that he suspend the mission may well have strengthened his
determination to send it. It appeared to Adams that the entire leadership
of the Federalist party was exerting pressure on him. Soon after he
arrived in Trenton he was astonished to learn that Ellsworth and Hamilton
were also there. "I transiently asked one of the heads of departments,"
he recalled, "whether Ellsworth and Hamilton had come all the way from
Windsor and New York, to persuade me to countermand the mission.
. . . I know of no motive of Mr. Ellsworth's journey. . . . Unsuspicious
as I was, I could not resist the evidence of my senses . . . Hamilton
unasked, had volunteered his influence. . . . I know of no business he
had at Trenton. Indeed I know, that in strict propriety he had no right
to come to Trenton at all without my leave. . . ."[68] However cautious
historians should be in unveiling secret motives, it is difficult to escape
the conclusion reached more than a century ago by the arch-Federalist
historian George Gibbs: "Again had HAMILTON risen up like a spectre
in his path. To meet *him,* the intriguer, there, with his coadjutors, Pickering, Wolcott, and McHenry; to find Ellsworth coming on to join them,
had roused the lurking demon of suspicion in his breast, and from that
moment he was ungovernable. He had nearly been the victim of a plot,
but the chief actor had too soon discovered himself."[69]
Adams' behavior at least had the virtue of consistency. Just as he had
chosen in February, 1799, to take his advisers by surprise in announcing
the appointment of the mission, so eight months later he chose to shock
them by ordering it to depart after he had intimated it would be suspended. In neither case was the substance of his decision censurable;

in both cases the manner in which it was done alienated not only his advisers but an important wing of his party.[70] The parallel goes further. Just as he had tried to take the political sting out of his decision in February by subsequently announcing that the envoys would not proceed until definite assurances of their reception had been received from France, so he now "declared his opinion that no treaty will be formed " and "even told the envoys that it would not be injurious to the interests of the United States, if they should be treated with indignity."[71] Some Federalists undoubtedly agreed with Timothy Pickering's and Hamilton's strained argument that the main objection to the mission was that its success might jeopardize United States relations with England,[72] others were mistakenly convinced that only a war with France could save the nation's wounded pride, but a goodly number of the so-called "High Federalists" objected on political grounds. Their dilemma was expressed by Jedidiah Morse, stalwart New England Federalist, who wrote soon after the mission sailed: "We know not how to order our speech aright, on this most interesting of all political subjects by reasons of darkness. *Dissent* is painful, open *opposition* might be fatal and dangerous. *Silence* is hardly expected from republicans. . . .[73] Adams' mistake in dispatching the envoys, James McHenry wrote to Washington, was not diplomatic but political. It would "become an apple of discord to the federalists that may so operate upon the ensuing election of President," he explained, "as to put in jeopardy the fruits of all their past labours, by consigning to men, devoted to French innovations and demoralizing principles, the reins of government. It is this dreaded consequence which afflicts, and calls for all the wisdom of, the federalists."[74] "The effects upon our domestic interests appear to me incapable of mitigation," echoed Oliver Wolcott. "It is certain that the federal party will be paralyzed . . . the President will gain no new supporters; his former friends will be in disgrace with the public, and the administration of John Adams, so much extolled, will end by the transfer of the powers of government to the rival party."[75]

Adams himself believed that the dispatch of the envoys and the Convention of 1800 which they subsequently negotiated was "the most disinterested, the most determined and the most successful of my whole life."[76] Although this has been virtually the unanimous opinion of historians for the past century or more, pro-Federalist historians writing in the decades before the Civil War did not agree.[77] There is, I think, more substance to their position than even they realized. In the first place, it is altogether likely, as I have suggested earlier, that peace negotiations would have taken place even had Adams not put country above party and sped the envoys on their way. In the second place, the Convention did not secure redress for French spoliations of American commerce—the major grievance over which the Americans had fought an undeclared war and which had been made a condition of any treaty. Third, the Convention of 1800 brought a pause and not an end to the Franco-American dispute. Within less than a decade Napoleon would adopt the discredited policies of the Directory and Jefferson and Madison would confront the same kind of French aggression and bellicosity which they had refused to credit in 1798.

The decision to seek a truce in the undeclared war was made by the French and was based on (1) a recognition of the increasing military capability of the United States; (2) a realization that their American policy had been predicated on the false premise that French intransigence might lead to the defeat of the Federalist party; (3) a sudden awareness that the American policy of the Directory had not promoted the economic or military advantages of France; (4) a realization that to prod America into an undeclared war was to push her into the arms of England; and (5) Napoleon's desire to beguile the United States while he secretly acquired Lousiana from Spain as the first step in building a colonial empire in the Mississippi Valley.

E. Wilson Lyon, the authority on the Convention of 1800, has said that "The publication of the XYZ dispatches in America in 1798 so alarmed Talleyrand, then Secretary for Foreign Affairs, that he became a veritable apostle for peace."[78] Throughout the spring and summer of 1799, the French government steadfastly manifested its determination to reach a rapprochement with the United States. In the autumn of 1799, as the Directory tottered, Talleyrand, never one to remain loyal to lost causes, resigned. His replacement as foreign minister, Reinhard, concluded that the negotiations should take place in the United States and proposed that a French minister be sent there.[79] The Directory never had a chance to act on Reinhard's recommendation for it was overthrown by Napoleon in the coup d'etat of November 9, 1799, and Talleyrand, resuming his old position of foreign secretary, continued the peace offensive begun more than a year earlier, including the assurances that American envoys would be courteously received in France. He deserves, as Lyon has said, "the principal credit for restoration of normal relations between the countries."[80]

The decision of the Directory to seek a negotiated peace was owing in part to the military build-up in the United States, but more importantly to the fact that French policy was self-defeating. By issuing retaliatory decrees designed to drive neutral commerce from the seas, particularly the notorious law of January 18, 1798, the Directory was unwittingly imposing a self-blockade. France, the country most urgently in need of supplies carried in neutral ships, was following a policy calculated to destroy neutral shipping. As Admiral Mahan commented, "Every blow against a neutral was really, even though not seemingly, a blow for Great Britain."[81] Napoleon was quicker to see this fallacy in French policy than the Directory had been, and in December, 1799, he repealed the notorious decree of January, 1798, and a few weeks later sought to curb the power of the prize courts which so flagrantly had violated neutral rights.

The French would have been singularly obtuse had they not seen that hostilities with the United States were strengthening the ties between the latter and England. Although some Federalists flirted with the idea of an Anglo-American alliance, neither the Administration nor Congress was receptive to a formal entanglement. But, in fact, as Bradford Perkins has pointed out, "the period from the publication of the XYZ dispatches to the Mortefontain convention was marked by common action and mutual assistance in the military field that was not equalled for more than a century."[82] Such a de facto alliance was far from fitting into Napoleon's plans. Aware that the French navy was all but destroyed, he determined to form a maritime league against Great Britain and to make peace with the world's leading neutral carrier was a necessary prerequisite to his ambitious schemes. The Convention of 1800 was, in short, one aspect of Napoleon's grand design for crushing British maritime supremacy. It is difficult to escape the conclusion that France would have abandoned the suicidal policy of the Directory even had John Adams not accepted its first peace-feelers.

That many New England Federalists should have viewed the Convention of 1800 as a betrayal of the interests of their section is understandable. Indeed, it is scarcely going too far to say that peace was purchased at the expense of the country's Federalist strong-hold. The United States had gone to the brink of war because of French attacks on their commerce and to Federalists a sine qua non of any treaty was payment for the losses American shipowners had sustained. To their great disappointment the Convention of 1800 failed to guarantee indemnity for spoliations committed upon American vessels and cargoes.[83]

Although the U.S. commissioners has been instructed to demand compensation for the maritime losses of American citizens as "an indispensable condition of the treaty," they found the French adamantly opposed to grant it. For their part, the French negotiators insisted that the U.S.

renounce its unilateral abrogation of the Franco-American treaties, a demand that the Americans stubbornly resisted. Finally, after months of wearying negotiations, the French suggested a quid pro quo—in exchange for French agreement to postpone discussion of the annulment of the Franco-American treaties, the Americans would agree to defer their demand for indemnities. When the treaty was signed at Paris on September 30, 1800, this compromise was contained in Article II which provided for renewed negotiation "at a convenient time on the problem of indemnities, the treaties of 1778, and the consular convention of 1788."[84] However imperative peace may have been for the Americans, the French had struck an undeniably shrewd bargain. To offset claims which even Talleyrand admitted were justified, they had set up treaties whose guarantees, as they well knew, had proven illusory.[85]

On February 5, 1801, the U.S. Senate, still controlled by Federalists, approved the convention with the significant reservations that it remain in force for only eight years and that Article II be expunged. Doubtless welcoming the opportunity thrust upon him by the United States, Napoleon agreed to accept the reservations only on condition that the United States abandon the indemnities. The efforts of William Vans Murray to salvage the claims made no dent in France's determination to avoid paying them. After Talleyrand sharply warned him that the patience of the French was wearing thin and that the United States must, in effect, accept Napoleon's counter-proposal or do without a treaty, Murray acquiesced. To obtain a treaty with France, as a nineteenth century pro-Federalist historian lamented, "The American government . . . sacrificed the rights of its own citizens" by taking "away all possibility of indemnity for spoliations committed upon American vessels and cargoes."[86] The U.S. Congress, it should be noted, tardily admitted the validity of this charge. An act of January 20, 1885, authorized the U.S. Court of Claims to ascertain claims "arising out of illegal captures, detentions, seizures, condemnations, and confiscations prior to the ratification of the Convention" of 1800.[87] In 1915 the Court of Claims awarded damages of $7,149,306.10. By the year 1955 Congress had appropriated $3,910,860.61 toward their payment.[88]

Historians, with their fondness for periodization, tend to divide the history of early American foreign policy into two distinct periods—the Administrations of Washington and Adams and the Administrations of Jefferson and Madison. In point of fact, "the problems of English and French violations of American commerce remained unsolved from 1793 until the close of the War of 1812 and of the Napoleonic epoch."[89] The Convention of 1800 did not, in fact, inaugurate a new era of Franco-

American relations. On October 1, 1800, one day after the signing of the treaty of Mortefontain, Bonaparte and Talleyrand secured the retrocession of Louisiana from Spain and the presence of the tricolor at New Orleans again embroiled the two countries in dispute.

When news of the Treaty of San Ildefonso reached the United States some six months later the hostility to France which had been quashed by the convention signed the previous September was revived. "I find men, formerly the most vehement in their politics," said Edward Thornton, British chargé des affaires in the United States, "asserting in the most unqualified terms the necessity of an union among all the members of the civilized world to check her [France's] encroachments, and to ensure the general tranquility."[90] Confronted with Napoleon's plans for a magnificent empire on the banks of the Mississippi, Jefferson and Madison reacted just as Adams and Pickering had responded to French plunder of American commerce in 1798 and 1799. By the spring of 1802, Jefferson was proposing measures which even John Adams had balked at adopting. French possession of New Orleans, he said in his famous letter to Robert R. Livingston, would seal "the union of two nations who in conjunction can maintain exclusive possession of the ocean. From that moment we must marry ourselves to the British fleet and nation."[91] Jefferson was saved from an Anglo-American alliance and war against France by Napoleon's timely concession of Louisiana.[92] But it was clearly the Louisiana Purchase rather than the Convention of 1800 which ended the Franco-American quarrel.

Even this magnificent diplomatic triumph brought a truce rather than peace. Napoleon soon adopted the very policies he had renounced in 1800, and from 1806 until 1812 his open contempt for American rights presented Presidents Jefferson and Madison with the same situation which had led to the naval war of 1798-1800. The significant differences were two: the United States now had to endure simultaneously the systematic plunder of her commerce by the British, and the American people, as Samuel E. Morison has said, now "preferred a foreign policy of debility and inaction to the Federalist policy of defense and reprisal."[93] When the Republicans finally adopted the latter policy and applied it against England, the Federalists, aping their former opponents, took refuge in states' rights and schemes of disunion. It is at least curious that the Republicans brilliantly accomplished what the Federalists had unsuccessfully tried to do: they attached to their opponents the stigma of disloyalty from which the Federalist party never recovered.

Whatever other merits Adams may have had (and they were numerous), historians should hesitate before endorsing his claim that the Convention of 1800, its preliminaries and aftermath, "must be transmitted to posterity as the most glorious period in American history, and as the most disinterested, prudent, and successful conduct in my whole life."[94] It may have averted a war, although this is unlikely since France as early as the summer of 1798 had decided not to fight one. Far from settling the differences between France and the United States, it was at best a temporary settlement, as the stormy relations between them from 1801 to 1803 and from 1806 to 1812 abundantly attest. In combination with the Louisiana Purchase, the Convention of 1800 did for a time postpone war, which when it came was with England rather than France. Until we are able to weigh imponderables, we cannot be sure that it was better this way.

NOTES

[1] See, for example, John Spencer Bassett, *The Federalist System, 1789-1801* (New York, 1906), pp. 248-49; Samuel E. Morison, *The Life and Letters of Harrison Gray Otis* (Boston, 1913), I, 162-63.

[2] One exception is Edward Hake Phillips, "The Public Career of Timothy Pickering, Federalist, 1745-1802" (unpublished Ph.D. dissertation, Harvard University, 1950).

[3] George Gibbs, *Memoirs of the Administrations of Washington and John Adams, Edited from the Papers of Oliver Wolcott . . .* (New York, 1846), II, 508 ff. (hereafter cited as Gibbs, *Wolcott*); Charles W. Upham, *The Life of Timothy Pickering* (Boston, 1873), III, 449, 490-93; John T. Morse, Jr., *John Adams* (Boston, 1897), p. 305; Henry Cabot Lodge, *Life and Letters of George Cabot* (Boston, 1870), p. 197.

[4] James D. Richardson, ed., *A Compilation of the Messages and Papers of the Presidents* (New York, 1897), I, 282.

[5] Sedgwick to Hamilton, February 22, 1799. Hamilton Papers, Library of Congress.

[6] Pickering to Hamilton, February 25, 1799. Hamilton Papers, Library of Congress.

[7] Upham, *Pickering*, III, 439.

[8] Richardson, *Messages and Papers*, I, 256.

[9] *Ibid.*, I, 262-63. In his message of December 8, Adams attempted to take a middle ground between the demands of his own party leaders that he refrain from offering to send another minister to France and the demands of Republican leaders that he scrap his preparedness program and reopen negotiations, with or without assurances. By combining the offer to reopen negotiations with a call for the vigorous prosecution of his defense program he pleased no one—the Federalists concluded that he was being irresolute and Republicans charged that he was a warmonger.

[10] *Ibid.*, I, 269.

[11] *Ibid.*, I, 266.

[12] December 12, 1798. *Ibid.*, I, 267.

[13] See "An Act suspending commercial intercourse with France," February 9, 1799 *(I Stat.,* 613-16); "An Act augmenting the Navy," February 25, 1799 *(I Stat.,* 621-22); "An Act regulating the medical establishment," March 2, 1799 *(I Stat.,* 721-23); "An Act for better organizing the troops of the United States," March 3, 1799 *(I Stat.,* 749-55); "An Act augmenting the Army," March 2, 1799 *(I Stat.,* 725-27). Although most of these measures were passed after Adams' nomination of the peace mission they had been introduced and were on the way to passage before then.

[14] On January 15, 1799, Adams wrote to his Secretary of State: "The President of the

United States requests the Secretary of State to prepare the draught of a project of a treaty and consular convention, such as in his opinion might at this day be acceded to by the United States, if proposed by France. It is his desire, that the Secretary of State would avail himself of the advice and assistance of all the heads of department in the formation of this composition, to be completed as soon as the pressure of other business of more immediate necessity, will permit. The necessity of inviolable confidence will be obvious.'' Charles Francis Adams, ed., *The Works of John Adams* (Boston, 1853), VIII, 621. This letter was sent several days after the return of Adams' son, Thomas, from Europe. Thomas Adams had brought with him official dispatches from William Vans Murray and John Quincy Adams and information on their personal views of the sincerity of French proposals for a reopening of negotiations.

[15] *American State Papers: Foreign Relations,* II, 229-38. Since Adams carefully went over the report, deleting passages to which he objected and suggesting changes, and since he submitted it to Congress, most Federalists reasonably assumed that it expressed his own views. See Pickering to Adams, January 18, 1799 (Adams, *Works,* VIII, 621-23).

[16] The French decree, dated October 20, 1798, stated that any person, whether the citizen of a neutral country or not, found upon a British warship "shall by this single fact be declared a pirate, and treated as such, without being permitted, in any case, to allege that he had been forced into such service by violence, threats, or otherwise" (*American State Papers: Foreign Relations,* II, 238).

[17] Article III of the decree of March 2, 1797, provided that ". . . every individual known to be an American, who shall hold a commission given by the enemies of France, as well as every seaman of that nation making a part of the crew of enemy ships, shall, by that act alone, be declared a pirate, and be treated as such, without being allowed in any case to allege that he was forced to it by violence, menaces, or otherwise" (*Ibid.,* II, 31).

[18] Richardson, *Messages and Papers,* I, 272.

[19] See, for example, Page Smith, *John Adams* (New York, 1962), II, 1001; Bassett, *Federalist System,* p. 248.

[20] Stephen Higginson and George Cabot were among those New Englanders who strongly urged war (see Higginson to Pickering, January 1, 1799. *American Historical Association Report,* 1896, I, 817; Cabot to Wolcott, October 6, 1798. Lodge, *Cabot,* pp. 168-70). Until we know much more than at present we do about public opinion in the 1790's it cannot be categorically asserted that they represented the opinion of even the New England wing of the Federalist party. Henry Cabot Lodge's observation that "between the partisans who favored peace on any terms and the war-Federalists were a portion of the Democratic and the larger part of the Federalist party" (*Cabot,* p. 192) is closer to the truth. Indeed, even James McHenry, who himself desired a declaration of war but realized its inexpediency, pointed out that many Federalists "dread an actual state of war" (To John Adams, November 25, 1798. Adams Papers, Massachusetts Historical Society). More importantly, if a war party existed in Congress it had been clearly defeated two months before Adams announced his intention to renew negotiations. In an answer to Adams' charges against his Cabinet, written a decade after the event, Benjamin Stoddert said that "A majority of a caucus, composed entirely of Federal members of the two Houses, would not agree to a declaration of war" (October 12, 1809. Quoted in Lodge, *Cabot,* p. 202).

[21] McHenry's and Stoddert's opinions are in the Adams Papers, Massachusetts Historical Society.

[22] Pickering to Adams, November 27, 1798. Adams Papers, Massachusetts Historical Society.

[23] November, 1798, Gibbs, *Wolcott,* II, 170. Page Smith (*Adams,* II, 989) repeats the assertion made in the 1850's by Charles F. Adams (*Works,* VIII, 610) that Hamilton wrote Wolcott's opinion. Although Jefferson expressed such an opinion in January, 1799, no proof of Hamilton's authorship has ever been given and neither the papers of Wolcott nor Hamilton contain even a reference to it. Stephen G. Kurtz asserts that it was dictated at

a conference which Pickering held with "the army high command when Pinckney, Hamilton, and Washington arrived in Trenton . . . in early November" 1798 (*The Presidency of John Adams: The Collapse of Federalism* [Philadelphia, 1957], p. 342), but he offers no proof for the allegation. He presumably credited Jefferson's charge that "The President's speech . . . is supposed to have been written by the military conclave, and particularly Hamilton" (To James Madison, January 3, 1799. Paul Leicester Ford, ed., *The Works of Thomas Jefferson* [New York, 1904], IX, 3).

Adams' message of December 8 incorporated verbatim Wolcott's statement on U.S.-French relations with one significant exception. The crucial difference was this: Wolcott wrote that "the sending another minister to make a new attempt at negotiation would be an act of humiliation to which the United States ought not to submit without extreme necessity; no such necessity exists, it must therefore be left with France, if she is desirous of accommodation, to take the requisite steps . . . if France shall send a minister to negotiate, he will be received with honour and treated with candour . . ." (Gibbs, *Wolcott,* II, 171). Adams said: "But to send another minister, without more determinate assurances that he would be received, would be an act of humiliation to which the United States ought not to submit. It must, therefore, be left with France, if she is indeed desirous of accommodation, to take the requisite steps. The United States will steadily observe the maxims by which they have hitherto been governed. They will respect the sacred right of embassy" (Richardson, *Messages and Papers,* I, 263). The difference between the two statements is not so great as has been believed. Adams wanted France to agree to receive an American minister; Wolcott wished the French to send an accredited envoy to this country.

24 *Correspondence of the Late President Adams Originally Published in the Boston Patriot . . .* (Boston, 1809), Letter XVIII, 85. (Cited hereafter as *Boston Patriot Letters*).

25 Broadus Mitchell, *Alexander Hamilton* (New York, 1962), II, 459.

26 January 6, 1799. Hamilton Papers, Library of Congress.

27 To cite a single example—Stephen Kurtz (*Presidency of John Adams,* p. 349) has used Rufus King's statement in a letter of September 23, 1798 (Charles R. King, ed., *The Life and Correspondence of Rufus King . . .* [New York, 1894], II, 424-25) that "You will have no war" as evidence that Hamilton and the "High" Federalists continued to whoop it up for a war despite their knowledge that France was willing to end the difficulties between the two nations. Such an interpretation is not valid. Months before King had written Hamilton the same thing. On June 6, 1798, he wrote: "Be upon your guard; France will not declare war against us . . ." (*Ibid.,* pp. 337-38). But more important than the bare statement in King's letter of September 23 was his qualification of it. "No," he went on to say, "her policy will be to pursue with us the same course she already has done, and which has served her purpose in Italy and among the honest but devoted and ruined Swiss." In other words, far from believing that France wanted peace, King believed that she would attempt to gain her ends by subversion rather than formal war and therefore concluded that the Americans should redouble their defense preparations. As he wrote to Hamilton on October 20, 1798: "I am gratified in receiving your opinion of the good condition of our public affairs, but do not feel confident that we are as safe as you appear to think we are. It is fraud not force that I fear . . ." (*Ibid.,* p. 454).

28 Adams first hinted that he was considering a new departure in foreign policy on October 20, 1798, when he requested Pickering's advice on the reopening of negotiations. Adams, *Works,* VIII, 609.

29 *Ibid.,* IX, 243-44. Gerry had returned to the United States on October 1, 1799, and had given his opinions on French policy to the President in conversations held at Quincy. Barlow's views had been sent to Washington who, in turn, enclosed them in a letter he wrote to Adams on February 1, 1799. Adams was uninfluenced by Barlow's opinions. "The wretch has destroyed his own character to such a degree," he told Washington, "that I think it would be derogatory to you to give any answer at all to his letter" (February 19, 1799. *Ibid.,* VIII, 624). Logan, a Philadelphia Quaker, had gone to France as a self-

appointed emissary of peace. In an interview with Merlin, the President of the Directory, Logan was assured that France wanted peace. Adams was not impressed by Logan's tidings of peace. "The officious interference of individuals without public character or authority is not entitled to any credit," he said (Richardson, *Messages and Papers,* I, 267). Codman and Cutting sent word through Harrison Gray Otis that "France sincerely wished a reconciliation with America" (Phillips, "Pickering," p. 349).

[30] *Boston Patriot Letters,* II, 10.

[31] Talleyrand's letter, dated September 28, and intended for conveyance to Adams, is in *American State Papers: Foreign Relations,* II, 239. It was enclosed in a letter which William Vans Murray wrote to Adams on October 7, 1798 (Adams, *Works,* VIII, 688-90). The date on which the President received this letter is unknown. Charles Francis Adams concluded that "it must have been received by the early part of February, as the inclosure, which accompanied it, made the basis of the nomination of Mr. Murray to the Senate on the 18th of that month." (*Ibid.,* VIII, 688). Phillips ("Pickering," p. 356) states that "these letters arrived in January, according to Pickering's endorsement on the rear of them."

Samuel Flagg Bemis argues that Talleyrand's assurances were a crucial factor in the President's decision but believes that "John Quincy Adams' counsel tipped the scale in favor of still another negotiation with France" (*John Quincy Adams and the Foundations of American Foreign Policy* [New York, 1950], pp. 99-101). Other historians have been enterprising in discovering the unavowed motives for Adams' decision. George Gibbs attributed it to suspicion of Hamilton's military ambition and to an effort to woo the support of Republican opponents for the election of 1800 (*Wolcott,* II, 220-22). Adams' latest biographer, Page Smith, argues that whatever the "direct and practical considerations" which prompted Adams' decision he was, in fact, "casting off inveteracy," that "unwavering devotion to a policy which, however necessary and right at the time of its initiation, may, if persisted in too long, become dangerous and destructive." Adams was thus able, Smith says, "to see better and to judge more wisely" (*Adams,* II, 987).

Many contemporary Federalists were disturbed by the role which they believed Elbridge Gerry had played in the decision. Adams himself, writing ten years later, said his decision was based on information from Gerry who "brought home the direct, formal and official assurances, upon which the subsequent commission proceeded and peace was made (*Boston Patriot Letters,* XIII, 65). Adams' willingness to lend credence to Gerry's opinions, it should be added, dismayed his contemporaries and has puzzled historians. The President had censured Gerry for remaining in Paris after Marshall and Pinckney left and had authorized his peremptory recall. Yet, two months later, when Gerry, by this time the *bête noire* of the Federalists and the hero of the Republicans, returned to the United States, Adams warmly welcomed him and paid more attention to his opinions than to those expressed by Marshall and Pinckney.

Although one should doubtless try to avoid the pitfall of attributing hidden motives, in Adams' case it is difficult to avoid the inference to which the evidence so clearly points—that he was prompted by motives which he did not avow. It is not only the suddenness of his reversal in policy but the contrast between the position he took in the summer of 1798 and that assumed only a few months later. In the summer of 1798 he had advocated war and had gone so far as to say to Jefferson "that he would not unbrace a single nerve for any treaty France would offer, such was their entire want of faith and morality" (quoted in Gibbs, *Wolcott,* II, 215). It is possible that Adams, suspicious as he was of his Cabinet, Hamilton, and Washington, was determined to undermine his enemies by a shrewd shift in diplomacy. Because his overture for peace was successful does not mean that his motives in pursuing it were as altogether selflessly patriotic as he made them out to be. They may, moreover, have been tinged with political considerations. Although I take strong exception to the type of evidence on which Stephen Kurtz relies to buttress his argument that Adams "saved the nation from Hamiltonian militarism and prevented the outbreak of the civil war," I find his argument that "motives of political expediency existed that Adams would have been blind to have overlooked and not acted upon" persuasive (*Presidency of John Adams*, pp. 353, 373). One can agree with Page Smith that "presidential elections were not a popularity contest in the 1790's" (*Adams*, II, 1002) and yet believe, as Smith does not, that Adams' nomination of Murray was in part a political maneuver designed to promote his chances for election in 1800. He may well have believed that by out-flanking his own official family and undermining Hamilton's influence within the party he could reassert his own leadership. Since he could anticipate the support of southern Federalists, he might reasonably have concluded that his decision to appoint Murray would win him as much support as he would lose. The retention of Wolcott and Pickering in his Cabinet, moreover, would serve to placate New England Federalists. Finally, he would with one bold act remove an issue which the opposition was using to discredit his administration.

32 Richardson, *Messages and Papers*, I, 272-73.

33 *Ibid.*, I, 274.

34 To Timothy Pickering, February 23, 1811. Lodge, *Cabot*, p. 206.

35 To Thomas Dwight, February 27, 1799. Seth Ames, ed., *Works of Fisher Ames . . .* (Boston, 1854), I, 252.

36 *Boston Patriot Letters*, X, 47-48. Benjamin Stoddert, Secretary of the Navy, disagreed with Adams' statement. He was unable to "perceive on what ground the five heads of departments, or any of them, would have given their advice against the measure, had they been consulted. All might not have agreed in the nomination of Mr. Murray, but I am convinced there would have been a majority for his appointment" (Stoddert to Adams, October 12, 1809. Lodge, *Cabot*, p. 202).

37 *Adams*, II, 1001.

38 In reply to a letter from Charles Lee, Attorney General of the U.S., supporting Adams' nomination of Murray, the President said that those who believed he would bow to the will of his party because he was elected President by only a three vote majority were in for a surprise. He was determined to be as independent and aggressive a leader as the Constitution would permit and would resign "if combinations of senators, generals, and heads of departments" should be formed too powerful to resist. He was determined, however, to "try my own strength at resistance first" (March 29, 1799. Adams, *Works*, VIII, 629).

39 As John S. Basset has said: Adams should have taken "a ruling attitude in the beginning; and this would have prevented much of the friction . . ." (*Federalist Era*, pp. 248-49). Moreover, as Page Smith remarks, Adams was dependent primarily on the Hamiltonians for his nomination" (*Adams*, II, 1002), and political expediency alone should have initiated the search for a policy which would achieve his goal without alienating them.

40 Bemis, *John Quincy Adams*, p. 100.

41 Washington went on to explain: "Had we said to Mr. Talleyrand through the channel of his communication, we still are, as we always have been, ready to settle by fair Negotiations, all differences between the two Nations upon open, just and honourable terms; and it rests with the Directory (after the indignities with which *our* attempts to effect this, have been treated if they are equally sincere) to come forward in an unequivocal manner, and prove it by their Acts. Such conduct would have shown a dignified willingness on our part to Negotiate; and would have tested their sincerity, on the other. Under my present view of the subject, this would have been the course I should have pursued; keeping equally in view the horrors of War and the dignity of the Government" (Washington to Timothy Pickering, March 3, 1799. John C. Fitzpatrick, ed., *The Writings of George Washington* [Washington, 1940], XXXVII, 142-43).

42 *The Public Conduct and Character of John Adams, Esq., President of the United States* (Henry Cabot Lodge, ed., *The Works of Alexander Hamilton* [New York, 1904], VII, 343-44). See also Mitchell, *Hamilton*, II, 460.

43 *Ibid.*, pp. 345-46. The difference between such recommendations and the course Adams pursued is, of course, one of procedure and not substance. Adams first appointed the mission and then demanded assurances before they should embark; Washington and

Hamilton would have required the pledge before the appointment. As for Hamilton's belief that the French should send an envoy to the U.S., the President, for all his staunch resistance to the proposal in December, 1798, suggested it to Talleyrand only three months later as an alternative (Pickering to Murray, March 6, 1799. *Boston Patriot Letters*, VII, 31-32).

⁴⁴ Elections held in the months following the appointment of the mission, suggested that Adams' peace program was popular. Smith, *Adams*, II, 1003.

⁴⁵ Lodge, *Cabot*, p. 196.

⁴⁶ See, as examples, Bassett, *Federalist System*, pp. 249-50; Claude G. Bowers, *Jefferson and Hamilton* (Boston, 1945), pp. 434-36; Gilbert Chinard, *Honest John Adams* (Boston, 1933), pp. 286, 289; Morrison, *Otis*, I, 167; Edward Channing, *A History of the United States* (New York, 1917), IV, 204; Smith, *Adams*, II, 1010-15; Kurtz, *Presidency of John Adams*, pp. 370, 384, 388.

⁴⁷ *Boston Patriot Letters*, VI, 26-27.

⁴⁸ "Notes on the Negotiations with France," January, 1800. Gibbs, *Wolcott*, II, 279.

⁴⁹ *Boston Patriot Letters*, XV, 73.

⁵⁰ Hamilton to Theodore Sedgwick, February 19, 1799. Massachusetts Historical Society.

⁵¹ *Correspondence between the Hon. John Adams . . . and . . . Wm. Cunningham . . .* (Boston, 1823), Letter XXX, 93. (Cited hereafter as *Cunningham Letters*).

⁵² See Phillips, "Pickering," p. 379.

⁵³ On March 6, 1799, Timothy Pickering had written to William Vans Murray enclosing his commission as U.S. envoy to France and directing him to secure from the French "direct and unequivocal assurances . . . that the envoys shall be received in character . . ." (*American State Papers: Foreign Relations*, II, 243). Murray received this letter on May 4 and in accordance with its directive wrote to Talleyrand on the following day. The French minister replied on May 12 (*Ibid.*, pp. 243-44). For Murray's letter to Timothy Pickering, May 7, 1799, see *Boston Patriot Letters*, VII, 32-36.

⁵⁴ Pickering to Oliver Wolcott, August 2, 1799. Pickering Papers, Massachusetts Historical Society.

⁵⁵ Adams, *Works*, IX, 10-12.

⁵⁶ *Ibid.*, IX, 18.

⁵⁷ *Ibid.*, IX, 23. Adams received the letter on September 14.

⁵⁸ Pickering to Adams, September 11, 1799 (*Ibid.*, IX, 23-25). All the Cabinet members except Charles Lee, the Attorney General, concurred in the opinion. Lee was not present in Trenton, having returned to Virginia. On October 6, 1799, he wrote to Adams dissenting from the Cabinet opinion that the mission should be suspended (*Ibid.*, IX, 38).

⁵⁹ On September 16, Stephen Higginson wrote to Oliver Wolcott: "We are here all wondering at the new mission to France. . . . The language used by the President *and his lady*, is in direct opposition to such a measure, and she has expressed much surprise that the intimations given in the papers of preparations for the envoys should be believed. This singular opposition of sentiment to conduct perplexes people very much, and many will not believe that the President intends they shall go on. . . . I confess that I cannot in any way or degree, reconcile his general language on that subject, with a settled and persevering intention to send them forward . . ." (Gibbs, *Wolcott*, II, 262-63). Higginson's conclusion is substantiated by a letter which the President wrote to his Secretary of the Navy on September 4. Replying to Benjamin Stoddert's plea that he come to Trenton immediately Adams wrote: "I have no reason nor motive to precipitate the departure of the envoys. If any information of recent events in Europe should arrive, which, in the opinion of the heads of departments, or of the envoys themselves, would render any alteration in their instructions necessary or expedient, I am perfectly willing that their departure should be suspended, until I can be informed of it, or until I can join you. I am well aware of the possibility of events which may render a suspension, for a time, of the mission, very proper . . ." (Adams, *Works*, IX, 19-20).

[60] *Ibid.,* IX, 30.

[61] It has been said that Stoddert's letters to Adams of Aug. 29 and Sept. 13 (*Ibid.,* IX, 18-19, 25-29) were an attempt to warn the President against the intrigues of Pickering, Wolcott, and McHenry (Smith, *Adams,* II, 1013). Such an inference cannot fairly be drawn from the Secretary of Navy's letters. "I have been apprehensive," he explained to Adams on September 13, "that artful designing men might make such use of your absence from the seat of government, when things so important to restore peace with one country, and to preserve it with another, were transacting, as to make your next election less honorable than it would otherwise be" (Adams, *Works,* IX, 28). What Stoddert meant by this remark is explained in the preceding paragraph of the same letter. If the instructions were prepared and the mission departed while Adams was still at Quincy, he said, responsibility for them might be attributed to the Cabinet rather than the President. Since the former "however high their merit, and however respected, . . . are not enough known to inspire the same degree of confidence" as the President, Adams' presence was politically necessary (*Ibid.*).

[62] As late as September 16, Adams wrote to Pickering that "I presume the whole business (of the envoys) may be as well conducted by letter and the post" (*Ibid.,* IX, 30). But receipt of Stoddert's letter of September 13 (see the above note) presumably convinced Adams that he should go to Trenton so that the decision, whatever it might be, would have the obvious stamp of presidential authority.

[63] Doubtless to the dismay of Pickering, he dropped a hint that he again had changed his mind about dispatching the envoys and would order them to proceed (September 21, 1799. *Ibid.,* IX, 33). Yet on the following day, he informed Oliver Ellsworth that "the convulsions in France . . . will certainly induce me to postpone for a longer or shorter time the mission to Paris (*Ibid.,* IX, 35). Taking this statement at face value, Ellsworth concluded that his mission had been suspended (see his letters to Oliver Wolcott of October 1, and to Adams of October 5, 1799. Gibbs, *Wolcott,* II, 266-67, 275).

[64] *Boston Patriot Letters,* VI, 27.

[65] Wolcott to Hamilton, October 2, 1800. Gibbs, *Wolcott,* II, 277-78.

[66] Adams to Timothy Pickering, October 16, 1799. Adams, *Works,* IX, 39.

[67] *Boston Patriot Letters,* XV, 76.

[68] *Boston Patriot Letters,* XVI, 78-79. Adams gave two accounts of his meeting with Hamilton in Trenton (see *Boston Patriot Letters,* VI, 24-30 and *Cunningham Letters,* XIV, 48). Hamilton explained his presence in Trenton as follows: "The truth most certainly is, that I went to Trenton with General Wilkinson, pursuant to a preconcert with him of some week's standing to accelerate, by personal conferences with the Secretary of War, the adoption and execution of arrangements which had been planned between the General and myself, for the future disposition of the western army; that when I left New York upon this journey, I had no expectation whatever, that the President would come to Trenton, and that I did not stay at this place a day longer than was indispensable to the object I have stated" (quoted in Gibbs, *Wolcott,* II, 276-77). McHenry in writing to Timothy Pickering on February 3, 1811, gives this account of Hamilton's presence in Trenton: "I have, be assured, no reason or ground for supposing that the General was appraised or had any knowledge of the President's approach; and I know the business that occasioned his coming to Trenton was with my department. . . . Being in Trenton, it was proper he should visit Mr. Adams. . . . The fact is, to complete his instructions to General Wilkinson, who was to be disposed on the frontiers, it was necessary to consult my department. For this purpose, General Hamilton had my permission to come to Trenton, and I certainly had the right to give it" (Lodge, *Cabot,* pp. 209-10).

[69] *Wolcott,* II, 276.

[70] New England Federalists had believed that the mission would be suspended. See Jedidiah Morse to Oliver Wolcott, November 8, 1799. Gibbs, *Wolcott,* II, 287; Fisher Ames to Timothy Pickering, October 19, 1799. Ames, *Works,* I, 257; Stephen Higginson to Oliver Wolcott, September 16, 1799. Gibbs, *Wolcott,* II, 262-63.

[71] Oliver Wolcott, "Notes on the Negotiations with France," January, 1800. *Ibid.,* II,

279. Wolcott also wrote that the President "said he did not believe that France would agree to the conditions which had been proposed, and that the nomination of the envoys, was the only way in which the insidious views of the French government could be detected, and explained to the American people" (*Ibid.*, IX, 278).

⁷² Timothy Pickering to George Washington, October 24, 1799. *Ibid.*, II, 280. See also George Cabot to Oliver Wolcott, October 16, 1798. Lodge, *Cabot,* pp. 244-46; Hamilton to Washington, October 21, 1799. Lodge, *Hamilton's Works,* X, 356.

⁷³ To Oliver Wolcott, November 8, 1799. Gibbs, *Wolcott,* II, 287.

⁷⁴ November 10, 1799. Jared Sparks, ed., *The Writings of George Washington* (Boston, 1840), XI, 575.

⁷⁵ To George Cabot, November 7, 1799. Gibbs, *Wolcott,* II, 286-87.

⁷⁶ *Cunningham Letters,* XXXIV, 101.

⁷⁷ See, for example, Gibbs, *Wolcott,* II, 438-41.

⁷⁸ "The Franco-American Convention of 1800," *Journal of Modern History,* XII (September, 1940), 305.

⁷⁹ *Ibid.,* p. 307. It is true, as Lyon points out, that Reinhard was bent on imposing stiff peace terms. But the significant point is French willingness to open negotiations by sending an envoy to the United States.

⁸⁰ *Ibid.,* p. 308. John Spencer Bassett wrote of the new approach in French policy that "the policy of nursing a French interest in America, which for seven years had been followed by Republican leaders in Paris, was now abandoned" (*Federalist System,* p. 250). To the contrary, there well may have been substance to the Federalist charge that Talleyrand was again seeking to strengthen the pro-French group in the United States. If so, his diplomacy was a brilliant success.

⁸¹ Quoted in Eli F. Hecksher, *The Continental System: An Economic Interpretation* (Oxford, 1922), p. 50.

⁸² *The First Rapprochement: England and the United States, 1795-1805* (Philadelphia, 1955), p. 95. For Perkins' convincing proof of close Anglo-American cooperation during the Quasi-War see pp. 95-105.

⁸³ There were two categories of American claims against France. The first consisted of "spoliations at the hands of French warships" and amounted to a total damage of $7,149,306.10. The second included "claims for embargoes, seizure of cargoes in French ports, arbitrary purchases, etc., which accumulated between 1793 and 1800" and amounted to $5,000,000. The Convention of 1800 made no provision for the payment of either class of claims. The first class was ultimately assumed by the U.S. and more than a century later ascertained by the U.S. Court of Claims. The second class of claims "were assumed in 1803 by the U.S. Government" to the limited amount of 20,000,000 francs, as part payment for Louisiana (Bemis, *Diplomatic History of the United States* [New York, 1955], pp. 114-115).

⁸⁴ Hunter Miller, ed., *Treaties and Other International Acts of the United States of America,* II, 457-87. The negotiations which resulted in the Convention of 1800 can be followed in John B. Moore, ed., *International Adjudications* . . . (New York, 1933), V, 203-210.

⁸⁵ Lyon, "Franco-American Convention," pp. 313, 316. The negotiations were from the beginning complicated by knotty questions of international law. For a discussion of some of these questions see Brooks Adams, "The Convention of 1800," *Massachusetts Historical Society Proceedings,* XLIV, (1911), 377-428. Had the two countries actually been at war, for example? If so, the treaties would have been annulled and the claims of the United States for spoliations permissible only in so far as the French might choose to admit them in the peace treaty. Both sides, therefore, denied that they had been engaged in a war. The Americans took the position that the guarantee in Article XII of the Treaty of 1778 which stated that "in case of rupture between France and England the reciprocal guarantee . . . shall have its full force and effect the moment such war shall break out" was inoperative in the Anglo-French war (Francis Wharton, ed., *A Digest of the Interna-*

tional Law of the United States . . . [Washington, 1887], II, 721). The United States contended that the *casus foederis* could never occur except in a defensive war and the French, it was argued, were not so engaged. France alleged on the other hand that American refusal to honor its treaty obligations had contributed to the loss of her West Indian possessions and thus constituted a French claim against the United States. This claim the American envoys consistently denied, arguing that "A Treaty being a mutual compact, a palpable violation of it by one party did, by the law of nature and of nations, leave it optional with the other to renounce and declare the same to be no longer obligatory. . . . The remaining party must decide whether there has been such violation on the other part as to justify its renunciation . . ." *(Ibid.,* p. 723). What was the validity of these conflicting claims in international law? Perhaps the most satisfactory answer to the problem was given in 1886 by Judge John Davis in a Court of Claims decision on the French spoliation cases: "Our claims were good by the law of nations, and we had no need to turn back to the treaties for a foundation upon which to rest our arguments. Not so with France. Her national claims must necessarily rest on treaty provisions . . ." *(Ibid.,* p. 725). But the American commissioners were forced either to give credence to the French contention or return home with no treaty. The point is, as I have said above, that the French managed to rid themselves of justified American claims by surrendering treaty obligations that were in fact of little national advantage to them. That the Americans were forced to accept the French interpretation of international law is doubtless a measure of France's superior bargaining position. The Convention of 1800, in other words, was more a French than an American diplomatic triumph.

[86] Upham, *Pickering,* III, 446.

[87] Wharton, *A Digest of the International Law,* II, 714.

[88] Bemis, *Diplomatic History,* p. 115.

[89] Morison, *Otis,* I, 50.

[90] Quoted in Perkins, *The First Rapprochement,* p. 163.

[91] April 18, 1802. *Works,* VIII, 145.

[92] Convincing evidence that Jefferson was willing to go this far to prevent the establishment of a French empire in Louisiana and that the Addington Ministry would have been receptive to American overtures is offered in Perkins, *The First Rapprochement,* pp. 160-170. According to Perkins, Jefferson raised the subject of an Anglo-American alliance at a Cabinet meeting in April, 1803, "and a majority was willing to bind the United States not to make a separate peace, a far more important restriction on American freedom of action than any responsible Federalist had considered in 1798" *(Ibid.,* p. 164).

[93] Morison, *Otis,* I, 180.

[94] *Cunningham Letters,* XXX, 93.

POLITICS AND LIBEL, 1800*

Dumas Malone

By far the most distinguished contemporary Jefferson scholar, Professor Dumas Malone has achieved a rare understanding of Jefferson's complex personality. In his definitive biography, Jefferson and His Times, *he has interpreted Jefferson anew for the present generation in warmly human terms. The chapter from the third volume,* Jefferson and the Ordeal of Liberty, *reprinted in this collection, concentrates on the political situation on the eve of the election of 1800. Malone's Jefferson, at this point, is subtle, yet effective as party leader. Sensitive to political developments in such key states as Virginia and Pennsylvania and keenly alert to the political significance of the Sedition Act trials, Jefferson nevertheless avoids direct participation in the growing party battles. He is the center of party activity and direction, yet at the same time remains the symbol of Republican principles. In his long and varied career, Professor Malone has been editor in chief of the* Dictionary of American Biography *and director and chairman of the Board of Syndics of Harvard University Press. Formerly a professor of history at Columbia University, he has been Jefferson Foundation Professor of History at the University of Virginia and, since 1962, resident biographer.*

Since the Federalists dominated all branches of the general government in 1800, the continuing struggle of the Republicans against them was waged more effectively on the state than the national level. Control of state governments was of crucial importance because the determination of the manner in which presidential electors should be chosen lay with the various legislatures. At this time there was no uniform practice,

* Reprinted by permission of Little, Brown and Co. From *Jefferson and the Ordeal of Liberty* by Dumas Malone (Boston, Little, Brown and Co., 1962). Copyright © 1962 by Dumas Malone. Chapter XXIX, "Politics and Libel, 1800," pp. 459-483.

and as a rule the dominant political group in a particular state prescribed the method which promised to be to its own advantage.[1] A full story of the presidential election of 1800, therefore, would comprise accounts of the struggles over the control of the legislatures in all sixteen states, and the various actions with respect to the method of choosing electors. Since Jefferson himself played virtually no direct part in these local struggles, there would be no real point in attempting to describe them here even if it were practicable to do so. Reference may be made, however, to a few of them, beginning with his own commonwealth and Pennsylvania, a state which always bulked large in his political thinking and about whose affairs he was well informed because he was spending part of each year in Philadelphia.

In Virginia the Republicans consolidated their position during the winter of 1799-1800 at the session of the General Assembly. It was then that Madison, emerging from retirement to assume a dominant legislative role, presented the renowned Report which closed the cycle of the Kentucky and Virginia Resolutions by strongly reaffirming the opposition of the Assembly to the Alien and Sedition Acts and clarifying the constitutional position of the dominant party.[2] He and other persons in thorough sympathy with the universally recognized leader of that party were in full control of the situation. Jefferson's disciple James Monroe was now governor, and another neighbor and intimate friend, Wilson Cary Nicholas, was elected to the United States Senate after the death of Henry Tazewell. In the light of history the most important action of this Assembly was the adoption of Madison's Report, but in the immediate political situation the most significant thing it did was to change the election law. In 1796, when presidential electors were chosen in Virginia by districts, supporters of Jefferson carried all the districts but one. In later congressional elections, however, the Federalists made marked gains. The majority party now sought to assure itself of the entire electoral vote of the state by providing for the choice of electors on a general ticket, as is the rule in our own time. This was not an undemocratic move, such as provision for election by the legislature would have been, but it was clearly in the interest of the majority vis-à-vis the minority.

There is no reason to believe that the idea of changing the law was Jefferson's in the first place, but he expressed himself privately to Monroe, and through Monroe to Madison and other leaders, as favorable to it under existing political circumstances. He said that election by districts would be the best method if it were general throughout the country, but in view of the fact that ten states chose electors by means of the legislatures or on a general ticket, he thought it folly for the others not to do likewise. "In these ten states," he said, "the minority is entirely unrepresented."[3] Judging from the returns of the congressional elections, the Republicans would have gained considerably in the country as a whole if choice by districts had been universal—that is, if every state had had a law like the one in effect in Virginia in 1796. Their present action in that state seemed desirable on purely political grounds in view of the immediate local situation, but the vote on the general-ticket law was embarrassingly close and there were many objections to the change in procedure. Hitherto Virginians had voted viva voce for a single candidate whom they knew personally, rather than for a long list, and the change involved numerous practical difficulties. Before there was actual voting under the new law, the Republican organization devised means to relieve the individual voters by having written lists prepared in advance for distribution among the freeholders, who could deposit them after signing their names. Madison believed that since the avowed object of the change was to give Virginia "fair play," it would become popular after proper explanation. That it did become so may be questioned, but the least valid of the objections to it were raised by the Federalists, who conveniently disregarded the high-handed actions of their own party in other states.[4]

Writing Monroe, Jefferson added this observation to his comments on the proposal: "Perhaps it will be thought I ought in delicacy to be silent on this subject. But you, who know me, know that my private gratifications would be most indulged by that issue which should leave me most at home." Even with reference to political activities within his own state he generally was silent. His role was one of acquiescence in the judgment of his friends rather than that of organizer. These friends and supporters created an elaborate organization for this campaign before the legislators dispersed. To begin with, they adopted an impressive ticket of electors, drawn from all parts of the state. This included George Wythe, Edmund Pendleton, and James Madison. They set up a central committee of five in Richmond, under the chairmanship of Philip Norborne Nicholas, and a committee of the same number in each county. Informing Jefferson of these actions, Nicholas said that the objects of establishing the committees were "to communicate useful information to the people relative to the election; and to repel every effort which may be made to injure either the ticket in general or to remove any prejudice which may be attempted to be raised against any person on that ticket."[5] Correspondence between the general committee and the subcommittees was begun immediately and became increasingly important in the heat of the summer campaign.[6]

Jefferson explained his delay of nearly two months in acknowledging the letter from the man who was virtually his campaign manager in Virginia on the ground that he was waiting until he could send him certain pamphlets containing views which he was anxious to have generally distributed.[7] These were papers by Joseph Priestley's friend Thomas Cooper, on the subject of "political arithmetic," of which he sent eight dozen copies so that one or more might go to every county in the state. Cooper, who afterwards gained considerable note as an economist and advocate of *laissez-faire*, was attacking foreign commerce in a way which Jefferson would not have wholly liked while Secretary of State, but which he now approved as a critic of the administration. He wanted the various committees to be agencies of information, which they unquestionably became, though some thought this particular item too heavy for the popular digestion.[8] Only to this degree does he appear to have co-operated directly with Nicholas's organization, and he left no doubt that he wanted his co-operation kept secret. At this stage there was no need for him to do anything for the Republican cause in his state, where things were going well. In the spring elections for the Assembly and Congress, his party made marked gains in Virginia.

Things were also going well in Pennsylvania. Before he returned to Philadelphia, soon after Christmas in 1799, the Republicans had gained a substantial victory in the fall elections in the state, after a campaign in which the Federalists considerably surpassed them in rancor. Judge Thomas McKean, who defeated United States Senator James Ross in the gubernatorial race, was a rather conservative Republican whose victory can be best explained as the result of rather more effective organization than that of his opponent and as a revulsion against the excesses of Federalist national policy.[9] His margin of victory was provided by the counties identified with the Fries Rebellion against federal taxes. Jefferson neither anticipated nor approved this particular revolt, but he had clearly foreseen the general reaction against taxation and repression. He viewed developments in Pennsylvania as a party man. When John Beckley, former clerk of the federal House of Representatives and an incessantly active Republican, made application to Governor McKean for an appointment, he supported it. McKean rewarded Beckley with the clerkship of two local courts, regarding these offices as roughly equivalent to the clerkship of which he had been "unjustly deprived." Jefferson had a high opinion of Beckley's competence, but he gave here one of the first signs of his acceptance of the idea of a degree of spoilsmanship in politics. This is hardly to be wondered at since the Federalists proceeded on the assumption that only members of their persuasion were fit for office. He was amply repaid by Beckley, one of whose pamphlets in his behalf appeared in an edition of five thousand.[10]

The Federalists did not recover from their defeat in Pennsylvania, but by obstructive tactics in the legislature, where they retained control of the Senate, they threatened to rob the Republicans of the fruits of victory so far as the approaching presidential contest was concerned. They blocked the Republican attempt to pass an election law, with the result that there was no provision for the casting of the electoral vote of this state. The Republicans, therefore, could only bide their time until the fall elections of 1800, in which they hoped to gain control of both houses. Early in the year Jefferson himself recognized the possibility that Pennsylvania might be deprived of her vote in the presidential contest. This proved to be virtually the case, for the Republicans did not quite carry the state Senate in the fall, though they made gains there and were decisively victorious in other contests. To get ahead of the story, what finally happened was that, as a result of a legislative compromise, the Republican ticket got eight electoral votes and the Federalist seven, despite a clear Republican majority in the state.[11]

The notorious electoral count bill of Senator Ross arose directly out of the political situation in Pennsylvania. Sensing that there might well be a dispute about the vote of his state in the presidential contest, the recently defeated candidate for governor introduced into the United States Senate in January, 1800, a measure which would have assured Federalist victory there and elsewhere. It would have set up a committee of thirteen to pass on electoral returns, determining which votes should be counted or disallowed and who should be President—all this without the possibility of appeal from its decision. This committee would consist of six members elected by the House of Representatives, six by the Senate, and the Chief Justice—that is, it would have been dominated by the Federalists. Thus the issue would have been resolved quite simply in their favor.[12] Though this flagrantly partisan measure was passed by the Senate, and in amended form by the House, it died because of the intransigence of the extremists in the upper chamber.[13] Besides offering a striking example of arrogance and self-righteousness, this bill provided the occasion of a clash between the body over which Jefferson presided and William Duane of the *Aurora,* the Republican newspaperman the Federalists were most anxious to punish and silence. The Vice President was a firsthand witness of this affair, a thing which cannot be said of any of the trials under the Sedition Act.[14]

The Federalist executioners had been cheated of their prey when Benjamin Franklin Bache died of yellow fever in September, 1798, before he could be prosecuted for seditious libel. Duane, who succeeded him as editor of the *Aurora*, the most important single Republican paper, proved to be the most effective of the journalists of the opposition in this era and was supremely objectionable to the group in power for just that reason. Though the Ross bill was debated behind closed doors, Duane quickly got wind of it and denounced it. Then, receiving a copy of it from certain Republican senators, he published this in the *Aurora* with further caustic comments on senatorial conduct.[15] Some of his statements about what had happened were inaccurate but he correctly sensed the import of the measure.

This publication was regarded as a high breach of the privileges of the Senate by two-thirds of the members of that body—which in the opinion of at least Uriah Tracy of Connecticut could not be questioned by anybody at any time, anywhere. Despite the objections of the small Republican minority, who reminded their colleagues of severe criticisms of their actions which had been previously voiced by the Federalist *Gazette of the United States*, Duane was condemned by resolution without a hearing. He was then ordered to appear under a prescribed procedure which involved Jefferson.[16] When the culprit appeared, the presiding officer was to address him in specifically prescribed words, charging him with "false, scandalous, and malicious assertions" tending to defame the Senate and bring it into disrepute. Jefferson was to be spared from reading the Senate resolution of condemnation, since that task was committed to the clerk, but afterwards he was to ask if Duane had anything to say in excuse or extenuation. If there was no answer, the editor was to remain in custody of the sergeant at arms until the Senate should reach a decision—that is, a sentence. When reached, this was to be pronounced by the presiding officer.

If the intolerant majority had in mind the embarrassment of Jefferson, as well as the punishment of Duane, their plans were circumvented by the ingenuity of the journalist and two Republicans whom he called into consultation—Alexander James Dallas and Thomas Cooper—and by Duane's subsequent elusiveness. The Federalist senators would undoubtedly have charged Jefferson with collusion had they known of the private letter in which Cooper informed him of the plan of campaign the trio had devised against the body over which he presided.[17] But, since this in no way affected the Vice President's official conduct, the chief purpose it served, no doubt, was to relieve his mind.

The upshot was that Duane, appearing before the Senate, requested that he be permitted to advise with counsel and withdrew. According to his plan, he then addressed letters to Dallas and Cooper, asking them to serve as counsel. This they both declined to do on the ground that the Senate had already prejudged the case and that they would only degrade themselves by appearing before the Senate under the limitation and restrictions that body had imposed. Duane submitted the entire correspondence to Jefferson as president of the Senate, with a statement that he declined to appear under the existing circumstances and that the Senate might proceed to do whatever it saw fit. All this he published in the *Aurora*.[18] The Senate then declared Duane guilty of contempt though by a smaller majority than heretofore, and issued a warrant for his arrest. Jefferson signed this in his official capacity, but Duane absolved him of all blame for this formal action.[19]

Duane evaded the process server until after the adjournment of Congress, continuing to write for his paper all the while. After some weeks of hide and seek, a petition and remonstrance in his behalf from citizens of Philadelphia was presented by Senator William Bingham of Pennsylvania, who was himself quite out of sympathy with it. On the question whether or not it should be read, the vote was 12 to 12. Enjoying one of his rare opportunities to break a tie, Jefferson decided in the affirmative.[20] The Senate rejected the petition that it reconsider its action against Duane, but, apparently aware of its own impotence, it requested the President to prosecute him under the Sedition Act.[21] This was the last action of the session, after the Vice President had excused himself to go home; Senator Tracy, who would tolerate no criticism, was in the chair. The criticism by Duane had no apparent effect, for, as Jefferson noted, the electoral count bill as passed by the Senate was more extreme than the one that appeared in the *Aurora,* since it extended the powers of the grand committee to "*all* subjects of enquiry."[22] Because of a succession of delays, however, nothing ever came of the prosecution of Duane, against whom proceedings were finally dropped after the former Vice President had become President. In this episode Jefferson consistently manifested respect for the Senate, though his sympathies lay elsewhere and his patience must have been sorely tried.

The Republicans rightly regarded the proceedings against Duane as more arbitrary and tyrannical than those in the federal courts under the Sedition Act, but all these proceedings were similar in purpose. It is noteworthy that a large proportion of the sedition trials did not occur until 1800, when the war danger which had provided the original occasion and excuse for repressive measures had receded. The timing of the trials was in part accidental, for the mills of justice (or injustice) ground slowly, but it became increasingly obvious that these were in fact political trials in a crucial election year. Their object, as Jefferson had perceived from the beginning, was the silencing of the opposition press.[23] During the course of the actual trials his recorded comments on them were few. He gave them blanket condemnation, regarding the men convicted in them as victims of political persecution. No doubt he was informed of the various individual trials during what he described as a reign of witches, but the two that came closest to him were those of Thomas Cooper and James Thomson Callender. The former, which was a direct consequence of Cooper's activities in behalf of Duane although the charges were based on things he had said about John Adams some months earlier, occurred in Philadelphia. The latter took place in Virginia, where Callender had sought refuge but where Justice Samuel Chase sought to provide the Republican gentry with an object lesson in federal authority.

The names of Duane, Cooper, and Callender were frequently conjoined in the Federalist newspapers of the time, especially in Philadelphia. They were often castigated as "foreign emissaries." Cooper was English while Callender was Scottish, and both of them could be properly regarded as refugees. Duane's case was much disputed, for although born in the province of New York he had grown up in Ireland and spent years in various parts of the British Empire. The Federalists made no bones about designating him as an Irishman of dubious American patriotism. A more important allegation was that these three "emissaries" took their orders from Jefferson as "Chief Juggler."

The case was thus presented in a communication to a Federalist paper:

> With respect to the organization of their political plan, it commenced by a subdivision of their business in detail, into three Grand Departments. Callender takes the southern, Duane the eastern, and Cooper, with Priestley for his aid major, has the whole of the Jacobin interest of the western country under his immediate controul; all the doings of these three *chiefs of division,* are subject to the controul of the Chief Juggler and his select council.[24]

The charge that Jefferson directed the Republican editors and pamphleteers followed the line that Hamilton had laid down at the time of Freneau, but neither at that time nor at any other in this decade is it borne out by available records, and, in fact, he would have been out of character had he done so. He was not that sort of party leader. He encouraged the Republican press and at times urged particular persons, like James Madison and Edmund Pendleton, to write on specified topics. Upon occasion he provided information on request, but he would have done this for anybody, and there is no suggestion that he was responsible for the leakage of any official information. This advocate of the freedom of the press left the party writers to their devices, and if he erred he did so in trusting them too much.

This year marked the beginning of an intellectual friendship between him and Thomas Cooper, then of Northumberland, Pennsylvania, which lasted the rest of his life. Though Jefferson tended to overrate the abilities of Priestley's friend, Cooper was a man of impressive learning whose contributions to campaign literature were of an unusually high order.[25] Though an inveterate controversialist, he served only temporarily as a journalist—relieving the editor of the *Sunbury and Northumberland Gazette* for a few months in 1799. In the volume of *Political Essays* which he published soon thereafter he declared himself to be in America as he had been in England "a decided opposer of political restrictions on the liberty of the press, and a sincere friend to those first principles of republican government, the sovereignty of the people and the responsibility of their servants."[26] His discussion of freedom of the press was broadly philosophical, and this, with his economic philosophy of *laissez-faire,* showed him to be a man after Jefferson's own heart. In the election campaign of 1799 in Pennsylvania his services were comparable to those of Duane.

Tried on the charge of seditious libel in April, 1800, Cooper was sentenced on May 1 to pay a fine of four hundred dollars and spend six months in jail.[27] The specific remarks about John Adams which led to his conviction were drawn from a handbill he had published the previous autumn. Some of these remarks were extravagant, but the statement of Justice Samuel Chase that this was the boldest attempt he had known "to poison the minds of the people" was much more so. Quite obviously, Cooper was punished because he had made himself conspicuous in the Duane affair and was politically objectionable to the ruling group. When Chase voiced the suspicion that his fine would be paid by his party, Cooper repudiated the suggestion, saying that he was no party writer but spoke out of his own convictions. His later career was not wholly consistent, but the sincerity of this statement need not be doubted. By the same token, he sought no aid from Jefferson or anybody else, willingly accepting martyrdom for the cause. This was not the most ludicrous of the sedition cases—that honor belongs to the case of Luther Baldwin of New Jersey, who in a state of inebriation expressed the wish that a cannon shot, fired in salute to Adams, had struck the President's posterior.[28] It may not have been the most cruel, though Cooper's wife died while he was in prison. But, most clearly of them all, it was an attack on the freedom of intelligence.

Ironically, the case of James Thomson Callender, the needy hack writer who, as time was to show, was willing to blacken anybody's reputation, touched Jefferson more directly. In the summer of 1798, in fear of the Sedition Act and perhaps because of other troubles, Callender had quitted Philadelphia. Jefferson's old landlord, the merchant Thomas Leiper, promised to take care of Callender's four children, and Senator Stevens Thomson Mason offered him safe lodging in Virginia. Accordingly, he walked all the way to Mason's place, Raspberry Plain in Loudoun County.[29] Leiper advised him not to come back, and he was sick of even the Republicans, he said, since so many of them had treated him badly. He also said that the aristocracy of his present neighborhood, "one of the vilest in America," had incessantly abused him and Mason. The plight of this hunted and impoverished creature who had no weapon but his pen was sad indeed, and when informed of it Jefferson sent him fifty dollars. That is, he asked Mason to draw on his agent in Richmond, George Jefferson, for that amount, keeping Callender's name out of the business. It was a humane act and no doubt this excessively generous man would have reproached himself if he had not done something of the sort. Like the two others who had specially befriended Callender, he was fully aware that the journalist had brought trouble on himself because of his attacks on the Federalists. In a letter which he wrote before he got the money, and which Jefferson received after he had ordered the money sent, Callender implied that the "assistant writer" of a party was entitled to support.[30] Jefferson would have been wise to challenge that statement for the record, but at a time when he was inordinately careful about his letters he obviously avoided writing this dubious character unless he had to.

While he was still enjoying the hospitality of Senator Mason and had the use of a good library, Callender, whose health had improved, formulated plans for other writing which would itself bring in money while stimulating the sale of the works he had already published. He would give his readers "such a tornado as no government ever got before."[31] Jefferson made no response to this prophecy, but by the summer of 1799, when Callender had found employment on the Richmond *Examiner,* there was promise of its fulfillment. Callender wrote Jefferson late in August, saying that he was to be a subscriber to his (Callender's) next volume, though there is no record of Jefferson's having said so, and reminding him that the fashion in Virginia was to pay for such things in advance. At the same time he dilated on the dangers to which he was subjected.[32] Actually there was an organized attempt to run him out of town. Replying from Monticello, Jefferson said that his agent in Richmond would give him fifty dollars on account of the book he was about to publish. He was to send two or three copies when it came out and hold the rest until Jefferson called for them. Reporting that the violence meditated against Callender had aroused indignation in his own part of the country, Jefferson reassured him by saying that Virginia had always been noted for lawful conduct and good order.[33]

Jefferson had put his latest gift in the guise of payment for copies of a publication. This turned out to be *The Prospect Before Us*, on the basis of which its author was afterwards convicted of seditious libel.[34] Jefferson saw this work, presumably in page proof, during the autumn of 1799—at just the time that his spirits were at their lowest point with respect to public prospects. He gave Callender at a very late date certain information which he could legitimately have given anybody, but there is no indication that he influenced the contents of the volume. Here as elsewhere Callender said precisely what he wanted to. Just how many pages Jefferson had seen when he expressed himself about the work is uncertain—perhaps sixteen, though Callender sent him upwards of a hundred eventually. At any rate he left these words on record: "Such papers cannot fail to produce the best effect. They inform the thinking part of the nation; and these again, supported by the taxgatherers as their vouchers, set the people to rights."[35] He commended nothing specifically and he had not seen the whole work, but he said enough to permit the author to associate the acknowledged leader of the Republican party with this publication if he chose to. Callender, who had considerable recourse to the bottle in later years, may then have deteriorated further, but if he was "a poor creature, . . . hypochondriac, drunken, penniless and unprincipled," as Jefferson said toward the end of his own life, he himself was blind and exceedingly gullible in not realizing this sooner.[36]

The facts do not support the later Federalist claim that he hired Callender to calumniate Hamilton and Adams: that is a gross distortion. But his later justification of his own conduct, after Callender had indeed shown "base ingratitude" by publishing far more scandalous false charges against him than that writer ever made against John Adams, leaves something to be desired.[37] Like most mortals he was not beyond rationalization and self-deception. His actions, as we have reported them thus far, do not bear out the later statement that, while still considering Callender a proper object of benevolence, "no man wished more to see his pen stopped." This sounds like an afterthought. The simplest explanation of the matter is that he did not want the attacks on Adams's public acts stopped, since he essentially agreed with these, despite the vehemence of Callender's language. He was warranted in saying that he no more sanctioned the "calumnies and falsehoods" against Adams than, as he supposed, Adams sanctioned the far more numerous ones hurled by Peter Porcupine and others against him, but he needed to allow for the influence of political excitement on anybody's judgment. He probably regarded some degree of personal attack, as distinguished from attack on public policy, as inescapable in view of the way the game was being played. Actually, the particular comments of Callender's about Adams which led to his trial and conviction could have been matched in the writings of Peter Porcupine and others, not to speak of a letter Alexander Hamilton was to write ere long. As for the praise lavished on him himself by Callender at this stage, Jefferson would not have been in character if he had not found this embarrassing.

In the full sense Callender's trial for sedition in Richmond in May and June, 1800, before Justice Samuel Chase, was political. A copy of his latest work with marked passages was given Chase by the Federalist bulldog Luther Martin when the Justice was on circuit, and he had determined to punish the author before he got to Richmond, where he also expected to put the Virginia lawyers in their place. Haranguing the grand jury, he struck a left-handed blow at Jefferson by asserting that he would allow no atheist to give testimony. The alleged atheist himself said that coming from Chase, the calumny would have less effect than from any other man in the country. Early in the year Monroe had predicted to Jefferson that an attempt would be made to carry the Sedition Law into Virginia as an electioneering trick. The Governor now hoped that the people would behave with dignity and was determined to prevent any public protest against Callender's arrest. He inquired of his friend, however, if it would not be proper for him to employ counsel to give the accused man legitimate defense. Jefferson's reply appears to be his only recorded comment on this trial at the time. "I think it essentially just and necessary that Callender should be substantially defended," he said. "Whether in the first stage by public interference [that is, by state-appointed counsel], or by private contributors, may be a question."[38] In view of the condemnation of the Sedition Act by the General Assembly, he regarded this case as a challenge to the state, but at the same time he wanted respect to be shown the Union.

Actually, the procedure that was followed was private: subscriptions were sought and lawyers volunteered their services. Among these, however, were Philip Norborne Nicholas, recently appointed attorney general of the state; William Wirt, clerk of the House of Delegates; and Monroe's son-in-law, George Hay. They proved useless, for Chase contradicted and overruled them so persistently that they withdrew. The presiding judge was the central figure in these proceedings, not the accused.

Republicans believed that they had sufficient political reason to support Callender against him from the start, and, before he got through, Virginians in general regarded him as insulting to their state. Callender, who was sentenced to a nine months' imprisonment and fine of two hundred dollars after a trial in which he was virtually defenseless, had more friends in jail than when at liberty. He served the Republican cause more effectively as a victim than as a writer.

While incarcerated he wrote part of the *Prospect*. He sent Jefferson sheets of this, saying he flattered himself that "although neither the style nor matter could be exactly conformable" to Jefferson's "ideas or taste, yet that upon the whole, they would not be disagreeable."[39] Jefferson did not acknowledge receipt of them or answer any of the numerous letters Callender wrote him in the fall and winter. But he instructed his agent in Richmond to take fifty dollars to the prisoner on the understanding that two copies of the proposed work would be sent him when published and further copies on convenience. He was again cloaking his charity in the guise of a purchase and was being as secretive as possible about the entire transaction. In view of past actions, political realities, and Callender's plight it would doubtless have been difficult to do otherwise.[40] It is hard to escape the impression that he had let himself become the victim of a species of blackmail. He did not destroy the documents, however, and for any mistakes of heart and head he may have made in dealing with this unfortunate and unscrupulous journalist time was to exact superabundant retribution.

i i

Before Callender was brought to trial in Richmond there were important political developments elsewhere which were distinctly encouraging to the Republicans. Jefferson, who thought the presidential contest hinged on the middle states, recognized the crucial importance of the election of members of the New York legislature, which chose the presidential electors on joint ballot. Despite the Federalist assertion that the victory of their foes would cause the music of the hammers on the wharves and the hum of busy industry to cease, while the temple of the Most High was being "profaned by the impious orgies of the Goddess of Reason," the party which Aaron Burr marshalled swept the city elections in New York City on May 1 sufficiently to ensure a majority in the legislature.[41] Jefferson got the news about the time that he heard of party victories in his own state, and when the intelligence reached the Federalist Senate that body, in no mood for business, quickly adjourned. These events brought gloom to every Tory countenance, according to Republican Edward Livingston. Also, they bore out the earlier comment of Governor John Jay that some were persuaded that George Washington had been taken away from *evil to come*.

They occasioned the extraordinary suggestion of Hamilton that Jay call into session the existing legislature, which had a Federalist majority, with a view of changing the law so that presidential electors would be chosen by districts. In such times of extraordinary peril it would not do to be overscrupulous, he said. Instead, every legal and constitutional step should be taken "to prevent an atheist in religion, and a fanatic in politics, from getting possession of the helm of state."[42] Jay wisely declined to adopt for party purposes so unbecoming a measure, and an immediate consequence of this election was to boost the political stock of Burr, who was credited on every hand with the result. Gallatin's father-in-law, James Nicholson, attributed the miraculous issue to "the intervention of a Supreme Power and our friend Burr the agent."[43]

By this time the Republican congressional leaders had already decided on sound political grounds that Jefferson's running mate should be a New Yorker. Gallatin, who had been delegated to make the necessary local inquiries, asked Nicholson to see George Clinton and Burr. The net result was the report that the former declined and that the latter, who was approved by all whom Nicholson talked with, could probably be induced to stand if assured of fair treatment in the southern states, where he had received such indifferent support four years before. At the same time Mrs. Gallatin, then in New York, wrote her husband: "Burr says he has no confidence in the Virginians; they once deceived him, and they are not to be trusted."[44] Burr was undisposed to give up the certainty of being elected governor for the uncertainty of becoming vice president, and some of his friends thought the chief state office more important anyway. His name "must not be played the fool with," said Nicholson, and the business of the last election must be smoothed over.

At a very large meeting of Republicans—that is, a caucus—on the night of May 11, it was unanimously agreed to support Burr for vice president.[45] There never had been any question about the candidate for President. In a memorandum of a conversation with Burr shortly after the latter was replaced on the Republican ticket in 1804 by George Clinton, Jefferson said that Burr claimed he had accepted the nomination in 1800 to promote Jefferson's fame and advancement and from a desire to be with him, "whose company and conversation had always been fascinating to him." Jefferson did not swallow that, and on his own part he now said that he had distrusted the man from the time he had first observed him as a senator.[46] If this was not an afterthought he cloaked his distrust during his years as leader of the opposition, when he established and maintained friendly political relations with the useful New Yorker. There is no reason to doubt his statement that there never was any intimacy between them, much as Burr may have enjoyed his conversation. Nor need it be doubted that he played a wholly passive role in the matter of Burr's nomination. He shared the determination of his own friends, however, that his running mate should get a full vote in Virginia as an evidence of good faith, bringing some personal influence to bear for that end. Under his benign leadership the Republicans really closed ranks in this campaign. "The Jacobins appear to be completely organized throughout the United States," lamented a High Federalist.[47] These "base plotters against the peace, safety and felicity" of the country acted in unison, he said, seeking to introduce into the state governments "unprincipled tools" of faction, and to assure the election to the chief office of "the great arch priest of Jacobinism and infidelity." To this purpose Burr had already proved himself an invaluable accessory.

Writing his son-in-law a few days before the Republicans decided on their second man, Jefferson, after saying that the Federalists did not conceal their despair because of the results of the election in New York, reported that they had held a caucus and determined on some "hocus-pocus maneuvers." That is, they were running Charles Cotesworth Pinckney to draw off votes in South Carolina, and possibly in North Carolina. A week later he commented that they were not without hope of giving Pinckney preference over Adams, reporting at the same time the resignation of McHenry, the dismissal of Pickering, and the succession of John Marshall to the latter's post as secretary of state.[48] His recorded contemporary references to these events are sparse, but they show that he perceived the dissension in the other camp and the purposes the High Federalists so fully expressed in private correspondence which naturally he did not see.[49]

They named Adams by force of political necessity, but the ultras preferred Pinckney, who was not himself a party to this intrigue. Their feelings were acerbated further when Adams cleared his Cabinet of two of his secret enemies and assumed at this late date undisputed command of his own official household. Hamilton had written Theodore Sedgwick: "To support *Adams* and *Pinckney* equally is the only thing that can possibly save us from the fangs of *Jefferson*." After receiving further information, he wrote that he would never more be responsible for Adams by direct support, even though the result would be the election of Jefferson. He was sure the government would sink under either man, but if they had to have an enemy at the head of it he preferred an open one. If convinced that Pinckney would be supported equally with Adams in the East, he would go along, but otherwise he would pursue Pinckney as his "single object."[50] Adams suspected as much, no doubt, and among the ultras he was reported to have said that he would sooner serve as vice president under Jefferson than to be indebted to "*such a being* as Hamilton," whom he did not hesitate to call a bastard and as much an alien as Gallatin.[51]

These references to "billingsgate language" were made on heresay by prejudiced reporters, but this feud was destined to surpass the one between Jefferson and the former Secretary of the Treasury. Rumors were also current in these same circles of a coalition between Jefferson and Adams, though the former appears to have made no reference to them and the latter denied them.[52] The real cause of complaint on the part of the High Federalists was that Adams, while critical of them, acted "as if he did not hate nor dread Jefferson." At times, indeed, he and the good lady his wife spoke of him with much regard, affecting indignation at the charge of irreligion against him and making no mention of his "wild philosophy and gimcrackery in politics."[53] Under existing political conditions, it is hard to see how any coalition between these two old friends could possibly have been effected, and neither could now have been expected to consent to serve under the other, but developing circumstances had blurred the issue between them. As things turned out, they were both against Hamilton and what he stood for.

The caucuses and John Adams's housecleaning took place at the very end of the congressional session—the last to be held in Philadelphia. In the middle of May, Jefferson, who had had many painful experiences in this place in the last three years, along with some delightful associations with men of learning, made his final departure in an optimistic state of mind. Even the news from abroad was good, for word had come that the American envoys to France had been favorably received and he believed that a settlement could not be avoided. He and one of his sons-in-law had some financial troubles, because of the state of the tobacco market, but he was going to see Maria and her husband, to visit the Eppes family and his Sister Bolling, and take his younger daughter back with him to Monticello where he was above the storms of politics.

Originally he planned to go by the Eastern Shore, a route he had never taken, proceeding up the south side of the James to Eppington. Then he would go straight home, missing Richmond altogether. He wanted to avoid ceremony everywhere and to keep his name out of the papers. In the end he did go by Richmond, where he stayed with James Monroe, but he seems to have been spared distasteful ceremony. It was while he was at Eppington that Governor Monroe asked his advice about the defense of the wretched Callender.[54] He got home toward the end of May and there, by July 4, he harvested the best wheat crop he had ever had. Not until the end of October, when he visited Poplar Forest, did he leave the county, and not until the last week in November of this election year did he set out for the new Federal City of Washington.

During these months he gave himself to the rural employments which always attracted him so much, and when at his writing desk he was considerably occupied, no doubt, with the manual of parliamentary practice which he was putting into final shape. He received letters from supporters in various parts of the country and kept in constant touch with the course of political affairs, but he maintained the policy of engaging in a minimum of political correspondence—assuming the attitude of passivity which, in his opinion, propriety required while he was being subjected to the free discussion of his countrymen. It is impossible to determine just how much of this discussion he was aware of, but it certainly should not be supposed that he read all, or even a substantial part, of the pamphlets and papers to which modern students of this age have access. The chances are that he read relatively few of them. Some things unquestionably came to his personal attention, however—such as the report of his death which got out before the Fourth of July.[55]

Oddly enough, this report was communicated to a friendly paper by a writer who referred to its subject as "the man in whom is centered the feelings and happiness of the American people," and who was himself convinced of its falsity.[56] The form in which it was circulated in the press thereafter, and the degree of credence given to it, depended largely on the politics of the particular newspapers. Supposedly the report was brought to Baltimore in the first place by three gentlemen from Winchester, who were said to have learned from a man from Charlottesville that Jefferson had died at Monticello after an illness of forty-eight hours. It was taken up by papers in Philadelphia and New York and then in New England at a time when Virginia papers were taking no note of it or were actually denying it. The rumor ran faster than the denials, and the *Aurora* quickly scented ulterior Federalist designs. Duane's paper described this as "a fabrication intended to damp the festivity of the 4th of July and prevent the author of the Declaration of Independence from being the universal toast" of that festival. Indeed, the *Aurora* claimed that the Federalists had shown marked indifference to the celebration in Philadelphia this year, while the Republicans rejoiced in it as usual. One Republican, charging the Federalists with exulting over the false report, said: "When lions fall, asses bray." That is, "the asses of aristocracy, fearing the paws of this republican lion, reported his death—because they wished him so!"[57]

This may be regarded an extreme and unwarranted assertion, but in the Federalist papers there was a notable absence of expressions of regret, though the conjunction of this report with the celebrations of American independence would certainly have led one to expect them even if good manners alone did not. Meanwhile, Du Pont de Nemours, after several days of "indescribable unhappiness," congratulated Jefferson and the United States on the falsity of the news. Other prominent supporters and friends, while disposed to believe that the report was political in origin, wondered if he had suffered any indisposition. Replying to Du Pont, he said: "I am much indebted to my enemies for proving, by their recitals of my death, that I have friends. . . . I have never enjoyed better nor more uninterrupted health."[58]

Since Jefferson was the living symbol of Republicanism and the rallying center of his party, his reputation as well as his life was precious to his partisans, and it was actively defended by them. He himself played no more direct part in the furious battle of words in the summer and autumn of 1800 than he did in matters of local organization, and for that reason we need not describe it in detail. The principles and policies which his supporters proclaimed were those he had set forth bit by bit, and sometimes in summarized form, in private letters.[59] He had never ceased talking about the "spirit of 1776," and he must have liked the language of the dignified address to the citizens of his own state which was printed so many times by the committee of which Philip Norborne Nicholas was chairman. Among other things this said: "As a friend of liberty, we believe Jefferson second to no man, and the experience of no man has afforded better lessons for its preservation." Therefore, the committee offered him to the affections of his fellow countrymen as the ablest guardian of their "peace, freedom, and constitution."[60] To this he himself would probably have added some reference to economy. But the party principles had been largely arrived at by consensus during the years of opposition, and he made no public pronouncement until his first inaugural, when he expressed essentially the same ideas in more moving language.

The verbal campaign of 1800 in the country as a whole, falling far below the level of the official Virginia address, surpassed that of 1796 in both quantity and scurrility. It has been estimated that upwards of a hundred pamphlets were issued on one side or the other, and there were far more communications to the newspapers, a large majority of which supported the party in power.[61] Whether the Federalist pot or the Republican kettle was the blacker, one would hesitate to say, but at least the opposition could attack the actual policies of the administration, while their opponents were emphasizing vague fears and dread future dangers. And it seems safe to say that the charges hurled against Jefferson, who was shielded by no sedition law, were more reckless than those against Adams and much less relevant. Indeed, it may be claimed that the personal attacks on the chief Republican were the most vicious in any presidential campaign on record.[62] One may doubt if a more distorted picture of a candidate for the first office has ever been presented by his foes. Many of these attacks were mere repetitions or elaborations of what had been said four years earlier. Many followed the line that Hamilton had laid down for his supporters in 1792, when writing as CATULLUS, he attacked his colleague in Washington's official family as an intriguing incendiary and secret enemy of the Constitution. But, to a greater extent than previously, Jefferson was assailed on religious grounds.

Though the main themes were the old ones, with increased emphasis on his "infidelity," there were minor ones which were played up in particular localities. Thus in South Carolina, where until now the Federalists had been stronger than in any other southern state, his liberal views on slavery were brought up against him. Evidence was drawn from his *Notes on Virginia*, where he described his vain early attempt to start gradual emancipation in his state, and from a kindly letter to a Negro almanac maker which had long been in print. He had gladly recognized and been encouraged by the achievements of Benjamin Banneker, giving them more praise in fact than he afterwards thought warranted.[63] Ironically, the slave revolt in Virginia that goes by the name of Gabriel was put down in the last summer of this year by Jefferson's friend the Governor, who wrote him several times about it, as Callender did from the Richmond jail. His advice to Monroe was on the side of mercy to the insurrectionists. At the summer's end he thought there had been hangings enough and was inclined to favor deportation of the remaining rebels, but there were more executions after he wrote, including that of the ringleader. One High Federalist, a close friend of Hamilton, sarcastically remarked that the Virginians were beginning to feel "the happy effects of liberty and equality," but Jefferson, fully aware of the extreme difficulties and dangers of the situation which slavery had created, wrote his friend Benjamin Rush, "We are truly to be pitied."[64]

Charges of personal immorality against Jefferson, who was in fact one of the most moral of men, appear to have entered into the campaign of 1800, especially the whispering campaign, but not until Callender turned on him in mad fury when he was President were these widely and gleefully publicized. Reflections on his financial integrity were nothing new, for the Federalists had long been asserting that his political attitude and that of his fellow planters was owing to their British debts, and unjust allegations of improper financial practice on his part had been made before. In the light of his heroic efforts during a quarter of a century to meet his inherited obligations honorably, and in view of his excessive personal generosity, these could not have failed to gall him when called to his attention. This summer he received a report that the Reverend Cotton Mather Smith, whose very name suggested the implacable New England clergy, had charged him with obtaining his property by fraud and robbery, and, more particularly, with defrauding a widow and her children as the executor of an estate. To his well-meaning informant he replied that every tittle of the tale was fable. Then, after demonstrating this in some detail, he suggested that if Mr. Smith regarded the precepts of the gospel as applicable to preachers as well as others, he might well repent and make some acknowledgment of his own error. Jefferson wrote this private letter for the satisfaction of his correspondent and others whom that gentleman might choose to speak to, but as usual he urged that under no circumstances was it to get into the papers.[65]

In the last of the letters signed BURLEIGH and originally published in Connecticut, the author asked a question: "Do you believe in the strangest of all paradoxes—that a spendthrift, a libertine, or an atheist is qualified to make your laws and govern you and your posterity?"[66] The charge of atheism was the one most pressed in this campaign: it was not only made in the public press; it was hurled from pulpits in various places, most of all probably in Connecticut. As the story goes, the time was approaching when Bibles were to be hidden in New England's wells. The long-lived conflict which the dominant clergy of that region and certain other wearers of the cloth waged against this apostle of religious freedom cannot be conveniently or appropriately treated here. We are chiefly concerned with its immediate political significance and with Jefferson's own reaction to it.

The attitude of his clerical foes can be partly explained on grounds of misunderstanding, for he made no effort to clarify his own position or make his personal religious opinions known. On the contrary, he regarded this as a wholly private matter which was nobody's business but his. Actually, he was a deist, not an atheist. His general position might well have been compared to that of John Adams, who discussed religious questions with him at great length and with utter candor in later years and who, even in the heat of a campaign, was critical of his clerical persecutors. In religion as in economics Jefferson was an advocate of *laissez-faire.* His ideas had been carried into effect in Virginia to a greater extent than elsewhere, and the example of revolutionary France, which his opponents so often held up as a terrible warning of things to come, was in fact quite irrelevant. But no theological absolutist could have been expected to like his views, and an entrenched clerical body, like that in New England where the alliance of church and state was still so strong, not unnaturally feared him. One at least of his public critics said that he objected to him solely because of his "disbelief" in the Scriptures and his deism, but we may safely assume that the overwhelming majority of those who raised the religious issue against him were also Federalists on other grounds.[67] They probably would not have supported him if he had had the simple faith and piety of Robert E. Lee.

One of his most notable clerical critics, the Reverend John M. Mason of New York, said that while his infidelity had long been undisputed, proof of it was at ready hand. "Happily for truth and for us," he said, "Mr. Jefferson has *written*; he has *printed.*"[68] But the detaching of single phrases or passages from the *Notes on Virginia,* without regard to their total context, seems less a pursuit of truth than of another objective. The obvious object of all this was to discredit the man and scare voters from his side. Exaggeration is to be expected in a political campaign, but the invocation of God in behalf of the Federalists is a striking example of the conjunction of self-righteousness with arrogance which they so often effected. The final words of Burleigh were: "GREAT GOD OF COMPASSION AND JUSTICE, SHIELD MY COUNTRY FROM DESTRUCTION."

Noting that Jefferson had been fiercely attacked on religious grounds, Hamilton's friend Robert Troup, more realistic at the moment than most of his High Federalist fellows, expressed doubt that anything said on that subject would deprive the Republican leader of a single vote.[69] He attributed this presumable failure to the irrevocable determination of Jefferson's supporters, but it might be attributed to public reaction against excess.

Jefferson's own reaction to these attacks has proved far more memorable than they have. It was not made known to the public but was revealed in what has come to be regarded as one of the most notable of his private letters. This he addressed affectionately to Dr. Benjamin Rush.[70] It is a sign of his intimacy with this friend that he was willing to discuss religion with him. He had promised him a letter on Christianity, he said, and would send it some day. He believed that his view of the subject ought to displease neither the rational Christian nor deist, and that it "would reconcile many to a character they have too hastily rejected." He doubted if it would reconcile him to the irritable tribe of clergy who were in arms against him—on grounds of their own interest, as he was convinced. He believed that certain groups of them wanted an establishment of their particular form of Christianity. The real danger may have been considerably less than he had thought, but, since freedom of the press had been so successfully attacked, there had surely been grounds to fear for freedom of religion. With renewed confidence he now said: "The returning good sense of our country threatens abortion to their hopes, and they believe that any portion of power confided to me will be exerted in opposition to their schemes. And they believe truly. for *I have sworn upon the altar of God eternal hostility against every form of tyranny over the mind of man.*" [71]

That was all they had to fear from him, he said, but that was enough to cause them to print lying pamphlets. Time has largely relegated those pamphlets to oblivion, while painting in bold letters on the walls of his national monument what is perhaps the most characteristic of all his single utterances. He spoke as a champion of the freedom of the human spirit, not as the leader of a party, and at the moment nobody heard him except Dr. Rush. But his record already spoke for itself to anyone who would listen.

NOTES

[1] For precise information about the prescribed methods in the 16 states in 1796 and 1800 see the chart in C. O. Paullin, *Atlas of the Hist. Geography of the U. S.* (1932), p. 89. In 10 states choice lay with the legislatures in 1800, which was a larger number than in 1796. In this period the trend was away from popular choice, on a general ticket or by districts.

[2] See Malone, *Jefferson and the Ordeal of Liberty* (1962) ch. XXVI, note 34.

[3] To Monroe, Jan. 12, 1800 (Ford, VII, 401). When the electors were actually chosen the number was even higher.

[4] Entire matter well discussed by Ammon, "Republican Party in Virginia," pp. 229-232. A circular, dated Aug. 9, 1800, giving a form of the Republican ticket with suggestions about the preparation of written lists in advance, is printed by Cunningham in *Jeffersonian Republicans*, p. 196.

[5] Nicholas to TJ, Feb. 2, 1800 (Library of Congress, 18171). Minutes of the meeting of Jan. 21, 1800, in which 93 members of the legislature were joined by others, are reproduced by W. E. Hemphill in *Virginia Cavalcade*, Summer 1952, pp. 28-29. At the meeting electors were chosen and the form of organization was decided on. This caucus met several times thereafter.

[6] For example, an address to the citizens of the state, dated July 7, 1800, appeared at regular intervals in the *Virginia Argus*. Cunningham (p. 194, note 82) gives eight dates, July 11-Oct. 24, 1800. My own reference is to the issue of Sept. 12.

[7] TJ to P. N. Nicholas, Apr. 7, 1800 (Ford, VII, 439).

[8] Ammon, p. 234, citing L. W. Tazewell to TJ, Mar. 29, 1800, from Mass. Hist. Soc. (MHS).

[9] H. M. Tinkcom, *The Republicans and Federalists in Pennsylvania, 1790-1801* (1950), ch. XII.

[10] TJ to McKean, Jan. 9, 1800; McKean to TJ, Mar. 7, 1800 (LC, 18163, 18210). On the circulation of Beckley's *Address to the People of the U.S.: with an Epitome and Vindication of the Public Life and Character of Thomas Jefferson,* see Cunningham, pp. 197-198.

[11] Tinkcom, ch. XIII; TJ to Madison, Mar. 4, 1800 (Ford, VII, 433-434).

[12] Jan. 23, 1800 (*Annals,* 6 Cong., I sess., pp. 29-32, giving the first debate).

[13] TJ to Edward Livingston, Apr. 30, 1800, and to Madison, May 12, 1800 (Ford, VII, 443-444, 446-447).

[14] It is admirably described by J. M. Smith in *Freedom's Fetters,* pp. 288-300. My own account of it in *Cooper,* pp. 113-116, is more restricted.

[15] *Aurora,* Feb. 19, 1800.

[16] Form of proceedings, presented by Senator Dayton, Mar. 22, 1800 (*Annals* 6 Cong., I sess., p. 117).

[17] Cooper to TJ, presumably Mar. 23, 1800 (LC, 20951).

[18] Mar. 27, 1800.

[19] *Annals,* 6 Cong., I sess., pp. 121-124 (Mar. 26, 1800); Duane in *Aurora,* Apr. 1, 1800.

[20] This is shown by the account in the *Aurora,* May 13, 1800, though not in the account in the *Annals* (May 10). Bingham voted against reading the petition.

[21] May 14, 1800 (*Annals,* 6 Cong., I sess., p. 184).

[22] To L. W. Tazewell, Apr. 10, 1800, quoted by Smith, p. 300, note 70, from Mass. Hist. Soc.

[23] An excellent summary of the enforcement of the Sedition Act is given in Smith, *Freedom's Fetters,* ch. IX. He treats individual cases afterward. According to his estimate, there were at least 14 indictments under the Act and 3 at common law.

[24] A FEDERAL REPUBLICAN, in Philadelphia *Gazette,* Mar. 12, 1800.

[25] I have discussed these in *Cooper,* pp. 92-110.

[26] *Political Essays* (1799), preface. A 2nd edn. appeared early in 1800.

[27] Account of trial in *Cooper,* ch. IV, and Smith, ch. XIV.

[28] Smith, pp. 270-274.

[29] Virtually the entire correspondence between TJ and Callender in this period was published by W. C. Ford in *N.-Eng. Hist. and Geneal. Register,* Vol. 50 (1896), pp. 321-333, 445-458; Vol. 51 (1897), pp. 19-24. Unless otherwise indicated, reference is to this collection, letters being cited by dates. Smith covers Callender and his trial admirably in ch. XV.

[30] Callender to TJ, Oct. 26, 1798. His first letter from Raspberry Plain was dated Sept. 22. TJ gave instructions to Mason on Oct. 11 (Ford, VII, 282).

[31] To TJ, Nov. 19, 1798.

[32] Callender to TJ, Aug. 10, 1799. On the threat to Callender, see Smith, p. 338, note 18.

[33] TJ to Callender, Sept. 6, 1799 (Ford, VII, 392).

[34] Extracts from the correspondence bearing on the work can be conveniently seen in Sowerby, III, 421-427. The first volume sold for a dollar.

[35] Oct. 6, 1799 (Ford, VII, 395).

[36] To Robert Richardson, Apr. 20, 1824 (Sowerby, III, 427).

[37] To Monroe, July 15, 1802 (Ford, VIII, 164-166); to Abigail Adams, July 22, 1804 (*A.-J. Letters,* I, 275).

[38] May 26, 1800 (Ford, VII, 448). The promptness of his reply was made possible by the fact that he was visiting at Eppington.

³⁹ To TJ, Oct. 11, 1800.

⁴⁰ To George Jefferson, Oct. 24, 1800; from George Jefferson, Nov. 3, 1800; to George Jefferson, Nov. 7, 1800; from George Jefferson, Jan. 12, 1801 (all Mass. Hist. Soc.). Later developments, relating to Callender's fine, his unsuccessful application for office, and his slanderous attacks on Jefferson, belong in the story of the latter's presidency, even though some of the documents antedate his inauguration.

⁴¹ Good brief account in S. I. Pomerantz, *New York, An American City, 1783-1803* (1938), pp. 126-130.

⁴² To Jay, May 7, 1800 (Lodge, VIII, 549-551). Also, E. Livingston to TJ, received May 3 (LC, 18297); Jay to Rev. Dr. Morse, Oct. 24, 1800 (*Correspondence and Public Papers*, IV, 266-267).

⁴³ Nicholson to Gallatin from N.Y., May 6, 1800 (Adams, *Gallatin*, p. 241).

⁴⁴ Nicholson to Gallatin, May 7, 1800, and Mrs. Gallatin to her husband, May 7 (*ibid.,* pp. 242-243). A fuller account, prepared by Nicholson in 1803, is in *Amer. Hist. Rev.,* VIII, 511-513 (April, 1903).

⁴⁵ Gallatin to his wife, May 12, 1800 (*ibid.,* p. 243). No proceedings of this or of the Federalist caucus were published. The standard account is in F. W. Dallinger, *Nominations for Elective Office in the U.S.* (1916 edn.), pp. 14-16.

⁴⁶ Memo. of Jan. 26, 1804 (Ford, I, 301-304).

⁴⁷ T. Parsons to John Jay, May 5, 1800 (Jay, *Correspondence and Public Papers,* IV, 269).

⁴⁸ To TMR, May 7, 14, 1800 (LC, 18277, 18215).

⁴⁹ These matters are discussed in detail by Dauer, ch. 16; Kurtz, ch. 17; and by other writers.

⁵⁰ Hamilton to Sedgwick, May 4, 1800; Sedgwick to Hamilton, May 7; Hamilton to Sedgwick, May 10 (J.C.H., VI, 436-438, 441-442).

⁵¹ Pickering to Rufus King, June 26, 1800 (King, III, 262).

⁵² In later years Pickering revived talk of this, but the resulting correspondence of the year 1811 between Adams, Benjamin Stoddert, and Samuel and Robert Smith of Md. (Adams, *Works,* X, 3-9) revealed only a shadowy episode which in my opinion, can be dismissed from consideration.

⁵³ Fisher Ames to R. King, Aug. 26, Sept. 24, 1800 (King, III, 296-297, 304-306).

⁵⁴ TJ to Monroe, Mar. 26, Apr. 13, 1800 (LC, 18230, 18231-18256); Monroe to TJ, Apr. 23, May 25, 1800 (S.M.H., III, 173-174, 179-180); TJ to TMR, May 7, 14, 1800 (LC, 18277, 18215). His various stopping places are shown in his Account Book.

⁵⁵ This interesting minor episode is well described by Charles Warren in *Odd Byways of American History* (1942), ch. VII.

⁵⁶ *Baltimore American,* June 30, 1800, quoted by Warren, p. 129.

⁵⁷ *Aurora,* July 3, 7, 1800, quoted by Warren.

⁵⁸ Du Pont to TJ, July 6, 1800, and TJ to Du Pont, July 26 (*Correspondence,* pp. 17-18); Elijah Griffith to TJ, July 8, 1800 (LC, 18315); S. T. Mason to TJ, July 11 (LC, 18317-18318). Warren cites (p. 132) a newspaper item attributing the rise of the report to the fact that a slave named Thomas Jefferson had died at Monticello. I have found no such slave listed in the *Farm Book* and doubt the use of the surname by any slave still in TJ's possession.

⁵⁹ Most notably, perhaps, in his letter of Jan. 26, 1799, to Elbridge Gerry (Ford, VII, 327-329). Cunningham, after quoting the most pertinent part of this, reprints from the *Aurora* a contrasting list of Federal policies and Republican promises, designating the latter and TJ's letter as in effect a party platform (pp. 211-214).

⁶⁰ *Virginia Argus,* Sept. 12, 1800, and other dates.

⁶¹ The estimate is that of C. O. Lerche, Jr., in his excellent article "Jefferson and the Election of 1800: A Case Study in the Political Smear," in *William and Mary Quarterly,* Oct. 1948, pp. 467-491. A more journalistic treatment is Coley Taylor and Samuel Middlebrook, *The Eagle Screams* (1936), ch. III.

[62] So Charles Warren says in *Odd Byways in American History*, p. 127.

[63] W. S. Jenkins, *Pro-Slavery Thought in the Old South* (1935), pp. 61-62, referring to *Address to the Citizens of South Carolina, by a Federalist* (Charleston, 1800). See also TJ to Banneker, Aug. 30, 1791 (Ford, V, 377-378), the letter which was printed, and TJ to Joel Barlow, Oct. 8, 1809 (Ford, IX, 261).

[64] A sympathetic account of the Gabriel insurrection is in Herbert Aptheker, *American Negro Slave Revolts* (1943), pp. 219-223. Gabriel himself was captured on Sept. 25 and hanged on Oct. 7. TJ wrote Monroe on Sept. 20, 1800 (Ford VII, 457-458) and made the comment to Rush in his famous letter of Sept. 23 (Ford, VII, 461). Robert Troup spoke of the matter to King on Oct. 1 (King, III, 316).

[65] To Uriah McGregory of Derby, Conn., Aug. 13, 1800 (*Domestic Life*, pp. 269-270), replying to a letter of July 19, received Aug. 7.

[66] Quoted by Warren, p. 128, from N.Y. *Commercial Advertiser*, Oct. 9, 1800. This noted attack by BURLEIGH, first published in the *Connecticut Courant*, appeared in the N.Y. paper in 15 numbers, beginning July 11.

[67] The reference is to the author of *Serious Questions on the Election of a President* (New York, 1800); see Lerche, p. 471. In the *Virginia Argus*, Sept. 8, 1800, this emphasis on the religious issue in disregard of others was objected to.

[68] Quoted by Lerche, p. 473, from *The Voice of Warning, to Christians on the Ensuing Election* (New York, 1800).

[69] R. Troup to R. King, Sept. 14, 1800 (King, III, 299-300).

[70] J. P. Boyd, in "Mr. Jefferson to Dr. Rush With Affection" (*Library of Congress: Quarterly Journal of Current Acquisitions*, Vol. I, No. I, Oct.- Dec. 1943) presented for the first time the full and authentic text of the famous letter of Sept. 23, 1800, with perceptive comments.

[71] Italics inserted.

CHARGE AND COUNTERCHARGE:

THE ELECTION OF 1800*

Morton Borden

    Replete with dramatic events, an unexpected electoral tie, and overtones of intrigue, the election of 1800 has a continuing fascination for the historian. Why were Adams and the Federalist Party defeated? How did Jefferson win the Presidency? Did he, as well as his rival, Aaron Burr, bargain for the necessary electoral votes? Did a Delaware Senator influence the outcome? According to Morton Borden's carefully researched and explicit analysis in The Federalism of James A. Bayard, *Burr played a more honorable role in the postelection crisis than has been generally thought. Borden maintains, further, that Senator Bayard was the central figure in negotiations between Federalist and Republican leaders. Assurances to Bayard that Jefferson's policies would not adversely affect major Federalist interests, led to his switching his vote from Burr to Jefferson. Party politics clearly were as complicated as the plot of an intricate play. Chiefly interested in political history of the Early National Period, Borden is a professor of history at the University of California at Santa Barbara and is general editor of this series on the American political party.*

    In the early months of 1801 all eyes were on Washington and more particularly upon Bayard. The United States had recently experienced a monumental presidential election which had ended in a tie between the two Republican candidates, Thomas Jefferson and Aaron Burr. The House of Representatives, as prescribed by the Constitution,[1] had the task of selecting between these two men. Bayard, as the sole representative of Delaware in the lower house, was a key figure in this election.

---

   * Reprinted by permission of Columbia University Press. From *The Federalism of James A. Bayard* by Morton Borden (New York, Columbia University, 1955). Copyright © 1954 by Columbia University Press: Chapter VII, "Charge and Countercharge: The Election of 1800," pp. 73-95.

It had been a strenuous campaign. In the decade preceding 1800, popular opinion had oscillated between two quickly emerging political parties. Jay's Treaty had aroused a storm of resentment against the Federalists. The XYZ affair had caused an uproar of protest against the "French faction." The lines were being drawn more closely, the focus sharpened and heightened, as it was realized that the battle for power would take place in 1800: simplicity against ostentation, economy and retrenchment against expenditure and debt, civil liberties guaranteed by the states against Alien and Sedition laws enforced by the federal government.[2] Would this infant nation break apart if the rich, the wise, and the well-born were defeated? What crazy theoretical notions would Jefferson try to impose? How were the Federalists to retain—constitutionally or otherwise—national power? All revolved around the important election of 1800. Had Jefferson's victory over Adams not been complicated by his equality with Aaron Burr, the event would have been monumental—indeed, revolutionary—enough. Those who look back on these decades from the vantage point of the twentieth century, who know of Jefferson's policies during his eight years in office, can see nothing "revolutionary" about this election. That the Republican leader adopted many Federalist policies and tactics is true enough; that the natural law philosopher had to become a utilitarian politician no one denies. But in 1800-1801, people could not see things with the same clarity of the modern historian, and *they* regarded it as a revolution. Federalists were not engaging in idle chatter, nor were they speaking for effect, when they predicted many dire consequences if Jefferson were elected. This was Jefferson the atheist, Jefferson of the Virginia and Kentucky Resolutions, Jefferson the lover of France, Jefferson the representative of Virginia's power and influence, Jefferson the demagogue, against whom they were fighting. And Republicans fought back with equal venom, watching carefully for tricks and subterfuge, threatening to march on Washington if the Federalists attempted somehow to stop Jefferson from taking his oath of office.

But Burr and Jefferson did have an equal number of electoral votes, and this complicated the picture, raising political passions to new heights. So intricate and involved are the charges and countercharges of intrigue and bribery concerning this election, that all through the nineteenth century men argued their occurrence—the schemes, the plots, the deals that did or did not take place. It is the purpose of this chapter to carefully detail the roles played by Bayard, Samuel Smith, Aaron Burr, and Jefferson in this election.

No Republican congressional caucus ever met to select Thomas Jefferson as their presidential candidate in 1800. It was unnecessary. Jefferson was the logical and inevitable choice of the party opposed to the administration. The Republicans waited, however, until the all-important New York City election for the state legislature was completed before they decided on a vice-presidential candidate. The Federalists, likewise, waited for the results before selecting their candidates. The entire national election, according to Jefferson, depended on it: "If the city election of N[ew] York is in favor of the republican ticket, the issue will be republican; if the federal ticket for the city of N[ew] York prevails, the probabilities will be in favor of a federal issue."[3]

Aaron Burr displayed his political acumen in this election, guiding his smoothly oiled ward machine to victory over the Federalists. At midnight on May 1, 1800, Matthew Davis, the young and loyal aide to Burr, joyously wrote to Albert Gallatin: "REPUBLICANS TRIUMPHANT," and then added, "To Colonel Burr we are indebted for everything."[4] The news then spread through Philadelphia and throughout the country. John Dawson wrote Monroe: "To his [Burr's] exertions we owe much—he attended the place of voting within the city for 24 hours, without sleeping or eating."[5] The Federalists were gloomy. Alexander Hamilton wrote to John Jay, the Governor of New York, asking him to void the election or suffer the consequences of an atheist President.[6] For most Federalists would agree with Gouverneur Morris's diary notation: "It is from thence concluded that Jefferson will be the president."[7]

On Saturday night, May 3, 1800, shortly after the results of the New York City elections were heard, the Federalists in Congress at Philadelphia held a caucus to select their candidates for the executive posts in the coming national elections. They decided upon some "hocus-pocus maneuvers" (as Thomas Jefferson termed it) by choosing John Adams and Charles C. Pinckney as running mates.[8] The slate was undoubtedly designed to attract both northern and southern votes. Adams, although he had antagonized the Federalist chieftains by his mission to France, still had the main body of New York voters solidly behind him.[9] It was not till Monday morning, May 5, moreover, that James McHenry, the Secretary of War, resigned, after being soundly berated by Adams; not until May 12 that Secretary of State Pickering was dismissed.[10] One wonders whether the congressional caucus would have selected Adams had this schism occurred before their meeting. Pinckney was selected because his name would surely (so the Federalists thought) carry South Carolina—and, perhaps, attract some other southern votes.

The Republicans were yet to meet in order to decide upon a vice-presidential candidate. Matthew Davis wrote to Gallatin before their meeting: "I believe it is pretty generally understood that Mr. Jefferson is contemplated for President. But who is to fill the Vice-President's chair?"[11] Davis suggested Burr. He had been the candidate for that position in 1796, when Jefferson narrowly lost the presidential seat to Adams. He had worked hard to defeat the Federalists in New York City. On Sunday evening, May 12, the Republican members of Congress held "a very large meeting," Gallatin wrote, "in which it was unanimously agreed to support Burr for Vice-President."[12] No formal distinction, however, was made between President and Vice-President.[13]

As it progressed, the contest became more and more virulent.[14] The newspapers screamed their abuse to a politically alert America. How did Thomas Jefferson feel about George Washington? about Christianity? about the Army and Navy? about France? The opposing faction responded: Will you vote for lovers of monarchy? of England? of aristocracy? of wealth? of national power? A typical rumor had John Adams uniting "his house to that of his majesty of Britain" through intermarriage, and "the bridegroom was to be king of America."[15]

The Republicans, meanwhile, were jubilant over the break-up of the President's cabinet. Stevens T. Mason jocularly reported to Monroe: "The Adams cabinet is splitting and falling to pieces in all its parts. . . . Pickaroon (as Chisholm calls him) . . . was of necessity dismissed."[16] Six months later, across the Atlantic seaboard, the people were buzzing about a remarkable pamphlet which described the incompetency of the Federalist presidential candidate, John Adams.[17] The author of this pamphlet was Alexander Hamilton, the brilliant New York Federalist leader. How could the Federalist party, then, succeed? Republican stalwarts would nod knowingly and quote the maxim: "When thieves fall out, honest men come by their own."

The Republicans, however, could not be too sanguine about the results. These Federalists were desperate men—what might they not do to retain power? So the letters flowed in an ever increasing number; every other topic became secondary. South Carolina: "Will Major Butler take part in the election? . . . What are the prospects in [New] Jersey?"[18] Tennessee: "Politics at present occupy much of [our] attention."[19] Delaware: "Our political horizon wears rather an unfavorable aspect in this State."[20] "Ill news from Virginia," reported John Marshall. "To succeed me has been elected by an immense majority one of the most decided democrats [John Clopton] in the union."[21] Philadelphia: "The intelligence from Rhode Island keeps the issue of the election there in doubt. . . . if we lose . . . [there] I am afraid we have lost the Republican candidate."[22] Pittsburgh: "Our Fed[eralist]s here . . . will be nearly as much mortified at Adams's election as at J[efferson]s. Adams has sinned before heaven."[23] Albany: "If North Carolina gives a majority and Maryland is entire and Pennsylvania withholds her votes . . . Jefferson cannot succeed."[24] Baltimore: "There remains no doubt in my mind of Mr. Jefferson's election."[25] "Never has any question occurred," wrote Jonathan Roberts of Pennsylvania, "which has involved more serious consequences than the present."[26]

In Delaware, as everyone expected, Bayard had a relatively easy time in his campaign for reelection. By this time he was a major figure in national political circles.[27] The Republicans looked about for a figure to contend with the renowned Bayard. They offered the nomination to Thomas Rodney who declined. "I told . . . [them]," Rodney noted, "they would not be able to carry any heavy man ag[ains]t Bayard."[28] The Republicans then attempted to persuade the venerable John Dickinson to run, but he also declined.[29] They finally settled on Major John Patten, who "was brought from political retirement . . . in the hope that his Revolutionary War record would garner . . . votes for his party."[30] Bayard was attacked for supporting the Alien and Sedition Acts, the war on France, and federal military expenditures. The Republicans also circulated a rumor of an alleged Bayard statement "that the people of Delaware were not half taxed." This story, wrote Bayard's friend Outerbridge Horsey, "I understand is the most formidable weapon against us."[31]

The Federalist friends of Bayard conducted a vigorous campaign in his behalf, but Bayard (as far as is known) made no speeches and engaged in no electioneering. The southernmost county of Delaware, Sussex, a consistently Federalist area, gave Bayard a huge majority over Patten. The middle county, Kent, also agricultural and usually Federalist, voted rather evenly, Bayard obtaining a majority of only ninety-one votes. "I am very sorry to inform you," John Fisher of Kent wrote Caesar A. Rodney,

> that after every fair exertion on the part of the Republicans in this county, we have, as usual, been completely beaten. We have not been so entirely distanced as formerly, but have lost every man in our ticket. Our chance for success was good, but there is most indubitably, a Majority here against us and when a change will take place we cannot divine. . . . I am not for opposition at any future period unless a great change takes place in the public mind. . . . [but] we calculate on succeeding in our Rep[resentative] to Congress, relying upon the republicanism of your county

[New Castle]. Bayard's majority of 91 we hope even when added to his majority in Sussex will not exceed your majority for Patten.[32]

New Castle County, the commercial region and most heavily populated area of Delaware, usually voted Republican and Bayard was beaten there.[33] But the Republican triumph in that county was not large enough to offset the downstate majorities for Bayard. The *National Intelligencer*, a Republican newspaper, commented: "The results of the Delaware election is federal. But the tenor by which federalism is held in that State must be viewed as precarious when it is observed that Mr. Bayard's majority was only 364, and when it is recollected that both its neighbors, Pennsylvania and Maryland, are decidedly Republican."[34]

But neither Pennsylvania nor Maryland was *decidedly* Republican; nor did the national scene warrant an attitude of easy victory on the part of the Republicans. As the letters of the day indicate, this was to be a close election. Added to the anxiety and doubt expressed in these letters was the touchy problem of Aaron Burr. The Jeffersonians had to be sure that Burr would not receive an equal amount to, or a majority over, Jefferson. This was complex. If they withheld a vote or two in some southern states, Burr might accuse them of bad faith. In fact, intimations that this had occurred in 1796 were broadcast by Burr's agents. Besides, the election would be very close. Burr might even lose the vice-presidency, if the Republicans did not give him every single vote.

Yet, at an early date, Republican party leaders were worried about the eventual issue. James Madison, an exception, was optimistic: "I can not apprehend any danger of a *surprise* that w[oul]d throw Mr. J[efferson] out of the primary station. . . . The worst . . . that could possibly happen would be a tie that w[oul]d appeal to the H[ouse] of R[epresentatives] where the candidates would certainly I think be arranged properly, even on the recommendation of the secondary one."[35] Others, however, were not so confident: "You know it has sometimes happened that a proposed secondary has become chief."[36] Haphazard plans, informal and sudden, were made in several Republican states to detract one vote from Burr. Peter Freneau wrote from South Carolina: "The vote tomorrow I understand will be Jefferson 8, Burr 7, Geo. Clinton 1. *You will easily discover why the one vote was varied.*"[37] Stevens T. Mason reported that in Kentucky and Tennessee "in each . . . a vote will be diverted from Mr. Burr."[38] These plans were not carried out, and by late December, 1800, it was apparent that Jefferson and Burr would have an equality of electoral votes.

The Federalists were jubilant. "Our Tories begin to give themselves airs already in expectation of a *tie,*" reported John Randolph, Jr. "I fear that, in this event, they will give us some trouble."[39] And Jefferson wrote to his friend Breckenridge: "The federalists in congress mean to take advantage of this, and either to prevent an election altogether, or reverse what has been understood to have been the wishes of the people as to their President and Vice President, wishes which the constitution did not permit them specially to designate. The latter alternative still gives us a republican administration; the former a suspension of the federal government for want of a head."[40]

The Republicans were nervous and worried, angry and dogmatic. Anxiously they surveyed the membership of the House of Representatives, for that body would now choose between Jefferson and Burr. At this stage the political movements become more intricate. Therefore, for the purpose of clarity and despite some duplication, it is best to continue our story by outlining three questions, which have long been matters of historical contention, and their answers. The first of these is:

Did Aaron Burr actively plot to become President after the electoral tie with Thomas Jefferson?[41]

Aaron Burr, residing in Albany, was always well informed of political trends across the nation. He well knew, at an early date, that the vote would be equal. On December 16, 1800, he addressed a carefully written note to Samuel Smith:

> It is highly probable that I shall have an equal number of votes with Mr. Jefferson; but, if such should be the result, every man who knows me ought to know that I would utterly disdain all competition. Be assured that the federal party can entertain no wish for such an exchange. As to my friends, they would dishonor my views and insult my feelings by a suspicion that I would submit to be instrumental in counteracting the wishes and expectations of the United States. And I now constitute you my proxy to declare these sentiments if the occasion should require.[42]

The day before the above letter was written, on December 15, 1800, Jefferson wrote to Burr. He explained, cautiously and diplomatically, the possibility of a Tennessee or Georgia electoral vote being diverted from Burr. Jefferson admitted that "it was badly managed not to have arranged with certainty what seems to have been left to hazard." He went on to outline the hopes of their enemies: "It was the more material because I understand several of the highflying federalists have expressed their

hope that the two republican tickets may be equal, and their determination
in that case to prevent a choice by the H[ouse] of R[epresentatives]
(which they are strong enough to do), and let the government devolve
on a President of the Senate."[43]

In answer to this, Burr responded: "I do not . . . apprehend any embarrassment even in case the voter comes out alike for us—my personal
friends are perfectly informed of my wishes on the subject and can never
think of diverting a single vote from you—on the contrary, they will
be found among your most zealous adherents. I see no reason to doubt
of you having at least nine States if the business should come before
the H[ouse] of Rep[resentatives]."[44] Thus the two Republican candidates
kept up an amicable and frank correspondence. Had not Burr specifically
designated Samuel Smith, one of Jefferson's closest friends, his official
spokesman to decline any competition?

Republicans, generally, accepted Burr's disclaimer. Stevens T. Mason
commented that "I have no doubt [Burr] will cordially cooperate with
us."[45] Caesar A. Rodney wrote to his Maryland friend Nicholson: "I
think Col. Burr deserves immortal honor, for the noble part he has acted
on this occasion."[46] The Federalists, on the other hand, believed Burr's
official letter to Smith to be mere window-dressing. "Burr is a cunning
man," wrote Uriah Tracy. "If he cannot outwit all the Jeffersonians I
do not know the man."[47] One Federalist, Robert Goodloe Harper,
believed that Burr was a Federalist at heart. On December 24, 1800,
he wrote to Burr:

> The votes of Tennessee are come in and decide the tie. The lan-
> guage of the Democrats is, that you will yield your pretensions
> to their favorite; and it is whispered that overtures to this end
> are to be, or are made to you. I advise you to take no step what-
> ever, by which the choice of the House of Representatives can
> be impeded or embarrassed. Keep the game perfectly in your own
> hands, but do not answer this letter, or any other that may be
> written to you by a Federal man, nor write to any of that party.[48]

By this time it had become apparent (as shown by Harper's letter)
that the Federalists would seriously support Burr, despite his letters
renouncing all competition. Had he written to them secretly? Would their
attempt succeed? On January 5, 1801, Benjamin Hichborn, a Republican
from Philadelphia, penned a hastily written note to Jefferson: "Col. Burr
is in the house with me and Gen. Smith from Baltimore has been here.
I am convinced that some of our friends . . . are willing to join the

other party, in case they should unite in favor of Col. Burr.''[49] Hichborn
need not have been alarmed. The meeting was anything but secret. The
Philadelphia *Aurora,* in fact, contained rumors about it.[50] Samuel Smith
had gone to meet with Burr with the knowledge of his Republican
superiors.

The purpose of his trip was serious. It was Smith's job to obtain a
second positive declination from Burr—that he had absolutely no aspirations towards the presidency; that he would not serve if elected. Smith
returned to Washington a sadly disappointed man. What had occurred
at the Philadelphia meeting is told in a letter written two years later by
Gabriel Christie (who had been a member of the House of Representatives from Maryland in 1801):

> You [Smith] informed us [Gabriel Christie and George Dent] that
> you went to Phila[delphia] on the day appointed and was much
> disappointed that Col. Burr did not come to Town at the time
> of day agreed on, however he arrived in the evening and you
> had a long conversation with him on the subject of the election
> . . . but you could not imagine what Col. Burr meant for some
> time as he . . . [did] not make any observations but what might
> as well have been made by letter, at length you inquired of Col.
> Burr what was to be done if the Federal members would not give
> up. . . . Col. Burr (greatly as you said to your surprize) told
> you that at all events the House could and ought to make a deci-
> sion, meaning if they could not get Mr. Jefferson they could take
> him. you told Col. Burr that that could not be done for the repub-
> licans would not give up on any terms. . . . you told *us* you
> came away much mortified as when you went up to Philadelphia
> you expected that Col. Burr would give you full authority to say
> that he would not serve if Elected. . . . but instead of that [he]
> gave you to believe that it would be best not to rise without mak-
> ing a choice even if that choice should be him. Thus far I have
> stated to the best of my recollections what passed between Mr.
> Dent and you and myself.[51]

The testimony of this letter is corroborated by Jefferson's diary of
1804. He therein describes a conversation with Col. Hichborn which
almost parallels Christie's account:

> He [Hichborn] was in company at Philadelphia with Col. Burr
> and General Smith (when the latter took his trip there to meet

Burr . . .) that in the course of the conversation on the elections,
Col. Burr said "we must have a President & a const[it]u[tion]al
one in some way." "how is it to be done," says Hitchburn, "Mr
Jefferson's friends will not quit him, & his enemies are not strong
enough to carry another." "Why," said Burr, "our friends must
join the federalists, and give the president." The next morning
at breakfast Col Burr repeated nearly the same, saying "we cannot
be without a president, our friends must join the federal vote."
"but," says Hitchburn, "we shall then be without a vice president: who is to be our vice president?" Col Burr answered "Mr
Jefferson."[52]

One week after this meeting with Burr, Smith penned a long letter
to him. It concerned a man named Ogden, who, claiming "that he had
your confidence," had "addressed the [New York] members on your
account directly and boldly, representing how much New York would
be benefited by having you for the President." Selecting his words carefully, Smith assured Burr that neither Jefferson nor any other Republican
believed that Ogden was an agent for Burr: "Mr Ogden's conduct was
considered as one of many attempts practiced by his party to disunite
[us] and treated accordingly."[53] But Ogden was only one of many. A
few years later, it was reported by Matthew Lyon that "John Brown
of Rhode Island, urging him to vote for Col. Burr, used these words:
'What is it you want Col Lyon, is it office, is it money? only say what
you want & you shall have it.' "[54]
    The evidence looks very damaging to Burr. He had refused to discour-
age any movement in his behalf; "lobbyists" were approaching key political figures of [supposedly] doubtful natures, all in behalf (so they said)
of Burr.[55]
    It is apparent that Burr's first letter to Samuel Smith had been written
when he believed it impossible to best Jefferson in a contest. When
reports, however, arrived of a solid Federalist phalanx behind him, Burr
refused to reiterate his disinterestedness. In late January, Bayard had
informed his cousin Andrew that "it is . . . certainly within the compass
of possibility that Burr may ultimately obtain nine states."[56] Nine states
meant the presidency.
    We come now to the crucial point. Burr had decided upon a policy
of watchful waiting. More significant, however, is the question of
whether Burr went to any further lengths to secure the chief executive's
position. On February 12, 1801, while the House of Representatives was
in a deadlock between Jefferson and Burr, the former noted in his diary

that Bayard had been approaching various Republicans *in the name of Burr.* [57] Two days later, on February 14, Jefferson again confided to his diary: "General Armstrong tells me that Gouverneur Morris, in conversation with him today on the scene which is passing, expressed himself thus: 'How comes it,' he says, 'that Burr, who is 400 miles off (Albany), has agents here at work with great activity, while Mr Jefferson, who is on the spot, does nothing?' "[58]

What, then, is the truth? Did Burr actually send agents to Washington? Did he actively scheme and plot with the Federalists for the presidency? The evidence overwhelmingly indicates that he did not. The following paragraphs will attempt to substantiate that conclusion.

Both from the letters of the day and from evidence which arises out of subsequent litigation, the picture becomes very clear. Bayard wrote to his father-in-law, that "Burr has acted a miserable paultry part. The election was in his power, but he was determined to come in as a Democrat, and in that event would have been the most dangerous man in the community. We have been counteracted in the whole business by letters he has written to this place."[59] To his wife, Bayard repeated that "Burr had refused the offers of the Federalists."[60] To Alexander Hamilton, Bayard wrote the identical thing: "I was enabled soon to discover that he [Burr] was determined not to shackle himself with federal principles."[61]

Two years later, because of political charges that Burr had tried, in 1801, to capture the presidency by fair or foul means, Edward Livingston wrote a letter in defense of Burr: "In consequence of certain insinuations lately circulated, I think it proper to declare, that you [Burr] did not, in any written or verbal communication to me, during the late presidential election, express any sentiments inconsistent with those contained in your letter to General Smith."[62] Other interested parties wrote similar letters in praise of Burr's actions. Burr himself wrote to Governor Bloomfield of New Jersey:

> You are at liberty to declare for me, that all those charges and insinuations which aver or intimate that I advised or countenanced the opposition made to Mr Jefferson pending the late election & balloting for president, that I proposed or agreed to any terms with the federal party; that I assented to be held up in opposition to him, or attempted to withdraw from him the vote or support of any man, whether in or out of congress; that all such assertions or intimations are false & groundless.[63]

*   *   *

Still one year later, in 1803, political enemies of Samuel Smith charged him with conspiring with Burr—and pointed to his hurried trip to Philadelphia as evidence! Once again many letters of rebuttal were called for and received, clearing Smith of this charge. Finally, in 1806, a series of trumped-up trials in New York City (*Burr* v. *Cheetham, Gillespie* v. *Smith*, etc.), calling for depositions concerning the election of 1801, evoked this reply from Bayard: "I cannot tell whether Mr. Burr was acquainted with what passed at our [Federalist] meetings. But I never knew or heard of any letter written to him on the subject. . . . It was . . . determined by the party, without consulting Mr. Burr, to make the experiment."[64]

The experiment, then, was made without Burr's knowledge. As this evidence indicates—although Burr refused to formally renunciate any competition with Jefferson when the Federalists decided to support him—the charges against him seem to be unwarranted. With these charges against Burr considered, it is now possible to investigate another facet of this complex and important election, and so we reach the second question of our outline:

Did Thomas Jefferson accept Bayard's "terms" in order to achieve the presidency?

Mr. Jefferson is our President. Our opposition was continued until it was demonstrated that Burr could not be brought in, and even if he could he meant to come in as a Democrat. In such case to evidence his sincerity he must have swept every officer in the United States. *I have direct information that Mr Jefferson will not pursue this plan.* The New England gentlemen came out and declared they meant to go without a constitution and take the risk of a Civil War. They agreed that those who could not agree to incur such an extremity ought to recede without loss of time. We pressed them to go with us and preserve unity in our measures.

After great agitation and much heat, they all agreed but one. But in compliance of his standing out, the others refused to abandon their old ground. . . . *I have taken good care of you, and think if prudent, you are safe.*[65]

This letter by Bayard to his friend, Col. Allen McLane, Collector of the Port of Wilmington, contains allegations which, if true, mar the reputation of Thomas Jefferson.

When the election was thrown into the House of Representatives, the validity of the motto "politics make strange bedfellows" was clearly exhibited. Alexander Hamilton had to choose between two evils. He wrote letters to all important Federalists—vote for Jefferson! To Bayard, for example, he said: "I admit that his politics are tinctured with fanaticism; that he is too much in earnest in his democracy; that he had been a mischievous enemy to the principal measures of our past administration; that he is crafty and persevering in his objects; that he is not scrupulous about the means of success, nor very mindful of truth, and that he is a contemptible hypocrite."[66] But, if Jefferson was all this, Burr was twice as bad! The adjectives used to describe him included: extreme, irregular, selfish, profligate, and artful. Burr was, in short, "a complete Cataline."[67] John Adams, about to retire to the quiet of Quincy, thought that the House should comply "with the will of the people."[68] At a later date he asked: "What pretensions had Aaron Burr to be President or [even] Vice President?"[69]

Against these views were those who were "determined to oppose the election of Jefferson *at all hazards*." It looked "like desperate works."[70] These men, explained George W. Erving to Monroe, were "Harper, Otis, Rutledge, etc. . . . [who] flatter themselves that they can bring their federal troops to act as heretofore in an united Phalanx."[71] These die-hards made a courageous attempt to rally the moderate and the timid to their banner.

At this point in the early months of 1801, Bayard, whose recent triumph at the polls had reassured him a seat in Congress, took the national spotlight. As the sole representative of Delaware, with the election at a deadlock, he could, if he desired, keep Jefferson out of office. Before Bayard left Wilmington to take his seat at Washington, he had already expressed his intention of voting for Jefferson. Caesar A. Rodney, Bayard's best friend and political enemy, wrote to Jefferson:

I do not know what intrigues under various shapes may be going on at headquarters [Washington] or what influence . . . the Federal Partizans, may have on the mind of my friend Bayard (I call him my friend, widely as we differ in our political course, with great truth and justice for in private life I have never met with a better) when he arrives, but I have lately heard him say repeatedly and in company, that in case of an equality of votes between yourself and Col. Burr he should not hesitate to vote for you and he has spoken frequently of the dignified impartiality observed by you in your conduct as President of the Senate with much approbation.'[72]

Bayard had received many letters from Hamilton asking him to follow
this path. Once in Washington, however, Bayard felt the pressure of the
Federalist supporters of Burr: "The federal gentlemen have generally
declared in favor of Burr, and if Delaware be added to those who have
declared—Jefferson cannot be elected."[73] "Your friend Jefferson cannot
be elected against the will of the federal party; and tho' the course which
will be taken is not absolutely decided upon, yet the inclination is much
in favor of Burr."[74] Gradually, from the many letters Bayard wrote, we
can see him giving way to Federalist pressure: "At present I am by no
means decided as to the object of preference. If the federal party should
take up Mr. Burr, I ought certainly to be impressed with the most
undoubting conviction before I separated myself from them."[75] "The
federal party certainly incline in favor of Mr. Burr, but no determination
has yet been made as to the course they will pursue."[76] By the time
the first ballot was cast, Bayard has decided to go along with his New
England colleagues. Delaware voted for Burr. John Vaughan's advice
to Jefferson that "our political destiny is suspended by a slender thread,
while dependent on the integrity of Mr. Bayard," seemed to be correct.[77]
     It was Bayard who now controlled any chance Burr had for the pres-
idency. There were eight states for Jefferson, six for Burr, and two tied.
The votes of nine states were needed for the presidency. Conjectures
of all sorts were made: "Be assured that the election depends on one
of three persons: Bayard from Delaware; and Craik and Baer from
Maryland—the former there are reasonable hopes from—the 2d full as
good—Mr. Craik's lady . . . will renounce her husband if he does not
vote for Mr. Jefferson."[78] And Jefferson himself said: "There are three
. . . states, Maryland, Delaware, and Vermont, from either of which
if a single individual comes over, it settles the matter."[79] But these key
figures, the four members from Maryland (Thomas, Craik, Dennis, and
Baer) and Morris of Vermont, had agreed to act in concert with Bayard.
As Bayard later explained to his cousin Samuel: "By the arrangements
I had made I became encircled of all the doubtful votes and made myself
responsible for the issue."[80]
     The Federalists now looked over the Republican ranks for "doubtful
votes." New Jersey's ten members were split, six being for Jefferson.
If one of the Republicans, James Linn, changed his vote, New Jersey
would at least be neutralized, if not Federalist. The Republicans were
worried: "Mr. Linn of [New] Jersey is . . . at present with us, which
gives the vote of that State—but might be thrown off."[81] The New York
Republicans followed the lead of Edward Livingston. Bayard is said to
have approached him.[82]

Against this Federalist attempt, the Republican ranks stiffened. "We wait with a great degree of anxiety," wrote Caesar A. Rodney to Jefferson, "confident . . . that it will meet the wishes of every . . . friend to American liberty."[83] "I think there is no fear of our friends giving way."[84] "We are resolved never to yield, and sooner hazard every thing."[85] "We never more adjourn but to proclaim Jefferson for President."[86]

The balloting continued far into the night of February 12. Joseph Nicholson of Maryland, sick with a high fever, had been carried into Congress on a stretcher to maintain the tied vote of his state. The tension mounted; the situation became increasingly desperate. Many of the "high flying" Federalists were willing to see the young nation collapse rather than have Jefferson as their President. Bayard decided, at this time, to divorce himself from his former associates. On Saturday night, February 14, after the balloting had been stalemated and deadlocked, Bayard let it be known that he would change his vote to Jefferson when the next ballot was taken on Monday afternoon. On Monday, however, as Albert Gallatin explained to John Nicholson, "he . . . acted otherwise. But [it] is supposed that the cause of his delay is an attempt on his part and some others to prevail on the whole federal party to come over [to Jefferson]."[87] Another witness, however, explained Bayard's hesitancy to the arguments of other Federalists who "prevailed on [Bayard] to postpone it [his change to Jefferson] until tomorrow [Tuesday, February 17], before which letters are expected . . . from Mr. Burr. . . . [then visiting Baltimore]."[88] Gallatin's supposition was incorrect. John Cotton Smith, a Federalist from North Carolina, describes the caucus at which this one day delay was decided:

Mr. Bayard of Delaware, requested a meeting of his Federal brethren for further consultation and it was held accordingly. He began by inquiring whether any gentlemen present had received any communication from Mr Burr touching the pending election or could inform us why he tarried at Baltimore, when his appearance here would undoubtedly secure his elevation to the presidency? But not one of us could give him the information desired, as no one of us had held any intercourse with him either before or during the session in relation to the subject. [It is impossible to determine whether Harper was at this meeting.] He then observed, that unless Burr made his appearance here, there was no prospect of our prevailing in the present contest; that the opposite party, he was well assured, would persevere to the 4th

of March before they would renounce their candidate, undismayed
by whatever disasters might result from leaving the nation without
a president, and, consequently, without a government, an event
which, so far from exciting any fearful apprehensions on their
part, would rather accord with their disorganizing principles; that
he would continue to vote as he had done until some one of the
gentlemen present of Burr's personal acquaintance would address
a letter to him on the point at issue, and wait a reasonable time
to receive an answer; but that, holding, as he did the vote of
a state, he could not consent that the 4th of March should arrive
without a chief magistrate.[89]

Bayard recounted the story of his struggle to end the election by giving
his vote to Jefferson, to his cousin Samuel:

When it was perfectly ascertained that Burr could not be elected
I avowed that the only remaining object was to exclude Jefferson
at the expense of the Constitution. According to an arrangement
I had made with Maryland I came forward and avowed my intentions of putting an end to the contest. The clamor was prodigious.
The reproaches vehement. I procured a meeting—explained
myself and declared an inflexible intention to run no risk of the
constitution. I told them that if necessary I had determined to
become the victim of the measure. They might attempt to direct
the vengeance of the Party against me but the danger of being
a sacrifice could not shake my resolution. Some were appeased:
other furious, and we broke up in confusion. A second meeting
was no happier in its effect: In the end however there was a
general acquiesence and the whole Party agreed to vote alike,
except Mr Esmonds of Connecticut. His persisting in voting for
Burr induced the four New England States to do the same thing.
Morris retired—Vermont in consequence voted for Jefferson—four members of Maryland voted blank,—the result of
the Maryland vote was the same with Vermont. South Carolina
and Delaware voted in blank. As I had given the *turn* to the election, it was impossible for me to accept an office [Minister to
France] which would be held on the tenure of Mr Jefferson's
pleasure.[90]

There is no doubt that Bayard switched to Jefferson, as he subsequently
stated in Congress, because of "imperious necessity."[91] A young nation,

like a young child, cannot survive if deprived of parents. The United States, Bayard well knew, needed a constitutional President before March 4. Bayard, however, wanted some assurance that Jefferson would be a proper parent, that he would not destroy the child. Bayard therefore approached John Nicholas of Virginia, a close friend of Jefferson:

> I [Bayard] stated to Nicholas that if certain points of the future administration could be understood and arranged with Mr Jefferson, I was authorized to say that three states would withdraw from an opposition to his election. He asked me what these points were: I answered, First, Sir, the subject of the public credit; secondly, the maintenance of the naval system; and, lastly, that subordinate public officers employed only in the execution of details established by law shall not be removed from office on the ground of their political character, nor without complaint against their conduct.[92]

Nicholas, according to Bayard, believed these points to be reasonable, but refused to approach Jefferson directly. With this Bayard was not satisfied. He wanted Jefferson's word. He then approached Samuel Smith and repeated these queries, adding the names of specific office holders he would like protected: "George Latimer, collector of the port of Philadelphia, and Allen McLane, collector of Wilmington."[93] Smith answered in the same vein as Nicholas. Bayard, again, was not satisfied; he wanted Jefferson's own statement. Smith promised to speak to Jefferson: "The next day, upon our meeting, General Smith informed me that he had seen Mr. Jefferson, and stated to him the points mentioned, and was authorized by him to say that they corresponded with his views and intentions, and that we might confide in him accordingly. The opposition of Vermont, Maryland, and Delaware was immediately withdrawn."[94]

It was after this assurance was received, and Bayard had given Jefferson the presidency, that Bayard wrote the tell-tale letter to Col. Allen McLane: "I have taken good care of you." These facts are all taken from Bayard's deposition in the case of *Gillespie* v. *Smith,* in the year 1806. Jefferson, aware of Bayard's allegations, noted in his diary:

> Bayard pretends to have addressed to me, during the pending of the Presidential election in Feb. 1801 through Genl. Samuel Smith, certain conditions on which my election might be obtained, and that Genl. Smith after conversing with me gave

answers for me. This is absolutely false. No proposition of any
kind was ever made to me on that occasion by Genl. Smith, nor
any answer authorized by me. And this fact Genl. Smith affirms
at this moment.[95]

To add to the controversy, Smith's deposition corroborates Bayard's!
According to Smith, Bayard, in 1801, asked:

What would be Mr Jefferson's conduct as to the public officers?
He said he did not mean confidential officers, but, by elucidating
his question, he added, such as Mr. Latimer, of Philadelphia, and
Mr. McLane of Delaware. I answered, that I never had heard
Mr Jefferson say anything on that subject. He requested that I
would inquire, and inform him the next day. I did so. And the
next day [Saturday] told him that Mr Jefferson had said that he
did not think that such officers ought to be dismissed on political
grounds only, except in cases where they had made improper use
of their offices under them to vote contrary to their judgment.
That, as to Mr. McLane, he had already been spoken to in his
behalf by Major Eccleston, and, from the character given him
by that gentleman, he considered him a meretorious officer: of
course, that he would not be displaced, or ought not to be displaced. I further added that Mr Bayard might rest assured (or
words to that effect) that Mr Jefferson would conduct, as to these
points, agreeably to the opinions I had stated as his.[96]

These depositions both aver that Jefferson accepted Bayard's terms in
order to end the contest in the House of Representatives. Actually, this
is not the entire story. In 1830, Jefferson's papers were published; his
notes in reference to the election of 1800 showed Bayard in a bad light.
Bayard's two sons, Richard H. Bayard and James A. Bayard, sent letters
across the country to the few people, intimately connected with the election, who were still alive. George Baer (one of the Maryland representatives in 1800) responded that he had "no hesitation in stating that the
facts stated in the deposition of your father . . . are substantially correct;
and although nearly thirty years have elapsed . . . my recollection is
vivid as to the principal circumstances."[97] Samuel Smith's own letter,
however, gives us the key to the mystery, and shows the villain to be
Smith himself: "I [Smith wrote] lodged with Mr. Jefferson, and that
night had a conversation with him, *without his having the remotest idea
of my object*. Satisfied with his opinion on the third point, I com-

municated to your father the next day—that, from the conversation that I had had with Mr. Jefferson, I was satisfied in my own mind that his conduct on that point would be so and so."[98]

Albert Gallatin, a very old man in 1848, explained succinctly and precisely what had occurred, in a letter to Henry Muhlenberg: "One of our friends [undoubtedly Samuel Smith], who was very erroneously and improperly afraid of a defection on the part of some of our members, undertook to act as an intermediary, and confounding his own opinions and wishes with those of Mr Jefferson, reported the result in such a manner as gave subsequently occasion for very unfounded surmises."[99]

We now come to the last question, one which we can answer only by conjecture: *Did Bayard attempt to influence, by promise of future office, several Republican members of Congress to vote for Aaron Burr pending the election in the House of Representatives?*

The basis of this charge is contained in the diary of Thomas Jefferson. The entry for February 12, 1801, reads:

> Edward Livingston tells me that Bayard applied today or last night to Genl. Samuel Smith and represented to him the expediency of his coming over to the states who vote for Burr, that there was nothing in the way of appointment which he might not command, and particularly mentioned the Secretaryship of the Navy. Smith asked him if he was authorized to make the offer. He said he was authorized. Smith told this to Livingston and to W. C. Nicholas who confirms it to me. Bayard in like manner tempted Livingston, not by offering any particular office, but by representing to him Livingston's intimacy and connection with Burr, that from him he had everything to expect if he would come over to him.[100]

Logically, there are many reasons we could list to give credence to this entry. Bayard did support Burr consistently until all opposition was futile. The vote of Samuel Smith meant the vote of Maryland; that of Edward Livingston would surely have given the state of New York to Burr; and the election would undoubtedly have gone to the "complete Cataline." To further support Jefferson's account, there is no direct evidence in the papers of 1801 that Bayard did *not* approach Smith or Livingston.

It is palpably false, however, when we consider it in a different light. After 1800, there were many charges against Aaron Burr and Thomas Jefferson concerning the election. But from 1801 until 1830, when Jef-

ferson's diary was published, there was not an inkling that Bayard had
approached either Samuel Smith or Edward Livingston.
The publication of the diary caused an uproar. John M.
Clayton, Senator from Delaware, took the floor to call for rebuttals by Smith and
Livingston. Both men denied that Bayard had ever attempted any such
overture.[101] Bayard's sons received letters from other figures who had
lived into 1830. Judge Paine of Vermont wrote to the editor of *Niles
Weekly Register:*

> Noticing, in the papers of the day, the memorandum of the late
> President Jefferson, of the communication of Mr Livingston. . . .
> I determined immediately to communicate to you my knowledge
> of the views and sentiments of Mr Bayard, in relation to that elec-
> tion. And first permit me to say, that probably I possess more
> knowledge on the subject, as it relates to Mr Bayard, than any
> person now living.

Judge Paine goes on completely to exonerate Bayard. "I have no belief
that Mr Bayard would . . . have made, what amounts to a proposition
to corrupt another."[102] James Madison claimed that Jefferson's notation
ought to be considered more correct than "the probability of . . . failures
of memory." He admitted that "there has been a great error some-
where." He concluded that *if* the error was to be attributed to Mr Jefferson, "it must have proceeded from misapprehensions."[103]
On January 31, 1855, James A. Bayard read into the Senate record
a complete account of the election of 1800 and later published this record
under the title "Vindication of Bayard." This pamphlet was again
reprinted, under different auspices, in 1907.[104]
Whether Bayard approached Livingston and Smith on the question of
voting for Aaron Burr and offered rewards for this change in allegiance
will not, it appears, be answered completely. Samuel Smith, of course,
is again the central figure in these intrigues. Perhaps Jefferson confused—since he received the rumor of Bayard's alleged overture from
a third-hand source—the actual details of the rumor. Perhaps Jefferson
was accurate in his diary entry, the alleged overture being the concoction
of Smith's imagination, a concoction designed to prove the Marylander's
devotion to Jefferson. Thus the three charges—against Burr, Jefferson,
and Bayard—all intimately involve Samuel Smith, all lack conclusive
evidence. The first derives from Burr's shadowy character; the second
from a misinterpretation of Samuel Smith's language; the third, probably,
from a misunderstanding by Jefferson of the many rumors of the day.

Bayard allowed Jefferson, a man whom the Delawarean hated through-out his life, to become President. Jefferson, to Bayard, was not only the leader of the Republican party, but the symbol of Republican thought. He saw in the Virginian a lover of revolution, a spokesman for states rights, an opponent of economic legislation he considered invaluable to the wealth and welfare of the national government. Jefferson was a Virginian, and Bayard—as a Delawarean—was wary of Virginia's power. Only the thought of disunion which would result in further sup-port of Burr caused the Delawarean to withdraw that support. It is there-fore due to his memory, said Albert Gallatin in 1848:

> to say that although he was one of the principal and warmest leaders of the Federal party and had a personal dislike for Mr. Jefferson, it was he who took the lead and from pure patriotism directed all those movements of the sounder and wiser part of the Federal party which terminated in the peaceable election of Mr. Jefferson.[105]

NOTES

[1] Article II, Section 1.

[2] See Thomas Jefferson's letter to William Short, April 13, 1800, William Short MS, Library of Congress; for other treatments of this election, see Morison, *Otis*, I, 199-216; William B. Hatcher, *Edward Livingston* (University, Louisiana, 1940), p. 339; Richard Hofstadter, *American Political Tradition* (New York, 1948), p. 33; Claude Bowers, *Jefferson and Hamilton* (New York, 1946), p. 504; Beard, *Jeffersonian Democracy*, pp. 353-414; Isaac Jenkinson, *Aaron Burr* (Cleveland, 1902), pp. 70-71. This listing, it is to be understood, is merely a representative sample; many other works touch upon the election of 1800.

[3] Jefferson to Madison, March 4, 1800, quoted in Paul L. Ford, *The Writings of Jefferson* (New York, 1892-1899), VII, 434. Hereafter cited as Ford, *Jefferson*.

[4] Davis to Gallatin, May 1, 1800, Adams, *Gallatin*, pp. 237-38.

[5] Dawson to Monroe, May 4, 1800, Monroe MS, New York Public Library.

[6] See Henry S. Randall, *The Life of Thomas Jefferson* (Philadelphia, 1871), III, 548-49. Hereafter cited as Randall, *Jefferson*.

[7] MS Diary of Gouverneur Morris, May 3, 1800, Library of Congress.

[8] Jefferson to Thomas Mann Randolph, May 7, 1800, Jefferson MS, Library of Con-gress. For these early caucuses, see M. Ostrogorski, "The Rise and Fall of the Nominating Caucus, Legislative and Congressional," *American Historical Review*, V (January, 1900), 259-60.

[9] Gallatin wrote to his wife, May 6, 1800: "Last Saturday evening the Federal members of Congress had a large meeting, in which it was agreed that there was no chance of carrying Mr. Adams, but that he must still be supported ostensibly in order to carry the votes of New England." Adams, *Gallatin*, pp. 240-41. It might be noted that the large number of votes Adams received in the election, despite the attempts of Hamilton, the Essex Junto, and other Federalists to promote Pinckney over him, lends credence to the belief that many people trusted and believed in Adams's actions while President.

[10] Beveridge, *Marshall*, II, 485-86.

[11] Davis to Gallatin, May 5, 1800, Adams, *Gallatin*, p. 239.

[12] Gallatin to Mrs. Gallatin, May 12, 1800, *ibid.*, p. 243.

[13] The twelfth amendment was a direct result of this election.

[14]. For this virulence, see the MS Diary of Lewis Beebe, June 10, 1800, Historical Society of Pennsylvania, which describes a typical stump-speech political debate; also, Sophia Carroll to her mother, August 14, 1800, Gough MS, Maryland Historical Society.

[15] Alexander Graydon, *Memoirs of a Life* (Harrisburg, 1811), p. 360.

[16] Mason to Monroe, May 15, 1800, Monroe MS, Library of Congress.

[17] Monroe to Madison, November 7, 1800, in Stanislaus M. Hamilton, *The Writings of James Monroe* (New York, 1898-1903), III, 219-20. This pamphlet was circulated and talked about a great deal. See, for example, John E. Howard to John Galloway, November 5, 1800, Galloway-Maxcy-Markoe MS, Library of Congress.

[18] Joseph Nicholson to Alexander Dallas, July 20, 1800, Dallas MS, Historical Society of Pennsylvania.

[19] Theodoric Bland to Sophia Bland, September 7, 1800, Bland MS, Maryland Historical Society.

[20] Caesar A. Rodney to Joseph Nicholson, September 28, 1800, Nicholson MS, Library of Congress.

[21] Marshall to Harrison G. Otis, August 8, 1800, Marshall MS, Library of Congress.

[22] Alexander Dallas to Thomas McKean, November 28, 1800, McKean MS, Historical Society of Pennsylvania.

[23] Tarleton Bates to Frederick Bates, August 17, 1800, Bates MS, Detroit Public Library.

[24] William P. Beers to Ebenezer Foote, August 27, 1800, Foote MS, Library of Congress.

[25] George Salnor to Sylvanus Bourne, December 16, 1800, Bourne MS, Library of Congress.

[26] Jonathan Roberts to his father, December 3, 1800, Roberts MS, Historical Society of Pennsylvania.

[27] Bayard had won the campaign of 1798, for reelection to Congress, apparently without much trouble. See John Batson to William H. Wells, September 23, 1798, quoted in Turner, *Sussex County*, p. 299. In 1800 John Rutledge, Jr. told Hamilton of Bayard's power in Delaware: "The Governor [Bassett] is all powerful in Delaware, but he is very much influenced by his Son in Law Bayard." July 17, 1800, Hamilton MS, Library of Congress.

[28] MS Diary of Thomas Rodney, August 6, 1800, Historical Society of Delaware. This author is unsure of the meaning of the word "heavy" in this quotation of Rodney. Perhaps it should read "any [but a] heavy man." In either case, the implication of Bayard's political power is plain.

[29] Munroe, "Delaware," pp. 391-92.

[30] *Ibid.*

[31] Horsey to William H. Wells [n.d., c.1800], quoted in Turner, *Sussex County*, pp. 303-4.

[32] Fisher to Rodney, October 8, 1800, Fisher MS, Historical Society of Delaware.

[33] See Borden, *The Federalism of James A. Bayard*, in Chapter I, footnotes 6 and 7 for distinctions in politics of the three counties of Delaware. The lower counties, agricultural, first settled, and therefore "oldest," strongly Anglican and Methodist in religion, were Federalist throughout this period. They were composed of conservative farmers, to whom Jefferson was an atheistic radical. The northern county was more fluid in population—and in thought—strongly Presbyterian, and consistently Republican.

[34] *National Intelligencer*, October 31, 1800; Caesar Rodney to Jefferson, October 13, 1800, Jefferson MS, Library of Congress.

[35] Madison to Monroe, November 10, 1800, Madison MS, Library of Congress.

[36] J. Williamson to Monroe, November 6, 1800, Monroe MS, Library of Congress.

[37] Freneau to Jefferson, December 2, 1800, Jefferson MS, Library of Congress. Italics my own. See also John Randolph's letter to Joseph Nicholson, December 17, 1800, Nicholson MS, Library of Congress.

[38] Mason to Monroe, December 22, 1800, Monroe MS, Library of Congress.

[39] Randolph to Nicholson, December 16, 1800, Nicholson MS, Library of Congress.

[40] Jefferson to Breckenridge, December 18, 1800, Ford, *Jefferson*, VII, 468-69; Jonas Platt to James Kent, December 17, 1800, in William Kent, *Memoirs and Letters of James Kent* (Boston, 1898), p. 140; Gouverneur Morris to Alexander Hamilton, December 19, 1800, in Jared Sparks, *The Life of Gouverneur Morris* (Boston, 1832), III, 132. Hereafter cited as Sparks, *Morris*; Lewis R. Morris to William Meredith, December 22, 1800, Meredith MS, Historical Society of Pennsylvania.

[41] For a view opposite to the one reached in this chapter, see John S. Pancake, "Aaron Burr: Would-Be Usurper," *The William and Mary Quarterly*, VIII (April, 1951), 204-13.

[42] Burr to Smith, December 16, 1800, quoted in Matthew Davis, *Memoirs of Aaron Burr* (New York, 1836), II, 75. Hereafter cited as Davis, *Burr*.

[43] Jefferson to Burr, December 15, 1800, Ford, *Jefferson*, VII, 466-68.

[44] Burr to Jefferson, December 23, 1800, *ibid.*

[45] Mason to Monroe, January 2, 1801, Monroe MS, Library of Congress.

[46] Caesar A. Rodney to Nicholson, January 3, 1801, Nicholson MS, Library of Congress.

[47] Tracy to James McHenry, December 30, 1800, McHenry MS, Library of Congress. McHenry, in turn, wrote to Rufus King, January 2, 1801: "[Federalists] do not consider that in it [Burr's letter to Smith] he has committed himself, not to accept of the office of President, if elected by the House of Representatives. They think they understand Burr." King MS, New York Historical Society.

[48] Harper to Burr, December 24, 1800, J. Fairfax McLaughlin, *Matthew Lyon, The Hampden of Congress* (New York, 1900), pp. 385-86. This letter was published in the Philadelphia *Aurora* (a reprint from the *Baltimore American*) on July 12, 1808. It seems to have passed by unnoticed at this time. It was again reprinted in *Niles Register*, January 4, 1823, at which time Harper remarked that he ". . . supposes it was received [by Burr]; but he does not know the fact, and has never heard a word from the said Aaron Burr . . . on the subject."

[49] Hichborn to Jefferson, January 5, 1801, Jefferson MS, Library of Congress. The name "Hichborn" is spelled differently from letter to letter. See Pickering to King, January 5, 1801, King MS, New York Historical Society.

[50] *Aurora*, January 6, 1801, contains a comical account of the rumors circulating about the meeting.

[51] Gabriel Christie to Samuel Smith, December 19, 1802, Samuel Smith MS, Library of Congress.

[52] Anas, January 2, 1804, Ford, *Jefferson*, I, 301.

[53] Smith to Burr, January 11, 1801, Samuel Smith MS, Library of Congress.

[54] Anas, December 31, 1803, Ford, *Jefferson*, I, 300-301.

[55] The key figures—"key" in that their votes controlled an entire state—were: Edward Livingston of New York; James Linn of New Jersey; and the four Marylanders—Samuel Smith, Joseph Nicholson, Gabriel Christie and George Dent. Not one of these, of course, went over to the Federalists.

[56] Bayard to Andrew Bayard, January 26, 1801, Donnan, *Report*, pp. 120-21.

[57] Anas, February 12, 1801, Ford, *Jefferson*, I, 291. Italics my own.

[58] Anas, February 14, 1801, *ibid.* Burr, in fact, had recently arrived in Baltimore, Maryland.

[59] Bayard to Bassett, February 16, 1801, Donnan, *Report*, pp. 126-27.

[60] MS Diary of Thomas Rodney, February 21, 1801, Library of Congress.

[61] Bayard to Hamilton, March 8, 1801, in John C. Hamilton, *The Works of Alexander Hamilton* (New York, 1850-1851), VI, 522-24. Hereafter cited as Hamilton, *Hamilton*.

[62] Livingston to Burr, July 27, 1802, quoted in James Cheetham, *A Letter to a Friend on the Conduct of the Adherents to Mr. Burr* (New York, 1803), p. 50.

[63] Burr to Bloomfield, September 21, 1802, quoted in William Van Ness, *An Examination of the Various Charges Exhibited Against Aaron Burr* (New York, 1804), p. 80. Burr sent a copy of this letter to Gallatin. Gallatin to Jefferson, September 21, 1802, Jefferson MS, Library of Congress.

[64] Davis, *Burr,* II, 123-25.

[65] Bayard to McLane, February 17, 1801, Jefferson MS, Library of Congress. Italics my own.

[66] Hamilton to Bayard, January 16, 1801, Lodge, *Hamilton,* X, 419.

[67] Hamilton to Bayard, December 27, 1800, *ibid.,* 412.

[68] Jefferson recounted Adams's views in a letter to Thomas Mann Randolph, January 23, 1801, Jefferson MS, Library of Congress.

[69] Adams to Jefferson, June 14, 1813, Adams, *Works,* X, 43.

[70] MS Diary of Thomas Rodney, February 11, 1801, Library of Congress. The terms in this quotation from Thomas Rodney are apparently culled from a letter written by Bayard to someone in Philadelphia. For the Philadelphia *Aurora* reported, February 6, 1801: "We are credibly informed that Mr. Bayard of Delaware, has written to a gentleman in this city stating that it is the intention of the Federalists *at all hazards* to attempt the defeat of *Mr. Jefferson's election.* This information the Editor had direct two days ago."

[71] Erving to Monroe, January 25, 1801, Monroe MS, Library of Congress.

[72] Caesar Rodney to Jefferson, December 28, 1800, Jefferson MS, Library of Congress; for confirmation of this letter, see Thomas McKean to Jefferson, January 10, 1801, Jefferson MS, Library of Congress.

[73] Bayard to Bassett, January 3, 1801, Donnan, *Report,* pp. 116-17.

[74] Bayard to Rodney, January 5, 1801, *ibid.,* pp. 117-18.

[75] Bayard to Hamilton, January 7, 1801, Hamilton, *Hamilton,* VI, 505-7.

[76] Bayard to Andrew Bayard, January 8, 1801, Donnan, *Report,* p. 119; see also MS Diary of Thomas Rodney, February 8, 1801, Library of Congress.

[77] John Vaughan to Jefferson, January 10, 1801, Jefferson MS, Library of Congress; Caesar Rodney's letters to Joseph Nicholson, December 29, 1800, February 9, 17, 19, 1801, Nicholson MS, Library of Congress; Mrs. Samuel H. Smith to Mary Ann Smith, February 27, 1801, Samuel H. Smith MS, Library of Congress.

[78] Samuel Tyler to James Monroe, February 9, 1801, quoted in Lyon G. Tyler, *The Letters and Times of the Tylers* (Richmond, 1884-1885, Williamsburg, 1896), III, 14-15. Hereafter cited as Tyler, *Tylers.* The name of Craik is spelled sometimes as Craig or Craick.

[79] Jefferson to Randolph, January 9, 1801, Jefferson MS, Library of Congress.

[80] Bayard to Samuel Bayard, February 22, 1801, Donnan, *Report,* pp. 131-32.

[81] John Dallas to Alexander Dallas, January 15, 1801, Dallas MS, Historical Society of Pennsylvania; G. Jackson to Madison, February 5, 1801, Madison MS, Library of Congress.

[82] For attempts to persuade a change in allegiance, see Gallatin to Alexander Dallas, February 13, 1801, in George M. Dallas, *Life and Writings of Alexander James Dallas* (Philadelphia, 1871), p. 112.

[83] Rodney to Jefferson, February 10, 1801, Jefferson MS, Library of Congress.

[84] Stevens T. Mason to John Breckenridge, February 12, 1801, Breckenridge MS, Library of Congress.

[85] John Dawson to Madison, February 12, 1801, Madison MS, Library of Congress.

[86] Littleton W. Tazewell to Monroe, February 12, 1801, Monroe MS, Library of Congress; Joseph Heister to John Heister, February 14, 1801, Gregg MS, Library of Congress.

[87] Gallatin to Nicholson, February 16, 1801, Adams, *Gallatin,* p. 262; see Gaillard Hunt (ed.), *The First Forty Years of Washington Society* (New York, 1906), pp. 9-10, for an enlightening anecdote of a near accident Bayard experienced at this time. Hereafter cited as Hunt, *Washington Society.*

[88] Col. Brook to Monroe, February 16, 1801, Monroe MS, Library of Congress; Leven Powell to Burr Powell, February 16, 1801, in "Correspondence of Col. Leven Powell, M.C., Relating to the Election of 1800," *The John P. Branch Historical Papers of Randolph-Macon College,* I (June, 1903), 250-51.

[89] William W. Andrews (ed.), *The Correspondence and Miscellanies of the Hon. John Cotton Smith* (New York, 1847), pp. 219-20. Hereafter cited as Andrews, *Smith.*

[90] Bayard to Samuel Bayard, February 22, 1801, Donnan, *Report,* pp. 131-32. Esmonds is William Edmond of Connecticut.

[91] Speech by Bayard in Congress, quoted in Randall, *Jefferson,* II, 130-33.

[92] Deposition of Bayard in case of *Gillespie v. Smith,* given April 3, 1806, quoted in Davis, *Burr,* II, 130-33. Compare this to the points mentioned by Alexander Hamilton in his letter to Oliver Wolcott, December 17, 1800, Lodge, *Hamilton,* X, 396-97.

[93] Davis, *Burr,* II, 130-33.

[94] *Ibid.*

[95] Anas, April 15, 1806, Ford, *Jefferson,* I, 311-14.

[96] Deposition of Samuel Smith in *Gillespie v. Smith,* April 15, 1806, Davis, *Burr,* II, 133-37.

[97] George Baer to Bayards, April 19, 1830, *ibid.,* II, 115.

[98] Samuel Smith to Bayards, April 3, 1830, *ibid.,* II, 107-9.

[99] Gallatin to Muhlenberg, May 8, 1848, in Henry Adams, *The Writings of Albert Gallatin* (Philadelphia, 1879), I, 250. Hereafter cited as Adams, *Writings of Gallatin.* Yet, in 1801, the rumor circulated that Jefferson had accepted certain Federalist terms to become President. Gallatin had to relieve the mind of Burr on this point; and Burr wrote back to Gallatin, February 25, 1801, assuring the Pennsylvanian that the rumors "would gain no credit with me." Gallatin MS, New York Historical Society; in 1809, Timothy Pickering, looking for an issue, asked Gouverneur Morris to furnish him with information about this deal. But Morris refused to commit by letter any information he may have had on that subject. Morris to Pickering, February 16, 1809, Sparks, *Morris,* III, 249-50; Thomas Rodney noted in his MS Diary, February 25, 1801: "The fed[eralist]s siffted [sic] Jefferson to know if they Voted for him Whether he would Turn out the present officers of Government but only obtained in reply 'that he would govern according to the mind of the people.' " Rodney MS, Library of Congress. Thus the rumor did spread at a very early date, but was corrected (as Rodney's diary notation indicates) at the same time. Nevertheless, Bayard always believed that he had bribed Jefferson; that Jefferson never fulfilled his part of the bargain.

[100] Anas, February 12, 1801, Ford, *Jefferson,* I, 291.

[101] *Register of Debates in Congress,* VI (Washington, 1830), 93-95.

[102] Paine to *Niles Weekly Register,* June 1, 1830, *Niles Weekly Register,* XXXVIII (June 12, 1830), 293-94.

[103] January 25, 1835. A memorandum in Madison MS, Library of Congress.

[104] Various copies in the Library of Congress and the Historical Society of Delaware.

[105] Gallatin to Henry A. Muhlenberg, May 8, 1848, quoted in Adams, *Writings of Gallatin,* I, 250.

Part IV

THE REPUBLICAN TRIUMPH, 1801-1816

To jubilant Republicans the accession of Jefferson to the Presidency seemed like the long-awaited clearing of the dark skies of Adams' administration. The change was more than that of personalities; for many it signified that a "revolution" in political orientation had indeed taken place. Liberal ideals—the rights of man and government by the people—had triumphed over the narrow parochialism and monarchical leanings of the Federalists. In contrast, the Federalists, shattered in spirit, vacillated between retreat from public life and hopefulness that the fortunes of their party were not entirely lost. The Republicans now held the executive office, had a sizable majority in both houses of Congress, and, in addition, were in a commanding position in many state legislatures. Clearly the Federalists had suffered a major defeat.

During the period of Republican ascendancy, the first party system continued to grow and concurrently began to disintegrate. Republican power and influence expanded in these years but also reached their zenith; Federalists reorganized, revived momentarily, yet failed to regain their former political stature. By the end of the War of 1812 the old parties were no longer able to meet the changing interests and needs of the nation. New political allegiances emerged after 1816, and the first parties, often epitomizing local or statewide political forces, gradually disappeared.

The following readings give evidence of a more mature party system but one that was also being weakened by divergence. In the first article Carl E. Prince reinterprets Republican patronage policies as a calculated thrust at Federalists in public office, suggesting that Jefferson gave greater impetus to the spoils system than has been recognized. James S. Young's thesis, presented in "Community and Society," is that various sociological forces in early Washington encouraged the formation of regional cliques rather than party groupings among Congressional members, seriously affecting the patterns of action of Congress in the Jeffersonian era. A selection from James M. Banner, Jr.'s study of the Massachusetts Federalist Party focuses on the social and political values of Federalist leadership, revealing the effect on the party of a transfer of power after 1800 from the older, entrenched elite to younger political activists. The increasing professionalization of Republican Party efforts to keep voters loyal is the theme of a chapter from Noble E. Cunningham, Jr.'s *The Jeffersonian Republicans in Power*. In the last essay Harry Ammon discusses the stirring election campaign of 1808 in Virginia. He considers the severe tensions between the regular Republican backers of Madison, the challenge offered by Old Republican supporters of Monroe, and the tactics used to ensure victory for Madison.

The election of 1800 did not dispel the doubts which still hung over the concept of a party system. Before the House of Representatives chose between Jefferson and Burr, Republicans had lively fears that dissident Federalists would overturn the Constitution by blocking the decision on the Presidency. Republican declarations, such as that of Pennsylvania Governor McKean who threatened to call out the militia in the event of an interregnum, were an overreaction to the situation. The very nature of Federalist leadership, in which men of prominence, means, and sense of public obligation were loosely organized, militated against usurpation. Subsequently, in the wake of victory, Jefferson's efforts at conciliation of the Federalists were directed toward ending party contention by winning over the moderates and isolating the extremists. The idea of the legitimacy of a continuing opposition was only tenuously accepted.

Antiparty opinions lay close to the surface and were emphatically expressed by public figures who were steeped in the political thought and practices of the past. They continued to regard parties as unnecessary—if not an evil which detracted from establishing the ideal state. Only when the party structure began to offer opportunities for advancement to the nonelite with the fading away of deference politics did parties become acceptable organizations. Older attitudes and modes of political operation persisted as long as the revolutionary generation remained active in public affairs. Newer concepts regarding parties, altered political techniques, and, above all, a new breed of dedicated party men were coming into prominence by 1816.

Republican gains during Jefferson's administration reflect more than a triumph over a fragmented and moribund Federalist Party whose fundamental ideas had been resoundingly rejected by the electorate. In his correspondence in 1802 John Quincy Adams commented about the Federalist program: ". . . there never was a system of measures more completely and irrevocably abandoned and rejected by the popular voice. It never can and never will be revived."[1] His dictum, however, was somewhat premature. Actually the Federalists continued to be active at the state level, challenging the Republicans and spurring them to organize, to adopt new party methods, and to fight vigorously. The increase in Republican Party organization and machinery was closely connected to the existence of Federalist opposition. Massachusetts' Republicans turned to an interrelated structure of state, county, and town committees under the direction of a central committee to counter the Federalist caucus in the General Court. The quest for victory which eluded the Republicans until they won control of the Massachusetts legislature in 1806 prompted efforts to unify the party ticket, to encourage voter turnout, and to utilize the pro-Republican newspapers to the fullest extent. In New Jersey the Republicans organized carefully in the face of Federalist resistance, originating the idea of a state nominating convention and resorting to a legislative caucus to guide the party. Yet in the South and West, where Federalism was much weaker, the growth of parties as institutions was appreciably slower. Adroit leadership, skillful use of patronage and the party press, appeal to voters' discontents, and recognition of the public's role in politics helped secure the Republicans in power.

Party methods alone did not ensure Republican supremacy. Although Republicans reflected a wide spectrum of ideals and political objectives, varying from John Taylor's strict constructionist views to De Witt Clinton's practical political outlook, there was a substratum of accepted principles. For many Republicans the ideological goal was to keep the nation true to the Spirit of '76 and, above all, to protect a fragile republicanism from its enemies. The Republican interest was based on the belief, expressed succinctly by a Pennsylvania party meeting in 1808, "that the people are capable of self government."[2] To this end the Republicans continued to emphasize increased opportunities for all, popular rule ensured by universal suffrage, election in the hands of the people, and opposition to special privilege.

The Republican organization was far from a monolithic structure; diffusion of power, rather than centralization, prevailed. The national party was limited in scope, while the state parties, diverse in structure, often appeared to be autonomous and not subordinate units. Yet Jefferson clearly established himself as head of his party, exerting a subtle, informal direction in Republican affairs which his successor, Madison, was unable to maintain. According to Dumas Malone, Jefferson's reluctance to wield obvious control was an important ingredient in the President's leadership. "Through his many correspondents he was informed of developments everywhere, and he always kept his finger on the public pulse, but rarely did he intervene in local matters, and with relatively few exceptions he recognized the party leaders who were locally approved.''[3]

Even during the difficult embargo crisis of 1807-1808, Jefferson continued to have an effective hold over his party. He was not able, however, to strengthen links with Congressional Republicans by means of a party leader acting as the administration spokesman in Congress. His efforts to work with the temperamental John Randolph and subsequent floor leaders in the House were both painful and disappointing. Madison, in keeping with his view of the Presidency, allowed Congress to lead. As a consequence, aggressive legislators wrested authority over party activities away from him. Through the nominating caucus, the standing committee system, and the speakership of the House, Republican Congressmen were able to exert a determining influence on the party.

Discontented Federalists were convinced that a highly disciplined Republican Party in Congress controlled its members through the dictatorship of its caucus. In its primacy, between 1800 and 1824, this assemblage of legislators held occasional meetings to direct the choice of Presidential and Vice Presidential nominees and to conduct other party business. In actuality its operations were far less sinister than the Federalist opposition contended. Jefferson had been the logical choice of the caucus in 1800 and was again in 1804, although there was dissatisfaction with George Clinton as the 1804 Vice Presidential nominee. By 1808 much political infighting took place between the supporters of Monroe, Madison, and George Clinton before Madison received a majority of caucus votes. Criticism of the system increased, but no serious challenge developed before 1816. Far from bringing about unanimity within the party, the caucus system had the effect of subordinating the President to members of Congress, and in a self-consciously democratic era it smacked too much of political intrigue.

In spite of the extension of Republican influence, the unity of the party was seriously undermined, almost from the beginning of its tenure, by a chronic factionalism. With the overall decline of Federalist strength, there was less force to impel party cohesiveness and a process of fragmentation occurred. Dissident Republicans took issue with Jefferson's moderate interpretation of party principles, contending that the President had abandoned true Republican ideals and was recruiting support from the Federalists. These Old Republicans fulminated, coalesced, and changed membership in kaleidoscopic fashion but never formed a genuine anti-Jefferson third party. Often they were called Quids, although the term was so loosely used at the time that it is more of a misnomer than an accurate designation.

John Randolph's breach with Jefferson in 1806 remained the defection of a maverick with only a minimal following. New York politics was ridden with factions which were the product of personal clashes and political maneuvering on the part of Burr, De Witt Clinton, Daniel D. Tomkins, and others. Republicans in Pennsylvania quarreled as frequently and vociferously not only over offices and patronage but also over fundamental issues such as the revision of the state judiciary system. Virginia Republican factionalism, more than in other states, reflected the deep ideological split between the conservative Old Republican advocates of a strict construction of the Constitution and limited government and the more flexible concepts of the party majority.

Jefferson himself was not overly concerned about these cleavages since he was convinced that they reflected a natural diversity of opinion among "freemen." He commented to Wilson Cary Nicholas that "the opinions of men are as various as their faces, and they will always find some rallying principle or point at which those nearest to it will unite, reducing themselves to two stations, under a common name for each. . . ."[4] The defections from the "regular" party ranks were, however, serious enough to rouse the concern of many Republicans who had come to regard party regularity as essential to the well-being of their organization. In essence the intraparty disputes were symptomatic of a gradual realignment of political forces, which was discerned as early as 1806 by some of the Old Republicans, who foresaw that a fusion between moderate Republicans and moderate Federalists would take place.

What of the Federalist Party in its time of defeat? Immediately after Jefferson's election its status was at best dubious. New England Federalists were convinced that they would regain their rightful place when the public awoke to the iniquities of the Republicans. Federalists must be prepared to rule; otherwise, as Noah Webster observed in 1807, "if *they* do not lead the people, fools and knaves will."[5] Those oriented to the "Washington school" of politics—elite direction and acceptance of this by the electorate—often abhorred the rough-and-tumble of political strife and, in the face of "Jacobin" gains, retreated hastily from public life. Other Federalists were unwilling to abandon the struggle or to cross over to the Republicans.

While older Federalists considered electioneering with distaste and resented catering to the voter, a more professionally minded group among the leaders chose to revitalize the party. Conscious that former political practices were rapidly being outmoded, they had no reservations about rejecting the original Federalist leadership or in adopting the techniques of their rivals. The newer and younger leaders, wherever contingents of Federalists remained, were as elite-minded as their predecessors. Astutely they minimized their own sense of social and intellectual superiority when dealing with voters, wishing to control the multitude for political purposes but not to entrust it with power. Their concept of the proper political structure was direction from above with participation of the average voter in party activity at the lower level. The new Federalists, to express it in harsh terms, sought the image of democratization, not the substance.

Rapidly the active Federalists developed party associations, varying in different states but often having a common core. A systematic, hierarchical organization took the place of the informal, often haphazard personal political methods of an earlier day. Based frequently on the power of a controlling caucus of Federalist leaders and legislators, the new arrangements were more broadly inclusive as the state committees encouraged the formation of county, local, and ward committees. In Massachusetts the control of the party rested securely in the hands of the legislative caucus, even though county committees held annual nominating meetings. In turn the caucus chose a state central committee of Bostonians which functioned as the directorship of the party. Until such states as Maryland, Delaware, and Virginia turned to statewide nominating conventions after 1810, the caucus was the heart of the party.

The need to have effective communication and contact with the voter was increasingly important to the Federalists. Under the insistent prompting of Fisher Ames, New England Federalists supported the (Boston) *New England Palladium,* which rapidly became a popular and influential party newspaper. The most successful political venture of the Federalists was to reach out to the voters through the numerous Washington Benevolent Societies. Based on an idea of Hamilton's, these fraternal organizations emphasized veneration of George Washington and the Constitution. The societies in their heyday between 1808 and 1816 were particularly appealing to the mechanics, small businessmen, and professionals of the New England and mid-Atlantic states.

How successful were the "new" Federalists during the Republican era? By restructuring the party and infusing it with new approaches and ideas, they kept it intact and in a position to challenge rivals in many local and state contests into the early 1820's. To some Federalists, although the party was unable to rule, it was unquestionably invaluable as a curb on the Republicans. The quest for a popular national issue and vote-getting candidates was elusive. Amid the rumbling of mounting discontent, first with the embargo and then with the war, the Federalists were able to regain a portion of their former strength. There was a resurgence of Federalism in New England and scattered increases in the mid-Atlantic states. Federalists made definite gains in Maryland, Delaware, and New Jersey; in both the Pennsylvania and New York assemblies they won control of about a third of the seats. Ultimately gains were ephemeral. Federalist elitism in an increasingly individualistic period proved a heavy political burden. In opposing the war and in furthering the Hartford Convention of 1814 with its overtones of secession, they lost public support and were tinged with the odium of treason.

Under the aegis of new leadership the party had undergone a metamorphosis even though it failed to achieve national victory. As David Hackett Fischer has aptly expressed it, "The contrast between the two generations of American conservatives was itself a measure of change in the political structure of the new republic."[6]

In summation, the party system experienced numerous stresses and underwent substantive change before 1816. Both parties moved steadily away from old moorings in the direction of a popularly centered, professionally led system. Each in the process was buffeted by internal storms—the Republicans through factionalism and the Federalists through the dissidence of archconservatives attempting to counter the extension of democracy in secession movements. Many of the political approaches of the eighteenth century had fallen by the way in the first decades of the nineteenth; in the next years after 1816 the parties themselves would fade away.

NOTES

[1] John Quincy Adams to Rufus King, October 8, 1802, Worthington C. Ford, ed., *Writings of John Quincy Adams* (New York, Macmillan, 1914), Vol. III, p. 9.

[2] Quoted in Sanford W. Higginbotham, *The Keystone in the Democratic Arch; Pennsylvania Politics, 1800-1816* (Harrisburg, Pa., Pennsylvania Historical and Museum Commission, 1952), p. 13.

[3] Dumas Malone, *Jefferson the President, First Term, 1801-1805* (Boston, Little, Brown and Company, 1970), p. 141.

[4] Thomas Jefferson to Wilson Cary Nicholas, March 26, 1805, Paul L. Ford, ed., *The Works of Thomas Jefferson* (New York, G. P. Putnam's Sons, 1905), Vol. X, p. 137.

[5] Noah Webster to Rufus King, July 6, 1807, Harry R. Warfel, ed., *Letters of Noah Webster* (New York, Library Publishers, 1953), p. 278.

[6] David Hackett Fischer, *The Revolution of American Conservatism: The Federalist Party in the Era of Jeffersonian Democracy* (New York, Harper and Row, 1965), p. 29.

THE PASSING OF THE ARISTOCRACY:

JEFFERSON'S REMOVAL OF THE FEDERALISTS, 1801-1805*

Carl E. Prince

A new interpretation of President Jefferson as party leader emerges from the investigations of Carl Prince into the operations of the Republican Party. In this article Prince denies that Jefferson attempted to ameliorate the extreme party tensions upon becoming President. Despite Jefferson's famous inaugural statement that "we are all republicans; we are all federalists," Republican policy was designed to eliminate an elite element from power by removing Federalists from appointive office wherever possible. By a quantitative method, Prince has determined that Jefferson dismissed a much larger percentage of incumbents, often for inconsequential reasons, than historians have recognized. In Prince's opinion, Jefferson was indeed very much a partisan President. Carl Prince, who is an associate professor of history at New York University, has been especially interested in the evolution and inner workings of the Democratic-Republican Party in New Jersey. He is the author of New Jersey's Democratic-Republicans *(1967) and the editor of* The Papers of Albert Gallatin, *a microfilm edition of which appeared in 1971.*

Every difference of opinion is not a difference of principle. We have called by different names brethren of the same principle. We are all republicans: we are all federalists.

On March 4, 1801, Thomas Jefferson uttered these celebrated words as the keynote to his first administration, and historians from Henry Adams to Marshall Smelser, with surprising uniformity, have accepted the inaugural statement as a reasonable reflection of the President's policy

* From Carl E. Prince, "The Passing of the Aristocracy: Jefferson's Removal of the Federalists, 1801-1805," *Journal of American History*, Vol. LVII (December, 1970), pp. 563-75. Copyright 1970 by The Organization of American Historians. Reprinted by permission of the Managing Editor, *Journal of American History*.

toward the Federalists whom he found entrenched in the first federal civil service. In spite of the numerous reinterpretations and shifts in emphasis through which the age of Jefferson has passed and in the face of many remarkable new insights into the operation of the first American party system, the treatment of Jefferson's dealings with the Federalists—a foundation stone upon which any interpretation of Jefferson the President as politician must rest—has remained consistent in placing the seal of moderation and forbearance on the third President's conduct.

"Moderation," in fact, was just the word Henry Adams used, adding that Jefferson "could afford to make few removals for party reasons."[1] Historians writing on the subject since Adams have agreed that moderation was more or less an accurate characterization of Jefferson's patronage policies. No recent writer, moreover, has had any doubts that Jefferson meant what he said with regard to "republicans" and "federalists" in his inaugural address. They have credited Jefferson not only with moderation but also with sincerity.

Two historians have attempted systematically to measure Jefferson's management of the civil service he inherited. More than half a century ago Carl Russell Fish came closest to a precise assessment, when he totaled up the removals from the service that were listed in the *Journal of the Executive Proceedings of the Senate of the United States of America*.[2] Fish concluded that once Republicans occupied a due proportion (50 percent) of the federal offices at Jefferson's disposal, the President, who rarely turned anyone out for political reasons alone, ordered removals to cease. Thus, under the first Democratic-Republican President, Fish concluded, "the character of the civil service was really not much changed" and only "technically" can one assign to Jefferson any responsibility for introducing a "spoils system" in the federal service.[3]

In a more detailed and comprehensive, though not a quantitative analysis, Noble E. Cunningham, Jr., was in general agreement. Concluding that "complete and reliable statistics on appointments and removals under Jefferson are impossible to obtain," Cunningham recognized that, "under the pressure of Republican demands and the influence of continuing Federalist opposition, the President's earlier sentiments of moderation and conciliation had undergone noticeable modification." Yet, he added, "on removals his practice and policy were not so clear cut," and Cunningham concluded that, "in general, Jefferson tried to steer a middle-of-the-road course" with regard to removals—"less moderate" at first, "more cautious later."[4] All other modern historians of the Jeffersonian Republican era agree that the Virginian followed a reasonable line with regard to his treatment of the Federalist civil service.[5]

The implications of these appraisals are that Jefferson placed a premium on the right to political opposition, fixed on a policy resting mainly on merit, refused to stoop to sweeping the political stables clean, and avoided the pitfalls inherent in politicizing the civil service. Jefferson, in short, was no Andrew Jackson when it came to spoils.

The fact is, however, that Jefferson's patronage policy during his first term was as decisive as it was thoroughly partisan. Removals in one form or another for purely political reasons constituted the backbone of his effort to break the Federalists' power, particularly that party's stranglehold on the sensitive and politically potent second-level United States offices in the states.

Jefferson had to deal with 316 second-level offices in 1801:[6] the inferior federal judges serving during good behavior and not normally subject to removal, the federal law enforcement establishment in the states, the customs department, the internal revenue service, and some civil appointments in the war and navy departments. Using the figure 316—the total number of federal offices in the states subject directly to presidential discretion—as an accurate base, it is possible to draw some conclusions that differ markedly from the present conception of Jefferson the party leader in the White House. The founder of the Virginia dynasty in one way or another forced out 146 incumbents (46 percent), at least 118 (37 percent) of whom can be identified as hardcore Federalist party cadre occupying the most politically useful offices in their respective states. It is probable that virtually all of the 146 deposed officeholders were Federalists. For the sake of accuracy, however, only those will be counted who can positively be singled out as Federalists engaged actively in partisan activities even while holding office in the 1790s and through the election of 1800. They were men who electioneered, chaired party meetings, engaged in Federalist propaganda programs, coordinated political activities, or sought systematically and continuously to use their official positions and private influence to affect the politics of others in their respective communities.[7] Of the 146 who were deposed in Jefferson's first term, 118 clearly conform to this definition of Federalist party activist.

The relatively partisan nature of Jefferson's actions become clear when Jefferson's removals are compared with Jackson's. Jefferson displaced 46 percent; Old Hickory eliminated 252 of 610 federal officeholders, or 41.3 percent.[8] Although an intensive analysis of Jackson's patronage policies would certainly raise Jackson's percentage appreciably, Jackson never professed to believe "we are all Adams men, we are all Jackson men."

Historians have heretofore accepted as complete the removal statistics derived from the *Journal . . . of the Senate of the United States.*[9] The fact is that for strategic reasons Jefferson did not always list as displaced the men he removed from office for political causes. It not only was indelicate to do so in many cases but also might have proved politically damaging to the Jeffersonians inasmuch as the *Journal* was a public document available to members of both parties. Publication of the complete statistics would have confirmed Federalist allegations about Jefferson's partisanship. That an individual was indeed removed, however, was sometimes noted on his private file folder in the archives of the state department, where all personnel files were kept (see note 7). Moreover, several Federalist incumbents—publicly for political reasons, or privately, either pleading for their jobs or writing to associates—disclosed that they were forced to resign under threat of being turned out. Jefferson used this tactic extensively, although no one has ever taken note of this fact.[10] Finally, even though a few Republicans appointed early in Jefferson's administration had to be otherwise provided for (they almost always were), Jefferson ruined more than a few Federalist fortunes when in 1802 he forced the repeal of the Judiciary Act of 1801 and "reorganized" the revenue service. In sum, not only were many Federalists displaced by a variety of devices but also, invariably, the party men occupying the key posts were the ones dismissed.

Undoubtedly the federal circuit and district judges filled the most prestigious offices open to presidential appointment in the states. The United States Circuit Court, although planned much earlier, had not been created until the final days of the Adams administration; its promulgation resulted in extended political controversy and the appointment of the "midnight judges."[11] The Federal District Court was established in 1789. Its judges, like those on the circuit court, usually served in their home states and were appointed during good behavior. These posts were not ordinarily subject to presidential dismissal.

The fact that these judges were not normally removable did not deter Jefferson. Counting the "midnight judges," the President found thirty-two inferior federal judges presiding in their respective states when he took office.[12] Jefferson set out to establish a political balance in the federal judiciary. The most difficult and controversial result of his efforts involved the impeachment and removal of United States District Judge John Pickering of New Hampshire. Although the allegations that by 1803 Pickering was either mentally ill, perpetually drunk, or both, were probably true, efforts to impeach and convict him, according to Lynn W. Turner, were inspired by political considerations. Turner described Pickering's removal as "a political rather than a legal issue"—impeachment became "a convenient political weapon." It was, moreover, a "tragic blunder which reflected discredit upon everyone connected with it." Turner's assessment of the case rests on the fact that, although the judge's incapacity was serious and clearly evident, existing law did not provide grounds for impeachment. When efforts by the President initially to secure Pickering's resignation failed, Jefferson, Turner concluded, could then have taken more subtle measures to relieve the judge of his duties, but "neither the President nor his opponents were in a mood to subordinate partisan spirit to statesmanship in 1803." At Jefferson's instigation Pickering was impeached and removed by the Senate.[13]

Two other district court judges suffered similar though less spectacular fates. Ray Green of Rhode Island, a Federalist United States senator who had resigned to accept a last-minute appointment to the bench from John Adams, was removed by Jefferson on the grounds that a technical flaw invalidated his hastily drawn commission—a blatant political removal.[14] Jacob Read of South Carolina, another Federalist United States senator, was appointed belatedly to the district bench by President Adams to replace Thomas Bee who had been elevated to the circuit court. Bee, however, declined his new appointment, and John Adams' term expired before he could deliver a second circuit court commission to Read. Read was out of luck. Jefferson refused to recognize his commission to the district bench on the grounds that no vacancy existed, inasmuch as Bee had never properly resigned. The President made no appointment of his own to the new circuit court, presumably because he knew it would soon be abolished.[15] The repeal of the Judiciary Act of 1801 eliminated fifteen more judges at one time, all presiding in the United States Circuit Court and all of them Federalists.[16]

All-in-all, then, of the thirty existing inferior federal judges who Jefferson found to be Federalists, three serving in the district court were dropped for essentially political reasons, and fifteen more fell by the wayside in 1802 as a result of the repeal of the Judiciary Act. A sweeping political removal had occurred. Eighteen of thirty Federalist partisans were cleared from the bench by 1803, even though the President lacked the removal power in every instance. In view of these circumstances, the repeal of the Judiciary Act of 1801 must be seen as part of a larger effort to unhinge the Federalist party.[17]

The President did possess the power to replace officials within the United States judicial substructure in the states, and here Jefferson acted decisively. That substructure contained some of the most politically oriented positions under the federal government. Recognizing this, he displaced thirteen of twenty-one United States attorneys, at least eleven of whom were Federalists. He then rooted out eighteen of twenty United States marshals in the states, at least thirteen of them were part of the Federalist cadre. Political power was a hallmark of both positions. The United States attorney for a given state was responsible for prosecuting federal cases (for example under the Sedition Act), compiling evidence on all government suits originating in his state, and farming out investigations to lawyers whose fees he assigned at his discretion. The marshal was charged with impaneling grand and petit juries for government cases (again, for example, in trials under the Sedition Act), and controlled extensive personal patronage in that he designated all assistant marshals serving outlying areas of his state.[18] Both positions were highly visible, highly political posts—hence the excessively large turnover. Only the sixteen United States district court clerks, occupying politically innocuous offices, remained unscathed after Jefferson turned over the judicial establishment.[19]

The upper reaches of the internal revenue service consisted of sixteen supervisors of the revenue (one for each state) and twenty-one inspectors (three more were also acting as supervisors). The inspectors served in the largest states. Of the supervisors, fifteen were Federalists. Six party men were released in 1801 and 1802, and nine more Federalists found their offices eliminated when Jefferson and Albert Gallatin reorganized the service in 1802.[20] Twelve of the twenty-one inspectors whose positions were abolished can be identified as Federalists. All twelve were either displaced prior to the reorganization of the service, or dislodged by the cutback.[21]

Of the 146 customs officers subject to presidential removal, Jefferson replaced fifty, of whom forty-one can be identified as Federalists. The President dropped all but one of the customs officers in the ports of New York and Philadelphia, where party activity abounded.[22] All five New Jersey port collectors were turned out for the same reason. Collectors occupied the most sensitive posts politically, in both large ports and small, because of their visibility and the patronage in the lower echelons of the customs at their disposal.

The story was much the same for New England. Portsmouth, New Hampshire, was swept clean of its Federalist officers. The collectors of New Haven and Middletown, Connecticut, were also removed. In Massachusetts, no less than ten politically active collectors were deposed; Boston Port, where General Benjamin Lincoln of Revolutionary fame presided, remained untouched, however.

In the South, four Maryland collectors (excluding Baltimore), six Vir-

ginia customs collectors (including those at Alexandria and Norfolk), and
the collector at Savannah, Georgia, all fell victim to Jefferson's patronage
program.[23] The political significance of the removal of these Federalist
collectors was enhanced because the forty-one known Federalists who
were dislodged had at their disposal some 271 other customs positions
in the lower reaches of the service; most of these, naturally, also passed
into Republican hands.[24]

The major moderating circumstance introduced first by the President
and later by the historians to justify those removals to which Jefferson
admitted was the presence of cause—apart from that of Federalist activity. Undefined "Misconduct" or "delinquency" was often the reason
he or his subordinates assigned to justify dismissals. Of the sixty-nine
removals Jefferson acknowledged, only nineteen, he said, could be
considered political.[25] But Jefferson's own annotations or those of his
subordinates on personnel folders indicate that only political reasons were
offered as causes for most of the replacements. There are only seventeen
cases where the annotations disclose causes other than purely political
for dismissal, discounting of course instances where offices were legislated out of existence.

In four of these seventeen cases, excessive use of alcohol was the
assigned cause for vacating public offices—a valid justification by almost
any standard. Yet examination of individual circumstances in each case
indicates that unsubstantiated allegation was enough to move the President to action. In one instance, the Pickering case, impeachment by the
Senate at the President's instigation has been adjudged a political
removal.[26] The other three cases involved only presidential action. It was
reported to Jefferson in 1803 by local Republican party leaders that Alexander Freeland, collector of customs at Great Egg Harbor, New Jersey,
had "taken to excessive hard drink . . . and is frequently intoxicated."
Another complaint against Freeland is perhaps more illuminating. After
explaining Freeland's service to the Federalist party and then alluding
to his drunkenness, the writer added that Freeland's removal "will be
highly recommendable [to] . . . the Republicans of the County at Large
. . . at this critical time in consequence of the approaching election."[27]
Jefferson displaced him without further investigation, and the "cause"
can only be regarded as essentially political in nature. Aaron Dunham,
supervisor of the internal revenue for New Jersey, suffered a similar fate
in 1801. The cause for his removal is listed as "intemperance," yet all
of the complaints were from Republicans. The Republican governor of
the state disclosed at the time of Dunham's dismissal that the supervisor
"has gone all lengths to support the late election of our political oppo-

nents, more by the characters and electioneering abilities of his Deputys in the several counties than by his own influence.'' Dunham was, in short, ''subordinate to the will of the aristocratic Junto,'' and that was why he had to be removed.[28]

Perhaps the most revealing case of removal for excessive drink was that of Joseph Tucker, collector of customs at York, Maine. He was reported to the administration as being ''constantly drunk and incapable of business, and a violent *federalist*.'' Tucker was turned out. The town of York immediately convened a town meeting and voted 106 to 0 to refute the allegation and to support Tucker's appeal for restoration of his office. Every selectman in town, in addition to the citizens, added his signature to a petition to the President that concluded by pointing out that Tucker ''has held every office in the Town of which he would accept.'' In spite of this impressive denial of the charge no further investigation was made, and a Republican succeeded to the collector's post.[29] It is clear that even a legitimate cause for dismissal was usually bound up with a man's politics; in some cases, moreover, it is evident that the ''cause'' was simply a pretext to remove a Federalist.

Four more of the seventeen dismissals for cause involved the charge of Toryism during the American Revolution. Richard Rogers, John W. Leonard, and Richard Harison of New York, and Andrew Bell of New Jersey were removed on that score.[30] It is questionable whether by 1801 Toryism itself constituted a legitimate cause for removal. However that may be, the credibility of that stigma as a reason for dismissal was impaired by Jefferson's appointment of three Tories who happened to be Republicans even as he dismissed four loyalists who were Federalists. Woodbury Langdon of New Hampshire was designated navy agent for the district of Portsmouth in 1801. Langdon, an active Tory for at least part of the Revolution, was also brother to an influential Jeffersonian, United States Senator John Langdon. Moreover, Daniel Ludlow, an acknowledged Tory for the whole of the Revolution, was appointed to the same post for the port of New York. Finally, in 1803 Jefferson named Tench Coxe the purveyor of public supplies in Philadelphia even though his loyalism during the war was widely acknowledged among his contemporaries.[31]

The remaining nine cases of dismissal for cause involved allegations of neglect of duty or financial peculation. These charges may have been valid, although in each instance the allegations were coupled with denunciations of the officer's political activism.[32] Whatever the cause, whether it involved a purely political removal, politics in combination with another allegation, or abolition of the office by statute, the 118 Federalists shared in common an active involvement in the leadership of their party in their particular states.

That Federalist leadership, in turn, constituted an American social and political aristocracy—an elite that Jefferson meant to remove from the sources of its political power. Nor was it a dying aristocracy. There are indications that most of the removals involved younger Federalists, in their most productive years, who continued to engage the Jeffersonians long after 1801. Of the fifty-seven dismissed Federalists whose ages could be uncovered (there were 118 known party men removed in all), forty-one (35 percent) had been born after 1750, while only sixteen (14 percent of the 118) were born before that date. It was not, in David Hackett Fischer's words, primarily "old school" Federalists who suffered but the younger, "second generation" party men who bore the cutting edge of Jefferson's patronage axe.[33]

There can be no doubt that the displaced, by several definitions, constituted a slice of an authentic and very old American gentry. Of the eighty of 118 whose occupations could be determined, no less than seventy (59 percent) were engaged in callings of the highest stature in the nation. There were thirty-six lawyers, twenty-four merchants, and ten more who were ship's masters, physicians, bankers, or planters. Of the eighty, only ten (8 percent of the 118) were artisans or farmers. The appellation "wealthy" applied to at least thirty-five (30 percent).

In determining elitism other criteria also apply. At least sixty (51 percent of the 118) of those removed were either scions of long-standing aristocratic American families, or kin to such families. Forty-three (36 percent) fall into the first category and seventeen more (14 percent) into the second.[34] At least twenty-five (21 percent of the 118) were graduates of ranking American or English colleges. The officers corps of the Continental Army contributed at least thirty-two (27 percent) of those dropped; some eighteen (15 percent) were or had been officers in the Society of the Cincinnati, the presumably nonpolitical fraternity of veteran officers of the Continental line.[35] Among the deposed there were also thirteen of the 118 (11 percent) former members of the Congress of the United States, including five United States senators, and nine who were members of the Continental Congress. Taking all of the elite categories enumerated and discounting any overlapping, there were at least eighty-eight of the 118 (75 percent) who could claim elite station. Jefferson, in sum, not only moved decisively in ridding his administration of Federalists but also attacked a very impressive and influential political and socio-economic elite.[36]

Thomas Jefferson in his first years in office was clearly touched by the burdens of power and responsibility; he was affected, perhaps, far more than either he and his followers cared to admit, or historians have heretofore acknowledged. Examinations of what he said have proven somewhat misleading. To arrive at a more accurate assessment of his political leadership in the White House, it is important to take into account more substantially what he did. The President was not the moderate party leader in power that historians have depicted him. Far from binding the ideological wounds of the nation, his actions defined more clearly than ever the dichotomy prevailing within the existent two-party structure of American politics. In some ways the emergent party system stood out with much greater clarity after 1800 than it had in the 1790s. The extent of the socio-economic gulf separating the two parties was dramatized in a way it had never been before and would not be again until the age of Jackson. In this light, the Federalists' extreme view of Jefferson as a partisan leader may not have been altogether misguided. In short, the changing of the guard, though not for the reasons offered by Henry Adams, can indeed be viewed as "the revolution of 1800."

It was a revolution in the sense that it led to the systematic elimination of a long-standing, heretofore well-anchored aristocracy from the second line of the federal government. That the Republicans perhaps replaced the old with a new, modified aristocracy does not detract from the purposeful and degrading damage inflicted on the existent elite, representing as it did many of the oldest and best-established families in America. The removal of the old guard from the second level of government, where it thought itself secure despite the election returns of 1800, can be viewed in two ways that are not necessarily mutually exclusive. On the one hand, it marked the beginning of the end of Federalist power in the several states by seriously impairing the power base and prestige of the entrenched Federalist leadership; on the other hand, it hastened the advent of the second generation Federalists' reorganization of the party structure by stirring them, perhaps for the first time, to greater machine-oriented efforts. In any case, Jefferson's sweeping removals policy had a shattering impact on the American elite and thus marked a decisive turning point in the maturation of the first American party system.

NOTES

[1] Henry Adams, *History of the United States of America During the Administrations of Thomas Jefferson and James Madison* (9 vols., New York, 1889-1891), I, 200-01, 238.

[2] Carl Russell Fish, "Removal of Officials by the Presidents of the United States," *Annual Report of the American Historical Association for the Year 1899* (2 vols., Washing-

ton, D.C., 1900), I, 67-70; Carl Russell Fish, *The Civil Service and the Patronage* (New York, 1905), 29-51.
  ³ Fish, *The Civil Service and the Patronage*, 42, 51.
  ⁴ Noble E. Cunningham, Jr., *The Jeffersonian Republicans in Power, Party Operations, 1801-1809* (Chapel Hill, 1963), 12-70, particularly 25, 60-62, 69-70.
  ⁵ William Nisbet Chambers, *Political Parties in a New Nation: The American Experience, 1776-1809* (New York, 1963), 179; Leonard D. White, *The Jeffersonians: A Study in Administrative History 1801-1829* (New York, 1951), 379; Paul Goodman, "The First American Party System," William Nisbet Chambers and Walter Dean Burnham, eds., *The American Party Systems: Stages of Political Development* (New York, 1967), 87; Morton Borden, *Parties and Politics in the Early Republic, 1789-1815* (New York, 1967), 59; Adrienne Koch, *Jefferson and Madison: The Great Collaboration* (New York, 1950), 223; Sidney H. Aronson, *Status and Kinship in the Higher Civil Service: Standards of Selection in the Administrations of John Adams, Thomas Jefferson, and Andrew Jackson* (Cambridge, Mass., 1964), 13. Even a recent authoritative study of the Jefferson years by Marshall Smelser is no exception to the general tenor established by recent historians. While admitting that Thomas Jefferson removed some Federalists from office to secure a Republican balance and in response to great pressures from below, Smelser concluded: "None were to be removed for difference of principle only." Marshall Smelser, *The Democratic Republic 1801-1815* (New York, 1968), 49. The most recent work, Dumas Malone, *Jefferson the President: The First Term 1801-1805* (Boston, 1970), has the impression that Jefferson resisted the pressure of his own partisans to remove Federalists from office on purely political grounds.
  ⁶ Jefferson used the figure himself. It is accepted by Smelser and Noble E. Cunningham, Jr., and generally tallies with the source for that figure which Jefferson must have employed: Albert Gallatin, "Roll of the Officers, Civil, Military, and Naval of the United States," Walter Lowrie and Walter S. Franklin, eds., *American State Papers, Miscellaneous: Documents, Legislative and Executive of the Congress of the United States* (2 vols., Washington, D.C., 1834), I, 260-319. See also Smelser, *The Democratic Republic,* 50; Cunningham, *The Jeffersonian Republicans in Power,* 61. Carl Russell Fish, for the categories herein defined, listed 313—close enough to accept the former figure without quibble. Fish, "Removal of Officials by the Presidents of the United States," 67-70. Postmasters did not fall specifically into the category of those subject to presidential removal because, like his predecessors, Jefferson delegated the removal authority to his postmaster general—with orders to remove Federalist activists.
  ⁷ Knowledge of the party activities of the 118 was derived from a variety of sources. In general, a great deal of biographical data and new information on political activism was garnered from Applications For Office Under President Washington, Series VII, George Washington Papers (Manuscript Division, Library of Congress); Letters of Application and Recommendation During the Administration of John Adams, General Records of the Department of State, RG 59 (National Archives); Letters of Application and Recommendation During the Administration of Thomas Jefferson, *ibid.*
  ⁸ Fish, "Removal of Officials by the Presidents of the United States," 74.
  ⁹ *Journal of the Executive Proceedings of the Senate of the United States of America* (111 vols., Washington, D.C., 1828-   ), I-III.
  ¹⁰ There are many examples of federal officeholders who chose to resign rather than accept the stigma of dismissal. For the case of George Latimer, collector of customs at Philadelphia, see Gallatin to William Duane, July 5, 1801, Albert Gallatin Papers (New-York Historical Society); Stephen Sayre to Jefferson, Feb. 5, 1801, Stephen Sayre Entry, Letters of Application and Recommendation During the Administration of Thomas Jefferson, General Records of the Department of State. For the case of Matthew Clarkson, commissioner of loans for New York, see Clarkson to Jefferson, Sept. 18, 1801, Resignations and Declinations Among the Records of the Department of State, 1789-1827, General Records of the Department of State. For the case of Henry Bogert, surveyor of customs

at Albany, New York, see Gallatin to Jefferson, Dec. 10, 1802, Thomas Jefferson Papers (Manuscript Division, Library of Congress). For the case of Philip Bradley, marshal for Connecticut, see Gallatin note, undated [1801], Aaron Burr Entry, Letters of Application and Recommendation During the Administration of Thomas Jefferson, General Records of the Department of State. For the case of Joseph Hiller, collector of customs at Salem, Massachusetts, see Jacob Crowninshield to Jefferson, Dec. 15, 1801, John Bigaut Entry, *ibid.*, Gallatin to Jefferson, Dec. 10, 1801, Thomas Jefferson Papers. For the case of Charles B. Cochran, marshal for South Carolina, see Ephraim Ramsey to Jefferson, May 10, 1801, Alexander Moultrie Entry, Letters of Application and Recommendation During the Administration of Thomas Jefferson, General Records of the Department of State; Robert E. Cochran to James Madison, undated [1802], Robert E. Cochran Entry, *ibid.*

[11] Kathryn Turner, "Federalist Policy and the Judiciary Act of 1801," *William and Mary Quarterly,* XXII (Jan. 1965), 3-32.

[12] Two of that number, Harry Innes of Kentucky and Richard Law of Connecticut, were Republicans, the remainder were Federalists who fit the earlier definition of political activist.

[13] Lynn W. Turner, "The Impeachment of John Pickering," *American Historical Review,* LIV (April 1949), 485-92.

[14] Fish, *The Civil Service and the Patronage,* 32; Jeremiah Olney to Oliver Wolcott, Jr., Oct. 30, 1797, David Barnes Entry, Letters of Application and Recommendation During the Administration of John Adams, General Records of the Department of State.

[15] Kathryn Turner, "The Midnight Judges," *University of Pennsylvania Law Review,* CIX (Feb. 19, 1961), 514-15.

[16] Turner, "Federalist Policy and the Judiciary Act of 1801," 3-32; Turner, "The Midnight Judges," 494-523; Gallatin, "Roll of the Officers, Civil, Military, and Naval of the United States," 302.

[17] Richard Bassett of Delaware, William Griffith of New Jersey, Philip Barton Key of Maryland, William McClung (John Marshall's brother-in-law) of Kentucky, Joseph Clay of Georgia, Samuel Hitchcock of Vermont, Benjamin Bourne of Rhode Island, Jeremiah Smith of New Hampshire, Wolcott of Connecticut, John Lowell of Massachusetts, and Egbert Benson of New York represented some of America's long-standing first families and were all widely acknowledged Federalist leaders in their respective states.

[18] Leonard D. White, *The Federalists: A Study in Administrative History* (New York, 1948), 406-15.

[19] The removals of district attorneys and marshals involved such highly important party operatives as Richard Harison and Aquila Giles of New York; Lucius Stockton of New Jersey; William Rawle, John Hall, and John Kittera of Pennsylvania; Charles Marsh and Jabez Fitch of Vermont; E. S. L. Livermore and Bradbury Cilly of New Hampshire; Daniel Davis, Harrison Gray Otis, Isaac Parker, and Samuel Bradford of Massachusetts; David M. Randolph of Virginia; George Woodruff and Ambrose Gordon of Georgia; and Samuel McDowell of Kentucky.

[20] Victimized also were five Republicans (one post was vacant at the time of the reorganization). Jefferson had appointed them to supervisors' posts to replace the Federalists removed earlier. Three of the Republicans, Ephraim Kirby of Connecticut, James Linn of New Jersey, and Peter Muhlenberg of Pennsylvania, were promptly placed in even more lucrative positions in other branches of the federal service.

[21] Nine cannot be identified as belonging to either party. Among the key Federalists turned out were Edward Carrington and William Gaines of Virginia; Nicholas Fish of New York; John Neville and Henry Miller of Pennsylvania; George Truitt of Delaware; Nathaniel Brush of Vermont; John Chester of Connecticut; Jonathan Jackson, John Brooks, and Ebenezer Storer of Massachusetts; John Kilty of Maryland; William Polk of North Carolina; and Daniel Stevens of South Carolina.

[22] Those removed in New York City were Joshua Sands the collector, Richard Rogers the naval officer of customs, and John W. Leonard the captain of the revenue cutter. At

Philadelphia, Latimer the collector, William McPherson the naval officer, and William Jackson the surveyor were displaced.

[23] Some of the Federalist cadremen removed from the customs service in New England and the South were: Thomas Martin of New Hampshire; Elizur Goodrich and Chauncey Whittlesey of Connecticut; Joseph Otis, William Watson, Joseph Wallace, Joseph Hiller, Samuel Gerry, Samuel Whittemore, and John Lee of Massachusetts; James Lingan, William Selby, James Frazier, and Robert Banning of Maryland; William Heth, Otway Byrd, and Charles Simms of Virginia; and James Powell of Georgia.

[24] Gallatin, "Roll of the Officers, Civil, Military, and Naval of the United States," 260-319. Four of fourteen commissioners of loans were also removed: Clarkson of New York, John Pierce of New Hampshire, Thomas H. Perkins of Massachusetts, and John Hopkins of Virginia. Among the removals in the war, navy, and state departments were Israel Whelan, purveyor of public supplies in Philadelphia; Stephen Higginson and William Crafts, naval agents in Boston and Charleston respectively; and Rufus Putnam, surveyor general of the United States. The political affiliations of two men dropped in the navy and war departments cannot be identified.

[25] Cunningham, *The Jeffersonian Republicans in Power*, 61-62. Several recent historians tend to take Jefferson at his word, utilizing as important evidence of his moderation the President's own analysis of the vacancies he created.

[26] Turner, "The Impeachment of John Pickering," 485-92.

[27] Benjamin B. Cooper to Jefferson, Sept. 7, 1803, Joseph Winner Entry, Letters of Application and Recommendation During the Administration of Thomas Jefferson, General Records of the Department of State; John Holmes *et al.* to Jefferson, Dec. 14, 1803, Alexander Freeland Entry, *ibid.*

[28] Joseph Bloomfield to Aaron Burr, April 8, 1801, William Rossell Entry, *ibid.*

[29] Moses Lyman *et al.* to Jefferson, Jan. 18, 1803, Joseph Tucker Entry, *ibid.*; Richard Cutts to Jefferson, Nov. 25, 1802, Samuel Derby Entry, *ibid.*

[30] For the removal of Richard Rogers, see Arthur Alexander, "Federal Patronage in New York State, 1789-1805" (doctoral dissertation, University of Pennsylvania, 1944), 37. For John W. Leonard's dismissal, see Caleb Brewster to Henry Dearborn, April 27, 1801, Caleb Brewster Entry, Letters of Application and Recommendation During the Administration of John Adams, General Records of the Department of State. For Harison's displacement, see George Ludlow to Harison, Sept. 29, 1801, Richard Harison Papers (New-York Historical Society); Albert Gallatin note, undated [1801], David Gelston Entry, Letters of Application and Recommendation During the Administration of Thomas Jefferson, General Records of the Department of State. For Andrew Bell's removal, see the manuscript sketch of Bell's life by J. Lawrence Boggs, Andrew Bell Papers (New-York Historical Society); Thomas Jefferson note, undated [1801], Oliver Barnet Entry, Letters of Application and Recommendation During the Administration of Thomas Jefferson, General Records of the Department of State.

[31] Gallatin, "Roll of the Officers Civil, Military, and Naval of the United States," 318; Dumas Malone and Allen Johnson, eds., *Dictionary of American Biography* (22 vols., New York, 1928-1958), X, 590; Lawrence Shaw Mayo, *John Langdon of New Hampshire* (Concord, N. H., 1937), 86-89, 155-64; Harold C. Syrett, ed., and Jacob E. Cooke, assoc. ed., *The Papers of Alexander Hamilton* (15 vols., New York, 1961-1969), XIV, 203-04, 541-45.

[32] These nine were John C. Ten Broeck of New York, William Watson of New Jersey, David Russell of Vermont, Thomas Foster of Pennsylvania, Elisha Hinman and Richard Dickinson of Connecticut, William Watson and Nathaniel Fosdick of Massachusetts, and Robert Banning of Maryland.

[33] See David Hackett Fischer, *The Revolution of American Conservatism: The Federalist Party in the Era of Jeffersonian Democracy* (New York, 1965), 25-49.

[34] Among the elite families touched by the stigma of removal from the federal services were the Fishes and Clarksons of New York; the Stocktons and Frelinghuysens of New

Jersey; the Tilghmans and Keys of Maryland; the Bassetts of Delaware; the Greens of Rhode Island; the Livermores of New Hampshire; the Wolcotts of Connecticut; the Perkins, Otises, Lowells, Jacksons, and Higginsons of Massachusetts; the Taylors, Randolphs, Carringtons, and Byrds of Virginia, and the Clays of Georgia. Examples of the kin to first families dropped from the civil service were the son-in-law of merchant Thomas Willing, the uncle of Harrison Gray Otis (who was himself deposed), and two brothers-in-law of Chief Justice Marshall.

[35] Among those active in the affairs of the Order were Aquila Giles, Fish, and Clarkson of New York; Anthony W. White of New Jersey; William McPherson, William Jackson, and Edward Hand of Pennsylvania; Daniel Lyman of Rhode Island; Philip Bradley of Connecticut; John Brooks of Massachusetts; Kilty of Maryland; and William Heth and Edward Carrington of Virginia.

[36] These findings with regard to socio-economic status compare most favorably with other important recent surveys of leadership status groupings; Paul Goodman, "Social Status of Party Leadership: The House of Representatives, 1797-1804," *William and Mary Quarterly*, XXV (July 1968), 465-74; Aronson, *Status and Kinship in the Higher Civil Service*, 164. Sidney Aronson indicates that the status and origins of federal civil servants under Jackson differed from those of the men appointed by John Adams—and that the major change took place during Jefferson's tenure. See also P. M. G. Harris, "The Social Origins of American Leaders: The Demographic Foundations," *Perspectives in American History*, III (1969), 159-346. P. M. G. Harris' data, drawn for this period from a survey of leaders whose biographies appear in the *Dictionary of American Biography*, show that, of 415 leaders with careers in government, law, and the military born between 1736 and 1771, approximately 77 percent derive from elite origins. The emergent pattern for the early national period, Harris concludes, was a continued "slope towards broader and more open sources of leadership. . . . That is, the social origin of this kind of leadership democratized." Harris' suggestive findings posit an extension of Aronson's data in that "the government of James Madison may have been still more democratically recruited than that of Jefferson before it, while the Monroe administration may have been somewhat less 'open' in this sense than both the Jacksonian and Madisonian eras of federal government." *Ibid.*, 199-202.

COMMUNITY AND SOCIETY*

James S. Young

From the beginning Washington politics has been enigmatical. There still are numerous inadequately resolved questions relating to the political process in spite of repeated investigation and much speculation. As a sociologically trained political scientist, James S. Young of Columbia University has been concerned with the fundamental political issue of acquiring and using power. In his prizewinning book The Washington Community, 1800-1828, *he has overturned many stereotyped interpretations relating to the interworking of social and political forces affecting the behavior of the ruling body within the national government.*

The chapter of his book chosen for this collection emphasizes a sociological approach to Congressional politics of the Republican era. Inescapable social conditions, the product of a raw, unformed capital city and also of the developing American political system, led to a unique legislative response to national issues. A heterogeneous, constantly changing Congressional membership, legislators' regional interests, absence of leadership in Congress—all precluded efficient resolution of national problems. As a consequence, "boardinghouse" allegiances transcended party cohesiveness, further exacerbating the confusion along the Potomac.

Outwardly, and in certain aspects of its inner life, the Hill resembled nothing so much as an early New England community.[1] The ground plan was similar: instead of the church on the village green with houses huddled round, the Capitol on its plaza, encircled by lodginghouses. The Capitol, like the village church, was the community center, gathering place for Sunday worship and political meetings. No other public building

* Reprinted by permission of Columbia University Press. From *The Washington Community, 1800-1828* by James Sterling Young (New York and London, Columbia University Press, 1966). Copyright © 1966 by Columbia University Press: Chapter 5, "Community and Society," pp. 87-109.

than a meetinghouse being provided in the settlement, the modest, look-alike houses clustered around it suggested a congregational, equalitarian society as unmistakably as the President's mansion, the town houses, and the nondescript shacks of the executive community bespoke hierarchy and status differences. As in the town-meeting villages of New England, it was the collectivity of individuals in the congressional community that made the binding decisions, with the ultimate authority vested not in particular social roles but in a numerical entity, the majority of those voting.

The intensity of the social exposure that was the lot of the New England villager, the experience of living constantly under the eye and in the presence of one's peers, was even more the lot of the legislator on Capitol Hill. Self-sufficient on their summit, the lawmakers lived the winter wholly in each other's company save as they might venture across the wastes of the Tiber to the executive quarter. They worked together, daily assembled in the noisy auditoriums of the Capitol, with no offices but their desks on the floor itself. They lived together in the same lodginghouses. They took their meals together around the same boardinghouse tables. Privacy was no more to be found during leisure than at work, not even privacy when they retired; in their lodginghouses "they lay two in a room, even the Senators."[2]

Here, however, the resemblance ends. For life on the Hill imposed upon a crowd of citizen delegates a communal discipline fit for Calvinists or monks. It threw together, under conditions of social intimacy not easily endured even by men long disciplined to it, a group which utterly lacked binding ties of the sort that reinforced, rationalized, and made tolerable the intensely communal life of the New England villagers. Common membership in the legislative institution they had, and common subjection to the ordeal of election: these were binding ties of sufficient strength, apparently, to draw them into a society apart from executives. Career officeholders they were, too. More than four fifths of the members of one Congress had government experience before coming to Washington (see Table 3), and of 439 Senators and Representatives whose careers have been investigated more than two thirds continued their political careers in other public jobs after leaving the congressional community.[3] But the stability of group membership, the social sameness, the habituation of the members to each other, and the fraternal feelings that usually distinguish congregational communities were conspicuous by their absence in the community on Capitol Hill.

Instead of a stable community membership, one finds a society of transients. Almost none of the members acquired homes in the capital or established year-round residence there.[4] They merely wintered in

TABLE 3
PREVIOUS GOVERNMENT SERVICE OF
MEMBERS OF THE 13TH CONGRESS,
1813-1815 *a*

Government experience	Senators (N=36)	Represen- tatives (N=174)	Percent of total mem- bership (N=210)
All categories	35	139	82.9
Federal	5	6	5.2
Executive	5	6	5.2
Judiciary	0	0	
State	32	124	74.3
Legislative	30	115	69.0
Executive	9	16	11.4
Judiciary	6	18	11.4
Local	3	36	18.6

Source: Biographical sketches appearing in the *Biographical Directory of the American Congress* and the *Dictionary of American Biography*.

a Previous government service means service prior to becoming members of Congress irrespective of when or which chamber of Congress the members first entered.

Since many members had previous service in more than one institution of government (e.g., in both the state legislature and the state judiciary), no two of the above job categories are mutually exclusive.

Washington, spending more time each year with constituents than with each other. Each new Congress, moreover, brought a host of new faces to the community, drastically reconstituting its membership every two years. For the first four decades of national government between one third and two thirds of the congressional community left every two years not to return (see Table 4). New faces appeared and familiar ones departed with considerably greater frequency than in today's Congress; on the average, the biennial turnover was 41.5 percent of the total membership, as compared with 15.8 percent turnover from the 78th to the 79th Congress and 22.4 percent from the 79th to the 80th Congress.[5] While there were a few for whom the Hill was more than a way station in the pursuit of a career, a man's affiliation with the congressional community tended to be brief.[6] Roughly two thirds of the Representatives on the roster of the 13th Congress, for example, did not serve for more than two terms, and two thirds of the Senators failed to serve more than

TABLE 4
BIENNIAL TURNOVER IN CONGRESS

Congress	Percent of total membership failing to return
1st to 2d	39.6
2d to 3d (Washington) a	35.9
3d to 4th	47.8
4th to 5th (John Adams)	42.5
5th to 6th	42.7
6th to 7th (Jefferson)	52.0
7th to 8th	39.6
8th to 9th (Jefferson)	33.4
9th to 10th	32.4
10th to 11th (Madison)	43.7
11th to 12th	37.9
12th to 13th (Madison)	47.4
13th to 14th	49.4
14th to 15th (Monroe)	63.1 b
15th to 16th	48.1
16th to 17th (Monroe)	46.5
17th to 18th	33.3
18th to 19th (John Quincy Adams)	40.1
19th to 20th	37.4
20th to 21st (Jackson)	40.8
21st to 22d	38.9

Source: Personnel rosters for each Congress appearing in the *Biographical Directory of the American Congress*.

a Parentheses enclose the names of the Presidents elected with these Congresses.

a This unusually high turnover apparently resulted from widespread citizen indignation against a Congress which had voted a pay increase for itself.

one term—quite a few of them resigning before they completed even that (see Table 5).

Thus, for all the forced social intimacy of their community life, the rulers on Capitol Hill were largely strangers to each other. "We never remain long enough together to become personally acquainted."[7] "There are many individuals in this House whom I do not know, for I have never met them in the House or out of it."[8] "Friendships . . . we had few and limited opportunities to cultivate," recalled another legislator, and those "were soon broken by our subsequent separation in different and often far-distant states."[9]

TABLE 5

LENGTH OF CONTINUOUS SERVICE OF
MEMBERS OF THE 13TH CONGRESS, 1813-1815 a

	REPRESENTATIVES		SENATORS	
	Number	Percent	Number	Percent
1-2 years	65	37.4	6	16.7
3-4 years	47	27.0	5	13.9
5-6 years	24	13.8	13	36.1
7-8 years	15	8.6	2	5.6
9-10 years	3	1.7	2	5.6
11 years or more	20	11.5	8	22.1
	174	100.0	36	100.0

Source: Biographical sketches of the members of the 13th Congress appearing in the *Biographical Directory of the American Congress.*
a The table includes all continuous service of which service in the 13th Congress was a part.

Not only was the cast of characters constantly changing but it embraced a most improbable variety of men and interests. Here was none of the social homogeneity that ordinarily characterizes communities organized on congregational and equalitarian principles, and that seems essential to peaceful coexistence between men thrown into such intensive interaction.

No English person who has not travelled over half the world, can form an idea of such differences among men forming one assembly for the same purpose, and speaking the same language . . . [forming] a society singularly compounded of the largest variety of elements . . . all . . . mixed up together in daily intercourse, like the higher circle of a little village.[10]

There was, needless to say, the political sectarianism of their different constituency ties, sharpened by the legislators' self-appointed roles as "advocates, retained expressly to support the particular views of particular parties" among their electorates at home.[11] There were differences in occupational background, although lawyers predominated in the same proportion as in the modern House of Representatives (see Table 6). The congressional community mixed together men widely apart in age, and

TABLE 6

CIVIL OCCUPATIONS OF LEGISLATORS,
9TH AND 13TH CONGRESSES *a*

Professions	Senators		Represen- tatives		Percent of total mem- bership (N=338)	
Law	42		142		54.4 *b*	
Other	6	48	34	176	11.8	66.2
Agriculture		9		48		16.9
Trade, commerce, finance		3		45		14.2
Other occupations		1		8		2.7
		61		277		100.0

Source: Biographical sketches appearing in the *Biographical Directory of the American Congress* and the *Dictionary of American Biography*.

a The table excludes 64 members whose civil occupations could not be ascertained. A small number of members who served in one chamber in the 9th Congress and the other chamber in the 13th Congress are counted twice.

b The proportion of lawyers increased by 13.2 percentage points from the 9th to the 13th Congress, while the proportion of farmers and planters dropped by 8.7 percentage points.

many sat as equals at work and at board beside colleagues young enough to have been their sons.[12] The land-rich were mingled with the money-rich, and both with the inaffluent. A variety of ethnic strains represented a nation which had been populated by transatlantic migration—Dutch, French, Scotch, English, Irish, "brought together out of law-courts, sugar-fields, merchants' stores, mountain-farms, forests and prairies."[13]

Most conspicuous of all were the behavioral contrasts associated with the various regions of the country from which the members came, where they spent the better part of each year, and to which they acknowledged their deepest loyalties. To speak of "regional differences" in the new nation is to put too mildly the gulf that separated men from North and South, from the seaboard and from the mountains and the frontiers of the West. For in the Jeffersonian era men from different regions were men from different cultures, with different ways of speaking and acting and thinking, with differing standards of behavior, even with differing concepts of right and wrong.[14] There were those from the plantation culture and the courthouse politics of the southeast—mercurial, proficient at oratory and duels, "ready to construe contradiction into insult"[15] and "great aristocrats in their . . . habits, if not in their politics."[16] The products of an almost totally different culture and life experience were the New Englanders, cultural aliens in the slaveholding southland. Austere, moralistic, inner-directed, they "keep to their lodgings,"[17] "an unmixed people . . . and used only to see neighbors like themselves."[18] From the homesteader culture of the frontier came David Crockett and cultural kinsmen—brash, boastful, elemental types, "accustomed to speak at barbecues and electioneering canvassings,"[19] at home in Washington's woods but not in its society. Upon them all the new American nationality sat lightly. "We come from every stage of civilization, fresh from the people, and bring with us the manners and tastes of [our] different regions. We never remain long enough together to . . . acquire, by much intercourse, that uniform system of . . . deportment, without which crowded societies could not get on for a moment."[20] The distinct provincial cultures that more than a century of prenational existence had nurtured on American soil and that primitive means of communication after nationhood still preserved from contact, Capitol Hill brought together. Power made a community of cultural strangers. And power, shared, was hardly a thing to bind strangers together.

To achieve political accord among men of such disparate interests and different acculturation would not have been an easy task even under the most auspicious circumstances. For those gathered to govern on Capitol Hill in the Jeffersonian era, the circumstances were anything but auspicious.

To the political cleavages inherent in any representative assembly were added the deeper social tensions that are generated when men of widely diverging beliefs and behaviors are thrust upon each other in everyday living. Close-quarters living gave rise to personal animus even between "men whose natural interests and stand in society are in many respects similar. . . . The more I know of [two New England Senators] the more I am impressed with the idea how unsuited they are ever to co-operate," commented a fellow lodger; "never were two substances more completely adapted to make each other explode."[21] As social intimacy bared the depth of their behavioral differences, tolerance among men from different regions was strained to the breaking point. Political coexistence with the South and the frontier states was hard enough for New Englanders to accept. Social coexistence was insufferable with slaveholders "accustomed to speak in the tone of masters" and with frontiersmen having "a license of tongue incident to a wild and uncultivated state of society.

With men of such states of mind and temperament," a Massachusetts delegate protested, "men educated in . . . New England . . . could have little pleasure in intercourse, less in controversy, and of course no sympathy."[22] Close scrutiny of their New England neighbors in power could convince southerners, in their turn, that there was "not one [who] possesses the slightest tie of common interest or of common feeling with us,"[23] planters and gentlemen cast among men "who raised 'beef and pork, and butter and cheese, and potatoes and cabbages' " and carried on "a paltry trade in potash and codfish."[24] Cultural antipathies, crowded barracks, poor rations, and separation from families left at home combined to make tempers wear thin as the winters wore on, leading to sporadic eruptions of violence. In a sudden affray at the table in Miss Shields's boardinghouse, Randolph, "pouring out a glass of wine, dashed it in Alston's face. Alston sent a decanter at his head in return, and these similar missiles continued to fly to and fro, until there was much destruction of glass ware."[25] The chambers of the Capitol themselves witnessed more than one scuffle, and, though it was not yet the custom for legislators to arm themselves when legislating, pistols at twenty paces cracked more than once in the woods outside the Capitol.[26]

To those who would seek political agreement in an atmosphere of social tensions, the rules of proceeding in Congress offered no aid at all. On the contrary, contentiousness was encouraged by Senate and House rules which gave higher precedence to raising questions than to deciding them and which guaranteed almost total freedom from restraint to the idiosyncratic protagonist.

The Americans, observed an astonished Britisher, have taken "the principle of democracy . . . [and] applied [it] to a legislative body."[27] It was not given to some to initiate action and to others to respond. Any legislator had "the privilege of bringing forward, at any moment, such measures as suit his fancy";[28] and any other legislator could postpone action on them indefinitely by the simple expedient of talking. There was no Rules Committee of the House to control the legislative proposals that got to the floor, and no other body served that function. Not even a mild cloture rule such as that in today's Senate existed in either chamber. Garrulity was the rule, and orations of two or three days' length were not uncommon. There was "a universal tolerance of long speeches,"[29] curtailed by "no coughing—no cheering—no hear! hear!—none of those indefinable, but significant sounds, which are so irresistibly efficacious in modifying the debates in the House of Commons."[30] No limits were placed on the number of times a member might speak on the same bill. There were no rules requiring a member's remarks to be germane to the issue, and "no attempt is ever made to restrict the range of argument or declamation, within the limits even of remote connexion with the subject of debate."[31]

Leadership, power to stop or control debate, was nowhere evident. There were no seniority leaders, seniority not being recognized as a basis for rank or prerogative either socially or politically on Capitol Hill.[32] There were no elective or formally recognized party leaders such as are found in the modern Congress: "absolutely no persons holding the station of what are called, in England, Leaders. . . . Persons of ability and address do, of course, acquire a certain degree of unsteady influence . . . but this never appears to entitle them to the character of leading men. The bare insinuation of such pretensions, indeed, would inevitably lead to the downfall of the man so designated."[33]

With permissiveness of the rules and lack of formally recognized leadership went no spirit of cooperation, conciliation, or deference to the opinions of others. On the contrary, individuation of behavior and opinion was approved and valued, while following the lead of others was scorned as a sign either of weakness of character or of ulterior motives for personal gain. To accommodate was to compromise one's principles. To "disdain the idea of relying . . . [on] any man or set of men" was doctrine;[34] and manifestoes of personal independence so suffused the legislative liturgy that the stenographer reported them in paraphrase for the official record: "He had, he said, a right to his opinion. . . . He held himself responsible for it to no man . . . but at his own will and pleasure. . . . I will express my opinion on this and every other subject, without restraint."[35] Men who agreed on an issue felt constrained to adduce different reasons for arriving at their opinions: "The actual practice is to acknowledge no . . . guidance; each member taking good care . . . to let [others] . . . see that he is independent."[36] As speaker after speaker would arise to put his own personal stamp on the measure in question and to expound his individual reasons for support or opposition, the logic, the reasons, the motives behind their opinions became themselves the subject of controversy. Debate would veer in unexpected directions; amendments would accumulate; involvement in the conflict would widen and deepen; agreement would fade, and firm majorities might go to pieces.

> The number of amendments had now become very great, and the accumulation of obstacles was increasing with every speech. I was assured,—and from the tenor of the debate, I have no doubt it was so,—that a majority was decidedly in favour of the . . .

[measure], but minor discrepancies of opinion were found to be irreconcilable. . . . The result was that . . . no money was granted at all, and the matter left for farther debate in another Congress.[37]

Legislators "are not yet sufficiently aware of the necessity of accommodation & mutual sacrifice of opinion for conducting a numerous assembly," President Jefferson complained. In a policy-making body which required some degree of collaboration to accomplish anything,

> the object of the members . . . seemed to be merely to thwart, by every means, the wishes of their political antagonists, and to wear one another out by persevering opposition . . . every man who has had to transact real business, must have found that even [when all sides are in agreement] . . . there must generally be some compromise—some mutual concessions,—something of what is familiarly called "giving and taking," in order to smooth away the difficulties incident to the very nature of our being, and the boundless complication in our interests. But [here] a deliberative body come to discuss a question in a spirit of avowed misunderstanding, without the smallest wish to agree.[38]

"Political hostilities are waged with great vigour," commented another observer, "yet both in attack and defence there is evidently an entire want both of discipline and organization. There is no concert, no division of duties, no compromise of opinion. . . . Any general system of effective co-operation is impossible."[39]

The result was a scene of confusion daily on the floor of House and Senate that bore no resemblance to the deliberative processes of either the town meeting or the parliamentary assemblies of the Old World. Congress at work was Hyde Park set down in the lobby of a busy hotel—hortatory outcry in milling throngs, all wearing hats as if just arrived or on the verge of departure, variously attired in the fashions of faraway places. Comings and goings were continual—to the rostrum to see the clerk, to the anterooms to meet friends, to the Speaker's chair in a sudden surge to hear the results of a vote, to the firesides for hasty caucuses and strategy-planning sessions. Some gave audience to the speaker of the moment; some sat at their desks reading or catching up on correspondence; some stood chatting with lady friends, invited on the floor; others dozed, feet propped high. Page boys weaved through the crowd, "little Mercuries" bearing messages, pitchers of water for parched throats, bundles of documents, calling out members' names, distributing mail just arrived on the stagecoach. Quills scratched, bond crackled as knuckles rapped the sand off wet ink, countless newspapers rustled. Desk drawers banged, feet shuffled in a sea of documents strewn on the floor. Bird dogs fresh from the hunt bounded in with their masters, yapping accompaniment to contenders for attention, contenders for power.[40] Some government! "Babeltown," a legislator called it.[41]

Instability of membership; the constant circulation of short-time servers through the community; cultural, political, temperamental, occupational, ethnic, and age disparities between the members, inflamed into personal animosities by close-quarters confinement on Capitol Hill; permissive rules of debate and dogged adherence to the practice of internal democracy; the absence of formal leadership roles; a compulsion to garrulity and contention; policy-making conducted in a hubbub of irrelevant activities—all these would seem more than enough to offset whatever advantages smallness of size and negligibility of citizen pressures upon the legislative establishment gave to those who would mobilize Congress for policy action. There was another aspect of the congressional community, however, which inhibited the processes of majority formation perhaps as severely as all these combined. This was a social structure which tended to institutionalize the sectional or regional differences among the members, and which probably aggravated the problems of achieving consensus far beyond any internal sources of cleavage to be found in the modern Congress.

Outside the chambers themselves the members did not, for all the closeness of their confinement, intermingle freely or associate widely. Instead they segregated into mutually exclusive, closely knit voluntary associations, forming a segmented social structure of face-to-face peer groups. These were the boardinghouse fraternities which almost all legislators joined when they came to Washington—the members who took their meals together, who lived together at the same lodginghouse, and who spent most of their leisure time together. Originating before the move to Washington and continuing at least until the Civil War, the congressional messes, as the members called their fraternities, were the basic social units of the Capitol Hill community. It is likely, as will shortly be seen, that they were the basic units of its political structure as well.

Within the larger governmental community, members segregated on the basis of branch affiliation. Within the congressional subcommunity, members segregated principally on the basis of sectional affiliation. Legislators had a decided aversion to sharing their mess table, their living quarters, and their leisure hours with colleagues from regions other than their own and much preferred to live in groups restricted to men having

TABLE 7

COMPOSITION OF BOARDINGHOUSE GROUPS *a*

	1807 (N=154)	1809 (N=163)	1816 (N=194)	1822 (N=219)	1828 (N=249)
Percent living in groups repre- senting: *b*					
a. one state	11.3	13.4	7.7	11.4	4.0
b. one region	72.4	69.4	74.2	66.8	68.9
c. different regions	13.2	14.7	15.0	15.5	18.5
Percent living alone	3.1	2.5	3.1	6.3	9.6
	100.0	100.0	100.0	100.0	100.0

Source: *Congressional Directories* for 1807, 1809, 1816, 1822, 1828.

a Percentages are of the total number of legislators with known residence.

The purpose here being to demonstrate patterns, category *a* includes larger boardinghouse groups in which there was no more than one "outsider" from another state; category *b* includes larger boardinghouse groups in which there was no more than one "outsider" from another region, as "region" is defined in note *b* below.

b Subject to the modifications noted below, the regional categories used here are as follows:

New England: Massachusetts, Connecticut, Rhode Island, Vermont, New Hampshire, Maine

Middle Atlantic: New York, New Jersey, Pennsylvania, Delaware, Maryland

South: Virginia, North Carolina, South Carolina, Georgia, Florida, Alabama, Mississippi, Louisiana

West: Tennessee, Kentucky, Ohio, Illinois, Indiana, Missouri, Arkansas, Michigan

Strict adherence to these categories would assign many states having a common border and sociocultural complex to different regions. The better to reflect common geocultural ties between members of the same boardinghouse group, messes are considered to represent a single region where all but one of the states represented in the group are of the same region, and that one exception is a state having a common boundary with one or more of the other states represented in the group. For example, a mess composed of four men each from New Jersey, New York, and Connecticut (the last a New England state but having a common boundary with New York) is considered to represent a single region.

approximately the same geocultural affiliation[42] (see Table 7). While most members saw to it that they had at least one companion from the same state in their mess, and while it was not unusual for a substantial portion of a state's delegation to gather under the same roof, few boardinghouse groups were comprised exclusively of members from the same state, and only rarely did an entire state delegation reside together.[43] Living in regionally mixed groups was preferred to living alone, but the truly cosmopolitan groups were few. Even when members from distant parts of the country formed a mess group, most often the group was dominated by a majority from the same state or region.

Ranging in size to as many as thirty members in one mess, the typical boardinghouse group was, then, a party of southerners or of westerners or of New Englanders, a conclave of New Yorkers, Jerseymen, and Pennsylvanians, or perhaps "a sett" of Virginians and Marylanders.[44] .Within the congressional messes, Senators and Representatives mixed freely, bridging in their extraofficial life their constitutional separation in official life. The young mixed with the old, the newcomers with the old-timers, the lawyers with the farmers, and the farmers with the merchants. But politics did not, for all this, make strange bedfellows on Capitol Hill. For these were not the important differences among sojourners in power, outward bound to the varied cultures of a new nation. In a heterogeneous society most members sought provincial companionship, setting themselves apart from men different in their places of origin and differently acculturated. They transformed a national institution into a series of sectional conclaves.

As their predominantly sectional composition suggests, few messes were chance groups of men who happened to find themselves at the same lodginghouse. Some legislators from the same state or region would travel together to the capital each fall and form themselves into a boardinghouse group upon arrival, perhaps recruiting others into their group to fill up the house.[45] Others "made up" their groups after arrival, sometimes with the boardinghouse proprietor or proprietress acting as intermediary.[46] Persons not members of Congress were rarely accommodated in the same house with legislators even in the early years when accommodations were scarce, and by 1828 a handbook for newcomers noted that "it has become an invariable custom for the members of Congress to mess by themselves."[47]

Mess group affiliation was recognized as a mark of identification among legislators. Conversationally members might be referred to as one of innkeeper "Dowson's crowd" or as a member of keeper "Coyle's family." Some boardinghouse groups were given distinctive names, such as the "Washington Mess" (so identified in the *Congressional Directory* for 1809) and the "War Mess," a fraternity of War Hawks in 1810-12. In further recognition of the importance of the boardinghouse groups the early *Congressional Directories,* rather than listing members in alphabetical order or by state, listed them by boardinghouse, each group roster headed by the name of the boardinghouse keeper and the groups listed in order of the proximity of their lodgings to the Capitol.[48] One surmises, therefore, that mess membership was regarded as a permanent affiliation for the duration of a session, with little shifting of individuals from one fraternity to another. The tendency was, moreover, for certain lodging-houses to be regarded as the "property" of certain regions from one Congress to the next, and take-over by an alien group was cause for ill feeling.[49]

Life within the boardinghouses combined the qualities of the fraternity house with those of the political club, bringing "together around the common mess-table kindred spirits engaged in the same pursuit"[50] and "insuring comradeship at all hours, and spirited but seldom acrimonious talk at meal-times."[51] It was a thoroughly communal existence. Since very few legislators brought their wives or families to Washington, boarding-house society was for the most part one of "unvarying masculinity."[52] Manners were informal: members "threw off their coats and removed their shoes at pleasure. . . . The formalities and observances of society were not only disregarded, but condemned as interferences with the liberty of person and freedom of speech and action."[53] Summoned to the dining hall by the breakfast or dinner bell "like scholars in a college, or monks in a monastery,"[54] messmates took their meals seated at one long table called the "ordinary," served by the proprietor or major-domo on plates handed down from the head of the table. All members of the group were placed on an equal footing, considerations of rank and precedence being entirely absent. At Conrad and McMunn's boardinghouse on Capitol Hill, Vice President Jefferson, recalled one of his friends,

> lived on a perfect equality with his fellow boarders, and ate at a common table. Even here, so far from taking precedence of the other members of Congress, he always placed himself at the lowest end of the table. Mrs. Brown, wife of the senator from Kentucky, suggested that a seat should be offered him at the upper end, near the fire, if not on account of his rank as vice-President, at least as the oldest man in the company. But the idea was rejected . . . and he occupied during the whole winter the lowest and coldest seat at a long table at which a company of more than thirty sat down.[55]

Characterized by the distinctive manners and customs of its region, "each mess was an organized community in itself," with social distance maintained between the messes.[56] Within the group, "our association on the floor, and . . . in our . . . lodgings, led to the reciprocation of friendships which remained intimate and cordial during the con-

TABLE 8

BOARDINGHOUSE GROUPS AS VOTING BLOCS, HOUSE OF

REPRESENTATIVES, 1807-1829 *a*

	1807	1809	1816	1828	1829	ALL CONGRESS	
	10th Cong.,	11th Cong.,	14th Cong.,	20th Cong.,	21st Cong.,		
	1st sess.	1st sess.	2d sess.	2d sess.	1st sess.	Number	Percen
Number of roll calls	32	17	28	19	20	116	
Number of groups	17	21	23	28	29		
Number of cases	544	357	644	532	580	2,657	
Cases of unanimity	44.7%	70.9%	38.5%	47.4%	42.4%	1,243	46.8
Cases of no more than							
one dissent in the group	26.3%	20.2%	28.9%	25.8%	33.1%	729	27.4
Totals: Cases of group							
"agreement"	71.0%	91.1%	67.4%	73.2%	75.5%	1,972 *b*	74.2 *b*
Cases in which two-							
thirds or more of group							
members agreed	87.0%	98.0%	90.5%	89.2%	83.3%	2,365	89.0

a Only groups of three or more Representatives were analyzed. "Absences" were dis
regarded with the following exception: where more than half a group's members faile
to vote, this was considered to be the group's "vote" and any members casting an actua
vote were considered dissenters. In the case of groups having only three Representatives
"agreement" in the above table means that at least two members voted similarly (or faile
to vote).

b Table 9 analyzes the distribution of these agreements on roll calls of high and lov
House cohesion.

tinuance of our mutual Congress life"; outside the group, "intercourse for the most part was polite, but cold and general."[57] Encounter between members of different fraternities appears to have been limited largely to the five or six hours daily when everyone was assembled for work in the Capitol, and even then some accounts suggest that mess groups selected a bloc of neighboring desks on the floor itself.[58]

Visiting between the messes after hours was said to be infrequent. "The company is good enough," wrote a Representative of mess life, "but it is always the same, and . . . I had rather now and then see some other persons."[59] If not avoided by choice, visiting was discouraged by lack of privacy and space within the boardinghouses. "Our not being able to have a room each is a great . . . inconvenience," wrote one of the party activists in the early Congress.[60] Guests would have to be received in the common room or parlor, a "hot oven full of senators and representatives"[61] and "abounding with noise and intrusion,"[62] where the members assembled after dinner to play cards, tell tales, talk over the events of the day, "& then for politics."[63]

It is precisely on this point of greatest interest, "politics," that the descriptive accounts of boardinghouse life tantalize, abounding with allusions but devoid of specific information on the "consultations" or "conferences" or "parlor assemblages" that seem to have been a regular feature of mess life.[64] Perhaps because these gatherings were so much a part of the routine or perhaps because they were meant to be clandestine, the community record reveals no more about the inner political life of the congressional messes than it reveals about the conferences of the Supreme Court justices at their lodginghouse. The official record of roll call votes, however, offers evidence which persuasively argues that the after-dinner "parlor assemblages" in the congressional boardinghouses were "caucuses" in fact if they were not so in name, and which explains why legislators occasionally applied the term "party" to their boardinghouse fraternity.[65]

For the members who lived together, took their meals together, and spent most of their leisure hours together also voted together with a very high degree of regularity. One hundred sixteen roll call votes in the House of Representatives were selected for study, and the voting behavior of each boardinghouse group on each roll call was analyzed.[66] In almost 75 percent of the resulting 2,657 cases analyzed, messmates voted unanimously or with only one dissenting vote within the group (see Table 8). In only 11 percent of the cases did as many as one third of the members of a group dissent from their group's vote.[67]

Moreover, boardinghouse fraternities voted as blocs quite independ-

TABLE 9

BOARDINGHOUSE GROUP AGREEMENTS ON
ROLL CALLS OF HIGH AND LOW COHESION,
HOUSE OF REPRESENTATIVES, 1807-1829 *a*

	Number of roll calls	Number of agreements	Percent of agreements
Low cohesion set	29	531	27.0
Range of indexes: 0.6-10.0			
Mean of indexes: 5.0			
Low-intermediate cohesion set	29	535	27.1
Range of indexes: 10.4-23.0			
Mean of indexes: 15.4			
High-intermediate cohesion set	29	441	22.3
Range of indexes: 23.2-37.4			
Mean of indexes: 30.0			
High cohesion set	29	465	23.6
Range of indexes: 37.8-76.8			
Mean of indexes: 50.3			
	116	1,972	100.0

a The 116 roll calls here analyzed are the same as those analyzed in Table 8. Table 8 also indicates how the 1,972 boardinghouse group agreements here analyzed were distributed as between different Congresses. (See Table 8, note *b*.) As indicated in Table 8, note *a*, "agreement" means cases where, half or more of the members of a boardinghouse group voting, they voted in unanimity or with only one dissenting vote; and cases where all members or all except one member of the group failed to cast a vote.

The Rice Index of Cohesion is used here, as throughout this work. (See Stuart A. Rice, *Quantitative Methods in Politics*.) Arithmetically this index is the difference between the percent favoring and the percent opposing a motion. Thus, an index of o.o. indicates a tie vote; an index of 50.0 indicates a 75 percent majority on the issue decided; and an index of 100.0 indicates a roll call on which no dissenting vote was cast. As the range of indexes indicated above suggests, roughly three quarters of the roll calls selected for analysis involved issues on which less than a two-thirds majority was mustered in the House.

To construct the "sets" used in this table, the cohesion index of each roll call was figured, and the roll calls were then arranged in ascending order of cohesion. The 29 roll calls having the 29 lowest indexes of cohesion were segregated as the "Low Cohesion Set" in the table above; as the range of indexes identified for this set indicates, these were roll calls on which the issues were decided by very close votes in the House. The next 29 roll calls in ascending order of cohesion were then segregated as the "Low-intermediate Cohesion Set," and so on for the other two sets. The number of boardinghouse group agreements in each set of roll calls is entered in the second column in the table; the percentage of agreements each set contributed to the total number of agreements is entered in the third column in the table.

ently of the size of the majority vote in the whole House—independently, it would therefore appear, of the voting cohesion of the majority and minority parties in the House.* Since a unanimous vote in the whole House would necessarily mean perfect unanimity in all boardinghouse groups, it might be expected that, as the size of the House majority increased, so would the incidence of agreement significantly increase within the subgroups that were the congressional messes. If such had been the case, the high incidence of group agreement shown in Table 8 would be less significant as a measure of the importance of these groups in the voting structure of the early Congresses. Table 9 demonstrates that this was not the case, however, on the 116 roll calls analyzed here. Boardinghouse groups voted as blocs on the closely contested issues in the House just as they did on the less controversial issues, decided by a large majority margin. Moreover, the incidence of bloc voting by messmates not only failed to rise but tended to decline slightly as the size of the majority vote in the whole House increased. The more evenly divided the House sentiment and the more closely contested the issue, the greater, apparently, was intrabloc "discipline" and the reliance upon messmates for political cues.[68]

The voting performance of the congressional messes clearly suggests, then, that legislators looked for policy guidance, as they did for companionship, to colleagues from the same locale or region, and that these intralegislative fraternal associations were influences of major significance upon the members' voting behavior.† This is not to assert that boardinghouse fraternities were the only source of guidance nor the only

---

* The assumption here is that fluctuations in the size of the House majority from issue to issue meant fluctuations in the cohesiveness of both the parties. It is not reasonable to infer that one of the parties was consistently cohesive, while the other was erratic.

† As with Representatives, Senators who were messmates tended to vote together. Thus, for example, of the six groups of Senators living together in 1809, two groups voted with perfect unanimity on all ten roll calls taken in the shortest session of the 11th Congress; one group voted unanimously on nine of the ten roll calls; two groups voted unanimously on eight; and the remaining group voted unanimously on five. Perfect unanimity was thus achieved in 83.3 percent of the sixty cases.

Any extended analysis of boardinghouse group cohesion for the Senate, however, would include too few of the total membership, and the groups analyzed would be too small, to yield significant comparisons with the House of Representatives. The reason is that most Senators preferred to share living quarters only with Representatives; and when they did share with colleagues in the upper chamber, usually only two, and rarely more than four, were affiliated with the same mess.

The fact that few Senators had boardinghouse fraternity ties with other Senators, and the small size of the senatorial contingents in any one fraternity, probably conduced to greater flexibility and fluidity of voting patterns in the Senate. It seems reasonable, however, to infer a similar importance for sectional influences in Senate voting patterns as in the House, given the predominantly sectional composition of the messes with which most Senators were affiliated.

politically significant associations on Capitol Hill.* But no other grouping of legislators was institutionalized in the social structure of the congressional community. No other grouping was reinforced by such con-
stancy and intensiveness of social interaction between the members as
the boardinghouse fraternities. And, as the following quotation illustrates,
for no other type of grouping was political conformity asserted to be
the moral obligation of the individual member, nor individual deviation
from the group attended with such drastic sanctions. When the presidential election of 1824 was thrown to the House, Representative Stephen
Van Rensselaer of New York violated an agreement among his messmates to cast their votes for Crawford, and voted for Adams instead.
What ensued is best told in the words of one of General Van Rensselaer's
messmates:

> When the election was over, as I was leaving the House, I saw
> [Van Rensselaer] coming to me, I hurried forward to avoid him
> . . . when I got home, I ran up in my own room, but had not
> been long there when he followed, he came in, he looked wretch-
> edly, tears were running down his cheeks, "forgive me,
> McClean," said he, stretching out his hand. "Ask your own con-
> science General and not me," said I turning away. Since then
> he has been in coventry. A similar scene took place with V.B.
> [Van Buren] and the other gentlemen of the mess, we let him
> continue with us, sit at the same table with us, but we do not
> speak to him. He is beneath anything but contempt. . . . He has
> betrayed those with whom he broke bread.[69]

By seeking primary-group affiliations at Washington with colleagues
most like their own constituents at home, legislators not only built
parochial influences into the structure of the congressional establishment
but made their responsiveness to these influences a matter of moral
obligation.

While legislators might disdain a posture of servility to constituents,
there can be little doubt, then, that they preferred those community arrangements which would enhance their ability to play the constituency
agent in Washington. Such, indeed, was the value they placed on the
role of the legislator as constituency agent that they appear to have
organized their entire community around it. Permissive procedures

---

* The voting cohesion of boardinghouse groups and state delegations is compared in
Table 10. That of boardinghouse groups was, on the whole, higher on the 24 roll calls
there analyzed.

afforded maximum freedom for advocating different constituency interests. Internal democracy conferred equality of status, prerogatives, and
power opportunities upon the surrogates of those interests. Denial of recognition for leadership roles and avoidance of interbranch and interregional associations protected them from personal influences which might
have conflicted with those interests. Chosen cycles of rendezvous at
Washington and dispersal to the hinterlands ensured more exposure to
constituents than to colleagues. And personal associations were chosen
at Washington which reinforced constituency allegiances outside
Washington: sectional fraternities put legislators in a primary field of
influence within the governmental establishment which tended to dup-
licate the sectarian influence of their constituencies at home.

A system more superbly adapted to the articulation of constituency
needs, more exquisitely sensitive to the mandates of provincial electorates, could scarcely be imagined. The remarkable thing is that such
a system took root on Capitol Hill at a time when the level of constituency attention to the doings of the Washington community, and the
level of constituency demands upon it, were perhaps at their lowest point
in history. Political utility for the members partially explains it, to be
sure. Boardinghouse fraternities tended to ensure that decisions made at
Washington would not be so out of line with constituency sentiment as
to endanger chances of reelection—for those who wished to stay in
Washington. Permissive rules of proceeding provided needed opportunities to particularize, clarify, or obscure one's position for the official
record, as constituency mood or local election prospects dictated. Yet
rules so utterly permissive of obstructionism seem quite to exceed the
electoral survival needs of legislators so remote from their constituents.
And a social system which went to such extremes in insulating legislators
from personal influences not in harmony with constituency allegiances
seems quite to exceed any objective need they had for keeping themselves
attuned to the moods of a distant and undemanding electorate.

Their isolation at Washington and the relative freedom of behavior this
afforded invite attention, therefore, to the sources of such a social system
in the values and attitudes of the legislators themselves, and especially
in their psychology about power. For surely it can be no coincidence
that power-holders who shared the cultural stereotype of power as evil
should choose community roles and arrangements at Washington which
tended to identify them with persons and interests outside the institutions
of power. The antipower values of the governors would seem to explain,
better than citizen demands upon them, the emergence of a constituency-
oriented culture and social organization on Capitol Hill. Ambivalence

about power among men in power would seem to explain, better than their needs for political survival, why they preferred the behavior of constituency agents to the behavior of rulers.

Causes aside, what emerges from the community record of the legislative branch is a social system which tended to ensure the integrity of the constitutional principle of representative government, just as the social system of the larger community tended to ensure the integrity of the constitutional principle of "separation of powers." But the dogged commitment to internal democracy and the fragmentation into sociopolitical blocs that have been discovered on Capitol Hill also raise—even more cogently for the congressional community—the same question that was raised by the antipower values and the fragmented structure of the larger governmental community. How could a system pregnant with such sources of conflict within itself perform the task of resolving conflict outside itself, in the nation at large? For it does not suffice for legislators at Washington merely to reflect, in their own values and organization, the varied and conflicting interests of the society they represent. What it takes to govern a people is something quite distinct from what it takes to represent a people; and the needs of rulership are not the needs of constituency spokesmanship. If a representative body is to perform adequately as an institution of governance, there must be some means for reconciling conflict among the representatives themselves. There must be some means for subordinating conflict to accomplishment of common goals.

What machinery was there, then, in the congressional community of Jeffersonian times for resolving the conflicts made inevitable by its structure, its values, its work, its composition? What was there to prevent an anarchy of groups in a community of segregated sectional conclaves? What was there to bind those conclaves, and the fragments of the nation they represented, together in a functioning whole? What resources were available to mobilize Congress for action when action was needed?

NOTES

[1] See Arensberg, "American Communities," *American Anthropologist*, LVII, No. 6, Part 1 (December, 1955), 1148-51.

[2] Foster, *Jeffersonian America*, p. 83.

[3] The 439 legislators whose careers were studied include 210 members of the 13th Congress and 229 other Senators and Representatives who resigned from Congress from the 5th through the 20th Congresses. Among the members of the 13th Congress, 58.6 percent held other public jobs after leaving Congress. Among the resigners the percentage was 76.9. Of all 439, 288 or 67.9 percent held public jobs subsequent to their congressional service.

[4] Busey, *Pictures of Washington,* Chapter 8.

[5] There was considerable variation among states in the rate of turnover in their delegations. Two of the largest state delegations, Pennsylvania and New York, were conspicuous
for their massive turnover with each of most congressional elections. John Quincy Adams
noted in his diary in 1821 that "the State of New York has got into a practice of changing
almost the whole of her delegation at every Congress. . . . They come with little knowledge
of the general affairs of the whole Union . . . and by the time they have acquired experience
necessary for the discharge of their duties their two years of service expire, and they are
heard of no more." *Memoirs,* V, 457. A study of the *Biographical Directory of the American Congress* reveals that almost none of the one-term servers from New York ever returned
to Congress at a later time. It would therefore seem that the high rate of turnover was
due to factors other than an evenly balanced party competition in this populous state. See
also McCormick, "New Perspectives in Jacksonian Politics," *American Historical Review,*
LXV (January, 1960), 288-301.

[6] Based on the membership of the 13th Congress, Representatives averaged 5.1 years'
continuous service in the House, and Senators 6.3 years' service in the Senate.

[7] Basil Hall, *Travels,* III, 29.

[8] AC, XXX (14th Congress, 2d sess.), 503.

[9] Quincy, *Life,* pp. 186-87.

[10] Martineau, *Western Travel,* I, 238, 301.

[11] Basil Hall, *Travels,* III, 27.

[12] Senators in the 13th Congress averaged forty-seven years of age; Representatives,
forty-six.

[13] Martineau, *Western Travel,* I, 301.

[14] On the cultural diversity of the early nation, see Arensberg, "American Communities," *American Anthropologist,* LVII, No. 6, Part I (December, 1955), 1143-62.

[15] Quincy, *Life,* p. 187.

[16] Foster, *Jeffersonian America,* p. 83.

[17] *Ibid.,* p. 84.

[18] Maclay, *Journal,* p. 5.

[19] Quincy, *Life,* pp. 187-88.

[20] Quoted in Basil Hall, *Travels,* III, 29.

[21] Quincy, *Life,* p. 125.

[22] *Ibid.,* pp. 187-88.

[23] Henry Adams, *Randolph,* p. 275.

[24] Quincy, *Life,* p. 158.

[25] Bruce, *Randolph,* I, 362.

[26] See John Quincy Adams, *Diary,* p. 53; Green, *Washington,* pp. 109-10, 216; Quincy,
Life, pp. 168 ff.; Galloway, *History of the House,* p. 46.

[27] Basil Hall, *Travels,* III, 26.

[28] *Ibid.,* p. 25.

[29] Hamilton, *Men and Manners,* II, 78.

[30] Basil Hall, *Travels,* III, 25.

[31] Hamilton, *Men and Manners,* II, 79.

[32] Galloway, *History of the House,* p. 70.

[33] Basil Hall, *Travels,* III, 32.

[34] AC, XXX (14th Congress, 2d sess.), 510.

[35] *Ibid.,* p. 519.

[36] Basil Hall, *Travels,* III, 25-26.

[37] Hamilton, *Men and Manners,* II, 90-91.

[38] Basil Hall, *Travels,* III, 56-57.

[39] Hamilton, *Men and Manners,* II, 82-83.

[40] D'Arusmont, *Views of Society,* p. 377; Plumer, *Life,* p. 342; AC, XXX (14th Congress, 2d sess.), 520; Margaret B. Smith, *First Forty Years,* p. 148; Basil Hall, *Travels,*

III, 6-7; Hamilton, *Men and Manners*, II, 82-83; Pope-Hennessy, ed., *Aristocratic Journey*, p. 175; Bruce, *Randolph*, I, 565-66, 568.

[41] Bruce, *Randolph*, I, 559.

[42] The sources for all descriptive statements hereafter concerning composition, size, location, and numbers of boardinghouse groups are, except where otherwise specified, the *Congressional Directories* for the years 1807, 1809, 1816, 1822, 1828, and 1829. (The *Directory* for 1807 is the earliest available.)

[43] The number of members who shared living quarters with one or more legislators from their own state decreased steadily from 81.5 percent of the total membership in 1807 to 56.4 percent in 1828. The political implications of this change in associational preferences of the members are discussed in Young, *Washington Community*, Chapter 9.

[44] Boardinghouse groups decreased in size but increased steadily in number as the Jeffersonian era progressed. Albert Gallatin identified the total number of boardinghouse groups in 1801 as eight or nine, with his own mess being "twenty-four to thirty . . . at table." Henry Adams, *Gallatin*, p. 253. In 1807, 50.5 percent of the members lived in boardinghouse groups of 10 or more members, as against 25.3 percent in 1828; and in the same period the number of groups had increased from 17 to 28. More detailed information on these changes is presented in Table 11.

[45] "Our little [traveling] party," wrote a member of the Connecticut delegation upon arriving at Washington, "took lodgings with a Mr. Peacock in one of the houses on New Jersey Avenue, with the addition of Senators Tracy, of Connecticut, and Chipman and Paine, of Vermont; and Representatives Thomas, of Maryland, and Dana, Edmond, and Griswold, of Connecticut." Busey, *Pictures of Washington*, p. 293.

[46] "I dined today at Mrs. Coyles," wrote Daniel Webster in 1824. "Her house is not yet full. She says she has never had so much difficulty in making up a mess." Webster, ed., *Correspondence*, I, 355.

[47] Cooley, *Etiquette*, p. 59.

[48] By the end of the Jeffersonian era, however, the *Congressional Directory* had changed format, listing the members by state delegation group and only individually by boardinghouse.

[49] Quincy, *Life*, p. 320.

[50] Busey, *Pictures of Washington*, p. 317.

[51] Nicolay, *Our Capital*, p. 292.

[52] Webster, ed. *Correspondence*, I, 234. Among the few who did bring their wives, however, boardinghouse life was preferred to the isolation of a private dwelling, the couples taking a room or a suite to themselves in the boardinghouse but eating at a common mess table.

[53] Busey, *Pictures of Washington*, p. 321.

[54] Gibbs, *Memoirs*, II, 377.

[55] Margaret B. Smith, *First Forty Years*, p. 12.

[56] Busey, *Pictures of Washington*, p. 321.

[57] Quincy, *Life*, p. 187.

[58] Cooper, *Notions*, II, 30.

[59] Henry Adams, *Gallatin*, p. 253.

[60] *Ibid.*

[61] Nicolay, *Our Capital*, p. 294.

[62] Quincy, *Life*, p. 142.

[63] Nicolay, *Our Capital*, p. 296.

[64] Busey, *Pictures of Washington*, p. 321.

[65] *Ibid.*, p. 293; Plumer, *Life*, p. 352.

[66] As indicated in Table 8, roll calls were selected from the following five Congresses: 10th, 1st session (1807), 11th, 1st session (1809); 14th, 2d session (1816); 20th, 2d session (1828); 21st, 1st session (1829). Selection of roll calls in the above Congresses was determined by the following criteria. (*a*) Roll calls on procedural questions involving no apparent

substantive issues were not analyzed. (b) Where the same issue was consecutively voted on, only the final vote was analyzed. (c) Only two roll calls on private bills in each congressional session were included. (No patterned differences in group voting behavior on these motions were apparent.) (d) Only those roll calls were included on which there was a substantial division in the House (see Table 9, note a). (e) Roll calls on which absenteeism or nonvoting was unusually high—typically toward the beginning or the close of a session—were not included. (f) All roll calls qualifying under these criteria in the 10th Congress, 1st session, and the 11th Congress, 1st session, were included in the analysis. For the remaining Congresses, the analysis, taking roll calls in the sequence in which they occurred, was stopped when group voting performance on each became sufficiently repetitive to establish the pattern. (No roll calls prior to 1807 could be analyzed because no boardinghouse lists before 1807 could be located.)

On these criteria, 2,657 group-votes (number of boardinghouse groups multiplied by number of roll calls) were yielded as the basic data for analysis.

It should be noted that 116 House roll calls fall far short of a statistically representative sample of roll calls over a period of twenty-eight years. For this reason the findings presented here should be regarded as tentative for the Jeffersonian period as a whole, and conclusive only for the specific time-periods of the congressional sessions selected for analysis. It goes without saying that the use of a statistically representative sample of roll calls for the entire Jeffersonian era would require a separate study of a scope unprecedented in the analytic literature on congressional voting. The number of group-votes analyzed here approaches the maximum that can be handled practically, short of resorting to the kind of elaborate machine methods that would be warranted only by a separate study. Roughly eighteen thousand visual scannings of 116 House vote rosters, for example, were required in order to carry out the single mechanical operation of transposing these rosters into boardinghouse vote rosters, before analysis could begin.

[67] Errors in the *Congressional Directories* may account for some cases of ostensible nonagreement. Thus, for example, one Representative in the 21st Congress is listed as having been a member of two mess groups, and two legislators in other Congresses were found to be listed in the *Directory* with groups of which they were not, by direct evidence, members. It is also probable that some of the groups showing a high incidence of nonagreement were not true "messes" but rather hotel "groups," associated merely by coresidence and having none of the communal life style of the messes. In the 21st Congress, for example, the eleven Representatives living in Gladsby's Hotel agreed on only three of the twenty roll calls analyzed for that Congress in Table 8. Because it is impossible on present evidence to make a reliable distinction between hotel groups and mess groups, all groups have been included in the analysis, even where the evidence strongly suggests that a particular group lived in the hotel style. It is known, however, that there were but a very few hotel-style groups in the Jeffersonian era. See Busey, *Pictures of Washington,* Chapter 8.

[68] Exploration of the voting behavior of boardinghouse groups has been limited in this study mainly to the facts demonstrating that the groups regularly voted together (Table 8) independently of the size of the majority margin in the whole House (Table 9). Further investigation is in progress on the dynamics of group agreement, including its relationship to such variables as size of the group, composition of the group, and nature of the policy issue involved. Preliminary impressions from the data might be noted here. One is that the size of the group did not have any consistent relationship to the number of times the group agreed on policy issues. Another is that a high proportion of the disagreements occurred among a relatively few groups. In the 20th Congress, for example, a mere one fifth of the boardinghouse groups supplied two thirds of the cases of nonagreement. A third impression is that interregional groups tended to vote more often in disagreement than regional groups. In the 20th Congress, for example, five of the six groups manifesting the highest incidence of internal disagreement were markedly interregional.

[69] Margaret B. Smith, *First Forty Years,* pp. 191-92.

FEDERALIST LEADERSHIP*

James M. Banner, Jr.

A reinterpretation of the Federalists, through biographical studies and searching analyses of the party's politics, has, in recent years, dispelled the image that the Federalist Party was the bête noire of early national history. No longer is it valid to see the Federalists solely as the extremist antagonists of early American democracy. The scholarly work of James M. Banner, Jr., of Princeton University has provided a new understanding of the party in Massachusetts through an extensive consideration of the sociological and ideological background of the party's adherents. In his book To the Hartford Convention: The Federalists and the Origins of Party Politics in Massachusetts, 1789-1815, *Banner sees the Federalist Party as the institutionalization of a political creed designed to achieve stability within a revolutionary world. In the selection presented here he explores the generation gap between the party's first leaders, whose concern was to provide effective government in the postrevolutionary years, and the aggressive younger leaders, whose penchant was for practical politics.*

From the beginning of its history, the Massachusetts Federalist Party spoke with many voices, not one. It was a coalition of men, interest groups, religious persuasions, and regional blocs which attracted a heterogeneous following, pitched its message to a wide assortment of people in all quarters of the state, and moved to the commands of a variety of men. Because we have grown accustomed to confining our vision to the limited context of party activity and because we have for so long ignored the remarkable growth in voting participation after 1800,

* From *To the Hartford Convention: The Federalists and the Origins of Party Politics in Massachusetts, 1789-1815* by James M. Banner, Jr. Copyright © 1969 by James M. Banner, Jr. Chapter IV, Sections I and II, "Federalist Leadership: Politicians and the Federalist Clergy," pp. 122-47. Reprinted by permission of Alfred A. Knopf, Inc.

it has been easy to believe that Massachusetts Federalism was under the lone direction of experienced politicians somehow isolated from the society about them. But party leaders never alone controlled the party's fate, and none were immune from popular sentiment. Beyond the orbit of the party organization were many well-placed and would-be statesmen, only remotely experienced in partisan politics, who aspired to direct the temporal affairs of men. Important differences existed between those on the one hand whose distinguishing and shared trait was seasoning in the political arts, and those on the other who had little knowledge of secular politics and less sympathy for its concerns. These differences arose less from age and ideology than from calling and station in the larger community. And in the dissimilarity of the politicians' and would-be politicians' roles lay one of the principal features of the history of Massachusetts Federalism.

For a quarter-century after Independence, the dominant figures of Massachusetts Federalism were the original members of the original party. Known in their own day as "gentlemen of the old school," they were the party's elders, esteemed for talent and integrity and set apart in men's minds by the eminence which accrues to a life of accomplishment and service.[1] With age, they had developed a distinctive manner of expression and a characteristic bent of mind which set the party's tone and deeply affected the thought and action of a younger generation of leaders. To the nation at large, they were the party's most representative and prestigious type.

Yet style and state of mind were not the chief sources of their commanding position. What gave them a superior claim upon the loyalty of other Federalists, and what explains the unique station they occupied, was that they had been "young men of the Revolution," the makers of rebellion and the architects of independence.[2] Their good fortune to have just entered upon their mature careers when war broke out and when the demand for capable and industrious leadership was so acute says much about their rapid rise to prominence and their influence in party affairs long after they had retired.

Born before 1760, the old-school gentlemen had come of age by the time of Yorktown and had taken part in the heady events of the Revolutionary cause. Capable and worthy of preferment in their own right, benefited by family, genteel comfort, and education, they had been in an unparalleled position as young men to exploit the opportunities of rapid change and to assume leadership in the young nation. By any measure they were cautious rebels who from the beginning frowned on the excesses of revolution and lent their efforts to the maintenance of domestic stability and tranquillity. From an early age they were drawn to order and repelled by variety and change.

In any other revolutionary setting their moderation would have impeded their advance, but in the American Revolution it only helped their rise to positions of power and strategic advantage. Indeed, such was their prudence that their Revolutionary record comes as a disappointment. A few of the future old-school gentry, like Henry Knox, Benjamin Lincoln, and Timothy Pickering, assumed military command and hazarded their lives for the republic. But for the most part, the party's future captains preferred, like Francis Dana, Nathan Dane, John Lowell, Theophilus Parsons, and Caleb Strong, to remain conveniently close to the centers of power and preferment, or they tried, like George Cabot, Benjamin Goodhue, Stephen Higginson, and the Derbys of Salem, to do well while doing good.[3] When peace came, these someday Federalists were better stationed than they had been before the war. They had advanced further than most contemporaries, and they confidently expected to rule the new nation. They had become early manifestations of a recurrent breed of American: upward-moving beneficiaries of change and new opportunity, eloquent in justification of the new order and jealous of their new-found place.

Not only did the Federalists-to-be possess that hypersensitivity toward change and that pervasive fear of competition characteristic of the *arriviste*, but they had a pride of unique station. Because of their intimate association with the events of the Revolution, these old-school figures enjoyed an advantage which comes to few men. They possessed a clearly defined and exclusive status. It could not be shared, nor passed on, nor reproduced. Successors might invoke the Revolution, but they, after all, had made it. And they believed it their right to define what it meant. "The American Revolution was in fact, after 1776," wrote Fisher Ames, "a resistance to foreign government." Its purpose was not to reshape society but to preserve it. Moreover, the claim of what Timothy Pickering called the "antifederalist-republican-democrats" to the succession of the Founding Fathers was illegitimate. "Who adopted the National Constitution?" inquired a Federalist legislator. "Federalists. Who opposed it? Democrats."[4]

In addition to trying to monopolize the definition of the national purpose, the old-school gentry believed that their very membership in the circle of men who had helped establish the institutions of the new nation gave them a transcendent claim upon public office. In the new governments they came to occupy official posts almost by prescriptive right. Unlike their successors, they did not have to "run" for office; they "stood" for it, certain of long tenure and contemptuous of those who questioned their qualifications. Because they staffed the governments they had constructed, they also refused to acknowledge a distinction between the government and its personnel. Assaults upon their administration of affairs appeared to them as attacks upon the framework of government. Republican opposition to their policies and against their repeated candidacies seemed more than a slur upon their class. It was an affront to the whole Revolution.

Yet the same experiences that made the old-school gentlemen resistant to change also made them sensitive and responsive to it. As trustees of the new government, their job was not only to preserve it but to make it work. In this endeavor, the setting and direction of their lives predisposed them to pragmatism and flexibility. Before the emergence of parties, these old-school patriots had become public figures, accustomed to the arena of state and national affairs. First as merchants and lawyers, then as political leaders, they had developed friendships and connections in distant towns and cities and had begun to move, if they did not already do so, in national and cosmopolitan circles. Their practice at the bar, their commercial transactions, their investments, and their travels were to an ever-mounting degree premised on the existence of a national community, national laws, and national institutions, which gave them a perspective on public affairs which transcended the parochial boundaries of village and town.

The men of maritime Massachusetts, born and raised in the varied and informed world of the coast, adapted perhaps most easily to the enlarged perspective of affairs. But others did so no less completely. The greatest change of view took place among the leading men of the interior, whose provincial beliefs were sharply challenged in the orbit of state and national politics. After a few years of life in the large commercial towns where governments convened and people from all over the world congregated, men like Caleb Strong and Theodore Sedgwick found their views altered and their affinity for local politics considerably diminished. They had become members of a national political elite, responsible to larger constituencies and charged with governing the new national order.

Whatever the varied forces which elevated these Revolutionary figures to positions of responsibility, the fact is that their rise was capped by the achievement of great authority. And the possession of such power at the meridian of their careers could scarcely fail to have an effect upon their attitudes toward government and leadership. Most political figures of the early republic may have deeply mistrusted the uses of the power; yet as men practiced in the business of public affairs, the old-school

Federalists, like many good Jeffersonians, never showed quite the same
fear of it when they held it as when they did not. When Caleb Strong
wrote that power was "of an encroaching nature," he added, as much
in the spirit of confession as rebuke, that "we think there is no danger
from it while it is exercised by us, or by those in whom we have great
confidence, and are apt to forget it may soon pass to others with whom
we should be unwilling to trust it."[5]

Thus, as much as they decried the abuse of power, by the 1780's they
had become experienced in its application and confident of their ability
to use it wisely. As framers of the new order, they were unable in good
conscience to escape involvement in its government. Indeed, their belief
that the wise and good alone must direct the affairs of men was accompanied by a compulsion to govern, a habit rooted in the long tradition
of stewardship upon which they had been raised. Old-school gentlemen
may have recoiled from the idea of politics in a partisan sense, but they
were never known to disdain the idea of politics conceived as impartial
statesmanship. And much as they assailed the costs and burdens of public
service, it never crossed their minds that it was a defective calling,
unworthy of their participation.

The old-school politicians were deeply committed to the notion that
effective government was the essential guarantor of public order and happiness. Though they called for education and moral discipline and worried that a society so deeply shot through with moral transgression could
not survive, they doubted that regeneration of the spirit could rescue the
nation unless its government were first reformed and "an aristocracy of
experience" placed in charge. There are many ways to read the Federalist
proposition that men capable of governing the state are to be found only
among the "natural aristocracy," "those, and those only, who by nature,
education, and good disposition, are qualified for government."[6] But if
by this they meant to offer a justification for upper-class rule, they also
had in mind the virtues of government by students of political science
and men of practical experience. What we can expect from the natural
aristocracy, Theophilus Parsons wrote, is "a thorough knowledge of the
interests of their country, when considered abstractly, when compared
with the neighboring States, and when with those more remote, and an
acquaintance with its produce and manufacture, or its exports and
imports. All these are necessary to be known, in order to determine what
is the true interest of any state; and without that interest is ascertained,
impossible will it be to discover, whether a variety of certain laws may
be beneficial or hurtful." In much the same vein, Parsons counseled
young aspirants to public office to avoid an education in theoretical and

useless subjects. "Look after the politics of the country," he admonished them, "as you look after your ships, your banks, your mills, your business." To parents, he gave the same utilitarian advice. "Educate your children in practical subjects," he told them, "and teach all those things . . . before Latin and Greek; or the calculus."[7]

This may sound like strange advice from one of the most learned men of Massachusetts, a master of ancient languages, astronomy, and mathematics. But Parsons' attitude was typical of most Federalists, and by 1800 one of the dominant motifs of the Federalist ideology was an attack upon politicians' visionary schemes. By then, the old-school gentry were convinced that the nation had fallen into the hands of impractical theoreticians who would toss away the experience of the ages to engage in the folly of social experimentation. Governing a republic called for caution and a regard for the accumulated knowledge of man's past, not for some utopian vision beyond the capacities of fractious, imperfect men. "One fact," said Ames, "is better than two systems." The Republican advocacy of popular rule of the state was the hallmark of "modern philosophism," and it caused old-school Federalists to assail the rationalist spirit and on their own behalf offer a defense of men who would "prefer the wisdom of *experience* to the illusions of *theory*."[8]

Jefferson gave them their chief target. They had many things in mind when they attacked him, but among their chief concerns was his supposed disregard for practical realities, well-tried procedures, and institutional forms. Jefferson seemed to them to ignore the restraints of law, to tamper lightly with the basic structures of government and society, to dabble in the curious and useless—all out of devotion to some philosophical vision. "Those are not the wisest of men who undertake to act always by rule," Fisher Ames reasoned with Jefferson in mind. "In political affairs there are no more self-conceited blunderers than the statesmen who affect to proceed, in all cases, without regard to circumstances, but solely according to speculative principles."[9] So well did they know Jefferson: inventor, architect, city planner, drafter of the decimal coinage system, and master politician!

If the old-school Federalists of Massachusetts assailed Jefferson's "philosophism" as the wellspring of his misguided attitudes toward executive leadership, they held it even more responsible for his supposed attachment to "levelling principles." And of all the threats to republicanism in their thinking, popular government was among the most dangerous. Cabot spoke the mind of all Federalists in holding "democracy in its natural operation to be the *government of the worst*." And Ames repeatedly warned that the nation would "sacrifice the essence of liberty to the spirit of democracy." Conceived in this way as an attitude of spirit rather than one of the institutional arrangements of society, democracy repelled every good Federalist of the state.[1]

Yet, when defined more strictly as limited participation in the electoral process, democracy was something which old-school Federalists endorsed. After all, government was built upon consent, and consent meant the approval of the citizenry. In this spirit, George Cabot admitted that "the people must have a share in every good government. . . . No government can be relied on that has not a material portion of the democratic mixture in its composition." But what Cabot had in mind as the "people" was not the whole body of adult males, nor did he mean by a "share" in government what we would call the opportunity to govern. Instead, he meant the concurrence of a limited portion of the adult male population in the selection of government officials. While on the one hand "I deprecate every system which should exclude the people from a share," he wrote, "I am satisfied that no system can stand where they preponderate," adding, "There is no security for a good government without some popular mixture in it; but there will be neither justice nor stability in any system, if some material parts of it are not independent of popular control."[2]

According to these standards, elections should, on the one hand, be referendums in which sober and responsible citizens signified their approval of the government's past actions and, on the other, commissions to the wise and good to rule according to their own judgment. Democracy, thus conceived, was a legitimizing process. It was a procedure and not, as the Republicans emphasized, an end of government. To the old-school Federalist mind, democracy was little more than the appurtenance of the most rigid and elitist republicanism.

Old-school Federalists were satisfied that if democracy could be confined to its legitimate but narrow orbit, the threat of excessive leveling could be countered. Yet, in the light of what eventually occurred, their optimism was misplaced and their conception of democracy fatally flawed. In the first place, their definition of democracy as minimal participation did not resolve the troublesome question of how to make people accept their limited role. Elitists assumed without much question that a well-informed public, instructed in the dismal logic of the natural inequalities among men, would defer to their betters. Their political opponents, however, were quick to exploit the pluralization of Massachusetts society to demonstrate their error.

In the second place, by construing democracy principally as a measure of participation, Federalists became accustomed to encouraging greater voting participation. By defining elections as referendums, Federalists invited attempts to solicit votes in order to win them. Only Ames, with characteristic insight, saw—and despaired—that "the body of the Federalists were always, and yet are, essentially democratic in their political notions"; but, like the rest, even he surrendered to the temptation to act the democrat in political methods.[3] After 1800, most old-school gentlemen worked hard to get out the vote and demonstrate the people's consent to Federalist rule. As they would have occasion to ponder by 1814, the price of seeking consent at the polls was nothing less than excessive democracy, Federalist style.

Try as they might, the old-school gentry knew that theirs was a losing struggle. By the time of Jefferson's election, they had few illusions about the irresistible advance of uncontrolled democracy. "We are sliding down into the mire of a democracy," groaned Ames, "which pollutes the morals of the citizens before it swallows up their liberties." Cabot agreed: "The spirit of our country," he wrote, "is doubtless more democratic than our principles; and those principles of necessity place power in the worst hands."[4]

Yet, pessimistic and bitter as they were, the party's elder statesmen never lapsed into hopelessness and apathy. If anything, the inroads of democracy only determined them all the more to impede its further advance. Here, two alternatives seemed to present themselves. The party could either try to modify the effects of democracy, a course which had by 1804 proven ineffective, or it could seek to capture democracy for elitist ends.[5] Of the practiced old-school statesmen, a few were of a mind to take the first course. Cabot, for example, flirted with the idea of placing tighter restrictions upon the suffrage. In addition, the old-school gentry who controlled the party caucus well past 1800 carefully, if misguidedly, preserved for themselves the right to select presidential electors in the General Court.[6]

Most old-school Federalists, however, and eventually even Cabot himself, recognized that these expedients, however desirable, could only offend the average voter and further sow the democratic germ. The problem, they were coming to see, was not to reduce the vote but to control it, not to prohibit the people's participation but to mobilize it. Whatever these practical statesmen might say about "our supreme Lord, the rabble," the people could vote; and the potentialities of the suffrage had begun to impress all but the most rigid of the older men. So too the need for organization, used with such effectiveness in 1776 and 1788, which once again recommended itself as a means of putting down a threat. At the same time that Cabot was contemplating counting the people out, he was deeply involved in preparations for the election of 1800, coordinating efforts among Federalists in many states, trying in the face of party disintegration to develop some sort of national plan, and groping, perhaps not fully consciously, toward a realization of the need for further organizational innovations.[7]

Cabot was not alone. Theodore Sedgwick, among the most conservative of the old-school sort, spoke for many of his kind in writing that he "would treat the people as if they were wise and virtuous." He would propagandize them and seize the initiative from the Republicans. ". . . The federalists are not only torpid & indifferent but their principles of defense are of a nature to be eternally attended with disgrace and defeat. It is a mere system of defence against the attacks of their adversaries." Appeals to reason will be unavailing, for "the people have neither a heart to fail nor a head to understand." Revealing vividly how the impulse to action and organization might arise from the deepest antagonism to democracy, Sedgwick concluded that "the party which hopes for victory or even safety must apply to fears & jealousies; it must raise passion & direct it." Ames was of the same mind. "The agents that move politics," he wrote, "are the popular passions." "Truth ought to be made popular, if possible." The Federalists, he was convinced, had for too long concerned themselves with what had to be hindered, not what must be done. "We must court popular favor, we must study public opinion, and accommodate measures to what it is and still more to what it ought to be."[8]

To Ames, it was also a question of action and organization. What was needed was something less than full-scale political mobilization but something considerably more than the mere elucidation of principle. "A party inactive," he declared, "is a party half-conquered." "Is it not, therefore, proper, and indispensably necessary," he asked, "to be active, in order to prevent the destruction of the feeble ties by which the federal party is held together?" The keys were energy and innovation; the public must be aroused; political resources must be organized; men must, above all, act. "We must animate the federalists. We must try to raise their zeal high."[9]

As early as 1798, Ames organized party festivities, wined and dined the community, entertained Dedhamites with toasts and speeches, and loftily announced, "The progress of Federalism seems to have begun." And it was Ames who, with Cabot's encouragement, took the lead in revitalizing a moribund Massachusetts newspaper and transforming it for a time, as the *New England Palladium*, into a vehicle for old-school politics. Party elders contributed discreet essays to its columns and underwrote efforts to give it the widest possible circulation throughout New England. Ames, a student of Jeffersonian practices, patterned his project after the Republican press, which he believed instrumental in securing the Presidency. He fully understood the role of popular attitudes. "Public opinion governs our country, the newspapers govern *it*, and it is very possible to govern the newspapers." He conceived of his newspaper as a defense against the party's "entire dissolution." It would be a first step in marshaling the "compactness, energy, and intelligence of the party."[1]

Although his project ultimately failed and Ames wearied of his participation in it, the effort was not in vain. In their desire to activate an apathetic following, to arouse popular understanding of the party position, and to coordinate party actions, Ames and other old-school figures revealed to their party the potentialities of the press as an instrument of political control. That their newspaper turned out to be a weak weapon in the party arsenal is not half so significant as the impulse behind it. By emphasizing action and seeking an appropriate response to the democratic spirit, the old-school gentlemen were laying the foundation of a new party-wide effort to update Federalist operations and discover a modus vivendi with democracy.

In this search, a partisan press was not their only contribution to Federalist politics. Another was the party's legislative caucus, which the old-schoolmen adopted initially in order to resolve a deep leadership crisis around 1800. Soon outgrowing its original function, the caucus wielded sovereign power over the Massachusetts party for roughly twenty-five years, and it called into being and ultimately controlled a broad committee hierarchy which had day to day administrative responsibility for Federalist affairs.

In other words, Massachusetts Federalism would not have lasted out Jefferson's administration without the constant encouragement of the old-school gentry and without their willingness to assume places in the new committee system. Christopher Gore, one of the stiffest of the breed, became a member of the original state Central Committee, and Israel Thorndike, a realist of the old school, joined the Committee later on. Other party elders staffed the system's lower echelons. Fisher Ames was first chairman of the Norfolk County Committee, Stephen Codman became first head of the Suffolk Committee, and such others as old-school congressmen Dwight Foster and Elijah Brigham served regularly on county and town committees. For every old-school gentleman who refused to take part in new-style Federalism, there was one who joined and helped set the tone of organization politics.

Most of those who failed to play a continuous and active role in the type of politics whose foundation they had helped lay withdrew from public life out of no quarrel with the new politics. Their disengagement was motivated as often as not by age, illness, or a desire to realize other ambitions. Cabot, for example, never known to enjoy public service, resigned his Senate seat in 1796 and retreated gloomy but rich to his Brookline estate at the age of forty-five. Many of his associates curtailed their activities for reasons of health and family. Cabot's Senate successor, Benjamin Goodhue, retired in 1800 after two decades of public responsibilities, ill and probably alcoholic at fifty-two. Nathan Dane, co-author of the Northwest Ordinance, member of the Continental Congress and the General Court, withdrew in 1797, afflicted with deafness at the early age of forty-five. Ames gave up his House seat in 1796, the victim at thirty-eight of chronic illness and depression. Some, of course, withdrew simply out of a refusal to suffer the trials and indignities of party strife. But most waited until worthy and willing younger men came along to take their places, and only then, like Parsons, Sedgwick, John Lowell, Samuel Sewall, Nathan Read, and George Thacher, exchanged the life of partisan politics for other promising and public careers.[2]

Because this was a time of shifting perspectives and new careers for all Americans, what is more noteworthy is the number of old-school gentlemen who did not withdraw from politics but remained active long after 1800. In addition to those who helped organize and administer the committee system, others served energetically for another two decades. Caleb Strong, governor for eleven years between 1800 and 1815, was succeeded by John Brooks, who served until 1823. Pickering was active in the federal House and Senate until 1817, and Samuel Taggart sat in the House for the same years. Many of those who intended to retire found, like Cabot, that they could not remain permanently inactive. They continued to exert considerable influence within party councils and maintained a link with affairs through correspondence, newspaper pieces, and occasional forays into the public forum.[3]

None of them refrained from assailing the new politics and the slim rewards of public service, but we should not assume that by scoring democratic politics they meant to impugn the actions of their successors. What they lamented was the necessity for organized politics, not the fact that Federalist politicians engaged in it. There is every reason to believe that had a systematic party organization recommended itself at an earlier date, most of the old-school gentry would have become its officers. That they did not act to create a formal party system in the 1790's was not so much out of resistance to the idea of organized politics but because circumstances did not earlier force such a departure upon them.

Ultimately, old-school politics served as a bridge between the decorous deference politics of colonial America and the more modern and aggressive politics of the new generation. The old-school gentlemen trained their successors in the ethos of public service and gave them an example of pragmatic leadership. They suggested that action and style were two necessary ingredients of any politics, and they laid the groundwork for the organization which would emerge after 1800. They could take satisfaction in having created the practical and intellectual underpinnings for their successors' actions. Though they bemoaned popular government and regretted any flirtation with its ways, they nevertheless encouraged efforts to discover political weapons to combat the democratic disease. Resisting the twin snares of apathy and amateurism, they set the stage for Federalist ventures in organized popular politics.

II

As the party elders gradually vacated their places in public life, they were succeeded by younger men whose thinking bore the unmistakable stamp of the old school. The new party leaders identified themselves with the Revolutionary generation, spoke of themselves as members of a natural aristocracy, and deplored the pretensions of "the most profligate and contemptible portion of society." They assumed the justice of monopoly government by the wise and good and assailed "government by acclamation." Like the first Federalists, they claimed the Constitution for their own; it was, said young Josiah Quincy, "almost wholly the work of men called Federalists, and was also opposed, almost to a man, by those, who now a days call themselves Republicans." With an asperity equal to their fathers', they scored the muddle-headed theorizing of modern political scientists and called for a regeneration of practical statesmanship. The Hartford Convention Report, which Harrison Gray Otis reputedly wrote, reviewed "the state of this nation under the advantages of a wise administration, contrasted with the miserable abyss into which it is plunged by the profligacy and folly of political theorists" and called on the people to "discard the influence of visionary theorists, and recognize the benefits of a practical policy."

How stiff a draught of anti-rationalism young Federalists took in from their fathers is perhaps nowhere better exhibited than in the perverse and uninhibited verse of fifteen-year-old William Cullen Bryant. "Go, Wretch, resign the presidential chair," he admonished Jefferson in 1809:

> Disclose thy secret measures, foul or fair.
> Go, search with curious eye, for horned frogs,
> Mid the wild wastes of Louisianan bogs;
> Or, where Ohio rolls his turbid stream,
> Dig for huge bones, thy glory and thy theme.
> Go, scan, Philosophist, thy [Sally's] charms
> And sink supinely in her sable arms;
> But quit to abler hands the helm of state,
> Nor image ruin on thy country's fate!

As Republicanism entrenched itself, contempt turned into deep pessimism. Between the resignation of old-schoolman Cabot and young Federalist Otis there was little difference. "The precipitate course of the dreadful torrent will finally overwhelm and perhaps destroy us," wrote Otis of the democratic advance. "You know I am a fatalist upon this subject. My fears are indeed great & my convictions strong: The struggle between a populace and the *natural aristocracy* of a country is a fearful clash, and where the latter is unsupported by a firm executive, it must fall."[4]

Yet if the young Federalists placed a rhetorical emphasis upon the coming national apocalypse, they were as cautious in action as their elders. Taking their cue from the old-school politicians, they conceived their stewardship of the common good in the most instrumental terms and devoted a major portion of their energies to the struggle for electoral success. And because they had come to political maturity within the party system and had adopted the norms of two-party politics from the earliest date, they readily appreciated the advantages of organized political activity and were little disposed to risk them for the alluring but vain prospects of nullification or disunion.

It is useful to compare these practical statesmen with those who might be called the true Federalist radicals, men who, like Pickering in Massachusetts and Roger Griswold in Connecticut, not only foresaw an apocalypse but did their best to provoke one. In almost all cases, the extremists who encouraged secessionist sentiment and countenanced plans for disunion were recruited from outside the ranks of the politically experienced young Federalists. Either, like Timothy Pickering, they had come of age well before the emergence of a party system and, differing from the likes of Cabot and Gore, had never succeeded in getting right with it, or like amateur politicians, they had never been a part of the political system and had never known the restraints and sanctions of organized partisan activity.

In contrast, the young Federalists, as charter members of the party organization, quickly discerned its possibilities and understood its limits. Though they struck out at the misuse of power and scored the excesses of party, they perceived that, no matter its shortcomings, the party was one means to control and apply power efficiently and responsibly. They did not believe, as they suspected so many amateurs did, that power was an end in itself. To them, power and politics were instruments in the service of larger goals. Wise enough to fear the perversion of authority, they nevertheless believed that, on balance, they were its best custodians: well prepared, high stationed, skilled, and endowed for stewardship.

The young and old politicians' common attitudes toward government, democracy, and politics were reinforced by a sense of status solidarity. Young Federalists were as well circumstanced as their elders and were drawn from the same circles. Cabot and Otis in eastern Massachusetts, Sedgwick and Henry Van Schaack in the western towns frequented the same parlors, directed the same banks, placed their monies in the same lands and cargoes, and worshipped the same distant God. In the maritime communities and their hinterlands, the legal profession and mercantile trades provided the majority of the party's cadre, young as well as old, and in the interior the farming gentry joined the men of bench and bar to staff the party posts.

To the bonds of status and calling were added those of blood and family. Young and old party captains were bound together in a vast cousinage which reached across the Commonwealth and oiled the machinery of government and society. Within the party, fathers and sons, uncles and nephews, and cousins and brothers exchanged the same posts and enforced the same ethic. The party, as Republicans liked to point out, had many aspects of a fiefdom, and its roster was the state's social and professional register.[5]

That young and old-school Federalists shared so many of the same circumstances and attitudes is not to say, however, that they were indistinguishable. But it is to suggest that what marked them off from each other was a difference of degree rather than of kind, a difference not in their ideas about democracy but in their notions of what to do about it. More than anything, this was a distinction grounded in the peculiar circumstances of each generation's political baptism, revolving around tactics, not goals; means, not ends.

When the old-school gentlemen had received their initiation into public affairs, they had bent every effort to prevent the rise of parties and counted among the triumphs of the Constitution a division of powers so clear that national parties were unthinkable. It was not until the late 1790's, when their careers were already on the wane, that they began to perceive that in order to coordinate the separate branches of government and make the presidential system work, parties were not only inevitable under the Constitution but indispensable. This realization marked a signal change in their attitude toward party, but it came too late in their political lives for them to act. Before they retired they could make only tentative beginnings toward organizing the party system.

In contrast, the second-generation Federalists opened their careers confronted by organized opposition to the wise and good and the stark alternative of surrender to the adversary or combat on his novel terms. By the accident of birth, most second-generation Federalists were just entering politics for the first time around 1800.[6] Few were past their thirties. Most had been born after 1760, had reached maturity only shortly before the Treaty of Paris and, even if they could recall the Revolution, had not taken part in it. Rather than making revolution, theirs was the different task of preserving and consolidating it.

Young Federalists justified their fitness to rule in the same elitist terms as their elders, but their availability was grounded in conditions altogether different from those of the old-school figures. Rather than getting in on the formation of a party and claiming their right to place and prominence, they had first to join the party and then prove their fitness to direct it. Rather than having created the government, they could only try to demonstrate superior talents in administering it. Instead of membership in the Patriot cause, they could only show membership in the Federalist Party. While their elders' careers depended on the success of the Revolution, their own rode with the success of a party. Under these conditions, they took their cue from their elders, moved beyond the old politics, and struck a bargain with the democratic way not because they wished to but because they had to.

Unwilling to preside over the liquidation of their party and desirous of protecting their own public careers, the young party captains had to give a new meaning to political action. Such were the altered political circumstances of the new century that, in comparison with their elders' public careers, the young Federalists' commitment to politics had to be far more continuous, dedicated, and expert—in short, far more professional. It could be said of all, as Otis said of Josiah Quincy, that they "intended ab initio to pursue politics as a profession."[7] To a much great-er extent than the old-school captains, they devoted most of their lives to politics. Like most other professionals, they were spurred on by an ideal of public service, considered their labors to be impartial, and came to believe that their calling demanded definable professional qualifica-tions. Except for the remunerative occupations needed to support their families, politics was their chief activity and interest. For the energetic young politician, life was a ceaseless round of travels and meetings, planning and fund raising, correspondence and speechmaking. Most young Federalists not only served in elective or appointive office at one time or another but concurrently managed parts of the party organization.

Because they were convinced that the fate of the republic and of an entire class of men was at stake, they did not conceive of their political activities as a sacrifice. Nor was it necessary to do so, because political service was coming to have widespread advantages to young men on the make. A highly articulated organization brought them into frequent contact with men of similar economic interests in all parts of the Com-monwealth. Politics gave them increased exposure in the centers of wealth and preferment and added new avenues of advance. The old restraints against political organization which had inhibited the old-school figures had diminished appreciably by 1800 and, given the Republican challenge, there were more compelling reasons than ever to go forward with party-building programs.

Thus the young Federalists gave a broader interpretation to action and propaganda than Ames and Sedgwick had done. Considering the party caucus as only a first step toward a party system, they conceived the full panoply of organized politics: its pyramidal structure of committees, its calculated fund raising, its central direction. It did not concern them that organization and demagogy smacked of the very system they sought to destroy. After all, had not Federalism always taught that the people were docile and easily led? What better way to save Federalism than to embrace democracy?

Not surprisingly, some members of the two political generations dis-trusted each other. But we seriously misconstrue the history of Mas-sachusetts Federalism to see a sharp disassociation between them. Many of the misunderstandings that existed can be credited to the natural differ-ences between generations. Many others were limited to the strategic but relatively small circle of maritime Federalism. More important, most of the friction was personal, and rarely did it affect party operations.

The principal targets of old-school suspicions were Otis and Quincy, both eloquent and powerful representatives of the younger breed and both always suspected of opportunism. From the very beginning of his political career, well before the rise of the party apparatus which he came to direct, Otis—charming, polished, witty, urbane—was charged with uncommon ambition and aggressiveness. First the old-school gentry accused him of seeking Pickering's spot in the State Department. When that office went to John Marshall, it was rumored that Otis planned to resign from Congress to accept appointment under the Convention with France of 1800. He also lost favor for endorsing Adams's peace mission to France in 1799 and for standing by Adams during the bitter election of 1800. Stephen Higginson dourly warned his friends that Otis would betray any trust for preferment. "For the sake of an additional vote, or the rise of one grade in the scale of promotion, [he] would sell any and all parties or persons in succession till he reached the top. Whoever trusts him will be betrayed." Even Ames, who had better reasons to appreciate Otis's talents, thought him "ardent and ambitious," and "eager in the chase of fame and wealth. . . . He sighs for political office—he knows not what, and he will file off the moment opportunity offers."[8] Christopher Gore singled out Otis and Quincy for his scorn. He scoffed at their "anxiety for office, distinction, & popularity," assailed them for believing that by "courting the prejudices of the mob, they should enter the seats of office & direct the whirlwind & the storm," and accused them of trying to preempt party offices and keep them from their party rivals.[1]

In moments of pique, the young objects of old-school suspicion reciprocated these feelings. Otis had little sympathy for the silly casuistry of men who "would sacrifice their party to save their theory," and he once condemned them for lacking the politician's touch. But his condemnations were directed more against the extremist Pickering than against the moderate Ames and Gore, and he was quick to grant that the elder statesmen were men "of probity, of talent, of influence" indispensable to the party.[2] All things considered, there was relatively little friction between old-school and young Federalists when it came to initiating the new-style politics after 1800.

Moreover, the older men never challenged the younger men's leadership. And, for their part, the younger men sedulously cultivated the favor of their elders, encouraged their continued participation in party affairs, and left aside strategic places for them in the party's highest councils. Quincy, for his part, stayed on close terms with Cabot, Ames, Parsons, and Higginson, and Otis remained an intimate of Cabot. In return, as I have tried to indicate, the elder statesmen made important contributions to the new-style politics and, like Cabot, tried to dampen any signs of radicalism and extremism outside the party hierarchy. The older men continued well into the new century to serve throughout the committee system with the younger men and remained at their posts about as long as their younger colleagues. . . .

NOTES

[1] For the Federalists' own use of the designation "old school," see David Hackett Fischer, *The Revolution of American Conservatism: The Federalist Party in the Era of Jeffersonian Democracy* (New York, 1965), p. 1 n.

[2] I borrow the term "young men of the Revolution" from Stanley Elkins and Eric L. McKitrick, "The Founding Fathers: Young Men of the Revolution," *Political Science Quarterly*, LXXVI (June 1961), 181-216.

[3] Fischer, *Revolution of American Conservatism,* Appendix II *passim.*

[4] [Boston] *New England Palladium* (hereafter *Palladium*), June 7, 1808; Ames, "Political Thoughts," *Monthly Anthology and Boston Review* (hereafter *Monthly Anthology*), II (Nov. 1805), 566; and Pickering to Samuel Williams, Jan. 9, 1810, Pickering MSS, Massachusetts Historical Society (hereafter MHS). For the latter-day statement of the Federalist argument, see Charles A. Beard, *Economic Origins of Jeffersonian Democracy* (New York, 1915).

[5] Strong to Pickering, Feb. 7, 1815, Pickering MSS, MHS.

[6] The phrases are Jonathan Jackson's in [Jackson], *Thoughts Upon the Political Situation of the United States of America* . . . (Worcester, Mass., 1788), pp. 55, 57.

[7] [Theophilus Parsons], *Result of the Convention of Delegates Holden at Ipswich in the County of Essex* (Newburyport, Mass., 1778), pp. 18-20; and Theophilus Parsons [Jr.], *Memoir of Theophilus Parsons* (Boston, 1859), pp. 120-21. This point is made in a different context by Norman Jacobson, "Class and Ideology in the American Revolution," in *Class, Status, and Power: A Reader in Social Stratification,* eds. Reinhard Bendix and Seymour Martin Lipset (Glencoe, Ill., 1953), pp. 550-51, and Linda K. Kerber, *The Federalists in Dissent, Imagery and Ideology in Jeffersonian America* (Ithaca, N.Y., 1970), Chap. IV.

[8] [Boston] *Columbian Centinel* (hereafter *Centinel*), Aug. 14, 1802; and Ames in *The Debates and Proceedings in the Congress of the United States* (Washington, 1834-56), usually cited as *Annals of Congress,* 3rd Cong., House, 1st Sess., 330. See also the Federalist toast in *Centinel,* June 3, 1801: "*May experience exemplify* what *precept* has *promised.*"

[9] *Works of Fisher Ames,* ed. Seth Ames (2 vols., Boston, 1854), II, 334. For Ames's comments in a similar vein on Madison, the "book politician," see *ibid.,* I, 35-50 *passim.* And for a more extended analysis of the Federalist view of science and theoretical thought, see Kerber, *Federalists in Dissent,* Chap. III. See also Sedgwick to Harmanus Bleeker, Jan. 23, 1812, Sedgwick MSS, MHS: The Jeffersonian era shows "the dominion of philosophy in opposition to common sense, and of theory against experience." Cabot to Pickering, Feb. 17, 1806, Henry Cabot Lodge, *Life and Letters of George Cabot* (Boston, 1878), pp. 352-53: "Great philosophers and men of distinguished talents will be often found the most zealous defenders of the most monstrous follies,—a good lesson for human pride."

[1] Cabot to Wolcott, Aug. 3, 1801 to Pickering, Feb. 14, 1804, Lodge, *Cabot,* pp. 322, 341; and Ames to Thomas Dwight, Jan. 25, 1804, Ames, *Works,* I, 338; II, 228.

[2] Cabot to Pickering, Feb. 14, 1804, to King, Mar. 17, 1804, to Gore, Apr. 10, 1801,

Lodge, *Cabot*, pp. 342, 345, 318; and Cabot to King, Nov. 6, 1801, King MSS, New York Historical Society (hereafter NYHS).

[3] Ames, *Works*, II, 348.

[4] Ames, "Political Thoughts," in *Monthly Anthology*, II (Nov. 1805), 556; and Cabot to King, July 30, 1801, King MSS, NYHS.

[5] Their assumption was, of course, that the party was worth saving. We must, said Ames, "preserve our being as a party." Ames to Wolcott, Mar. 18, 1801, Ames MSS, Dedham, Mass., Historical Society. The party, he repeated on another occasion, is "our only resource." The question was how to activate it. Ames to Wolcott, Dec. 2, 1802, Wolcott MSS, Connecticut Historical Society (hereafter CHS).

[6] Cabot to Pickering, Feb. 14, 1804, Lodge, *Cabot*, p. 344.

[7] See, e. g., Cabot to Rutledge, Oct. 22, 1800, Rutledge MSS, University of North Carolina (hereafter UNC). My argument in this chapter and elsewhere is at variance with that expressed by Max Weber that, especially in England and America, the members of the high social and political elite in the older static and deferential society (whom Weber called the "notables") were incapable of becoming "professional" politicians in an organization *outside* the legislature. See Weber, "Politics as a Vocation," in *From Max Weber*: *Essays in Sociology*, eds. H. H. Gerth and C. Wright Mills (New York, 1958), esp. pp. 102-3.

[8] Sedgwick to Rutledge, June 27, 1801, Rutledge MSS, UNC; and to Theodore Sedgwick, Jr., May 17, 1804, to Harmanus Bleeker, Jan. 23, 1812, Sedgwick MSS, MHS. On Sedgwick's highly practiced talent for politicking and manipulation, see Joseph Charles, *The Origins of the American Party System* (Williamsburg, Va., 1956), p. 114.

[9] Ames to Gore, Dec. 13, 1802, to Theodore Dwight, Mar. 19, 1801, Ames, *Works*, I, 309-11, 292; and to Thomas Dwight, Feb. 19, 1804, Ames MSS, Dedham.

[1] Ames to Wolcott, July 6, 1798, George Gibbs, *Memoirs of the Administrations of Washington and John Adams* (2 vols, New York, 1846), II, 69; Ames to Wolcott, Mar. 18, 1801, Ames MSS, Dedham; to Wolcott, Dec. 2, 1802, Wolcott MSS, CHS; and Cabot to Gore, to Alexander Hamilton, Oct. 11, 1800, to Wolcott, Oct. 5, 1800, Lodge, *Cabot*, pp. 292, 294, 295. Early Massachusetts backers and contributors to the *Palladium* included elder Federalists Jedidiah Morse, Cabot, John Lowell, John Thornton Kirkland, Eliphalet Pearson, and David Tappan. Robert Edson Lee, "Timothy Dwight and the Boston *Palladium*," *New England Quarterly* (hereafter NEQ), XXIV (June 1962), 229-39.

[2] Many of those who claimed to have retired for reasons related to the rise of democracy more probably did so for a complex set of reasons, many of them unstated. Sedgwick, for instance, declared in 1802 that he would not have abandoned his political post had he not been convinced that the people wished to experiment with democracy and that his comfort would have to be sacrificed. But a closer look at Sedgwick's actions suggests that he would not have given up his place in the House had he not been satisfied at having found a worthy successor to his Berkshire seat. Only when his Federalist successor failed to be elected did Sedgwick pour out his bitterness. Significantly, he could not himself resist public life and soon accepted an appointment to the Massachusetts Supreme Judicial Court. Sedgwick to Rufus King, Mar. 24, 1801, June 15, Aug. 24, 1802, King MSS, NYHS.

[3] In 1801, Cabot wrote that he had little contact with the world except, as he put it, through "*our own sect* exclusively." Cabot to Wolcott, Aug. 3, 1801, Lodge, *Cabot*, pp. 320-22. Yet Cabot's "sect" was a wide one, embracing the leading political figures of both generations. See Cabot to Wolcott, Mar. 26, 1798, Gibbs, *Memoirs*, II, 42-43, in which Cabot writes that despite his reclusiveness he retains a keen interest in public affairs, writes for newspapers, and speaks frequently to others. And for similar evidence, see also Lodge, *Cabot*, pp. 588-89, and Ames to Pickering, Mar. 24, 1806, Ames, *Works*, I, 378. Gore listed the most pragmatic reasons for his return to public life and office holding. Gore to Rufus King, Apr. 15, 1806, King MSS, NYHS.

[4] Otis to Rutledge, Oct. 18, 1801, Dec. 2, 1804, Rutledge MSS, UNC; [Josiah Quincy],

An Answer to the Questions: Why Are You a Federalist? and Why Shall You Vote for Gov. Strong (n.p., 1805), pp. 3, 5-6; and William Cullen Bryant, *The Embargo* (2nd ed. corrected and enlarged, Boston, 1809), pp. 12-13. Another of the poem's passages suggests the kind of sentiments toward democracy which Bryant imbibed from his father, a Federalist officeholder from the arch-Federalist town of Cummington in Berkshire County:

> Enter, and view the thronging concourse there,
> Intent, with gaping mouth, and stupid stare;
> While in their midst their supple leader stands,
> Harangues aloud, and flourishes his hands;
> To adulation tunes his servile throat,
> And sues successful for each blockhead's vote.

In later years, Bryant was embarrassed enough by the poem—on political grounds as well —to exclude it from his collected works; but he never explicitly repudiated it.

[5] For further evidence, see Banner, *To the Hartford Convention*, Chap. V, Secs. ii and iii.

[6] For brief sketches of some of the state's leading young Federalists, see Fischer, *Revolution of American Conservatism*, Appendix II, pp. 262-77. I have benefited greatly from Fischer's suggestive and ambitious work. Yet as provocative as is his thesis of a marked division between the older and younger Federalist generations and as refreshing as is his rediscovery of Federalist Party politics, he seriously overstates the disjunction between political generations and fails to do justice to the dynamics and sociology of Federalism. There is little doubt, as Fischer argues and as I have shown in detail in Chapter VII, of *To the Hartford Convention*, that an active two-party system was crucial to the process of political democratization and, even more, to the creation of truly representative government. Yet what is most arresting about the early politics of Massachusetts is the continuity between the political generations. Without the support of the old-school gentlemen, as much the seasoned practitioners of politics as any young contemporary, the efforts of their successors would have come to nothing. Rather than hobbling the organizational efforts of the young party captains, the old-school figures provided the intellectual foundations and the personal incentives for their successors' political departures and then joined them in fashioning a new-style politics for a new political age.

[7] Otis to John Phillips, 1818, Edmund Quincy, *Life of Josiah Quincy* (Boston, 1868), p. 376.

[8] Wolcott to Ames, Dec. 29, 1799, Gibbs, *Memoirs*, II, 315; Higginson to Pickering, Jan. 12 & Apr. 16, 1800, Pickering MSS, MHS; and Ames to Gore, Oct. 5, 1796, Ames, *Works*, I, 202. See also Samuel Eliot Morison, *The Life and Letters of Harrison Gray Otis, Federalist, 1765-1848* (2 vols., Boston, 1913), I, 166-67, 237-38. Higginson had a special dislike for Otis. See also Higginson to Pickering, May 11, 1797, Nov. 24, 1798, Pickering MSS, MHS.

[1] Gore to ?, May 7, 1822 (photostat), Misc. MSS Colls, New York Public Library; Gore to Rufus King, Oct. 5, 1812, King MSS, NYHS. How risky it is to hypothesize a clear split among generations is made apparent by examining the movement to line up Federalist support behind New York Republican DeWitt Clinton in 1812. George Cabot encouraged Otis's, Quincy's, and other young Federalists' participation in a Clinton convention, while Gore steadfastly refused to have anything to do with a scheme linking him with Otis. In Gore's case, like Higginson's, his distrust of the younger men was more personal than political. See Banner, *To the Hartford Convention*, Chap. VIII.

[2] Otis to Sedgwick, Apr. 13, 1800, Sedgwick MSS, MHS; and Otis to Quincy, [1811?], Edmund Quincy, *Josiah Quincy*, p. 242.

THE PARTY AND THE VOTER*

Noble E. Cunningham, Jr.

In investigating the oligarchic tendencies in modern party politics the French sociologist Robert Michels pointed out that parties were often based on majority principles and always incorporated the concept of the mass of people. Even those parties basically aristocratic in origin and principles were pushed to adopt democratic means if they were to remain alive. While Michels' various "iron laws" of politics would be difficult to apply to the Republican era, they do invite further consideration of the means by which the early parties attempted to relate to the "mass" of the day—namely, the voter.

Noble E. Cunningham, Jr., in the chapter reprinted from The Jeffersonian Republicans in Power, *emphasizes that the continued Republican successes were, in large measure, due to the party's ability to win and hold the allegiance of the average voter. However much the direction of the party came from local oligarchies such as the Richmond Junto or from personal followings such as that of the New York Clintonians, the Republicans had recognized, at an early stage, the importance of the electorate in party affairs. Cunningham explores, in vivid detail, the electioneering methods used by the Republicans and their adroit techniques of denigrating the Federalists to considerable political advantage.*

The machinery and organization of the Jeffersonian party and the methods and practices of its leaders reflected, in the final analysis, the power of the American voter. The devices of party, geared to the functioning of democratic government, reaffirmed the voter's ultimate authority. By the nature of the American political system, the party's record

* Reprinted by permission of the University of North Carolina Press. From *The Jeffersonian Republicans in Power: Party Operations, 1801-1809* by Noble E. Cunningham, Jr. (Chapel Hill, University of North Carolina Press for the Institute of Early American History and Culture, 1963). Copyright © 1963 by the University of North Carolina Press: Chapter XI, "The Party and the Voter," pp. 275-98.

and program were always presented to the electorate in the form of political candidates aspiring to office. Just as party machinery varied from state to state, so the methods and campaign practices of candidates seeking political preferment were adapted to the customs and practices of local political life. Persons from one section of the country were frequently surprised by the campaign and election practices of other regions. Observing a day of electioneering in South Carolina, Edward Hooker, a Connecticut-born Yale graduate, found himself "an astonished spectator of a scene, the resemblance of which I had never before witnessed." On the other hand, Henry W. DeSaussure, a South Carolinian attending an election in Hartford, Connecticut, observed that "it was a singular spectacle, unlike all other elections I ever saw."[1] The South Carolina scene which astonished Hooker, as it would have equally amazed many other New Englanders, was direct solicitation of votes by political candidates. It was Saturday afternoon in Pickensville, in western South Carolina, in September 1806, and the fall campaign was in full swing. Let Hooker describe the day:

> Several hundreds of people came together: the houses and streets were thronged. The three candidates for Congress, Alston, Hunter and Earle were present electioneering with all their might —distributing whiskey, giving dinners, talking, and haranguing, their friends at the same time making similar exertions for them. Besides these, there was a number of Candidates for the Assembly. It was a singular scene of noise, blab and confusion. . . . Handbills containing accusations of federalism against one, of abuse of public trust against another—of fraudulent speculation against a third—and numerous reports of a slanderous and scurrilous nature were freely circulated. Much drinking, swearing, cursing and threatening—but I saw no fighting. The minds of uninformed people were much agitated—and many well-meaning people were made to believe that the national welfare was at stake and would be determined by the issue of this back-woods election.[2]

Hooker, who had attended church services in the region on the previous Sunday, had also witnessed an electioneering scene outside the church door: "The candidates had stationed themselves conveniently, and were now very busy in saluting every man in the crowd, taking care to call by name as many as possible, and putting themselves on the terms of old acquaintance. Col. Alston was perfect master of the art, and played his game with so much adroitness as almost to persuade one that nobody could have a more cordial attachment to him, or feel a greater interest in his welfare."[3] At another time, Hooker expressed surprise that "a person told me he had seen letters from a person to several voters, announcing himself a candidate, and soliciting their patronage and influence. To such a height does the fondness for office and power rise."[4] Although a New Englander might be shocked at such electioneering practices in South Carolina, open campaigning by candidates in their own behalf was common in most of the region from Delaware and Maryland southward.

In Maryland, the stump-speaking political canvass was the accepted practice. Candidates for office toured the state or district, speaking at public meetings, militia reviews, barbecues, or wherever a crowd could be assembled. Opposing candidates frequently spoke or debated from the same platform. A contemporary report of one of these campaign gatherings near Baltimore in 1808 described a Saturday militia review followed by electioneering speeches. "A considerable number of citizens had collected both from the city and county," it was reported. "Between 3 and 4 o'clock, a circle was formed around a stump, on which Mr. Pollock mounted, and addressed the auditory in his usual vein of humor and pertinacity declaring himself a candidate for a seat in Congress." Pollock was followed by a Mr. Winder who also offered himself as a candidate for Congress and "commenced a philippic on the great *stalking horse* of federalism, the Embargo." Several other candidates also spoke soliciting suffrages.[5] So accepted had such campaign practices become in Maryland that one candidate felt called upon to explain: "My present engagements, and the necessary attention to my private affairs, will not allow me to appear at every public meeting which is held for the purpose of *Electioneering*." It was therefore his hope that "as Free and Independent Men, you are not to be *cajoled* by the show of great *personal respect*, nor caught with the miserable bait of *entertainment*."[6] This candidate was not elected, however, and most men who sought public favor in Maryland found it necessary to engage in a canvass.

Campaign practices in Delaware followed those in Maryland, as Caesar A. Rodney explained in writing to Madison in October 1801. "I returned late last evening from a political tour of about two weeks in the lower counties of this State," he reported. "I travelled with the acts of Congress, the annual reports of the Secretary of the Treasury and other documents in my hands to meet the Federalists on their strongest grounds. We have followed the example of the worthy Duvall and the other Republicans of Maryland in addressing the people on the state of affairs at the various public assemblies and I trust with the same good effect."[7] Self-nomination which was acceptable in Maryland, however, was considered improper in Delaware.

Political candidates in Virginia campaigned openly, making speeches, attending county court days, and soliciting the suffrages of the voters on the day of the election.[8] A successful candidate for the state legislature in 1801 explained:

> Two months before the Election were almost exclusively appropriated to electioneering. I traversed every part of the County, and became acquainted with almost the whole of the people, with whom before that Time I was wholly unacquainted. I had a good opportunity of observing the state of their Manners, and Sentiments. Many of them I found to be ignorant, brutified and totally indifferent to the Exercise of their most important Rights. The only stimulus with them to that Exercise was through the medium of their palates. Grog, strong Grog was to them of much more Consequence than the giving their Votes for this or that man. These persons I generally neglected, having determined not to gain my Election by such means, and I succeeded, for I believe I did not spend two Dollars during the two Months, in which I canvassed. Some I found to be extremely independent, and intelligent, and it was by the Votes of these men, and the neighborhood Influence which they possessed, that I was elected. Others again, not so bad as the first, although they put on the appearance of Independence, yet possessing it not in Reality, required a great Deal of courting.[9]

This candidate found a two-month canvass more successful than treating the voters with grog; but it was clear that he found campaigning necessary for election.

John Randolph in 1805 boasted: "I have been to none of the election or public meetings since my return, but the *good people* have again deputed me to serve them."[10] However, in 1808 when a strong opposition was made to his re-election, Randolph was compelled to campaign. His opponent, as a friend warned Randolph, adopted the practice of "following you about in your District, replying at one Court-House to speeches which you had made at another."[11] Randolph disclosed more about the campaigning in this election when he reported in regard to his opponent that "an electioneering barbacue was given to him (or rather against me) where at he was present and declared off. I was not there."[12]

Something of the conduct of a Virginia candidate can be concluded from a contemporary comment on current political practices in the state published in the Richmond *Examiner* in 1803, in which the writer declared that "in choosing a representative, we look for qualities, often adverse to, and at best, accidentally associated with political merit. Has a candidate an easy exterior, condescending manners, and is he equally polite to all? Does he recollect your names, the names of your wives and children, and greet you with the meretricious smile of continued placidity and universal good humour? He is too often the man of your choice."[13]

In Kentucky, "flattery" and "barbecues" were listed by a contemporary observer as high among the "electioneering arts" in that state,[14] and one Kentucky politician recalled in regard to Matthew Lyon's success in winning elections to four terms in Congress: "He was a man of Herculean frame and constitution—could drink Grog all the day long without getting drunk; tell pretty good rough anecdotes and take him altogether was a good 'Electioneerer.' "[15] Robert H. Grayson, an unsuccessful candidate for Congress, condemned "the practice of treating and feasting for votes, a practice which I think every independent voter will condemn, and which however it may be smoothed over is the worst kind of corruption in elections." Grayson's remarks on election practices in Kentucky afford a rare contemporary commentary:

It is a misfortune, sir, for this country, that electioneering (as it is called) has been so compleatly reduced to a science, as with us. Candidates are in the habit of making appeals to the passions and prejudices, not the reason of the voter. Duplicity, flattery and the most shameful political and religious hypocricy are frequently resorted to. To prevent a *fair expression* of the public voice, they frequently act over the whole comedy of tricks and maneuvres, and he who plays his part the best is praised for his *address*. Cameleon like, you see them changing colors, and in order to please, they are saints and sinners by turns, as occasion may require. Treating some of the voters, in open violation of the laws of our country, is practised under pretence of *sociability*. The whole dictionary of insipid jokes is consulted and these jokes dealt out with great profusion upon all occasions and in all companies', as if men were to be sent to Congress, or to the assembly, to act the part of Buffoons or jesters. Intemperance, it seems, is not always an improper qualification for a candidate. A pack of cards, a keg of whisky, and a game cock, have on some occasions (it is said) been a good electioneering apparatus, for a man, who if elected, was to assist in making laws for a nation. But this is not all, the candidate according to the present mode of electioneering, if he wishes to succeed, must, for at least a year before the election, totally neglect his private affairs, however inconvenient it may be to him, and instead of having that necessary time for preparing himself, to discharge properly the trust reposed in him by the people, if elected, he has perpetually to take the rounds, through the district with the velocity of a race rider. If he does not do this, there are not wanting men to accuse him of neglect and pride. These measures to obtain an election cannot long be countenanced. They are pursued in no other state in the Union. The people will open their eyes, and ask why men adopt these extraordinary means to obtain success if they had nothing in view but the good of their country?[16]

In Tennessee, as in Kentucky, campaigning for office was openly conducted, and the outcome of elections depended heavily on the exertions of a candidate, his friends, and party supporters in directly soliciting votes. Considerable last-minute canvassing appears to have taken place at the polls, and these activities were not always above suspicion. "To vote by ballot is subject to corruption which more than viva voce suffrages," wrote one Tennessee observer who witnessed the canvassing on election day at Rutledge and "understood the carryings on at most other Court-Houses in this District was much the same." He concluded: "An active impudent Man with some address and could write with facility and always have pen, ink, and paper at hand, was worth more than fifty common Voters to his party."[17]

In North Carolina, electioneering speeches were made "at the Courthouse door," candidates "spoke on the fence" in support of their elections, and active solicitation of votes on election day at times became clamorous.[18] Nathaniel Macon, a popular and often re-elected congressman from North Carolina, could write: "I have never solicited any man to vote for me or hinted to him that I wished him to do so, nor did I ever solicit any person to make interest, for me to be elected to any place."[19] But though Macon adhered to such a mode of political conduct, most candidates in North Carolina by 1800 did not appear to have regarded open electioneering activities as improper.

In Georgia, political candidates and their friends also campaigned openly. John Milledge was supported in his race for Congress in 1801 by friends who "rode day and night" and "worked like a Horse," as one of them said, to promote his election.[20] Joseph Bryan, running for Congress in 1803, was advised by a close political friend to make a campaign tour. "I think you would do well to spend a few weeks in the *upcountry* the latter part of this summer," wrote Obadiah Jones, "in which case, I give it as my opinion your Election would be pretty certain." And Jones himself proposed to visit the "upcountry" before the election: "I wish much to get up, before the great day of the feast . . . for I conclude I should do your Election no injury."[21] Bryan evidently made an electioneering tour, and so did his opponent, for Jones reported after Bryan's victory that Bryan's opponent "had gone over the same ground after you electioneering, and had made use of means that I think very unjustifiable, I mean that of lying (at least telling untruths) and publishing some specious pieces in the papers."[22] During another election it was a matter of political concern that "Mr. Spalding has been a Considerable time in the up Country; he is a man of talents and information, of smooth and insinuating manners and address."[23] Electioneering in Georgia also took place at county seats when courts were in session, at militia musters, and at the polls on election day.[24]

Electioneering by the candidates themselves was more open and direct in the South than in the middle states or in New England. In these regions, self-nomination—widely accepted in the South—was regarded as improper. A meeting of Republicans in Woodbury, Pennsylvania, in 1804, resolved: "That this meeting highly disapprove of the practice, so inimical to republican principles of individuals announcing themselves to oppose, by all proper means in their power, the election of any person persisting in such indelicate practice."[25] But although the candidate himself maintained a more reserved position in these states, the voters were no less exempt from some form of electioneering than the electorate in the southern states. The growth of political parties had brought electioneering to all parts of the union. A New England writer protested early in 1801: "Elections to office, in New England, have been always, till very lately, *free* beyond any example that can be found elsewhere. . . . It was not prudent for any man to express a wish for promotion . . . . Unhappily, however, our democrats have already had some influence in changing this truly republican state of things among us. The detestable practice of electioneering is, by their means, indirectly gaining ground, in these states."[26]

The development of party machinery in the New England states brought well-organized electioneering campaigns to that region. Although stump speaking does not appear to have yet become acceptable, the solicitation of suffrages by a candidate's friends and by party committees, employing personal contacts, party handbills, and the press, was extensive. Dr. Nathaniel Ames in his diary, March 20, 1808, noted: "Electioneering opened. Pamphlets flying like wild geese in a storm."[27] Massachusetts elections were becoming particularly tumultuous. Thomas Dwight confessed in 1802: "If my conscience would allow me to be the occasion of losing one vote in the federal cause I would not go into Boston to attend the Election—it is always a noisy business of parade. To have seen this scene acted over once is enough—enough—to see it done over and over year after year is painful or at the least irksome to me."[28] Another explained: "So loud and so indecently rude, is the noise made by the distributers of ballots for the different candidates, and such the illiberal reflections and uncandid remarks upon their respective characters, as cannot but excite painful sensations in every delicate mind."[29] Although Federalists claimed to disdain electioneering, both parties were actively engaged. James Sullivan, Republican candidate for governor in 1806, protested: "The arts, frauds, bribes and calumnies used by the federalists this year were never equalled but in one instance. Bribery is boasted of without a blush, and the most attrocious slanders smoothed over with an apology that they were only for an electioneering purpose."[30]

Election campaigns in New York and Pennsylvania were consistently among the most vigorously contested races in the country. The divisions between Federalists and Republicans had early turned these states into party battlefields. Party machinery was extensive, newspapers were numerous and politically active, and public participation in party affairs was unusually extensive. There are far more extant political handbills from New York elections than from any other state, attesting to the extensive use of that method of campaigning in New York. Handbills were also widely circulated in Pennsylvania. Campaigns in which there were party splits with Republicans fighting Republicans were among the most bitter of the period, and nowhere were Republicans more plagued by divisions than in New York and Pennsylvania. Perhaps the most abusive campaign waged during the period was the gubernatorial election of 1804 in New York when Burr and his followers challenged the regular Republican organization.[31]

In New Jersey, elections were accompanied by considerable campaigning by party committees, and, as a result of last-minute electioneering and the availability of grog on election days, there was frequent tumult at the polls.[32] One New Jersey observer declared in 1804:

Look at an election scene and the steps preparatory to it. Behold characters torn into tatters and scattered to the winds. Committees of lies to tell the truth to the people. . . . What changing of votes and tricks and impositions upon electors? . . . What bribery, perjury, and corruption? Lo! a voter, brimful of freedom and grog, marching up to the election box, guarded by two or more staunch patriots, lest the honest soul should mistake, lose his way or be surprised by the other party and lost.[33]

Although party machinery varied and election procedures and campaign practices differed, there were certain common patterns of political behavior that can be ascribed to party workers in all parts of the country. The immediate aim of every party worker was, of course, to win the election at hand and in so doing to contribute to the over-all success of the party in securing or maintaining control of the state and national administrations. To accomplish this purpose the party machinery described in earlier chapters was put into operation. Whatever its construction, Republican party machinery aimed at common objectives through similar means: nominating or approving of party candidates, publicizing the party program and defending the party record, familiarizing the electorate with the party's candidates and appealing to the interests and the sentiments of the voters to support them, arousing public interest especially in getting out to vote, and maintaining party unity.

Appeals to voters to exercise their suffrage were frequent in Republican party literature. An editorial in the Newark *Centinel of Freedom*, on the eve of the election in November 1804, urged:

Let it be remembered that one hour, or a day spent in making the choice of proper persons to represent us in our national councils, and electing persons for to chuse the President and Vice-President of the U. States, is of more importance to a farmer than the same time spent following his plow, or a mechanic at his anvil, or the merchant behind the counter. If our information is true, our opponents are organizing in secret, with a view of making a bold push, at a late hour, in hopes of finding the republicans off guard. Fellow freemen of the state of New Jersey, we again intreat you to come out; do not sleep, do not slumber on the days of election. However secure we may feel ourselves; let it be remembered that we have enemies.[34]

In Connecticut, where Federalists were firmly in control of the state government, a circular issued by the Republican party state manager in 1805 declared: "Those, who talk against federalism through the year, and yet neglect to attend proxies, do worse than nothing. Those, who profess to be republicans, and yet vote for federalists on any occasion, do us irreparable mischief. Federalism cannot be talked down or flattered down; IT MUST BE VOTED DOWN."[35] Republicans were regularly urged by party spokesmen to vote the party ticket. "It is our duty, *one and all*, to be *vigilant and united* in support of the [Republican] ticket," Republicans were told;[36] and one of the most frequently repeated party slogans was "United we stand, divided we fall."[37]

That Republican leaders sought to encourage a feeling of popular participation in the affairs of the party and to keep alive popular enthusiasm for the party was well demonstrated by the frequency of party celebrations held throughout the country. Many of the Republican celebrations which accompanied the inauguration of Jefferson on March 4, 1801, were well-planned, elaborate demonstrations which featured parades, dinners, orations, balls, and other festivities.[38] These celebrations were repeated in many places in March of each year throughout Jefferson's administration.[39] "The 4th of March forms an epoch in the political history of the United States, which ought always to awaken the purest sensations of the American Patriot," declared a Richmond Republican meeting in announcing "the celebration of that day, which restored to us the genuine principles of '76, and removed the alarms which had clouded the fairest prospects of American Liberty and Independence."[40] Reporting the Republican celebration in New Haven in March 1803, Abraham Bishop enthusiastically pointed out that "the procession extended in close columns through two sides of the public square and consisted of 1108 men. The whole company far exceeded that on commencements and Elections."[41] The Boston *Independent Chronicle* on Monday, March 5, 1804, announced: "This Day, the anniversary of the renovation of *Republicanism* in the United States, in the inauguration of the patriot, the sage, the inflexible Republican, will be celebrated in the most splendid manner."

In addition to the March 4th celebrations, there were also the July 4th festivities which came to be separately observed by the two parties in many places.[42] A July 4th celebration planned and controlled by Republicans meant, as explained by Levi Lincoln, "a republican orator, republican prayers, republican music, republican toasts, and republican songs."[43] Special celebrations were also held, the most elaborate and extensive being the celebration of the acquisition of Louisiana. From Washington, Federalist Congressman Manasseh Cutler reported in

January 1804: "There is a *Jubilee* proclaimed here by the Democrats.
. . . There is to be such a feast, it is said, as was never known in
America, on account of taking possession of *Louisiana*. There is to be
diners—suppers—balls—assemblies, dances, and I know not what. . . .
The *Jubilee* is to begin here—but they expect it will run—like *wildfire*,
to every dark and benighted corner of America."[44] And spread it did.
Republican newspapers called for a national festival, and Republicans
in many parts of the country organized celebrations. So tremendous was
the Philadelphia celebration that it must have dominated the life of the
city for days, even weeks, before the May 12 festival.[45]

Federalists replied to the Republican celebrations by observing
Washington's birthday, just before the March 4th festivals, and in other
ways calling attention to the first President. The Worcester *Massachusetts
Spy*, obviously trying to counteract recent Republican demonstrations,
devoted most of the issue of March 7, 1804, to publishing Washington's
Farewell Address.

Although every election had its own peculiar set of circumstances and
many voters were influenced in their suffrages by considerations often
of a local or personal nature, there were certain appeals voiced sufficiently frequently and universally by Republican candidates and party
spokesmen that they may be correctly referred to as party appeals. These
Republican appeals reveal the issues or lack of issues which were presented to the voters, as well as the methods by which party workers
sought to advance the Republican cause.

First of all, the Republicans who had successfully turned out John
Adams in 1800 campaigned against Adams as long as they could keep
alive the memories of the unpopular measures of his administration. A
circular in support of Republican candidates for the legislature of Maryland in September 1802 declared:

Sir, you cannot have forgotten the unjust and oppressive
measures of the late administration.

WHO imposed, unnecessarily, upon the people a debt of
upwards of ten millions?—The Federalists.

WHO laid and continued the tax on your stills?—The Federalists.

WHO taxed your dwelling houses?—The Federalists.

WHO taxed your lands?—The Federalists.

WHO imposed on you a Stamp-Act, and created an *host of
officers* to collect the excise duties?—The Federalists.

> WHO imposed on you an alien law, a Sedition Act, and a new
> and unnecessary Judiciary law . . . ?—The Federalists.
> WHO raised a useless standing army?—The Federalists. . . .
> The *principal* actors in the Federal measures approve of the
> former, and are dissatisfied with the present administration. . . .
> The question before you is, do you wish those measures of
> extravagant Taxation pursued by the Federalists re-established?[46]

Republican delegates from the various counties of New Jersey in
recommending the Republican ticket for Congress in 1803 explained: "It
is not necessary . . . to recall to the recollection of their fellow-citizens,
the extravagant, oppressive, and unconstitutional measures of the late
administration; or to direct their attention to the economical, pacific, and
equitable conduct of the present. Every friend to a republican government, in form and substance, must wish to avert a recurrence of the
scenes that marked Mr. Adams's administration, and to perpetuate the
system practised by the administration of Mr. Jefferson."[47] The Democratic Republican Corresponding Committee of New-Castle County,
Delaware, in 1804, announced that "the Committee would be willing
to rest the fate of the approaching general election in the State of
Delaware on the comparative review . . . of the measures and policy
of the *former* and *present* administrations, believing that the public suffrages will give a decided preference to the friends of the *latter* who
are candidates for office—and this on the score of economy alone, if
there were no other reasons."[48] The Democratic Republicans of Gloucester County, New Jersey, in 1807, authorized the printing and distribution
of five hundred copies of an address, "containing a brief narrative of
the most oppressive laws passed during the federal administration, their
extravagant expenditure of the public money, prosecutions, fines and
imprisonments, to prevent freedom of speech, or an investigation of their
conduct; contrasted with the conduct of the present administration."[49]

In the election of 1808, when the Federalists, hoping to take advantage
of the unpopularity of the Embargo, made their strongest efforts thus
far to regain popular support, the issues of the Adams administration
were revived with increased vigor. A Republican reply to William Gaston, who was running as a Federalist elector in support of Charles Cotesworth Pinckney in North Carolina, concluded:

> General Pinckney, as to political principles, is just such a man,
> Fellow-Citizens, as you dismissed from office eight years ago,

on account of those principles. If you elect Mr. Gaston, he will endeavor to give you a Federal President. If this should take place, it is reasonable to conclude, that under similar circumstances, he would act as the former President did. Therefore . . . you must expect—"Alien and Sedition Laws—Direct,— Stamp, —Still and other Internal TAXES."[50]

A notice printed in Republican newspapers called attention to the difference between the Adams and Jefferson administrations in the following comparison:

LOOK ON

THIS PICTURE   AND ON THIS.

During *four* years of Adams' administration the National Debt was *augmented* eleven millions of dollars; a host of judges appointed to receive large salaries and carry the sedition law, etc., into execution, and so intimidate a free people; four hundred tax-gatherers were employed to collect the internal direct taxes on lands, houses, stills, carriages, sugar, and domestic distilled spirits. Navies were built, armies were raised; and loans were obtained at the enormous interest of eight per cent.—to maintain the system of direful waste and extravagance.

During Jefferson's republican administration, the *whole system* of internal taxes has been abolished; the superfluous and useless judges dismissed; and even the duties on imports in some cases diminished. No tax is paid to the general government;—yet near 30 *millions* of the public debt has been redeemed; and Louisiana purchased for *fifteen* millions of dollars—though it is worth sixty millions of dollars, renders us secure on the S.W. border of the Union, and produces cotton and sugar in great abundance. And of the 15 millions, three went to compensate our merchants for spoliations.[51]

The preceding illustrations not only indicate how Republicans throughout the country campaigned against the previous administration, but they also show how Republicans in both national and state elections stood on the record of the administration. Printed circular letters sent by Republican congressmen to their constituents also were filled with glowing praise of the accomplishments of the administration which they supported and which they pledged themselves to continue to support if re-elected.[52]

As the presidential election of 1804 approached, party spokesmen and the party press called attention to the accomplishments of Jefferson's first years in office. The following summary published in the Republican press included the major points which Republicans emphasized when appealing for the support of the electorate. The record of the administration, Republicans claimed, showed:

It has taken off the whole internal taxes, among which were the duties on stills, on stampt paper, etc. and the people now pay no tax, only to support their state Governments.

It has dispensed with several thousand unnecessary officers, who were before fattening upon the labor of the people.

It has reduced the land forces employed on our frontiers, and as much of the navy as could safely be dispensed with.

It has lessened the expences in every department of Government, by employing no unnecessary agents, and allowing no improper expenditures.

It has reduced, several millions of dollars, the National Debt, which had increased under Mr. Adams; and has made provision by law for its entire discharge in about fifteen years.

It has preserved peace, even when its opposers declared for instant war; and has effected by negotiation in a few months what it would have taken years of hostilities to acquire; and have purchased for fifteen millions of dollars, a territory which is worth ten times the sum, and which would have cost an hundred millions of dollars, and thousands of lives, if it had been taken by force, as its opposers proposed and insisted.[53]

The conscious Republican emphasis on the Jeffersonian retrenchment policies was succinctly confessed by James Cheetham, editor of the New York *American Citizen*, when he remarked: "The reduction of our taxes and the diminution of the public debt, are arguments which the worst reasoner in the union can justly appreciate."[54]

Seeking election as a Jeffersonian elector in the presidential contest of 1804, Montfort Stokes appealed to North Carolina voters to "take a retrospective view of the successful operations of our Government for the last four years," affirming:

We enjoy peace and respect abroad, happiness and tranquility at home. With many burdens lightened, and no new impositions laid we have yet been enabled . . . to diminish the public debt. . . . Without the aid of a standing army or a burthensome naval force, our commerce is less embarrassed by the depredations of foreign powers, and our frontiers less disturbed by our Indian neighbours, than at any period since we became an Independent nation. . . . We have no alien or sedition law. . . . By the repeal of the excise laws and other internal taxes, we have got rid of a host of revenue officers, who were fattening on the spoils of the industrious.

Much praise was also lavished on the Louisiana purchase. These were but "a few of the many blessings we have experienced by the wise policy of Mr. Jefferson."[55]

Republicans campaigned on the administration record not only in presidential elections but also in state contests. Robert H. Grayson, a Kentucky candidate for Congress in 1804, announced in an electioneering circular reviewing the accomplishments of Jefferson's administration:

I am a friend to those political measures recommended and pursued by the enlightened statesman who now fills the presidential chair; a statesman who has given us the best theory, and is now exhibiting the best practical exposition of the essential principles of our free government ever attempted. It would exceed the limits, and perhaps be travelling a little out of the usual course of an address, to pass in review the various benefits we have received from his administration. My solicitude, however that they should be known to every American citizen, will, I hope, plead my apology for noticing some of the most important, and contrasting them with the evils we sustained from those unwise principles of policy pursued by the last administration.[56]

Caesar A. Rodney, seeking re-election to Congress in 1804, assured the President: "I stand upon the single and solid ground of being a supporter of you and your administration."[57] A Republican convention in New Jersey in 1808 nominated candidates for Congress who had "uniformly and steadily, supported the measures of the present administration of our General Government:—Measures, in our opinion, founded in wisdom and sound policy."[58]

Standing on the administration's record was a position easy to adopt during Jefferson's first term, when the President enjoyed an immense popularity climaxing in the enthusiastic reception given to the purchase of Louisiana; but it was a stand more difficult to take during his last years in office, when the administration was burdened with increasing problems in regard to foreign affairs. The President's handling of the crisis with England over neutral rights provided a major issue which the Federalist opposition could effectively exploit, and it also became an issue among Republicans. The Embargo Act of December 1807, the capstone of the administration's attempt to bring England to terms through economic coercion, was a measure which demanded much sacrifice while conferring only the negative benefit of avoiding something worse—war or the surrender of the American position in regard to neutral rights.

The Embargo was unquestionably the most prominent issue in the election of 1808; it pervaded not only the presidential contest but state elections as well. It was a principal issue in the gubernatorial elections in Massachusetts and in Pennsylvania, in both of which contests the Republicans defended the administration's foreign policy and the Embargo.[59] There was probably no state election in 1808 in which the Embargo issue did not play a part. Federalists clearly hoped to profit from the distress created by the halting of trade, and Republican opponents of Secretary of State Madison likewise used the issue, especially in support of Clinton in New York. Despite some open Republican attacks and considerable equivocation on the Embargo policy, the majority of Republicans still campaigned on the Jeffersonian record, standing by the Embargo; and Madison emerged victorious in the election of 1808 as the candidate running squarely on the administration's record.

The prominence of the Embargo issue and the repeated attacks on the administration's foreign policy resulted in widespread Republican efforts to make it clear to the voters that the party supported the administration. Numerous party meetings throughout the country passed resolutions expressing confidence in the administration and support for the Embargo. In Essex County, Massachusetts, a Republican county convention "*Resolved*, That we fully approve of the present administration under the direction of THOMAS JEFFERSON, in whom we recognize the inflexible patriot, the great philosopher, and the friend of Man." It also "*Resolved*, That we consider the embargo, at the present crisis, as a measure best calculated to preserve our property from plunder, our Seamen from impressment, and our nation from the horrors of War."[60] In September 1808, "A General Meeting of the Republicans of the City of New York" passed the following resolutions "with but few dissenting voices":

> *Resolved,* That this meeting continues to repose full confidence in the patriotism and wisdom of the PRESIDENT and of the

Republican majority in both houses of the Congress of the United States.

Resolved, That in our opinion the EMBARGO is a prudent, just and politic measure, rendered necessary by the rapacity and depredations of the principal belligerent nations, and not originating from any events within the power of our government to have controuled—that a repeal of the same, under existing circumstances, would probably involve us in the calamities of WAR; and, that it is therefore the duty of every faithful citizen to afford the Administration his firm and decided support.[61]

Similar resolutions were passed elsewhere.[62]

Although the Republican party was at times seriously disturbed by party disunity, Republican factions ordinarily claimed to be supporters of the national administration when the divisions were confined to state politics. John Randolph's schism and the Republican divisions in the election of 1808 conspicuously extended party divisions into national politics, and Republicans then took conflicting stands on the Jeffersonian record. However, John Randolph failed to attract any sizable Republican following in his anti-administration movement; and the anti-administration position adopted by the supporters of George Clinton in the election of 1808 won him but six presidential electoral votes.

Republicans who appealed to the voters on the basis of principles, politics, and interests also spoke to their passions and prejudices. In the election of 1808, the Federalists were denounced as attached to Great Britain, and frequent reminders of the Revolutionary War, designed to arouse anti-British sentiment, appeared in Republican party literature. A Republican handbill circulated in the Massachusetts gubernatorial election in 1808 made a passionate appeal:

As in the days of HANCOCK and ADAMS, you have among you the emissaries of Britain. They are anxious to restore the DESCENDANTS of the OLD TORIES, and degrade the patriots of our Revolution. They are in favor of men who wish to hazard our Commerce to the depredation of the European powers—who are desirous to have our ships BURNED ON THE OCEAN—who wish to expose our SEAMEN to every outrage of impressment and murder, just to gratify their British masters. They seek to DIVIDE YOU FROM YOUR GOVERNMENT, so that British Aggressions may find less opposition. They even have the audacity to declare, in *recommendation* of their candidate, that he is opposed to our national government—at this time, too, when foreign encroachments make union so necessary. These men are devoted friends to the nation who set CHARLESTOWN in flames—who destroyed thousands of American prisoners on board the British GUARD Ships—who attempted to starve the people of Boston by a cruel PORT bill. They are familiarized to massacres and murder. They advocated the Boston Massacre. They approve the sanguinary action of KILLING AMERICAN SEAMEN. They thirst for the Blood of Republicans.[63]

Although this was an exceptionally extreme appeal, similar efforts to associate the Federalists with British sympathizers and the Tories of the Revolution were common Republican tactics.[64]

Republicans also sought to direct sentiment in favor of national unity to party advantage by arguing that state governments should have the confidence of the national administration. A Republican appeal in support of Israel Smith for governor of Vermont in 1807—the year of the Burr trial and of the *Chesapeake* affair—explained:

At this eventful period, when we are on the eve of a war with Great Britain, when rebellion stalks abroad in our land, union of sentiment, union of energies of the nation are peculiarly necessary. United, we have nothing to fear from any nation on earth—divided, we may become an easy prey to any invader.

You cannot be insensible of the necessity at all times, but more especially in the time of war and rebellion, that a perfect confidence subsist between the general and the respective state governments. . . .

. . . Let it be remembered that the question is not men but principles; that is, not whether Israel Smith or Isaac Tichenor shall be Governor; but whether Vermont will unite and cooperate with the government of the United States in the present moment, or whether in the hour of danger we will basely desert our country's rights, and by our vile example excite discord and division, and thereby encourage the machinations of foreign foes and domestic traitors.[65]

A circular, distributed by the Republican Central Committee of Massachusetts in 1806, opposing the re-election of Federalist Governor Caleb Strong similarly argued:

* * *

The Last Day.

Every shot's a vote, and every vote kills a **TORY !**

This is the last day of the election—Shall it close gloriously for Republicans, or in TORY triumph?

Every American will cling to his
COUNTRY ;

Every true whig will oppose with all his might
The Tories ;

Every man in whose veins there runs a drop of republican blood will
SUPPORT THE
Republican Ticket :

He who wishes not this State and the Union to be governed by
Britiſh Politics,

Will leave no honorable effort untried to defeat the
Britiſh Ticket,

at the head of which stands the name of
RUFUS KING,

The friend of Tory principles—the pander, of the British government—the enemy of our republican institutions.
Bad Weather

Will be no excuse for the triumph of a
Bad Cause ;

Every man to his tent, O Israel !
An Old Soldier.

APRIL, 1807

Republican Campaign Handbill, New York, 1807
(Courtesy of the New-York Historical Society)

It is a fact, which neither our present Chief Magistrate, or those who support him, will deny, that he never has, and we confidently believe, never will, harmonize with the present Administration of our National Government. And at a time when our foreign Relations with the Belligerent powers of Europe have become extremely critical . . . we hold it to be most essentially necessary, that every State Government in the Union should be ready cordially to unite, in support of the measures, which may be adopted by the National Administration.

Knowing, as we do, that the Republican Candidates for the two first offices for the Executive department in this State have the disposition to unite their Energies with those of the General Government, and possess their Confidence, and that their Opponents have neither the one, nor possess the other; we consider this alone to be a sufficient reason for a Change at the present moment.[66]

Although Republicans were anxious to keep the name of John Adams associated with the Federalists, they were unwilling to allow the Federalists to claim President Washington. Federalists made repeated efforts to keep Washington's name before the public in connection with their party. They conspicuously celebrated Washington's birthday. Federalist party tickets were labeled the "Washington Ticket," the "Washington and Anti-Embargo Ticket," and "Washington and Adams Nominations."[67] Recommending the Washington ticket for Congress, New Hampshire Federalists claimed: "The political principles of these gentlemen are those which ever actuated our beloved and revered Washington, during his administration of the Federal Government. They are all Federalists—they are all Republicans: Not of the *French* school, but of that of WASHINGTON."[68] Republicans in Vermont reacted to Federalist use of Washington's name by designating their ticket the "Washington and Jefferson Ticket" and referring to the Federalist slate as the "Adams and Hamilton Ticket."[69] The Boston *Columbian Centinel* however, replied:

The democrats still continue to *profane* the revered name of WASHINGTON, by opposing it to that of JOHN ADAMS, and uniting it with that of JEFFERSON. *Let it be remembered,* that in 1796, JOHN ADAMS was the Federal, and THOMAS JEFFERSON, the antifederal candidate for President of the United States. In that year, all the electors of *Virginia, save only one*—voted for THOMAS JEFFERSON:—That one was Colonel POWELL, and he

voted for JOHN ADAMS—*And be it also remembered,* that
GEORGE WASHINGTON, then in the 66th year of his age, rode
from *Mount Vernon,* to *Alexandria*, a distance of 8 miles to give
his vote for Col. POWELL, *the Federal Candidate. Facts are
knotty things!*[70]

Federalists were still using this same appeal in 1808.[71]

Federalist claims of having received the blessing of the "immortal
Washington" brought Republican reminders that Jefferson had been
Washington's Secretary of State and that Madison had been active in
support of the Constitution.[72] Aroused by the use of Washington's name
by South Carolina Federalists, the Charleston *Carolina Gazette* vigorously protested:

> The Tories and Disorganizers who have constantly abused and
> vilified the government and its laws . . . now have the impudence
> to call themselves *Followers of Washington*—this fetch will not
> do, gentlemen Tories; disguise yourselves under what names you
> please, you are, in fact, nothing else than followers and faithful
> servants of George the third. You know not Washington but as
> a man whose life was spent in freeing his country from such evil
> doers as yourselves.[73]

Republicans flatly refused to give up claims to Washington. Declared
the Boston *Independent Chronicle*:

> The most glorious things of which our country can boast, claim
> Washington, Jefferson, and Madison for their authors:
> Washington fought and conquered for Liberty:
> Jefferson composed the Declaration of Independence, and con-
> firmed its principles by his administration—
> Madison originated the present admirable constitution of the U.
> States, and has victoriously supported it against all its foes.[74]

Party leaders and active party workers fully realized that the voter was
influenced in sundry ways, and they hoped not to leave any means of
arousing his support neglected. Effective organization and aggressive
campaigning through newspapers, party literature, and personal contacts
were directly aimed at winning and maintaining the support of the voter,
who made the ultimate decisions in the American political system. The
meaningfulness of the alternatives from which the voter had to choose

varied according to local contests; but, in the broad perspective, the Republican party offered to the voter a program of government action with which the voter could identify and of which a majority could, and did, approve.

NOTES

[1] J. Franklin Jameson, ed., "Diary of Edward Hooker, 1805-1808," entry of Sept. 27, 806, American Historical Association, *Annual Report, 1896* (Wash., 1897), I, 900; DeSaussure to John Rutledge, Sept. 21, 1802, Rutledge Papers, Univ. of N.C.

[2] Jameson, ed., "Diary of Edward Hooker," entry of Sept. 27, 1806, Amer. Hist. Assn. *Annual Report, 1896*, I, 900.

[3] *Ibid.*, entry of Sept. 21, 1806, 897.

[4] *Ibid.*, entry of Sept. 6, 1806, 892.

[5] Baltimore *American*, Sept. 26, 1808; for details of similar electioneering practices in Maryland in 1800, see Cunningham, *Jeffersonian Republicans, 1789-1801*, 190-94.

[6] David Kerr, *To the Voters of Talbot County*, Aug. 11, 1803, Broadside, Md. Hist. Soc.

[7] Rodney to Madison, Oct. 5, 1801, Madison Papers, Lib. Cong. See also Rodney to Jefferson, Aug. 11, 1801, John Vaughan to Jefferson, Oct. 10, 1801, Rodney to Jefferson, May 16, June 19, 1802, Jefferson Papers, Lib. Cong.

[8] Richmond *Enquirer*, Apr. 26, 1805; John W. Eppes to Jefferson, Feb. 10, 1803, Edgehill-Randolph Papers, Univ. of Va.; John G. Jackson to Madison, Apr. 29, 1803, Madison Papers, Lib. Cong.

[9] William Brockenbrough to Joseph C. Cabell, June 18, 1801, Cabell Papers, Univ. of Va. Harry Ammon quotes this letter in *The Republican Party in Virginia, 1789 to 1824* unpubl. Ph.D. diss., Univ. of Va., 1948), 33-34.

[10] Randolph to Joseph H. Nicholson, Apr. 18, 1805, Nicholson Papers, Lib. Cong.

[11] Randolph to James M. Garnett, May 27, 1808, Garnett to Randolph, Aug. 12, 1808, Randolph Papers, Garnett Transcripts, Lib. Cong.

[12] Randolph to Garnett, July 24, 1808, *ibid.*

[13] *Examiner*, Mar. 23, 1803.

[14] James Brown to Wilson C. Nicholas, Aug. 23, 1803, Nicholas Papers, Univ. of Va.

[15] "Memoirs of Micah Taul," Kentucky State Hist. Soc., *Register, 27* (1929), 364-65.

[16] Robert H. Grayson, [Circular], Mason County, June 5, 1806, broadside, Filson Club. The Kentucky Constitution of 1799 contained a prohibition against treating which apparently was frequently circumvented. This was indicated in the following resolution passed by the Kentucky House of Representatives in 1809: *"Resolved,* That the provision in the constitution, against a treating by candidates for the House of Representatives, as much forbids an union and agreement amongst all the candidates of a county, to treat, and divide the expence equally between themselves, with a view of affecting the election, as it does a treating by an individual candidate." Hopkins, ed., *Papers of Henry Clay*, I, 429-30.

[17] Arthur Campbell to David Campbell, Aug. 22, 1803, Campbell Papers, Duke Univ.

[18] William Lenoir, Memorandum Book from Mar. 1, 1802, to Mar. 15, 1804, in Fletcher Green, ed., "Electioneering 1802 Style," *North Carolina Historical Review,* 20 (1943), 243-44.

[19] Macon, brief autobiographical sketch, Macon Papers, Duke Univ.

[20] James Jackson to Milledge, Apr. 2, 1801, Salley, ed., *Correspondence of John Milledge,* 70-71.

[21] Jones to Bryan, June 25, Sept. 24, 1803, Arnold-Screven Papers, Univ. of N.C.

22 Jones to Bryan, Jan. 20, 1804, *ibid*.
23 Jones to Bryan, July 18, 1804, *ibid*.
24 Nicholas Ware to Thomas Carr, Sept. 28, 1806, Carr Papers, Univ. of Ga.; Obadiah Jones to Joseph Bryan, Jan. 20, 1804, Sept. 1, 1802, Arnold-Screven Papers, Univ. of N.C.
25 Wilmington *Mirror of the Times*, Sept. 15, 1804.
26 Hartford *Connecticut Courant*, Feb. 2, 1801.
27 Warren, *Jacobin and Junto*, 243.
28 Dwight to John Williams, May 21, 1802, Dwight Papers, Mass. Hist. Soc.
29 Boston *New-England Palladium*, Feb. 10, 1801.
30 Sullivan to Jefferson, Apr. 21, 1806, Jefferson Papers, Lib. Cong. See also Barnabas Bidwell to Jefferson, June 21, 1806, *ibid*.
31 See collections of broadsides for 1804 at N.Y. Pub. Lib. and N.Y. Hist. Soc.; see also Dixon Ryan Fox, *The Decline of Aristocracy in the Politics of New York* (N.Y., 1919), 63-67.
32 McCormick, *History of Voting in New Jersey*, 114.
33 New Brunswick *Guardian*, Sept. 27, 1804, quoted in *ibid*., 115.
34 *Centinel of Freedom*, Nov. 6, 1804.
35 [Circular], Nov. 1, 1805, printed in Hartford *Connecticut Courant*, Nov. 27, 1805. For other examples, see Elizabeth-Town *New-Jersey Journal*, Sept. 27, 1808; Newark *Centinel of Freedom*, Nov. 1, 1808.
36 Baltimore *American*, Aug. 31, 1808.
37 Boston *Independent Chronicle*, Feb. 23, Mar. 29, 1804, Mar. 24, 1808; *United We Stand—Divided We Fall*, Boston, Feb. 20, 1807, broadside, Hist. Soc. of Pa.
38 Richmond *Examiner*, Feb. 6, 27, Mar. 13, 1801; Richmond *Virginia Argus*, Mar. 13, Apr. 14, 1801; *Alexandria Advertiser*, Mar. 5, 16, 1801; *Raleigh Register*, Apr. 14, 1801. See Cunningham, *The Jeffersonian Republicans in Power*, pp. 5-6.
39 See Richmond *Examiner*, Mar. 2, 30, 1803, Richmond *Virginia Argus*, Feb. 22, Mar. 7, 1804; Hartford *American Mercury*, Mar. 7, 1805; Washington *National Intelligencer*, Feb. 9, 1803; New Haven *Connecticut Journal*, Feb. 24, 1803; Portland *Eastern Argus*, Mar. 9, 1804. See also Cunningham, *op. cit.*, pp. 127-28.
40 *Petersburg Intelligencer*, Feb. 17, 1804.
41 Bishop to————, Mar. 23, 1803, Misc. Coll., N.Y. Hist. Soc.
42 *Raleigh Register*, July 20, 1802; Boston *Independent Chronicle*, July 7, 1808; Boston *Columbian Centinel*, July 6, 1808; [Circular], Worcester, June 20, 1808, signed by Edward Bangs and others, broadside, Amer. Antiq. Soc.; Nathaniel Cogswell to Jefferson, July 11, 1808, Jefferson Papers, Lib. Cong.
43 Lincoln to Madison, July 5, 1801, Madison Papers, Lib. Cong.
44 Cutler to Francis Low, Jan. 21, 1804, "Cutler Letters," Essex Institute, *Hist. Collections*, 39 (1903), 325; see also Simeon Baldwin to Mrs. Baldwin, Jan. 22, 1804, Baldwin Family Papers, Yale Univ.
45 Philadelphia *Aurora*, Mar. 29, Apr. 6, 20, 26, May 10, 14, 1804; Richmond *Virginia Argus*, Feb. 25, 1804; New York *American Citizen*, Jan. 11, Feb. 3, 1804; Lexington *Kentucky Gazette*, May 15, 1804; Bishop, *Oration in Honor of the Election of President Jefferson, and the National Festival, in Hartford on the 11th of May, 1804*, pamphlet, Lib. Cong.
46 *Circular*, Frederick-Town, Sept. 23, 1802, broadside, Lib. Cong. For other examples of campaigning against the Adams administration see *To the Electors of the Middle District*, Poughkeepsie, Apr. 3, 1801, *To the Electors of the Southern District of the State of New York*, By order of the General Committee in New York, N.Y., Apr. 7, 1801, broadsides, Lib. Cong.; *Authentic Information relative to the Conduct of the Present and Last Administrations of the United States* (Wilmington, Del., 1802), pamphlet, Lib. Cong.; Washington *National Intelligencer*, Sept. 17, 1802; Chillicothe *Scioto Gazette*, Oct. 29, 1804; Thomas Sumter, [circular to his constituents], Washington, May 1, 1802, Sumter Papers, Lib.

Cong.; Richard Stanford, [circular to his constituents], Washington, Feb. 26, 1803, broadside, Lib. Cong.

⁴⁷ Newark *Centinel of Freedom*, Nov. 29, 1803.

⁴⁸ *The Address of the Democratic Republican Corresponding Committee of New-Castle County*, pamphlet, Lib. Cong.

⁴⁹ *At a Meeting of the Democratic Republicans of the County of Gloucester . . . 31st day of August, 1807*, pamphlet, Lib. Cong.

⁵⁰ *Remarks, on Mr. Gaston's Address to the Freemen of Wayne, Green, Lenoir, Jones, Craven and Cateret* (Newbern, N.C., 1808), pamphlet, Lib. Cong., replying to William Gaston, *To the Freemen of the Counties of Wayne, Green, Lenoir, Jones, Craven and Carteret* (Newbern, N.C., 1808), pamphlet, Univ. of N. C.

⁵¹ Charleston *Carolina Gazette*, Oct. 14, 1808, reprinted from Baltimore *Whig*.

⁵² Thomas Sumter, [circulars to his constituents], Washington, May 1, 1802, Mar. 4, 1803, Sumter Papers, Lib. Cong.; John Clopton, [circulars to his constituents], Washington, Feb. 24, 1803, Feb. 19, 1805, broadsides, Va. State Lib.; Richard Stanford, [circular to his constituents], Washington, Feb. 26, 1803, broadside, Lib. Cong.; John Claiborne, [circular to his constituents], Washington, Apr. 18, 1806, broadside, Duke Univ.

⁵³ Windsor *Spooner's Vermont Journal*, Oct. 25, 1803, reprinted from *Alexandria Expositor*.

⁵⁴ Cheetham to Jefferson, May 30, 1803, Jefferson Papers, Lib. Cong.

⁵⁵ Stokes, *To the Freemen of the Counties of Rowan, Randolph, and Cabarrus, in the State of North Carolina*, Sept. 6, 1804, broadside, Univ. of N.C.

⁵⁶ Robert Harrison Grayson, *To the Voters of the Sixth Congressional District . . .* , April 14, 1804, broadside, Filson Club.

⁵⁷ Rodney to Jefferson, June 14, 1804, Jefferson Papers, Lib. Cong.

⁵⁸ Elizabeth-Town *New Jersey Journal*, Sept. 27, 1808.

⁵⁹ Boston *Independent Chronicle*, Feb. 29, Mar. 28, 1808; Boston *Democrat*, Feb. 27, Mar. 26, 1808; Delegates of the Democratic Citizens of the Fourteen Wards of Philadelphia, *The New Crisis of American Independence* (Phila., 1808), pamphlet, Amer. Antiq. Soc.

⁶⁰ Boston *Independent Chronicle*, Feb. 29, 1808; Boston *Democrat*, Feb. 27, 1808.

⁶¹ New York *Public Advertiser*, Sept. 16, 1808; *Address of the Republicans of the City and County of New-York, to their Republican Fellow-Citizens of the United States* (N.Y., 1808), pamphlet, N.Y. Hist. Soc.

⁶² For other examples of meetings at which resolutions were passed in support of the Embargo see: Philadelphia *Aurora*, June 22, Aug. 9, 1808; Newark *Centinel of Freedom*, Aug. 23, 1808; *At a Very Numerous . . . Meeting of the Democratic Citizens of New-Castle County*, Sept. 3, 1808, broadside, Lib. Cong.; [Circular], State of New Hampshire, July 4, 1808, signed by Richard Evans, broadside, N.Y. Hist. Soc.; Portsmouth *New Hampshire Gazette*, Aug. 23, 1808; *Republican Convention*, Essex County, Massachusetts [1808], pamphlet, Amer. Antiq. Soc.

⁶³ *National Honor and Permanent Peace, or a Glorious Struggle for Independence*, [April 4, 1808], broadside, Amer. Antiq. Soc.

⁶⁴ See Bennington *World*, Aug. 8, 1808; Philadelphia *Aurora*, Oct. 10, 1808; Boston *Independent Chronicle*, Nov. 7, 1808; *British Barbarity and Piracy!!*, Boston, Mar. 25, 1808, broadside, Lib. Cong.; *The Last Day*, Apr. 1807, broadside, N.Y. Hist. Soc.

⁶⁵ *To the Freemen of Vermont*, [1807], broadside, N.Y. Hist. Soc.

⁶⁶ [Circular], Boston, Feb. 20, 1806, signed Thompson J. Skinner and others, broadside, Amer. Antiq. Soc. For other examples, see: *United We Stand—Divided We Fall*, Boston, Feb. 20, 1807, signed "The Central Committee," broadside, Hist. Soc. of Pa.; *To the Electors of the Southern District of the State of New York*, New York, Apr. 7, 1801, broadside, Lib. Cong.; *New York Address: To the Republican Electors for Governor and Lieutenant Governor. . .* , [1804], broadside, N.Y. Hist. Soc.; Hartford *American Mercury*, Mar. 21, 1805.

[67] Concord *Courier of New Hampshire,* July 25, Aug. 1, Oct. 3, 1804; Boston *Columbian Centinel,* Mar. 3, 1804, Oct. 8, 1808; *Trenton Federalist,* Oct. 10, 1803; *Providence Gazette,* Oct. 29, 1808, *Newport Mercury,* Oct. 8, 1808.

[68] Concord *Courier of New Hampshire,* July 25, 1804. For similar examples see Boston *Columbian Centinel,* Sept. 5, Nov. 3, 1804.

[69] Bennington *Vermont Gazette,* Aug. 22, 1804; Walpole (N.H.) *Political Observatory,* Aug. 25, 1804.

[70] *Columbian Centinel,* Oct. 3, 1804; see also *ibid.,* Nov. 3, 1804.

[71] *Ibid.,* Sept. 3, Apr. 2, 1808.

[72] *Republican Address to the Electors of New-Hampshire, on the Choice of Electors of President and Vice-President* (Walpole, N.H., 1804), pamphlet, N.Y. Hist. Soc. This pamphlet was written in reply to [William Plumer], *An Address to the Electors of New Hampshire* [n.p., 1804], pamphlet, N.Y. Hist. Soc.

[73] *Carolina Gazette,* Aug. 12, 1808; see also Charleston *Times,* Oct. 7, 1808; *Now or Never! Disciples, Pupils, Friends of Washington,* Charleston, Oct. 14, 1806, broadside, Lib. Cong.

[74] *Independent Chronicle,* July 14, 1808.

JAMES MONROE AND THE ELECTION
OF 1808 IN VIRGINIA*

Harry Ammon

  *The election of 1808, like that of 1796, signified the end of
a political phase. Jefferson's retirement from public office meant
opening the floodgates for Presidential aspirants. Republicans
vied with Republicans—Madison, Monroe, and George Clinton
contested for the Republican caucus nomination. Federalists saw
hope in the medley of Republican rivals and tried to recoup their
losses by choosing their former candidate of 1804, Charles Cotesworth Pinckney.*

  *What in the election campaign merits attention? In the follow-
ing selection, Harry Ammon assesses the conflicting crosscurrents
in Virginia politics, clarifying the reasons Monroe's bid for the
Presidential nomination in Virginia was abortive. He finds that
Monroe's ambivalence about seeking office undercut his chances,
yet in a larger sense it was the strength of the regular party
organization which curbed the Old Republicans. Professor
Ammon, author of the definitive biography of the fifth President,*
James Monroe: The Quest for National Identity *(1971), is cur-
rently a member of the Department of History at Southern Illinois
University.*

The presidential election of 1808 ranks as one of the least familiar
elections in the history of the United States; yet, in many ways, it is
one of the most curious presidential contests of the nineteenth century.
It presented for the edification of the voters the most unusual spectacle
of George Clinton running as both vice-presidential nominee on the regular Republican ticket and as presidential candidate on his own ticket
in New York state. In Virginia two of President Jefferson's closest

* Reprinted by permission from Harry Ammon, "James Monroe and the Election of
1808 in Virginia," *William and Mary Quarterly*, 3d Ser., Vol. XX (January, 1963), pp.
33-56.

friends—James Madison and James Monroe—were offered to the voter as regular Republican candidates for the presidency. This strange state of affairs was the aftermath of the numerous factional quarrels which shook the Republican party during Jefferson's second term and which contrasted painfully with the unity and solidarity that had been in evidence prior to 1800. In New York, Pennsylvania, and Virginia the Republicans displayed a new talent for disagreeing among themselves.

Of all these factional disputes the one which most seriously disturbed the national leaders took place in Virginia. Unlike the conflicts in New York and Pennsylvania where personal ambition and the spoils of office were at stake, the dispute in Virginia involved fundamental differences. It was of little importance which faction dominated in New York or Pennsylvania, since continued support of party policies seemed assured. Such was not the case in Virginia, where the members of the opposition group were raising basic issues which threatened to split the party permanently. This conflict, which had been developing since Jefferson's first inauguration, did not reach alarming proportions until 1808, when the Virginia dissidents supported Monroe as a presidential candidate against the administration favorite. Monroe's association with the opposition presented a far more serious threat to party unity in Virginia than had John Randolph's earlier frontal onslaughts on the administration. Monroe, in contrast to Randolph, commanded a wide personal following in his home state, had a national reputation, and was considered a man of broad experience and sound judgment. Under his guidance the rather amorphous opposition threatened to develop into a full-fledged split which might open the way for a Federalist resurgence.

I

The opposition within the Virginia party which came to the surface after 1805 has been variously labeled "Quid" and "Old Republican." The latter phrase was largely preferred by the Virginia dissidents, for it emphasized their adherence to what they deemed the true principles of the party from which Jefferson had by implication departed—those formulated during the 1790's. To some degree the two terms have been used interchangeably, but to be fully accurate the term "Quid" is most properly used in connection with the hardy band of Congressmen who joined John Randolph of Roanoke in opposing Republican policies during and after the Congressional session of 1805-6. Old Republican is a much broader term, embracing not only the Quids, but all those Republicans critical of the administration.[1]

Most Virginians, including those who considered that the President had departed from strict Republican dogma, were devoted to him and could not approve of Randolph's personal rancor. Hence, John Randolph did not operate as a cohesive force among the Old Republicans. Prior to 1808 they did not form a distinct party or faction, tending instead to operate as individuals. Although there was a certain amount of understanding and contact among them, they were restrained from any effort to organize an open opposition by their fear of splitting the party and risking a Federalist victory. This, as they saw it, would be a far greater disaster than the perpetuation of erroneous doctrines within the Republican party. Prior to 1808 the Virginia critics of the administration—always excepting Randolph and the Quids—confined themselves to attempting to capture the control of the party machinery in order to ensure the nomination of a presidential candidate more favorable to their point of view.[2]

Although Randolph's eruption in Congress during the winter of 1805-6 was the first public indication of trouble within the Republican party, it was not the first intimation the national leaders had that some Virginia Republicans were complaining about laxity in applying Republican principles. Indeed, even before Jefferson's first inauguration, rumors were circulating that he had made concessions to the Federalists in order to ensure victory. These reports were given special credence in Virginia, for they were ascribed to Wilson Cary Nicholas, one of Jefferson's principal lieutenants during the election. Among those most disturbed by such reports was the influential John Taylor of Caroline, who expressed his concern to both Nicholas and Monroe. They in turn warned the President-elect that he must be cautious in his efforts to conciliate the Federalists, or many Republicans would be alienated. Jefferson, acknowledging the seriousness of Taylor's remarks and recognizing the wisdom of the advice his friends were giving, optimistically assured them that his inaugural address would dispel all apprehensions.[3] Accepting Jefferson's pledge that no commitments had been made to the Federalists, Taylor awaited measures which would positively embody the principles of the party. He fully expected the President to propose amendments to the Constitution restricting the power to borrow money and making the power to raise armies contingent upon the approval of the states. When he pressed these amendments upon Nicholas, he received what he regarded as the astonishing reply that the President had no power to make such recommendations. Taylor's reaction to this was to inform Nicholas somewhat tartly that if this were true then the only safeguard for the liberties of the people was for Jefferson to remain permanently in office.[4]

The principles which Taylor and others believed to be basic to the Republican program were given public formulation in an essay published by Edmund Pendleton in October 1801. Pendleton's distinction as an elder statesman naturally lent much weight to his statement, and, unquestionably, its publication was inspired by John Taylor, his nephew and adopted son. Significantly entitled "The Danger Not Over," the essay was not only the first but remained the only clear-cut exposition of the Old Republican program. Singling out certain defects of the Constitution, Pendleton warned that unless they were remedied the liberties of the people could never be regarded as truly secure. He proposed a series of amendments, the most important of which restricted the President to one four-year term and shortened the term of senators, who in the future should be directly elected by the people. He condemned the appointive power of the President as a source of particular danger, since it opened the way to arbitrary power through the corruption of the legislature. As a safeguard he proposed an amendment forbidding members of Congress and judges to receive appointments while in office. Finally he recommended amendments to spell out the powers of the federal government more precisely and thus eliminate once and for all the "wiles of construction."[5] In particular he stressed the need of placing limitations on the power to borrow money. Reflecting as they did the party issues and slogans which the Republicans had reiterated interminably during the 1790's, these proposals met with widespread approval and received the public endorsement of Jefferson's son-in-law, John Wayles Eppes.[6] Were these not the very proposals for which Jefferson had campaigned? The Virginia House of Delegates during the session of 1801-2 gave its approval to a list of seven amendments closely resembling those outlined by Pendleton. However, for reasons which cannot be ascertained, they were not adopted by the state Senate and hence were never submitted to Congress.[7]

During the remainder of Jefferson's first administration his critics were silenced by the success and prosperity of those years. At the earnest solicitation of Jefferson, who possibly felt that Taylor's abstract opinions might well be tempered by contact with political reality, Taylor entered the Senate in 1803.[8] Along with other Republicans in Congress, Taylor, normally a paragon of strict constructionism, discovered that his principles were sufficiently elastic to approve of the Louisiana Purchase. Fundamentally a scholar in taste and habit, Taylor did not care for the burden of legislative service and retired after serving a year. He gave tangible expression of his good will to the administration by publishing a defense of its measures with particular emphasis upon the constitutionality of the Louisiana Purchase.[9] Yet, if one accepts the testimony of two active Old Republicans, Littleton W. Tazewell of Norfolk and John Taylor, the absence of public criticism of the administration did not mean that there was no feeling of dissatisfaction. Many Virginians continued to be perturbed by Jefferson's failure to carry out a truly Republican program. Their sense of disappointment was heightened by specific policies, both foreign and domestic, upon which the Republicans embarked after 1805.[10] Affection and loyalty to Jefferson understandably led them to place the blame for the betrayal of Republican principles elsewhere, chiefly on James Madison. The malcontents regarded Madison as the evil genius of Republicanism, responsible for the introduction of Federalist principles into the Republican party (his authorship of the *Federalist* was recalled) and some even suspected him of monarchical tendencies. They blamed him for the Yazoo compromise, for the deteriorating relations with England, and, ultimately, for the Embargo, a measure most unpopular in Virginia where it had led to serious agricultural stagnation.[11] In what seems a desperate effort to shift the onus of the Yazoo settlement (which nearly all the Virginia delegation in Congress had voted against) from Madison, Thomas Ritchie, editor of the Richmond *Enquirer*, solemnly maintained that Madison had been deceived by Albert Gallatin—a suggestion hardly flattering to Madison's abilities as a statesman.[12] By mid-1806 such an effective whispering campaign was underway in Virginia that Wilson Cary Nicholas informed Madison of the rumors and urged him to do everything he could to dispel the allegation that he was tainted with Federalism.[13] The goal of the Old Republicans at this time was to secure control of the party machinery—in Virginia at least—and force the selection of a candidate other than Madison. The expectation that this could be achieved quietly and without conflict was abruptly shattered when Randolph went openly into opposition in 1806.[14]

Randolph's sudden blowup in Congress was most embarrassing to the Old Republicans, for he not only called public attention to the critics of the administration, but he was forcing the very issue they were most anxious to avoid—an open rupture with the party. The regular Republicans took immediate steps to strengthen their position, urging influential men of orthodox views to enter politics.[15] Randolph's conduct tended to place a premium on party regularity and rendered the position of those who sought to block Madison as Jefferson's successor most difficult. Any person who now criticized the administration rendered himself suspect as a member of the Randolph faction and risked the loss of all influence within the party. Old Republicans were doubly embarrassed by the fact that they fundamentally agreed with both Randolph's state rights principles and his opposition to the administration's foreign policy, yet they were unable to rally under his leadership. In deciding to let Randolph go his own way, the Old Republicans were governed primarily by two motives: their determination to reform the party from within and their unswerving loyalty to Jefferson. They could not stomach the personal rancor Randolph exhibited towards the President. To have accepted Randolph as their titular leader would have compromised the Old Republican movement beyond all recovery in Virginia. Even those who admired his oratorical abilities and his unrivaled mastery of parliamentary procedure, realized that most contemporaries looked upon Randolph as lacking in one of the most important qualifications for leadership—a sound judgment of men and events. Moreover, in spite of his prominence in Congress, he had no real following among the most influential leaders within his home state. In an age when personal contacts were of prime importance in shaping a political career, Randolph could not rely upon the support of any substantial group.

Although Randolph made the task more difficult, the Old Republicans continued their quiet operations to supplant Madison by advancing a candidate with the qualifications which Randolph so conspicuously lacked. Their choice fell upon James Monroe, who not only possessed a wide circle of friends and was well known on the national scene, but had the additional recommendations of being a Revolutionary War veteran, a founder of the party, and a close friend of Jefferson. Of Monroe's soundness of judgment and wide knowledge of public affairs his contemporaries have provided ample testimonials. Their first tentative approaches to Monroe were made in 1804; but, as befitted a loyal party member, he declined to take these suggestions seriously, pushing them aside with the observation that others had prior claims. On this matter, he informed his correspondents, he would be guided by Jefferson's preferences.[16] Undeterred, the Old Republicans continued to advocate his superiority over Madison and to urge that he be nominated. In 1807, the proposals which Monroe had so quickly dismissed three years earlier found a quite different and favorable response. His change of heart did not result from any commitment on his part to the principles of Old Republicanism, but stemmed from a breach in his personal ties with the administration.

II

In 1803 when Monroe departed on the special mission that resulted in the purchase of Louisiana, he took with him the warm wishes of Jefferson and Madison, whom he regarded as his intimate friends and devoted patrons. Yet when he returned to the United States in December 1807, this happy atmosphere had dissipated. In its stead were suspicion and distrust engendered by Monroe's conviction that he was being reduced to a subsidiary rank in the Republican hierarchy from which there would be no further advancement. Although there was never any open break between Jefferson and Monroe, their relations for some years were awkward and uneasy and without that free and frank interchange which had previously marked their association. With Madison the situation was far worse; a complete rupture took place in the spring of 1808 and lasted until the middle of 1810. During this time they neither wrote nor saw one another. Indeed, when Madison was staying with Jefferson at Monticello in the autumn of 1808 he pointedly refrained from visiting Monroe, who lived only a few miles away, and Monroe with equal emphasis avoided all contact with Monticello as long as the Madisons were there.[17]

The estrangement between Monroe and his old friends had its roots in Monroe's displeasure at having William Pinkney joined to him as co-commissioner in the treaty negotiations which Monroe had inaugurated as minister to England. Regarding this act as a reflection upon his own abilities, Monroe was all the more embittered because he had specifically requested that no one be associated with him during his mission.[18] Undoubtedly Jefferson's explanation—rendered somewhat belatedly in 1808—that he had not received Monroe's letter in time to withhold the appointment was correct, but it came too late to solace the disappointed minister.[19] Jefferson maintained that the sole motive in appointing Pinkney had been to enable Monroe to return to the United States in accordance with his own request.[20] The ill feeling which arose from this episode was partly the result of the slowness of transatlantic communication and partly from the fact that Monroe seems to have forgotten that the decision to remain abroad was his own. Certainly Jefferson would have explained the reasons for sending Pinkney much sooner had he been asked, but Monroe, although freely voicing his annoyance to some of his correspondents (among them John Randolph) said nothing to his old friend.[21] Monroe might not have been quite so concerned about the implications behind Pinkney's appointment had he not at the same time been the recipient of letters from Taylor, Randolph, and other Old Republicans warning him that there was a movement underfoot to damage his reputation among Republicans in order to enhance that of Madison and to ensure the latter's nomination.[22] While Jefferson was fully aware of the approach which was being made to Monroe, he did not know that Monroe's wounded sensibilities were making him receptive to such suggestions. Consequently when Jefferson warned Monroe about such a "so-distant" friend as Randolph, he made no reference to the Pinkney appointment. His prime concern was to caution Monroe that Randolph's views were not to be taken as those of the public, which completely endorsed the policies of the administration. He pointedly concluded by observing that all those who had Monroe's best interests at heart fully supported the administration's policies. Under the impression that Monroe was anxious to return to the United States, Jefferson offered him the governorship of Louisiana, an act which Monroe interpreted as an obvious device for relegating him to political obscurity.[23] Monroe declined the post on the grounds that his personal affairs would require his complete attention upon his return later in the year. As to his association with Randolph, he made no comment, declining to discuss these "delicate topicks" raised by Jefferson.[24]

Since he fully expected to conclude a treaty with Great Britain, Monroe repressed his resentment over Pinkney's appointment and remained in London. The treaty which was eventually concluded late in 1806 was regarded by Monroe as a fitting conclusion to his diplomatic service in England, for it would serve to preserve peace between the two nations. It is easy to imagine his dismay and indignation when the news reached him that Jefferson considered the treaty so unsatisfactory that he would not submit it to the Senate. This decision, which Jefferson regarded as a kindness since it would spare Monroe the humiliation of a rejection by the Senate, was completely misunderstood. Monroe harshly and unreasonably attributed Jefferson's rejection of his treaty to the influence of those in the party who were seeking to lower his prestige. Although Jefferson and Madison had excellent grounds for discarding the treaty—Monroe and Pinkney had specifically violated their instructions by negotiating a treaty without any provision concerning impressment—they seem to have forgotten Monroe's peculiar sensitivity to any action which questioned his integrity or his judgment. Both failed to realize that he would be deeply offended, and, consequently, they neglected to send the kind of explanations which would remove the bitterness he now felt towards his old friends.

Although Monroe rather freely expressed to his Old Republican friends his distress over the conduct of the administration, he declined to make any commitment prior to his return as to his willingness to allow his name to be placed in opposition to that of Madison. Understandably, his arrival in Virginia in December 1807 was awaited eagerly by the Old Republicans and uneasily by the party regulars. In both Norfolk and Richmond he was greeted warmly by the citizens and presented with a laudatory address by the House of Delegates. These testimonials revealed none of the party's inner tensions. Only in the Governor's Council, where a majority of the members supported Monroe, was friction apparent. Here Governor William C. Cabell refused to sign a highly complimentary address on the grounds that such actions were improper for the Council. According to Lieutenant Governor Alexander McRae, a prominent backer of Monroe, the Governor's refusal was prompted exclusively by his fear of advancing Monroe's political fortunes.[25] After lingering for ten days in Richmond, Monroe journeyed to Washington where he met with a reception which he considered unsatisfactory. It was not that Jefferson and Madison neglected any proper manifestations of friendship or confidence, but, as Monroe reported, they made no effort to seek his advice on current policy with England, a subject on which he considered himself an expert. Throughout his stay in the capital he received no indication of what his future preferment would be nor was he included in any political discussion. To the overly sensitive Monroe it seemed as if he were being deliberately excluded from the inner circle of leadership.[26] Consequently, when he returned to Virginia he made no further objections to allowing his supporters to advance his candidacy.

III

At this time Monroe formulated a precise stand regarding his nomination which he reiterated throughout the campaign. In the familiar language of politicians, he declared that he was not an active candidate and would do nothing to seek the nomination, but if he were nominated he would run and if elected he would serve.[27] With his tacit permission, his backers at once began a drive to secure his nomination, rallying not only the Old Republicans but those regular party members known to have a strong personal preference for Monroe.

The struggle over the Republican nomination was waged in two theaters—Washington and Richmond—and in neither were Monroe's friends successful. The drive in Washington failed almost at once, for too much reliance had been placed on the hope that Congressmen personally friendly to Monroe would be willing to lead a drive for his nomination. (For obvious reasons Randolph could not be used to perform this task.) A rapid survey left no doubt that the Madison forces were well organized and commanded such an overwhelming majority that any effort in behalf of Monroe was doomed.[28] This solid Congressional phalanx was shaped by Wilson Cary Nicholas and William Branch Giles, two masters of political manipulation as practiced in the gentlemanly environment of the Richmond Junto. Nicholas had been summoned to return to Congress by Jefferson in 1806 to counteract the divisive influences affecting the party in Congress.[29] Long before Monroe's arrival in Virginia, Giles and Nicholas had been patiently toiling behind the scenes to guarantee that Madison would be nominated by both the Richmond and Washington caucuses without any counternominations and thus present an outward show of party unanimity. Their original plan, which miscarried to some extent, was to hold the Washington caucus prior to that in Virginia (contrary to the usual custom) and thus make it possible for the decision reached in Washington to influence that in Virginia. Madison's backers were clearly unwilling to run the risk that an early Virginia caucus might damage his chances in Congress by endorsing Monroe.[30] This strategy had the further advantage of weakening Monroe's following in Virginia. The problem faced by Giles and Nicholas was not limited to the exclusion of Monroe; it was equally important that the supporters of Clinton should not further embarrass the party by attempting to disrupt the caucus. To ensure that only Madison's name would be brought before the caucus and that he would receive a nearly unanimous vote required careful preliminary work on the part of Madison's managers. On January 21 notices were sent to all Republican members of Congress, with the exception of the Quids, notifying them that a caucus would be held on January 23. Although a public notice was subsequently posted, it was ignored by the Quids, who later published a joint address protesting the failure of the Republican leaders to notify them.[31] When the caucus met and Giles, as prearranged, was made chairman, a motion was promptly passed providing that the balloting for a presidential candidate should proceed without placing any names in nomination. This motion enabled Madison's backers to avoid any unpleasant surprises which might be attempted by either the Monroe or the Clinton camp. Of the eighty-nine votes cast (five members abstained from voting) eighty-three were for Madison, while Clinton and Monroe each received three. Outwardly the caucus indicated a united party, but there were seventy-nine Republican members of Congress who did not attend. The absentees were largely Clintonians, who apparently abstained in order to keep Clinton on the regular ticket as vice-presidential candidate while leaving themselves free to run him independently. Before the meeting adjourned a motion was made by Nicholas to appoint a Congressional corresponding committee with one member from each state—Giles, significantly, was entrusted with the delicate task of directing the Madison forces in Virginia.[32]

The Republicans in Virginia were by no means as easily directed as those in Congress. Until mid-January, forces in the legislature remained evenly balanced, while in the Governor's Council a majority continued to favor Monroe.[33] His backers were divided into two groups—Old Republicans and personal friends and admirers. Most of the latter were willing to support him only as long as this could be done within the ranks of the party. Consequently a substantial number of his friends, such as the rising young lawyer William Wirt, regarded themselves as pledged to Monroe only until it was obvious that he would not win the nomination of the party.[34] Giles and Nicholas fully understood this division in the Monroe ranks and concentrated their efforts at this vulnerable point. Every effort was made to detach those who were supporting Monroe only for reasons of friendship and who had never been associated with the Old Republicans. The principal tactic employed was that of creating a firm impression that Madison had such powerful backing outside of Virginia that continued opposition to his candidacy would not only seriously damage Monroe's prestige but also place Virginia in the unenviable position of being the only state resisting Madison. Early in January letters were sent from Washington, some of which were printed, stressing the extent of Madison's Congressional support. These same letters asserted that Monroe's sponsors in Washington had agreed to yield Clinton first place on a joint ticket. To stir the feelings of all those passionately loyal to the President, it was alleged that Monroe was intimately allied with John Randolph.[35]

Although these letters were successful in alienating many from the Monroe campaign, they did not deter his most ardent backers, who fully intended to contest openly for his nomination in the state caucus. In view of the anticipated conflict, Madison's Virginia organizers concluded that it would be unwise to wait for the news of the Washington caucus of January 23 to arrive in Richmond before summoning the state caucus which had been scheduled for January 28. Following the Washington plan, they decided to exclude Monroe's supporters by circulating private invitations to those favorable to Madison summoning them to a caucus on January 21 at the Bell Tavern. Monroe's friends got wind of this and attempted to introduce a resolution in the legislature calling for a general caucus on the same day, but they were blocked by an adjournment. Consequently two caucuses met on January 21. One, at the Bell

Tavern, was attended by 124 regular Republicans who nominated Madison unanimously and appointed the necessary committee for the campaign. The second met at the Capitol (the usual meeting place for caucuses) and nominated Monroe by a vote of fifty-seven to ten.[36]

Surprised by the sudden maneuver to hold the caucus on January 21, Monroe's managers had no opportunity to select the members of the county committees nor to prepare a slate of electors and hence had to reassemble for this purpose several days later. These lists were improvised hastily and without the prior consent of those appointed, and in the weeks following their publication there were numerous resignations as the force of the argument of party solidarity exercised its influence. The central committee, responsible for the over-all conduct of the campaign and for the replacement of all county committee members and electors who might resign, was composed of George Hay (who became Monroe's son-in-law in September), John Clarke, Edward C. Stanard, William Robinson, and John Brockenbrough, all of whom were members of the Junto and possessed considerable influence in the state. The roster of electors contained many well-known names—Littleton W. Tazewell, Richard Brent, Creed Taylor, John Taylor of Caroline, Henry St. George Tucker, General John P. Hungerford, and Daniel Sheffey. Of these, all but the two last named were personal friends of Monroe, and only two—John Taylor and Tazewell—were identified with the Old Republicans. Sheffey and Hungerford were nominally Federalists—the only ones to be found on the list of electors.[37]

Once nominated, Monroe neither accepted nor declined, confining himself to the formula developed earlier in the year. In the face of efforts made to persuade him to withdraw, he adopted the position that the voters had the right to choose between two Republican candidates. Although he would do nothing to secure his election, he would not decline to serve if elected. This was substantially the answer Monroe made to Jefferson when the latter sadly commented: "I see with infinite regret a contest arising between yourself and another, who have been very dear to each other, and equally so to me."[38] Throughout the campaign Monroe remained in touch with the members of the central committee. He did not actively direct them, but on occasion he gave advice and undoubtedly the restraint shown by his followers in making personal attacks on Madison and in condemning the foreign policy of the administration was in conformity with his wishes.

In allowing his name to be entered in the presidential campaign, Monroe was not under any illusion that he could defeat Madison. Had he seriously believed in such an outcome, he would have launched a far more aggressive campaign and made serious attempts to reach an understanding with the Clintonians and the Federalists. No such efforts were made in either direction, although one of his more ardent supporters, Littleton Waller Tazewell, strongly urged them.[39] Monroe's objective in 1808 was to vindicate himself by demonstrating that he commanded the loyalty and confidence of a substantial number of his fellow citizens.

The campaign which began immediately after the caucuses had met was in many ways a most unusual one. Perhaps its most remarkable feature was the generosity of Thomas Ritchie, editor of the most important Republican newspaper in the state, in opening the columns of the *Enquirer* to Monroe's advocates. In an age of intense partisan journalism, such conduct was nearly unprecedented, and had it not been for him the minority element would have been without a public forum. It was not until late in the summer that Old Republicans established a paper—the *Spirit of '76* (Richmond)—edited by Edward Stanard, a member of Monroe's corresponding committee.[40] The other Republican papers in the state, and in particular the Richmond *Virginia Argus*, edited by the public printer, Samuel Pleasants, Jr., gave no space to minority views. The moribund Federalist press gave little space to politics. Ritchie's liberality at the time is especially baffling when it is contrasted with the bitter intensity with which he persecuted the Old Republicans—particularly John Taylor—after the election was over. Ritchie's conduct was prompted neither by any sympathy for the Old Republican cause, nor by affection for Monroe, but seems to have stemmed from his involvement in the obscure friction over state banking which took place in the legislature during 1805-6. Ritchie had given his support to the defeated faction and as a result was deprived of the lucrative post of public printer until 1808. Although he endorsed Madison and served on the Madison corresponding committee, Ritchie, for reasons which are far from clear, declined to close the columns of his paper to Monroe.[41]

During the first phase of the campaign, which lasted until September, the major emphasis on both sides was upon matters which were entirely peripheral. The very issues which had given rise to the Old Republican movement as well as those which had been responsible for Monroe's misunderstanding with the administration were scarcely touched upon. In particular both sides handled the whole question of foreign policy with the utmost delicacy. It is true that in April Monroe's treaty and accompanying documents were released for publication, an act which might be construed as a blow against him. However, Monroe and his backers were so confident of the correctness of his diplomacy that they looked upon the publication as a vindication. In particular the inclusion of his long letter to Madison of February 8, 1808, defending his conduct seemed to answer his critics fully. This letter had been regarded as sufficiently important by party regulars to induce Giles to attempt to exclude it from the documents which were released with the treaty.[42] Whether the publication of the treaty led to any substantial decline in Monroe's following is difficult to say.[43] Its appearance was not followed by any general discussion of its merits. Both sides throughout this phase of the campaign were obviously reluctant to place this issue in a central position.

Since the central issues were only lightly touched upon, the early phases of the campaign had a curious air of unreality. The innumerable and tedious pseudonymous writers concentrated their attention on an extensive denunciation of the way in which the Washington and Richmond caucuses had been rigged by a handful of politicians to deprive the people of a proper voice in the nominations. They argued that the caucuses had been used to lead the voters to the incorrect conclusion that Madison was the choice of the nation. Much was made of allegedly false reports emanating from Washington shortly before the state caucus met, which had created the impression that Monroe's supporters in Congress were yielding to Madison's prior claims. Naturally the rebuttals of the Madisonians occupied an even larger space.[44] There was almost no attempt to define the positions of the candidates. In March, the Monroe corresponding committee published its first address, a lengthy exposition of the arguments against the caucus and a bald assertion that Monroe was better suited for the office of the President than his rival. The Madison propagandists were as cautious as their opponents—saying little about the rejected treaty or the sins of the Old Republicans. Indeed it was obvious that both sides feared to enter the area of foreign policy. The prospect that a broadside on the Monroe treaty might unleash a counterattack on the Embargo compelled the Madisonians to be cautious.

Equal delicacy was displayed in all personal references to the candidates. Only on one occasion did the *Enquirer* print items which struck at Madison in a rather personal way. On March 18, Ritchie published two short letters, the first of which accused Madison of being a Federalist in principle and of having employed a former private secretary of Alexander Hamilton in the State Department. The second letter reminded the public that a man who had approved of the Yazoo settlement could scarcely be regarded as a true Republican. In printing these letters, Ritchie observed that they would only arouse disgust in those who read them.

During the summer, when many Virginians fled to the cool quiet of the springs, there was a relaxation in the political campaigning. Apart from endless letters defending the Embargo,[45] only one important political item made its appearance—a letter from Wilson Cary Nicholas to his constituents, which appeared late in June. This letter is of particular interest because it was the first bluntly worded denunciation of Monroe's treaty and a direct attack on his ability as a diplomat. Nicholas pointed out that Monroe had specifically violated his instructions in negotiating a treaty which had no provision on the impressment issue and that the conditions attached to the ratification of the treaty by the British government had humiliated this nation in the eyes of the world. Nicholas's lengthy and harshly worded condemnation—all the more significant because he published it without the disguise of a pseudonym—was most galling to Monroe.[46] Later in the year his anger at Nicholas was intensified when Nicholas called for the payment of money which Monroe had borrowed while in England. Monroe was convinced that this had been done deliberately in order to inconvenience him. These two circumstances produced a rupture between the two men which was never to be healed in spite of the good offices of Jefferson.[47] Less violent but equally long enduring was the personal dislike which developed between Monroe and Giles. Giles did not publish any of his attacks on Monroe, but he wrote many private letters to Monroe's influential backers criticizing in sharp terms Monroe's diplomatic career.[48]

When Nicholas's letter appeared, Monroe was absent in Kentucky, but if Nicholas anticipated that the letter would provoke the Monroe committee to act rashly, he was disappointed, for it waited to hear from Monroe before issuing a statement. In accordance with his unvarying policy throughout the campaign Monroe instructed his friends not to launch a violent counterattack, recommending instead that Nicholas's remarks be ignored except in anonymous publications.[49]

Shortly after Monroe's return from the West in September the committee issued a circular—the first since March.[50] After recapitulating the caucus issue, the address broke new ground when it informed the people of Virginia that the major objection to the election of Madison was the present state of foreign affairs, which was largely the result of his policy as Secretary of State. The committee, however, did not draw up any bill of particulars, merely pointing out that Monroe's greater experience as a diplomat made it more likely that he would be able to solve the nation's difficulties. Monroe, the committee observed, was not committed to either war or Embargo and hence was free to pursue new policies.[51] In this statement the committee implied, although most carefully avoiding categorical terms, that Monroe opposed both the Embargo and war, and that he was the advocate of an entirely different (though unstated) policy. As numerous critics pointed out, Monroe's opinions on these topics were quite unknown, for he had, as the editor of the *Argus* acidly remarked, remained "indignantly mute" since his return.[52] Apart from letters calling on Monroe and his friends to state their views on foreign policy, the address did not provoke debate on the issue itself.[53]

As the summer drew to an end the newspapers abounded with letters urging Monroe to withdraw his name in the interest of party unity, and it was to answering these appeals that the Monroe corresponding committee devoted its next and final address, which appeared in the *Spirit of '76* on October 17.[54] Once again Monroe's managers denied that there was any split in the party, insisting that they were merely exercising their rights as citizens to support the candidates whom they preferred. Independent action had been forced upon them by the maneuvering of the Madisonians who denied them an opportunity to express a preference in an open caucus. Affirming their Republicanism and denying any affiliation with the Federalists, the members of the committee pledged full support to whichever candidate should be elected. With this curious affirmation of party loyalty, the Monroe committee ceased its activities, leaving the final word to the candidate himself.

A scant two weeks before the election, Monroe finally broke his long silence by releasing to the press—with Jefferson's somewhat reluctant consent—a lengthy exchange of letters between the President and himself.[55] In this interchange, which had taken place in the spring, Monroe had defended his conduct and Jefferson had offered explanations for the supposed slights experienced by Monroe. Since neither could well admit that the other had been correct on matters of policy, the correspondence had a decidedly inconclusive atmosphere, but it was friendly in tone. The object in releasing these letters was to let the voters know that Jefferson and Monroe were still close friends, and hence a vote for Monroe was not a vote against Jefferson. Reprints were widely distributed in those counties where Monroe forces had a local organization, but they were published too late to have much effect on the campaign.[56]

What of the Federalists in this intramural struggle? Although they were naturally pleased at the sight of the conflict within the ranks of the rival party, they were in no position to derive any advantage from the situation unless one of the Republican factions should make a bid for their support. Since, as John Marshall sadly observed, the Federalists were a permanent minority in Virginia, holding less than 10 per cent of the seats in the legislature, they had no expectation that they could carry the state as a result of the Republican split.[57] Neither the representatives of Madison nor those of Monroe sought any aid from the Federalists—indeed in accordance with the custom of the day both Republican factions denounced them. The Federalists, with that lack of harmony so characteristic of the party even when it was to their advantage to remain united, were unable to agree upon a common course of action. Some, such as the wealthy Richmonder, Edward Carrington, were inclined to support Monroe, deeming him to be "less bigotted [sic] to the errors which have enthralled us to our present difficulties," although as Carrington sarcastically added, this opinion was founded entirely upon "unexplained circumstances."[58] Others preferred to endorse the national Federalist candidates, Charles Cotesworth Pinckney and Rufus King. Still a third group seems to have concluded that they might as well vote for Madison as the candidate known to be attached to the principle of a strong federal government.[59] Unable to unite in common action, the Federalists eventually held two separate conventions, one endorsing Monroe, the other, Pinckney.[60]

The Madison forces, as was to be expected, were overwhelmingly victorious with 14,665 votes for their ticket to 3,408 for the Monroe slate. The Federalists seem to have cast their votes for the Republican candidates, for Pinckney trailed far behind with only 760 votes.[61] Although the vote cast for Monroe may seem rather small, it should not be forgotten that his supporters were opposed by a powerfully organized body of regular Republicans, who brought great pressure to bear to ensure party orthodoxy. Indeed it was no mean achievement to be able to hold one-sixth of the electorate in view of the complete inactivity of Monroe and the rather desultory way in which his campaign was handled. Although he made no comment on the results, Monroe cannot have been disappointed at the showing. Assuredly he was too much of a realist to have expected to carry the state, even though some of his more sanguine followers, such as Tazewell, seem to have expected this to be possible.[62]

Once the returns were in and Madison's election was assured, the long suppressed animosities of the regular Republicans were released. The first object of their wrath was George Clinton about whom little had been said in Virginia during the campaign. It was much resented that he had run against Madison in New York, while at the same time running as vice-presidential candidate on the Madison ticket. As a result of Clinton's tactics, Madison had been deprived of part of the electoral vote of New

York. A number of local leaders in Virginia felt that the Virginia Republicans should retaliate by persuading the state's electors not to cast their vote for Clinton as Vice-President. This plot had such active backing that Wilson C. Nicholas and Giles, who were both in Washington, were called upon by Judge Spencer Roane and Philip Norborne Nicholas to prevent this awkward denouement. Giles and Nicholas dispatched letters which were to be read to the assembled electors frankly admitting that in many ways Clinton did not deserve the election. They argued, however, that unless the electors voted for Clinton as the candidate chosen by the Congressional caucus, they would merely add further discredit to the system of nomination. This plea for the preservation of the established order was sufficient to bring the electors into line. Distasteful as they found it, the electors of Virginia cast all their second ballots for Clinton. Before the electors balloted it was agreed that the doubts of the electors would never be revealed and all pledged themselves to secrecy.[63] So well kept was this pledge that not the slightest hint made its way into the press.

Although Clinton escaped the wrath of the Republicans in Virginia, not all who had opposed Madison escaped so lightly. Monroe was spared any direct reprisal, but pressure was brought upon Madison to preclude his elevation to the cabinet. Lesser figures fared worse. When the legislature assembled in December 1808, the triumphant Madison majority struck out at all those within its reach. The principal victims were two members of the Governor's Council, Alexander McRae and John Guerrant, who were removed from their posts solely because of their activities in behalf of Monroe. George Hay, federal attorney for Virginia who had served as chairman of Monroe's corresponding committee, was subjected to sharp criticism for failing to prosecute violators of the Embargo. Jefferson seems to have contemplated removing him, but he never did so. Hay, McRae, and Guerrant had given their support to Monroe out of personal preference; consequently their punishment was relatively mild, and within a few years they were restored to good standing in the ranks of the Junto.[64] Taylor and Randolph, two of the outstanding Old Republicans, were singled out for special retribution. Randolph became a constant target for the *Enquirer*, which made every effort to secure his defeat as a member of Congress, eventually succeeding in that task in 1813 when Jefferson's son-in-law, John W. Eppes, unseated him. That Randolph should have been proscribed is fully understandable, but the virulence which was displayed against John Taylor of Caroline seems quite inexplicable. Taylor had taken no active part in the campaign and was loyal to Jefferson, yet the attack on him which was launched by the

Enquirer on February 7, 1809, can only be explained on the assumption that the local leaders in Virginia feared that Taylor would now assume a more active role in directing the Old Republicans.[65]

In denouncing Taylor, Ritchie confined himself to matters which had little relation to the recent campaign. The consequences were rather embarrassing. After labeling Taylor a "weak and wavering politician" who "had not enough energy to continue in the army during the American revolution," Ritchie proceeded to expose what he considered to be the basis of Taylor's animosity towards Madison. It sprang, he maintained, from Taylor's offense at having been told that Madison had referred to him as a "wild and visionary politician," and from his resentment that Madison's Report of 1800 was more highly praised than Taylor's Resolutions of 1798. To cap his demolition of Taylor's reputation Ritchie dismissed Taylor's celebrated pamphlet attacking the Hamiltonian system as a work of "confused perplexities." One can readily imagine Ritchie's shock a few days later when he received Taylor's reply informing him that Madison was the true author of the Resolutions of 1798 for which Taylor had served solely as an agent. Equally dismaying was Taylor's enclosure of an excerpt of a letter from Madison praising the bank pamphlet in enthusiastic terms.[66] After some delay, during which he undoubtedly verified these facts, Ritchie resumed combat with a venomous attack on Taylor as a "trimmer." He disposed of Taylor's awkward revelations by remarking: "That you are not the author of the famous Resolutions of 1798, is really *'news'* to the world. I candidly confess, that it struck me as a stroke of electricity. . . . And it is thus, I exclaimed, that perish the reputations of men! What then remains to prop his tottering reputation?"[67] With this skillful evasion Ritchie closed the columns of his paper to any further discussion lest there be more unpleasant "news." On this bitter note the postcampaign reprisals ended. As the principal victim, Taylor remained outside the main stream of party politics until the 1820's when the Virginia Republicans, having espoused extreme state rights doctrines, restored him to his rank of party theorist.[68] Monroe's return to good standing was far more rapid, culminating in his appointment as Secretary of State in 1811. Yet, in spite of his rapid restoration to national prominence many Virginia leaders never fully forgave him for his departure from party regularity.

NOTES

[1] This distinction was recognized by contemporaries. See James M. Garnett to Monroe, Mar. 19, 1806, Monroe Papers, Library of Congress, Washington, D. C.

[2] As defined by John Taylor in a letter to Monroe, Oct. 26, 1810, *ibid.*

[3] John Dawson to Monroe, Feb. 23, 1801, Jefferson to Monroe, Mar. 7, 1801, Monroe Papers, New York Public Library, New York; Monroe to Jefferson, Mar. 3, 1801, Mar. 18, 1801, in Stanislaus Murray Hamilton, ed., *Writings of James Monroe* (New York, 1898-1903), III, 262-274.

[4] Taylor to Nicholas, Aug. 3, Sept. 5, 1801, Coolidge Papers, Massachusetts Historical Society, Boston.

[5] Pendleton's essay is printed in full in David John Mays, *Edmund Pendleton, 1721-1803,* II (Cambridge, Mass., 1952), 333-336.

[6] J. W. Eppes to his constituents, June 25, 1802, *Virginia Artus* (Richmond), July 3, 1802.

[7] *Journal of the House of Delegates . . . of Virginia . . . 1801* (Richmond, 1801), Jan. 26, 1802, pp. 82-83; *Virginia Argus,* Feb. 12, 1802.

[8] Taylor to Jefferson, Aug. 29, 1802, Coolidge Papers.

[9] Henry H. Simms, *Life of John Taylor of Caroline* (Richmond, 1932), 96-113.

[10] Tazewell to Monroe, Oct. 8, 1808; Taylor to Monroe, Oct. 26, 1810, Monroe Papers, Lib. Cong.

[11] John Taylor to W. C. Nicholas, May 14, June 6, 1806, Edgehill-Randolph Papers, University of Virginia, Charlottesville; W. C. Nicholas to J. Taylor, Nov. 19, 1807, Carter-Smith Papers, Univ. of Va.

[12] *Enquirer* (Richmond), Feb. 11, 1808.

[13] Wilson Cary Nicholas to Madison, July 6, 1806, Madison Papers, Lib. Cong.

[14] Tazewell to Monroe, Oct. 8, 1808, Monroe Papers, Lib. Cong.

[15] *Ibid.*; Jefferson to Nicholas, Apr. 13, 1806, in Paul L. Ford, ed., *Writings of Thomas Jefferson* (New York, 1892-99), VIII, 434-435. The attention of party leaders to the possibility of a split was also aroused by a conflict which took place within the Republican ranks in the Virginia legislature during the session of 1805-6. This factional conflict centered about the selection of state-appointed directors to the chartered banks and the efforts made to terminate the monopoly enjoyed by Richmond banking interests. Personalities rather than principles seem to have been the guiding forces. The contest also involved the choice of the governor—William C. Cabell being chosen by a narrow majority over Alexander McRae. It is true that McRae was a supporter of Monroe in 1808 (probably from motives of personal attachment), but he does not seem to have been identified with the Old Republicans at this time. What is most interesting is that neither McRae nor Cabell (who owed his election to the support of 20 Federalists) was the choice of the regular party members. The exact nature of the conflict in the legislature was not only obscure today, but even contemporary observers, such as W. A. Burwell and John Taylor, were unable to explain the issues clearly. Taylor categorically stated that it had no connection with the Old Republican movement. The whole question of the political importance of banking interests at this time in Virginia which was of great consequence seems to defy modern elucidation. See *Enquirer*, June 25, Dec. 10, 1806; Manuscript memoir of W. A. Burwell, Lib. Cong.; John Brockenbrough to Fulwar Skipwith, Dec. 10, 1805, Causten-Pickett Papers, Lib. Cong.; John Taylor to Monroe, Feb. 17, 1806, Monroe Papers, Lib. Cong.; Charles Henry Ambler, *Thomas Ritchie* (Richmond, 1913), 27-32.

[16] Samuel Tyler to Monroe, May 13, 1804, Larkin Smith to Monroe, June 7, 1805, L. W. Tazewell to Monroe, Aug. 16, 1804, Monroe Papers, N.Y. Pub. Lib.; George Joy to Madison, Jan. 20, 1808, Madison Papers; Monroe to Randolph, June 16, 1806, in Hamilton, ed., *Writings of Monroe*, IV, 466-467.

[17] Elizabeth Trist to Mary Gilmer, Sept. 1, 1808, Gilmer Papers, Univ. of Va.

[18] Monroe to Madison, Feb. 2, 1806, in Hamilton, ed., *Writings of Monroe,* IV, 400. Pinkney was appointed early in Mar. and undoubtedly before this letter was received.

[19] Jefferson to Monroe, Mar. 10, 1808, in Ford, ed., *Writings of Jefferson,* IX, 178-180; same to same, Apr. 11, 1808, Monroe Papers, Lib. Cong.

[20] Monroe made this request originally in a letter to Jefferson, Sept. 26, 1805, in Hamilton, ed., *Writings of Monroe,* IV, 334-335.

[21] To Randolph, Nov. 12, 1806, *ibid.,* 491-492.

[22] Randolph to Monroe, Mar. 20, 1806, Joseph Nicholson to Monroe, May 5, 1806, James M. Garnett to Monroe, Mar. 19, 1806, Monroe Papers, Lib. Cong.

[23] Jefferson to Monroe, May 4, 1806, in Ford, ed., *Writings of Jefferson,* VIII, 447-448. Two of Monroe's close friends, William Wirt and John Beckley, were also pressed into service to write Monroe warning him of the danger of too close an association with Randolph. Wirt to Monroe, June 10, 1806, Monroe Papers, N.Y. Pub. Lib.; Beckley to Monroe, July 13, 1806, Monroe Papers, Lib. Cong.

[24] Monroe to Jefferson, July 8, 1806, in Hamilton, ed., *Writings of Monroe,* IV, 477-478.

[25] Alexander McRae to Monroe, Dec. 22, Dec. 23, 1807, Monroe Papers, N.Y. Pub. Lib.

[26] Undated Memorandum in Monroe's hand in an account book dated 1794-1801 (Lib. Cong.) in which he reviewed the grounds of his discontent. This does not seem to have been intended for publication.

[27] Monroe to Dr. Walter Jones, Jan. 24, 1808, in Hamilton, ed., *Writings of Monroe,* V, 22-23. Monroe also contemplated a public statement of his position, and a draft declaration following the lines of his private correspondence is to be found among his papers in the Lib. Cong.

[28] John Clopton to Alexander McRae, Dec. 25, 1807, Mathew Clay to Monroe, Feb. 29, 1808, Walter Jones to Monroe, Jan. 18, 20, 1808, Monroe Papers, Lib. Cong.

[29] Jefferson to Nicholas, Apr. 13, 1806, in Ford, ed., *Writings of Jefferson,* VIII, 434-435.

[30] Memoir of W. A. Burwell, Lib. Cong.

[31] Protest of John Randolph and others, Feb. 27, 1808, printed in the *Virginia Argus,* Mar. 11, 1808.

[32] *Enquirer,* Jan. 28, 1808; Jan. 20-23, in Charles Francis Adams, ed., *Memoirs of John Quincy Adams . . . ,* I (Philadelphia, 1874), 504-506; Irving Brant, *James Madison, Secretary of State, 1800-1809* (New York, 1953), 422-429; Dice Robins Anderson, *William Branch Giles . . .* (Menasha, Wisc., 1914), 123-124; *Aurora* (Philadelphia), Jan. 26, 1808. The Clinton Delegates did not attend, although they presumably received invitations. One is strongly inclined to suspect their absence was the result of a prior agreement which enabled them to retain Clinton as the vice-presidential candidate on the Madison ticket in return for refraining from nominating Clinton in the caucus.

[33] *Proceedings of the Executive Council of Virginia, 1806-1808,* July 9, 1808, p. 150, Dec. 12, 1808, p. 261, Virginia State Library, Richmond.

[34] Wirt to Monroe, Feb. 8, 1808, Monroe Papers, Lib. Cong.; Alexander McRae to Monroe, Dec. 31, 1807, Monroe Papers, N.Y. Pub. Lib.

[35] "Powhatan," "A.B." [George Hay], *Enquirer,* Jan. 19, Feb. 23, 1808. After Monroe was nominated by his caucus in Virginia, an effort was made to persuade the Clintonians to accept the second place on his ticket, but this fell through. E. C. Stanard to Monroe, Feb. 19, 1808, Monroe Papers, N.Y. Pub. Lib.

[36] *Enquirer,* Jan. 23, 1808; "Hortensius" [probably George Hay], *ibid.,* Jan. 30, 1808. At the Madison caucus the leading roles were those of James Barbour, Robert B. Taylor, and Thomas Ritchie. Madison's corresponding committee was composed of William Foushee, Peyton Randolph, Samuel Pleasants, Thomas Ritchie, and Gervais Storrs. All could be considered party stalwarts and members of the Junto. Official notice that the caucus would be held on Jan. 28 had appeared in the *Enquirer* on Jan. 16.

[37] *Ibid.*, Jan. 26, Sept. 30, Oct. 11, Oct. 25, 1808.

[38] Jefferson to Monroe, Feb. 18, 1808, in Ford, ed., *Writings of Jefferson,* IX, 177.

[39] Tazewell to Monroe, Oct. 8, 1808, Monroe Papers, Lib. Cong.

[40] This paper survives only in incomplete files in the Lib. Cong. and the Va. State Lib. From its contents it is clear that it was established by the Old Republican element among Monroe's supporters who wanted a more forceful attack on the administration. It was not a successful journal and eventually was moved to Washington where it expired in 1811 as a Federalist organ. See John Taylor to Monroe, July 27, 1811, Monroe Papers, Lib. Cong.

[41] Ambler, *Ritchie,* 27-32; see n. 15 for additional comment on the controversy over the state banks.

[42] Mar. 25, 1808, in Adams, ed., *Memoirs of John Q. Adams,* I, 523.

[43] Monroe's backing had been weakened by the caucus decision more than anything else. It is true that three members of the Governor's Council—Alexander Stuart, William Munford, and W. W. Hening—asserted that they had supported Monroe immediately after his return but upon seeing the treaty had changed their views. *Proceedings of the Executive Council of Virginia, 1806-1808,* Dec. 12, 1808, p. 261.

[44] *Enquirer,* Mar. 18, 19, 22, Apr. 1, 26, 1808.

[45] The Embargo was widely unpopular in Virginia, where the planters blamed the low agricultural prices upon its operation. Party loyalty alone led them to sustain this measure. The editor of the *Enquirer,* who was in other ways so generous to the opposition, never carried any attacks on the Embargo. Indeed during the summer of 1808 the columns of his paper were full of elaborate defenses of this measure. This massive effort to defend the Embargo was launched by Wilson Cary Nicholas, who recognized the necessity of justifying a measure known to be so little liked. See files of the *Enquirer* and *Virginia Argus* for Mar.-Oct. 1808. Nicholas to Madison, Apr. 11, 1808, Rives Papers, Lib. Cong.

[46] Nicholas's letter, which is undated, appeared in the *Enquirer,* June 24, 1808.

[47] Monroe's reactions are to be traced in Monroe to ————[probably George Hay], July 19, 1808, Monroe to John Randolph [Dec. 1808], Monroe Papers, Lib. Cong.; Nicholas to Jefferson [ca. 1816], Edgehill-Randolph Papers, Univ. of Va.

[48] Giles to Creed Taylor, Mar. 27, 1808, Creed Taylor Papers, Univ. of Va. This particular letter was subsequently published as part of Giles's running feud with Monroe, *Enquirer,* Apr. 21, 1826; Creed Taylor to Giles, Apr. 2, 1808, Creed Taylor Papers; Notes on Mr. Giles' letter, memo in Monroe's hand, n.d., Monroe Papers, Lib. Cong.; Anderson, *Giles,* 123-125.

[49] Monroe to [George Hay], Bedford Co., July 13, 1808, Monroe to [John Taylor], July 19, 1808, in N.Y. Pub. Lib., *Bulletin,* V (New York, 1901), 371-376.

[50] Monroe to Tazewell, Sept. 25, 1808, Draft, Monroe Papers, Lib. Cong.

[51] *Enquirer,* Sept. 30, 1808, reprinted from the *Spirit of '76,* Sept. 24, 1808.

[52] Oct. 18, 1808.

[53] *Enquirer,* Oct. 7, 11, 1808.

[54] *Ibid.,* Sept. 30, 1808; *Virginia Argus,* Aug. 23, 26, 1808. None of the Richmond papers reprinted the address from the *Spirit of '76.* The above account is taken from the *American Citizen* (New York), Oct. 26, 1808, which reprinted it.

[55] *Virginia Argus,* Nov. 1, 1808, reprinted from the *Spirit of '76* in which they first appeared.

[56] *Ibid.,* Nov. 24, 1808, quoting a letter from Halifax Co.; Samuel Tyler to Monroe, Nov. 30, 1808, Monroe Papers, Lib. Cong.

[57] John Marshall to C. C. Pinckney, Richmond, Oct. 19, 1808, in Jack L. Cross, "John Marshall on the French Revolution and on American Politics," *William and Mary Quarterly,* 3d Ser., XII (1955), 648-649.

[58] To Timothy Pickering, Jan. 30, 1808, Pickering Papers, Mass. Hist. Soc.

[59] John Corbin to Madison, Oct. 29, 1808, William Pope to Madison, Oct. 31, 1808, both in Madison Papers.

[60] *Enquirer,* Oct. 4, 18, 1808; *Virginia Argus,* Oct. 18, 1808. The meeting to endorse Pinckney was held in Staunton. The Federalists in Richmond endorsed Monroe.

[61] Returns are from *Virginia Argus,* Nov. 8, 11, 15, 18, 25, 1808. Geographically the vote is not revealing. Of the 10 counties Monroe carried, five were in the Tidewater, which suffered severely from the effects of the Embargo, two in the Trans-Allegheny region, and three in northern Virginia.

[62] Tazewell to Monroe, Oct. 8, 1808, Monroe Papers, Lib. Cong.

[63] Wilson C. Nicholas to [Philip N. Nicholas], Dec. 3, 1808, P. N. Nicholas to W. C. Nicholas, Dec. 17, 1808, Nicholas Papers, Lib. Cong.; Spencer Roane to W. B. Giles, Nov. 24, 1808, Virginia Historical Society, Richmond. Roane and P. N. Nicholas (brother of Wilson C. Nicholas) were major figures in the Junto.

[64] For a full account of these reprisals see Harry Ammon, "The Richmond Junto, 1800-1824," *Virginia Magazine of History and Biography,* LXI (1953), 403-405.

[65] Taylor blamed W. C. Nicholas for the attack on him and accused Nicholas of permitting Ritchie to use their private correspondence for material for the articles denouncing Taylor. See Taylor to W. C. Nicholas, Apr. 6, June 16, 1809, Edgehill-Randolph Papers.

[66] *Enquirer,* Feb. 7, 1809; Taylor to Ritchie, Feb. 10, 1809, but not printed in the *Enquirer* until Mar. 14.

[67] *Ibid.,* Mar. 17, 1809.

[68] See Ammon, "Richmond Junto," 411-412.

Part V

PARTIES IN TRANSITION,
1816-1828

In the wake of the war years, party politics substantially changed as the constituent elements of the first party system disintegrated and political institutions themselves underwent a reformation, determined by the degree of economic and social growth. By the mid 1820's Federalist and Republican parties alike had ceased to be definable; both had lost their cohesiveness, ending their period of effective contribution to public life. In place of contending parties, firm in their ideological opposition, only fragments remained. Yet by 1824 new political combinations were arising phoenixlike out of the ashes of the old. Four years of shifting patterns followed before reintegration into new and different political entities gave substance to the emergence of the second party system. The period between 1816 and 1824, often misdesignated as the Era of Good Feelings, was a time of political erosion, of factional and aggressively personal politics, symptomatic of the inability of the earliest versions of American parties to adjust to the realities of a changing milieu. Innovations in the concept of party, largely connected with the rise of professional politicians, were being felt by the 1820's. By Jackson's first administration the shift away from the party structure and methods of the patrician period was well under way.

The four selections of readings which follow serve to illustrate major strands of party history involving the dissolution of existent parties, the rise of new leaders, and the organization of parties in the transitional period. Robert V. Remini's article accentuates the emergence of a new type of party leader, often of relatively humble origin, who was to exercise increasing influence and control of parties. In "Jackson Men with Feet of Clay," Charles Greer Sellers, Jr., turns his attention to the origins of Andrew Jackson's political career, effectively dispelling the myth of Jackson's "democratic" stance. Shaw Livermore, Jr., in *The Twilight of Federalism* has been primarily concerned with the political fate of the later Federalist Party. In the segment of his work reprinted here, he suggests that there was a marked continuity of personnel between the first and second party systems as ambitious Federalists tried to carry on their political careers within the National Republican or Democratic parties. The major objective of Richard P. McCormick in *The Second American Party System* is to examine the process of party formation in the Jacksonian era. A systematic state by state analysis—in this anthology only the case of Massachusetts has been included—shows that the new parties were largely established by self-aggrandizing politicians more preoccupied with power than ideological principles.

The decline of the first party system became obvious immediately after the War of 1812. Nominally, two parties continued to exist, yet actually the fading away of unified, politically alert, competing organizations was significant. Despite persistent attempts to invigorate their party, the Federalists were losing political strength and were effective only in scattered areas. By the election of 1816, as the veteran Federalist Gouverneur Morris pointed out, "no federal Character can run with Success."[1] In the public eye Federalists continued to be doubly suspect; they symbolized upper-class social and political rule, and they persisted in their pro-English attitudes. Increasingly they seemed to be an anachronism to an ebullient nation proud of its achievements in the war with Great Britain.

Why, then, did the party not quickly disappear from the political scene? Frequently entrenched in public positions, the Federalists did not easily abandon the field of their longtime rivals. In New England, where Republicans had not been considered respectable, Federalist strength ebbed only slowly. The local party kept control of the Massachusetts governorship until 1823 and lingered as a state organization for another two years. In Connecticut the Federalists conducted a rearguard action, losing to reformers rallying under the banner of the "Toleration" party in 1817. Outside of New England, the once-formidable Federalists retained only a portion of their former position, yet in isolated areas in Pennsylvania and New Jersey they continued to be active and occasionally victorious until the mid-1820's.

Federalists no longer were as flexible as they had been after 1800 in redirecting their party efforts, seeming unable to cope with changing political realities. As the Republican Party adopted nationalist ideas and programs, the Federalists found it increasingly difficult to remain politically distinctive in their principles and actions. On such issues as taxation, the Army, the Navy, and the National Bank, the Republicans had taken over the Federalist position, claiming it as their own. One of the most eminent Federalists, Rufus King, regarded "the practice of the Republicans . . . to be the same as that of the Federalists formerly; with this difference however, that now the measures are carried further, than the Federalists carried them; thus while things are essentially the same, names are different."[2]

In the final analysis the Federalists did not rebuild their party on a national basis despite their momentary revival in certain states during the upheaval of the war years. A rapidly altering political climate, as the nation turned away from previously significant foreign issues, undermined the Federalist position. Long-term deficiencies in political methods, as well as a generally pessimistic view of the future of American society, further contributed to the decline of the Federalist Party.

As the only national party the Republicans had a commanding position, drawing many of the politically ambitious to them; at the same time they were weakened by the absence of opposition. To the public, the Republican party was intimately identified with democratic values—a perennially useful political talisman—but the former crusading zeal of the party had irretrievably deteriorated. Stresses within the party, long a reality on both national and state levels, became more evident as the Republicans lost their vitality and innovativeness. In various states they suffered continuing internal dissension and factionalism. Pennsylvania Republicans were torn between an "Old School" faction and the new nationalists with Hamiltonian proclivities, yet those who renounced political conflict in an effort to establish a nonpartisan position were quickly isolated. In New York the fragmentation of the Republicans and the long internecine war between the personal faction of DeWitt Clinton and Van Buren's Bucktails embittered politics.

A conflict of values was all too apparent among the Republicans. With the decline of the Federalists, old antiparty attitudes found new nourishment. In the emotional climate of the "Era of Good Feelings," the dream of a nation united in its goals and free of the contentiousness of party strife seemed desirable and attainable to the older generation of leaders brought up with the eighteenth-century attitudes toward party, as well as to others satiated with interparty conflict. President Monroe gave his support to the idea of a one-party nation, firmly convinced that Federalism must be uprooted and an all-inclusive Republicanism allowed to triumph in order to maintain a free government.

As growing jealousies transcended the spirit of nationalism, the Republican Party came under new tension. Once a highly effective voice of Southern and also Northern interests, the party no longer had the commanding role, no longer spoke authoritatively for its major adherents. Continued control of national politics by the Virginia Dynasty evoked restiveness among Northern elements in 1816. By 1819 the panic and the resultant agricultural depression led to a resurgence of Old Republicanism in the upper South and to the spread of states' rights doctrines elsewhere in the South. More and more aware of its fragile position, the South realized that it "could not long survive in a majoritarian democracy that had the power of the national government at its disposal."[3] Losing their responsiveness as a party, the Republicans were adversely affected by the divisive Missouri statehood controversy of 1819-1820. As contemporaries grimly acknowledged, the issue of slavery entwined with politics was a hydra-headed monster which could only temporarily be allayed. In the view of Richard H. Brown, the crisis resulted in the forging anew of a political alliance between New York and the South by Van Buren. "It handed the keys to national party success thereafter to whatever Northern leader could surmount charges of being pro-Southern and command the necessary Northern votes to bring the party to power."[4]

With the passage of time the party leadership of Jefferson, Madison, and Gallatin had been replaced by utilitarian-minded politicians who bowed to democratic principles but worshiped in actuality party loyalty and party organization. Younger leaders basically rejected the patrician direction of party, so much the hallmark of the passing generation. Many of the new men in politics regarded the party as a unifying rather than as a divisive force in the nation. They were drawn to party organization because of its political usefulness and because it afforded them, as individuals, unusual opportunities for advancement. Success in politics was no longer a matter of family position or inherited wealth. Instead, it was dependent on incessant work, political astuteness, and dedication to the party.

A powerful organization in which the party faithful subverted their wishes to the interests of the whole and to the continuity of the party became a political imperative. Irrespective of specific members, the party had an ongoing life of its own. As Michael Wallace suggests about early nineteenth-century New York parties, "the practices that tended to preserve the party became the real 'principle' of the party for the ultimate 'principle' was self-preservation."[5] The new order took into account the need to perpetuate political opposition rather than to gain a total victory. Events in recent years had dramatically emphasized the fatal consequences of declining party competition and voter apathy. Unending contest between the elements of a party system was therefore normative and highly desirable. A central factor in the rebirth of the party system was the widespread recognition of the efficacy of the political party; still, the underground spring of antiparty attitudes continued to flow. Van

Buren reflected the changing outlook in his autobiography when he commented, "But knowing . . . that political parties are inseparable from free governments, and that in many and material respects they are highly useful to the country, I never could bring myself for party purposes to deprecate their existence."[6]

In discarding old patterns of political behavior, the new leadership was keenly aware of democratic trends and sought to build their organizations and political machines on the secure base of large popular support. Ostensibly the existent caucus method would afford the public opportunities to exert its will in the nominating process. Yet vociferous protests at its undemocratic nature and the proliferation, in some states, of independent tickets induced perceptive politicians to drop it. By the end of the 1820's the convention was becoming an effective replacement for the caucus. Control of the party, however, remained in the sure hands of a cadre of professionals who were adept at creating an aura of party democracy.

The much-heralded elections of 1824 and 1828 are too complex in the interplay of personalities and political maneuvering to be discussed at length within the scope of this essay. They are important as bell buoys to mark the shoals in the twisting channel of party development. Early in 1820, John Quincy Adams gloomily commented in his diary that the breakdown of old party lines had resulted in a continuous effort of Congress to subjugate the executive while political principles were in abeyance and personal opposition to President Monroe flourished. Symptomatic of these fragmenting party ties, the campaign of 1824, with seven Republican candidates at the outset, became a pell-mell rush for the Presidency. Each aspirant reached out for national support, muting sectional issues, while trying not to alienate his own sectional backing. The election stalemate and the choice of John Quincy Adams by the House of Representatives were indicative of the state of parties. Personal politics—Clay's accord with Adams to exert influence in the House on behalf of Adams—proved to be the determining factor in the outcome rather than party unanimity.

The dramatic events and the furor accompanying the national election merely fostered the development of the second party system. Public interest was still largely centered on state political activity; in New Hampshire, to cite a case, the gubernatorial election commanded more votes than the Presidential contest of 1824. Yet the controversy over Adams' succession to the Presidency and the "corrupt bargain" charge had the effect of turning attention to the Presidential election and party involvement in it. Among a growing number of professionally focused politicians, pressures were leading increasingly to a broadening emphasis on the party as the only viable means to achieve political objectives. The drive for political success, the search for office, the continuing challenge of rival groups, the need to tap the political support of an enlarging populace—all were factors pushing in the direction of a new form of party.

During the intense election campaign of 1828 new party formation gained momentum when disparate elements within the crumbling Republican organization combined in a series of alliances out of which the Jacksonian and National Republican parties grew. Amid discussion of restoring the Republican Party to its early Jeffersonian principles, Van Buren adroitly led the North-South entente he had engineered into the Jacksonian Presidential camp. His skillful political management added anti-Adams Republican Congressmen and even ex-Federalists to the developing Jacksonian party. At this particular state, the Jacksonians were directed by a small corps of professional politicians carefully planning a political victory under the banner of a national hero. While the Jacksonian Presidential campaign was based on the political involvement of the mass of the people, it is now very evident that it was not a democratic crusade. As Robert V. Remini indicates in his *The Election of Andrew Jackson,* "the revolution did not emanate from the people despite the powerful groundswell of popular enthusiasm for Jackson. The real revolution came from the politicians; it moved in one direction only— from the top down."[7]

By 1827 New England supporters of Adams, "administration" men in other regions, friends of Henry Clay, and the ubiquitous former Federalists were developing a coalition to reelect John Quincy Adams. Mocked at by some Jacksonians as the "Amalgamation Party," the new entity was becoming known as the National Republican Party.

The members of the emerging parties were aware of the need to establish a secure organization,working tenaciously to raise money, to build interstate party unity, and to cultivate a favorable press. While the National Republicans resolved many problems of party building, it was their rivals who, in various states, showed the superiority of their organizational talents. Recognizing the need for meticulous planning and operations in local party units, they succeeded in stirring popular enthusiasm for Jackson and converting it into party loyalty which proved to be an outstanding ingredient in the Democratic victory of 1828.

As parties broke out of the pupa stage in the late 1820's, it was evident that even though they incorporated many of the political ideas and party procedures of the past, they were new institutions. The rising generation of politicians responded to new issues by accepting the challenge of party confrontation, endeavoring to gain victory at the polls and continuity in office by developing a unique concept of a functioning party. In the process, by 1828, the new party leaders had broken largely with the traditions of the Federalist-Republican era and were moving in the direction of the modern political party.

NOTES

[1] Gouverneur Morris to Rufus King, March 15, 1816, *The Life and Correspondence of Rufus King*, Charles R. King, ed. (New York, G. P. Putnam's Sons, 1900), Vol. VI, p. 15.

[2] Rufus King to Christopher Gore, June 26, 1816, *ibid.*, p. 27.

[3] Norman Risjord, *The Old Republicans: Southern Conservatism in the Age of Jefferson* (New York and London, Columbia University Press, 1965), p. 175.

[4] Richard H. Brown, "The Missouri Crisis, Slavery, and the Politics of Jacksonianism," *South Atlantic Quarterly*, Vol. LXV (Winter, 1966), p. 58.

[5] Michael Wallace, "Changing Concepts of Party in the United States: New York, 1815-1828," *The American Historical Review*, Vol. LXXIV (December, 1968), p. 469.

[6] Martin Van Buren, *The Autobiography of Martin Van Buren*, John C. Fitzpatrick, ed. (New York, Augustus M. Kelley, 1969), p. 125.

[7] Robert V. Remini, *The Election of Andrew Jackson* (Philadelphia and New York, J. B. Lippincott Company, 1963), p. 87.

NEW YORK AND THE PRESIDENTIAL
ELECTION OF 1816*

Robert V. Remini

Politics at the conclusion of the War of 1812 were taking on a different cast with the rise to prominence of a new element—the professional politician. The advent of self-made leaders dedicated to party politics, adept at political maneuvers, and shrewd in their understanding of men, signified the passing of the era of patrician direction of party. In "New York and the Presidential Election of 1816," Robert Remini, a distinguished Jacksonian analyst, emphasizes that it was Martin Van Buren, leader of the Bucktail faction of New York's Republicans, who became kingmaker in the choice of Monroe as Presidential nominee. The election campaign, with its three-way contest between Virginia's Monroe, New York's Tompkins, and Georgia's Crawford, gave Van Buren the unique opportunity of strengthening his national stature while at the same time thwarting his arch political rival in New York. Remini indicates that, in spite of the Northern hostility to a continuation of the Virginia Dynasty, Van Buren adroitly shifted his support to Monroe while ostensibly aiding the candidacy of D. D. Tompkins. National issues were clearly subordinate to the demands of the intense conflict for control of the New York Republican Party. It was out of such manipulations that Van Buren was able to forge his party machine, the Albany Regency.

Professor Remini, former chairman of the History Department at the University of Illinois at Chicago Circle, has written, among other works, Martin Van Buren and the Making of the Democratic Party *(1959), and* The Election of Andrew Jackson *(1964).*

The election of James Monroe to the presidency in 1816, partially obscured in mystery, was actually brought about by an involved political

* Reprinted by permission of Robert V. Remini and the New York State Historical Association, Cooperstown, New York. From "New York and the Presidential Election of 1816," *New York History,* Vol. XXXI (July, 1950), pp. 308-22.

intrigue and the irresoluteness of one man. Jefferson and Madison, long accredited with having secured Monroe's election, in reality contributed less to it than the "Little Magician" from Kinderhook, New York—Martin Van Buren.

With the realization that James Madison's two terms in office as President were drawing to a close, considerable speculation developed throughout the country as to his possible successor. The Federalist party lay in ruin because of its close association with the extremists of the Hartford Convention, some of whom advocated the dissolution of the Union. Though it continued to exert tremendous influence in many States, on the national level it could not hope successfully to sustain a candidate for the presidency. Consequently the rival Republican party had merely to agree upon a single individual and the election was assured. The decision, for all practical purposes, would be made in a Congressional caucus and the voting in November would do no more than place a stamp of approval on that selection.

Believing the unbeatable Virginia-New York combination, that had chosen the Republican ticket since 1800, was still in force, Jefferson, Madison and a majority of Virginians offered their favorite son and "heir," James Monroe, the Secretary of State. Disregarding the fact that their plans meant the domination of the Union by the "Virginia Dynasty" for another two terms—bringing the total period to twenty-four years—they sincerely believed that Monroe would receive the "undivided support of the Republican party."[1] They had failed to measure the temper of the other States.

The North, during the past number of years, had grown steadily restless under Southern influence. Not since 1796 had there been a President who resided north of the Potomac. While Northerners were permitted to select the Vice-President, the very fact that they were expected to rest content with second place infuriated them. They convinced themselves, therefore, that the moment had arrived in 1816 for a reversal of policy, and no matter how "meritorious" might the past services of Monroe appear, his candidacy was unacceptable.[2]

Aaron Burr circulated the information among his friends that Monroe was "the most improper and incompetent [man] that could be selected. Naturally dull and stupid; extremely illiterate; indecisive to a degree that would be incredible to one who did not know him; pusillanimous, and, course, hypocritical. . . ."[3] The North accepted this vilification as fact, for "it seems Mr. M is unfortunately a Virginian."[4]

Considering that New England had literally cut herself off from the rest of the country by her participation in the Hartford fiasco, the choice, as far as the North was concerned, was limited to the Middle States. New York, in the past, had been rewarded for her continued loyalty to Virginia with an approving pat on the head and permission to choose the Vice-President. No longer satisfied with this, she now began beating the drums for the right to name the next executive. "Virginia has ruled long enough," was the cry continually raised.[5] Ambrose Spencer, one of the more powerful politicians in the State, wrote that "the republicans of our Legislature are unanimously opposed to another President from Virginia & have made it known to our Representative in Congress. Indeed the sentiment against Monroe is universal, & if he knew the effects his nomination would produce in this State & had any patriotism, he would decline."[6] De Witt Clinton joined the general tumult stating: "I fully agree with you that the transfer of the Executive authority from Virginia is required by every consideration of justice and policy. . . ."[7] Clinton's words gave much encouragement since he was not seeking the nomination himself. His attempt to unseat Madison in 1812 and his flagrant cavorting with Federalists during that election made his present candidacy impossible.

Instead, New York looked to her governor, Daniel D. Tompkins, to carry the party standard. Affectionately known as "The Farmer's Boy," Tompkins had risen quickly in the ranks of State politics largely through his unrivalled popularity with the electorate and the active support of Clinton. The two eventually parted, however, when the governor favored Madison's re-election in 1812. As a judge, Tompkins was "rarely incorrect" and whether his decisions were favorable to the suitor or not, they were "gratefully remembered . . . and ensured respect."[8] As governor, he had done creditable work during the war with England, despite the opposition of a Federalist Assembly and his carelessness in dispersing public funds. Dignified, tall "though somewhat inclined to corpulency," possessed with a valuable memory for names and faces, this was the man behind whom New Yorkers rallied in their quest for the presidency.

Nevertheless, there were difficulties to his candidacy, the greatest being the fact that he possessed little or no backing in the South. "I have no doubt," remarked one Congressman, "that Mr. Tompkins is a good governor. We, also, have a good governor in North Carolina, but we do not, on that account, expect you to support him for the office of president."[9] In reply, Tompkins' friends argued that neither experience nor reputation should be the sole basis in the selection of a candidate. New York was entitled to consideration for her position and power and that whomever she chose must be acceptable to the other States, whether he was known or not.

They rightfully suspected, however, that the true cause of opposition was the decision of a large segment of the West and South to elevate William H. Crawford of Georgia. Certainly the most popular man in Congress, he would more than likely be nominated in the caucus with ease, provided he permitted the use of his name.[10] He had served in the Senate and was elected president *pro tempore* of that body when the Vice-President, George Clinton, died. In 1813 Crawford became Minister to France and two years later was appointed Secretary of War. His affable manner, keen judgment and imposing presence had won the requisite following in Congress necessary to raise him to the highest rank in the nation.

With three candidates—Monroe, Tompkins and Crawford—vying with each other for the Republican nomination, the state was set for the entrance of a master politician to settle the question. That man was Martin Van Buren.

Elected a State Senator in 1812, when he arrived in Albany to take his seat in the Legislature, Van Buren was described as dressed in a "green coat, buff breeches, and white-topped boots, and, withal, bearing himself somewhat jantily, he looked much more like a sportsman than a legislator."[11] But the facade was soon pierced revealing an expert political tactician and organizer. For a short while Van Buren was one of DeWitt Clinton's ablest lieutenants. Familiarity however, led first to an estrangement and then to open warfare. As a result, Van Buren joined forces with Tompkins and assumed control of that portion of the Republican party, although ostensibly the governor was still in command.[12]

In bitter opposition to the pretensions of the Tompkins-Van Buren alliance stood Clinton and his chief advisor and relative, Ambrose Spencer. The latter was almost Van Buren's match when it came to politics. A judge of the State Supreme Court, Spencer travelled on circuit duty about the countryside and made it a point to see all the leading Republicans in the various counties. By granting appointments within his jurisdiction with a free but discriminating hand, he "exercised an almost uncontrolled influence throughout the state. . . ."[13] "With a large frame, and a commanding person, tall, straight . . . and with a countenance indicative of strong thought . . . it certainly was not a light thing to encounter his displeasure."[14] Consequently, New York was little more than a battleground upon which Van Buren and Spencer engaged in a

fierce political struggle to the death, fashioning elections and appointments as weapons to club one another into submission. They were each
aware of the enormous possibilities of the coming national election and
eagerly reached out for it as another instrument in their uncompromising
warfare.

Spencer early enlisted himself within the ranks of the supporters of
the Secretary of War, William H. Crawford.[15] In return, he expected
the federal patronage in New York to be given him to dispose of as
expediency dictated. "I am more & more convinced," he wrote, "that
we must have new hands to conduct the ship, from Commander in chief
down to the cabin boys. . . ."[16] Crawford, a realistic and practical man,
was amenable to all such demands. That accomplished, the spoils would
then be used to chasten Van Buren and bring his ascendency to a halt.

In Washington, every sign indicated that Crawford would receive the
nomination.[17] So concerned were the friends of Monroe that they
threatened to refuse a caucus nomination.[18] Van Buren knew the situation
all too well. He was repeatedly told by his adherents in Congress that
Tompkins had little or no prospects.[19] Many of those throughout the
country who opposed a Virginia President, wrote one, "acknowledge the
weight of New York and her claims to a full share of public consideration, but they also say, that the people in the different states do not know
our Candidate, that his reputation is local or at most not established as
to those qualities indispensible in our political head. . . ."[20] "Our
friends," the writer went on, "concede that it is now impossible for
Gov. T—to be elevated."

Faced with this knowledge and fearful of the consequences that would
accrue should Crawford succeed, Van Buren searched for a solution to
free himself from this predicament. If he abandoned Tompkins in favor
of another, he would lose the vote-getting power "The Farmer's Boy"
possessed in New York. Such a move would also jeopardize his own
position and require a re-orientation of his policies at home. At this stage
of the game, he could not sacrifice his standing in New York to the
interests of national politics. To remain completely aloof from the question held little attraction and would, at the same time, undoubtedly
threaten his relations with Tompkins.

But were he willing to drop the governor, Van Buren must choose
between Monroe and Crawford. The former was out of the question
because of the opposition by New York to the "Virginia Dynasty." If
Van Buren supported the latter, it required, as a preliminary step, his
submission to the stern, vindictive and arrogant Judge Spencer, who

would not hesitate to bring his political career to an abrupt end. Van Buren was, therefore, stuck with Tompkins, like it or not.

Rather dejectedly Van Buren made a trip to Washington. It was early in the Congressional session and immediately upon his arrival he was set upon by a number of New York Republicans questioning him as to the candidate they ought to support. "We say Tompkins, *of course*," was the curt reply.[21] He then quickly passed to another subject.[22] One close friend later claimed that it was Van Buren's habit to turn a discussion elsewhere when he did not wish to give an opinion.[23]

The bewildered Congressmen who heard the words but thought they understood a hidden meaning were at a loss as to their next move. Were they to begin a campaign in Crawford's favor? Monroe, they knew, was unthinkable. Certainly it would necessitate a general meeting to determine their choice. Some went to Van Buren's lodgings on repeated occasions to get his advice, only to find him out.[24] Then, before they realized it, Van Buren had gone back to New York.

The subsequent events that occurred during the next two months indicate clearly that the "Little Magician" finally found a way out of his dilemma by a daring and unique plan. Recognizing that Crawford's election would bring about Spencer's triumph in New York, and worse, his own defeat, coupled with the fact that Tompkins was now out of the picture, he decided to work secretly towards bringing about Monroe's nomination, at the same time maintaining the aspect of total allegiance to "The Farmer's Boy."

Letters from his friends at once convinced him of the necessity of coming around to this new course and the method by which its goal could be attained. Samuel R. Betts, who kept Van Buren in touch with all developments in the Capitol, wrote:

> Our delegation will meet in a day or two and decide the course we shall pursue. We shall immediately apprize you. If we are satisfied that Gov T—cannot succeed I for one shall be strongly in favor of Mr. Crawford. He will serve if elected—but he will not suffer his name to be brought forward & a canvass made upon it, unless it is certain that New York goes for him. So say all his intimate friends.
>
> I am strongly impressed with a persuasion that M—can now be opposed by no other competitor but Crawford. If we will all unite we can secure his election.
>
> Possibly, should there be no possibility of carrying Gov T—you

would prefer nominating Crawford for Pres & Gov T (if he will consent) for Vice Pres in your Legislature[25] to having it done here in Caucus. Such nominations would start the ticket with a high character.[26]

If New York openly espoused Crawford's cause in sufficient time to produce the desired effect upon the country as a whole, the nomination would assuredly be his. In view of the subsequent tremulous and vacillating conduct of Crawford and his friends, Betts was probably correct when he said the Secretary of War "will not suffer his name to be brought forward & a canvass made upon it, unless it is certain that New York goes for him." For his own self-preservation, and in order to strike at Spencer, Van Buren was required, therefore, to employ all possible effort to preclude any such maneuver from taking form and direction.

Betts proposed that the Legislature might be an excellent sounding board for the sentiments and intentions of the State. The procedure had much to recommend it and Van Buren concluded that with a variation or two of the original suggestion, it might prove highly advantageous. What, for example, would result if instead of nominating Crawford, New York should insist upon Tompkins? Betts answered with conviction.

We have never, till within a few days, been able to ascertain what course would eventually be taken by those *in the abstract* opposed to Virginia's giving us another President.

These gentlemen *profess* a great regard for Gov Tompkins and think he merits much from the country for his exertions & patriotism . . . but they also say [that he is unknown] and that if *we press him*, they shall acquiesce in the Virginia claims & make common cause against us. I know these to be the resolutions of the members from Georgia, N. Carolina, two from S. Carolina—Tennessee & a majority of those from Kentucky.[27]

Thus, according to Betts, while New York could settle the issue in Crawford's favor by nominating him at Albany, at the same time she could decide it for Monroe by pressing Tompkins. Here was a neat little plot which Van Buren doggedly followed until the election was over.

The meeting of the New York delegation at Washington, mentioned in Betts' letter, might have ruined Van Buren's plan had the members announced a preference for Crawford. But it was too early in the session for them to abandon their favorite son and after much haggling decided unanimously "to support Gov Tompkins."[28] One of their number, Jabez

Hammond, remembering Van Buren's coolness while at the Capitol, sadly remarked: "I had supposed that our true policy was to support the pretentions of Mr. Crawford in preference to Mr. Monroe. . . . The Majority of our Delegation however have determined that we are to push exclusively the nomination of Gov. T. What little I can do therefore will be in his behalf, but I am sorry to say I have very little expectation of success."[29]

Crawford then made one of the greatest mistakes in his life. Beset with doubts as to his own adequacy, of the possibility of Monroe's victory and its effect upon his future career, to say nothing of the timidity he found everywhere displayed by his supposedly ardent partisans, he unsuccessfully attempted to withdraw from the race. Foolish though it was, he authorized his close friend and advisor, Dr. W. W. Bibb, Senator from Georgia, to make his decision known. As reported in the newspapers the contest appeared to be over, but Crawford's friends swore they would never consent to it. Van Buren, in possession of the information for some time, wrote to Bibb that when "at Washington I understood from you in a manner which left no doubt on my mind of its correctness that Mr. Crawford would not be brought forward as a candidate for the Presidency . . . I had no hesitation in communicating it to my friends here. . . ."[30] This new development, because of its suddenness and possible consequences, he declared, "renders it of infinite importance that we should be correctly informed as to the views and wishes of our republican friends from the South & West."

Bibb replied that from "the commencement of the discussions concerning the presidential election I have been (as I now am) fully satisfied that Mr. Crawford is desirous not to be brought forward for the presidency. I have been (as I now am) opposed to his name being put in competition for the office."[31]

The election, therefore, might have ended in February had not a new rumor been circulated that Crawford himself did not wish the nomination under any circumstances. Bibb, feeling obliged to set the record straight, denied the accuracy of the report explaining that Crawford had merely said that he "did not think *he ought* to be included among the number of those spoken of as likely to fill the office."[32] Though their confidence was shaken, most of Crawford's friends paid no heed to the rumor and continued campaigning for him. For one thing, the New York Congressmen were expected to come to his rescue by abandoning Tompkins, since a majority of them wanted to declare for Crawford.[33] But Van Buren's plans were too well laid to go askew at this late date. He was happily informed that there was division in the ranks of the delegation, and if continued, the "probability is that Monroe must from that obtain the nomination. . . . They, some of them, declare openly that they will vote for Monroe in preference to Crawford—and yet endeavor to inculcate a belief that it is all out of regard for Gov. Tompkins. They say our State will be disgraced in giving any support to Crawford as Monroe must prevail etc etc."[34]

The time had now arrived for New York to quit its hedging about and take some stand. "If *you all* wish Mr. Crawford to be pushed," Van Buren was told, "he must be nominated at Albany. The secession in our Delegation will jeopardize—probably destroy the practicability of nominating him here."[35] With orderliness characteristic of regimentation, the Republican members of the State Legislature in Albany were now ordered to assemble and execute the will of their master. When they met on February 14, 1816, Van Buren was in complete domination.[36] Resolutions were passed instructing the New York delegation in Congress to oppose the nomination of another Virginian and recommended that they throw their entire weight to Daniel D. Tompkins.

Considering Spencer's strength in the Legislature it would have been comparatively simple to propose Crawford, had Van Buren so decreed.[37] By insisting upon Tompkins, despite the repeated warnings of his friends of the probable results, Van Buren knew that he was in fact assuring Monroe's candidacy though denouncing it at the same time.[38]

The arrival of the instructions in Washington prompted one man to comment: "If, at Albany, Mr. Van Buren was ardent in the support of Tompkins, at Washington, to say the least, he was philosophically calm and cool."[39] The delegation immediately convened to consider the resolutions. Because the members were required to support a man they knew to be unacceptable to most others, there was a good deal of discussion as to the advisability of preventing a caucus nomination altogether.[40] But this brought an impasse and the meeting was postponed for three days.

The very evening the New Yorkers met, a committee was in session, composed of Congressmen from all the States opposed to Virginia, endeavoring "to arrange some general mode of operation" to win the nomination for Crawford.[41] The Secretary of State's friends were also active. The "overwhelming influence of *patronage*" was said to be in evidence, with the object being to "decide the matter in favor of Monroe."[42]

Three days later, when the New York members of Congress reconvened, a committee was appointed

*   *   *

to ascertain the practicability of effecting a nomination of Gov. Tompkins for the Presidency. In preferring Gov. Tompkins for our candidate the delegation is unanimous—but it is not believed by any of us that his nomination can be effected at this place. If the committee should so report of which there is no doubt, a difference of opinion is known to exist in regard to the other candidates. Knowing this fact & highly appreciating the counsel of our friends at Albany as contained in their last resolution of the 14th instant it was proposed on Monday evening that in case Gov Tompkins' nomination could not be effected that we should unanimously agree to support such other candidate as a majority of our delegation should approve.[43]

Had this proposal been agreed to, the choice of the majority would have fallen to Crawford.[44] Similarly it would appear to the nation that New York was renouncing her claim to the presidency; that her support of Tompkins was merely perfunctory to be abandoned with time; that she considered Crawford and Monroe the only true candidates; and that of the two she preferred the Secretary of War. This, in turn, would automatically produce Crawford's nomination in the caucus. As one New Yorker put it: "If Gov. Tompkins & Mr. Crawford & Mr. Monroe are candidates, Col. Monroe would have more votes than either of the other gentlemen."[45] On the other hand, many of the "most informed" declared that if Tompkins withdrew and gave his support to Crawford, the combined votes would "certainly exceed those of the friends of Mr. Monroe."[46]

It was absolutely necessary, therefore, that the proposal be voted down and Tompkins kept in the race. A small band of Van Buren's friends, including Peter B. Porter, John W. Taylor and Enos T. Throop, in desperation, broke up the meeting before the resolution could be adopted.[47] The information then circulated abroad was that the delegation unanimously agreed with the resolutions from Albany to sustain Tompkins.

It is interesting to note that shortly thereafter, when Monroe was President, Peter B. Porter was appointed Commissioner of the United States under the sixth and seventh articles of the Treaty of Ghent that concluded the War of 1812, to determine the boundary from the St. Lawrence River to the Lake of the Woods. Enos Throop became a circuit court judge. Taylor, greatly disappointed at not being rewarded, complained to John Quincy Adams that he understood "as a promise from Mr. Monroe of the appointment of District Judge for the Northern District of New York" for his invaluable work.[48]

With each passing week Monroe continued to gain ground. The Legislature of Pennsylvania and a State Convention in Rhode Island came out strongly for him. Realizing that each day brought further reversals, the Crawfordites determined to call a caucus and scotch the reports that one would not be held during that session of Congress. On March 10th, an anonymous notice was published announcing a meeting to be held two days hence in the House of Representatives, at seven o'clock in the evening. Monroe's partisans, keenly aware that delay improved their candidate's position, refused to recognize the unsigned order. Nevertheless, the meeting was held, but only fifty-seven—less than half the number in Congress—were present. A postponement until March 16th was voted. A new summons, duly authorized and properly signed, was distributed. Still the Virginia men were undecided as to whether or not they should attend, because "the better opinion of the day, is that Mr. Crawford will be nominated President, by the caucus."[49]

Crawford, in the meantime, had long since agreed to put an end to the contest. It was known only by his most intimate advisors. Ever since February when he declared that he was reluctant to oppose Monroe, his friends had refused to consent to his withdrawal. Conscious that they had the strongest man in Congress as their candidate, but indecisive as to the best means of overcoming the many obstacles placed in their path, they suggested instead a scheme by which they could ride with the current of popular opinion. They refused to take "open and unqualified ground" in Crawford's behalf.[50] They played on his ego, fears and desires. "Their plan I understand to be," Crawford wrote, "to attend the caucus, and vote for Mr. Monroe and state the facts in the Intelligencer,[51] which would, as they believed, place me on higher ground than could be occupied in any other way, as I did not wish to be elected."[52] Actually he had been scared out of running, surrounded as he was by meek and timid men. He was also fearful lest his chances for nomination in 1824 be placed in jeopardy. To gracefully bow out at this point would presumably clear the way of all opponents eight years hence. And he was willing to wait.

When the second caucus met on March 16th, one hundred and eighteen Republicans appeared. Approximately twenty-four men were missing, of whom nine were absent from the city.[53] The other fifteen either objected to the method of nominating a candidate or absented themselves because Crawford would be defeated.[54] Five others refrained from attending, but were represented by proxies.

General Smith of Maryland was elected chairman and Colonel Richard M. Johnson of Kentucky appointed secretary. Futile efforts were made by John W. Taylor of New York and Henry Clay to stop the caucus, since the friends of Monroe had agreed at a meeting held a few days before, to attend the caucus but prevent a nomination.[55] Some warned that "the parties are so nearly equally divided that if Mr. M. obtains a victory . . . it will be like the Victory of Pyrrhus over the Romans—it will politically ruin him."[56] One competent observer suspected that Clay, supposedly a Crawfordite, had come to an understanding with Monroe.[57]

Tompkins, now convinced his candidacy was futile and having waited until the last possible moment, let it be known that he would accept the Vice Presidency under either candidate.[58] The New York delegation, in a complete quandary, voted as their own predilections dictated.

Within a short time after the balloting began it was obvious to everyone that something had happened. All along the line Crawford's supporters began deserting him. Taul and Barry of Kentucky, Wilson from Pennsylvania, Henderson, Thomas and Powell of Tennessee, one from North Carolina and Wilson along with "one other" from New Jersey—men "who had always declared their decided preference for Crawford, voted for Monroe. They assign as the reason that they believe their constituents wish Monroe."[59] The *Washington City Weekly Gazette* observed that a number of New York Crawford men also voted for Monroe.[60] Four other friends of the Secretary of War, including Bibb, Tait, Macon and Hall, refused to attend.[61] The total known defection amounted to thirteen. When the balloting was concluded it showed that Monroe had been nominated by the narrow margin of eleven votes. The final count was 65 to 54. Tompkins, rather handily, won the Vice Presidency over Simon Snyder of Pennsylvania.

Most of the New York Congressmen, with Tompkins eliminated, voted for Crawford, but it was too late to prove effective. Their instructions from Albany requested that they use the entire bloc of twenty-one votes against the Virginian. They cast four votes for Monroe and fourteen for Crawford, leaving a balance of ten against Virginia instead of twenty-one.

To complete Crawford's humiliation, he found that his friends failed to carry out their agreement. They had absented themselves, and many changed their votes. Nevertheless, the plan "was eventually abandoned, without any explanation ever having been given."[62] They were to have explained in the newspapers that Crawford all along "did not wish to be elected" and was not responsible for his name being brought before the caucus. But no statement was forthcoming. In despair, Crawford wrote: "I think I have serious cause of complaint against my particular friends."[63]

The Federalists went on to support Rufus King for the presidency but in the election, the following November, Monroe achieved an overwhelming victory. The electoral vote stood at 183 to 34, with King carrying but three States, Massachusetts, Connecticut and Delaware. It had not been expected to be otherwise.

Because of her preferred position, New York could have decided the election in Crawford's favor on numerous occasions. However, the consequences upon Van Buren, who controlled the State, were such as to force him to put the Secretary of War out of the running. Crawford always maintained that the presidency "was clearly in my reach if I had been ambitious of it."[64] The statement is partially correct. What he needed were real supporters who would be willing to buck Jefferson, Madison and the entire "Virginia Dynasty" in their desire to nominate him. Unfortunately, Van Buren at this time was not one of Crawford friends. Instead, he labored diligently for Monroe. And he lived to regret it.

NOTES

[1] James Barbour et al., to the Virginia Legislature, February 9, 1816, Miscellaneous Papers, New York Public Library.

[2] John Rird to James Monroe, March 12, 1816; Matthew Lyon to James Monroe, March 15, 1816, Monroe Papers, New York Public Library. John B. McMaster, A History of the People of the United States, IV, 363.

[3] Aaron Burr to Governor Joseph Alston, November 20, 1815, Matthew L. Davis, Memoirs of Aaron Burr, II, 434.

[4] John Rird to James Monroe, March 12, 1816, Monroe Papers, New York Public Library.

[5] William W. Van Ness to Rufus King, January 31, 1816, The Life and Correspondence of Rufus King, Charles R. King, ed., V, 502.

[6] Ambrose Spencer to Jacob Brown, March 2, 1816, Jacob Brown Papers, Massachusetts Historical Society.

[7] DeWitt Clinton to Jabez D. Hammond, April 19, 1816, Clinton Papers, Columbia University Library.

[8] John S. Jenkins, Lives of the Governors of New York, 164.

[9] Jabez D. Hammond, The History of Political Parties in the State of New York, I, 408.

[10] Christopher Hughes to Jonathan Russell, February 5, 1816, Miscellaneous Papers, Massachusetts Historical Society. James Barbour et al., to the Virginia Legislature, February 9, 1816, Miscellaneous Papers, New York Public Library.

[11] Jenkins, op. cit., 374.

[12] James Emott to Rufus King, December 28, 1816, King, op. cit., VI, 39.

[13] Levi Beardsley, Reminiscences, 206. William H. Seward, Autobiography of William H. Seward, 48.

[14] William Raymond, Biographical Sketches of the Distinguished Men of Columbia County, 64.

[15] De Alva S. Alexander, *A Political History of the State of New York*, I, 237.

[16] Ambrose Spencer to Jacob Brown, March 2, 1816, Brown Papers, Massachusetts Historical Society.

[17] Martin Van Buren, *Autobiography*, 122. Henry Adams, *History of the United States*, IX, 123.

[18] Christopher Hughes to Jonathan Russell, February 5, 1816, Miscellaneous Papers, Massachusetts Historical Society.

[19] Jabez D. Hammond to Van Buren, January 23, 1816; Samuel R. Betts to Van Buren, January 19, 1816, Van Buren Papers, Library of Congress.

[20] Samuel R. Betts to Van Buren, January 19, 1816, Van Buren Papers.

[21] Hammond, *op. cit.*, 411.

[22] *Ibid.*

[23] Beardsley, *op. cit.*, 306.

[24] Jabez D. Hammond to Van Buren, January 23, 1816, Van Buren Papers.

[25] State Legislature in Albany.

[26] Samuel R. Betts to Van Buren, January 19, 1816, Van Buren Papers.

[27] *Ibid.*

[28] Jabez D. Hammond to Van Buren, January 23, 1816, Van Buren Papers.

[29] *Ibid.*

[30] Van Buren to W. W. Bibb, January 29, 1816, Van Buren Papers.

[31] W. W. Bibb to Van Buren, February 5, 1816, Van Buren Papers.

[32] Christopher Hughes to Jonathan Russell, February 5, 1816, Miscellaneous Papers, Massachusetts Historical Society.

[33] Betts to Van Buren, February 5, 1816; Nathan Sanford to Van Buren, March 14, 1816, Van Buren Papers.

[34] Betts to Van Buren, February 5, 1816, Van Buren Papers.

[35] *Ibid.*

[36] John Q. Adams, *Memoirs*, C. F. Adams, ed., V, 439. Hammond. *op. cit.*, 412.

[37] *Ibid.*

[38] *Ibid.*, 411. Alexander, *op. cit.*, 240. Henry Adams, *op. cit.*, 123. Van Buren, at a later date, stated that he never understood that Tompkins expected or desired "his friends should attempt to bring him forward for the Presidency. . . ." *Autobiography*, 122. This would tend to prove that there was a plot.

[39] Hammond, *op. cit.*, 412.

[40] Betts to Van Buren, February 24, 1816, Van Buren Papers.

[41] *Ibid.*

[42] Betts to Van Buren, February 5, 1816, Van Buren papers.

[43] John W. Taylor to John Tayler, February 28, 1816, John W. Taylor Papers, New York Historical Society.

[44] Hammond, *op. cit.*, 411. Henry Adams, *op. cit.*, 123. Alexander *op. cit.*, 240.

[45] John W. Taylor to E. Cowen, March 4, 1816; John W. Taylor to John Tayler, February 28, 1816, Taylor Papers.

[46] Nathan Sanford to Van Buren, March 14, 1816, Van Buren Papers.

[47] Hammond, *op. cit.*, 409.

[48] John Quincy Adams, *op. cit.*, 440.

[49] Nathan Sanford to Van Buren, March 14, 1816, Van Buren Papers.

[50] Van Buren, *Autobiography*, 122.

[51] *National Intelligencer*, a Washington newspaper.

[52] William H. Crawford to Albert Gallatin, May 10, 1816, Gallatin Papers, New York Historical Society.

[53] *National Intelligencer*, March 18, 1816.

[54] *Niles' Weekly Register*, March 23, 1816. Betts to Van Buren, March 23, 1816, Van Buren Papers.

[55] Betts to Van Buren, March 23, 1816, Van Buren Papers.

[56] Jabez D. Hammond to Van Buren, March 10, 1816, Norcross Collection, Massachusetts Historical Society.

[57] Rufus King to C. Gore, February 16, 1817, King, *op. cit.*, VI, 56.

[58] Victory Birdseye to John W. Taylor, March 13, 1816, Taylor Papers.

[59] Betts to Van Buren, March 17, 1816, Van Buren Papers.

[60] March 16, 1816, quoted in the *Albany Advertiser*, March 27, 1816.

[61] Betts to Van Buren, March 17, 1816, Van Buren Papers.

[62] Crawford to Albert Gallatin, May 10, 1816, Gallatin Papers.

[63] *Ibid.*

[64] Crawford to Charles Tait, September 4, 1821, quoted in J. E. D. Shipp, *Giant Days or The Life and Times of William H. Crawford*, 149.

JACKSON MEN WITH

FEET OF CLAY*

Charles Grier Sellers, Jr.

The shock waves generated by Arthur M. Schlesinger, Jr.'s famous work, The Age of Jackson, have not subsided but have resulted in a continuing, intensive investigation of numerous facets of the period, greatly altering previously accepted interpretations. Charles Grier Sellers, Jr., noted as a scholar of the Jacksonian period, has critically explored the beginnings of Jackson's Presidential campaign in the provocative article which follows. Plunging into the intricacies of Tennessee politics of the early 1820's, Sellers finds, in local political controversies, an explication of the motivation of the early Jacksonian movement. Democratic ideals, high personal impulses, and friendship for Jackson fade as acceptable political motives. The general's rise to political prominence was primarily the product of efforts on the part of ambitious, conservative Tennessee politicians to use the popular hero as a means of achieving supremacy over a rival faction. The movement, once launched, quickly merged with the democratic ambitions of the populace at large to become a dynamic force in politics. Jackson, in turn, became a new political symbol to the dismay of his original backers, most of whom eventually opposed him politically.

The author of several important studies of Jacksonian politics, among them, James K. Polk, Jacksonian, 1795-1843 *(1957)*, James K. Polk, Continentalist, 1843-1846 *(1966)*, Charles Grier Sellers, Jr., is a professor of history at the University of California at Berkeley.

The contagious enthusiasm for General Andrew Jackson that in 1824 swept thousands of voters for the first time out of their accustomed tutelage to the established leaders demands careful study as a major

* Reprinted by permission from Charles G. Sellers, "Jackson Men with Feet of Clay," *American Historical Review, Vol. LXII (April, 1957), pp. 537-51.*

phenomenon in the history of political democracy. It demands study also as an example of the frequently neglected influence of local political maneuvers on national developments. Though a few historians have intimated that Old Hickory's popularity could not have been converted into an electoral plurality without the aid of disgruntled politicians pursuing conventional factional and personal advantages in the various states,[1] little attention has been paid to the Tennessee politicians who brought him before the country in the first place.

The accepted interpretation assumes that the men behind Jackson's candidacy—principally Judge John Overton, Senator John H. Eaton, Felix Grundy, and Major William B. Lewis—were moved by sincere admiration and affection for their friend. They are also credited with a shrewd perception that the ground swell of democratic discontent building up beneath the surface of American politics might be mobilized to make the popular general President.[2] A close scrutiny of the events of 1821-1823 in Tennessee reveals, however, that the objectives of Judge Overton and most of his associates were by no means so large and disinterested. There is evidence to show that Jackson was nominated for the presidency only in order that specific local political advantages could be achieved and that "the original Jackson men" actually favored other nominees.

When General Jackson retired to private life in the winter of 1821-1822, seven years had elapsed since his victory over the British at New Orleans had made him a national hero. The sporadic talk that he might be a presidential possibility had never been entertained seriously in any responsible quarter, and Jackson himself had never taken it seriously. President-making was still left exclusively to the political leaders, and they were already grooming more than enough entries for the presidential sweepstakes of 1824. Already in the field, or soon to be there, were the major contenders: President Monroe's Secretary of State, John Quincy Adams of Massachusetts; the Secretary of the Treasury, William H. Crawford of Georgia; the Secretary of War, John C. Calhoun of South Carolina; and the Speaker of the national House of Representatives, Henry Clay of Kentucky. Among the long shots being mentioned were Congressman William Lowndes of South Carolina, soon to be removed by death, and Governor DeWitt Clinton, leader of the opposition to Martin Van Buren's pro-Crawford Bucktail faction in New York.

Jackson's attitude toward these candidates was dictated mainly by personal considerations. Grateful to Adams and Calhoun for their defense of his violent incursion into Spanish Florida in 1818, he was hostile to Crawford and Clay, whose friends had attacked the Florida expedition in Congress. Crawford was slated by the old-line Republican leaders to receive the nomination of the regular congressional caucus, but Jackson declared that he "would support the Devil first."[3] The Georgian had earlier impugned some of Jackson's Indian treaties, and he was being supported by the general's personal and political enemies in Tennessee.

The exigencies of factional politics largely controlled the attitudes of Tennesseans generally toward the presidential candidates. Overton, Eaton, and Lewis were associated with a faction that had dominated Tennessee for most of its history. Founded by William Blount, the architect of a fabulous land speculation involving most of the acreage in the state, this faction had been concerned primarily with making good its land claims and later with exploiting the possibilities of the banking business. Jackson had worked with this loosely knit group in his early days of political activity, and he was still personally intimate with Overton, now its unofficial leader, Eaton, Lewis, and their principal allies in East Tennessee, Overton's brother-in-law, Hugh Lawson White, and Pleasant M. Miller, a son-in-law of William Blount.

John Sevier had led the opposition to the Blount-Overton faction in the state's first years; more recently his mantle had fallen on a group of vigorous men who were all deadly personal enemies of Andrew Jackson. They included Senator John Williams and several congressmen, while their principal strategist was a Middle Tennessee planter and land speculator, Colonel Andrew Erwin, with whom Jackson was, in 1822, engaged in a bitter litigation that brought Erwin to the brink of financial ruin.[4]

Since Erwin and his friends were solidly in the Crawford camp, the Blount-Overton men were certain to be anti-Crawford, and Jackson undoubtedly hoped to line them up behind Adams or Calhoun. This hope was threatened, however, when Henry Clay entered the presidential competition as the first western candidate in the history of the office, attracting strong support that cut across factional lines in Tennessee. Judge Overton had visited Clay in the summer of 1821, and as soon as the Kentuckian became a candidate, the judge promised him Tennessee's electoral votes. Clay got additional support from another important Tennessee politician, Felix Grundy, who a decade before had worked closely with him as one of the congressional War Hawks in precipitating the War of 1812. Grundy, like Overton, had been in communication with Clay during 1821, urging him to become a candidate and assuring him of Tennessee's support. Still another Clay backer was Governor William Carroll.[5]

Overton, Grundy, and Carroll spanned the political spectrum in Tennessee, and a union of their followers for the Kentuckian would have ensured his success in the state. Overton and his faction had been in eclipse since the Panic of 1819, which had generated a storm of public resentment against the banks they operated. Grundy, the only important Tennessee politician not identified with either major faction, had shrewdly capitalized on this popular discontent to become the dominant figure in the legislature, while veering back and forth between the two factions. Carroll was the ultimate beneficiary of the panic-generated discontent. Running as the Erwin faction's candidate for governor in 1821, he won a smashing victory over the Blount-Overton candidate. It was, in fact, the Overton men's desperate efforts to regain their ascendancy that led to Jackson's nomination for President.

The accounts left by Major Lewis and Judge Overton both indicate that the movement to nominate Jackson developed in the winter of 1821-1822, hard on the heels of Carroll's election. According to Lewis, the general's friends around Nashville "began now to speak of him as a candidate and, in *good earnest*, to take the necessary steps to place his name prominently before the country." The first public manifestation of the movement, Lewis continues, was an article in one of the Nashville newspapers in January, 1822, and soon afterward the Nashville *Gazette*, organ of the Blount-Overton faction, "took the field openly and boldly for the General."[6]

Overton's account is similar, but he claims credit for originating the movement. Early in 1822, says the judge, "it forcibly struck me that he [Jackson] ought to be the next President and by proper means might be made so." Overton goes on to recall that he had "praises thrown out" in the Nashville *Gazette*. "They were lightly thought of," he says, "but that made no difference with me."[7]

Contemporary evidence makes it clear, however, that Overton was not the first to envision Jackson as a presidential candidate. Indeed, even after the Jackson talk had started, the judge preferred another. In a letter of January 16, 1822, he assured Clay that "as far as I know the public mind, you will get all the votes in Tennessee in preference to any man whose name has been mentioned." Though Overton reported "some whispering conversation here that Jackson would suffer himself to be run," he was "almost certain that he will not, and my information is derived from good authority." The judge added that Jackson could probably "beat you himself" in Tennessee, but that the general could not induce the voters to prefer Adams or Calhoun over Clay. Overton particularly requested Clay to keep his remarks confidential. "Inasmuch as I, and our family have always been friendly with Jackson," he wrote,

"I should not like him to know of any interposition of mine on this subject."[8]

The apparent conflicts in the foregoing evidence are not irreconcilable. It would seem that the Jackson-for-President talk actually started with a group of politically ineffectual men around the general, most notably Major Lewis, that Overton was converted to the idea shortly after he wrote to Clay, and that Overton then instructed the *Gazette's* editor to launch the public campaign. If things happened this way, Overton's claim that he initiated the movement is essentially valid, since without his support it would never have gotten beyond the stage of talk. At any rate, the movement was certainly being pushed "in *good earnest*" by February, when Jackson's wife complained that "Major Eaton, General Carroll, the Doctor and even the Parson and I can't tell how many others—all of his friends who come here—talk everlastingly about his being President."[9]

Why did Overton throw his great influence behind the Jackson movement? Much of the answer to this question may be found in a letter he received about the time he must have been making his decision. On January 27, Pleasant M. Miller of Knoxville, leader of the Blount-Overton forces in the lower house of the legislature, wrote to the judge suggesting that Jackson should be run for governor in 1823.[10] Though Miller's epistolary style was highly ambiguous, the most casual reader could hardly miss his reiterated suggestions that Jackson's popularity might be used to effect certain local political objectives. Overton would have had no trouble understanding Miller's intimations that Governor Carroll, whose overwhelming strength was the chief obstacle to a Blount-Overton comeback, might thus be defeated at the state elections of 1823, that a new legislature purged of Jackson's enemies from the Erwin-Carroll faction might be elected at the same time, and that the various legislative purposes of the Blount-Overton men might thus be achieved.[11]

A single paragraph of Miller's long letter will sufficiently suggest its tone:

> 1st is there any man whose personal popularity is so likely to assist in fixing the seat of government permanently at any given point as Andrew Jackson, if so why should he not be the next governor, or why should this not be wish[ed] for by those who desire this result. I am satisfied that this cannot be done with the present legislature.

*   *   *

A more reliable legislature could be elected along with Jackson in 1823, Miller was suggesting. Even in Bedford County, Andrew Erwin's stronghold, Miller was confident the Jackson question would be potent enough to ensure the right kind of representation. In addition, Senator John Williams, whose term was expiring, could be replaced by a reliable Blount-Overton man. Miller had himself in mind for this position, as subsequently appeared.

At the time Miller wrote, there was talk of calling a special session of the legislature to meet during the summer. This legislature, having been elected along with Carroll the previous year, was untrustworthy from the Blount-Overton point of view. Hence Miller was anxious to prevent a special session, or if it were called, to keep it from acting on the matters he mentioned.

Miller had got wind of the talk about running Jackson for President, and he was by no means opposed to the idea, his comments implying that the general had no chance to be elected, but that his candidacy might yield certain collateral advantages. Miller was reported to favor Adams for the presidency about this time,[12] and though his meaning is obscure, his letter of January 27 seems to suggest that Tennessee and other southern states cooperate with the smaller northeastern states in electing the New England candidate. Jackson's nomination would actually help Adams in the electoral college by depriving Crawford and Clay of votes from Tennessee, Alabama, Mississippi, and Louisiana, in most of which the New Englander had no chance anyhow. Crawford's defeat would aid in prostrating the Erwin-Carroll faction in Tennessee. Miller knew that Grundy "has different views at the called session," which doubtless meant a plan to nominate Clay. But, he told Overton, "I know that if you fall in with my notions that you will know how to act." He particularly urged the judge to "take time to consider of these matters so far as they concern our local affairs & ascertain how far certain persons will act on them," and concluded by promising to visit Nashville in March, when "we can converse more freely."

Overton's desertion of Clay and endorsement of the Jackson movement was substantially a fulfillment of Miller's hope that the judge would "fall in with my notions." The project of running Jackson for governor was found impracticable, but his nomination for President was to serve the same purposes. Although it was Miller who actually conceived the essential strategy first, Overton was doubtless responsible for abandoning the plan to run Jackson for governor and concentrating on his presidential candidacy. Early in the spring, Miller made his promised trip west to concert strategy with Overton. The special session had now been called for July, and it was agreed that this body should nominate Tennessee's hero formally.

Miller's subsequent letters to Overton throw further light on the motives of Jackson's two principal managers. "I have Jackson's interest deeply at heart," he wrote on June 8.[13] "I think I know how bringing him forward is to operate upon the next congressional election &c. &c. I should not have went to the west when I did but with this view, & I think the effects of my visit will shew itself in some shape." The time had come, he thought, "for the papers to come directly forward" and call on the legislature to nominate Jackson at the special session. "Tell Jackson to come up Wednesday of the first week while people are all in a good humour—ask his friends to see him," Miller advised. "He can say he feels proud he has once returned to private life. If he has any redgmental coat were it, put on little milletary dress &c. You know more I need say no more."

Miller did not hesitate to admit that "I have motives for this matter." Jackson's nomination was the best way of frustrating Senator Williams' plan to win reelection at the special session. "There ought not to be an election for Senator at this time," Miller insisted, "—these good people must be held in check & this is all the hold we have—in a state of excitement publick opinion will keep them down unless that election is over." Should Williams be reelected, he predicted, there would be "a prodigious struggle" to realign Tennessee's congressional districts so as to favor Erwinite congressmen who "will in caucus vote for you knowho [Crawford]. I believe however I understand this matter tolerable well & expect to frustrate these views," Miller continued. "If I fail it will be the first time[.] keep your eye on [the] fidler & work even a head & let me alone for the rest." Almost parenthetically he reported talk that "I am a candidate for the Senate, & that my visit to the west was to promote that view."

Several weeks later, Miller wrote again,[14] in terms indicating that he and Overton were working closely together toward mutually agreeable objectives. "I have rec[eive]d your two letters," he told the judge, "& things will be attended to to your satisfaction in part or in whole. I am using all my exertions to bring old hickory to view during the approaching session."

Meanwhile Overton and Miller had acquired an important recruit. Felix Grundy had become estranged from the Erwin-Carroll men and, in danger of political isolation, was ready to jump aboard any band wagon that happened along. The Jackson movement offered him a perfect opportunity to reinstate himself in the good graces of the Blount-Overton faction, and he did not hesitate. It was Grundy who on June 27 signed the note asking Jackson whether he had any objection to the proposed nomination.[15] Jackson seems not to have replied, but silence was as good as open assent.

The last possible obstacle removed, Overton, Miller, and Grundy now made their final preparations, and the Nashville newspapers endorsed the plan for a legislative nomination. State pride kept even the Erwin-Carroll men from opposing Jackson publicly,[16] though the editorial of endorsement in their organ, the Nashville *Clarion*, had a sarcastic ring. When the special session assembled on July 22, Miller was able to push his nominating resolutions through the lower house promptly, though the Erwin-Carroll men delayed action in the senate for two weeks.[17]

The reactions to Jackson's nomination by well-informed politicians outside the circle of Jackson managers were significant. All the comments that have been discovered agree in predicting that Jackson would not remain in the race as a serious contender. A month before the nomination, one of Governor Carroll's associates, Colonel Andrew Hynes, had informed Clay that Jackson had no hope of being elected and that he was being brought forward "not so much with view of promoting his own elevation, as to subserve an Eastern or Northern interest."[18] The same explanation was advanced as late as the summer of 1823 by that astute politician, Thomas Hart Benton, following a two-month tour of Tennessee in the interest of Clay. "Jackson out of the way the state will go for you," Benton told the Kentuckian, "and there is hardly anyone who thinks he has any chance, and many see in his offering nothing but a diversion in favor of Adams."[19]

During the special session of 1822, Colonel Hynes discovered an additional explanation for the nomination. According to a "secret rumor that is afloat in the air," he informed Clay, Jackson's nomination was designed mainly to affect the senatorial election.[20] This was corroborated by a Colonel McClung, one of the leading citizens of Knoxville, who asserted that Pleasant Miller had "played off his manouvre to bring Jacksons name to bear, & make a point in the election of Senator." McClung was confident that Williams would be reelected by the special session despite the Jackson movement and that "so soon as the election of Senator is over, we shall hear no more of a Tenn. candidate for the office of President."[21] McClung's judgment was wrong, for Miller's strategy succeeded in blocking Williams' reelection at the special session, and the senatorial election was postponed to the regular session of 1823.

Meanwhile, Governor Carroll was spreading reports that Jackson would probably not remain long in the running and telling Clay that he still had a good chance for Tennessee. The governor also informed the Kentuckian that Grundy had promised to support him "if the prospects of Jackson became hopeless . . . and that he would indeavour to have you nominated at the next meeting of our legislature."[22] About the same time, Colonel Hynes was in New Orleans assuring the Louisiana politicians that Tennessee would ultimately go for Clay.[23]

Skepticism about the seriousness of Jackson's candidacy was also expressed by one of his sincere admirers. "Whatever may be the estimate in which he is held by the people of this State (and surely even here he is very differently estimated)," wrote Thomas Claiborne to a friend in Virginia, "I confess that I fear he will not be likely to unite sufficient strength in other States to secure his election. There are too many great men in other States to suffer a man from the young & small State of Tennessee at the present day to be made President of the United States."[24]

Whatever their ultimate purposes or expectations, Miller and his allies did everything they could to raise a Jackson excitement in the state campaign of 1823. Meetings to endorse Jackson were organized all over the state; pro-Jackson candidates for Congress and the legislature were put up in most districts; office seekers were called upon to say whether they would vote against Williams for senator and for Jackson in the presidential election; and an unsuccessful effort was made to induce Jackson to aid his supporters by touring East Tennessee.[25]

One of the hottest contests was in the Knoxville district, home of Williams, Miller, and Judge Hugh Lawson White, where Miller had entered a Doctor Wiatt as the pro-Jackson candidate for the legislature against the senator's brother, Thomas L. Williams.[26] This placed Judge White in a particularly embarrassing position. One of Jackson's oldest friends, a brother-in-law of Overton, and long a leader of the Blount-Overton faction, White was also related to Senator Williams and reluctant to oppose him. When he took the Williams' side in the Knoxville legislative campaign, he and his sons became involved in such a bitter personal broil with the Miller-Wiatt party that several duels were barely averted.

"If Genl Jackson has any wishes or prospects of success, I never was more disposed to aid him than now," White explained to Overton; "but I will not, as far as I can prevent it, permit scoundrels by the use of his name, to effect their dishonest or dishonorable purposes." White never doubted that Miller's senatorial aspirations lay at the root of the Jackson-for-President movement. "The whole cry is that Jackson must be President," he complained. "They have no more notion of trying to make him President than of making me. If he had a wish that way, and there was any prospect of success no three persons in this State would aid him more zealously than me and my sons; but I will not consent that scoundrels under a pretense of that kind shall rule, or tyrannize, over me and mine."[27] Recalling these events later, White maintained that Wiatt was in reality for Clay, while Miller wished "to use the name of Gen. Jackson, only for the purpose of securing the election of Mr. Adams, by dividing the western vote."[28]

When the state election finally occurred in August, 1823, the results were inconclusive. The Williamses defeated Miller's pro-Jackson candidate for the legislature in the Knoxville district, but Andrew Erwin lost to a pro-Jackson candidate for Congress, and a pro-Jackson legislator was elected in Erwin's bailiwick, Bedford County.

Meanwhile there had been two important new developments. First, an astonishing and unprecedented upsurge of grass roots support for Jackson had manifested itself in various places outside Tennessee. A veritable "contagion" of Jacksonism was spreading over Alabama, as an alarmed Clay backer had to admit, and it rapidly attained sufficient proportions to block the expected election of a Crawford man as United States senator.[29] Major Lewis had been sounding out North Carolina and Mississippi politicians with surprisingly gratifying results.[30] Most startling of all was the outburst of Jackson sentiment in Pennsylvania, stemming, as one of Calhoun's lieutenants sneered, from "the grog shop politicians of the villages & the rabble of Philadelphia & Pittsburgh."[31] But contempt quickly turned into intense concern when the swelling Jackson enthusiasm prevented the anticipated nomination of Calhoun by the state Republican convention in March.[32] Major Lewis was virtually the only member of Jackson's inner circle who seems to have anticipated anything like this. As early as October, 1822, he had predicted that Jackson's popularity with the masses would give him such states as Pennsylvania and North Carolina, that Calhoun would be forced to withdraw, and that Jackson would fall heir to the South Carolinian's following.[33] At the time it was written, Lewis' estimate had been the wildest optimism, but by the summer of 1823 it was a sober statement of a reality that was daily becoming more apparent.

Simultaneously with these surprising indications of his national strength, Jackson began demonstrating a disturbing independence of the Blount-Overton faction on state issues. Entering Tennessee politics many years before under the aegis of William Blount, Jackson had joined the Blount men in land and mercantile speculations based on paper credit and political power. But his business ventures had ended in a bankruptcy that cured him of all sympathies for the speculative system. He was outraged, therefore, when Grundy, Overton, and Miller induced the special session of 1822 to pack the state supreme court with judges who would overturn an earlier ruling adverse to the land speculators and to pass a punitive law aimed at Patrick H. Darby, a self-educated attorney who had been bringing suit against the speculators' doubtful titles. When Darby established a newspaper in self-defense and announced for the legislature against Grundy from the Nashville district, Jackson upheld him warmly, which "put Judge Overton in a great state of fretfulness" and produced a perceptible coolness with Grundy.[34]

Banking was an even more important issue than land speculation in 1823. The banks, which were controlled by Blount-Overton men, had not paid specie on their notes for four years, and the new legislature would finally decide their fate. Here too Jackson's views were inimical to his managers, and he egged Darby on to expose the fraudulent misuse of federal pension funds by the Overton ally who headed one of the principal banks. Jackson was telling all who would listen, in fact, that he opposed all banks on principle.[35]

Thus by the time the new legislature met in 1823, Jackson's conservative managers were in a dilemma. Their candidate had begun to display his dangerous tendencies just at the moment when he unexpectedly became a major contender. Most mortifying of all, they had initiated the whole business. But Jackson's candidacy might still be killed. John Williams' reelection to the Senate would indicate that Jackson did not control his own state and keep worried politicians in states like Pennsylvania from jumping aboard the Jackson band wagon. Even Tennessee might be held for Clay after all.

The crucial importance of the Tennessee senatorial election was appreciated far beyond the borders of the state. Senator Ninian Edwards came down from Illinois to represent Calhoun's interests, while Thomas Hart Benton of Missouri spent several months in Tennessee on a similar mission for Clay.[36] When the legislature assembled at Murfreesborough in September, the little village was crowded with "extra members," who had flocked in from every part of the state to influence the legislators in the senatorial election. Judge White had come from Knoxville to "spread himself against Jackson,"[37] and was frequently seen with Senator Williams "in deep consultation on the woodpiles about the square."[38] The pro-Jackson delegation on hand to ensure Williams' downfall included Senator Eaton, Major Lewis, Thomas Claiborne, fresh from his defeat for the legislature on the anti-Grundy ticket, and Sam Houston, the dashing young lawyer who had just won a seat in Congress as Jackson's protégé.

During the preceding weeks, John Williams had been touring the state to line up his supporters, and despite Miller's active campaign the senator reached Murfreesborough with the assurance of a comfortable majority over the announced opposition. Much of his advantage arose from the fact that Miller was not the only politician hoping to ride into the Senate on Jackson's coattails. William G. Blount, son of the great speculator and a former congressman from East Tennessee, threatened to enter the race, while Jackson's old crony, the veteran East Tennessee politician, John Rhea, had actually abandoned his seat in Congress to offer as a candidate. Neither Miller nor Rhea would withdraw, and the Jackson men were forced into desperate efforts to stave off the election until they could unite on one of their two candidates. The least division would ensure the election of Jackson's notorious enemy and almost certainly destroy his presidential prospects.[39]

There is strong evidence that Overton and Grundy were now working for just this result, with the important assistance of Judge White. Since January, Senator Williams had been writing familiarly to Overton about his chances,[40] and now Thomas L. Williams implored Overton to come to Murfreesborough and help his brother. "As the friends of our opponents assemble to influence members and to promote the views of their favourite I think ours should be permitted an equal liberty," he wrote, betraying not the slightest doubt of Overton's sympathy. "Will you come up next week."[41]

Grundy, meanwhile, was leading the fight to bring on the election at once. "His vote had been firmly fixed from shortly after his arrival here," a newspaper reported him as saying in debate; "previous to that time a difficulty had existed with him on the subject which but one man [John Williams] could remove; and he now could say that the difficulty had been removed fully and satisfactorily, and he was now ready to give his vote."[42] This was merely part of a concerted effort to convince members that Williams was not unfriendly to Jackson and would not oppose his presidential aspirations. Simultaneously, Grundy introduced resolutions instructing Tennessee's senators to do their best to prevent the congressional nominating caucus. All of this convinced Jackson's friends that Grundy was leading the Williams forces and had introduced his caucus resolutions to obviate the most serious objection to Williams, the expectation that he would attend the caucus and help nominate Crawford.[43]

The suspicious Jackson men now sent a delegation to question Williams on his attitude toward the general, and when he equivocated, they dispatched a messenger urging Jackson to hasten to Murfreesborough and save the situation. Jackson refused to come, but he did insist on Williams' defeat and denounced Grundy and the other "schemers of the opposition."[44] By this time, as Governor Carroll reported to Clay, the situation was extremely "strange and uncertain."[45] When it became clear that Miller had too many personal enemies to overcome the well-organized Williams forces, the Jackson men persuaded the general to endorse Rhea, but even this left them three votes short of a majority. Jackson again refused to come personally to their aid, and the election could be staved off no longer.

Finally, in desperation, Eaton and Lewis had Jackson's name placed before the legislature as Williams' competitor for the Senate. When the messenger bearing this news reached the Hermitage, Jackson mounted up and left posthaste for Murfreesborough, arriving in the middle of the night preceding the election. Even with Jackson as a candidate and present at the election, Williams was beaten and Jackson elected senator by a vote of only thirty-five to twenty-five.

In Washington the following winter, Senator Jackson charmed friend and foe alike. Pennsylvania soon endorsed Tennessee's hero, most of Calhoun's support shifted to Jackson when the South Carolinian was forced to withdraw, and everywhere the popular enthusiasm for Old Hickory mounted.

Though Grundy, Overton, Miller, and White now joined Lewis and Eaton in the five-year campaign that carried Jackson into the White House, their situation was ironical. A movement started by obscure Tennessee politicians for their own local purposes had unexpectedly been caught up by a deep ground swell of democratic aspiration. The original Jackson promoters found themselves uncomfortably astride a whirlwind of their own devising.

None of these conservative men were fundamentally sympathetic to Jackson's social philosophy, as it began to manifest itself in the 1820's or as it was implemented in the 1830's. Old Hickory was hardly inaugurated before Miller went into opposition. Overton and Eaton evidenced their discomfort by trying to block Van Buren's vice presidential nomination in 1832. Overton died shortly afterward, while Eaton opposed the Jackson party covertly in 1836 and openly in 1840. Major Lewis dissembled from about 1833 on, professing friendship to Jackson but actually aiding his enemies. Judge White ran for President against the Jackson party's candidate in 1836. Only the adaptable Grundy, acutely sensitive to Old Hickory's popularity, managed to remain loyal until his death in 1840.

Since the foregoing account depends at some points on inference from rather ambiguous documents, it has been necessary to present much of the evidence in relatively raw form. This evidence each reader may evaluate for himself; but to the writer the following conclusions are clearly indicated:

1. Major Lewis and a few other politically inconsequential personal friends were the first Tennesseans to think seriously of making Jackson President, and these men could never have initiated the Jackson movement by themselves.

2. Jackson's nomination by the Tennessee legislature in 1822 was the work of Pleasant M. Miller, John Overton, and Felix Grundy, none of whom preferred Jackson personally and none of whom thought he had a chance to be elected, or even to be a major contender. Miller seems to have favored John Quincy Adams, while Overton and Grundy hoped ultimately to carry Tennessee for Henry Clay.

3. The primary motive of these "original Jackson men" was to use Jackson's popularity to achieve certain local political advantages. Miller, who apparently sold this strategy to Overton in January, 1822, was particularly motivated by a desire to succeed John Williams in the United States Senate.

4. Overton and Grundy, surprised by the ground swell of Jackson sentiment outside Tennessee and dismayed by Jackson's increasingly manifest social philosophy, sought to kill his presidential candidacy by securing John Williams' reelection to the Senate in 1823.

American history is full of ironies, but surely few are more striking than the situation of these conservative Tennesseans as they unwittingly launched the movement that carried popular democracy to victory in national politics. The episode in itself is hardly more than a fascinating footnote to the Jackson story, yet for historians it is significantly representative. Scholarly indifference to the local and particular ends that are often the springs of political behavior has shrouded much of our political history in a pervasive unreality. The Jackson movement originated in a curious amalgam of local machinations by obscure politicians and of broad national developments. The political system thus imposed on the country has continued to rest on just such an amalgam. We shall never understand that system and its history adequately so long as able scholars confine themselves to congressional and cabinet level materials, while regarding investigations at the base of political life as work for inferior talents.

NOTES

[1] See especially Philip S. Klein, *Pennsylvania Politics 1817-1832: A Game without Rules* (Philadelphia, 1940), pp. 117-24.

[2] Cf. James Parton, *Life of Andrew Jackson* (New York, 1861), III, 11-23; John Spencer Bassett, *The Life of Andrew Jackson* (New York, 1911), I, 326-29; Marquis James, *The Life of Andrew Jackson* (Indianapolis, 1938), pp. 335-53.

[3] Jackson to James Gadsden, Dec. 6, 1821, draft copy, Andrew Jackson Papers, Library of Congress.

[4] Charles G. Sellers, Jr., "Banking and Politics in Jackson's Tennessee, 1817-1827," *Mississippi Valley Historical Review*, XLI (June, 1954).

[5] Overton to Clay, Jan. 16, 1822, Henry Clay Papers, Library of Congress; Nashville *Constitutional Advocate*, Sept. 17, 1822.

[6] Lewis to Gov. Lewis Cass, undated letter, probably written in the 1840's, in the Henry L. Huntington Library.

[7] Overton to his nephew, Feb. 23, 1824, quoted in a sketch of Overton by Judge John M. Lea, a newspaper clipping in the Overton Papers on microfilm at the Joint University Library, Nashville. In the letter, Overton dates these events in early 1821, but this is an obvious slip, since he speaks of them as immediately preceding the legislature's nomination of Jackson, which did not occur until 1822.

[8] Overton to Clay, Jan. 16, 1822, Clay Papers.

[9] Augustus C. Buell, *History of Andrew Jackson: Pioneer, Patriot, Soldier, Politician, President* (New York, 1904), II, 157-58.

[10] Miller to Overton, Jan. 27, 1822, John Overton Papers, Claybrooke Collection, Tennessee Historical Society, Nashville.

[11] Among the issues to which Miller alluded were the location of the state capital and a proposed penitentiary, land legislation in which the speculators were vitally interested, and revision of the state judiciary. The judicial question was related to the land issue, the state supreme court having recently made a ruling disastrous to the speculators, and Overton was anxious to return to the supreme bench for the purpose of rectifying matters (see Patrick H. Darby to Jackson, July 4, 1821, Jackson Papers).

[12] Statement of Hugh Lawson White, in the Nashville *Union*, Sept. 25, 1835.

[13] Miller to Overton, June 8, 1822, Overton Papers.

[14] Miller to Overton, June 25, 1822, *ibid.*

[15] Grundy to Jackson, June 27, 1822, Jackson Papers. Grundy was probably enlisted during Miller's visit to Nashville in the spring. Miller had even foreseen Grundy's cooperation, having informed Overton in his letter of January 27 that Grundy had "abandoned the head of the department at Nashville [Govenor Carroll] & said that he would stick to me."

[16] Andrew Hynes (an associate of Carroll) to Henry Clay, June 30, 1822, Clay Papers; James, *Jackson*, p. 351.

[17] James, *Jackson*, pp. 352-53. Though inaccurate in details, Overton's account, cited in fn. 7 above, illuminates the roles of the principals. "The Legislature met," says the judge, "and then I communicated to a leading member my views which he gave into, communicated them to Grundy, who at first seemed a little surprised, but gave into the measure of recommending him by our Legislature which was done unanimously. The resolutions were preceded by a speech which I wrote for a member." Most of these negotiations took place, as we have seen, some time before the legislature met. The "leading member" was unquestionably Miller.

[18] Hynes to Clay, June 30, 1822, Clay Papers.

[19] Benton to Clay, July 23, 1823, *ibid.*

[20] Hynes to Clay, July 31, 1822, *ibid.*

[21] McClung's remarks were reported by one of Clay's correspondents, George C. Thompson, Thompson to Clay, Aug. 12, 1822, *ibid.*

[22] Carroll to Clay, Feb. 1, 1823, *ibid.*

²³ *Ibid.;* Isaac L. Baker to Jackson, Mar. 3, 1823, Jackson Papers.

²⁴ Claiborne to David Campbell, Sept. 9, 1822, David Campbell Papers, Duke University Library.

²⁵ Samuel Martin to Jackson, June 17, 1823, Jackson Papers; John Williams to Rufus King, Nov. 19, 1823, Rufus King Papers, New York Historical Society; James Campbell, to David Campbell, Apr. 3, 1823 [misplaced 1825], Campbell Papers.

²⁶ J. G. M. Ramsey to Francis P. Blair, Oct. 5, 1835, Blair-Lee Papers, Princeton University Library.

²⁷ White to Overton, Jan. 30, 1823, Overton Papers. White expressed similar sentiments in a letter to David Campbell, June 19, 1823, in the Campbell Papers.

²⁸ Quoted in the Nashville *Union,* Sept. 25, 1835.

²⁹ James, *Jackson,* p. 370; Charles R. King, ed, *The Life and Correspondence of Rufus King* . . . (New York, 1900), VI, 494.

³⁰ Albert Ray Newsome, *The Presidential Election of 1824 in North Carolina, James Sprunt Studies in History and Political Science,* XXXIII, No. 1 (Chapel Hill, 1939), 90-91; Lewis to George Poindexter, Oct. 10, 1822, J. F. H. Claiborne Papers, Mississippi Dept. of Archives and History (copy furnished the writer by Dr. Edwin Miles).

³¹ George McDuffie to Charles Fisher, Jan. 13, 1823, Charles Fisher Papers, Southern Historical Collection, University of North Carolina Library.

³² James, *Jackson,* p. 370.

³³ Lewis to George Poindexter, Oct. 10, 1822, Claiborne Papers.

³⁴ John Spencer Bassett, ed., *Correspondence of Andrew Jackson* (Washington, D. C., 1926-1935), III, 194.

³⁵ Sellers, *loc. cit.*

³⁶ Elihu B. Washburne, ed., *The Edwards Papers* (Chicago, 1884), p. 207; John Williams to Rufus King, Nov. 19, 1823, King Papers; Benton to Clay, July 23, 1823, Clay Papers; Jackson to [Eaton?], Oct. 4, 1823, draft copy, Jackson Papers.

³⁷ J. G. M. Ramsey to F. P. Blair, Oct. 5, 1835, Blair-Lee Papers.

³⁸ Nashville *Union,* Sept. 22, 1836.

³⁹ John Rhea to Jackson, June 18, 1823, Jackson Papers; R. G. Dunlap to Jackson, July 2, 1823, *ibid.;* John Williams to Rufus King, Nov. 19, 1823, King Papers; *Correspondence of Andrew Jackson,* III, 201n.; Tenn. *House Journal* 1823, pp. 20, 76-77; Tenn. *Senate Journal* 1823, pp. 29-30, 37, 59-60.

⁴⁰ John Williams to Overton, Jan. 14, 1823, Overton Papers.

⁴¹ Thomas L. Williams to Overton, Sept. 20, 1823, *ibid.*

⁴² Nashville *Whig,* Sept. 22, 1823.

⁴³ William Brady and Thomas Williamson to Jackson, Sept. 20, 1823, Jackson Papers.

⁴⁴ Jackson [to William Brady and Thomas Williamson], Sept. 27, 1823, draft copy, *ibid.;* Nashville *Union,* Sept. 22, 1836.

⁴⁵ Carroll to Clay, Oct. 1, 1823, Clay Papers.

AMALGAMATION FOR DEFEAT*

Shaw Livermore, Jr.

Often ignored by historians, often overshadowed by the emergence of the Jacksonians, the Federalist Party in its last years has remained in obscurity. What became of the old party leadership and organization during the period when the National Republicans and the Jacksonian Democrats were congealing as the elements of a new party system? Shaw Livermore, Jr., finds, as a result of his investigation, that the Federalists did not disappear into oblivion after the War of 1812 but were integral to the political process until the election of Jackson. Livermore's chapter, "Amalgamation for Defeat," from his extensive study, Twilight of Federalism, The Disintegration of the Federalist Party, 1815-1830, *concerns the denouement of the fragmenting party in the late 1820's. Alternately wooed and rejected by both the National Republicans and the Democrats, the Federalists were numerous enough to command respect, yet continued to be feared because of their aristocratic tendencies. For some Federalists "amalgamation" with the Republicans was the only solution; for others, perhaps more clairvoyant, fusion with the Democrats offered hope for future political preferment. The end result, however, was the inevitable extinction of the Federalist Party.*

Shaw Livermore, Jr., of the University of Michigan, has made the history of the Federalist Party in the early nineteenth century a major area for his research.

Federalists flowed freely into both presidential camps after 1824. Although the process varied in the several states, one characteristic stood out: The Adams Republicans tended to treat the Federalists as a bloc, whereas the Jacksonians tended to recruit them on an individual basis. Amalgamation, therefore, was a phenomenon associated with the Administration. Instead of being a mixture of the parties, amalgamation

---

* Reprinted by permission of Princeton University Press. "Amalgamation for Defeat," in Shaw Livermore, Jr., *The Twilight of Federalism: The Disintegration of the Federalist Party, 1815-1830* (Copyright © 1962 by Princeton University Press), pp. 223-41.

was really an alliance system. Being such, the Adams cause was made peculiarly vulnerable to Jacksonian charges of bargain and corruption (ironically, the "arrangements" Adams made with Clay and Webster before the election helped on the one hand to create the psychological "fix" that helped to determine the bloc approach and, on the other, to lend credence to the later Jacksonian charges that Adams was bargaining with Federalists). Reaction to this Jacksonian attack led the Administration to "pull back" at crucial times when an appointment or other action might have cemented an effective and vigorous alliance. The debilitating effects of indecision and confusion were but compounded by the suspicion that naturally arose within the ranks of Adams Republicans and friendly Federalists. Jacksonian leaders, ever alert and intelligent, fed upon the spoilage.

The state of New Hampshire was rocked by collisions between Federalists and Republicans in the late 1820's. The first moves toward amalgamation had floundered because of the way Jeremiah Mason and his friends had tried to win a Senate seat in 1824 and 1825. Tensions within the Republican party, however, caused two candidates, David Morril and Benjamin Pierce, to run in the gubernatorial race of 1826. Federalists, thus put in a decisive role, generally supported Morril on the ground that Pierce was backed by Isaac Hill, the *enfant terrible* of New Hampshire Republicanism.[1] Hill's constant concerns were the purity of his party and the fear of resurgent Federalism. A Crawford man in 1824 but soon for Jackson, he kept his *Patriot* bubbling with hatred of Federalists and emotional defenses of the caucus system, which he insisted was the only means of preserving Republican ideals. At the same time, Hill tried to control the formal party machinery in the state by encouraging his friends to dominate local caucus meetings.

Filial devotion intensified Daniel Webster's constant interest in New Hampshire politics. During long and earnest conversations with Senator Samuel Bell, a leading Adams Republican, Webster decried the caucus and held out the promise of a strong Adams party based solidly upon a majority of both Republican and Federalist voters. If Bell and his friends refused to break with Hill and the Caucus, Webster argued, the New Hampshire Federalists would not sit by quietly. Instead, they would take the lead in calling meetings of "all persons" friendly to the Administration, thereby leaving Bell's friends the unhappy choice of following the Federalists or joining Hill in opposition.[2] Since one-third of the legislature was Federalist in 1827 and an undoubted majority of New Hampshire citizens preferred Adams, the force of Webster's logic was compelling. Still, Bell was reluctant. The threat of Hill's fury hung like a pall.

The stage was thus set for the extraordinary events during and preceding the legislative session that began in June of 1827. Troubled by Webster's appraisal, Bell had returned from Washington, only to be swept into a meeting called by the "Republican friends of the Administration." The purpose of the meeting was to express approval of Adams' policies in the form of resolutions that would later be introduced in the legislature. One speaker in effect apologized for Rufus King's appointment, and another damned the Jacksonian tactics in other states of tantalizing undecided Federalists with Jackson's friendly advice to Monroe while assuring Republican friends that no danger would flow "from the fraternal embrace of the former rival political parties." The object of all the speakers, Webster's brother charged, "was to prove Mr. Adams to be a democrat, & his administration to be strictly democratic, & more purely & entirely so, than Mr. Munroe's or Mr. Madison's or even Mr. Jefferson's. They vindicated him from the charge of being a federalist, or inclining to favor the Federalists. *This was the substance of their story.*"[3]

New Hampshire's Federalists were furious. To a man, Federalists in the legislature voted for postponement of the resolutions, and they were, of course, joined by the Jackson Republicans. As his brother had instructed him, Ezekiel Webster rose to explain his action. "Let the cause of the Administration be supported," he bristled, "on just and liberal principles; not proscribing men by classes, not for past political opinions, honestly formed, independently expressed, and honorably throughout maintained—or let it not be supported at all."[4] News went out over the country that the New Hampshire legislature had snubbed the Administration by a resounding vote of 137-70. The effect, both public and private, of these proceedings was devastating. Senator Bell and Ezekiel Webster parted "under a good deal of excitement" after a heated meeting, and Levi Woodbury, a leading Jacksonian, observed happily that the stinging defeat had disclosed "a firmness & independence among us."[5] The ardently amalgamationist *Portsmouth Journal* tried desperately but vainly to repair the grievous damage.[6] Though angered, Daniel Webster kept at his friend Bell. If the Adams Republicans would not call a meeting of all friends of the Administration, Webster assured Bell that the Federalists would oppose every one of their candidates at the spring election in 1828.[7] Webster's words, alternately threatening and soothing, had their effect. Caught in a withering cross fire between Federalists on one side and the rampant Hill on the other, a group of Portsmouth Republicans finally issued a call of "all friends" to meet in December of 1827.[8]

This meeting marked the beginning of a slow and halting course of cooperation, made more painful by Hill's scathing editorials and the implacable insistence of the Jacksonians that the Republican party must stay pure. The Portsmouth meeting was followed by a "mixed" state convention which nominated a slate of state senators and put Senator Bell's brother at the head of their ticket. The Federalists had agreed not to put forward any of their men for these nominations, but they did so with the understanding they would be rewarded in the near future. Although the state senatorial slate generally succeeded, Bell lost. The *Portsmouth Journal* explained that the incumbent had only been in office a year and had not openly declared for Jackson. Added to this, the *Journal* confessed, were "some little remains of the old political prejudice against Mr. Bell because he was once a federalist."[9] By the fall elections in 1828 the Adams forces were acting in comparative harmony, but they had lost ruinously in numbers. The Jackson legions, working confidently and decisively since the debacle a year and a half earlier, succeeded in breaking off great chunks of the overwhelming New Hampshire support Adams had enjoyed when he was elected.

The amalgamation forces in Massachusetts enjoyed happier days. Governor Lincoln was re-elected in 1826 over a feeble opposition candidate put up by disgruntled Federalists, but the alliance was still shaky, and many waited eagerly for its proprietors to stumble. The rise in 1827 of small and ephemeral parties based on local issues had allowed bitter-end Federalists again to harass the amalgamationists. A confusing melange of tickets kept Boston from sending its full allotment of representatives to the General Court. Webster promptly denounced the Federalist obstruction as "folly," and "insanity," and in two major speeches pounded away at his central theme that all men of good will must stand together against the unsavory, slave-ridden Jacksonians.[10] Because the Bay State still backed Adams solidly, the Republican-controlled legislature later that year elected Webster, its second choice, to the U. S. Senate. Governor Lincoln was obviously the favorite, but he had declined to be a candidate.[11] No one else approached Webster as a talented and effective champion of the Administration. Only Adams' intervening election could have prompted Republicans, fresh from hard-fought victories in 1823 and 1824, to send Daniel Webster to the Senate in 1827.

For the masses of Massachusetts Republicans who supported Adams, however, the course of events after 1825 was deeply disquieting. They knew that the Federalists were gradually slipping back into power, yet they could find no way to curb them. The files of staunch Republican presses like the *Boston Patriot* and the *Springfield Republican* abounded with signs of this frustration. The *Republican* editor, Samuel Bowles, had dedicated himself in 1824 to maintaining pure Republicanism, which naturally included regular attacks on the Hartford Convention and the "aristocracy of wealth." A firm Adams supporter, he tried in succeeding years to fight both amalgamation and Federalism, in spite of his acknowledgment that most Massachusetts Federalists stood behind Adams. Gradually Bowles shifted his main battery fire away from Federalists in order to combat the onrushing Jacksonians.[12] He had been caught in the same dilemma as those Federalist editors who, while supporting Monroe, had tried to rouse Federalists to independent action on the state level. An influential Republican relayed to Henry Clay in 1827 the general anxiety of his colleagues. "I have felt," he fretted, "that a bad policy has been pursued in relation to our own State, most certainly one that has effectually displaced the old Republicans and given the power into hands, that may not abuse it, but not as reliable, as I could wish—I urged upon Mr. Webster's friends the impolicy of placing him in the Senate—I had various reasons for it, but the one most operative with me was, that he was too strong a man to be made too Independent. . . . It was moreover too soon to commit so great a violence upon the old Republican feelings of the State—I hope however that he may be faithful—I hope to acquire more confidence in him hereafter."[13] The God-like Daniel left in his powerful wake a sea filled with drifting men, depressed by suspicion and distrust.

The amalgamation movement in Massachusetts reached a zenith in 1828. Webster was advised by the *Boston Patriot* editor in March that a large meeting of local Republicans had unanimously agreed to act with Federalists in the presidential election. "*From your exertions last year,*" the editor cooed, "*we think we shall reap a full harvest this.*"[14] A month later, a prominent Boston Federalist assured Webster: "The Union Administration Cause here can boast of an organization equal in efficiency and unanimity to that of the good old days of 1814-16."[15] At an harmonious convention called in June to choose Adams electors, a central committee was formed, which included the names of Henry Shaw, Timothy Fuller, and Joseph Sprague, all prominent Republicans, and Leverett Saltonstall, Abbott Lawrence, and John Winthrop, each a notable Federalist.[16]

There remained a group of Federalists who could not tolerate Adams the apostate. They gathered at the Exchange Coffee House in Boston to appeal to those brethren who had supported Crawford in 1824 and who had not since succumbed to the blandishments of amalgamation. Theodore Lyman, Jr., in the chair, the assemblage listened to perfervid speeches by Francis Baylies and Lemuel Williams.[17] The latter confided to his friend Vergil Maxcy that afterwards most fellow lawyers would barely speak to him in court.[18] Undaunted by meager success in the spring elections, this coterie began publication, with Lyman as editor, of an attractive newspaper, blithely styled the *Boston Jackson Republican*. It competed with the *Boston Statesman*, chief organ of the little band of Boston Republicans who had steadily supported Jackson. David Henshaw, leader of the Jackson Republicans, took a dim view of his new Federalist allies, and suggested that they had not come out openly until certain that Jackson would win the national election. Henshaw hoped they would stir up resentment in Federalist circles, but he intended to have nothing to do with them.[19] The two groups squabbled constantly during the campaign, each suspecting, with some justification, that patronage was the chief incentive for the other's activities. Lyman and Henshaw both openly thirsted for the collectorship of customs at Boston.

Although amalgamation did not develop as early in Connecticut, the pattern was similar. An ardent Jackson Republican, Gideon Welles, reported in June 1827: "A dish of amalgamation is ere long to be served up here as in Massachusetts and New Hampshire."[20] Connecticut Federalists, not blessed with a dominant leader like Webster, had wallowed in hesitation and conflicting advice from old captains. Most came to favor Adams though few sincerely admired him. A substantial number, including the most prominent, continued to despise the President. These men made common cause with Andrew Jackson.[21]

Republicans in the state, still nursing bitter memories of the 1817 election, tried manfully to keep the party together. Animosities stemming from differing presidential choices, however, together with long-standing jealousies within the party, led to an open rift in 1828. The naming of two slates of presidential electors, both entirely Republican, opened the way for Federalists to press amalgamation. A disgusted Jacksonian charged: "The Federalists altho innately divided in sentiment on the presidential question will yet act together with a view to overthrow our Republican ranks. Alone they expect nothing under the national government. To divide & overthrow the republicans in the State is their whole object with us."[22] Jackson Republicans were well aware that Connecticut would go to Adams by a wide margin. Their hope lay in the prospect that Jackson would win nationally, in which case they would make it easy for the Hero "to distinguish between his friends & enemies in this State." Yet the desire to attract a respectable vote for Jackson led a surprising number of fervent Republican supporters to recommend in the last months of the campaign that their friends avoid unduly affronting Federalists in election addresses and newspaper broadsides.[23] The breakup of the Republican party in Connecticut had cast up rich provender for Federalists.

In other New England states too, amalgamation was among the chief topics of political controversy. Many of the Republican leaders in Maine who had supported Crawford in 1824 soon swung over to Jackson. In spite of taunts from Adams men that these former Crawfordites had once tried to get Federalist support, the Jackson campaign was skillfully managed. Amalgamation was cut apart by tireless appeals to old Republican sympathies.[24] During an Adams convention in February 1828, one participant observed with pride and evident relief that although several Federalists had attended, all the committees were wholly Republican. This fact, he suggested, "should effectively silence the clamor, that it was a federal convention."[25] Such language was a tribute to the effectiveness of Jacksonians in a state that had backed Adams generously in 1824. A limited suffrage and a deep interest in manufactures led to successful amalgamation in Rhode Island, though again there was a hard core of Federalists which stood behind Jackson. Because Vermont Federalists had ceased for many years to act as a body, amalgamation there was a relatively minor issue.

Federalists and the image of Federalism greatly complicated the efforts of New York state voters to adjust to emerging national alignments. The twisting course of state politics after 1824, when a substantial majority of the electorate favored Adams over Jackson, led New York to give a majority of its electoral vote to the Hero in 1828. A variety of favorable circumstances in 1824-25 had pointed to the building of a powerful Adams party, firmly grounded in New York Republicanism. Among these were the strong sectional preference for a Northern man, the interest of New York in a high tariff policy, and the triumph of Adams Republicans over the Van Buren-Crawford faction in the 1824 electoral battle. The force of these factors, nevertheless, was blunted by the maladroitness of the Adams Administration, the skillful maneuvering of the Red Fox, Van Buren, and—not least—the actions of New York Federalists.

Adams and his advisers could not make up their minds what group in New York state should receive the Administration's blessings. By first offering the English diplomatic mission to Clinton, it appeared that Adams intended to make the Clintonians his chief support. This view was quickly dispelled when, after Clinton's refusal, the mission was given to Rufus King, an anti-Clinton Federalist. The appointment of another "High-Minder," John Duer, to a high position seemed to confirm the feeling that the Administration specially favored this coterie, articulate but few in numbers, which revolved around Charles King and his *New York American*. Such a policy, though foolish, would have had at least the virtue of consistency, but other major appointments went in turn to Clinton Republicans and Van Buren Bucktails. The possible advantage from these moves was, of course, largely destroyed by the total effect of a frantic scramble for votes from any quarter. This bungling was bad enough, but the one group that believed itself most entitled to executive favor, those Republicans who opposed *both* Clinton and Van Buren and who had carried the day in November 1824, received little encouragement from Washington.

Frequent pleas for aid by this last group were shunted aside in favor of various schemes to placate other factions. "Those Republicans who seceded from the Party—& won the Electors in this State," James Tallmadge complained in 1826, "now find themselves opposed by Clintonians—unsupported by the Crawford men & unacknowledged by the Genl Administration."[26] Clintonians openly scoffed at Tallmadge and his friends for having been let down by Adams, and Bucktails condemned them as renegades from the Republican party. Other Adams men deeply resented the Administration's continued flirtations with Clintonians. One termed this policy "a most fatal error," and the discontent grew worse when in the spring of 1826 Van Buren and Clinton entered into an "intimate negotiation leading towards an anti-Adams coalition."[27] Clinton's increasingly open support for Jackson was painful to those of his followers who preferred Adams, but the Administration offered these men no clearly defined and rewarding alternative.

Martin Van Buren was firmly convinced by the spring of 1825 that he must lead his Bucktail forces from support of Crawford to Jackson. He was equally aware, however, that an abrupt shift to the Hero in the face of general satisfaction with Adams' election and Jackson's poor showing in New York during the 1824 campaign would be disastrous.[28] Accordingly, the Red Fox first set out to intimidate and harass the Adams Republicans. He sidled up to Clinton, his ancient enemy, with the purpose of confusing his Republican opponents and possibly laying the base for a strong Jackson coalition. Then, in a startling *volte-face*, Van Buren suddenly threw his full support behind an Adams Republican who opposed Clinton in the 1826 gubernatorial election. The object was to split sharply those Republicans who approved of the Administration but who disagreed violently about Clinton's merits. Not until the summer of 1827 did Van Buren feel strong enough to come out for Jackson openly. By appealing directly to Republican voters on the ground that Adams was the Federalist candidate, he further demoralized and weakened the Adams Republicans.[29] Their hopes of attracting Republican votes thus dimmed, the Adams forces began to listen to those Federalists who had offered their services to the Administration cause. The curse of amalgamation settled more firmly upon the Empire State.

A numerous body of New York Federalists, however, either supported Jackson openly or took no part for either candidate. The merchant community of New York City was nearly united in clamoring against Adams' tariff policy, and William Coleman's *Post* burnished rusting memories of John Quincy Adams' apostasy and his father's perfidy toward New York's adopted son, Alexander Hamilton. Jackson's advice to Monroe was not forgotten, nor were the many Federalists who had already gained prestige by following the Hero.[30] Of particular importance to the many Federalists who had become deeply attached to him was DeWitt Clinton's belief that his own fortunes would best be served by a Jackson victory. When Clinton stood behind one Enos Throop, for a vacant U. S. Senate seat in 1827, an Adams Republican bridled: "We cannot support our Clintonian Jacksonian candidate for the Senate. *We* prefer even a bucktail Jacksonian to a federal. Throop, you are aware I presume, is an old federalist, and then Clintonian, and his transition to Jacksonianism is natural and *necessary*."[31]

Clinton died before the 1828 election, which left many of his followers floundering about, though the intense loyalty Clinton inspired apparently caused many to do as "the great man" would have wished. More Clinton Federalists would probably have formed behind Adams if some of the "High-Minders," especially Charles King and other writers for the *New York American*, had relented in their abuse of Clinton.[32] Even among the "High-Minders," however, there was a schism as James Hamilton and Josiah Hoffman led a strong minority in support for Jackson.[33] A New York Federalist had to weigh many competing hates and desires in making his presidential choice. Many could make no firm judgment and remained aloof.

If Administration leaders were muddle-headed in directing New York affairs they were downright stupid in Pennsylvania, where sectional and economic factors (especially the tariff and internal improvements issues) were as favorable as in New York. Instead of forthrightly making every effort to built a strong organization rooted in Republican soil, letting Federalists come along if they wished, the powers at Washington harbored the strange notion that to amalgamate Philadelphians should be their chief concern. Adams made his Pennsylvania appointments with very few exceptions from among Republicans, but many of them had little influence or were outright Jacksonians. Often the impression got abroad that the Administration would rather have appointed Federalists.

Knowing Republicans suggested time and again that Jackson's many Federalist friends in Pennsylvania could be turned to advantage. Identifying Jackson with Federalism would, in the words of one supporter, "completely revolunize [sic] Penn in favour of the administration."[34] Samuel Ingham, a leading Jacksonian who lived in New Hope on the Delaware, hinted privately to Van Buren that there was substance to this theory. He lamented after a visit to a New Jersey county just across the river: "[There was] a good deal of torpor, owing to the fact of several active Federalists there having declared for Jackson—the Democrats seem yet at a loss and many are undecided."[35] A typical example of the Administration's foolishness was its treatment of John Binns, the tough Philadelphia Republican editor who had turned from Crawford to Adams during the winter of 1824-25. Obviously influential among Republican voters, Binns loaded his editorial salvos with charges that Jackson was remarkably popular in Federalist circles throughout the state. His sulphuric attacks upon Federalism itself brought howls of protest from Adams Federalists, who complained regularly to Administration leaders in Washington. Smitten with the will-o'-the-wisp of a triumphant liaison between Republicans and Philadelphia Federalists, these leaders treated Binns with less than candor and rarely heeded his pleas for money and perquisites.[36]

Philadelphia Federalists were among the most sensitive and prideful of the breed. They had maintained with outstanding success a tightly organized city machine in the fervent hope that at least one outpost of honor and respectability would survive the onslaught of Jeffersonianism. By 1826 they still retained a slight margin over the despised Republicans, but their whole focus, even more so than in past years, had become centered upon city affairs. Accordingly, cries of anguish drifted skyward when John Sergeant, after refusing a Federalist nomination for Congress, changed his mind upon meeting with a Republican delegation which was both friendly to the Adams Administration and amenable to working with Federalists in Sergeant's behalf. Always moderate and thus acceptable to many Republicans, Sergeant hoped to force a realignment of Philadelphia parties by pitching his campaign upon support for Adams. But the majority of Philadelphia Federalists were mortally offended by his action. Acting from injured pride they promptly put up another candidate who would properly represent their narrow interests.[37]

An exciting three-way contest followed when the Jacksonians happily entered their own man. Oddity and chance provided the dismal climax: Sergeant and the Federalist candidate got exactly the same number of votes—a flip of the coin went against Sergeant. "There is a positive loss in Pennsylvania," mourned Adams in his diary, "and those who call themselves friends of the Administration have neither concert nor courage."[38] A young Federalist friend in Philadelphia assured Henry Clay that the Republican and Federalist friends of the Administration would thereafter work in concert.[39] The assurance was premature, and Adams' friends could not shake the delusion that if Federalists and Republicans could at last get together in Philadelphia, victory in the state would be theirs.

The wounds had not yet healed by the fall of 1827 when another Congressional race impended. Sergeant once more announced that he would be a candidate on a platform of outright support for the Administration. Those who controlled the Federalist machinery again thought seriously of running their own votary, but they compromised by withholding their imprimatur from any candidate. The Jacksonians thereupon nominated a Federalist of their own with the hope of quietly drawing off dissidents. In spite of Sergeant's open preference, the speakers at a Federalist rally held in his cause avoided any mention of the presidential question. Sergeant felt called upon to apologize to Clay for the "politic" course.[40] Sergeant won, but still the Administration forces would not combine firmly. In July 1828 the Adams supporters called for a great peace meeting in Philadelphia to adjust their differences. Joseph Hopkinson and Sergeant were the main speakers at this highly publicized gathering, and each devoted most of his attention to the exhilarating effects of hoped-for amalgamation. Impressive resolutions were passed and tearful promises exchanged.[41] Here was prime grist for the Jacksonian mill and Adams' chances for winning the state slumped still lower.

The Jackson Federalists in Pennsylvania were led by James Buchanan, the leader of an efficient machine in Lancaster which could turn out a majority of 2,500 in a major election.[42] The *Lancaster Journal* followed

Buchanan in his support for the Hero, it being one of three such Federalist presses in the state to do so—only five favored Adams. Outside Philadelphia no major Federalist leaders in Pennsylvania supported Adams in 1828. James Ross, Henry Baldwin, and William Wilkins, the captains of Pittsburgh Federalism, were ardent Jacksonians. Even in Philadelphia, Jackson ran surprisingly well in traditionally Federalist wards, and Joseph Hemphill, a Jackson Federalist, overwhelmed Sergeant in the Congressional contest.[43] It has been variously estimated that there were fifty or sixty thousand "Federalist votes" in the state, a fact that led one investigator—apparently unaware of the wide Federalist support for Jackson—to write that since Adams got about that number of votes in 1828 they were probably all Federalist votes.[44] Much closer to the truth is an estimate that Federalists divided their votes about equally between Jackson and Adams, a depressing result for the eager amalgamationists.

Federalists were also about equally divided in the other middle states. After a careful study of New Jersey politics in this period, Walter Fee concluded that although Federalists had no firm choice in 1824 they afterwards turned increasingly to Jackson.[45] When Richard Stockton and his son both came out openly for Jackson in 1827 (the result of their disappointment in not getting a federal judgeship from Adams) it became eminently respectable for New Jersey Federalists to become Jacksonians. Fee found that the most common and telling political argument used by the Adams Republican newspapers in New Jersey was the fact that Federalists dominated the state leadership of the Jackson movement.[46] The majority of Delaware Federalists had by 1828 turned from Crawford to Jackson, a factor which encouraged Adams Republicans there. Old party discipline on both sides had remained firm until 1827, when, for the first time, a Congressional election turned on the question of supporting the Adams Administration. Both men who contested for the seat in 1827 were Federalists, the Jacksonian nominee being the son of James Bayard, Delaware's most distinguished contribution to the Federalist hagiology. The Adams candidate won in a close election, but a majority of Federalists probably aided young Bayard.[47]

Maryland Federalists not only split down the middle in their presidential preferences for 1828, but they also assumed commanding positions of leadership in both camps. At an Adams convention in 1827, Robert H. Goldsborough, a prominent Federalist, brought all the resolutions before the meeting and read the official address.[48] Appropriately, the semi-official Jacksonian reply to this address was written by Vergil Maxcy, Calhoun's Federalist protégé.[49] Maxcy was helped in his campaign for Jackson by such Federalist champions as Charles Carroll of Carrollton, Roger Taney, Charles Goldsborough, Benjamin Howard, and Charles C. Harper.[50] On the other side, Clement Dorsey, Henry Warfield, Daniel Jennifer, and George Hanson led the list of well-known Federalists who took an active part for Adams. Since the Federalists had given up their state organization before the 1824 election, formal amalgamation as such was not a pressing issue. Relations between Federalists and Republicans in their respective camps, accordingly, were more harmonious than was the case in most of the other New England and middle states. Adams and Jackson partisans, however, still tried on the one hand to stigmatize the enemy with the taint of Federalism and on the other to defend their own cause from such attacks. Contrary to its short-sighted policy in New York and Pennsylvania, the Adams Administration paid special attention to Maryland Republicans, particularly Governor Joseph Kent. He was in turn able to conduct a vigorous and effective campaign among Republican voters.[51]

By the spring of 1828, it was obvious to most observers that Andrew Jackson would be the next President. In spite of the unceasing anti-Federalist assaults that flowed from Jacksonian orators and presses, a large body of Federalists in the various states had enlisted with the Hero. Motivated by a number of factors, these Federalists found most compelling the hope that under Jackson old distinctions of party would be erased and Federalists could once more assume their "proper" place in the conduct of public affairs. This hope was based in part upon an estimate of Jackson's character, the tone of his letters to Monroe, and upon the willingness of Jackson Republicans to forgive any man's past sins if he would swear loyalty to their leader. After his election, Jackson proceeded to appoint more Federalists to important offices than had been appointed by all his Republican predecessors combined.

NOTES

[1] W. Plumer to L. Woodbury, March 9, and April 5, 1826, Plumer Letterbook, LC. See also, D. Morril to H. Clay, September 18, 1826, Clay Mss, LC.

[2] D. Webster to J. Mason, May 31, 1826, Hilliard, *Mason,* 304-305; Webster to Mason, April 10, 1827, Webster, *Webster,* XVII, 419.

[3] E. Webster to D. Webster, June 17, 1827, Clay Mss, LC.

[4] D. Webster to E. Webster, April 4, 1827, Webster, *Webster,* XVI, 152; *Portsmouth Journal,* June 30, 1827.

[5] E. Webster to D. Webster, June 17, 1827, Clay Mss, LC; L. Woodbury to R. Jarvis, August 27, 1827, Jarvis Mss, LC; D. Webster to J. Q. Adams, June 30, 1827, Webster, *Webster,* XVI, 154-56.

[6] See issues of June 30, July 7, 14, 1827.

[7] D. Webster to S. Bell, October 15, 1827, Webster Mss, LC.

[8] *Portsmouth Journal*, December 15, 1827.

[9] *Ibid.*, March 15, 1828. See also, E. Webster to D. Webster, March 17, 1828 and E. Evans to D. Webster, April 4, 1828, Webster Mss, LC.

[10] *Portsmouth Journal*, April 7, 1827, May 5, 1827; D. Webster to H. Clay, May 18, 1827, Clay Mss, LC.

[11] L. Lincoln to D. Webster, May 24, 1827, Clay Mss, LC.

[12] See files of the *Republican* through the period 1824-28, especially December 29, 1824, May 24, 1826, May 31, 1827, and April 9, 1828.

[13] H. Shaw to Clay, August 23, 1827, Clay Mss, LC.

[14] G. Fairbanks to Webster, March 12, 1828, Webster Mss, LC.

[15] B. Russell to Webster, April 14, 1828, *ibid.*

[16] *Address of the Central Committee . . . Friendly to the Election of John Q. Adams . . . Held . . . in Boston, June 10, 1828* (Boston, 1828).

[17] *Boston Columbian Centinel*, March 8, 1828; *New York Post,* March 14, 1828.

[18] Williams to Maxcy, April 1, 1828, Maxcy Mss, LC.

[19] Henshaw to R. Jarvis, March 5, and July 11, 1828, J. Boyd to Jarvis, March 5, 1828, Jarvis Mss, LC.

[20] G. Welles to H. Mitchell, June 26, 1827, Welles Mss, LC.

[21] T. Smith to R. Baldwin, March 14, 1827, Baldwin Mss, YL; J. Andrews to G. Welles, June 30, 1828, Welles Mss, LC.

[22] A. Sterling to G. Welles, June 22, 1828, *ibid.*

[23] See the Welles Mss, LC for the period June-October, 1828, especially R. Fairchild to Welles, June 23; R. Heinman to Welles, July 5; and J. Crawford to Welles, July 5.

[24] *Portsmouth Journal*, June 16, 1827, September 29, 1827.

[25] J. Hill to J. Bailey, February 4, 1828, Bailey Mss, NYHS.

[26] Tallmadge to J. Taylor, February 22, 1826, Taylor Mss, NYHS.

[27] J. Cramer to J. Taylor, January 10, 1827, *ibid.* Rufus King's son regarded the temporary Clinton-Van Buren alliance as a "coquette," which had assumed "The appearance of open prostitution." C. King to H. Clay, March 21, 1826, Clay Mss, LC.

[28] Fitzpatrick, *Van Buren,* 159.

[29] M. Van Buren to A. Jackson, September 14, 1827, Bassett, *Jackson Correspondence,* III, 381-82.

[30] H. Martindale to J. Taylor, November 13, 1827, T. Rudd to J. Taylor, February 27, 1828, Taylor Mss, NYHS; E. Baldwin to S. Baldwin, February 27, 1827, Baldwin Mss, YL; J. Morgan to A. Flagg, December 4, 1827, Flagg Mss, NYPL; J. Townsend to I. & J. Townsend, January 21, 1828, Townsend Mss, NYPL.

[31] H. Martindale to J. Taylor, October 16, 1827, Taylor Mss, NYHS.

[32] J. Thomas to H. Clay, May 13, 1827, Clay Mss, LC.

[33] J. Campbell to G. Verplanck, April 9, 1828, Verplanck Mss, NYHS.

[34] P. Markley to H. Clay, April 28, 1827, Clay Mss, LC.

[35] Ingham to Van Buren, July 31, 1828, Van Buren Mss, LC.

[36] J. Binns to H. Clay, May 10, 1826, B. Crowninshield to H. Clay, March 14, 1827, Clay Mss, LC; Binns, *Recollections,* 250.

[37] S. Breck to W. Meredith, September 21, 1826, Meredith Mss, PHS; E. Ingersoll to H. Clay, September 22, 1826, Clay Mss, LC; *Boston Courier,* October 5, 1827.

[38] Adams, *Memoirs,* VII, 154.

[39] R. Peters, Jr., to Clay, October 24, 1826, Clay Mss, LC.

[40] Sergeant to Clay, September 26, 1827, *ibid.* See also the several letters from Sergeant to Clay earlier in the month.

[41] *Report of the Proceedings of the Town Meeting in the City of Philadelphia, July 7th, 1828* (Philadelphia, 1828).

[42] Klein, *Pennsylvania Politics,* 214-15, 221, 225; S. Ingham to M. Van Buren, July 31, 1828, Van Buren Mss, LC.

[43] *New York Post,* Otober 7, 17, 1828.

[44] Florence Weston, *The Presidential Election of 1828* (Washington, 1938), 167.

[45] Fee, *New Jersey,* 272.

[46] *Ibid.,* 262.

[47] J. Sergeant to H. Clay, September 18, 23, 1827, Clay Mss, LC; *Boston Courier,* October 8, 1827.

[48] R. Goldsborough to H. Clay, August 9, 1827, Clay Mss, LC; *Proceedings of the Maryland Administration Meeting . . . 1827.*

[49] W. Grason to V. Maxcy, September 25, 1827, Maxcy Mss, LC.

[50] H. Niles to J. Taylor, May 10, 1827, Taylor Mss, NYHS; S. Smith to M. Van Buren, May 26, 1827, Steiner, "Van Buren's Correspondents," 142.

[51] C. Goldsborough to V. Maxcy, January 2, 1828, Maxcy Mss, LC.

PARTY FORMATION IN NEW ENGLAND:

MASSACHUSETTS*

Richard P. McCormick

The study of political parties, Richard P. McCormick asserts in his book The Second American Party System, *must go beyond considerations of party ideology or constituency to investigate the structure and function of the components of a party system. Regarding parties as organisms designed to win elections, McCormick maintains that they should be studied in light of the political and constitutional milieu in which they operated. Massachusetts, in the transitional period of the late 1820's when the National Republican and Democratic parties were emerging, was a state in which politics had reached a practical plateau. With the demise of the Federalist and Republican parties by 1828, new political demands led to new party groupings, often involving, however, party leaders who had recently shifted their allegiance from their former party. Neither a groundswell of popular enthusiasm for Jackson nor a dynamic democratic ideology was a major factor, at this time, in Massachusetts party formation.*

Massachusetts, unlike most states in 1824, possessed a still vigorous two-party system that had been in operation for more than a quarter of a century. When the voters went to the polls in April to cast their ballots in the gubernatorial election, they divided their suffrages between two candidates bearing Federalist and Republican labels. A year later, however, the familiar pattern began to alter. Old party distinctions lost their meaning as, for a brief period, support for the native son, John Quincy Adams, seemingly overbore all other considerations. Then, with the approach of the presidential election of 1828, partisan divisions again

* Reprinted by permission of the University of North Carolina Press. From *The Second American Party System: Party Formation in the Jacksonian Era* by Richard P. McCormick (Chapel Hill, University of North Carolina Press, 1966). Copyright © 1966 by the University of North Carolina Press: Chapter 3, "Party Formation in New England," pp. 36-49.

manifested themselves in both state and national politics and new party formations emerged.

The old party system that was to break down in 1824, had begun to take form in the first year of John Adams' presidency. Despite the aversion of the citizens of Massachusetts to overt partisan "interference" in the free choice of elective officials, party organization was well advanced by 1800 and had gained such a degree of public acceptance by 1804 that it was no longer necessary to hide party activity behind a thin veil of secrecy. Both parties acknowledged the use of elaborate apparatus for nominating candidates, managing campaigns, and conducting party affairs, and the voters in turn assumed partisan identities. Perhaps the most remarkable feature of this early party system was its stability. Federalists and Republicans alike, using similar techniques for centralizing party management, were extraordinarily successful in maintaining party unity and avoiding the factional discord that characterized parties in certain of the Middle States. Too, they remained well balanced and competitive almost from their inception down to 1824, a condition that was common to but one other state—Delaware.

The constitutional and legal framework within which elections were conducted in Massachusetts influenced the structure of party organization. Although the constitution of 1780 prescribed a small property qualification for voting, which was transformed into a taxpaying qualification in 1821, it would appear that in practice only a very small minority of adult males were actually disfranchised. State elections were held annually, and paper ballots—which, after 1830, might be printed—were used. With the town as the voting unit, the governor, lieutenant-governor, and senators were elected in April and the representatives in May, until 1831, when the state elections were shifted to November. The town was the constituency for representatives. Senators were elected initially from counties, but after 1812 (except from 1814-1816) were chosen from districts made up of one or more counties. Representatives were apportioned roughly on the basis of population and senators ostensibly on the basis of taxes paid. Congressmen were always elected under the district system, but the method of choosing presidential electors was subject to frequent changes until 1824, when the practice of state-wide elections on a general ticket was adopted. Although not peculiar to that state, Massachusetts election laws were unusual in the requirement that successful candidates must receive an absolute majority of the total vote cast.

Under this system of representation and election the town and the state were the most vital arenas of political activity. The county, the senatorial district, and the congressional district were secondary units that had somehow to be accommodated within the party structures. The fact that there was no competing focus of political power intermediate between the town and the state explains in part, at least, the remarkable authority wielded by party institutions at the state level in Massachusetts, as well as elsewhere in New England.

The management of party affairs at the state level was—in both parties—a function of the legislative caucus, or, more properly, the mixed legislative caucus. First used by the Federalists in 1800 to nominate their candidate for governor, the same mechanism was soon copied by the Republicans and was employed by both parties with great effectiveness throughout their existence. Often referred to in official party propaganda as a "Grand Convention of citizens from all parts of the Commonwealth," the caucus was in fact composed of party members within the legislature and an indeterminate number of party stalwarts who were co-opted to attend.

The Federalist caucus customarily met in February, during the legislative session, to nominate candidates for governor and lieutenant-governor and to draft an "address" to the voters. In addition it appointed a Central Committee, which appointed county committees, and these in turn appointed town committees. The Central Committee, made up of seven men from Boston and vicinity, not necessarily members of the legislature, issued political directives in the form of circular letters before election campaigns and generally determined party strategy. The county committees sponsored mass meetings at which the names of candidates for the senate would be presented and ratified, and the town committees functioned similarly with respect to the nomination of representatives.

The Republican caucus was closely patterned after the Federalist model.[1] At the level of the counties, senatorial districts, and congressional districts, however, the Republicans as early as 1808 were using what were referred to as conventions of delegates—rather than mass meetings—to nominate senators and congressmen. There is also some evidence to indicate that within the Republican party, party committees below the state level were elected, rather than appointed.

That both parties were under highly centralized direction is evident from their handiwork. What is far from clear, though, is the relationship between the Central Committee and the caucus. Whether the controlling influence of the state parties was in fact the caucus, or whether the caucus was largely controlled by the Central Committee—the membership of which changed little over the years—is a question worthy of further investigation.

There were definite conventions that regulated the style of politics in

Massachusetts. Elections were relatively orderly affairs, conducted with decorum, and corruption was all but non-existent. Personal solicitation of votes by candidates was regarded as improper, and there was no "stump speaking" or theatrical campaigning before 1840. Voters were appealed to through "addresses" and letters in the newspapers, through broadsides and pamphlets, and through personal solicitation by party committees in each town. Party members were inspired to action in town caucuses, county mass meetings or conventions, and by printed circular letters from the Central Committee. Federalists made effective use of the Washington Benevolent Societies to stimulate party enthusiasm while Republicans indulged themselves in celebrations of the Fourth of July and the anniversary of Jefferson's accession to the presidency. The conduct of politics, in brief, reflected the distinctive character of Massachusetts society and might properly be studied as a form of cultural expression as well as an aspect of government.

The stability, durability, and balance of the parties in Massachusetts was, by contrast with other states, most extraordinary. From 1800, when the parties became competitive, through 1824, the state elections were usually closely contested, and in most years the victorious candidate won by a margin of less than 10 per cent of the total vote. Never did a third-party candidate enter the lists, nor was there ever more than a scattering of votes for independent candidates for the governorship. The Federalists retained their dominance until 1807, when James Sullivan became the first Republican governor. The Republicans won the governorship again in 1808, 1810, and 1811, but could not score another victory until 1823. The only clear-cut Republican triumph in a presidential election was in 1804, when electors-at-large pledged to Jefferson were chosen by popular vote. Despite the vicissitudes of the party elsewhere, and despite the hopeless position of the party in national politics, the Federalists remained the dominant party in Massachusetts until 1823. Even then, they lost the gubernatorial elections of 1823 and 1824 by relatively small margins.

Although party competition was sustained and party organization was highly developed, voter interest in politics, as measured by participation in elections, was in general surprisingly low. Voter participation in gubernatorial elections, expressed in terms of the percentage of adult white males voting, rose from 30.8 per cent in 1800 to 41.8 per cent in 1804. It then climbed steadily to a peak of 67.4 per cent in 1812, which was to be the highest rate of voter participation in any state-wide election in Massachusetts through 1860. Participation remained near the 60 per cent level until 1817, when it began to decline, reaching a low of 40.6

per cent in 1822. In 1823 there was a revival, which brought the figure above the 50 per cent mark, and in 1824, 57 per cent of the adult white males participated in the election that was in fact to be the last for the old party system. In presidential elections, when electors were chosen by popular vote, participation tended to be at an even lower level than in state elections, except in 1804. Why the Massachusetts voter seemingly was apathetic about going to the polls I do not know, but this apathy was to continue to characterize the state in the decades after 1824 as well.

With the revival of the contest for the presidency in 1824, Massachusetts politics entered a distinctly new era. Old party distinctions had ceased to have any meaning by 1828, and two new parties, primarily oriented toward national politics but exhibiting as well the effects of local circumstances and personal rivalries, were forming. But the most important single factor bearing upon party formation in Massachusetts—and indeed throughout New England—was the candidacy of a native son, John Quincy Adams, in 1824 and 1828. As a sectional favorite, his strength was so great as to inhibit the formation of a genuine opposition party until near the end of his troubled administration.

In the presidential election of 1824, conducted for the first time with electors chosen at large by popular vote, Adams received five-sixths of the votes cast. Fewer than 30 per cent of the estimated electorate went to the polls, in contrast to the 57 per cent that had turned out for the gubernatorial election in April. Adams had the support of the leadership of the Republican party; most Federalists, recalling Adams' "apostasy" from the party in 1808, probably remained aloof from the election. An unpledged opposition slate of electors attracted its small support from a diverse array of Crawfordites, Calhounites, die-hard Federalists, and disgruntled Republicans. The low voter turnout may have been attributable to the one-sided nature of the contest or to the lack of compelling enthusiasm for any of the candidates, or both.

The election itself was not the signal for a reorganization of parties. Before the gubernatorial election of 1825, the old parties caucused as in the past, although the Federalist agreed to support the Republican nominee for governor, Levi Lincoln, who was all but unanimously elected. A similar attempt to end old conflicts was made in 1826, but dissident Federalist factions sponsored irregular candidates, who collectively polled nearly one-third of the total vote. In 1827 there was again only scattered opposition to the re-election of Lincoln, representing neither the continuance of old party loyalties nor the emergence of a new opposition party. Although relative harmony reigned at the state level, the Federalist and Republican parties retained their organizations, in spite of fusion movements in many areas and the irrelevance of such divisions to national politics. But in 1827 the Federalists ran their last candidates for office; a year later there was no Federalist party.

The most practical political question of the period was whether the old Republican party, which had now become in reality the Adams party, would remain "exclusive" or would permit former Federalists to "amalgamate." Both policies had supporters within the party leadership, and the issue was not determined until 1829. The first clear sign that amalgamation was under way came in 1827 with the election of Daniel Webster to the United States Senate by a predominantly Republican legislature. But early in 1828, separate caucuses were held by the "Republican members" of the legislature and the members "friendly to the national and state administrations" to renominate Lincoln for governor. By June 11, 1828, when the Administration-Republican members of the legislature met to choose an electoral ticket pledged to Adams and Rush, they also named a Central Committee, made up of former Federalists as well as Republicans.[2]

Still the issue of "amalgamation," as well as the future structure of the Administration-Republican (or National Republican) party, remained unsettled. On February 12, 1829, the "members of the legislature friendly to the present [Lincoln] State administration" met in the New Court House in Boston under the chairmanship of Robert Rantoul to renominate Lincoln for governor and to consider "what measures it is expedient to take for maintaining our party, and giving it organization and efficiency in the ensuing elections." After an adjournment, the session reconvened on February 16 and approved an "address" recommending a political organization throughout the state, on "liberal and national principles, which should not go to the exclusion of plain straight-forward republicans of any denomination." Thus was the National Republican party, as it must now be called, brought into existence. Although it called for unity of sentiment, as well as "liberal principles," the address did not specify what principles should be espoused.[3]

Vague though it was about principles, the new party caucus was explicit on the subject of organization. A Central Committee of nine men was chosen. Then the members present from each county nominated a man to be county chairman, and these nominees were elected by the full caucus. The county chairmen, at the request of the Central Committee, were to call county conventions—made up of delegates from the towns—for the purpose of electing county committees. They were also to correspond with the Central Committee on all matters affecting the interests of the party. In this manner a centralized type of party organization, much like that in existence before 1824, was ordained. Too, the new organization contemplated that, in keeping with long tradition, the legislative caucus of the party would annually make nominations for state offices, reconstitute the Central Committee, and appoint county chairmen.

One Republican faction endeavored to preserve the old party on an "exclusivist" basis. Meeting—perhaps significantly—in the Old Court House, with Benjamin F. Varnum as chairman and Horace Mann as secretary, a group of Republican legislators endorsed the nomination of Lincoln for governor but chose their own Central Committee and stated their abhorrence of amalgamation. In the ensuing state election these "Exclusivists," as they were termed, endeavored to run candidates for the legislature, but the movement produced slight results and appears to have been abandoned after the election. Despite subsequent vicissitudes, the new party that was formally launched on February 16, 1829, was to endure for a generation, first under the name of National Republican and later under the Whig label. At its core, the party represented a continuance of the old Republican party, but after 1824—and especially after 1827—it received accretions of strength from former Federalists and suffered losses to the emergent Democratic and Antimasonic parties.

Organized support for Andrew Jackson was slow to develop in Massachusetts. His name scarcely figured in the election of 1824, and it was not until 1827 that preliminary steps were taken to organize a pro-Jackson party by two very diverse elements. David Henshaw (Boston wholesale druggist, proprietor of the *Statesman*, and ambitious political manager) together with Marcus Morton (former Republican Congressman from Western Massachusetts and lieutenant-governor before ascending to the supreme bench of the state) constituted the leadership of what was to emerge as the dominant Jacksonian faction. Henshaw favored Crawford in 1824, shifted to support of Adams in 1826, and in 1827 turned to Jackson. It is not apparent that he admired the general or his policies, but he was, like Morton, enamoured of Calhoun and susceptible to his influence. He also appears to have wished to play a larger role in politics than that allotted him by the Administration-Republican party. A second faction, headed by the ultra-Federalist, Theodore Lyman, Jr., and with the *Jackson Republican* as its organ, supported Jackson out of detestation for Adams, but by 1829 this odd ally had been out-maneuvered by the energetic and astute Henshaw, who was recognized by the Jackson administration as the head of the party in Massachusetts.

Henshaw and his *Statesman* faction began their organizational activities

on behalf of Jackson with a dinner on January 8, 1828, the anniversary
of the general's victory at New Orleans. In the April election, Marcus
Morton was the unwilling candidate of the faction for governor, receiving
little more than a token vote. "Judge Morton was not regularly
nominated," explained the *Statesman*, "and there was not the least concert or arrangement to procure support or draw out strength." But the
Henshaw organ predicted that there would be concerted efforts put forth
in the presidential contest.[4] In preparation for that contest, a Jackson
Republican "Convention," composed of members of the legislature
friendly to Jackson and "delegates" from Boston and nearby towns, met
in the State House on June 10, 1828.[5] An electoral ticket, headed by
Henshaw, was adopted, and a Central Committee of nine members was
appointed, which was authorized to prepare and publish an address. Over
the succeeding few months, feeble attempts were made to stimulate party
organization at the levels of the counties and towns, but the movement
was not widespread. When the presidential election was held, the Jackson
ticket polled only one-sixth of the total vote cast; that the electorate was
indifferent to the contest is indicated by the low turnout of approximately
one voter in four. Despite this dismal showing, the Jackson-Democratic
party had in fact made its debut.

Fortified with an appointment as collector of the Port of Boston, and
with patronage for his henchmen, Henshaw displayed only moderate zeal
for building the strength of the party of which he was to be the "boss"
for a decade. In 1829, Marcus Morton, even though he was not formally
a candidate and no genuine party exertion was made in his behalf, polled
almost the same number of votes that Jackson had received in 1828.
In 1830, however, the Jacksonian members of the legislature caucused
in February, nominated Morton for the governorship, and adopted an
address and resolutions dealing with state issues. Conventions were held
in several counties to name senatorial candidates, and later in the year
congressional district conventions presented Jacksonian candidates for
Congress. As a result of these organizational efforts, Morton more than
doubled the number of votes he had received in 1829, although he had
less than half as many as the victorious Lincoln. Morton was again the
nominee of the caucus in 1831, but his vote fell below that of the previous year.

Doubtless with an eye to the presidential election of 1832, but also
because a change in the constitution made necessary a second gubernatorial election in November, 1831, the Jacksonian members of the legislature decided on June 9, 1831, that it was expedient "to organize the
Republican party in this Commonwealth" and issued a call for a state

convention, to be held in Worcester on September 1.[6] Each county was to send delegates equal in number to its representation in the General Assembly. The Worcester convention, attended by over two hundred delegates, nominated Morton for governor, appointed two delegates-at-large to attend the Democratic National Convention, and directed that conventions should be held in each congressional district at the call of the Central Committee to choose district delegates to the National Convention. Morton again went down to defeat, this time running third to Lincoln and the Antimasonic candidate.

By 1829, then, the old parties had been replaced by new ones, which contested on an extremely uneven basis both state and national elections. They did not represent the continuation of old allegiances under new names; they were new parties. The National Republicans owed their dominance largely to the fact that they were able to merge the ablest leadership elements in the older parties, initially on the popular issue of support for John Quincy Adams. Their opponents, lacking a popular program and led by figures who commanded little respect and who lacked both zeal and capacity, were doomed to remain for a decade in a position of weakness. Both parties were tightly controlled by their leaders, operating through a Central Committee ostensibly named by the legislature caucus, and both were content to conduct politics in the traditional restrained, conservative manner. Popular interest in the new political order was negligible. No election between 1825 and 1830 brought as many as 30 percent of the adult white males to the polls.

Scarcely had a new two-party system emerged when the Antimasonic enthusiasm assumed political form and complicated the scene. The first rumblings of the movement were felt in Bristol County in 1828, and by 1829 it had spread sufficiently to produce the state's first political convention, held in Faneuil Hall in December to form a party organization. By 1831 the party felt strong enough to enter the November gubernatorial contest behind Samuel Lathrop, nominated by a state convention in May. Lathrop ran second to Lincoln and was again the party's candidate in 1832. In that year he fell below Lincoln and Morton in the poll, although the Wirt electoral ticket took second place in the presidential voting. In 1833, after devious maneuvers designed to unite the National Republicans and the Antimasons behind a single candidate had foundered, the redoubtable John Quincy Adams, running as an Antimasonic candidate for governor, polled the highest vote the party was ever to secure, but he fell far short of victory. By 1834 the party had begun to crumble, and the disintegration was hastened by the decision in 1835 to support the Whig candidate for governor, the Democratic candidate for lieutenant-governor, and Van Buren for the presidency. By 1836 the party had ceased to be a factor of consequence, and the two-party system was restored.

The Antimasons did succeed in bringing to the polls men to whom the major parties had little appeal. Voter participation rose markedly after 1830, rising to over 45 per cent of the estimated electorate in 1834. When the party fell apart, these new voters apparently retained their political interest, and the major portion of them seem to have moved into the Democratic ranks. Too, the Antimasons may have had the effect of inducing the major parties to exhibit increased concern about the reform measures that were being agitated at the time. Neither the Whigs nor the Democrats were disposed to offer substantial concessions to the Antimasons, however, with the result that there was no "amalgamation," such as was to occur in certain other states. Basically, the Antimasonic party, like the Workingmen's party—which flourished briefly in the same years—reflected popular discontent or frustration with the two major parties.

After 1835 the Democrats steadily narrowed the margin that separated them from their opponents. In 1836 Van Buren received 45 percent of the popular vote, the strongest showing made by any Democratic presidential candidate until after the Civil War. Marcus Morton, the perennial candidate for governor, increased his vote from around fifteen thousand in 1833 to over fifty-one thousand in 1839, when he finally won an election. The Whig vote, meanwhile, had remained relatively stable. The Democrats obviously profited more than the Whigs from the demise of the Antimasons. Too, the party leaders were compelled to make concessions both to a "Workingmen" faction and a western "Country" faction, with the result that the image of the party as a spokesman for the "common man" was strengthened. In 1838 George Bancroft replaced Henshaw both as collector of the Port of Boston and as the party leader, and under his guidance the party was reorganized on "reform" principles and reached its peak effectiveness. As the parties became more competitive, voter participation rose to a new high of 66 percent in the 1840 elections.

The formal structure of the major parties underwent little change. Although both Whigs and Democrats resorted on occasion to the use of state conventions, especially in preparation for presidential elections, the caucus and the Central Committee were retained as the prime agencies of state party management.[7] Campaign practices remained relatively sedate, until the election of 1840 with its enormous mass meetings, popular oratory, and generally festive atmosphere, broke down the traditional reserve. It was, indeed, with the election of 1840 that the new order of politics that had its inception in the revival of the contest for the presidency sixteen years earlier finally reached maturity.

NOTES

[1] Federalist party machinery is described in Samuel Eliot Morrison, *The Life and Letters of Harrison Gray Otis, Federalist, 1765-1848* (2 vols, Boston and New York, 1913), especially I, 286 ff. For early references to the Republican organization, see the (Boston) *Independent Chronicle*, Mar. 1, 1804, Feb. 9, 20, 1809, Feb. 15, 1810; *Boston Patriot,* Mar. 31, 1810.

[2] *Hingham Gazette,* Mar. 14, June 20, 1828.

[3] There are full accounts of these caucuses in the (Boston) *Columbian Centinel,* Feb. 21, Mar. 14, 18, 25, 1829.

[4] *Boston Statesman,* June 3, 7, 1828.

[5] The convention was reported in the *Boston Statesman*, July 12, 1828, and in the (Concord) *New Hampshire Patriot,* July 21, 1828.

[6] *Boston Statesman,* June 25, 1831. For the report on the Worcester convention see *ibid.*, Sept. 10, 1831. The Jackson Central Committee named the county chairmen, who in turn appointed the township chairmen. Henshaw, with his extensive patronage as collector of the Port of Boston, functioned at least down to 1835 as the boss of the party.

[7] The National Republicans held their first state convention at Worcester, October 11-12, 1832. *Journal of the Proceedings of the [Massachusetts] National Republican Convention . . . Worcester, October 11, 1832* (Boston, 1832). The Whigs held state conventions in 1833, 1836, 1840, and regularly after 1843. In the intervening years nominations were made by mixed conventions, made up of Whig members of the legislature together with delegates from towns not represented by Whigs in the legislature. For reports of the mixed conventions, see *Boston Courier,* Mar. 28, 1836; Mar. 20, 1837; Mar. 4, 1839; Mar. 1, 1841.

BIBLIOGRAPHY

Part I: Introduction

Volumes currently in paperback editions are marked with an asterisk.

ADAIR, DOUGLASS, " 'That Politics May Be Reduced to a Science': David Hume, James Madison, and the Tenth *Federalist*," *Huntington Library Quarterly*, Vol. XX (August, 1957), pp. 343-360.

BINKLEY, WILFRED E., *American Political Parties: Their Natural History*, 4th ed. New York, Alfred A. Knopf, 1963.

BONE, HUGH A., *American Politics and the Party System*, 4th ed. New York, McGraw-Hill Book Co., 1970.

CHAMBERS, WILLIAM N., "Party Development and Party Action," *History and Theory*, Vol. III, No. 1 (1963), pp. 91-120.

The American Party Systems: Stages of Political Development. New York, Oxford University Press, 1967.

COMMAGER, HENRY S., "The American Political Party," *American Scholar*, Vol. XIX (Summer, 1950), pp. 309-16.

CROTTY, WILLIAM J., ed., *Approaches to the Study of Party Organization*. Boston, Allyne and Bacon, 1968.

———, "A Perspective for the Comparative Analysis of Political Parties," *Comparative Political Studies*, Vol. III (October, 1970), pp. 267-96.

*DAHL, ROBERT A., *A Preface to Democratic Theory*. Chicago, University of Chicago Press, 1956.

*DUVERGER, MAURICE, *Political Parties: Their Organization and Activity in the Modern State*. New York, Barnes & Noble, 1954.

*ELDERSVELD, SAMUEL J., *Political Parties: A Behavioral Analysis*. Chicago, Rand McNally & Co., 1964.

GRODZINS, MORTON, "American Political Parties and the American System," *Western Political Quarterly*, Vol. XIII (December, 1960), pp. 974-98.

KEY, VALDIMER O., JR., *Politics, Parties, and Pressure Groups*, 5th ed. New York, T. Y. Crowell, 1964.

*LA PALOMBARA, JOSEPH, and WEINER, MYRON, eds., *Political Parties and Political Development*. Princeton, Princeton University Press, 1966.

LEISERSON, AVERY, *Parties and Politics: An Institutional and Behavioral Approach*. New York, Alfred A. Knopf, 1958.

————, "The Place of Parties in the Study of Politics," *American Political Science Review*, Vol. LI (December, 1957), pp. 943-54.

MCCLOSKY, HERBERT, "Consensus and Ideology in American Politics," *American Political Science Review*, Vol. LVIII (June, 1964), pp. 361-82.

*MCDONALD, NEIL A., *The Study of Political Parties*. New York, Random House, 1955.

MERRIAM, CHARLES E., *The American Political Party System: An Introduction to the Study of Political Parties*, 4th ed. New York, Macmillan, 1949.

NICHOLS, ROY F., *The Invention of the American Political Parties*. New York, Macmillan, 1967.

RANNEY, AUSTIN, and KENDALL, WILLMOORE, *Democracy and the American Party System*. New York, Harcourt, Brace & World, 1956.

*ROSSITER, CLINTON, *Parties and Politics in America*. Ithaca, N.Y., Cornell University Press, 1964.

SCARROW, HOWARD A., "The Function of Political Parties: A Critique of the Literature and the Approach," *The Journal of Politics*, Vol. XXIX (November, 1967), pp. 770-90.

*SORAUF, FRANK J., *Political Parties in the American System*. Boston, Little, Brown and Co., 1964.

Part II: Nascent Parties, 1789-1796

Volumes currently in paperback editions are marked with an asterisk.

AMMON, HARRY, "The Formation of the Republican Party in Virginia, 1789-1816," *Journal of Southern History*, Vol. XIX (August, 1953), pp. 283-310.

————, "The Genêt Mission and the Development of American Political Parties," *Journal of American History*, Vol. LII (March, 1966), pp. 725-41.

*BAILYN, BERNARD, *The Origins of American Politics*. New York, Random House, 1968.

*BEARD, CHARLES, *Economic Origins of Jeffersonian Democracy*. New York, Macmillan, 1965.

BERNHARD, WINFRED E. A., *Fisher Ames: Federalist and Statesman, 1758-1808*. Chapel Hill, University of North Carolina Press, 1965.

*BORDEN, MORTON, *Parties and Politics in the Early Republic, 1789-1815*. New York, Thomas Y. Crowell, 1967.

BRANT, IRVING, *James Madison: Father of the Constitution, 1787-1800*. Indianapolis, Bobbs-Merrill Co., 1950.

BROWN, STUART G., *The First Republicans: Political Philosophy and Public Policy in the Party of Jefferson and Madison*. Syracuse, N. Y., Syracuse University Press, 1954.

*CHAMBERS, WILLIAM N., *Political Parties in a New Nation: The American Experience, 1776-1809*. New York, Oxford University Press, 1963.

COOKE, JACOB E., "The Compromise of 1790," *William and Mary Quarterly*, 3d Ser., Vol. XXVII (October, 1970), pp. 532-45.

CUNNINGHAM, NOBLE E., JR., *The Jeffersonian Republicans: The Formation of*

Party Organization, 1789-1801. Chapel Hill, University of North Carolina Press, 1967.

GOODMAN, PAUL, *The Democratic-Republicans of Massachusetts: Politics in a Young Republic*. Cambridge, Mass., Harvard University Press, 1964.

*HAMMOND, BRAY, *Banks and Politics in America from the Revolution to the Civil War*. Princeton, Princeton University Press, 1957, 1967.

HOWE, JOHN R., JR., "Republican Thought and the Political Violence of the 1790's," *American Quarterly*, Vol. XIX (Summer, 1967), pp. 147-65.

KENYON, CECELIA, "Alexander Hamilton: Rousseau of the Right," *Political Science Quarterly*, Vol. LXXIII (June, 1958), pp. 161-78.

KIRBY, JOHN B., "Early American Politics—The Search for Ideology: An Historiographical Analysis and Critique of the Concept of 'Deference,'" *The Journal of Politics*, Vol. XXXII (November, 1970), pp. 808-38.

*KOCH, ADRIENNE, *Power, Morals, and the Founding Fathers: Essays in the Interpretation of the American Enlightenment*. Ithaca, N. Y., Cornell University Press, 1961.

LERCHE, CHARLES O., JR., "Jefferson and the Election of 1800: A Case Study in the Political Smear," *William and Mary Quarterly*, 3d Ser., Vol. V (October, 1948), pp. 467-91.

*MALONE, DUMAS, *Jefferson and His Time*, Vol. 2, *Jefferson and the Rights of Man*. Boston, Little, Brown and Co., 1951.

*MILLER, JOHN C., *Alexander Hamilton and the Growth of the New Nation*. New York, Harper and Row, 1964.

*———, *The Federalist Era, 1789-1801*. New York, Harper and Row, 1960.

RYAN, MARY P., "Party Formation in the United States Congress, 1789 to 1796: A Quantitative Analysis," *William and Mary Quarterly*, 3d. Ser., Vol. XXVIII (October, 1971), pp. 523-42.

SMELSER, MARSHALL, "The Federalist Period as an Age of Passion," *American Quarterly*, Vol. X (Winter, 1958), pp. 391-419.

———, "The Jacobin Phrenzy: the Menace of Monarchy, Plutocracy, and Anglophobia, 1789-1798," *The Review of Politics*, Vol. XXI (January, 1959), pp. 239-58.

*SYDNOR, CHARLES S., *American Revolutionaries in the Making*. New York, Macmillan, 1965.

*TINKCOM, H. M., *Republicans and Federalists in Pennsylvania, 1790-1801*. Harrisburg, Pa., Pennsylvania Historical and Museum Commission, 1950.

WHITE, LEONARD D., *The Federalists: A Study in Administrative History*. New York, Macmillan, 1956.

*WILLIAMSON, CHILTON, *American Suffrage from Property to Democracy, 1760-1860*. Princeton, Princeton University Press, 1960.

Part III: Contending for Power, 1797-1800

Volumes currently in paperback editions are marked with an asterisk.

ABERNETHY, THOMAS P., *The South in the New Nation, 1789-1819*. Baton Rouge, Louisiana State University Press, 1961.

ARONSON, SIDNEY H., *Status and Kinship in the Higher Civil Service.* Cambridge, Mass., Harvard University Press, 1964.

*CHINARD, GILBERT, *Honest John Adams.* Boston, Little, Brown and Co., 1961.

*DAUER, MANNING J., *The Adams Federalists.* Baltimore, The Johns Hopkins Press, 1968.

*DECONDE, ALEXANDER, *The Quasi-War: The Politics and Diplomacy of the Undeclared War with France, 1797-1801.* New York, Charles Scribner's Sons, 1966.

*HOWE, JOHN R., JR., *Changing Political Thought of John Adams.* Princeton, Princeton University Press, 1966.

*KURTZ, STEPHEN G., *The Presidency of John Adams: The Collapse of Federalism, 1795-1800.* Cranbury, N.J., A. S. Barnes, 1961.

*MILLER, JOHN C., *Crisis in Freedom, The Alien and Sedition Acts.* Boston, Little, Brown and Co., 1952.

PURCELL, RICHARD J., *Connecticut in Transition: 1775-1818.*, new ed. Middletown, Conn., Wesleyan University Press, 1963.

RICHARDS, LEONARD L., "John Adams and the Moderate Federalists: The Cape Fear Valley as a Test Case," *North Carolina Historical Review,* Vol. XLIII (Winter, 1966), pp. 14-30.

RODDY, EDWARD G., "Maryland and the Presidential Election of 1800," *Maryland Historical Magazine,* Vol. LVI (September, 1961), pp. 244-268.

*SCHACHNER, NATHAN, *Aaron Burr.* Cranbury, N.J., A. S. Barnes, 1961.

*SMITH, JAMES M., *Freedom's Fetters: The Alien and Sedition Laws and American Civil Liberties.* Ithaca, N.Y., Cornell University Press, 1956, 1966.

STEWART, DONALD H., *The Opposition Press of the Federalist Period.* Albany, N.Y., State University of New York Press, 1969.

Part IV: The Republican Triumph, 1801-1816

Volumes currently in paperback editions are marked with an asterisk.

BROWN, DOROTHY M., "Embargo Politics in Maryland," *Maryland Historical Magazine.* Vol. LVIII (September, 1963), pp. 193-210.

*BROWN, ROGER H., *The Republic in Peril: 1812.* New York, Norton, 1971.

CUNNINGHAM, NOBLE E., JR., "Who Were the Quids?" *Mississippi Valley Historical Review,* Vol. L (September, 1963), pp. 252-63.

*EATON, CLEMENT, *Henry Clay and the Art of American Politics.* Boston, Little, Brown and Co., 1957.

FISCHER, DAVID H., "The Myth of the Essex Junto," *William and Mary Quarterly,* 3d Ser., Vol. XXI (April, 1964), pp. 191-235.

*FISCHER, DAVID H., *The Revolution of American Conservatism: The Federalist Party in the Era of Jeffersonian Democracy.* New York, Harper and Row, 1969.

FOX, DIXON R., *The Decline of Aristocracy in the Politics of New York, 1801-1840,* 2d ed. New York, Harper and Row, 1965.

*HIGGINBOTHAM, SANFORD W., *The Keystone in the Democratic Arch: Pennsyl-

vania Politics, 1800-1816. Harrisburg, Pa., Pennsylvania Historical and Museum Commission, 1952.

KASS, ALVIN, *Politics in New York State, 1800-1830.* Syracuse, N.Y., Syracuse, University Press, 1965.

*MALONE, DUMAS, *Jefferson and His Time,* Vol. 4, *Jefferson the President, First Term, 1801-1805.* Boston, Little, Brown and Co., 1970.

PANCAKE, JOHN S., "The 'Invisibles': A Chapter in the Opposition to President Madison," *Journal of Southern History,* Vol. XXI (February, 1955), pp. 17-37.

POLE, J. R., "Jeffersonian Democracy and the Federalist Dilemma: New Jersey, 1800-1812." *Proceedings,* New Jersey Historical Society, Vol. LXXIV (October, 1956), pp. 260-92.

PRINCE, CARL E., "Patronage and a Party Machine: New Jersey Democratic-Republican Activists, 1801-1816," *William and Mary Quarterly,* 3d Ser., Vol. XXI (October, 1964), pp. 571-78.

RISJORD, NORMAN K., "1812: Conservatives, War Hawks, and the Nation's Honor." *William and Mary Quarterly, 3d. Ser.,* Vol. XVIII (April, 1961), pp. 196-210.

————*The Old Republicans: Southern Conservatism in the Age of Jefferson.* New York, Columbia University Press, 1965.

ROBINSON, WILLIAM A., *Jeffersonian Democracy in New England.* New Haven, Yale University Press, 1916.

SAPIO, VICTOR, "Maryland's Federalist Revival, 1808-1812," *Maryland Historical Magazine,* Vol. LXIV (Spring, 1969), pp. 1-17.

TURNER, LYNN W., *William Plumer of New Hampshire.* Chapel Hill, University of North Carolina Press, 1962.

*WALTERS, RAYMOND, JR., *Albert Gallatin: Jeffersonian Financier and Diplomat.* Pittsburgh, University of Pittsburgh Press, 1969.

WHITE, LEONARD D., *The Jeffersonians: A Study in Administrative History, 1801-1829.* New York, Macmillan, 1959.

*WOLFE, JOHN H., *Jeffersonian Democracy in South Carolina.* Chapel Hill, University of North Carolina Press, 1940.

Part V: The Dissolution of the First Party System, 1816-1828

Volumes currently in paperback editions are marked with an asterisk.

AMMON, HARRY, "James Monroe and the Era of Good Feelings," *Virginia Magazine of History and Biography,* Vol. LXVI (October, 1958), pp. 387-98.

*BENSON, LEE, *The Concept of Jacksonian Democracy: New York as a Test Case.* Princeton, Princeton University Press, 1970.

BROWN, EVERETT S., "The Presidential Election of 1824-25," *Political Science Quarterly,* Vol. XL (September, 1925), pp. 384-403.

BROWN, RICHARD H., "The Missouri Crisis, Slavery, and the Politics of Jacksonianism," *South Atlantic Quarterly*, Vol. LXV (Winter, 1966), pp. 55-72.
*DANGERFIELD, GEORGE, *The Awakening of American Nationalism: 1815-1828.* New York, Harper and Row, 1965.
*———*The Era of Good Feelings.* New York, Harcourt, Brace and World, 1952.
DARLING, ARTHUR B., *Political Changes in Massachusetts, 1824-1848: A Study of Liberal Movements in Politics.* New Haven, Yale University Press, 1925.
DEWEY, DONALD O., "Madison's Views on Electoral Reform," *William and Mary Quarterly*, 3d Ser., Vol. XV (March, 1962), pp. 140-45.
FORMISANO, RONALD P., "Political Character, Antipartyism, and the Second Party System," *American Quarterly*, Vol. XXI (Winter, 1969), pp. 683-709.
HALLER, MARK H., "The Rise of the Jackson Party in Maryland, 1820-1829," *Journal of Southern History*, Vol. XXVIII (August, 1962), pp. 307-26.
HARRISON, JOSEPH H., JR., "Oligarchs and Democrats, The Richmond Junto," *Virginia Magazine of History and Biography*, Vol. LXXVIII (April, 1970), pp. 184-98.
HOFFMAN, WILLIAM S., *Andrew Jackson and North Carolina Politics.* Chapel Hill, University of North Carolina Press, 1958.
KLEIN, PHILIP S., *Pennsylvania Politics: 1817-1832, A Game Without Rules.* Philadelphia, Historical Society of Pennsylvania, 1940.
McCORMICK, RICHARD P., "New Perspectives on Jacksonian Politics," *American Historical Review*, Vol. LXV (January, 1960), pp. 288-301.
———"Suffrage Classes and Party Alignments: A Study in Voter Behavior," *Mississippi Valley Historical Review*, Vol. XLVI (December, 1959), pp. 397-410.
*MOORE, GLOVER, *The Missouri Controversy, 1819-1821.* Lexington, University Press of Kentucky, 1966.
NAGEL, PAUL C., "The Election of 1824: A Reconsideration Based on Newspaper Opinion," *Journal of Southern History*, Vol. XXVI (August, 1960), pp. 315-29.
*NEWSOME, ALBERT R., *The Presidential Election of 1824 in North Carolina.* The James Sprunt Historical Studies, Vol. XXIII, No. 1. Chapel Hill, University of North Carolina Press, 1939.
*REMINI, ROBERT V., *The Election of Andrew Jackson.* Philadelphia and New York, J. B. Lippincott Co., 1964.
SELLERS, CHARLES G., Jr., "Banking and Politics in Jackson's Tennessee, 1817-1827," *Mississippi Valley Historical Review*, Vol. XLI (June, 1954), pp. 61-84.
STEVENS, HARRY R., *The Early Jackson Party in Ohio.* Durham, N.C., Duke University Press, 1957.
SYUDNOR, CHARLES S., "The One-Party Period of American History," *American Historical Review*, Vol. LI (April, 1946), pp. 439-51.
*TURNER, FREDERICK J., *Rise of the New West, 1819-1829.* New York, Collier-Macmillan, 1962.
TURNER, LYNN W., "The Electoral Vote Against Monroe in 1820—An Ameri-

can Legend." *Mississippi Valley Historical Review*, Vol. XLII (September, 1955), pp. 250-73.

WALLACE, MICHAEL, "Changing Concepts of Party in the United States: New York, 1815-1828," *American Historical Review*, Vol. LXXIV (December, 1968), pp. 453-91.